D0073474

Blacks in the American West and Beyond—America, Canada, and Mexico

Recent Titles in
Bibliographies and Indexes in Afro-American and African Studies

Daddy Grace: An Annotated Bibliography
Lenwood G. Davis, compiler

African Studies Thesaurus: Subject Headings for Library Users
Freda E. Otchere

Chester Himes: An Annotated Primary and Secondary Bibliography
Michel Fabre, Robert E. Skinner, and Lester Sullivan, compilers

A Bibliographical Guide to African-American Women Writers
Casper LeRoy Jordan, compiler

Invisible Wings: An Annotated Bibliography on Blacks in Aviation, 1916–1993
Betty Kaplan Gubert, compiler

The French Critical Reception of African-American Literature: From the Beginnings to
1970, An Annotated Bibliography
*Michel Fabre, compiler, with the assistance of Rosa Bobia, Christina Davis, Charles
Edwards O'Neill, and Jack Salzman*

Zora Neale Hurston: An Annotated Bibliography and Reference Guide
Rose Parkman Davis, compiler

Roots of Afrocentric Thought: A Reference Guide to Negro Digest/Black World, 1961–
1976
Clovis E. Semmes, compiler

African American Criminologists, 1970–1996: An Annotated Bibliography
Lee E. Ross, compiler

Contemporary African American Female Playwrights: An Annotated Bibliography
Dana A. Williams

Rooted in the Chants of Slaves, Blacks in the Humanities, 1985–1997: A Selectively
Annotated Bibliography
Donald Franklin Joyce, compiler

The African-American Male: An Annotated Bibliography
Jacob U. Gordon, compiler

Blacks in the American West and Beyond—America, Canada, and Mexico

A Selectively Annotated Bibliography

George H. Junne, Jr.

Bibliographies and Indexes in Afro-American and African Studies,
Number 40

GREENWOOD PRESS
Westport, Connecticut • London

Library of Congress Cataloging-in-Publication Data

Junne, George H.
   Blacks in the American West and beyond—America, Canada, and Mexico : a selectively
   annotated bibliography / George H. Junne, Jr.
      p.   cm.—(Bibliographies and indexes in Afro-American and African studies, ISSN
   0742–6925; no. 40)
   Includes indexes.
   ISBN 0–313–31208–7 (alk. paper)
      1. Afro-Americans—West (U.S.)—History—Bibliography.   2. Afro-Americans—Canada,
   Western—History—Bibliography.   3. Afro-Americans—Mexico—History—Bibliography.   4.
   West (U.S.)—History—Bibliography.   5. Canada, Western—History—Bibliography.   6.
   Mexico—History—Bibliography.   I. Title. II.   Series.
   Z1361.N39 J86 2000
   [E185.925]
   016.978′00496073—dc21   00–020764

British Library Cataloguing in Publication Data is available.

Library of Congress Catalog Card Number: 00–020764
ISBN: 0–313–31208–7
ISSN: 0742–6925

First published in 2000

Greenwood Press, 88 Post Road West, Westport, CT 06881
An imprint of Greenwood Publishing Group, Inc.
www.greenwood.com

Printed in the United States of America

The paper used in this book complies with the
Permanent Paper Standard issued by the National
Information Standards Organization (Z39.48–1984).

10 9 8 7 6 5 4 3 2 1

In memory of Gertrude Gant Junne Phillips and Josefina Framil Freeland Sessions, my mother and stepmother, respectively.

Contents

Contents   ix

Acknowledgements

It would have been almost impossible for me to complete a project such as this without support from various colleagues and other interested people. My deepest appreciation for starting me on this research has to go to Professor Michael Welsh of UNC's (University of Northern Colorado) Department of History. His extension of an invitation for me to participate in a 1997 summer teachers' workshop moved me to investigate the subject of Blacks in the West in more depth.

Further continuous support came from colleagues in the Africana Studies Department, namely Professors Osita Afoaku and Hermon George, Jr. Dean of Arts and Sciences Sandra Flake has provided for a spin-off project related to this work. Ms. Shirley Soenksen of Government Publications in UNC's James Michener Library continues to provide me with information that she has uncovered. Ms. Mary Linscome and Ms. Evelyn Measner of the Michener Archives have continued to show interest and provide encouragement. Ms. Karen Moreira of CU-Boulder's Department of Ethnic Studies assisted with Spanish and French translations.

Professors Bruce A. Glasrud of Sul Ross State University, Patricia Nelson Limerick of the University of Colorado at Boulder, Quintard Taylor of the University of Washington and Elliott West of the University of Arkansas, all noted historians, have found time to encourage me to continue this work and seek its publication.

Two friends who have continually given me encouragement on all of my projects, Winston and Beryl Churchill of Powell, Wyoming, also deserve thanks.

The Hinckley Library at Northwest College, also in Powell, deserves acknowledgment for the days I spent using their resources.

I appreciate the support of friends Professors Michael Higgins of UNC and Jualynne Dodson of CU-Boulder, as well as various faculty members, staff and students who kept inquiring about the project.

Finally, I would like to acknowledge the receipt of a UNC Summer Research Professor Program award for 1999. That stipend was presented through the offices of Provost Marlene Strathe and Dean of the Graduate School Richard A. King, and allowed for timely completion of this work.

Introduction

What is the American West? Neither this bibliography nor any other will answer that question. The American West can be defined through various social, political, historical, and mythical interpretations. Many of them would be legitimate, depending on one's point of view. Once in American history, the West was western Pennsylvania, Kentucky and Ohio. After the Louisiana Purchase of 1803, the American West suddenly extended to the Pacific Ocean. Some historians talk of the Trans-Mississippi West while other define the West as those continental states through which the 98th longitude runs, plus the states west of that line. Therefore, most works on the American West do not include two of our most western states, Alaska and Hawaii.

The West of myth also helps to define the American West. In the minds of many, the West is the home of the "cowboys and Indians," despite the fact that some Native American tribes now in the West were forcibly removed to that part of the country and, previously, were Easterners. Further, the Hollywood-perpetuated myth of the cowboy only existed for a short period during the late 19th century.

For this work, the West includes the continental states, through which the 98th longitude runs, and states west of there to the Pacific Ocean. There are three states included that are east of the 98th—Arkansas, Iowa, and Missouri. Arkansas, formerly part of the Louisiana Purchase, was linked to Indian Territory (Oklahoma). When established as a territory, Oklahoma did not have a territorial government so Arkansas filled that function. Iowa, also once part of the Louisiana Territory, is more difficult to rationalize for its inclusion. However, some historians include Iowa when writing about the western frontier. Missouri, also carved out of the Louisiana Purchase, was politically linked with Kansas before and during the Civil War. It also became the gateway for pioneers heading west and was a terminus for the Pony Express.

Former slaves and free Blacks went to Canada and many helped to settle the western areas of that country, inviting its inclusion. Much of the territory in the West was once part of Mexico. Further, many Blacks who first migrated or settled in the West went there through Mexico or Mexican territory (formerly, Spanish territory or New Spain). For those and other reasons, Canada and Mexico have been included in the bibliography.

I began to put together a bibliography on Blacks in the West, including Canada and Mexico, during the spring of 1997. It is still mostly unannotated and is now over 600 pages in length. It soon became evident, as I attempted to research certain areas, that there were gaps and problems relating to the subject. It was apparent that the voices of Black Westerners themselves were missing from a lot of past and current books and articles. It is also clear that while many books, articles, and theses focused on Black men, there was little featuring the women. There were over twenty-five pages on Buffalo Soldiers while writing devoted solely to women covered only fifteen pages. There were only twenty-six entries for theses and dissertations that researched Black women.

There is a lot of focus on "problems" or high-profile subjects such as riots, segregation/integration, and occupational mobility. Examples of titles are:

"Discrimination, Poverty, and the Negro: Arizona in the National Context."
"Problems of Negro Youth in Tucson."
"The Los Angeles Riot Study."
"The Ugly Mood of Watts."
"Two Weeks of Racial Crisis in Richmond, California."
"A Night of Violence: The Houston Riot of 1917."

There is also a lot of writing on the Civil War and slavery, and a curious lack of longitudinal studies.

This bibliography was created to respond to the lack of a current and comprehensive work providing resources on the history and contributions of African Americans to the American West. The first objective was to provide an updated resource for faculty, students, teachers and others interested in the subject. I as compiler also wanted to make this resource accessible to both academic and non-academic users. Additionally, I attempted to incorporate areas not included in many bibliographies, including films and videos, and Black newspapers.

Second, this work is an attempt to serve the practical needs of departments and programs, plus graduate and undergraduate students who are conducting research on the Black West. Therefore, the work is divided into major and minor topics to facilitate that inquiry. For the most part, the work is unannotated except where the title of an entry seems insufficient to explain the topic adequately. Respecting the amount of effort that goes into annotating, others and I have found that research topics are sometimes so specific that the researcher still has to peruse the books or articles. In the case of books, sometimes one might glean more information from the index rather than the annotation. The comments should not be taken as an argument against annotated bibliographies, for that would be absurd. It is only a rationale of why I decided to present this bibliography in this fashion.

There have been many bibliographies that have preceded this one and which continue to remain valuable resources. They include works compiled by Bruce A. Glasrud, James de T. Abajian, Lenwood G. Davis, Roger D. Hardaway and others. Some focus on subject areas not covered by others (Glasrud's *African Americans in the West: A Bibliography of Secondary Sources* that also catalogued a list of fictional works, for instance) while others may omit subjects or may not be as comprehensive in specific areas. One contained a myriad of legal documents, an area that I felt obliged to omit.

One section that becomes an integral component of this work is that relating to Black newspapers. Newspapers are one of the most difficult resources to compile because many copies no longer exist, while some are only known from mention in other papers. Some papers only existed for a few editions and some, because of sale or other events, changed their names and reappeared with a new masthead. Some had several titles during their existence. Even annuals listing Black newspapers proved to be incomplete. Dates of the founding and extinction of the newspapers varied, sometimes as much as decades. Realizing that there may be some discrepancies in that information, it is still the most complete listing of Black newspapers of the West yet found. Newspapers are a significant reference for understanding what the Black community felt were important issues. They are also a treasure trove for genealogies, Black businesses and their locations, local news and gossip, and alternative interpretations of national and international events. Sometimes, one company might print several newspapers that they distribute in various communities. To assist the reader, I have boxed those papers using a single line. In the instances where newspapers changed names on their mastheads because of new ownership or for other reasons but continued publication, I have boxed them using double lines.

One goal is to present the fullest and the most accurate bibliography on Blacks in the American West to date. By using this work, researchers may be assisted in their reconstruction of the history and culture of that group. Another is to demonstrate the continuity of that history and culture from the earliest times to the present. Lastly, the work should encourage the researcher to raise questions concerning gaps or lack of information in topic areas. Perhaps those gaps will lead to investigations of new areas or new topics.

For instance, is the reason there is comparatively little information on Black women that there is so little or that so little has yet been researched or collected? Are there new areas that need expanded research, such as women's clubs in the West? Why is there such a dearth of information concerning Black professional women? Is there a lack of material, a lack of Black professional women, or a lack of interest on the subject by those responsible for guiding students through research projects? Observing the gaps in the research will hopefully not only lead researchers to increase our knowledge of Blacks in the West, but perhaps will also challenge some existing stereotypes of those people.

General Black Western History

Articles:

Abramowitz, Jack. "The Negro in the Agrarian Revolt." *Agricultural History* 24 (1950).

Anderson, Talmadge. "An Ideological Treatise on Black Publications and Black Writers: The Evolution of the Western Journal of Black Studies." *Serials Librarian* 9 (1984).

Armitage, Susan, Deborah Gallacci Wilbert. "Black Women in the Pacific Northwest: A Survey and Research Prospectus." Chapter in *Women in Pacific Northwest History: An Anthology*, ed. Karen J. Blair. Seattle: University of Washington Press, 1988.

Barker, Gordon H., and W. Thomas Adams. "Negro Delinquents in Public Training Schools in the West." *Journal of Negro Education* 32 (Summer 1963). A study of boys at the Lookout Mountain School for Boys in Golden, Colorado.

Barr, Alwyn. "Black Migration into Southwestern Cities, 1865–1900." Chapter in *Essays on Southern History Written in Honor of Barnes F. Lathrop*. Austin: General Libraries, University of Texas at Austin, 1980.

————. "Blacks in Southwestern Cities." *Red River Valley Historical Review* 65 (Spring 1981).

"Bass Reeves, Marshall in Old West, Name Included in National Cowboy Hall of Fame." *Jet*, 2 March 1992.

Bellson, Ford. "Labor Gains on the Coast: A Report on the Integration of Negro Workers into the Maritime Unions of the Pacific Coast States." *Opportunity: Journal of Negro Life* 17 (May 1939).

Berardi, Gayle K., and Thomas W. Segady. "Community Identification and Cultural formation: The Role of African American Newspapers in the American West, 1880–1914." *Griot* 10 (Spring 1991).

_____. "The Development of African-American Newspapers in the American West: A Sociohistorical Perspective." *Journal of Negro History* 75 (Summer-Fall 1990). Story of the Black newspapers, but figures are inaccurate.

Bergman, G. M. "The Negro Who Rode With Fremont in 1847 (Jacob Dodson)." *Negro History Bulletin* 28 (November 1964).

"Big Sky Country." *American Visions*, June 1990. Special issue presented by Greyhound Lines devoted to Black travelers. Focus on cemeteries, churches, cultural centers, forts, homes, monuments, museums, statues, etc., in Idaho, Iowa, Montana, Nebraska, North Dakota, South Dakota, and Wyoming.

"The Black Historical Journey." *American Visions*, June 1990. Special issue presented by Greyhound Lines devoted to Black travelers. Focus on cemeteries, churches, cultural centers, forts, homes, monuments, museums, statues, etc., in Missouri.

"Black History" *Prairie Pioneer* 14 (January 1995).

"Blacks on Yellow: Afro-Americans View Chinese-Americans, 1850–1935." *Phylon* 39 (March 1970). Much of the article focuses on the West.

Blake, Elias, Jr. "Color Prejudice and the Education of Low-Income Negroes in the North and West." *Journal of Negro Education* 34 (Summer 1965).

Brier, Stephen. "The Career of Richard L. Davis Reconsidered: Unpublished Correspondence from the National Labor Tribune." *Labor History* 21 (1980).

Brodie, James M. "Rounding Up the Truth: Black Scholars Push for 'Real History' of Old West." *Black Issues in Higher Education* 9 (26 March 1992).

Burroughs, John Rolfe. "Some Bad Men" and "Hair Brands and Hard Cases." Chapters in *Where the Old West Stayed Young*. New York: William Morrow and Company, 1962. The story of Isom Dart.

Burton, Arthur T. "Bass Reeves: A Legendary Lawman of the Western Frontier." *Persimmon Hill* 20 (Summer 1992).

Byrd, James W. "Afro-American Writers in the West." Chapter in *A Literary History of the American West*, ed. J. Golden Taylor. Fort Worth: Christian University Press, 1987.

Byrnes, Deborah A., and Gary Kiger. "Racial Attitudes and Discrimination: University Teacher Education Students Compared to the General Student Population." *College Student Journal* 22 (1988). Examination of racial tolerance of students at a university "in the Rocky Mountain region."

Carlson, Oliver. "The Negro Moves West." *Fortnight* 17 (6 October 1954).

Cashin, Joan E. "Black Families in the Old Northwest." *Journal of the Early Republic* 15 (Fall 1995).

Castles, Jean I. "The West: Crucible of the Negro." *Montana: The Magazine of Western History* 19 (Winter 1969).

Colbert, Robert E. "The Attitude of Older Negro Residents Toward Recent Migrants in the Pacific Northwest." *Journal of Negro Education* 15 (Fall 1946).

Colley, Charles C. "The Desert Shall Blossom: North African Influence on the American Southwest." *Western Historical Quarterly* 14 (July 1983). Plants from Africa brought to the New World by Spain.

Cooper, Gary. "Stage Coach Mary." *Ebony*, October 1959. Academy Award actor remembers Mary Fields.

Coray, Michael S. "Blacks in the Pacific West, 1850–1860: A View from the Census." *Nevada Historical Society Quarterly* 28 (Summer 1985).

_____. "Influences on Black Household Organizations in the West, 1850–1860." *Nevada Historical Society* 31 (1988).

_____. "Negro and Mulatto in the Pacific West, 1850–1860: Changing Patterns of Black Population Growth." *Pacific Historian* 29 (Winter 1985). Indicates that the mulatto population in the Pacific West was larger than any other area of the U.S.

"Dark Horse Operas: A Film Article." *Negro History Bulletin* 36 (January 1973). Black Westerns.

David, Joel. "The West and Westerns." *Journal of the West* 29 (April 1990). Black films included.

Davis, J. M. "We Said: Let's find the Facts." *Survey* 56 (1 May 1926). Survey of race relations on the Pacific Coast.

de Graaf, Lawrence B. "Recognition, Racism, and Reflections on the Writing of Western Black History." *Pacific Historical Review* 44 (February 1975).

_____. "Significant Steps on an Arduous Path: The Impact of World War II on Discrimination Against African Americans in the West." *Journal of the West* 35 (January 1996).

Decker, Beryl. "The Last Pioneers." *Negro Digest* (May 1963).

_____. "Significant Steps on an Arduous Path: The Impact of World War II on Discrimination Against African Americans in the West." *Journal of the West* 35 (January 1996).

Dempsey, Mary A. "The Bronze Buckaroo Rides Again: Herb Jeffries Is Still Keepin' On." *American Visions*, August-September 1997. Jeffries was star of all-Black cowboy movies.

Deutsch, Sarah. "Landscapes of Enclaves: Race Relations in the West, 1865–1990." Chapter in *Under an Open Sky: Rethinking America's Western Past*, eds. William Cronon, George Miles, and Jay Gitlin. New York: W. W. Norton, 1992.

Drotning, Phillip T. "Taming the Western Wilderness." Chapter in *Black Heroes in Our Nations's History: A Tribute to Those Who Helped Shape America.* New York: Cowles Book Company, 1969.

Du Bois, W. E. B. "The Great Northwest." *Crisis* 6 (September 1913).

Erlich, Karen Lynn. "Blacks in the Cattle Industry." Section in "Minorities in the Cattle Industry: A Historigraphic Analysis." *Journal of NAL Association* 4 (1979).

Forbes, Jack D. "Black Pioneers: The Spanish-Speaking Afro-Americans of the Southwest." *Phylon* 27 (Fall 1966). Author concludes that Spaniards of part-Black ancestry constituted 20% of the 1790 California population.

_____. "Race and Color in Mexican-American Problems." *Journal of Human Relations* 16 (1968). Racism against Blacks tied to racism against Indians and Mexican Americans.

"Forgotten Pioneers: Blacks in the West." *U.S. News and World Report* 117 (8 August 1994).

Garvin, Roy. "Benjamin or 'Pap' Singleton and His Followers." *Journal of Negro History* 33 (January 1948).

Greene, Harry W. "Negro Colleges in the Southwest." *Opportunity* 5 (November 1927).

Gwaltney, William W. "Black History in the Parks." *National Parks* 65 (1 January 1991).

Hansen, Klaus J. "The Millennium, the West, and Race in the Antebellum American Mind." *Western Historical Quarterly* 3 (October 1972).

Harris, William H. "Federal Intervention in Union Discrimination: FEPC and West Coast Shipyards During World War II." *Labor History* 22 (Summer 1981).

Harvey, James R. "Negroes in Colorado." *Colorado Magazine* 26 (April 1949). Based on Master's thesis.

Heuterman, Thomas H. "Racism in Frontier Journalism: A Case Study." *Journal of the West* 19 (April 1980).

Hickman, Christine B. "The Devil and the One Drop Rule: Racial Categories, African Americans, and the U.S. Census." *Michigan Law Review* 95 (1 March 1997).

Hill, Daniel Grafton. "The Negro in the Early History of the West." *The Iliff Review* 3 (Fall 1946).

Hodder, Frank H. "The Authorship of the Compromise of 1850." *Mississippi Valley Historical Review* 22 (1936).

_____. "The Railroad Background of the Kansas-Nebraska Act." *Mississippi Valley Historical Review* 12 (1925).

Hoffman, Donald. "Whose Home on the Range? Finding Room for Native Americans, African Americans, and Latino Americans in the Revisionist Western." MELUS 22 (Summer 1997). Examines *Dances with Wolves, Posse*, and *The Ballad of Gregorio Cortez*.

Hollis, Deborah. "Conducting Black Genealogical Research: The Story of Oliver and Lillia." *Colorado Libraries* 21 (Summer 1995).

Hoy, Jim. "Black Cowboys." *Kansas* 18 (November 1986).

Johnson, James Weldon. "Robert C. Owens: A Pacific Coast Successful Negro." *Colored American Magazine* 9 (July 1905).

Johnson, M. K. "'Strangers in a Strange Land': An African American Response to the Frontier Tradition in Oscar Micheaux's *The Conquest: The Story of a Negro Pioneer*." *Western American Literature* 33 (Fall

1998). Micheaux's literary attempt to demonstrate that legends of the West can be Black legends, and challenges anti-Black racism.

Kennedy, Tolbert H. "Racial Survey of the Intermountain Northwest." *Research Studies of the State College of Washington* 14 (September 1946).

_____. "Racial Tensions Among Negroes in the Intermountain Northwest." *Phylon* 7, (Winter 1946).

Lapp, Rudolph M. "Negroes in the Far West." Chapter in *The Reader's Encyclopedia of the American West*, ed. Howard R. Lamar. New York: Thomas Y. Crowell, 1977.*f*

Luchetti, Cathy. "Black Cookery in the Old West." *American Visions*, April–May 1993. Excerpted from the book *Home on the Range,* contains 19ᵗʰ century Black cuisine.

Luebke, Frederick C. "Ethnic Group Settlement on the Great Plains." *The Western Historical Quarterly* 7 (October 1977). Information of various ethnic groups including Blacks.

Makopfsky, Abraham. "Experience of Native Americans at a Black College: Indian Students at Hampton Institute, 1878–1923." *Journal of Ethnic Studies* 17 (Fall 1989).

"Mario Van Peebles Heads All-Star Cast in 'Posse,' a Film about Black Cowboys." *Jet*, 31 May 1993.

McChristian, Douglas C. "'Dress on the Colors, Boys': Black Noncommissioned Officers in the Regular Army, 1866–1898." *Colorado Heritage* (Spring 1996).

McConnell, Roland C. "Isaiah Dorman and the Custer Expedition." *Journal of Negro History* 33 (July 1948). The Black guide with Custer.

McWilliams, Carey. "Jim Crow Goes West." *Negro Digest* 3 (August 1945).

Merriam, Harold G. "Sign-Talker with Straight Tongue." *Montana: The Magazine of Western History* 12 (July 1962).

Miller, Loren R. "The Negro Voter in the Far West." *Journal of Negro Education* 26 (Summer 1957).

Minerbrook, Scott. "The Forgotten Pioneers." *U.S. News and World Report*, 8 August 1994. Blacks in the Old West.

Mogulof, Melvin B. "Black Community Development in Five Western Model Cities." *Social Work* 15 (January 1970). Examines the Fresno, Oakland, Portland, Richmond, and Seattle predominantly Black communities.

Montesano, Philip M. "A Black Pioneer's Trip to California." *Pacific Historian* 13 (Winter 1969). The 1849 trip from Missouri by Alvin Aaron Coffey.

Mooney, Ralph James. "Matthew Deady and the Federal Judicial Response to Racism in the Early West." *Oregon Law Review* 63 (1984).

"Nation's NAACP Chapters on Alert After Recent Attacks on West Coast." *Jet*, 16 August 1993. Examines situations in Sacramento and Tacoma.

O'Brien, Robert W. "The Changing Caste Position of the Negro in the North-west." *Research Studies* 10 (March 1942).

O'Brien, Robert W., and Bernard E. Squires. "The Negro in the Northwest before the Civil War." *Negro History Bulletin* 5 (June 1942).

O'Brien, Robert W., and Lee M. Brooks. "Race Relations in the Pacific Northwest." *Phylon* 7 (1946).

O'Carroll, Patrick W. , and James A. Mercy. "Regional Variation in Homicide Rates: Why is the West so Violent?" *Violence and Victims* 4 (1989).

Palmer, Colin A. "From Africa to the Americas: Ethnicity in the Early Black Communities of the Americas." *Journal of World History* (Fall 1995).

Paul, Rodman W., and Richard W. Etulain, comps. "Black Americans in the West." Chapter in *The Frontier and the American West*. Arlington Heights, IL: AHM, 1977.

Peltier, Jerome. "Moses 'Black' Harris." Chapter in *The Mountain Men and the Fur Trade of the Far West*, ed. LeRoy R. Hafen. Glendale, CA: Arthur H. Clark, 1968.

Pinkney, Alphonso. "Prejudice Toward Mexican and Negro Americans: A Comparison." *Phylon* 24 (Winter 1963).

Porter, Kenneth Wiggins. "Negroes and the Fur Trade." *Minnesota History* 15 (December 1934).

_____. "Negroes on the Frontier." Chapter in *The Reader's Encyclopedia of the American West*, ed. Howard R. Lamar. New York: Thomas Y. Crowell, 1977.

Quimby, George I. "Culture Contact on the Northwest Coast, 1785–1795." *American Anthropologist* 50 (April 1948.

"Race Riots on the Pacific Coast." *Outlook* 87 (21 September 1907).

"Rampages of Ku Klux Klan on Pacific Coast." *Messenger* 4 (June 1922). Activity in Bakersfield and Oregon.

Randolph, Asa Philip. "The Organization Tour West." *Messenger* 8 (April 1926). Randolphs's visit to major West Coast cities for his union.

Ravage, John W. "Blacks in the American West." *History of Photography* 16 (Winter 1992).

Reddick, Lawrence D., ed. "Race Relations on the Pacific Coast." *Journal of Educational Sociology* 19 (November 1945). Special issue.

Rice, Marc. "Frompin' in the Great Plains: Listening and Dancing to the Jazz Orchestra of Alphonso Trent, 1925–44." *Great Plains Quarterly* 16 (Spring 1966).

Riley, Carroll. "Blacks in the Early Southwest." *Ethnohistory* 19 (Summer 1972).

Savage, W. Sherman. "Early Negro Education in the Pacific Coast States." *Journal of Negro Education* 15 (Winter 1946).

_____. "The Negro in the History of the Pacific Northwest." *Journal of Negro History* 13 (July 1938).

_____. "The Negro in the Westward Movement." *Journal of Negro History* 25 (October 1940).

_____. "The Negro on the Mining Frontier." *Journal of Negro History* 30 (January 1945).

_____. "Slavery in the Pacific Northwest." *Oregon Native Son* (November 1900).

Schmitzer, Jeanne C. "Sable Riders of the American West: The Twenty-Fifth Infantry Bicycle Corps." *Journal of the Afro-American Historical and Genealogy Society* 13 (1994).

Schoenberger, Dale T. "The Black Man in the American West." *Negro History Bulletin* 32 (March 1969).

Seraile, William. "Saving Souls on the Frontier: A Chaplain's Labor." *Montana* 42 (1992).

Smith, Alonzo N., and Quintard Taylor. "Racial Discrimination in the Workplace: A Study of Two West Coast Cities During the 1940s." *Journal of Ethnic Studies* 8 (Spring 1980).

Smith, Duane. "We Are Equal: Racial Attitudes in the West." *Westerners Brand Book* (Chicago) 30 (January 1974).

Smith, Theodore C. "The Liberty and Free Soil Parties in the Northwest." *Harvard Historical Studies* 6 (1897).

Smurr, J. W. "Jim Crow Out West." Chapter in *Historical Essays on Montana and the Northwest: In Honor of Paul C. Phillips*, eds. J. W. Smurr and Ross Toole. Helena, MT: The Western Press, 1957.

Stowe, David W. "Jazz in the West: Cultural Frontier and Region during the Swing Era." *Western Historical Quarterly* 23 (February 1992).

"Success of 'Posse' Altered Blacks' View of Westerns." *Jet*, 19 July 1993.

Taylor, Quintard. "Bibliographic Essay on the African American West." *Montana: The Magazine of Western History* 46 (Winter 1996).

_____. "Blacks in the American West: An Overview." *Western Journal of Black Studies* 1 (March 1997).

_____. "The Emergence of Black Communities in the Pacific Northwest, 1865–1910." *Journal of Negro History* 64 (Fall 1979).

_____. "From Esteban to Rodney King: Five Centuries of African American History in the West." *Montana: The Magazine of Western History* 46 (Winter 1996).

Tetlow, Roger. "There Were Black Pioneers, Too." *Northwest Magazine* (October 5, 1969).

Toll, William. "W. E. B. Du Bois and Frederick Jackson Turner—The Unveiling and Preemption of America's Inner History." *Pacific North West Quarterly* 65 (April 1973). Differing viewpoints concerning the West.

Vincent, F. C. "Southern Nigger in the Northwest Woodpile." *Sunset: The Pacific Monthly* 41 (August 1918).

Voegeli, V. Jacques III. "The Northwest and the Race Issue, 1861–1862." *Mississippi Valley Historical Review* 50 (1963).

Walsh, Margaret. "New Horizons for the American West." *History Today* 44 (March 1994). Multifaceted view of the settlement of the American West.

Walters, Ronald. "The Great Plains Sit-In Movement, 1958–66." *Great Plains Quarterly* 16 (Spring 1996).

_____. "Standing Up in America's Heartland: Sitting-in before Greensboro." *American Visions*, February 1993.

Washington, Margaret. "African American History and the Frontier Thesis." *Journal of the Early Republic* 13 (Summer 1993). Turner's thesis omits Blacks, but Black historians found a deeper meaning for Blacks.

White, Richard. "Race Relations in the American West." *American Quarterly* 38 (1986).

White, W. Thomas. "Race, Ethnicity, and Gender in the Railroad Work Force: The Case of the Far Northwest, 1883–1918." *Western Historical Quarterly* 16 (July 1985).

Whittlesey, Lee. "A Brief History of Black Americans in the Yellowstone National Park Area, 1872–1907." *Annals of Wyoming* 69 (Fall 1997).

Wiggins, William H., Jr. "Juneteenth." *American Visions*, June–July 1993. June 19 celebration in Colorado, Kansas, Oklahoma, and Texas.

Wilkin, Ray. "The West in Wartime," *Crisis* 50 (May 1943).

Williams, Nudie E. "Bass Reeves: Lawman in the Western Ozarks." *Negro History Bulletin* 42 (April/May/June 1979).

_____. "Black Men Who Wore the Star." *Chronicles of Oklahoma* 59 (Spring 1981).

_____. "Black Men Who Wore White Hats: Grant Johnson, United States Deputy Marshal." *Red River Valley Historical Review* 5 (Summer 1980).

_____. "They Fought for Votes: The White Politician and the Black Editor." *Chronicles of Oklahoma* 64 (Spring 1986).

_____. "United States vs. Bass Reeves: Black Lawman on Trial." *Chronicles of Oklahoma* 68 (1990).

Woodson, Carter G. "The Exodus to the West." Chapter in *Century of Negro Migration*. Washington, DC: Association for the Study of Negro Life and History, 1918.

Woolsey, Ronald C. "The West Becomes a Problem: The Missouri Controversy and Slavery Expansion as the Southern Dilemma." *Missouri Historical Review* 77 (July 1983).

Work, Monroe Nathan. "A Negro Pioneer in the West." *Journal of Negro History* 8.

Cowhands

Allmindinger, Blake. "Deadwood Dick: The Black Cowboy as Cultural Timber." *Journal of American Culture* 16 (Winter 1993).

"Artist, Model, Cowboy." *Soldiers* 51 (July 1996). Veteran and artist researches roles of Blacks in the West.

"Black Cowboy Rides Horse From Texas to New Jersey Home." *Jet*, 1 July 1985.

"Black Cowboys." *Essence* 15 (April 1985).

Butruille, Susan G. "The American Cowboy: From Frontier to Fantasy." *Westways* 75 (1983).

"Carlos A. Foster, 76, Cowboy and Role Model." *New York Times*, 18 December 1998. Obituary.

Clayton, Lawrence. "Bill 'Tige' Avery." Chapter in *Cowboys Who Rode Proudly*, ed. J. Evetts Haley. Midland, TX: Nita Stewart Haley Memorial Library, 1992.

Dempsey, Mary A. "The Bronze Buckaroo Rides Again: Herb Jeffries is Still Keepin' On." *American Visions*, August-September 1997. Profile of Jeffries, star of all-Black westerns.

Durham, Philip. "The Lost Cowboy." *Midwest Journal* 7 (1955).

_____. "The Negro Cowboy." *American Quarterly* 7 (Fall 1955).

Durham, Philip, and Everett L. Jones. "Negro Cowboys." *American West* 1 (Fall 1964).

_____. "Slaves on Horseback." *Pacific Historical Review* 33 (1964). Black cowhands on the Great Plains from the 1850s to the 1870s.

Fleming, Elvis E. "Old Black Add from the LFD." *True West* 41 (August 1994). Profile of the "most noted Negro cowhand that ever 'topped off' a horse."

Gaines, Edith, and H. Lloyd. "Land of the Black Cowboy." *Sepia* 23 (June 1974).

Gill, Gale. "Texas Trail Ride, Negro Cowboys." *Ebony*, May 1963.

Gillespie. A. S. "More About Negro Cowmen." *Cattleman* 23 (June 1936).

Harmon, John H. "Black Cowboys are Real." *Crisis* 47 (1940).

Hendrix, John M. "Tribute Paid to Negro Cowmen." *Cattleman* 22 (February 1936).

Hicks, L. Wayne. "A Museum for Black Cowboys." *Western Horseman* 57 (March 1992). Denver's Black West Museum and Heritage Center.

Katz, William Loren. "Bose Ikard: Faithful Cowhand on the Goodnight-Loving Trail." Chapter in *Black People Who Made the Old West*.

_____. "Deadwood Dick (Nat Love): Wild Man of the Old West." Chapter in *Black People Who Made the Old West*.

_____. "Isom Dart: He Tried Mightily to Go Straight." Chapter in *Black People Who Made the Old West*.

Knox, Andrew P. "Before Hollywood Made the Myth: Negro Cowboys in the Old West." *Black World* 14 (September 1965).

Lewis, Jr., Richard. "Racial Position Segregation: A Case Study of Southwest Conference Football, 1978 and 1989." *Journal of Black Studies* 25 (March 1995). Race discrimination and race division in college football.

Lowry, Jack. "The Forgotten Cowboys." *Texas Highways* 38 (August 1991).

"Medicine Roles and Black Cowboys." *The New Yorker*, 17 March 1986.

Miller, Robert H. "The (Historical) Truth." *Teaching Pre K-8* 22 (1 February 1992). Visit to author Miller to learn about Black cowhands.

Porter, Kenneth Wiggins.   "Negro Labor in the Western Cattle Industry,
     1866–1900." *Labor History* 10 (Summer 1969); reprinted in *Black La-
     bor in America*, ed. Milton Cantor. Westport, CT: Negro Universities
     Press, 1970; reprinted in *Essays on the History of the American West*,
     ed. Stephen Salsbury. Hinsdale, IL: The Dryden Press, 1975; reprinted
     in *The Negro on the American Frontier* by Kenneth Wiggins Porter.
     New York: Arno Press and the New York Times, 1971; reprinted (ab-
     breviated) in *Major Problems in the History of the American West:
     Documents and Essays*, ed. Clyde A. Milner II. Lexington, MA: D.C.
     Heath and Company, 1989; reprinted (abbreviated) in *Peoples of Color
     in the American West*, ed. Sucheng Chan, Douglas Henry Daniels,
     Mario T. Garcia, and Terry P. Wilson. Lexington, MA: D.C. Heath
     and Company, 1994.   Profiles the conditions and experiences of the
     Black cowboys.
"A Potpourri." *Reunions: The Magazine* 4 (Spring 1994). Black cowhand re-
     unions included.
Preece, Harold. "American Negro Cowboys." *Real West* 9 (January 1966).
Richardson, Barbara J.   "Black Cowboys Also Rode." *Password* 31 (Spring
     1986).
Savage, William W., Jr. "History, Culture, and the Cowboy Image." Chapter
     in *The Cowboy Hero: His Image in American History and Culture*.
     Norman, OK: University of Oklahoma Press, 1979.   Argues that
     numbers cited for Black cowboys may be too high.
Schrum, Keith. "Of Myth and Men: The Trail of the Black Cowboy." *Colo-
     rado Heritage* (Autumn 1998). Profiles George McJunkin, Daniel Web-
     ster (80 John) Wallace, Bill Pickett, and Nat Love, plus provides a good
     overview of cowboy life.
Searles, Michael N. "The Black Cowboy—Yesterday and Today: A Hard Won
     Reputation." *Augusta Today Magazine* 4 (January-February 1997); re-
     printed, *Texas Illustrated: A Magazine of History and Folklore* 1 (Feb-
     ruary 1997).
Smith, Patricia Ann. "Negro Cowboys." *Negro History Bulletin* 29 (February
     1966). High school student writes about the Black cowhands.
Westermeier, Clifford P. "Black Rodeo Cowboys." *Red River Valley Historical
     Review* 3 (Summer 1978).
Weston, Jack. "Minority Cowboys and Women Cowhands." Chap. in *The Real
     American Cowboy*. New York: Schocken Books, 1985.
Wood, Collette. "Lou Rawls Stars in First All-Black Cowboy Movie." *Holly-
     wood Reporter* (September 17, 1969).

Slaves and Slavery

Baker, Julie Philips.   "Black Slavery Among the American Indians." *AB
     Bookman's Weekly* 89 (February 1992).

Berwanger, Eugene H. "Western Prejudice and the Extension of Slavery." *Civil War History* 12 (1966). Investigates failure to establish slavery in California, Illinois, Indiana, Kansas, and Oregon.

Creer, Leland Hargrave. "Spanish-American Slave Trade in the Great Basin, 1800–1853." *New Mexico Historical Review* 24 (July 1949).

Durham, Philip, and Everett L. Jones. "Slaves on Horseback." *Pacific Historical Review* 33 (1964). Black cowhands on the Great Plains from the 1850s to the 1870s.

Foley, William E. "Slave Freedom Suits before Dred Scott: The Case of Marie Jean Scypion's Descendants." *Missouri Historical Review* 79 (October 1984).

Foner, Eric. "The Wilmot Proviso Revisited." *Journal of American History* 56 (1969). The attempt by Van Burenite Democrats to stop the expansion of slavery.

Gamble, Douglas A. "Garrisonian Abolitionists in the West: Some Suggestions for Study." *Civil War History* 23 (1977).

Hansen, Klaus J. "The Millennium, the West, and Race in the Antebellum American Mind." *Western Historical Quarterly* 3 (1972). Opposition to slavery in the West to maintain it as a white domain.

Hart, Charles Desmond. "Slavery Expansion to the Territories, 1850: A Forgotten Speech by Truman Smith." *New Mexico Historical Review* 41 (October 1966).

Hubbart, H. C. "Pro-Southern Influences in the Free West, 1840–1865." *Mississippi Valley Historical Review* 20 (June 1923). Slavery influences.

Lynch, William O. "Antislavery Tendencies of the Democratic Party in the Northwest, 1848–1850." *Mississippi Valley Historical Review* 11 (1924).

Parish, John C. "An Early Fugitive Slave Case West of the Mississippi River." *Iowa Journal of History and Politics* 6 (1908).

Posey, W. B. "The Influence of Slavery upon the Methodist Church in the Early South and Southwest." *Mississippi Valley Historical Review* 17 (March 1931).

_____. "The Slavery Question in the Presbyterian Church in the Old Southwest." *Journal of Southern History* 15 (August 1949).

Potts, Alma G. "Slavery in the Old Northwest." *Social Studies* 33 (February 1942).

Ramsdell, Charles W. "The Natural Limits of Slavery Expansion" *Mississippi Valley Historical Review* 16 (1929–1930).

Schapsmeier, Edward L., and Frederick H. Schapsmeier. "Lincoln and Douglas: Their Versions of the West." *Journal of the West* 7 (1968). Two views on dealing with the slavery issue and the West.

Staughton, Lynd. "On Turner, Beard and Slavery." *Journal of Negro History* 48 (October 1963). Historiographers Frederick Jackson Turner and Charles Beard minimized the importance of slavery.

Books:

Abajian, James de T., comp. *Blacks and Their Contributions to the American West: A Bibliography and Union List of Library Holdings Through 1970*. Boston: G. K. Hall, 1974.

Abdul-Jabbar, Kareem. *Black Profiles in Courage*. New York: Avon Books, 1997. Profiles of Estevanico and Bass Reeves.

Alexander, Charles C. *The Ku Klux Klan in the Southwest*. Lexington: University of Kentucky Press, 1965.

Allen, Henry Wilson. *One More River to Cross: The Life and Legend of Isom Dart*. New York: Random House, 1967.

Anderson, LaVere. *Saddles and Sabers: Black Men in the Old West*. Champaign, IL: Garrard Publishing Company, 1975.

Anderson, Martha E. A. *Black Pioneers of the Northwest, 1800–1918*. Portland, OR: Pioneer Publishing, 1980.

Berwanger, Eugene H. *The Frontier Against Slavery. Western Anti-Negro Prejudice and the Slavery Extension Controversy*. Urbana: University of Illinois Press, 1971.

_____. *The West and Reconstruction*. Urbana: University of Illinois Press, 1981.

Billington, Monroe Lee, and Roger D. Hardaway, eds. *African Americans on the Western Frontier*. Niwot, CO: University Press of Colorado, 1998.

Blacks in the Western Movement. Anacostia Neighborhood Museum. Washington, DC: Smithsonian Institution Press, 1975.

Blacks in the Westward Movement. Washington, DC: Smithsonian Institution Press, 1975. Booklet with photographs.

Bogardus, Emory Stephen. *The Survey of Race Relations on the Pacific Coast*. Los Angeles: Council on International Relations, 1926.

Bontemps, Arna, and Jack Conroy. *Anyplace but Here*. New York: Hill and Wang, 1966.

Bruce, Howard C. *The New Man: Twenty-Nine Years a Slave, Twenty-Nine Years a Free Man, Recollections of H. C. Bruce*. Blacks in the American West Series. Lincoln: University of Nebraska Press, 1996.

Burt, Olive W. *Negroes in the Early West*. New York: Julian Messner, 1969. Juvenile.

Burton, Arthur T. *Black, Red, and Deadly: Black and Indian Gunfighters of the Indian Territory, 1870–1907*. Austin: Eakin Press, 1991.

Carney, Ellen. *The Oregon Trail: Ruts, Rogues and Reminiscences*. Wayan, ID: Traildust Publishing, 1993. Experiences of many people.

Chan, Sucheng, et al. *Peoples of Color in the American West*. Lexington, MA: D. C. Heath and Company, 1994.

Cromwell, Arthur. *The Black Frontier*. Lincoln: University of Nebraska Television (KUON), 1970. Booklet with detailed bibliography.

Davis, Lenwood G. *Blacks in the American West: A Working Bibliography*, 2^d ed. Exchange Bibliography, no. 661. Monticello, IL: Council of Planning Librarians, 1974.

_____. *Blacks in the Pacific Northwest, 1788–1974: A. Bibliography of Published Works and of Unpublished Source Materials on the Life and Contributions of Black People in the Pacific Northwest.* Monticello, IL: Council of Planning Librarians, 1975.

_____. *Blacks in the Pacific Northwest: 1788–1972. A Bibliography of Published Works and of Unpublished Source Materials on the Life and Contributions of Black People in the Pacific Northwest.* Monticello, IL: Council of Planning Librarians, 1972.

Early, Sarah J. *Life and Labors of Rev. Jordan W. Early: One of the Pioneers of African Methodism in the West and South.* Stratford, NH: Ayer, 1977.

Farmer, George Luther. *Education: The Dilemma of the Afro-American.* Los Angeles: University of Southern California, 1969. Education in the West.

Finkelman, Paul, ed. *Slavery in the North and West.* Articles on American Slavery Series, Vol. 5. New York: Garland Publishing, 1989.

Fletcher, F. Marion. *The Negro in the Drug Manufacturing Industry.* Philadelphia: Wharton School of Finance, 1970. Includes the West, and Los Angeles.

Foner, Philip S., and George E. Walker, eds. *Proceedings of the Black State Conventions, 1840–1865.* Philadelphia: Temple University Press, 1979. Vol. II includes conventions in California, Kansas, and Missouri.

Forbes, Jack D. *Afro-Americans in the Far West.* Washington, DC: Government Printing Office, 1969.

_____. *Afro-Americans in the Far West: A Handbook for Educators.* Berkeley: Far West Laboratory for Educational Research and Development, 1968.

Frazier, Edward Franklin. *Bourgeoisie Noire* (Black Bourgeoisie). Glencoe, IL: Free Press and Falcon's Wing Press, 1957.

Gibbs, Mifflin Wistar. *Shadow and Light: An Autobiography with Reminiscences of the Last and Present Century.* Washington, DC: 1902; reprinted, New York: Arno Press and the New York Times, 1968; reprinted, Lincoln: University of Nebraska Press, 1995. Autobiography of public official and newspaper editor.

Glasrud, Bruce A., and James A. Halseth, eds. *The Northwest Mosaic: Minority Conflicts in Pacific Northwest History.* Boulder: Pruett Publishing, 1977.

Gordon, Taylor. *Born to Be.* Blacks in the American West Series. New York: Civici, Friede, 1929; reprinted, Lincoln: University of Nebraska Press, 1995. Growing up in a Black community in White Sulphur Springs.

Grafton Tyler Brown: Black Artist in the West. Oakland Museum, Oakland,
California. February 11–April 22, 1972. Catalogue.

Hardaway, Roger D. *A Narrative Bibliography of the African-American Frontier: Blacks in the Rocky Mountain West, 1535–1912.* Studies in
American History, Vol. 9. Lewiston, NY: Edwin Mellen Press, 1995.

Harris, Theodore D., ed. *Negro Frontiersman: The Western Memoirs of Henry
O. Flipper, First Negro Graduate of West Point.* El Paso: Texas
Western College Press, 1963.

_____, ed. *Black Frontiersman: The Memoirs of Henry O. Flipper, First
Black Graduate of West Point.* Fort Worth: Texas Christian University Press, 1997.

Harris, William H. *The Harder We Run: Black Workers since the Civil War.*
New York: Oxford University Press, 1982.

Heard, J. Norman. *The Black Frontiersmen: Adventures of Negroes Among
American Indians, 1528–1918.* New York: John Day Company, 1969.

Howard, John C. *The Negro in the Lumber Industry.* Philadelphia: Wharton
School of Finance, 1970. Includes Arizona, California, Idaho, Montana, Oregon, and Washington.

Howell, Ann C., and Chandler White. *Old West: A Salute to Black Inventors.*
Chicago: Black Inventors Activity Books, 1992.

Johannsen, Robert W. *Frontier Politics and the Sectional Conflict: The Pacific
Northwest on the Eve of the Civil War.* Seattle: University of Washington Press, 1955. Chapter on settlers and slavery.

Johnson, Reginald A. *The West Coast and the Negro.* n.p., 1944.

Katz, William Loren. *Black People Who Made the Old West.* New York:
Crowell, 1977; reprinted, Lawrenceville, NJ: Africa World Press,
1992. Juvenile.

_____. *The Black West.* New York: Simon and Schuster, 1996.

_____. *The Black West: A Documentary and Pictorial History.* Garden
City, NY: Doubleday, 1973; reprinted, New York: Simon and Schuster, 1996.

_____. *The Black West: A Documentary and Pictorial History of the Afri-
can American Role in the Westward Expansion of the United States.*
New York: Simon and Schuster, 1996.

Koziara, Edward C. *The Negro in the Hotel Industry.* Philadelphia: Wharton
School of Finance, 1968. Los Angeles and San Francisco included.

Larrie, Reginald. *Corners of Black History.* New York: Vantage Press, 1971.
Short biographies include Cherokee Bill, Henry O. Flipper, Ben Hodges
and William A. Leidesdorff. Juvenile.

Lay, Shawn, ed. *The Invisible Empire in the West: Toward a New Historical
Appraisal of the Ku Klux Klan of the 1920s.* Urbana: University of Illinois Press, 1992.

Love, Nat. *The Life and Adventures of Nat Love: Better Known in the Cattle
Country as "Deadwood Dick."* Blacks in the American West Series.
Los Angeles, 1907; reprinted, New York: Arno Press and the New

York Times, 1968; reprinted, Lincoln: University of Nebraska Press, 1995.

Lovingood, Penman. *A Negro Seer: The Life and Work of Dr. R. S. Lovingood, Educator, Churchman and Race Leader, by Penman Lovingood.* Compton: The Lovingood Company, 1963. Biography of Lovingood, Wiley College instructor at Marshall, Texas.

Lynk, Miles V. *The Black Troopers.* New York: AMS Press, 1998.

McGowen, Tom. *African-Americans in the Old West.* Cornerstones of Freedom Series. Danbury, CT: Children's Press, 1998. Juvenile.

Middleton, Stephen. *Black Laws in the Old Northwest: A Documentary History.* Westport, CT: Greenwood Publishing Group, 1993.

Miller, Robert H. *Mountain Men,* Reflections of a Black Cowboy Series. Morristown, NJ: Silver Burdett Press, 1991.

_____. *Pioneers,* Reflections of a Black Cowboy Series. Morristown, NJ: Silver Burdett Press, 1991. Juvenile.

Monceaux, Morgan. *My Heroes, My People: African Americans and Native Americans of the West.* New York: Frances Foster Books, 1999. Portraits of Blacks, Native Americans, and mixed-heritage people. Juvenile.

Monographs: Blacks in the West. San Francisco African American Historical and Cultural Society Manuscript Series no. 1. San Francisco: The Society, 1976.

Morrison, Michael A. *Slavery and the American West: The Eclipse of Manifest Destiny and the Coming of the Civil War.* Chapel Hill: University of North Carolina Press, 1997. Territorial issues and the origins of the Civil War.

_____. *The Story of Nat Love.* Morristown, NJ: Silver Press, 1995. Juvenile.

Nasatir, A. P. *The Mountain Men and the Fur Trade of the Far West.* Glendale, CA: Arthur H. Clark Company, 1965. Chapters on Jacques Clamorgan and James Beckwourth.

Northrup, Herbert Roof. *The Negro in the Aerospace Industry.* Philadelphia: Wharton School of Finance, 1968. Includes California and Washington.

Northrup, Herbert Roof, and Alan B. Batchelder. *The Negro in the Rubber Tire Industry.* Philadelphia: Wharton School of Finance, 1969. Includes California cities.

Northwest Black Pioneers: A Centennial Tribute. Seattle, WA: BON, 1987.

Northwest Journal of African and Black American Studies.

Parry, Ellwood. *The Image of the Indian and the Black Man in American Art, 1590–1900.* New York: G. Braziller, 1974.

Peltier, Jerome. *Black Harris.* Fairfield, WA: Ye Galleon Press, 1986. Biography of trapper in the Rockies and Northwest.

Pelz, Ruth. *Black Heroes of the Wild West.* Seattle: Open Hand, 1989. Juvenile.

Porter, Kenneth Wiggins. *The Negro on the American Frontier*. American Negro, History and Literature Series. New York: Arno Press, 1971. Blacks, pioneer life and relations with Native Americans.

_____. *The Negro on the American Frontier,* ed. Jack Ravage. Stratford, NH: Ayer, 1996.

Quay, William Howard. *The Negro in the Chemical Industry*. Philadelphia: Wharton School of Finance, 1969. Includes the West, specifically Long Beach and Los Angeles.

Ravage, John W. *Black Pioneers: Images of the Black Experience on the North American Frontier*. Salt Lake City: University of Utah Press, 1997. Nearly 200 photographs of Blacks on the frontier.

Rawick, George P., ed. *The American Slave: A Complete Autobiography. Arkansas, Colorado, Minnesota, Missouri, Oregon and Washington Narratives*. Westport, CT: Greenwood Publishing Company, 1977. Transcriptions of narratives for the 1936–1938 Federal Writers' Project.

Redkey, Edwin S. *Black Exodus*. New Haven: Yale University Press, 1969.

Roumasset, Charles A. , and Edward N. Smith. *The Negro in the West, Some Facts Relating to Social and Economic Conditions: 1, the Negro Worker*. San Francisco: Bureau of Labor Statistics, Department of Labor, 1966.

_____. *The Negro in the West, Some Facts Relating to Social and Economic Conditions: 2, Negro Consumer*. San Francisco: Bureau of Labor Statistics, Department of Labor, 1966.

_____. *The Negro in the West, Some Facts Relating to Social and Economic Conditions: 3, Negro Family*. San Francisco: Bureau of Labor Statistics, Department of Labor, 1967.

Rowan, Richard L *The Negro in the Steel Industry*. Philadelphia: Wharton School of Finance, 1968. Includes Arizona, California, Colorado, Oregon, Utah, and Washington.

Russell, Ross. *Jazz Style in Kansas City and the Southwest*. Berkeley: University of California Press, 1971.

Sadoux, Jean-Jacques. *Racism in the Western Film from D. W. Griffith to John Ford: Indians and Blacks*. Brooklyn, NY: Revisionist Press, 1980.

Salsbury, Stephen. *Essays on the History of the American West*. Hinsdale, IL: The Dryden Press, 1975.

A Salute to Black Pioneers. Empak Black History Publication, Vol. 3. Chicago: Empak Publishers, 1996. Juvenile.

Samuels, Howard J. *Remarks to University of California Centennial Symposium on Prejudice and Industry, Berkeley, Calif., March 26, 1968*. Washington, DC: U.S. Government Printing Office, 1968.

Savage, W. Sherman. *Blacks in the West, 1830–1890*. Westport, CT: Greenwood Press, 1977.

Schlissel, Lillian. *Black Frontiers: A History of African American Heroes in the Old West*. New York: Simon and Schuster Books for Young Readers, 1995. Juvenile.

Smith, Theodore C. *The Liberty and Free Soil Parties in the Northwest.* n.p, 1897; reprinted, New York: Arno Press, 1970.

Suggs, Henry Lewis, ed. *The Black Press in the Middle West, 1865–1985.* Contributions in Afro-American and African Studies, 177. Westport, CT: Greenwood Publishing Group, 1996. Includes Iowa, Kansas, Nebraska, Oklahoma, and South Dakota.

Taylor, Quintard. *The Forging of a Black Community: Seattle's Central District, from 1870 through the Civil Rights Era.* Emil and Kathleen Sick Lecture-Book Series in Western History and Biography. Seattle: University of Washington Press, 1994.

————. *In Search of the Racial Frontier: African Americans in the American West, 1528–1990.* New York: W. W. Norton, 1998.

Thieblot, Armand J. *The Negro in the Banking Industry.* Philadelphia: Wharton School of Finance, 1970. Includes Denver, Los Angeles, Phoenix, San Francisco, and Seattle.

Trelease, Allen W. *White Terror: The Ku Klux Klan Conspiracy and Southern Reconstruction.* New York: 1971.

Turner, Herschell. *Black West Coloring Book.* Spring Lakes, MI: All Media Productions, 1992. Children.

————. *Black West Print Set.* Spring Lakes, MI: All Media Productions, 1992.

Turner, Herschell, and Gerald Blanchard. *The Black West Activity Guide.* Spring Lakes, MI: All Media Productions, 1992.

Underwood, Willard A. , and Ralph E. Ferguson. Black Americans in the Southwest. From the collected work, "The Current Status of Minorities in the Southwest" papers presented at the society for Intercultural Education, Training, and Research, Chicago, 24–27 February 1977. ERIC. ED 145 994. Migration patterns and population trends.

United States Bureau of Labor Statistics. *The Negro and the West...Some Facts Relating to Social and Economic Conditions.* San Francisco: U.S. Department of Labor, 1965-1967. Three volumes on (1) the worker, (2) the consumer, and (3) the family.

United States Department of Labor and Department of Commerce. *The Negro in the West.* Washington, DC: U.S. Government Printing Office, 1968.

Unseld, Teresa S., Bev Dana, et al., eds. *Portfolios: African-Americans of the Old West.* White Plains, NY: Dale Seymour Publications, 1997. Juvenile.

Wright, Courtni C. *Wagon Train: A Family Goes West in 1865.* New York: Holiday, 1995. Juvenile.

Young, Kenneth M. *As Some Things Appear on the Plains and Among the Rockies in Mid-Summer.* Spartanburg, SC: Press of W. Al. Fowler, lessee, Herald Printing Establishment, 189? Black traveler recounts cross-country visit. Library of Congress pamphlet.

Yount, Lisa. *Frontier of Freedom: African Americans in the West*. Library of African-American History Series. New York: Facts on File, 1997. Frontier and pioneer life. Juvenile.

Cowhands

Black Cowboys. African American Achievers Series. Broomall, PA: Chelsea House Publishers, 1997.

Christman, Harry E. *The River of Ladders: The Story of I. P. (Print) Olive*. Denver: Sage, 1962. Also discusses Black cowhand Jim Kelly.

Clark, Charlotte R. *Black Cowboy: The Story of Nat Love*. Eau Claire, WI: Em M. Hale, 1970. Biography for juveniles of implausible cowboy.

De Angelis, Gina. *The Black Cowboys*. Broomall, PA: Chelsea House, 1997. Juvenile.

Downey, Bill. *Tom Bass, Black Horseman*. St. Louis: Saddle and Bridle, 1975. Biography of horse trainer from Mexico, Missouri.

Durham, Philip, and Everett L. Jones. *The Negro Cowboys*. New York: Dodd, Mead, 1965; reprinted, Lincoln: University of Nebraska Press, 1983. The first major popular book on the subject.

————. *The Adventures of the Negro Cowboys*. New York: Dodd, Mead, 1966. Juvenile. Based on previous book.

Felton, H. W. *Nat Love: Negro Cowboy*. New York: Dodd, Mead, 1969. Juvenile.

French, Philip. *Westerns: Aspects of a Genre*. New York: Oxford University Press, 1981.

Knill, Harry. *The Black Cowboy*. Livonia, MI: Bellerophon, 1993. Juvenile.

McCafferty, Jim, and Florence S. Davis. *Holt and the Cowboys*. Gretna, LA: Pelican Publishing Company, 1993. Juvenile. Romanticized biography of Holt Collier.

McGowen, Tom. *African-Americans in the Old West*. Cornerstones of Freedom Series. Danbury, CT: Children's Press, 1998. Juvenile.

Miller, Robert H. *Cowboys*. Reflections of a Black Cowboy Series. Morristown, NJ: Silver Burdett Press, 1992.

————. *Reflections of a Black Cowboy*. Englewood Cliffs, NJ: Silver Burdett Press, 1991.

————. *Reflections of a Black Cowboy*, 2^d ed. Parsippany, NJ: Silver Burdett Press, 1998.

Randall, Lawanda. *Nelson Jackson-Cowboy*. Washington, DC: Directions, Production Services, Inc., 1997. Juvenile.

Stewart, Paul W., and Wallace Yvonne Ponce *Black Cowboys*. Broomfield, CO: Phillips Publishing Company, 1986. Biographical sketches of approximately 100 Black people presented in a "coffee table" book. Stewart is the founder of the Black American West Museum and Heritage Center in Denver.

Wukovits, John F. *The Black Cowboys*. Broomall, PA: Chelsea House, 1997.

Theses and Dissertations:

Alexander, Charles C. "Invisible Empire in the Southwest: The Ku Klux Klan in Texas, Louisiana, Oklahoma, and Arkansas, 1920–1930." Ph.D. diss., University of Texas, 1962.

Bailey, David Thomas. "Slavery and the Churches: The Old Southwest." Ph.D. diss., University of California, Berkeley, 1979.

Berwanger, Eugene H. "Western Anti-Negro Sentiment and Laws, 1846–1860: A Factor in the Slavery Extension Controversy." Ph.D. diss., University of Illinois at Urbana, 1964.

Casavantes, Edward Joseph. "Reading Achievement and In-Grade Retention Rate Differentials for Mexican-American and Black Students in Selected States of the Southwest." Ph.D. diss., University of Southern California, 1973.

Cavanagh, Helen M. "Anti-Slavery Sentiment and Politics in the Northwest, 1844–1860." Ph.D. diss., University of Chicago, 1938.

Class, Donna Kirty, et al. "Contributions by Blacks to Social Welfare History in the Early West: A Group Thesis." MSW thesis, University of Denver, 1974.

Hardaway, Roger D. "The African American Frontier: Blacks in the Rocky Mountain West, 1535–1912." DA thesis, University of North Dakota, 1995.

Hart, Charles Desmond. "Congressmen and the Expansion of Slavery into the Territories: A Study in Attitudes, 1846–61." Ph.D. diss., University of Washington.

Harvey, James R. "Negroes in Colorado." Master's thesis, University of Denver, 1941.

Henderson, Archie Maree. "Introduction of the Negroes into the Pacific Northwest, 1788–1842." Master's thesis, University of Washington, 1949.

Jackson, Joseph Sylvester. "The Colored Marine Employees Benevolent Association of the Pacific, 1921–1934; or Implications of Vertical Mobility for Negro Stewards in Seattle." Master's thesis, University of Washington, 1939.

Johnson, Lulu M. "The Problem of Slavery in the Old Northwest, 1787–1858." Ph.D. diss., University of Iowa, 1942.

Lack, Paul D. "Urban Slavery in the Southwest." Ph.D. diss., Texas Tech University, 1973.

Lamm, Alan K. "Buffalo Soldier Chaplains: A Case Study of Five Black United States Army Chaplains, 1884–1901." Ph.D. diss., University of South Carolina, 1995.

Organ, David Joseph. "The Historical Geography of African-American Frontier Settlement." Ph.D. diss., University of California-Berkeley, 1995.

Pohlmann, Bruce Edward. "Ethnicity, Class, and Culture: Multicultural Educa-
    tion in the Rural Northwest." Ph.D. diss., University of California,
    Berkeley, 1989.
Rankin, Dan F. "The Role of the Negro Office Holders in the Reconstruction of
    the Southwest." Master's thesis, North Texas State College, 1954.
Rhodes, Ethel C. "Negroes in Pacific Coast History Prior to 1865." Master's
    thesis, Howard University, 1940.
Scally, William. "The Question of National Power Over Slavery in The Terri-
    tory, 1846–1865." Master's thesis, University of California, Berkeley,
    1928.
Taylor, Quintard "A History of Blacks in the Pacific Northwest, 1788–1970."
    Ph.D. diss., University of Minnesota, 1977.
Thorpe, Reed. "The Southwest and Slavery." Master's thesis, University of
    Utah, 1943.
Voegeli, V. Jacques III. "The Northwest and the Negro During the Civil War."
    Ph.D. diss., Tulane University, 1965.
Wengi, Richard Adolf. "Slavery in the Trans-Mississippi West." Master's the-
    sis, Humboldt State University, 1964.
Young, Joseph A. "Oscar Micheaux's Novels: Black Apologies for White Op-
    pression." Ph.D. diss., University of Nebraska, Lincoln, 1984.
    Analysis of Micheaux's works that reflect some of his experiences in
    the West.

Black Newspapers and Periodicals:

Pittsburgh Courier. Pittsburgh, PA. 1910. West coast edition from W.W.II
    into the 1950s.

Other:

ABC's of Black American Cowboys, Trailblazers and Soldiers. Freehold, NJ:
    Afro-American Heritage House, 1983. Filmstrip-cassette.
The Black West. Norwood, MA: Beacon Films, 1982. Videorecording. Late
    1800s through early 1900s.
Don't Leave Out the Cowboys. San Francisco: AM Videos, 1988. Videore-
    cording.

Art and Artists

Articles:

"Artist, Model, Cowboy." *Soldiers* 51 (July 1996). Veteran and artist researches roles of Blacks in the West.

Balch, Jack. "Democracy at Work: The People's Art Service Center in St. Louis." *Magazine of Art*, February 1943. A WPA program for Blacks.

"The Black Man's Gallery." *Urban West* 1 (November/December 1967). San Francisco gallery devoted to works of Black artists.

Bracken, Lil. "The Lynching of Emmett Till." *New Odyssey* 1 (Spring 1992). Emmett Till, murdered in Mississippi in 1955, is memorialized in the Dr. Martin Luther King statue in Denver.

"Church Muralist." *Ebony*, June 1952. Aaron Miller's work at the Emanuel Church of God in San Francisco.

Clarke, George Elliott. "Contesting a Model Blackness: A Mediation on African-Canadian African Americanism, or the Structure of African Canadianite." *Essays on Canadian Writing*, no. 63 (Spring 1998). African Canadians have developed their own forms of art and literature.

"Dallas Boy Born Without Hands Excels as a Gifted Artist." *Jet*, 1 March 1999. Desmond Blair, age 12, is outstanding artist at the Dallas W. E. Greiner Middle School and the Academy For the Exploratory Arts.

Douglas, Emory. "Art in Service for the People." *Black Scholar* 9 (November 1977). Philosophy of Douglas, former artist for the Black Panther Party newspaper.

Dunitz, Robin J. "The African-American Murals of Los Angeles: Putting Art where People Live." *American Visions*, December-January 1994.

Ennis, Michael. "Shock Therapy: Austin Painter Michael Ray Charles." *Texas Monthly*, June 1997.

FitzSimons, Casey. "'Alchemy' at New Langton Arts." *Artweek* 29 (March 1998). Review of exhibition by Thomas Allen Harris and Lyle Ashton Harris in San Francisco.

Gite, Lloyd. "Artfully Inspired." *Black Enterprise*, September 1996.   Joyce
    Hunt, the owner of Mitchie's Fine Black Art in Austin, Texas.

Hall, Paula. "Vaquero: The First American Cowboy." *Gilcrease Magazine of
    American History and Art* 13 (1991).

Harris, Joanne. "Portfolio." *American Visions*, August–September 1996. Pro-
    files of artists Barbara Thomas and Marita Dingus of Seattle and Kira
    Lynn Harris of Los Angeles.

Johnston, Thomas F. "Blacks in Art Music in Western Canada." *Canadian
    Journal of Anthropology* 19/2 (1981). Blacks in classical and jazz mu-
    sic.

"K.C. in Swingtime and Now." *International Review of African American Art*
    14 (1997). Jazz music in Kansas City during the 1930s and its depic-
    tion in Black art.

Kandel, Susan. "Museum of African American Art, Los Angeles: Exhibit."
    Arts Magazine 66 (December 1991).

LeFalle-Collins, Lizzetta. "Grafton Tyler Brown Selling the Promise of the
    West." *International Review of African American Art* 12 (Winter
    1995).

————. "The Mexican Connection: The New Negro and Border Crossings."
    American Visions, December-January 1996. Black artists influenced by
    Mexican muralists.

"Lynching as a Japanese Sculptor Sees It." *Christian Century* 52 (13 February
    1935). Isamu Noguchi's bronze statue of a Black man lynched in
    Sherman, Texas.

Miller, Kelly. "Art as a Cure for Lynching." *Christian Century* 52 (17 April
    1935). Letter concerning article "Lynching as a Japanese Sculptor Sees
    It," above.

Mitchell, Charles Dee. "F. L. 'Doc' Spellmon and Ruth Mae McCrane at the
    Museum of African-American Life and Culture." *Art in America* 84
    (July 1996). Two Texas artists exhibit at the Dallas gallery.

Montgomery, Evangeline J. "Southern California Black Art Activities." *Phase
    II* (Spring 1970).

————. "Black Art Activities." *Phase II* (Summer 1970).

Myers, Chris. "View from South Central." *International Review of African
    American Art* 13 (Winter 1996). The Art Team of LA works with tal-
    ented youth.

Pipkin, Loretta. "Loretta Pipkin: Finding My Place." *International Review of
    African American Art* 13 (1996). Textile designer of Dallas.

Rabey, Steve. "Palette of Forgiveness." *Christianity Today*, 7 October 1996.
    Profile of painter Thomas Blackshear II of Blackshear Gallery, Colorado
    Springs.

Remington, Frederic. "Artist Rides with 10th U.S. Cavalry, A Scout With the
    Buffalo-Soldiers, Famous Negro Dragoons." *Butterfield Express: His-
    torical Newspaper of the Southwest* 14 (August—September 1966).

_____. "A Scout with the Buffalo Soldiers." *Century Magazine* 37 (April 1889); reprinted in *Pacific Historian* 12 (1968); reprinted in *Frederic Remington's Own West*, ed. Harold McCracken. New York: Dial Press, 1960; reprinted in *The Black Military Experience in the American West*, ed. John M. Carroll. New York: Liveright Publishing Corp., 1971; reprinted in *Pacific Historian* 12 (Spring 1968).

_____. "Two Gallant Young Cavalrymen." *Harper's Weekly* (March 22, 1890).

_____. "Vagabonding with the Tenth Horse." *Cosmopolitan Magazine* 22 (February 1897); reprinted in *The Black Military Experience in the American West*, ed. John M. Carroll. New York: Liveright Publishing Corp., 1971.

Story, Rosalyn M. "Guardians of Peace in Bronze." *American Visions*, October-November 1998. Freedman's Memorial burial site and sculpture park in Dallas, plus an article on its designer, sculptor David Newton.

Tarshis, Jerome. "San Francisco." *Artforum* 9 (October 1970). Works of five Bay area artists.

_____. "San Francisco." *Artforum* 9 (December 1970). Notes 3rd anniversary of Black Man's Art Gallery.

Taylor, Bob. "California Black Craftsmen." *Phase II* (Spring 1970).

"Thaddeus McCall: Impatient Young Artist." *Sepia*, August 1967. Profile of painter who owns Houston's Hemis Art Gallery.

Wright, Melanie. "Dallas Museum of Art: Showcasing African American Artists." *Time*, 18 January 1990.

Books:

Adele, Lynne. *Black History, Black Vision: The Visionary Image in Texas.* The Gallery: University of Texas at Austin, 1989. Exhibition catalog, Archer M. Huntington Art Gallery, University of Texas at Austin and the University of Texas Institute of Texan Cultures at San Antonio, 1989. Videorecording also available.

Arrowhead Allied Arts Council. *Arrowhead Allied Arts Council Presents Festival of Arts, May 2–12, 1968.* San Bernardino: The Arts Council, 1968. Catalogue of African American art exhibit.

Biggers, John Thomas, Carroll Simms, and John Edward Weems. *Black Art in Houston: The Texas Southern University Experience.* College Station: Texas A&M University Press, 1978.

A Black Community Album Before 1930. Halifax: Art Gallery, Mount Saint Vincent University, 1983. Photographic exhibition. Organized by Henry Bishop and Frank Boyd of the Black Cultural Centre for Nova Scotia.

The Black Military Experience in the American West (The Black Military Art Show, Fort Leavenworth, Kansas, Dec. 1973–Feb. 1974). John M.

Carroll military art collection: Fort Leavenworth Museum, 1973. Art catalog.

Blackman's Art Gallery, San Francisco. *Blackman's Art Gallery: Dedicated to Black Culture*. San Francisco: S. F. Golden Printers, 1970. Brochure.

Bunch, Lonnie G. *Black Angelenos: The Afro-American in Los Angeles 1850–1950*: [Exhibition] June 11, 1988–March 6, 1989. Los Angeles: California Afro-American Museum, 1988.

California Black Artists. College of Marin Art Gallery, Kentfield, California. March 13–April 10, 1970. Catalogue.

California Black Craftsmen. Mills College Art Gallery, Oakland, California. February 15–March 8, 1972. Catalogue.

Carroll, John M. *The U.S. Army Military History Research Collection Presents John M. Carroll's Collection: Illustrations of the Black Soldier in the West*. n.p., 1973. Illustrations for an October 1973 military art show, limited to 30 copies.

Cochran, Jo, et al., eds. *Gathering Ground: New Writing and Art by Northwest Women of Color*. Seattle: Seal Press, 1984. A cross-cultural anthology.

Dunitz, Robin J., and James Prigoff. *Painting the Towns: Murals of California*. Los Angeles: RJD Enterprises, 1997. Black and Latino public art.

Evans, Walter O. *The Walter O. Evans Collection of African American Art*. Detroit, MI: W. O. Evans Collection, 1991.

Grafton Tyler Brown: Black Artist in the West. Oakland Museum, Oakland, California. February 11–April 22, 1972. Catalogue.

International Review of African American Art. Los Angeles. 1991.

Kinfolks: A Collection of Art by Afro-American Artists: An Exhibition. Dallas: South Dallas Cultural Center, Art Gallery, 1990. Exhibit catalogue.

Lewis, Floyd. *African American Art and Artists*. Berkeley: University of California Press, 1990.

Los Angeles 1972: A Panorama of Black Artists. Los Angeles County Museum of Art, Los Angeles, California. February 8–March 19, 1972. Catalogue.

Mumford, Esther Hall. *Calabash: A Guide to the History, Culture, and Art of African Americans in Seattle and King County, Washington*. Seattle: Ananse Press, 1993.

Museum of African-American Life and Culture. *They Showed the Way: An Exhibit of Black Texas Women, 1836–1986*. Dallas: Museum of African-American Life and Culture, 1986.

Parry, Ellwood. *The Image of the Indian and the Black Man in American*.

Robbins, Carolyn C. *Lew Davis: "The Negro in America's Wars" and Other Major Paintings: Scottsdale Center for the Arts, Scottsdale, Arizona, September 13, 1990–November 11, 1990*. Scottsdale: Scottsdale Center for the Arts, 1990. Art exhibition catalogue.

Samuels, Willfred D. *Raymond Lark: American Artist of Tradition and Diversity*. Salt Lake City: Utah Museum of Fine Arts, 1989. Catalog of exhibitions.

The Negro in American Art. Los Angeles: California University Art Galleries, 1966. A catalogue of an exhibition.

Wardlow, Alvia J. *The Art of John Biggers: View from the Upper Room*. Houston: Museum of Fine Arts and Harry N. Abrams, 1995. Exhibit book.

West Coast 74, Black Image: 1974 Invitational Exhibition: [Exhibition Dates, E. B. Crocker Art Gallery, Sacramento, California, September 13–13 October, 1974, Los Angeles Municipal Art Gallery, Barnsdall Park, Los Angeles, California, January 22–16 February, 1975]. Sacramento: Crocker Art Gallery, 1974. 20th century Black art.

Willis, Deborah, ed. *J. P. Ball Daguerrean and Studio Photographer*. New York: Garland Publishing, 1993.

Theses and Dissertations:

Berry, Wilbert Lee. "The Effectiveness of Teaching Art in the Negro Elementary Schools in Missouri." Master's thesis, Colorado State College of Education, 1941.

Okelo, Arnethia Wright. "A Comparative Study of the Recommended Art Education curricula of Kenya and California in terms of Achieving the Perceived Goals/Needs of Kenyans and Afro-Americans." Ph.D., University of California, Berkeley, 1976.

Black Journal:

Phase II: Journal of Black Art Renaissance. Berkeley. 1970–? Black Heritage Class, University of California.

Other:

Black On Black: Forever Free. KMTV Omaha, James A. Nelson, producer, 1981. Review of exhibit "Forever Free," art by Black women, 1862–1980, Omaha's Josyln Museum. Videorecording.

Robert Colescott. University of Colorado-Boulder Department of Fine Arts interview of Tucson artist. Videorecording.

James Beckwourth and Edward Rose

Articles:

Blenkinsop, Willis. "Edward Rose." Chapter in *The Mountain Men and the Fur Trade of the Far West*, ed. LeRoy Hafen, Vol. 9. Glendale, CA: Arthur H. Clark, 1972.

Brooks, Jacqueline. "This is the Pass that Beckwourth Found." *National Motorist* 16 (August 1939). Includes short biography.

Burt, Olive W. "Edward Rose." Section in *Negroes in the Early West*. New York: Julian Messner, 1969. Juvenile.

————. James P. Beckwourth." Section in *Negroes in the Early West*. New York: Julian Messner, 1969. Juvenile.

Camp, Charles L. "Edward Rose." Section in *James Clyman: American Frontiersman, 1792–1881*. San Francisco: California Historical Society, 1928. Beckwourth's life between 1854 and 1866, following the years covered in his autobiography.

Ewing, Belle C. "Adventure was His Name." *California Highway Patrolman* 30 (June 1966). Information on Beckwourth.

Hafen, LeRoy. "The Last Years of James Beckwourth." *Colorado Magazine* 5 (August 1928).

Heard, J. Norman. "Jim Beckwourth, the Mountain Man." Chapter in *The Black Frontiersmen: Adventures of Negroes Among American Indians, 1528–1918*. New York: John Day Company, 1969.

————. "That Rascal Ed Rose." Chapter in *The Black Frontiersmen: Adventures of Negroes Among American Indians, 1528–1918*. New York: John Day Company, 1969.

Holmes, Reuben. "The Five Scalps." Edited by Stella M. Drumm. *Glimpses of the Past* 5 (January–March 1938). Article about Edward Rose. Holmes knew Rose whom he inexplicably calls "a white man."

Hughes, Langston. "James P. Beckwourth: Frontiersman." Chapter in *Famous Negro Heroes of America*. New York: Dodd, Mead and Company, 1966. Juvenile, but well-written.

Hutchinson, William H. "Mountain Man of Color." *Westways* 41 (July 1949).

"Jim Beckwourth and Ina Coolbirth." *Pony Express* 14 (July 1947).

Katz, William Loren. "James Beckwourth: Crow Chief and Fur Trader." Chapter in *Black People Who Made the Old West*. New York: Thomas Y. Crowell, 1977.

McClure, Galen. "James P. Beckwourth—Trail Blazer of the Sierra." *California Highway Patrolman* 13 (February 1950).

Morgan, Charles. "Huckster on Horseback." *Westways* 60 (November 1968).

Oswald, Delmont R. "James Beckwourth." Chapter in *The Mountain Men and the Fur Trade of the Far West*, Ed. LeRoy R. Hafen, Vol. 6. Glendale, CA: Arthur H. Clark, 1968: reprinted, chapter in *Trappers of the Far West*, ed. LeRoy R. Hafen. Lincoln: University of Nebraska Press, 1983.

Porter, Kenneth Wiggins. "Negroes and the Fur Trade." *Minnesota History* 15 (1934).

————. "On Jim Beckwourth: A Review Essay." *Journal of Ethnic Studies* 1 (Fall 1973). Though a review of two books on Beckwourth, Porter also critiques Beckwourth's life.

Savage, W. Sherman. "James Beckwourth—Negro Fur Trader." *Negro History Bulletin* 17 (March 1954).

"Varied Parts Played Negroes in the American Fur Trade." *Minnesota History* 15 (December 1934).

Wells, Harry L. "Beckwourth's Ride." *Pony Express Courier* 2 (October 1935).

Books:

Beckwourth, James P., and Thomas D. Bonner. *The Life and Adventures of James P. Beckwourth, Mountaineer, Scout, Pioneer, and Chief of the Crow Nation of Indians*. New York: Harper and Brother, 1856; reprinted, Charles G. Leland, ed., London: T. Fisher Unwin, 1892; reprinted, Bernard De Voto, ed., New York: Alfred A. Knopf, 1931; reprinted, Delmont R. Oswald, ed., Lincoln: University of Nebraska Press, 1972.

Blassingame, Wyatt. *Jim Beckwourth: Black Trapper and Indian Chief*. Champaign, IL: Garrard Publishing, 1973; reprinted, Broomall, PA: Chelsea House, 1991. Juvenile.

Burt, Olive W. *Jim Beckwourth: Crow Chief*. New York: Julian Messner, 1957. Juvenile.

Cleland, Robert G. *This Reckless Breed of Men: The Trapper and Fur Traders of the Southwest*. New York: Alfred A. Knopf, 1950. Jim Beckwourth profiled.

Cortesi, Lawrence. *Jim Beckwourth; Explorer-Patriot of the Rockies*. New York: Criterion Books, 1971. Historical inaccuracies and fantasy.

Dolan, Sean. *James Beckwourth*. Broomall, PA: Chelsea House, 1992.

Felton, H. W. *Edward Rose, Negro Trailblazer*. New York: Dodd, Mead, 1967. Juvenile.

_____. *Jim Beckwourth, Negro Mountain Man*. New York: Dodd, Mead, 1966; reprinted, 1996. Juvenile.

Hafen, Ann W. *The Lost Crow*. Denver: Aiken and Bagshaw, 1935. Jim Beckwourth.

Jim Beckwourth: Adventures of a Mountain Man. Mahwah, NJ: Troll Communications, 1992. Juvenile.

Mumey, Nolie. *James Pierson Beckwourth, 1856–1866: An Enigmatic Figure of the West: A History of the Latter Years of His Life*. Denver: The Old West Publishing Company, 1957. Limited edition of 500.

Place, Marian T. *Mountain Man: The Life of Jim Beckwourth*. New York: Crowell-Collier Press, 1970. Juvenile.

Shepard, Betty, ed. *Mountain Man, Indian Chief: The Life and Adventures of Jim Beckwourth*. New York: Harcourt, Brace, and World, 1968. Juvenile.

Wilson, Elinor. *Jim Beckwourth: Black Mountain Man and War Chief of the Crows*. Norman: University of Oklahoma Press, 1972. A scholarly attempt to accurately portray Beckwourth's life.

Theses and Dissertations:

Oswald, Delmont R. "James Pierson Beckwourth, 1798–1866." Master's thesis, Brigham Young University, 1967.

Black and Native American Relationships

Articles:

Andrews, Thomas F. "Freedmen in Indian Territory: A Post Civil War Dilemma. *Journal of the West* 4 (June 1965). The freed slaves and their relationship with the Chickasaws and Choctaws.

Baker, Julie Philips. "Black Slavery Among the American Indians." *AB Bookman's Weekly* 89 (February 1992).

Ballenger, T. L. "The Colored High School of the Cherokee Nation." *Chronicles of Oklahoma* 30 (1952).

Bateman, Rebecca Belle. "Africans and Indians: A Comparative Study of the Black Carib and Black Seminole." *Ethnohistory: The Bulletin of the Ohio Valley* 37 (Winter 1990).

Beninato, Stefanie. "Popé, Pose-yemu, and Naranjo: A New Look at Leadership in the Pueblo Revolt of 1680." *New Mexico Historical Review* 65 (October 1990). Black involvement in the revolt.

Bennett, Charles. "The Buffalo Soldiers and the Apache War Chief." *El Palacio* 101 (Summer 1996). Native American reactions to Black troops in New Mexico Territory.

Bentley, Martha M. "The Slaveholding Catawba." *South Carolina Historical Magazine* 92 (April 1991).

Billington, Monroe Lee. "Black Cavalrymen and Apache Indians in New Mexico Territory." *Fort Concho and the South Plains Journal* 22 (Summer 1990).

"Black and Indian Heritage." *Crisis* 101 (February 1994).

Bradley, John Ed. "Buffalo Soldier: In His Quest to become a Coach in the NBA, Kareem Abdul-Jabbar will go Anywhere to gain Experience—Even to an Apache Reservation in Arizona." *Sports Illustrated* 89 (30 November 1998).

Braund, Kathryn E. Holland. "The Creek Indians, Blacks, and Slavery." *Journal of Southern History* 57 (November 1991).

Britten, Thomas A. "The Dismissal of the Seminole-Negro Indian Scouts, 1880–1914." *Fort Concho and the South Plains Journal* 24 (Summer 1992).

_____. "The Seminole-Indian Scouts in the Big Bend." *Journal of Big Bend Studies* 5 (January 1993).

Brooks, James F. "Confounding the Color Line: Indian-Black Relations in Historical and Anthropological Perspective." *American Indian Quarterly* (Winter 1988). Focus on the "Black-Ute Clan."

Brown, Thomas Elton. "Seminole Indian Agents, 1842–1874." *Chronicles of Oklahoma* 51 (1973).

Burkey, Elmer R. "The Thornburgh Battle With the Utes on Milk Creek." *Colorado Magazine* 13 (1936).

Calhoun, Daniel H. "Strategy as Lived: Mixed Communities in the Age of New Nations." *American Indian Quarterly*, Winter 1988. Relationships in Mexico.

Carew, Jan. "United We Stand! Joint Struggles of Native Americans and African Americans in the Columbian Era." *Monthly Review* 44 (July/August 1992). Symposium: Columbus and the New World Order."

Chappell, Kevin. "Black Indians Hit Jackpot in Casino Bonanza." *Ebony*, June 1995.

Chase, D. "American Indians, African Americans: Their Common Histories." *JAMA* 268 (19 August 1992). Letter to the Editor.

Chávez, Fray Angélico. "Pohé-yemo's Representative and the Pueblo Revolt of 1680." *New Mexico Historical Review* 42 (April 1967); reprinted in *The Black Military Experience in the American West*, John M. Carroll, ed. New York: Liveright Press, 1971.

Cornell, Stephen. "Land, Labour and Group Formation: Blacks and Indians in the United States." *Ethnic and Racial Studies* 13 (July 1990).

Davis, John B. "Slavery in the Cherokee Nation." *Chronicles of Oklahoma* 11 (1933).

Dempsey, Mary A. "The Indian Connection" *American Visions*, August-September 1996. Racial mixing between Blacks and Native Americans.

Drotning, Phillip T. "Black Soldiers and Red Men." Chapter in *Black Heroes in Our Nations's History: A Tribute to Those Who Helped Shape America*. New York: Cowles Book Company, 1969. Overview of the 9th and 10th.

Du Chateau, Andre P. "The Creek Nation on the Eve of the Civil War." *Chronicles of Oklahoma* 52 (1974).

Ellison, Mary. "Black Perceptions and Red Images: Indian and Black Literary Links." *Phylon* 44 (March 1983). Looks at shared cultural standards.

Fischer, Leroy H., and Kenny A. Franks. "Victory at Chusto-Talasah." *Chronicles of Oklahoma* 49 (Winter 1971–1971). Civil War action.

Forbes, G. "Part Played by Indian Slavery in Removal of Tribes to Oklahoma." *Chronicles of Oklahoma* 9 (June 1938).

Forbes, Jack D. "The Evolution of the Term Mulatto: A Chapter in Black-Native American Relations." *Journal of Ethnic Studies* 10 (1982).

_____. "The Manipulation of Race, Caste, and Identity: Classifying Afroamericans, Native Americans, and Red-Black People." *Journal of Ethnic Studies* 17 (Winter 1990).

_____. "Mulattoes and People of Color in Anglo-North America: Implications for Black-Indian Relations." *Journal of Ethnic Studies* 12 (1984).

_____. "Mustees, Half-Breeds and Zambos in Anglo North America: Aspects of Black-Indian Relations." *American Indian Quarterly* 7 (1983).

Franks, Kenny A., and Leroy H. Fischer. "Confederate Victory at Chusto-Talasah." *Chronicles of Oklahoma* 49 (Winter 1971–1972).

Gammon, Tim. "Black Freedmen and the Cherokee Nation." *Journal of American Studies* 11 (December 1977.

_____. "The Black Freedmen of the Cherokee Nation." *Negro History Bulletin* 40 (July-August 1977).

Gwaltney, William W. "The Story of the Seminole-Negro Indian Scouts." *Lest We Forget* 4 (October 1996).

Halliburton, Janet. "Black Slavery in the Creek Nation." *Chronicles of Oklahoma* 56 (1978).

Halliburton, R., Jr. "Black Slave Control in the Cherokee Nation." *Journal of Ethnic Studies* 3 (1975).

_____. "Black Slavery Among the Cherokees." *American History Illustrated* 11 (1976).

_____. "Origins of Black Slavery among the Cherokees." *Chronicles of Oklahoma* 52 (Winter 1974–1975).

Hancock, Ian F. "Texas Gullah: The Creole English of the Bracketville Afro-Seminoles." Chapter in *Perspectives on American English*, ed. Joseph L. Dillard. The Hague: Mouton, 1980.

Helms, Mary W. "Negro or Indian? The Changing Identity of a Frontier Population." Chapter in *Old Roots in New Lands: Historical and Anthropological Perspectives on Black Experiences in the Americas*, ed. Ann M. Pescatello. Westport, CT: Greenwood Press, 1977.

Holland, Reid A. "Life in the Cherokee Nation, 1855–1860." *Chronicles of Oklahoma* 49 (1971). Aspects of antebellum slavery.

Huber, Donald L. "White, Red, and Black. The Wyandot Mission at Upper Sandusky." *Timeline* 13 (May 1996).

Hunt, H. F. "Slavery among the Indians of Northwestern America." *Washington Historical Quarterly* 9 (October 1918).

"J. D. Saul Charged with Murder of Indian Wife." *Oregon Spectator* (24 December 1846). Other articles appear on 6 August 1846; 30 December 1851; and 20 October 1853.

James, Parthena Louise. "Reconstruction in the Chickasaw Nation: The Freedman Problem." *Chronicle of Oklahoma* 45 (Spring 1967).

Jelz, Wyatt F. "The Relations of Negroes and Choctaw and Chickasaw Indians." *Journal of Negro History* 33 (January 1948).

Johnson, John Allen. "The Medal of Honor and Sergeant John Ward and Private Pompey Factor." *Arkansas Historical Quarterly* 29 (1970). Two Seminole-Indian Scouts win the Medal of Honor.

Johnston, James Hugo. "Documentary Evidence of Relations of Negroes and Indians." *Journal of Negro History* 14 (1929).

Jones, H. Conger. "Old Seminole Scouts Still Thrive on Border." *Frontier Times* 11 (1934).

Katz, William Loren. "Black and Indian Cooperation and Resistance to Slavery." *Freedomways* 17 (1977).

_____. "Interrace People: Black Indians." *Interrace* 6 (December 1994).

Kendrick, Robb. "The Black Seminole: A Tradition of Courage." *Smithsonian* 22 (August 1991).

Kimmel, Jean. "Rural Wages and Returns to Education: Differences Between Whites, Blacks, and American Indians." *Economics of Education Review* 16 (1997).

King, Wilma. "Multicultural Education at Hampton Institute—The Shawnees: A Case Study, 1900–1923." *Journal of Negro Education* 57 (Fall 1988).

Klos, George E. "Black Seminoles in Territorial Florida." *Southern Historian* 10 (Spring 1989).

_____. "Blacks and the Seminole Removal Debate, 1821–1835." *Florida Historical Quarterly* 68 (July 1989).

Krapf, Kellie A., and Floyd B. Largent, Jr. "The Black Seminole Scouts: Soldiers Who Deserve High Praise." *Persimmon Hill* 24 (Winter 1996).

Krogman, Wilton Marion. "The Racial Composition of the Seminole Indians of Florida and Oklahoma." *Journal of Negro History* 19 (1934).

Littlefield, Daniel F., Jr., and Mary Ann Littlefield. "The Beams Family: Free Blacks in Indian Territory;" *Journal of Negro History* 61 (January 1976). The antebellum family faced murder, enslavement, and forced flight to Mexico.

Littlefield, Daniel F., Jr., and Lonnie E. Underhill. "The Crazy Snake Uprising of 1909: A Red, Black or White Affair?" *Arizona and the West* 20 (Winter 1978).

_____. "Slave 'Revolt' in the Cherokee Nation, 1842." *American Indian Quarterly* 3 (Summer 1977).

Love, Edgar F. "Legal Restrictions on Afro-Indian Relations in Colonial Mexico." *Journal of Negro History* 55 (April 1970).

Lovett, Laura L. "African and Cherokee by Choice." *American Indian Quarterly*, Winter 1988. Race identity in North America.

Magnaghi, Russel. "The Role of Indian Slavery in Colonial St. Louis." *Missouri Historical Society Bulletin* 31 (July 1975).

McDonald, Dedra S. "Intimacy and Empire: Indian-African Interaction in Spanish Colonial New Mexico, 1500–1800." *American Indian Quarterly*, Winter 1988.

McLoughlin, William G. "Cherokee Slaveholders and Baptist Missionaries, 1845–1860." *Historian* 45 (February 1983).

————. "The Choctaw Slave Burning: A Crisis in Mission Work Among the Indians." *Journal of the West* 13 (January 1974). Black slave commits suicide over a murder and mistress is burned at the stake.

————. "Indian Slaveholders and Presbyterian Missionaries, 1837–1861." *Church History* 42 (1973).

————. "Red Indians, Black Slavery and White Racism: America's Slaveholding Indians." *American Quarterly* 26 (October 1974).

"Negro and White Man Fight Over Squaw." *Oregon Spectator* (20 October 1853).

Opala, Joseph A. "Double Homecoming: American Indians with African Roots Return to the 'Rice Coast.'" *West Africa* 3778 (January 22–28, 1990). Black Seminoles in the Gullah delegation to Sierra Leone.

Perdue, Theda. "Cherokee Planters, Black Slaves and African Colonization." *Chronicles of Oklahoma* 60 (Fall 1982).

Peterson, Iver. "Indians in West Turning to Voting Rights Took that Aided Blacks in the South." *New York Times* (3 July 1986). Crow and Northern Cheyenne in Montana.

Pew, Thomas W., Jr. "Boley, Oklahoma: Trial in American Apartheid." *American West* 17 (November-December 1980).

Poatgieter, A. Hermina. "Black Men in the Fur Trade with the Indians." *Gopher Historian* 23 (Winter 1968–1969).

Porter, Kenneth Wiggins. "Abraham." *Phylon* 2, no. 2 (1941). Runaway slave and Seminole leader.

————. "The Cowkeeper Dynasty of the Seminole Indians." *Florida Historical Quarterly* 30 (1952).

————. "The Episode of Osceola's Wife: Fact or Fiction?" *Florida Historical Quarterly* 26 (July 1947).

————. "Farewell to John Horse: An Episode of Seminole Negro Folk History." *Phylon* 8 (1947).

————. "Florida Slaves and Free Negroes in the Seminole War, 1835–1842." *Journal of Negro History* 28 (1943).

————. "The Hawkins Negroes Go to Mexico." *Chronicles of Oklahoma* 24 (Spring 1946).

————. "The Negro Abraham: His Life Among the Seminole Indians." *Florida Historical Society Quarterly* 25 (July 1946).

————. "Negro Guides and Interpreters in the Early Stages of the Seminole War." *Journal of Negro History* 35 (1943).

————. "Negroes and Indians on the Texas Frontier, 1831–1876." *Journal of Negro History* 41 (October 1956).

————. "Negroes and Indians of the Texas Frontier, 1831–1876." *Southwestern Historical Quarterly* 53 (October 1949).

————. "Negroes and the Seminole War, 1817–1818." *Journal of Negro History* 36 (1951).

_____. "Negroes and the Seminole War, 1835–1842." *Journal of Southern History* 30 (1964).

_____. "Notes Supplementary to 'Relations between Negroes and Indians.'" *Journal of Negro History* 18 (1933).

_____. "Relations Between Negroes and Indians Within the Present Limits of the United States." *Journal of Negro History* 27 (1932).

_____. "The Seminole in Mexico, 1850–1861." *The Hispanic American Historical Review* 31 (1951).

_____. "The Seminole in Mexico, 1850–1861." *Chronicles of Oklahoma* 29 (1951).

_____. "The Seminole in Mexico, 1850–1861." *Hispanic American Review* 31 (1951).

_____. "The Seminole-Negro Scouts, 1870–1881." *Southwestern Historical Quarterly* 55 (January 1952).

_____. "Wild Cat's Death and Burial." *Chronicles of Oklahoma* 21 (1943).

Rogers, B. Ann, and Linda Shcott. "'My Mother Was a Mover': African American Seminole Women in Brackettville, Texas, 1914–1964." Chapter in *Writing the Range: Race, Class, and Culture in the Women's West*, eds. Elizabeth Jameson and Susan Armitage. Norman: University of Oklahoma Press, 1997.

Roth, David D. "Lakota Sioux Terms for White and Negro." *Plains Anthropologist* 20 (1975). Etymological research into terms used by the Oglala and their ancestors on the Pine Ridge reservation.

Saunt, Claudio. "'The English has Now a Mind to Make Slaves of Them All': Creeks, Seminoles and the Problem of Slavery." *American Indian Quarterly*, Winter 1998.

Sefton, James E. "Black Slaves, Red Masters, White Middlemen: A Congressional Debate of 1853." *Florida Historical Quarterly* 51 (1972). Blacks, Seminoles, Creeks, the secretary of war, and Congress.

Smith, C. Calvin. "The Oppressed Oppressors: Negro Slavery among the Choctaw Indians of Oklahoma." *Red River Valley Historical Review* 2 (1975).

Smith, Charlotte Anne. "Freedmen of the Cherokee Nation." *Wild West* 8 (February 1996).

Speck, Frank G. "Negroes and the Creek Nation." *Southern Workman* 37 (1908).

Steacy, Stephen. "The Chickasaw Nation on the Eve of the Civil War." *Chronicles of Oklahoma* 49 (1971).

Sturtevant, William. "Creek into Seminole." In *North American Indians in Historical Perspective*, eds. Eleanor B. Leacock and Nancy O. Lurie. New York: Random House, 1971.

Swisher, C. Kevin. "Frontier Heroes." *Texas Highways* 39 (July 1992). Black Seminole scouts.

Taylor, Annan R. "Note Concerning Lakota Sioux Terms for White and Negro." *Plains Anthropologist* 21 (1976). Response to the above Ross article.

Thornton, Michael C., and Yuko Mizuno. "Religiosity and Black Adult Feelings Toward Africans, American Indians, West Indians, Hispanics and Asian Americans." *Sociological Focus* 28 (1995).

Thybony, Scott. "Against All Odds, Black Seminoles Won Their Freedom." *Smithsonian* 22 (August 1991).

_____. "The Black Seminole: A Tradition of Courage." *Smithsonian* 22 (April 1991).

Troper, Harold M. "The Creek-Negroes of Oklahoma and Canadian Immigration, 1901–1911." *Canadian Historical Review* 53 (September 1972). Creek Indian Negro and conflicts with Southern Blacks, plus development of Canadian anti-Negro immigration restrictions.

Tucker, Phillip Thomas. "John Horse: Forgotten African-American Leader of the Second Seminole War." *Journal of Negro History* 77 (Spring 1992).

Warren, Hanna R. "Reconstruction in the Cherokee Nation." *Chronicles of Oklahoma* 45 (1967). The Ridge and Ross factions and the status of former Negro slaves.

Watts, Jill. "We Do Not Live for Ourselves Only: Seminole Black Perceptions and the Second Seminole War." *UCLA Historical Journal* 7 (1986).

Wilson, Walt. "Freedmen in Indian Territory During Reconstruction." *Chronicles of Oklahoma* 49 (Summer 1971).

Woodhull, Frost. "The Seminole Indian Scouts on the Border." *Frontier Times* 15 (December 1937).

Wrone, David R. "The Cherokee Act of Emancipation." *Journal of Ethnic Studies* 1 (1973). The Cherokee people freed slaves on 21 February 1863, plus gave them a land base.

Books:

Abel, Annie Heloise. *The American Indian as Slaveholder and Secessionist: An Omitted Chapter in the Diplomatic History of the Southern Confederacy.* Cleveland: Arthur H. Clark Company, 1915; reprinted, Lincoln: University of Nebraska Press, 1992.

Baker, Julie Philips. *Black Slavery Among the American Indians.* Clifton, NJ: AB Bookman's Weekly, 1992.

Bowman, J. Wilson. *America's Black and Tribal Colleges.* South Pasadena, CA: Sandcastle Publications, 1994.

Britten, Thomas A. *A Brief History of the Seminole-Negro Indian Scouts.* Lewiston, NY: Mellen Press, 1999.

Burton, Arthur T. *Black, Red, and Deadly: Black and Indian Gunfighters of the Indian Territory, 1870–1907.* Austin: Eakin Press, 1991.

Campbell, J. B. *Campbell's Abstract of Creek Freedman Census Cards and Index*. Muskogee: Phoenix Job Printing Company, 1915.

Cunningham, Teresa, and Montez DeCarlo. *Black Indians: A Pictorial Essay of a Secret Heritage*. Natural Experience, 1996.

Debo, Angie. *The Road to Disappearance*. Norman: University of Oklahoma Press, 1967. Contains some history of Blacks in the Creek nation.

Dinnerstein, Leonard, Roger L. Nichlos, and David M. Reimers. *Natives and Strangers: Blacks, Indians, and Immigrants in America*, 2^d ed. New York: Oxford University Press, 1990.

Dramer, Kim. *Native Americans and Black Americans*. Broomall, PA: Chelsea House, 1997.

Flickinger, Robert Elliott. *The Choctaw Freemen and the Story of Oka Hill Industrial Academy, Valliant, McCurtain County, Oklahoma, now called the Alice Lee Elliott Memorial; Including the Early History of the Five Civilized Tribes of Indian Territory, the Presbytery of Kiamichi, Synod of Canadian, and the Bible in the Free Schools of the American Colonies, but Suppressed in France, Previous to the American and French Revolutions*. Pittsburgh, PA: Presbyterian Board of Missions for Freedmen, 1914.

Forbes, Jack D. *Africans and Native Americans: The Language of Race and the Evolution of Red-Black Peoples*. Urbana: University of Illinois Press, 1993.

_____. *Black Africans and Native Americans: Color, Race, and Caste in the Evolution of Red-Black Peoples*. New York: Blackwell, 1988.

Foster, Laurence. *Negro-Indian Relations in the Southeast*. Philadelphia: University of Pennsylvania, 1935; reprinted, New York: AMS Press, 1978. Though not about the West, it does provide a history of that relationship.

Griffin, Larry D. *Black Slaves in the Cherokee Nation*. Arlington, TX: University of Texas, 1974.

Halliburton, R., Jr. *Red Over Black: Black Slavery Among the Cherokee Indians*. Westport, CT: Greenwood Press, 1977.

Hancock, Ian F. *Creole Features in the Afro–Seminole Speech of Brackettville, Texas*. Society for Caribbean Linguistics Occasional Papers, No. 3. Mona, Jamaica: Society for Caribbean Linguistics, 1975.

_____. *Further Observations on Afro-Seminole Creole*. Society for Caribbean Linguistics Occasional Papers, No. 7. Mona, Jamaica: Society for Caribbean Linguistics, 1977.

_____. *The Texas Seminoles and Their Language*. Austin: University of Texas African and Afro-American Studies and Research Center, 1980.

Heard, J. Norman. *The Black Frontiersmen: Adventures of Negroes Among American Indians, 1528–1918*. New York: John Day, 1969. Juvenile.

Jairazbhoy, Rafique Ali. *Ancient Egyptians and Chinese in America*. London: George Prior Associated Publishers, 1974. Pre-Columbus contact and influences.

Katz, William Loren. *Black Indians: A Hidden Heritage.* New York: Atheneum, 1986.

Katz, William Loren, and Paula Angle Franklin. *Proudly Red and Black: Stories of Native and African Americans.* New York: Atheneum, 1993. Biographies, juvenile.

LaTorre, Felipe A., and Dolores L. LaTorre. *The Mexican Kickapoo Indians.* Austin: University of Texas Press, 1976.

Lancaster, Jane F. *Removal Aftershock: The Seminoles' Struggle to Survive in the West, 1836–1866.* Knoxville: University of Tennessee Press, 1994.

Laws of the Chickasaw Nation, I. T.: Relating to Intermarried and Adopted Citizens and Rights of Freedom. Wilmington, DE: Scholarly Resources, 1975. Tribal citizenship, legal status and law, including that of Black ex-slaves of the Chickasaws.

Littlefield, Daniel F., Jr. *Africans and Creeks: From the Colonial Period to the Civil War.* Westport, CT: Greenwood Press, 1979.

————. *Africans and Seminoles: From Emancipation to American Citizenship.* Westport, CT: Greenwood Press, 1977.

————. *Africans and Seminoles: From Removal to Emancipation.* Westport, CT: Greenwood Press, 1977.

————. *The Cherokee Freedmen: From Emancipation to American Citizenship.* Contributions to Afro-American and African Studies, no. 40. Westport, CT: Greenwood Press, 1978.

————. *The Chickasaw Freedmen: A People Without a Country.* Westport, CT: Greenwood Press, 1980. Traces the freedmen through Oklahoma statehood.

Marty, Martin E. *Native American Religion and Black Protestantism.* Austin: University Publications of America, 1993. Black religion missions.

May, Katja. *African Americans and Native Americans in the Creek and Cherokee Nations, 1830s to 1920s: Collision and Collusion.* New York: Garland Publishers, 1996. Creeks, Cherokees and Blacks.

Monceaux, Morgan. *My Heroes, My People: African Americans and Native Americans of the West.* New York: Frances Foster Books, 1999. Portraits of Blacks, Native Americans, and mixed-heritage people. Juvenile.

Mulroy, Kevin. *Freedom on the Border: The Seminole Maroons in Florida, the Indian Territory, Coahuila, and Texas.* Lubbock: Texas Tech University Press, 1993.

Noah, Belinda. *The Black Seminoles: The Little-Known Story of the First Seminoles.* Tallahassee, FL: B. Noah, 1995.

Olcione, Amos, and Thomas Senter, eds. *Kenneth Wiggins Porter's "The Black Seminoles: A History of a Freedom-Seeking People."* Gainesville, FL: University Press of Florida, 1996.

Opala, Joseph A. *A Brief History of the Seminole Freedmen*. African and Afro-American Studies and Research Center Papers Series 2, no. 3. Austin: University of Texas, 1980.

Perdue, Theda. *Slavery and the Evolution of Cherokee Society, 1548–1866*. Knoxville, TN: University of Tennessee Press, 1979; reprinted, Knoxville, TN: University of Tennessee Press, 1988.

Porter, Kenneth Wiggins. *The Black Seminoles: History of a Freedom-Seeking People*, eds. Alcione M. Amos and Thomas P. Senter. Gainesville: University of Florida, 1996.

_____. *Relations between Negroes and Indians*. Washington, DC: Association for the Study of Negro Life and History, 1932.

Promised Land on the Solomon: Black Settlement at Nicodemus, Kansas. Washington, DC: U.S. Government Printing Office, 1986. Frontier life and historic buildings and restorations.

Pulley, Clyde. *Blacks Who Pass for Indian and White*. n.p., 1978. Though focused on North Carolina, provides some insight into that phenomenon.

Sivad, Doug. *The Black Seminole Indians of Texas*, 2^d ed. Boston: Sivad Group, 1986.

Speck, Gordon. *Breeds and Half-Breeds*. New York: C. N. Porter, 1969.

Van Sertima, Ivan. *They Came Before Columbus*. New York: Random House, 1976. Pre-Columbus African contact and influence.

Walton-Raji, Angela Y. *Black Indian Genealogy Research: African-American Ancestors among the Five Civilized Tribes*. Bowie, MD: Heritage Books, 1993.

Willhelm, Sidney M. *Red Man, Black Man and White America: The Constitutional Approach to Genocide*. Andover, MA: Warner Modular Publications, 1969.

Wright, J. Leitch, Jr. *Creeks and Seminoles: The Destruction and Regeneration of the Muscogulge People*. Lincoln: University of Nebraska Press, 1986.

Theses and Dissertations:

Armstrong, Robert Plant. "Patterns in the Stories of the Dakota Indians and the Negroes of Paramaribo, Dutch Guiana." Thesis, Northwestern University, 1957.

Bales, Rebecca Anne. "The Black White Man." Master's thesis, University of Colorado, 1990.

Bateman, Rebecca Belle. "'We're Still Here': History, Kinship, and Group Identity Among the Seminole Freedmen of Oklahoma." Ph.D. diss., Johns Hopkins University, 1991.

Boyett, Cheryl Race. "The Seminole-Black Alliance During the Second Seminole War, 1835–1842." Master's thesis, California State University, Dominguez Hills, 1996.

Britten, Thomas A. "The History of the Seminole Negro-Indian Scouts." Master's thesis, Hardia-Simmons University, 1990.

Foster, Laurence. "Negro-Indian Relationships in the Southeast." Ph.D. diss., University of Pennsylvania, 1935.

Gallagher, Arthur, Jr. "A Survey of the Seminole Freedmen." Master's thesis, University of Oklahoma, 1951.

Hackney, Jami D. "Cherokee Culture and Racism: An Evaluation of Cherokee and Black Relations from 1800 to 1907." Honor's thesis, Southern Connecticut College, 1996.

Holman, Victor. "Seminole Negro Indians, Macabebes, and Civilian Irregulars: Models for Future Employment of Indigenous Forces." Master's thesis, U.S. Army Command and General Staff College, 1995.

Jackson, Nellie B. "Political and Economic History of the Negro in Indian Territory." Master's thesis, University of Oklahoma 1960.

Lancaster, Jane F. "The First Decades: The Western Seminoles from Removal to Reconstruction, 1836–1866." Ph.D. diss., Mississippi State University, 1986.

Lawuyi, Olatunde Bayo. "Seminole Freedmen's Identity in Plural Setting." Ph.D. diss., University of Illinois at Urbana-Champaign, 1985.

Miller, Susan A. "Wild Cat and the Origins of the Seminole Migration to Mexico." Master's thesis, University of Oklahoma, 1988.

Mulroy, Kevin. "Relations between Blacks and Seminoles after Removal." Ph.D. diss., University of Kelle, 1984.

Pisacka, Karen Kay. "The Cherokee Black Man, 1840–1907." Master's thesis, University of Texas at Arlington, 1973.

Roethler, Michael D. "Negro Slavery among the Cherokee Indians, 1540–1866." Ph.D. diss., Fordham University, 1964.

Wilson, Raleigh A. "Negro and Indian Relations in the Five Civilized Tribes from 1865 to 1907." Ph.D. diss., University of Iowa, 1950.

Other:

"Black Seminoles: A Celebration of Survival." Horizon Series, National Public Radio, 1981. Soundrecording.

"The Black West: Black Cowboys and Indians." Slide show and lecture by William Loren Katz. Montclair School, 1991. Videocassette.

Cherokee—Freemen (Tahlequah). Oklahoma Historical Society Contains lists of freedmen the Cherokee Supreme Court admitted to citizenship.

Choctaw Freedman information, including freedmen census data from 1885 and 1896, may be located through the Oklahoma Historical Society. Microfilm CTN 7.

The Final Rolls of Citizens and Freedmen of the Five Civilized Tribes. Washington, DC: National Archives Microfilm Publications. Microfilm T529.

List of Freedmen Entitled and Exercising Citizenship in the Cherokee Nation.
        Authenticated roll, 1880.   Oklahoma Historical Society.   Microfilm
        DC42.
Special Files. Chickasaw Freedmen. Washington, DC: National Archives.

Black Towns

Articles:

Bates, Angela. "New Promise for Nicodemus." *National Parks* 66 (July 1992).

Bentz, Donald N. "Nicodemus—the Promised Land?" *Golden West* 5 (November 1968).

Beran, Janice A. "Diamonds in Iowa: Blacks, Buxton, and Baseball." *Journal of Negro History* 75 (Summer, Fall 1990).

Bilger, Burkhard. "My Eyes Have Seen the Glory." *Oklahoma Today* 47 (February 1997). Black towns.

Bittle, William Elmer., and Gilbert L. Geis. "Racial Self-fulfillment and the Rise of an All-Negro Community in Oklahoma." *Phylon* 18 (Fall 1957). The establishment and destruction of political power in Boley.

Carney, George O. "All Black Towns." *Chronicles of Oklahoma* 69 (Summer 1991). Reviews the "bold experiment."

Chase, Henry. "Boley's Bank Robbed!" *American Visions*, December 1994.

Crockett, Norman L. "Witness to History: Booker T. Washington Visits Boley." *Chronicle of Oklahoma* 67 (Winter 1989). Booker T. Washington's two visits to Boley

Dillon, Merton L. "Benjamin Lundy in Texas." *Southwestern Historical Quarterly* 63 (July 1959).

Entz, Gary R. "Image and Reality on the Kansas Prairie: 'Pap' Singleton's Cherokee County Colony." *Kansas History* 19 (Summer 1996).

Fleming, Elvis E. "Collins Family." In *Roundup on the Pecos*, eds. Elvis E. Fleming and Minor S. Huffman. Roswell, NM: Chaves County Historical Society, 1978. Story of Monroe and Mary Collins and family, homesteaders of Blackdom and Roswell.

Fleming, Walter L. "Moses of the Colored Exodus." *Americana* 7 (October 1912). Profile of "Pap" Singleton.

———. "Pap Singleton, The Moses of the Colored Exodus." *American Journal of Sociology* 15 (July 1909).

Garvin, Roy. "Benjamin, or 'Pap,' Singleton and His Followers." *Journal of Negro History* 33 (January 1948).

Gibson, Daniel. "Blackdom." *New Mexico Magazine* 64 (February 1986). History of the small community of Blackdom which lasted from 1901 until almost 1930.

Gray, Linds C. "Taft: Town on the Black Frontier." *Chronicles of Oklahoma* 66 (Winter 1988).

Hamilton, Kenneth Marvin. "The Origins and Early Developments of Langston, Oklahoma." *Journal of Negro History* 62 (July 1977).

_____. "The Origins and Early Promotion of Nicodemus: A Pre-Exodus, All-Black Town." *Kansas History* 5 (1982).

_____. "Townsite Speculation and the Origin of Boley, Oklahoma." *Chronicles of Oklahoma* 55 (1977).

Harris, Andrew. "Deerfield [sic], A Negro Ghost Town in Weld County, Colorado." *Negro History Bulletin* 27 (1963).

Harvey, James R. "Negroes in Colorado." *Colorado Magazine* 26 (1949).

Haywood, C. Robert. "The Hodgeman County Colony." *Kansas History* 12 (1989–1990).

Herbert, Solomon J. "Blacks Who Migrated West between 1915 and 1945." *Crisis* 98 (February 1990). Migration from the South to Los Angeles.

Hickey, Joseph V. "'Pap' Singleton's Dunlop Colony: Relief Agencies and the Failure of a Black Settlement in Eastern Kansas." *Great Plains Quarterly* 2 (Winter 1991).

Hill, Mozell C. "The All-Negro Communities of Oklahoma: The Natural History of a Social Movement." *Journal of Negro History* 31 (July 1946).

Johnson, Frederick. "Agricultural Negro Colony in Eastern Colorado." *Western Farm Life* 17 (11 May 1915). An interview with Dearfield founder O. T. Jackson.

Kremer, Gary R., and Ann Jenkins. "The Town with Black Roots." *Missouri Life* (July-August 1983). Black town of Eldridge, Missouri.

Kremer, Gary R., and Lynn Morrow. "Pennytown: A Freedmen's Hamlet, 1871–1945." *Missouri Folklore Society Journal* 11 and 12 (1989–1990). Missouri community.

Law, Howard. "'Self Reliance is the True Road to Independence': Ideology and the Ex-Slaves in Buxton and Chatham." *Ontario History* 77 (1985). Life in two Canadian towns.

Magill, Dennis William. "The Relocation of Africville: A Case Study of Planned Social Change." Ph.D. diss., Washington University, 1974.

Malcomson, Scott L. "Having Their Say: Residents of Boley, Oklahoma Describe Conditions in the All-Black Town." *The New Yorker*, 29 April 1996.

McAuley, William J. "History, Race, and Attachment to Place Among Elders in the Rural All-Black Towns of Oklahoma." *Journals of Gerontology-Series B* 53 (January 1998).

McNutt, George L. "Race Question Solved in Buxton." *Independent* 62 (30 May 1907).

N'Namdi, Carmen A. "A Play in Three Acts: A Town You Could Bank On." *Learning* 19 (February 1991). Excerpt of a play about Boley to assist students in learning about Black history.

O'Brien, Claire. "'With One Mighty Pull'": Interracial Town Boosting in Nicodemus, Kansas." *Great Plains Quarterly* 16 (Spring 1996).

Olmsted, Frederick Law. "Organized Negro Communities: A North American Experiment." *Journal of Negro History* 48 (January 1962).

"Only All Negro Village in Kansas, Nicodemus, is Fading into History." *Kansas City Times* (28 May 1959).

Pease, William H., and Jane H. Pease. "Opposition to the Founding of the Elgin Settlement." *Canadian Historical Review* 38 (September 1957). Anti-Black sentiment.

_____. "Organized Negro Communities: A North American Experiment." *Journal of Negro History* 47 (January 1962). Examines some Canadian communities.

Pew, Thomas W., Jr. "Boley, Oklahoma: Trial in American Apartheid." *American West* 17 (June 1980).

Pittman, Ruth. "Allen Allensworth: Man of Ambition." *Crisis* 98 (February 1990).

Reese, Linda Williams. "Working in the Vineyard: African-American Women in All-Black Communities." *Kansas Quarterly* 25 (1992).

Rieke, Tom. "Triumph Over Tragedy: The Story of the Sons and Daughters of Buxton, Canada." *American Visions*, 1991.

Robbins, Arlie C. *Legacy to Buxton*. Chatham, ON: Ideal Printing, 1883; reprinted, North Buxton, ON: A. C. Robbins, 1983. Black community of North Buxton, Ontario.

Roberson, Jerri. "Edward McCabe and the Langston Experiment." *Chronicles of Oklahoma* 51 (Fall 1973).

Robinson, Louie. "Death Threatens Western Town." *Ebony*, June 1967. Arsenic in the water supply at Allensworth.

Rose, Harold M. "The All-Negro Town: Its Evolution and Function." *Geographical Review* 55 (July 1965).

Rye, Stephen H. "Buxton: Black Metropolis of Iowa." *Annals of Iowa* 41 (Spring 1972).

Schwendemann, Glen. "The 'Exodusters' on the Missouri." *Kansas Historical Quarterly* 29 (Spring 1963).

_____. "Nicodemus: Negro Haven on the Solomon." *Kansas Historical Quarterly* 34 (Spring 1968).

_____. "Wyandotte and the First 'Exodusters' on the Missouri." *Kansas Historical Quarterly* 26 (Autumn 1960).

Shiffer, Beverly. "The Story of Buxton." *Annals of Iowa* 37 (Summer 1964).

The Spirit of Africville. Halifax, NS: Formac Publishing Company, 1992.

The Spirit of Africville and Remember Africville. Halifax, NS: Maritext, 1993.

Steinberg, Stephen. "My Day in Nicodemus: Notes from a Field Trip to Black Kansas." *Phylon* 37 (September 1976). White New York sociologist takes a car trip to Nicodemus and goes to a service in the Black church.

Stiff, Cary. "Black Colorado." Black Colorado Series. *Denver Post Empire Magazine*, July 13–Nov. 16, 1969. Twelve installments. Barney Ford, Isom Dart, the Ku Klux Klan, Dearfield, etc.

Strubel, D. B. "Dearfield, Colorado: Population 1." *Denver Post Empire Magazine*, 8 August 1955.

Swisher, Jacob A. "The Rise and Fall of Buxton." *Palimpsest* 26 (June 1945). Profile of Buxton, Canada.

Tolson, Arthur L. "Black Towns of Oklahoma." *Black Scholar* 1 (April 1972).

Waddell, Karen. "Dearfield...A Dream Deferred." *Colorado Heritage* (1988). Story of O. T. Jackson and the community he founded.

Washington, Booker T. "Boley: A Negro Town in the West." *Outlook* 88 (4 January 1908).

————. "A Town Owned by Negroes." *World's Work* 14 (July 1907).

Wayne, George H. "Negro Migration and Colonization in Colorado, 1870–1930." *Journal of the West* 15 (January 1976).

Weiler, Kathleen. "The School at Allensworth." *Journal of Education* 17 (1990). California all-Black town.

Westermeier, Clifford P. "The Dream of Dearfield." *Denver Post Empire Magazine*, 2 November 1969.

Wiese, Andrew. "Places of Our Own: Suburban Black Towns Before 1960." *Journal of Urban History* 19 (May 1993).

Wiggins, William H., Jr. "The Emancipation of Nicodemus." *Natural History* 107 (July/August 1998). The August 1 emancipation celebration homecoming event.

Woodward, James E. "Vernon: An All Negro Town in Southeastern Oklahoma." *Negro History Bulletin* 27 (1964). Town founded in 1911.

Books:

Abucar, Mohamed Hagi. *Struggle for Development: The Black Communities of North and East Preston and Cherry Brook, Nova Scotia, 1784–1987*. Dartmouth: Black Cultural Centre for Nova Scotia, 1988.

Africville: A Spirit That Lives On. Halifax, NS: Art Gallery, Mount Saint Vincent University and the Black Cultural Centre for Nova Scotia, Africville, 1989. From the exhibition, 20 October–19 November 1989.

Africville Genealogical Society, ed. *The Spirit of Africville*. Halifax: Formac Press, 1992.

Alexander, Charles C. *Battles and Victories of Allen Allensworth*. Boston: Sherman, French, 1914. Black chaplain.

California, Resources Agency, Department of Parks and Recreation. *Allensworth Feasibility Study*. Sacramento: Department of Parks and Recreation, 1975.

Chambers, W. L. *Niles of Nicodemus: Exploiter of Kansas Exodusters, Negro Indemnity and Equality of Blacks with Whites His Obsession, Beats Bankers, Bench, and Barrister; Courter League to Post-War K.K.K. Riots and Finally Prison*. Los Angeles: Los Angeles Washington High School, Vocational Training Press, 1925. Exposé on John W. Niles, president of the town's self-governing organization.

Chu, Daniel, and Bill Shaw. *Going Home to Nicodemus: The Story of an African American Frontier Town and the Pioneers Who Settled It*. Englewood Cliffs, NJ: Silver Burdett Press, 1995. Juvenile.

Clairmont, Donald H., and Dennis W. Magill. *Africville, Relocation Report*. Halifax, NS: Institute of Public Affairs, Dalhousie University, 1971.

_____. *Africville Relocation Report and Supplement*. Halifax, NS: Institute of Public Affairs, Dalhousie University, 1973.

_____. *Africville: The Life and Death of a Canadian Black Community*. Toronto: McClelland and Stewart, 1974; reprinted, Toronto: Canadian Scholars' Press, 1987; reprinted, 1997. Blacks and social conditions in Halifax.

_____. *Nova Scotian Blacks: An Historical and Structural Overview*. Halifax, NS: Dalhousie University, 1970.

Crockett, Norman L. *The Black Towns*. Lawrence: Regents Press of Kansas, 1979.

Gradwohl, David M., and Nancy M. Osborn. *Exploring Buried Buxton: Archaeology of an Abandoned Iowa Coal Mining Town with a Large Black Population*. Ames: Iowa State University Press, 1984; reprinted, 1990.

Hamilton, Kenneth Marvin. *Black Towns and Profit: Promotion and Development in the Trans-Appalachian West, 1877–1915*. Blacks in the New World Series. Urbana: University of Illinois Press, 1991.

Kunkel, Peter, and Sara Sue Kennard. *Spout Spring: A Black Community*. New York: Holt, Rinehart and Winston, 1971.

Memorial and Other Papers of Caesar F. Simmons, Formerly Postmaster at Boley, Okfuskee County, Okla., to the 69th Congress of the United States. Boley: n.p., 1933.

Mikell, Robert S. *A Pictorial History of Allensworth: A Unique Black Town*. Fresno: n.p., 1985.

Morris, Ann, and Henrietta Ambrose. *North Webster: A Photographic History of a Black Community*. Bloomington: Indiana University Press, 1993. Missouri Black community.

Nicodemus: Kansas Special Resources Study. Kansas: National Park Service, U.S. Department of Interior, 1993.

Oliver, W. P. *Brief Summary of Nova Scotia Negro Communities*. n.p., 1964. Blacks in Nova Scotia.

Pease, William H. *Black Utopia: Negro Communal Experiments in America.* Madison: State Historical Society of Wisconsin, 1963. Colonization in the U.S. and Canada.

Robbins, Arlie C. *Legacy to Buxton.* Chatham, ON: Ideal Printing, 1883; reprinted, North Buxton, ON: A. C. Robbins, 1983. Black community of North Buxton, Ontario.

Schweider, Dorothy, Joseph Hraba, and Elmer Schweider. *Buxton, Works, and Racial Equity in a Coal Mining Community.* Ames: Iowa State University Press, 1987.

Smith, Leon E. *Hidden Heroes on the Checkerboard Plains: All Black Town's Bank Trap Terminated Notorious Bandits...The Pretty Boy Floyd Gang.* Diversified, 1980.

————. *High Noon at the Boley Corral (An Autobiographic Documentary).* Detroit: Leon E. Smith, 1980.

Wellington, Thomas. *The Land Time Forgot: Black Settlement at Nicodemus, Kansas.* Nicodemus, KS: Nicodemus, 1995.

Theses and Dissertations:

Ashley, Velma D. "A History of Boley, Oklahoma." Master's thesis, Kansas State College, 1940.

Bell, J. D. "A Study of a Negro City." Master's thesis, University of Kansas, 1930. Boley, Oklahoma.

Belleau, William J. "The Nicodemus Colony of Graham County, Kansas." Master's thesis, Fort Hays State College, 1950.

Brewington, Paulette F. "The Colored Page: A History of the African-American Communities of Bethel, Texas, and Happy Holler in Kannapolis, North Carolina: An Account Based on Oral Narratives and Other Sources." Master's thesis, North Carolina Agricultural and Technical State University, 1996.

Elahi, Larry. "A History of Boley, Oklahoma, to 1915." Master's thesis, University of Chicago, 1968.

Hamilton, Kenneth Marvin. "Black Town Promotion and Development on the Middle Border." Ph.D. diss., Washington University, 1978.

Harvey, James R. "The Negro in Colorado." Master's thesis, University of Denver, 1941.

Humphrey, Charles Allen. "Socio-Economic Study of Six All-Black Towns in Oklahoma." Thesis, Oklahoma State University, 1974.

Kirk, James H. "Kinloch, Missouri: A Study of an All-Negro Community." Ph.D. diss., St. Louis University, 1951.

Knight, Thomas. "Black Towns in Oklahoma: Their Development and Survival." Ph.D. diss., Oklahoma State University, 1975.

McDaniel, Orval. "A History of Nicodemus, Graham County, Kansas." Master's thesis, Fort Hays State College, 1943.

Norris, Melvin Edward, Jr. "Dearfield, Colorado—The Evolution of a Rural Black Settlement: An Historical Geography of Black Colonization on the Great Plains." Ph.D. diss., University of Colorado, 1980.

Passey, M. Louise. "Freedmantown: The Evolution of a Black Neighborhood in Houston, 1865–1880." Master's thesis, Rice University, 1993.

Picher, Margaret. "Dearfield, Colorado: A Story from the Black West." Master's thesis, University of Denver, 1976.

Ramsey, Eleanor Mason. "Allensworth: A Study in Social Change." Ph.D. diss., University of California, Berkeley, 1977.

Shaw, Van B. "Nicodemus, Kansas: A Study of Isolation." Ph.D. diss., University of Missouri, 1951.

Thomas, Chleyon Decatur. "Boley: An All-Black Pioneer Town and the Education of Its Children." Ph.D. diss, University of Akron, 1989.

Tolson, Arthur L. "A History of Langston, Oklahoma, 1890–1950." Master's thesis, Oklahoma State University, 1953.

Truxton, Virginia. "1918-1921: The All-Black Town Phenomenon Re-Visited at a Critical Juncture in its Evolution and Reconstruction of African-American Urban Historical Geography." Master's thesis, University of California, Berkeley, 1989.

Waldron, Nell Blyth. "Colonization in Kansas from 1861–1890." Ph.D. diss., Northwestern University, 1923.

Werner, Brian R. "Colorado's Pioneer Blacks: Migration, Occupations and Race Relations in the Centennial State." Master's thesis, University of Northern Colorado, 1979.

Wiley, Ben Wayne. "Ebonyville in the South and Southwest: Political Life in the All-Black Town." Ph.D. diss., University of Texas at Arlington, 1984. Study of five Black towns.

Other:

Cedric Page for Colorado Reflections. University of Colorado-Denver. 1983 or 1984. Geography professor talks about Denver and Dearfield. Sound recording.

Dearfield, The Road Less Traveled. HomeFolks Creative Works and Northeast Denver Women's Center, 1995. Donnie L. Betts, producer and director; Reynelda Muse, producer and writer; John Amos, narrator. The history of Dearfield, Colorado. Videorecording.

Happy Birthday, Mrs. Craig. A 102 year old woman, the daughter of slaves, recalls her family's journey to Nicodemus and then on to Colorado in 1915. She taught school for fifty-five years. Videorecording.

Historic Survey of the Townsite of Dearfield, Colorado: A Report. Denver: State Historical Society of Colorado, 1985.

The Need, The Dream, The Reality: Colorado Black Settlements. KOA-TV, Denver, 1989. Narrator–Reynelda Muse. Videorecording. Dearfield, Colorado.

Remember Africville. National Film Board of Canada, Shelagh Mackenzie, 1991. Residents of Halifax Black community discuss Africville's demolition and their relocation. Videorecording.

The Spirit of Allensworth. KTEH -TV with Spirit Productions. 1980. All-Black California town. Videorecording.

U.S. Congress, Senate. *Report and Testimony of the Select Committee of the United States Senate to Investigate the Causes of the Removal of the Negroes from the Southern States to the Northern States* [Voorhees Committee Report]. *Senate Reports*, no. 693. 46th Congress, 2d Session, 1880 (Serials 1899 [pt. 1] and 1900 [pts. 2 and 3]). Investigated why Blacks were leaving the South, many of whom moved West.

Black Women

Articles:

Anderson, Kathie Ryckman. "Era Bell Thompson: A North Dakota Daughter." *North Dakota History* 49 (Fall 1982). Account of the childhood of an editor for *Ebony*.

Anderson, Larry. "We Need Acceptance Where We Are: A Central Area Negro Leader Gives Her Views." *Seattle Times Magazine*, 18 September 1966.

Andrew, John A. "Betsey Stockton: Stranger in a Strange Land." *Journal of Presbyterian History* 52 (Summer 1974).

"The Anita Hill Chair: A New Chapter in the Long Racial History of the University of Oklahoma College of Law." *Journal of Blacks in Higher Education* 11 (Spring 1996).

"Anita Hill Resumes Teaching Post at University of Oklahoma Law School." *Jet*, 11 September 1995.

"Anita Hill Sabbatical Raises ire of Oklahoma Republicans." *Black Issues in Higher Education* 9 (10 September 1992).

"Anita Hill to Resign as Law Professor at Univ. of Oklahoma." *Jet*, 3 April 1995.

Armitage, Susan, Theresa Banfield, and Sarah Jacobus. "Black Women and Their Communities in Colorado." *Frontiers: A Journal of Women's Studies* 2 (Summer 1977). Interviews of six Black women who grew up in Colorado in the early 20th century.

Armitage, Susan, and Deborah Gallacci Wilbert. "Black Women in the Pacific Northwest: A Survey and Research Prospectus." Chapter in *Women in Pacific Northwest History: An Anthology*, ed. Karen Blair. Seattle: University of Washington Press, 1988.

Baker, F. M., et al. "Black, Middle-Class Women in San Antonio, Texas." *Journal of the National Medical Association* 84 (June 1992). Mechanisms through which women handled stress.

Beasley, Delilah L. "California Colored Women Trail Blazers." Chapter in *Homespun Heroines and Other Women of Distinction*, ed. Hallie Q. Brown. Xenia, OH: Aldine Publishing Company, 1926; reprinted, New York: Oxford University Press, 1988.

Bennett, Lerone, Jr. "A Historical Detective Story: The Mystery of Mary Ellen Pleasant." *Ebony*, April and May 1979.

Bibbs, Sushell. "Mary Ellen Pleasant: Mother of Civil Rights in California." *Historic Nantucket* 44 (1995).

"Black Women in Colorado: Two Early Portraits." *Frontiers: A Journal of Women's Studies* 7 (1984). Biographies of nurse Daisy Jones and cowgirl Beatrice Boyer Jones.

Blackburn, George M. , and Sherman L. Richards. "The Prostitute." Section in "The Prostitutes and Gamblers of Virginia City, Nevada: 1870." *Pacific Historical Review* 48 (1979). Four of the 138 prostitutes were Black, and are profiled.

Brady, Marilyn Dell. "Kansas Federation of Colored Women's Clubs, 1900–1930." *Kansas History* 9 (Spring 1986).

————. "Organizing Afro-American Girls Clubs in Kansas in the 1920's." *Frontiers* 9 (1987).

Brandenstein, Sherilyn. "*Sepia Record* as a Forum for Negotiating Women's Roles." Chapter in *Women and Texas History: Selected Essays*, eds. Fane Downs and Nancy Baker Jones. Austin: Texas State Historical Association, 1993.

Brooks, Christopher. "Coming Home: An Interview with Sippie Wallace." *Texas Humanist* (July/August 1985). Blues singer of the 1920s restarts her career.

Brown, Angela Darlean. "Women and the Black Panther Party: An Interview with Angela Brown." *Socialist Review* 26 (1996).

Broyles, William. "The Making of Barbara Jordan." *Texas Monthly*, October 1976.

Buckbee, Edna Bryan. "The 'Boys' Called Her 'Mammy' Pleasant." *The Pony Express* 20 (October 1953).

Burka, Paul. "Major Barbara [Jordan]." *Texas Monthly*, March 1996.

Butler, Anne Katherine M. "Still in Chains: Black Women in Western Prisons, 1865–1910." *Western Historical Quarterly* 20 (February 1989). Profiles prisoners in Kansas, Louisiana, Montana, Nebraska, and Texas.

"California Freedom Papers." *Journal of Negro History* 3 (January 1918). Copies of manumission papers, 1851–1856, including those of Biddy Mason and her children.

"California Representative Maxine Waters, Always Outspoken, Sounds Off on Homophobia among Blacks and Racism among Gays and Lesbians." *The Advocate* (26 January 1993).

Castañeda, Antonia I. "Women of Color and the Rewriting of Western History: The Discourse, Politics, and Decolonization of History." *Pacific Historical Review* 61 (1992).

Chaffin, Glenn. "Aunt Tish: Beloved Gourmet of the Bitter Root." *Montana: The Magazine of Western History* 21 (Autumn 1971). Former slave Tish Nevins of Hamilton, Montana, with accounts of her famous cooking.

Chaudhuri, Nupur. "'We All Seem Like Brothers and Sisters': The African-American Community in Manhattan, Kansas, 1865–1940." *Kansas History* 14 (Winter 1991).

Cochran, Elizabeth. "Black Women in Colorado: Two Early Portraits." *Frontiers* 7 (1984).

Cooper, Afua. "The Search for Mary Bibb." Chapter in *We Specialize in the Wholly Impossible: A Reader in Black Women's History*, eds. Darlene Clark Hine, Wilma King, and Linda Reed.

_____. "The Search for Mary Bibb, Black Woman Teacher in Nineteenth-Century Canada West." *Ontario History* 83 (March 1991).

Cooper, Gary. "Stage Coach Mary." *Ebony*, October 1959. Academy Award actor remembers Mary Fields.

Crawford, Ann Fears, and Crystal Sasse Ragsdale. "Congresswoman from Texas." Chapter in *Women in Texas: Their Lives, Their Experiences, Their Accomplishments*. Burnet, TX: Eakin Press, 1982. Barbara Jordan.

Crouch, Barry A. "Seeking Equality: Houston Black Women during Reconstruction." Chapter in *Black Dixie: Afro-Texas History and Culture in Houston*, eds. Howard Beeth and Cary D. Wintz. College Station: Texas A&M University Press, 1992.

Crowell, Evelyn Miller. "Twentieth Century Black Women in Oregon." *Northwest Journal of African and Black American Studies* I (Summer 1973).

Curtis, William J. "Emily Fisher, First Independence Black Business Woman." *The Kansas City Genealogist* 36 (Fall 1995).

Day, Ava Speese. "The Ave Speese Day Story." Chapter in *Sod House Memories*, ed. Frances Jacobs Alberts. Hastings, NB: Sod House Society, 1972.

de Graaf, Lawrence B. "Race, Sex and Region: Black Women in the American West, 1850–1920." *Pacific Historical Review* 49 (May 1980).

Devejian, Pat, and Jacqueline J. Etulain. "African Americans." Chapter in *Women and Family in the Twentieth-Century American West: A Bibliography*. Albuquerque: Center for the American West, 1990.

Dickson, Lynda Faye. "African-American Women's Clubs in Denver, 1890s–1920s." Chapter in *Peoples of Color in the American West*, ed. Sucheng Chan, et al. Lexington, MA: D. C. Heath and Company, 1994. Because of exclusion from white organizations, Black women created their own.

_____. "Towards a Broader Angle of Vision in Uncovering Women's History: Black Women's Clubs Revisited." *Frontiers: A Journal of Women's Studies* 9 (1987). Dickson discusses the research methods used to write her dissertation.

Diebel, Linda. "Black Women in White Canada." *Chatelaine* 46 (1973).

Dingus, Anne. "Angela Shelf Medearis." *Texas Monthly,* September 1997. Profile of Medearis, author of sixty children's books with Black themes.

_____. "Jo Long." *Texas Monthly*, September 1997. Profile of Long, community-arts organizer of the Carver Community Cultural Center.

Douglas, Pamela. "West Coast Wonder Women." *Black Enterprise*, November 1981.

Downs, Fane. "Tryels and Trubbles: Women in Early Nineteenth-Century Texas." *Southwestern Historical Quarterly* 90 (July 1986). Includes women slaves.

Everett, George. "Westerners." *Wild West* 8 (1 February 1996). Biography of "Black Mary" Fields.

Faust, Drew Gilpin. "Trying to Do a Man's Business: Gender Violence and Slaves Management in Civil War Texas." Chapter in *Southern Stories in Peace and War*, ed. Drew Gilpin Faust. Columbia: University of Missouri Press, 1992.

Frisch, Paul A. "'Gibraltar of Unionism': Women, Blacks and the Anti-Chinese Movement in Butte, Montana, 1880–1900." *Southwest Economy and Society* 6 (1984).

Fullilove, Mindy T., et al. "Black Women and AIDS Prevention: A View towards Understanding the Gender Rules." *Journal of Sex Research* 27 (1990). Examines patterns of sexual behavior.

Gilbert, Judith A. "Esther and Her Sisters: Free Women of Color as Property Owners in Colonial St. Louis, 1765–1803." *Gateway Heritage* 17 (Summer 1996).

Gill, Gerald R. "'Win or Lose—We Win': The 1952 Vice-Presidential Campaign of Charlotta Bass." Chapter in *The Afro-American Woman: Struggles and Images*, eds. Sharon Harley and Rosalyn Terborg-Penn. Port Washington, NY: Kennikat Press, 1978.

Gite, Lloyd. "Vanessa Gilmore: Stating Her Case in Texas." *Essence*, January 1995. The youngest federal judge in the country and the only Black woman on the federal bench in Texas.

Glasrud, Bruce A. "Josephine Leavell Allensworth." Section in *African American Women: A Biographical Dictionary*, ed. Dorothy C. Salem. New York: Garland Publishing, 1993.

_____. "Yvonne Brathwaite Burke." Section in *Encyclopedia of African American Civil Rights: From Emancipation to the Present*, eds. Charles D. Lowery and John F. Marszalek. Westport, CT: Greenwood Press, 1992.

Godard, Barbara. "A Writing of Resistance: Black Women's Writing in Canada." *Zora Neale Hurston Forum* 9 (Fall 1994).

Haiken, Elizabeth. "'The Lord Helps Those Who Help Themselves': Black Laundresses in Little Rock, Arkansas, 1917–1921." *Arkansas Historical Quarterly* 49 (Spring 1990).

Hamilton, Sylvia. "Our Mothers Grand and Great—Black Women of Nova Scotia." *Canadian Women Studies/les cashiers de la femme* 11 (Spring 1991).

Hardaway, Roger D. "African-American Women on the Western Frontier." *Negro History Bulletin* 60 (January-March 1997).

Harrigan, Stephen. "The Yellow Rose of Texas." *Texas Monthly*, April 1984.

Harris, Mark. "The Legend of Black Mary." *Black World* 8 (August 1950). Mary Fields.

Harris, Trudier. "'The Yellow Rose of Texas': A Different Cultural View." Chapter in *Juneteenth Texas: Essays in African-American Folklore*, eds. Francis Edward Abernethy, et al. Publication of the Texas Folklore Society, no. 54. Denton: University of North Texas Press, 1996.

Hay, Kenneth W. "I Remember Old Yogo and the Weatherwax: A Boyhood Idyll about Glory Holes and Bonanza Dreams." *Montana: The Magazine of Western History* 25 (Spring 1975). Includes information of former slave Millie Ringgold, a Black mine owner.

Hayden, Delores. "Biddy Mason's Los Angeles, 1851–1891." *California History* 68 (Fall 1989).

Henry, Annette. "African Canadian Women Teachers' Activism: Recreating Communities of Caring and Resistance." *Journal of Negro Education* 61 (Summer 1992).

Henson, Margaret. "She's the Real Thing." *Texas Highways* 33 (April 1986).

Herve, Julia Wright. "The Black Scholar Interviews Kathleen Cleaver." *Black Scholar* 3 (December 1971).

Howard, Vicki. "The Courtship Letters of an African American Couple: Race, Gender, Class, and the Cult of True Womanhood." *Southwestern Historical Quarterly* 100 (1996).

Hudson, Lynn M. "A New Look, or 'I'm Not Mammy to Everybody in California': Mary Ellen Pleasant, a Black Entrepreneur." *Journal of the West* 32 (July 1993).

Hulet, Diana. "McDaniel, 20-ish, Does Hollywood Her Way." *American Photo*, May–June 1995. Hollywood's Melodie McDaniel.

Hunton, A. W. "The Club Movement in California." *Crisis* 5 (December 1912). Black women's organizations.

Jackson, Elizabeth. "Toward a Multicultural History of Women in the Western United States." *Signs* 13 (Summer 1988). Feminist research with a multicultural emphasis.

Jackson, Lela. "Rachel Whitfield (1814–1908)." Chapter in *Women in Early Texas*, ed. Evelyn M. Carrington. Austin: Jenkins Publishing, 1975.

Johnson, Clifton H. "Mary Ann Shadd: Crusader for the Freedom of Man."
    Crisis (April-May 1971). Brief biographical sketch.

Jones, Mrs. Laurence C. "The Desire for Freedom." *Palimpsest* 7 (May 1927).
    Black abolitionist woman Charlotta Pyles.

Jones, Yvette. "Seeds of Compassion." *Texas Historian* 37 (November 1976).

"Juanita M. McDonald Wins Congressional Seat in California." *Jet*, 22 April
    1996.

Katz, Milton S., and Susan B. Tucker. "A Pioneer in Civil Rights: Esther
    Brown and the South Park Desegregation Case of 1948." *Kansas His-
    tory* 18 (1995–1996).

Lanza, Ruth Willett. "Aunt Clara Brown: Black Angel of Central City." *True
    West* 38 (April 1991).

Launius, Roger D. "A Black Woman in a White Man's Church: Amy E. Rob-
    bins and the Reorganization." *Journal of Mormon History* 19 (Fall
    1993).

Lemke-Santangelo, Gretchen. "African American Migrant Women in the San
    Francisco East Bay Area." Chapter in *American Labor in the Era of
    World War II*, eds. Sally M. Miller and Daniel A. Cornford. Westport,
    CT: Praeger, 1995.

Lind, Michael. "Obituary." *New Republic*, 12 February 1996. The death of
    Barbara Jordan.

Luchetti, Cathy, and Carol Olwell. "Minority Women." Chapter in *Women of
    the West*. New York: Orion Books, 1982.

Mathis, Annie Maie. "Negro Public Health Nursing in Texas." *Southern
    Workman* 56 (July 1927).

McCubrey, Joanne. "Trailblazer of Black History." *Westways* 82 (1 February
    1990). Profile.

McGraw, Dan. "Tackling Woes Others Won't." *U.S. News and World Report*,
    27 November 1995. Patricia Hogan Williams, church leader with the
    Windsor Village United Methodist Church of Houston, tackles social
    problems.

Min, Janice. "Hanging Tough." *People Weekly*, 15 May 1995. Feature on
    Miss USA Chelsi Smith, formerly Miss Houston and Miss Texas.

"Missouri Black Marriage Registers." *Ash Tree Echo* 28 (September 1993).

Moore, Shirley Ann. "'Her Husband Didn't Have a Word to Say.': Black
    Women and Blues Clubs in Richmond, California, during World War
    II." Chapter in *American Labor in the Era of World War II*, eds. Sally
    M. Miller and Daniel A. Cornford. Westport, CT: Praeger, 1995.

_____. "'Not in Somebody's Kitchen': African American Women Workers
    in Richmond, California, and the Impact of World War II." Chapter in
    Writing the Range: Race, Class, and Culture in the Women's West,
    eds. Elizabeth Jameson and Susan Armitage. Norman: University of
    Oklahoma Press, 1997.

Morris, Celia. "Changing the Rules and the Roles: Five Women in Public
    Office." Chapter in *The American Woman, 1992–1993*, eds. Paula

Ries and Anne J. Stone. New York: W. W. Norton and Company, 1992. Includes Maxine Waters.

Murphy, Lucretia P. "Black Women: Organizing to Lift...to Rise." *Texas Journal of Women and the Law* (4 (Summer 1995).

Nash, Sunny. "A Mission Completed for Doll." Chapter in *State Lines*, ed. Ken Hammond. College Station: Texas A&M University Press, 1993.

Newell, Linda King, and Valeen Tippets Avery. "Jane Manning James, Black Saint, 1847 Pioneer." *The Ensign* (August 1979).

Owens, M. Lilliana. "Julia Greeley, 'Colored Angel of Charity.'" *Colorado Magazine* 20 (1943). Biography of former slave Julia Greeley, later a servant to Governor Gilpin.

Perales, Marian. "Empowering 'The Welder': A Historical Survey of Women of Color in the West." Chapter in *Writing the Range: Race, Class, and Culture in the Women's West*, eds. Elizabeth Jameson and Susan Armitage. Norman: University of Oklahoma Press, 1997.

Pipkin, Loretta. "Loretta Pipkin: Finding My Place." *International Review of African American Art* 13 (1996).

Reese, Linda Williams. "Working in the Vineyard: African-American Women in All-Black Communities." *Kansas Quarterly* 25 (1992).

Riley, Glenda. "American Daughters: Black Women in the West." *Montana, the Magazine of Western History* 38 (February 1988); reprinted, "African American Women in the West." Section in *A Place to Grow: Women in the American West*. Arlington Heights, IL: Harlan Davidson, 1992. Riley calls on historians to increase their efforts in uncovering material on Black women.

Rodenberger, Lou Halsell. "A Developing Tradition: African-American Writers." Chapter in *Texas Women Writers: A Tradition of Their Own*, eds. Sylvia Ann Grider and Lou Halsell Rodenberger. College Station: Texas A&M University Press, 1997.

Rogers, B. Ann, and Linda Schott. "'My Mother Was a Mover': African American Seminole Women in Brackettville, Texas, 1914–1964." Chapter in *Writing the Range: Race, Class, and Culture in the Women's West*, eds. Elizabeth Jameson and Susan Armitage. Norman: University of Oklahoma Press, 1997.

Ruffin, Orolee. "'Jim-Crowing' Nurses." *Crisis* 37 (April 1930).

Sanders, Charles L. "Barbara Jordan: Texan Is a New Power on Capitol Hill." *Ebony*, February 1975.

Savage, W. Sherman. "Mary Ellen Pleasant." Section in *Notable American Women, 1607–1950*. Cambridge: Harvard University Press, 1971.

Schaffer, Ruth C. "The Health and Social Functions of Black Midwives on the Texas Brazos Bottom, 1920–1985." *Rural Sociology* 56 (Spring 1990).

Schwartz, Henry. "The Mary Walker Incident: Black Prejudice in San Diego, 1866." *Journal of San Diego History* 19 (1973).

Shadd, Adrienne. "Special Feature: 300 Years of Black Women in Canadian History." *Tiger Lily* 1 (1980).

Simond, Ada DeBlanc. "The Discovery of Being Black: A Recollection." *Southwestern Historical Quarterly* 76 (1973).

Smallwood, James M. "Black Freedwomen after Emancipation: The Texas Experience." *Prologue: The Journal of the National Archives* 27 (Winter 1995).

Smith, Gloria Lawsha. "Bessie Coleman: From the Cotton Fields to the Airfields." Chapter in *KenteCloth: African American Voices in Texas*, eds. Shery McGuire and John R. Posey. Denton: University of North Texas Press, 1995. Pilot born and raised in Texas.

Snapp, Elizabeth, and Harry F. Snapp, eds. "African American Women." Chapter in *Read All about Her!: Texas Women's History, a Working Bibliography*. Denton: Texas Woman's University Press, 1995.

Spickard, Paul R. "Work and Hope: African American Women in Southern California During World War II." *Journal of the West* 32 (July 1993).

"Stagecoach Mary." *Catholic Digest* (December 1959). Mary Fields, taken from the Gary Cooper article.

Taylor, Quintard "Mary Ellen Pleasant." Chapter in *By Grit and Grace: Eleven Women Who Shaped the American West*, eds. Glenda Riley and Richard W. Etulain. Golden, CO: Fulcrum Publishing, 1997.

Thompson, Cordell. "Mrs. Eldridge Cleaver Returns to U.S. to Give State of Revolution Message." *Jet*, 2 December 1971.

"Transmission and Use of an Illegal Syringe Exchange and Injection-Related Risk Behaviors among Street-Recruited Injection Drug Users in Oakland, California, 1992 to 1995." *AIDS Weekly Plus*, 5 October 1998.

White, Deborah Gray. "Mining the Forgotten: Manuscript Sources for Black Women's History." *Journal of American History* 74 (June 1987).

Williams, Lorece. "Lorece Williams." Chapter in *Growing Up in Texas: Recollections of Childhood*. Austin: Encino, 1972.

Williams, Patricia R. "Literary Traditions in Works by African-American Playwrights." Chapter in *Texas Women Writers: A Tradition of Their Own*, eds. Sylvia Ann Grider and Lou Halsell Rodenberger. College Station: Texas A&M University Press, 1997.

Williams, Rev. Cecil. "A Conversation with Angela." *Black Scholar* 3 (March–April 1973). Exclusive interview while Davis was still imprisoned for murder, kidnapping, and other charges.

Winegarten, Ruthe, and Merline Pitre. "Black Texas Women: 150 Years of Trial and Triumph." *The Journal of Southern History* 62 (1996).

Winegarten, Ruthe, and Rosanne M. Barker. "Black Texas Women: 150 Years of Trial and Triumph." *The Mississippi Quarterly* 50 (1997).

Wolfinger, Henry J. "A Test of Faith: Jane Elizabeth James and the Origins of the Utah Black Community." Chapter in *Social Accommodation in Utah*, ed. Clark Knowlton. Salt Lake City: University of Utah American West Center, 1975. Black servant of Joseph Smith lived a life of poverty and was a devout Mormon.

Womack, Ytasha L. "Teacher Gives Cues on Learning." *Emerge* 7 (September 1996). Actor Irma P. Hall of "A Family Thing" talks about teaching in Dallas.

Woodard, Helena. "Mary Ellen Pleasant." Chapter in *Notable Black American Women*, ed. Jessie Carney Smith. Detroit: Gale, 1992.

Wright, Roosevelt, Shirley W. King, William E. Berg, and Robert F. Creecy. "Job Satisfaction among Black Female Managers: A Causal Approach." *Human Relations* 40 (1987). Model developed for women in 5 southwestern states to report job satisfaction.

Yee, Shirley J. "Finding a Place: Mary Ann Shadd Cary and the Dilemmas of Black Migration to Canada, 1850–1870." *Frontiers: A Journal of Women Studies* 18, no. 3 (1997).

Young, Mary E. "Anita Scott Coleman: A Neglected Harlem Renaissance Writer." *CLA Journal* 40 (March 1997).

Books:

Asbaugh, Carolyn. *Lucy Parsons, American Revolutionary*. Chicago: Kerr, 1976.

Bass, Charlotta A. *Forty Years: Memoirs from the Pages of a Newspaper*. Los Angeles: Bass Publishers, 1960. Editor of the *California Eagle*.

Bass, Joseph Blackburn, and J. W. Duncan. *Butte's Colored Organizations: Churches, Lodges, Business Concerns, etc*. Helena: n.p., 1906.

Beals, Melba Pattillo. *Warriors Don't Cry: A Searing Memoir of the Battle to Integrate Little Rock's Central High*. New York: Pocket Books, 1994.

Blackwelder, Julia Kirk. *Women of the Depression: Caste and Culture in San Antonio, 1929–1939*. College Station, TX: Texas A&M University Press, 1984.

Braithwaite, Rella. *The Black Woman in Canada: A Book of Profiles on Black Women*. n.p.: Sister Vision, 1976.

Bramble, Linda. *Black Fugitive Slaves in Early Canada*. Vanwell History Project Series. St. Catherines: Vanwell, 1988.

Brand, Dionne, Lois De Shield, et al. *No Burden to Carry: Narratives of Black Working Women in Ontario 1920s to 1950s*. Toronto: University of Toronto Press, 1991.

Bristow, Peggy, et al. *We're Rooted Here and They Can't Pull Us Up: Essays in African Canadian Women's History*. Toronto: University of Toronto Press, 1994.

Brown, Elaine. *A Taste of Power: A Black Woman's Story*. New York: Pantheon Books, 1992.

Brown, Rosemary. *Being Brown: A Very Public Life*. Mississauga: Random House, 1989.

Bruÿn, Kathleen. *"Aunt" Clara Brown: Story of a Black Pioneer*. Boulder:
    Pruett Publishing Company, 1970. Combines fact and fiction with
    embarrassing "Negro" dialect.

Bryant, Ira B. *Barbara Charline Jordan: From the Ghetto to the Capitol*. Hous-
    ton: D. Armstrong Company, 1977.

Clark, Michael J. *U.S. Army Pioneers: Black Soldiers in Nineteenth Century
    Utah*. Fort Douglas, UT: Fort Douglas Military Museum, 1981.

Clayton, Sheryl H., ed. *Black Women Role Models of Greater St. Louis*. East
    St. Louis, IL: Essai Seay Publishers, 1982.

_____. *Black Women Role Models of Houston, Texas*. East St. Louis, IL:
    Essai Seay Publishers, 1986.

Cochran, Jo, et al., eds. *Gathering Ground: New Writing and Art by Northwest
    Women of Color*. Seattle: Seal Press, 1984. A cross-cultural anthol-
    ogy.

Coleman, Wanda. *Native in a Strange Land: Trials and Tremors*. Santa Rosa,
    CA: Black Sparrow Press, 1996.

Coughtry, Jamie, ed. *Lubertha Johnson: Civil Rights Efforts in Las Vegas,
    1940's–1960's*. Reno: Oral History Program, 1988.

Craft, Juanita. *A Child, the Earth, and a Tree of Many Seasons: The Voice of
    Juanita Craft*. Dallas: Halifax Publishing, 1982. Houston NAACP
    leader.

Crouchett, Lawrence P., Lonnie G. Bunch III, and Martha Kendall Winnacker.
    The History of the East Bay Afro-American Community, 1851–1977.
    Oakland: Northern California Center for Afro-American History and
    Life, 1989.

Crouchett, Lorraine Jacobs. *Delilah Leontium Beasley: Oakland's Crusading
    Journalist*. E. Cerrito, CA: Downey Place Publishing House, 1990.

Croxdale, Richard, and Melissa Hied, eds. *Women in the Texas Workforce:
    Yesterday and Today*. Austin: People's History of Texas, 1979.

Davis, Angela Y. *Angela Davis, An Autobiography*. New York: Random
    House, 1974. Collections of letters, poetry, essays.

Davis, Angela, and Bettina Aptheker. *If They Come in the Morning: Voices of
    Resistance*. New York: The Third Press, 1971. Collection of letters,
    poetry and essays.

Dr. Justina L. Ford House, Grand Opening and Dedication Ceremony. Denver:
    Black American West Museum and Heritage Center, 1988.

Elders, Jocelyn, and David Chanoff. *Jocelyn Elders, M.D.: From Sharecrop-
    per's Daughter to Surgeon General of the United States of America*.
    New York: Morrow, 1996.

Elgersman, Maureen G. *Unyielding Spirits: Black Women and Slavery in Early
    Canada and Jamaica*. New York: Garland, 1999.

Everett, Syble Ethel Byrd. *Adventures With Life: An Autobiography of a Dis-
    tinguished Negro Citizen*. Boston: Meador Publishing, 1945. Re-
    counts being raised in Oklahoma where she became a teacher. Also
    tells of experiences while a student at the University of Utah.

Finke, Blythe Foote. *Angela Davis: Traitor or Martyr of the Freedom of Expression*. Charlotteville, NY: Sam Har Press, 1972. Short book based on Davis' speeches.

Fisher, Ada Lois Sipuel, and Danny Goble. *A Matter of Black and White: The Autobiography of Ada Lois Sipuel Fisher*. Norman: University of Oklahoma Press, 1982; reprinted, 1996.

Govenar, Alan B. *The Life and Poems of Osceola Mays*. Racine, WI: Arcadian Press, 1989. Biography of a Texan woman.

Grant, Billie Arlene. *Black Women of the West: Success in the Workplace*. Denver: Billie Arlene Grant, 1982.

Hallman, Patsy. *A Psalm of Life—A Story of a Woman Whose Life Made a Difference—Willie Lee Campbell Glass*. Austin: Sunbelt Media, 1990. Blacks and education in Texas.

Holdredge, Helen. *Mammy Pleasant: San Francisco's Powerful and Sinister Ruler, 1815–1904*. New York: Ballantine, 1953.

————. *Mammy Pleasant's Cookbook*. San Francisco: 101 Productions, 1970. Includes biographical information. Sensationalized account.

————. *Mammy Pleasant's Partner*. New York: Putnam, 1954. Mrs. Pleasant's business partner Thomas Bell.

Hunt, Annie Mae, and Ruthe Winegarten. *I Am Annie Mae: An Extraordinary Woman in Her Own Words: The Personal Story of a Black Texas Woman*. Austin: Rosegarden Press, 1984; reprinted, Austin: University of Texas Press, 1996.

James, Joy, ed. *The Angela Y. Davis Reader*. Malden, MA: Blackwell Publishers, 1998. A collection of Davis' seminal writings.

Jones, Allene, Henry Lee Brown, Jr. and Michelle R. Brown. *The Memoirs of Elnora Brown*. Moab Community (Lexington), Texas: Mount Nebo African Methodist Episcopal Church, 1993. Brown's writings and recipes collected and printed to help with the renovation of the church she attended.

Jordan, Barbara, and Shelby Hearon. *Barbara Jordan, A Self-Portrait*. Garden City, NY: Doubleday, 1979.

Jordan, Julia K. Gibson, and Charlie Mae Brown Smith. *Beauty and the Best: Frederica Chase Dodd, the Story of a Life of Love and Dedication*. Dallas: Delta Sigma Theta Sorority, Dallas Alumnae Chapter, 1985. Texan educator, social worker, and sorority leader.

Katz, William Loren. *Black Women of the Old West*. New York: Atheneum Books, 1995. Juvenile.

Kennedy, Flo. *Color Me Flo: My Hard Life and Good Times*. New York: Prentice-Hall, 1976.

Ledé, Naomi W. *Precious Memories of a Black Socialite: A Narrative of the Life and Times of Constance Houston Thompson*. Houston: D. Armstrong Company, 1991. Life of a Houston socialite.

Lemke-Santangelo, Gretchen. *Abiding Courage: African American Migrant Women and the East Bay Community*. Chapel Hill: University of North Carolina Press, 1996. Rural-urban migration to the Bay area.

Levenson, Dorothy. *Women of the West*. New York: Watts, 1973.

Lowery, Linda. *Aunt Clara Brown*. Minneapolis: Lerner Publishing Group, 1998. Juvenile.

Luchetti, Cathy, and Carol Olwell. *Women of the West*. St. George, UT: Antelope Press, 1984. A cross-cultural study.

Malone, Ann Patton. *Women on the Texas Frontier: A Cross-Cultural Perspective*. El Paso: Texas Western Press, University of Texas at El Paso, 1983.

Miller, Robert H. *The Story of "Stagecoach" Mary Fields*. Stories of the Forgotten West Series. Englewood Cliffs, NJ: Silver Burdett Press, 1995.

Mock, Charlotte K. *Bridges: New Mexican Black Women, 1900–1950*. Albuquerque: New Mexico Commission on the Study of Women, 1985.

Montana Federation of Negro Women's Clubs, State Journal. Butte: Oates and Roberts, 1921. Proceedings of the first session of the Montana State Federation of Negro Women's Clubs held at Schaffer A.M.E. Chapel, Butte, Montana.

Mungen, Donna. *Life and Times of Biddy Mason: From Slavery to Wealthy California Laundress*. n.p., 1976.

Museum of African-American Life and Culture. *The Showed the Way: An Exhibit of Black Texas Women, 1836–1986*. Dallas: Museum of African-American Life and Culture, 1986.

Nadelson, Regina. *Who is Angela Davis: The Biography of a Revolutionary*. New York: P. H. Wyden, 1972.

Nash, Sunny. *Bigmama didn't shop at Woolworth's*. College Station: Texas A&M University Press, 1996.

Pitts, Lucia Mae. *One Negro WAC's Story*. Los Angeles: Lucia Mae Pitts, 1968. Includes experiences at Fort Huachuca, Arizona.

Ray, Emma P. *Twice Sold, Twice Ransomed: Autobiography of Mr. and Mrs. L. O. Ray*. Chicago: Free Methodist Publishing House, 1926. Southern and Western experiences of couple who became missionary workers in Seattle.

Reese, Linda Williams. *Women of Oklahoma, 1890–1920*. Norman: University of Oklahoma Press, 1997. Profiles some minority women.

Ropes, Hannah Anderson. *Six Months in Kansas, By a Lady*. Freeport, NY: Books for Libraries Press, 1972. Black woman writes about her life.

Scott, Victoria. *Sylvia Stark, a Pioneer: A Biography*. Seattle: Open Hand Publishing, 1991. Juvenile.

Silvera, Makeda, ed. *Silenced: Talks with Working Class West Indian Women About Their Lives and Struggles as Domestic Workers in Canada*. Toronto: Sister Vision, 1989.

Spann, Dorothy Bass. *Black Pioneers. A History of a Pioneer Family in Colorado Springs*. Colorado Springs: Little London Press, 1978; reprinted, Friends of the Colorado Springs Pioneer Museum, 1990.

Stanley, William David. *The Impact of the TV Event "Roots": A Case Study of East Texas Nonmetropolitan Black Women*. College Station, TX: Texas A&M University, 1979.

Thompson, Era Bell. *American Daughter*. St. Paul, MN: Minnesota Historical Society Press, 1946; reprinted, 1986. Social life and customs in North Dakota and Iowa from a future editor at *Ebony*.

Turner, Martha Anne. *The Life and Times of June Long*. Waco: Texian, 1969.

————. *The Yellow Rose of Texas: Her Saga and Her Song*. Austin: Shoal Creek Publishers, 1976.

————. *The Yellow Rose of Texas: The Story of a Song*. El Paso: Texas Western Press, 1971. Recounts the story of Emily, a slave woman captured by Mexican general Santa Ana, and how she inspired the song.

Who's Who Among Black Women in California. Inglewood: Who's Who Among Black Women in California, 1982.

Wiggins, Bernice Love. *Tuneful Tales*. El Paso: n.p., 1925.

Winegarten, Ruthe. *Black Texas Women: A Sourcebook: Documents, Biographies, Timeline*. Austin: University of Texas Press, 1996.

————. *Black Texas Women: 150 Years of Trial and Triumph*. Austin: University of Texas Press, 1995.

————. *Brave Black Women: From Slavery to the Space Shuttle*. Austin: University of Texas Press, 1997.

Women of Texas: A Brochure Honoring Miss Ellie Alma Walls, First Woman President of the Colored Teachers State Association of Texas. 65th Annual Convention, 24–26 November 1949, Houston.

Theses and Dissertations:

Abney, Lucille A. "Black Mothers' Perceptions of their Child-rearing Practices from 1945 to 1955: A Cohort of Southern Black Mothers Born in the 1930's." Ph.D. diss., Texas Woman's University, 1991. Galveston County, Texas.

Brandenstein, Sherilyn. "Prominent Roles of Black Womanhood in *Sepia Record*, 1952–1954." Master's thesis, University of Texas at Austin, 1989.

Brown, Angela Darlean. "Servants of the People: A History of Women in the Black Panther Party." AB thesis, Harvard University, 1992.

Brown, Bobby Joe. "The Relationship of Selected Biographical and Psychometric Characteristics for Disadvantaged Adolescent Females to Success in a Compensatory Education Program for Office Occupations." Thesis, University of Oklahoma, 1973. Vocational Education of women of Guthrie.

Butler, Anne Katherine M. "The Tarnished Frontier: Prostitution in the Trans-Mississippi West, 1865–1890." Ph.D. diss, University of Maryland College Park, 1979. Though Black women not the focus of this work, still an important study.

Dickson, Linda Faye. "The Early Club Movement Among Black Women in Denver, 1890–1925." Ph.D. diss., University of Colorado, 1982.

Evans, Eola Adeline. "Activity of Black Women in the Woman Suffrage Movement, 1900–1920." Master's thesis, Lamar University, 1987.

Gaston, John Coy. "The Denver, Colorado Area Black Professional/Businesswoman's Perception of Her Communication with the Black Male." Ph.D. diss., University of Colorado, 1979.

Gray, Pamela Lee. "Yvonne Brathwaite Burke: The Congressional Career of California's First Black Congresswoman, 1972–1978." Ph.D. diss., University of Southern California, 1987.

Hall, Ella. "The Development of the Kansas City, Kansas, Young Women's Christian Association." Master's thesis, University of Kansas, 1945.

Hudson, Lynn M. "When 'Mammy' Becomes a Millionaire: Mary Ellen Pleasant, an African American Entrepreneur." Ph.D. diss., Indiana University, 1996.

Kirk, Rita G. "Barbara Jordan: The Rise of a Black Woman Politician." Master's thesis, University of Arkansas, 1978.

Lemke-Santangelo, Gretchen. "A Long Road to Freedom: African American Migrant Women and Social Change in the San Francisco East Bay Area, 1940–1950." Ph.D. diss, Duke University, 1993.

LeSure, Lessie Lois Fowler. "Willa A. Strong: An Historical Study of Black Education in Southeastern Oklahoma." Ph.D. diss., University of Oklahoma, 1982.

London, Arcenia Phillips. "Determinants of Self-Acceptance of Black Female School Teachers Selected from the Syracuse Public School System and from Little Rock, Arkansas Public School System." Thesis, Syracuse University, 1976.

Miles, Merle Yvonne. "'Born and Bred' in Texas: Three Generations of Black Females: A Critique of Social Science Perceptions on the Black Female." Ph.D. diss., University of Texas at Austin, 1929.

Miller, Kate. "Some Pioneer Women Teachers in Texas before 1850." Master's thesis, University of Texas at Austin, 1929.

Neeley, Saran LeVahn. "A Study of the Rehabilitation Program at Crockett State School for Girls." Master's project, Texas Southern University, 1958.

Reese, Linda Williams. "Race, Class, and Culture: Oklahoma Women, 1890–1920." Ph.D. diss., University of Oklahoma, 1991.

Reynolds, James Talmadge. "The Preretirement Educational Needs of Retired Black Women Who Were Domestic Workers in Dallas, Texas." Ph.D. diss., East Texas State University, 1981.

Reynolds, Lois Arnell. "Sustenance Position of Texas Negro Domestic Servants in the Texas Economy." Master's thesis, Prairie View State Normal and Industrial College, 1942.

Royster-Horn, Juana Racquel. "The Academic and Extracurricular Undergraduate Experiences of Three Black Women at the University of Washington, 1935–1941." Ph.D. diss., University of Washington, 1980.

Shannon, Mary Gamble. "An Occupational Study of Negro Maids in Dallas." Master's thesis, Southern Methodist University, 1941.

Stanley, William David. "Southern Black Women's Orientation toward Interracial Relations: Study of a Small Nonmetropolitan-Urban East Texas Town, 1970–1977." Master's thesis, Texas A&M University, 1982.

Strong, Willa A. "The Origin, Development, and Current Status of the Oklahoma Federation of Colored Women's Clubs." Ph.D. diss., University of Oklahoma, 1957.

Yerwood, Ada Marie. "Certain Housing Conditions and Activities of Negro Girls Enrolled in Federally Aided Schools in Texas as One Index of Their Educational Needs." Master's thesis, Iowa Sate College, 1936.

Other:

Black on Black: Forever Free. KMTV Omaha, James A. Nelson, Producer, 1981. Review of exhibit "Forever Free," art by Black women, 1862–1980, Omaha's Josyln Museum. Videorecording.

"Dark Cowgirls and Other Prairie Queens." Linda Parris-Bailey, writer. Play about Black heroines of the West.

Older, Stronger, Wiser. By Dione Brand and Claire Prieto. National Film Board of Canada, 1989. Life stories of five women document the history of Black women in Canada. Videorecording.

Buffalo Soldiers

Articles:

Adde, Nick, and Leon Coates. "From the 'Buffalo Soldier' to the Astronaut." *Air Force Times* 44 (February 27, 1984).

Alexander, Thomas G., and Leonard J. Arrington. "The Utah Military Frontier, 1872–1912: Forts Cameron, Thornburgh, and Duchesne." *Utah Historical Quarterly* 32 (1964). Discusses the 9th Cavalry at Fort Duchesne.

Amos, Preston E. "Military Records for Nonmilitary History." Chapter in *Afro-American History: Sources for Research*, ed. Robert L. Clarke. Washington, DC: Howard University Press, 1981.

Andrews, George L. "The Twenty-Fifth Regiment of Infantry." *Journal of the Military Service Institution of the United States* 13 (1892); reprinted in *The Army of the United States: Historical Sketches of Staff and Line with Portraits of Generals-in-Chief*, eds. Theodore F. Rodenbough and William L. Haskin. New York: Argonaut, 1966.

"Army Historians Admit Racism Caused Downfall of Black Regiment." *Jet*, 14 August 1995. The 24th Infantry.

Arnold, Paul T. "Negro Soldiers in the United States Army." *Magazine of History* 10 (August—December 1909) and 11 (January—March 1910).

Bailey, Anne J. "Henry McCulloch's Texans and the Defense of Arkansas in 1862." *Arkansas Historical Quarterly* 46 (Spring 1987).

————. "A Texas Cavalry Raid: Reaction to Black Soldiers and Contrabands." *Civil War History* 35 (June 1989).

————. "Was There a Massacre at Poison Spring?" *Military History of the Southwest* 20 (Fall 1990).

Bailey, Sedell. "Buffalo Soldiers (Black Troops of the 9th and 10th Cavalries)," *Armor* 83 (January/February 1974); reprinted, *Lest We Forget* 4 (October 1996).

Banks, Leo W. "The Buffalo Soldiers." *Arizona Highways* 71 (January 1995).

Barr, Alwyn. "The Black Militia of the New South: Texas as a Case Study." *Journal of Negro History* 63 (1978).

Barrow, William. "The Buffalo Soldiers: The Negro Cavalry in the West, 1866–1891." *Black World* 16 (July 1967).

Baumler, Mark F., and Richard V. N. Ahlstrom. "The Garfield Monument: An 1886 Memorial of the Buffalo Soldiers in Arizona." *Cochise County Quarterly* 18 (Spring 1988).

Bennett, Charles. "The Buffalo Soldiers and the Apache War Chief." *El Palacio* 101 (Summer 1996). Native American reactions to Black troops.

Bigelow, John, Jr. "The Tenth Regiment of Cavalry." *Journal of the Military Service Institution of the United States* 13 (1892); reprinted in *The Army of the United States: Historical Sketches of Staff and Line with Portraits of Generals-in-Chief*, eds. Theodore F. Rodenbough and William L. Haskin. New York: Argonaut, 1966.

_____. "Tenth Regiment of Cavalry." *Journal of the Military Service Institution of the United States* 13 (January 1892).

Billington, Monroe Lee. "Black Cavalrymen and Apache Indians in New Mexico Territory." *Fort Concho and South Plains Journal* 22 (Summer 1990).

_____. "Black Soldiers at Fort Selden, New Mexico, 1866–1891." *New Mexico Historical Review* 62 (1987). About a thousand Blacks served at Fort Selden.

_____. "Civilians and Black Soldiers In New Mexico Territory, 1866–1900: A Cross-Cultural Experience." *Military History of the Southwest* 19 (Spring 1989).

"The Black Troopers." *Leisure House* 19 (1876).

Bond, Anne Wainstein. "Buffalo Soldiers at Fort Garland." *Colorado Heritage* (Spring 1996).

Bond, Horace Mann. "The Negro in the Armed Forces of the United States Prior to World War I." *Journal of Negro Education* 12 (1943).

Bowmaster, Patrick A. "Buffalo Soldier Emanuel Stance Received the Medal of Honor and Became a Legend." *Real West*, February 1997.

Bragg, Bea. "Calm 'Under Fire.'" *Highlights for Children*, February 1999. Biography of Henry Ossian Flipper.

Branley, Bill. "Black, White and Red: A Story of Black Cavalrymen in the West." *Soldiers* 47 (June 1981).

_____. "Black Soldiers at Fort Selden, New Mexico, 1868–1891." *New Mexico Historical Review* 62 (January 1987).

"Brief History of Troop 'K', Tenth U.S. Cavalry." *Colored American Magazine* 7 (December 1904). The 10th in Arizona and Montana.

Britten, Thomas A. "The Dismissal of the Seminole-Negro Indian Scouts, 1880–1914." *Fort Concho and the South Plains Journal* 24 (Summer 1992).

_____. "The Seminole-Indian Scouts in the Big Bend." *Journal of Big Bend Studies* 5 (1 January 1993).

Brown, Mark D. "The Negro in the Indian Wars." *Negro History Bulletin* 14 (March 1951).

Brown, Wesley A. "Eleven Men of West Point." *Negro History Bulletin* 19 (April 1956).

Buecker, Thomas R. "Confrontation at Sturgis: An Episode in Civil-Military Race Relations, 1885." *South Dakota History* 14 (Fall 1984).

_____. "Fort Niobrara, 1880–1906: Guardian of the Rosebud Sioux." *Nebraska History* 65 (Fall 1984).

_____. "One Soldier's Service: Caleb Benson in the Ninth and Tenth Cavalry, 1875–1908." *Nebraska History* 74 (February 1993).

_____. "Prelude to Brownsville: The Twenty-Fifth Infantry at Fort Niobrara, Nebraska, 1902–1906." *Great Plains Quarterly* 16 (1996).

_____. "10th Cavalry at Fort Robinson: Black Troops in the West, 1902–1907." *Military Images* 12 (May 1991).

_____. "The Tenth Cavalry at Fort Robinson: Black Troops in the West, 1902–1907." *Military Images* 12 (May-June 1991).

"Buffalo Soldiers." *The Golden Roots of the Mother Lode* 17 (Spring 1997).

"Buffalo Soldiers." *Soldiers* 45 (July 1990).

"The Buffalo Soldiers." *U.S. News and World Report* 120 (6 May 1996). Examination of the U.S. Army's last all-Black unit.

"Buffalo Soldiers Commemorated on U.S. Postage Stamp." *Stamps* 247 (2 April 1994).

"Buffalo Soldiers Help Open the West." *The NCO Journal* 5 (Summer 1995).

Bullard, Robert Lee. "The Negro Volunteer: Some Characteristics." *Journal of the Military Service Institution of the United States* 29 (July 1901).

Burkey, Elmer R. "The Thornburgh Battle With the Utes on Milk Creek." *Colorado Magazine* 13 (1936).

Butler, Ron. "The Buffalo Soldier." Section in *The Best of the Old West: An Indispensable Guide to the Vanishing Legend of the American West.* Austin: Texas Monthly Press, 1983.

_____. "The Buffalo Soldier, A Shining Light in the Military History of the American West." *Arizona Highways* (March 1972).

Carlson, Paul H. "William R. Shafter, Black Troops, and the Finale to the Red River War." *Red River Valley Historical Review* 3 (1978).

_____. "William R. Shafter, Black Troops, and the Opening of the Llano Estacado, 1870–1875." *Panhandle-Plains Historical Review* 47 (1974). Opening the Texas Panhandle for settlement.

_____. "William R. Shafter Commanding Black Troops in West Texas." *West Texas Historical Association Year Book* 50 (1984).

Carroll, H. Bailey. "Nolan's 'Lost Nigger' Expedition of 1877." *Southwestern Historical Quarterly* 44 (July 1940).

_____. "Lieutenant Henry Ossian Flipper." In *The Black Military Experience in the American West*, ed. John M. Carroll. New York: Liveright Publishing Corp., 1971.

Chase, Hal J. "Struggle for Equality: Fort Des Moines Training Camp for Colored Officers, 1917." *Phylon* 39 (Winter 1978).

Cholak, Carolyn. "The Buffalo Soldiers." *The Western Horseman* 58 (June 1993). Buffalo Soldier exhibit at the Kentucky Horse Park.

Choralian, Meg, ed. "Buffalo Soldiers." *Cobblestone* (February 1995).

Christian, Garna L. "Adding on Fort Bliss to Black Military Historiography." *West Texas Historical Association Year Book* 54 (1978).

_____. "The Brownsville Raid's 168th Man: The Court Martial of Corporal Knowles." *Southwestern Historical Quarterly* 93 (July 1989).

_____. "The El Paso Racial Crisis of 1900." *Red River Valley Historical Review* 6 (Spring 1981).

_____. "The Ordeal and the Prize: The 24th Infantry and Camp MacArthur." *Military Affairs* 50 (1986).

_____. "Rio Grande City: Prelude to the Brownsville Raid." *West Texas Historical Association Year Book* 57 (1981).

_____. "The Twenty-Fifth Regiment at Fort McIntosh: Precursor to Retaliatory Racial Violence." *West Texas Historical Association Year Book* 55 (1979).

_____. "The Violent Possibility: The Tenth Cavalry at Texarkana." *East Texas Historical Journal* 23 (Spring 1985).

Christian, Garna L., and Marvin E. Fletcher. "Black Soldiers in Jim Crow Texas, 1899–1917." *The American Historical Review* 102 (1997).

Clark, Michael J. "Improbable Ambassadors: Black Soldiers at Fort Douglas, 1896–99." *Utah Historical Quarterly* 46 (1978). The 24th in Utah. Before arriving at Fort Douglas, Salt Lake citizens were upset. After their arrival, citizens supported them and a newspaper that previously expressed contempt, apologized.

Clary, David A. "The Role of the Army Surgeon in the West: Daniel Weisel at Fort Davis, Texas, 1868–1872." *Western Historical Quarterly* 3 (January 1972). The 9th Cavalry and the 41st (later the 25th) Infantry were stationed there.

Clendenen, Clarence C. "The Punitive Expedition of 1916: A Reevaluation." *Arizona and the West* 3 (Winter 1961).

Cody, Michael A. "'Massacre Canyon': Buffalo Soldiers of the 9th Cavalry Regiment Who were Killed in an 1879 Clash with Apaches were Remembered during Ceremonies that Recognized their Heroic Action and Commemorated the New Mexico Battle in which They Fought." *Army* 47 (1 September 1997).1st

Coleman, Ronald G. "Blacks in Utah History: An Unknown Legacy." Chapter in *The Peoples of Utah*, ed. Helen Z. Papanikolas. Salt Lake City: Utah State Historical Society, 1976. From 1820s to the 1970s.

_____. "The Buffalo Soldiers: Guardians of the Uintah Frontier, 1886–1901." *Utah Historical Quarterly* 47 (1979). Examines relations between the Buffalo Soldiers, local whites and the Utes.

"The Colored Troops." *Army Navy Journal* 3 (February 1866).

Cornish, Dudley Taylor. "Kansas Negro Regiments in the Civil War." *Kansas Historical Quarterly* 20 (May 1953).

_____. "The Union Army as a Training School for Negroes." *Journal of Negro History* 37 (October 1952).

Cox, Clinton. "The Forgotten Heroes: The Story of the Buffalo Soldiers." *Scholastic* (1993).

Crimmins, Martin L. "Captain Nolan's Lost Troop on the Staked Plains." *West Texas Historical Association Year Book* 10 (October 1934); reprinted in *The Black Military Experience in the American West*, ed. John M. Carroll. New York: Liveright Publishing, 1971.

_____. "Colonel Buell's Expedition into Mexico in 1880." *New Mexico Historical Review* 10 (April 1935).

_____, ed. "Shafter's Explorations in Western Texas, 1875." *West Texas Historical Association Year Book* 9 (October 1933).

Czech, Kenneth P. "Reviews." *Wild West* 7 (October 1994). Buffalo Soldiers and battles with Indians.

Daniel, Wayne. "The Many Trials of Captain Armes." *Fort Concho Report* 13 (Fall 1981).

_____. "The 10th at Fort Concho, 1875–1882." *Fort Concho Report* 14 (Spring 1982).

Davis, Lenwood G., and George Hill, comps. "Blacks in the American West." Chapter in *Blacks in the American Armed Forces, 1776–1983: A Bibliography*. Westport, CT: Greenwood Press, 1985.

Davison, Michael S. "The Negro as Fighting Man." *Crisis* 76 (1969).

Dinges, Bruce J. "Colonel Grierson Invests on the West Texas Frontier." *Fort Concho Report* 16 (Fall 1984).

_____. "The Court-Martial of Lieutenant Henry O. Flipper: An Example of Black-White Relationships in the Army, 1881." *American West* 9 (January 1972).

_____. "The Irrepressible Captain Armes: Politics and Justice in the Indian-Fighting Army." *Journal of the West* 32 (April 1993).

_____. "New Directions in Frontier Military History: A Review Essay." *New Mexico Historical Review* 66 (1991).

_____. "Scandal in the Tenth Cavalry: A Fort Sill Case History, 1874." *Arizona and the West* 28 (Summer 1986). White officers of the 10th.

Dobak, William A. "Black Regulars Speak." *Panhandle-Plains Historical Review* 47 (1974). Veterans talk about their experiences for a 1930s project.

_____. "Civil War on the Kansas-Missouri Border: The Narrative of Former Slave Andrew Williams." *Kansas History* 6 (Winter 1983).

Dollar, Charles M. "Putting the Army on Wheels: The Story of the Twenty-Fifth Infantry Bicycle Corps." *Prologue* 17 (Spring 1985).

Drotning, Phillip T. "Black Soldiers and Red Men." Chapter in *Black Heroes in Our Nations's History: A Tribute to Those Who Helped Shape America*. New York: Cowles Book Company, 1969. Overview of the 9th and 10th.

East, Brenda K. "Henry Ossian Flipper: Lieutenant of the Buffalo Soldiers." *Persimmon Hill* 23 (Summer 1995).

Ege, Robert J. "Braves of all Colors: The Story of Isaiah Dorman, Killed at the Little Big Horn." *Montana: The Magazine of Western History* 16 (Winter 1966); reprinted in *The Black Military Experience in the American West*, ed. John M. Carroll. New York: Liveright Publishing, 1971.

_____. "Custer's Negro Interpreter." *Negro Digest* 14 (February 1965).

_____. "Isaiah Dorman: Negro Casualty with Reno." *Montana: The Magazine of Western History* 16 (Spring 1966).

Eppinga, Jane. "Henry O. Flipper in the Court of Private Land Claims: The Arizona Career of West Point's First Black Graduate." *The Journal of Arizona History* 36 (Spring 1995).

Fick, Janet. "Beyond the Call of Duty." *True West* 44 (1 June 1997). Fourteen Buffalo Soldiers and six of their white officers win the Medal of Honor.

Finley, James P. "Buffalo Soldiers at Fort Huachuca: Military Events in the American Southwest from 1910–1916." *Huachuca Illustrated* 1 (1993).

Fleming, Elvis E. "Captain Nicholas Nolan: Lost on the Staked Plains." *Texana* 4 (Spring 1966). Nolan and Negro cavalrymen searching for Comanches.

Fletcher, Marvin E. "Army Fire Fighters." *Idaho Yesterdays* 16 (Summer 1972).

_____. "The Black Bicycle Corps." *Arizona and the West* 16 (Autumn 1974). The 25th Infantry and the bicycle test for military transport included a 1,900 excursion.

_____. "The Black Soldier Athlete in the United States Army, 1890–1917." *Canadian Journal of History of Sport and Physical Education* 3 (December 1972).

Foner, Jack D. "Blacks in the Post-Civil War Army." Chapter in *Blacks and the Military in American History: A New Perspective*. New York: Praeger Publishers, 1974.

_____. "The Negro in the Post-Civil War Army." Chapter in *The United States Soldier Between Two Wars: Army Life and Reforms, 1865–1898*. New York: Humanities Press, 1970.

_____. "The Socializing Role of the Military." Chapter in *The American Military on the Frontier*, ed. James P. Tate. Washington, DC: Office of Air Force History, 1978. Foner posits that the experiences of the Buffalo Soldiers fit Turner's "safety valve" thesis better than any other group.

"Forgotten Heroes." *Airman* 39 (July 1995). Buffalo soldiers.

Galloway, Joseph L. "The Last of the Buffalo Soldiers: A New Look at the Army's Last All-Black Unit." *U.S. News and World Report*, 6 May 1996. A history of the 24th regiment, segregated through the Korean War.

Geary, James W. "Buffalo Soldiers and African-American Scouts on the Western Frontier, 1866–1900." *Ethnic Forum* 15 (Spring-Fall 1995).

Glasrud, Bruce A. "Western Black Soldiers Since *The Buffalo Soldiers*: A Review of the Literature." *Social Science Journal* 36, no. 2 (1999).

Glass, Edward L. N. "The Buffalo Soldiers in Arizona." Chapter in *The History of the Tenth Cavalry, 1866–1921*. Tucson: Edward L. N. Glass, 1921. Glass was an officer in the 10th Cavalry.

Good, Donnie D. "The Buffalo Soldiers." *American Scene Magazine10* (1970). This special issue is devoted to the cavalry.

Greene, Robert Ewell. "The Indian Campaigns, 1866–1890." Chapter in *Black Defenders of America, 1775–1973*. Chicago: Johnson Publishing Company, 1974.

Grinde, Donald, and Quintard Taylor. "Red vs. Black: Conflict and Accommodation in the Post Civil War Indian Territory." *American Indian Quarterly* 8 (1984).

Gustafson, Marsha L. "The Buffalo Soldiers: Heroes That History Forgot." *Persimmon Hill* 23 (Summer 1995).

Gwaltney, William W. "The Making of Buffalo Soldiers West." *Colorado Heritage* (Spring 1996).

————. "The Story of the Seminole-Negro Indian Scouts." *Lest We Forget* 4 (October 1996).

Gwaltney, William W., and Thomas Welle. "By Force of Arms: The Buffalo Soldiers of Colorado." *Colorado Heritage* (Spring 1996).

Hardaway, Roger D. "Buffalo Soldiers." Chapter in *A Narrative Bibliography of the African American Frontier: Blacks in the Rocky Mountain West*. Lewiston, NY: Mellen Press, 1995.

Hardeman, Nicholas P. "Brick Stronghold of the Border: Fort Assinniboine, 1879–1911." *Montana: The Magazine of Western History* 29 (Spring 1979). The descendant of a white lieutenant who served at the fort writes about the 10th Cavalry.

Harris, Theodore D. "Henry Flipper and Pancho Villa." *Password* 6 (Spring 1961).

Hayman, Perry. "Ten Years of Exciting Experiences and Hard Service in the Tenth Cavalry." *Winners of the West* (March 1925).

Haynes, Robert "The Houston Mutiny and Riot of 1917." *Southwestern Historical Quarterly* 76 (April 1973). White provocation leads to largest court martial in history.

————. "Unrest at Home: Racial Conflict between White Civilians and Black Soldiers in 1917." *Journal of the American Studies Association of Texas* 6 (1975).

Heini, Nancy. "Colonel Charles Young: Pointman." *Army* 27 (March 1977).

"Henry Ossian Flipper." *U.S. News and World Report*, 1 March 1999. Flipper receives pardon from President Clinton.

Hovey, H. W. "The Twenty-Fourth Regiment of Infantry." *Journal of the Military Service Institution of the United States* 15 (1894); reprinted in *The Army of the United States: Historical Sketches of Staff and Line with Portraits of Generals-in-Chief*, eds. Theodore F. Rodenbough and William L. Haskin. New York: Argonaut, 1966.

Hughes, Langston. "Charles Young: West Pointer, 1864–1922." Chapter in *Famous Negro Heroes of America*. New York: Dodd, Mead and Company, 1966. West Point graduate Young in the 10th Cavalry. Juvenile.

Hunter, John Warren. "Mutiny of Negro Soldiers at Fort Concho, 1882." *Hunter's Magazine* (December 1911).

_____. "A Negro Trooper of the Ninth Cavalry." *Frontier Times* 4 (April 1927); reprinted in *The Black Military Experience in the American West.*, ed. John M. Carroll. New York: Liveright Publishing, 1971. Reminiscences of Jacob Wilks, former slave who joined the 9th Cavalry in 1866.

Hurtt, C. M. "The Role of Black Infantry In the Expansion of the West." *West Virginia History* 40 (Winter 1979). Chronicles the exploits of the 24th and 25th infantry regiments.

Hutcheson, Grote. "The Ninth Cavalry." *By Valor and Arms* 1 (Spring 1975).

_____. "The Ninth Regiment of Cavalry." *Journal of Military Service Institution of the United States* 13 (1892); reprinted, chapter in *The Army of the United States: Historical Sketches of Staff and Line with Portraits of Generals-in-Chief*, eds. Theodore F. Rodenbough and William L. Haskin. New York: Argonaut, 1966.

_____. "The Ninth Regiment of Cavalry." *Journal of the Military Service Institution of the United States* 8 (1892); reprinted, *By Valor and Arms* 1 (Spring 1975).

Johnson, John Allen. "The Medal of Honor and Sergeant John Ward and Private Pompey Factor." *Arkansas Historical Quarterly* 29 (1970). Two Seminole-Indian Scouts win the Medal of Honor.

Jones, H. Conger. "Old Seminole Scouts Still Thrive on Border." *Frontier Times* 11 (1934).

Kachel, Douglas. "Fort Des Moines and Its African-American Troops in 1903/1904." *Palimpsest* 74 (Spring 1993).

Katz, William Loren. "The Black Infantry and Cavalry." Chapter in *The Black West: A Documentary and Pictorial History of the African American in the Westward Expansion of the United States*. New York: Simon and Schuster, 1996.

_____. "Six 'New' Medal of Honor Men." *Journal of Negro History* 53 (1968).

Keefe, Mark A. IV. "The Buffalo Soldier Rides Forever." *American Hunter* (October 1992).

Kesting, Robert W. "Conspiracy to Discredit the Buffalo Soldiers: The 92nd Infantry in World War II." *Journal of Negro History* 72 (Winter, Spring 1987). Problems stemmed from racist views of the U.S. Army command.

Knapp, George E. "Buffalo Soldiers: 1866 through 1890." *Military Review* 72 (July 1992).

Knuth, Priscilla, ed. "Cavalry in the Indian Country, 1864." *Oregon Historical Quarterly* 65 (March 1964).

Krapf, Kellie A., and Floyd B. Largent, Jr. "The Black Seminole Scouts: Soldiers Who Deserve High Praise." *Persimmon Hill* 24 (Winter 1996).

Lamkin, Patricia E. "Blacks in San Angelo: Relations between Fort Concho and the City, 1875–1889." *West Texas Historical Association Year Book* 66 (1990).

Langellier, John Phillip. "'Knowing No Fear': Buffalo Soldiers of the American West." *Kansas Heritage* 5 (Autumn 1997).

_____. "Walk-A-Heaps: Black Infantrymen in the West." *Wild West*, February 1997. Focus on the 24th and 25th infantry.

Langellier, John Phillip, and Alan M. Osur. "Chaplain Allen Allensworth and the 24th Infantry, 1886–1906." *Smoke Signal* 40 (Fall 1980); reprinted in *Brand Book 4*. Tucson: Tucson Corral of the Westerners, 1984.

Leckie, William H. "Black Regulars on the Texas Frontier, 1866–85." Chapter in *Texas Military Experience: From the Texas Revolution through World War II*, ed. Joseph G. Dawson III. College Station: Texas A&M University Press, 1995.

_____. "Buell's Campaign." *Red River Historical Review* 3 (Spring 1978).

"Lee Coffee, Jr. Tells the Buffalo Soldiers' Story." *Emerge* 7 (1 March 1996).

Lee, Irvin H. "The Indian Fighters." Chapter in *Negro Medal of Honor Men*. New York: Dodd, Mead and Company, 1967. Recounting of events that garnered the Medal of Honor for the Buffalo Soldiers.

Leiker, James N. "Black Soldiers at Fort Hayes, Kansas, 1867–1869: A Study in Civilian and Military Violence." *Great Plains Quarterly* 17 (Winter 1997).

Lemus, Rienzi R. "The Enlisted Man in Action or, The Colored American Soldier in the Philippines." *Colored American Magazine*, May 1902. Routines of the 25th Infantry

Leonard, John. "Television." *New York* 30 (8 December 1997). Television show "Buffalo Soldiers" rewrites the West.

Lindemeyer, Otto. "Black and Red: The Frontier Wars, 1870–1890." Chapter in *Black and Brave: The Black Soldier in America*. New York: McGraw-Hill, 1970.

"List of Actions, etc., With Indians and Other Marauders, Participated in by the Tenth U.S. Cavalry, Chronologically Arranged-1867–1897." *Journal of the U.S. Cavalry* (December 1897).

Longacre, Edward G. "A Philadelphia Aristocrat with the 'Buffalo Soldiers.'" *Journal of the West* 18 (April 1979).

Lowe, Albert S. "Camp Life of the Tenth U.S. Cavalry." *Colored American Magazine* 7 (March 1904).

Lowry, Jack. "Buffalo Soldiers." *Texas Highways* 36 (February 1989).

Maraniss, David. "Buffalo Soldiers: Forgotten Black Heroes of the Old West." *Washington Post Magazine* (20 January 1991).

Martinal, Doris. "The Negro Raid." *Texas History Teachers Bulletin* 14 (December 1927).

Marszalek, John F., Jr. "A Black Cadet at West Point." *American Heritage* 12 (August 1971).

Mattison, Ray H. "The Army Post on the Northern Plains, 1865–1885." *Nebraska History* 35 (1954).

Matthews, Jim. "Squarely Fought: Fort Concho and the Campaign Against Victorio, 1880." *West Texas Historical Association Year Book* 69 (1993).

May, Robert E. "Invisible Men: Blacks and the U.S. Army in the Mexican War." *Historian* 49 (1987).

McChristian, Douglas C. "'Dress on the Colors, Boys!': Black Noncommissioned Officers in the Regular Army, 1866–1898." *Colorado Heritage* (Spring 1996).

_____. "Grierson's Fight at Tinaja De Las Palmas: An Episode in the Victorio Campaign." *Red River Valley Historical Review* 7 (1982).

McClung, Donald R. Second Lieutenant Henry O. Flipper: A Negro Officer on the West Texas Frontier." *West Texas Historical Association Year Book* 47 (1971).

McConnell, Roland C. "Isaiah Dorman and the Custer Expedition." *Journal of Negro History* 33 (July 1948). The Black guide with Custer.

McDaniel, Reginald W. "Buffalo Soldiers Won their Spurs." *Wild West* 7 (February 1995). The 9th and 10th Cavalry overcome great odds.

McKaine, Osceola E. "The Buffaloes." *Outlook* 119 (22 May 1918).

Melzer, Richard. "On Villa's Trail in Mexico: The Experiences of a Black Cavalryman and a White Infantry Officer, 1916–1917." *Military History of the Southwest* 21 (Fall 1991).

Miles, Donna. "They Ranged the Old West as Buffalo Soldiers." *Soldiers* 45 (July 1990).

Miles, Susan. "The Soldiers' Riot." *Fort Concho Report* 3 (Spring 1981).

Monnett, John H. "Relief and Retribution." Chapter in *The Battle of Beecher Island and the Indian War of 1867–1869*. Niwot, CO: University Press of Colorado, 1992. The 10th Cavalry's pivotal involvement in the rescue during the affair.

Morey, Lewis S. "The Cavalry Fight at Carrizal." *Journal of U.S. Cavalryman* (January 1917).

Moss, James M. "Recent Experiments in Infantry Bicycling Corps." *Outings* (February 1897). The 25th Infantry Bicycle Corps at Fort Missoula, Montana.

Moulton, Candy. "Henry Ossian Flipper's Remarkable Journey From Slavery to West Point to the West." *Wild West*, June 1997. Interview with Jane Eppinga, author of *Henry Ossian Flipper: West Point's First Black Graduate.*

————. "Twenty-Three Buffalo Soldiers Received the Medal of Honor in the 19th Century." *Wild West*, February 1998. Interview with Frank Schubert, author of *Black Valor: Buffalo Soldiers and the Modal of Honor, 1870–1898.*

Murray, Robert A. "The United States Army in the Aftermath of the Johnson County Invasion: April through November 1892." *Annals of Wyoming* 38 (April 1966); reprinted in *The Black Military Experience in the American West*, ed. John M. Carroll. New York: Liveright Publishing, 1971.

Myers, Lee. "Mutiny at Fort Cummings." *New Mexico Historical Review* 46 (1971). The truth behind the 1867 mutiny, based on military records.

Nalty, Bernard C. "Reaction in the South, Action in the West." Chapter in *Strength for the Fight: A History of Black Americas in the Military.* New York: Free Press, 1986.

Nash, Horace Daniel. "Community Building on the Border: The Role of the 24th Infantry Band at Columbus, New Mexico, 1916–1922." *Fort Concho and the South Plains Journal* 22 (1990).

"A Negro Trooper of the Ninth Cavalry." *Frontier Times* 4.

"New Concepts in Tourism Development." *Business America* 113 (30 November 1992). Cultural diversity considerations in tourism, as evidenced by the Buffalo Soldier monument.

Nunn, W. Curtis. "Eighty-Six Hours Without Water on the Texas Plains." *Southwestern Historical Quarterly* 43 (January 1940). Account of Captain Nicholas Nolan and a company of the 10th Cavalry.

O'Connor, Richard. "'Black Jack' of the 10th." *American Heritage* 18 (February 1967). Traces the 10th before and during Pershing's command.

O'Neill, Alexis. "Welcome to Buffalo Soldier Country." *Cobblestone* 16 (1 February 1995).

Perkins, Frances Beecher. "Two Years with a Colored Regiment, A Woman's Experience." *New England Magazine*, January 1898.

Perry, Alexander W. "The Ninth United States Cavalry in the Sioux Expedition of 1890." *Journal of United States Cavalry Association* 4 (March 1891).

Phillips, Thomas D. "The Black Regulars." In *The West of the American People*, eds. Allen G. Bogue, Thomas D. Phillips, and James E. Wright. Itasca, IL: F. E. Peacock Publishers, 1970. Overview of the Buffalo Soldiers in the late 19th century.

Pickens, William. "Death Detail: Trial and Execution of Thirteen Negro Soldiers at Fort Sam Houston, Texas, December, 1917." *World Tomorrow* 13 (April 1930).

Pierson, Lloyd. "Buffalo Soldiers Come to Spanish Valley." *Canyon Legacy* (Winter 1996).

Pittman, Ruth. "Allen Allensworth: Man of Ambition." *Crisis* 98 (February 1990). Describes his career.

Porter, Kenneth Wiggins. "Negroes and Indians on the Texas Frontier, 1831–1876." *Journal of Negro History* 41 (July 1956).

_____. "Negroes and Indians on the Texas Frontier, 1834–1874." *Southwestern Historical Quarterly* 53 (1949).

_____. "The Seminole in Mexico, 1850–1861." *Hispanic American Historical Review* 31 (1951).

_____. "The Seminole Negro-Indian Scouts, 1870–1881." *Southwestern Historical Quarterly* 56 (January 1952).

_____. "The Seminole Negro Indian Scouts, Texas, 1870–1914." Chapter in *The Black Seminoles: History of a Freedom-Seeking People*, eds. Alcione M. Amos and Thomas P. Senter. Gainesville: University of Florida Press, 1996.

Price, Byron. "Mutiny at San Pedro Springs." *By Valor and Arms* 1 (Spring 1975).

Rackleff, Robert B. "The Black Soldier in Popular American Magazines, 1900–1917." *Negro History Bulletin* 34 (1971).

Rampp, Lary C. "Negro Troop Activity in Indian Territory, 1863–1865." *Chronicles of Oklahoma* 47 (1969). Includes exploits of the 1st Kansas Colored Volunteer Infantry Regiment.

"Record of the 24th Infantry." *Manila Times*, 29 June 1902.

Reddick, Lawrence D. "The Negro Policy of the United States Army, 1775–1945." *Journal of Negro History* 34 (January 1949). Covers the Buffalo Soldiers.

Reeve, Frank D., ed. "Frederick E. Phelps: A Soldier's Memoirs." *New Mexico Review* 25 (April 1950). Includes Buffalo Soldiers.

Remington, Frederic. "Artist Rides with 10th U.S. Cavalry, A Scout With the Buffalo-Soldiers, Famous Negro Dragoons." *Butterfield Express: Historical Newspaper of the Southwest* 14, August—September 1966.

_____. "A Scout with the Buffalo Soldiers." *Century Magazine* 37, April 1889; reprinted in *Pacific Historian* 12 (Spring 1968); reprinted in *Frederic Remington's Own West*, ed. Harold McCracken. New York: Dial Press, 1960; reprinted in *The Black Military Experience in the American West*, ed. John M. Carroll. New York: Liveright Publishing Corp., 1971; reprinted in *Pacific Historian* 12 (Spring 1968). The Black soldiers speak in a stereotypical style.

_____. "Two Gallant Young Cavalrymen." *Harper's Weekly*, March 22, 1890.

_____. "Vagabonding with the Tenth Horse." *Cosmopolitan Magazine* 22, February 1897; reprinted in *The Black Military Experience in the American West*, ed. John M. Carroll. New York: Liveright Publishing Corp., 1971. Remington accompanies the 10th Cavalry while they are on maneuvers near Fort Assiniboine, Montana.

Reynolds, George W. "Nature Sets the Stage as Defeated Men Pray for Quenching Rains." *Montana: The Magazine of Western History* 10 (Autumn 1960). Role of Black troops near Wallace, Montana, aid in fire fighting.

Rickey, Don. "An Indian Wars Combat Record." *By Valor and Arms* 2 (1975). Discusses the roles of the Black regiments.

Rippy, J. Fred. "Some Precedents of the Pershing Expedition into Mexico." *Southwestern Historical Quarterly* 60 (July 1956).

Robinson, Michael C., and Frank N. Schubert. "David Fagen: An Afro-American Rebel in the Philippines, 1899–1901." *Pacific Historical Review* 44 (February 1975). Some Buffalo Soldiers also fought in the Philippines.

Rolley, LaNelda. "Buffalo Soldiers Ride Again." *New Mexico Magazine* 72 (July 1994). Recognition for Black troops.

Ross, Leon Thomas. "Buffalo Soldiers." *The Far-Westerner* 33 (July 1992).

Rowe, Mary Ellen. "The Early History of Fort George Wright: Black Infantrymen and Theodore Roosevelt in Spokane." *Pacific Northwest Quarterly* 80 (July 1989).

"Samuel C. Coleman, November 10, 1980." *Jet*, 13 November 1995. Coleman honored on that date as the oldest Black war veteran.

Savage, W. Sherman. "Blacks in the Military." Chapter in *Blacks in the West*. Westport, CT: Greenwood Press, 1976.

_____. "The Role of Negro Soldiers in Protecting the Indian Frontier from Intruders." *Journal of Negro History* 36 (January 1951).

Schubert, Frank N. "Black Soldiers on the White Frontier: Some Factors Influencing Race Relations." *Phylon* 32 (Winter 1971). Author surmises that the proximity of Native Americans may have affected how the troops were embraced in Wyoming.

_____. "The Fort Robinson YMCA, 1902–1907: A Social Organization in a Black Regiment." *Nebraska History* 55 (Summer 1974). The importance of the YMCA for the 10th Cavalry.

_____. "The Suggs Affray: The Black Cavalry in the Johnson County War." *Western Historical Quarterly* 4 (January 1973). Demonstrates the racism against Black soldiers and how the military handled the incident.

_____. "Ten Troopers: Buffalo Soldier Medal of Honor Men Who served at Fort Robinson." *Nebraska History* 78 (Winter 1997).

_____. "Troopers, Taverns, and Taxes: Fort Robinson, Nebraska, and Its Municipal Parasite, 1886–1911." Chapter in *Soldiers and Civilians: The U.S. Army and the American People*, eds. Garry D. Ryan and Timothy K. Nenninger. Washington, DC: National Archives and Records Administration, 1987.

_____. "The Violent World of Emmanuel Stance." *Nebraska History* 55 (Summer 1974). Profile of Medal of Honor winner.

Seraile, William. "Fort Missoula, 1891–1898." Chapter in *Voice of Dissent: Theophilus Gould Steward (1843–1924) and Black America*. Brooklyn: Carlson Publishing Company, 1991. Chaplain Steward and the 25th Infantry at Fort Missoula, Montana.

_____. "Theophilus G. Steward, Intellectual Chaplain, 25th US Colored Infantry." *Nebraska History* 66 (Fall 1985).

Shafter, W. R. "Shafter's Explorations in Western Texas, 1875." Ed. Martin L. Crimmins. *West Texas Historical Association Year Book* 9 (1933).

Simmons, Charlie. "Thanksgiving Day in the Tenth Cavalry." *Voice of the Negro* 2 (January 1905).

Smith, C. Calvin. "The Houston Riot of 1917, Revisited." *Houston Review* 13 (1991).

_____. "On the Edge: The Houston Riot of 1917 Revisited." *Griot* 10 (Spring 1991).

Smythe, Donald. "John J. Pershing at Fort Assiniboine." *Montana, the Magazine of Western History* 18 (January 1969). Pershing was lieutenant with the 10th Cavalry.

_____. "John J. Pershing: Frontier Cavalryman." *New Mexico Historical Review* 38 (1963). Pershing with the 10th Cavalry at Fort Assiniboine.

"Soldier in Texas." *Crisis* 1 (May 1911).

Spiller, Roger J. "Honoring the Buffalo Soldiers." *American Heritage* 43 (February-March 1992).

Spratt, Stephen D. "Buffalo Soldiers Ride Again." *The American Legion* 142 (1 January 1997). Young Black males find role models in Buffalo Soldiers.

Starr, Michelle. "Buffalo Soldier." *Army* 31 (January 1981).

Stiles, T. J. "Buffalo Soldiers." *Smithsonian* 29 (December 1998).

Stover, Earl F. "Black Chaplains." Section in *Up From Handymen: The United States Army Chaplaincy, 1865–1920*. Washington, DC: Department of the Army, 1977. Roles of the five Black army chaplains in the West.

_____. "Chaplain Henry V. Plummer, His Ministry and His Court-Martial." *Nebraska History* 56 (Spring 1971).

Swisher, C. Kevin. "Frontier Heroes." *Texas Highways* 39 (July 1992). Seminole-Negro scouts.

Taylor, Quintard. "Comrades of Color: Buffalo Soldiers in the West: 1866–1917." *Colorado Heritage* (Spring 1996).

_____. "From Esteban to Rodney King: Five Centuries of African American History in the West: More than Cowboys and Buffalo Soldiers." *Montana: The Magazine of Western History* 46 (Winter 1996).

Temple, Frank M. "Colonel B. H. Grierson's Administration of the District of the Pecos." *West Texas Historical Association Year Book* 38 (1962).

_____. "Colonel B. H. Grierson's Victorio Campaign." *West Texas Historical Association Year Book* 35 (October 1959); reprinted in *The Black Military Experience in the American West*, ed. John M. Carroll. New York: Liveright Publishing, 1971.

_____. "Colonel Grierson in the Southwest." *Panhandle-Plains Historical Review* 30 (1957).

_____. "Discipline and Turmoil in the Tenth U.S. Cavalry." *West Texas Historical Association Year Book* 17 (Winter 1985).

_____. "The Tenth United States Cavalry in Texas." *Fort Concho Report* 17 (Winter 1985).

"The Tenth U.S. Cavalry...1867–1897." *Journal of U.S. Cavalry* (December 1897).

Theisen, Lee Scott, ed. "The Fight in Lincoln, N.M., 1878: The Testimony of Two Negro Participants." *Arizona and the West* 12 (Summer 1970).

Thompson, Erwin N. "The Negro Soldier and His Officers." In *The Black Military Experience in the American West*, ed. John M. Carroll. New York: Liveright Publishing, 1971. A condensed study of the Black regiments.

_____. "The Negro Soldiers on the Frontier: A Fort Davis Case Study." *Journal of the West* 7 (April 1968). Between 1867 and 1885, all Black units were stationed at Fort Davis at some time.

_____. "Private Bentley's Buzzard." Chapter in *The Black Military Experience in the American West*, ed. John M. Carroll. New York: Liveright Publishing, 1971.

Thybony, Scott. "Against All Odds, Black Seminoles Won Their Freedom." *Smithsonian* 22 (August 1991).

Troxel, Erwin N. "The Tenth Cavalry in Mexico." *U.S. Cavalry Journal* 18 (October 1916).

Utley, Robert M. "The Buffalo Soldiers and Victorio." *New Mexico Magazine* 62 (March 1984). The role of the 9th and 10th cavalries in ending the "Victorio War."

_____. "'Pecos Bill' on the Texas Frontier." *American West* 6 (January 1969).

Villard, Oswald Garrison. "The Negro in the Regular Army." *Atlantic Monthly* 91 (June 1903). Grandson of abolitionist William Lloyd Garrison and founder of the NAACP recounts that history.

Waide, C. D. "When Psychology Failed: An Unbiased Fact-Story of the Houston Race Riot of 1917." *Houston Gargoyle* (15, 22, and 29 May; plus 5 and 12 June 1928).

Wallace, Andrew. "The Sabre Retires: Pershing's Cavalry Campaign in Mexico, 1916." *Smoke Signal* 9 (Spring 1964).

Wallace, Edward S. "General John Lapham Bullis, Thunderbolt of the Texas Frontier, I." *Southwestern Historical Quarterly* 54 (April 1951).

_____. "General John Lapham Bullis, Thunderbolt of the Texas Frontier, II." *Southwestern Historical Quarterly* 55 (July 1951).

82   Blacks in the American West

Ward, C. H. "A Trip to the Cavalry Camps in Southern Arizona." *Cosmopolitan* 2 (October 1886). Black soldiers included.

Warner, Ezra J. "A Black Man in the Long Gray Line." *American History Illustrated* 4 (January 1970). Biography of Henry O. Flipper.

Weidman, Budge. "Preserving the Legacy of the United States Colored Troops." *Prologue* 29 (1997).

Wharfield, H. B. "The Affair at Carrizali: Pershing's Punitive Expedition." *Montana: The Magazine of Western History* 18 (October 1968). The 10th Cavalry at Chihuahua, Mexico.

————. "A Fight with the Yaquis at Bear Valley, 1918." *Arizoniana* 4 (1963). Skirmish of January 9, 1918, involving the 10th Cavalry and 30 Yaquis.

————. "Tenth Cavalry in the Early Days." Chapter in *10th Cavalry and Border Fights*. El Cajon, CA: The Author, 1965. Wharfield was a white officer who served with the 10th years afterward.

White, Lonnie J. "The Battle of Beecher Island: The Scouts Hold Fast on the Arickaree." *Journal of the West* 5 (January 1966).

Williams, Anthony. "The Buffalo Soldier Monument." *Army* 47 (1 February 1997). The tribute to the 9th and 10th at Fort Leavenworth.

Williams, Clayton W. "A Threatened Mutiny of Soldiers at Fort Stockton in 1873 Resulted in Penitentiary Sentences of Five to Fifteen Years." *West Texas Historical Association Year Book* 52 (1976).

Williams, Mary L. "Empire Building: Colonel Benjamin H. Grierson at Fort Davis, 1882–1885." *West Texas Historical Association Year Book* 61 (1985).

————. "Fort Davis, Texas: Key Defense Post on the San Antonio—El Paso Road." *Password* 31 (Winter 1986).

Wilson, Steve. "A Black Lieutenant in the Ranks." *American History Illustrated* 18 (December 1983).

Woodhull, Frost. "The Seminole Indian Scouts on the Border." *Frontier Times* 15 (1937).

Woolley, Bryan. "Freedom Fighters." *Dallas Life Magazine* (2 February 1992).

Young, Karl. "A Fight That Could Have Meant War." *American West* 3 (Spring 1966). The 10th Cavalry in New Mexico and Mexico.

Young, Richard. "The Brownsville Affray." *American History Illustrated* 21 (October 1986).

Zollo, Richard P. "General Francis S. Dodge and His Brave Black Soldiers." *Essex Institute Historical Collections* 122 (July 1986).

Books:

Alexander, Charles C. *Battles and Victories of Allen Allensworth*. Boston: Sherman, French, and Company, 1914. Allensworth of the 24th Infantry was one of five Black chaplains with the Buffalo Soldiers.

Amos, Preston E. *Above and Beyond in the West: Black Medal of Honor Winners, 1870–1890*. Falls Church, VA: Pioneer America Society Press, 1974.

Bailey, Linda C. *Fort Missoula's Military Cyclists: The Story of the 25th U.S. Infantry Bicycle Corps*. Missoula: The Friends of the Historical Museum at Fort Missoula, 1997. Monograph.

Baker, Edward I. *Roster of Non-Commissioned Officers of the Tenth Cavalry*. St. Paul: n.p., 1897.

Beef, Catherine. *Buffalo Soldiers*. New York: Twenty-First Century Books, 1993.

Bigelow, John, Jr. *On the Bloody Trail of Geronimo*. Los Angeles: Westernlore Press, 1968. Illustrations with maps concerning the 10th Cavalry in New Mexico.

Billington, Monroe Lee. *New Mexico's Buffalo Soldiers: 1866–1900*. Niwot, CO: University Press of Colorado, 1991.

Black, Lowell D., and Sarah H. Black. *An Officer and a Gentleman: The Military Career of Lieutenant Henry O. Flipper*. Dayton, OH: Lora Company, 1985.

The Black Military Experience in the American West (The Black Military Art Show, Fort Leavenworth, Kansas, Dec. 1973–Feb. 1974). John M. Carroll military art collection: Fort Leavenworth Museum, 1973. Art catalog.

Blocksom, Augustus P., et al. *Affray at Brownsville, Texas, August 13 and 14, 1900, Investigation of the Conduct of U.S. Troops*. Washington, DC: U.S. Government Printing Office, 1906.

Bowmaster, Patrick A. *Occupation—Soldier: The Life of 1st Sgt. Emanuel Stance of the 9th U.S. Cavalry Buffalo Soldiers, the First African-American to Win the Congressional Medal of Honor for Action in the Post-civil War Period*. 1995. An independent study project completed at Virginia Polytechnic Institute and State University, Dr. Hayward Farrar director.

Braddy, Haldeen. *Pershing's Mission in Mexico*. El Paso: Texas Western Press, 1966.

Buffalo Soldiers at Fort Leavenworth in the 1930s and Early 1940s. Fort Leavenworth, KS: Combat Studies Institute, U.S. Army Command and General Staff College, 1991. George E. Knapp, interviewer.

Buffalo Soldiers West. Mattituck, NY: Amereon, 1985.

Buffalo Soldiers. Broomall, PA: Chelsea House, 1997. Juvenile.

Buffalo Soldiers. Friends Series, Vol. 29, no. 9. Southfield, MI: Ceco Publishing Company, 1972.

Cage, James C., and James M. Day. *The Court Martial of Henry Ossian Flipper: West Point's First Black Graduate*. El Paso: El Paso Corral of the Westerners, 1981.

Carlson, Paul H. *"Pecos Bill": A Military Biography of William R. Shafter*. College Station: Texas A&M University Press, 1989.

Carroll, John M., ed. *The Black Military Experience in the American West.* New York: Liveright Publishing, 1971.

_____. *Buffalo Soldiers West.* Fort Collins, CO: Old Army Press, 1971; reprinted, Mattituck, NY: Amereon, 1995. Oversized picture book with over fifty full-page drawings by thirteen artists.

Cashin, Herschel V., et al, eds. *Under Fire with the Tenth U.S. Cavalry.* New York: F. Tennyson Neely, 1899, reprinted, New York: Arno Press, 1969; reprinted, Niwot, CO: University Press of Colorado, 1993. Primarily, the 10th Cavalry's role in the Spanish American War.

_____, et al. *Under Fire with the Tenth Cavalry. Review of the Negro's Participation in the Wars of the United States. The Ninth and Tenth Cavalries. Indian Campaigns.* Chicago: American Publishing House, 1899.

Chelsea, Taressa, ed. *The Buffalo Soldiers.* Broomall, PA: Chelsea House, 1997.

Chew, Abraham A. *A Biography of Colonel Charles Young.* Washington, DC: R. L. Pendleton, 1923.

Christian, Garna L. *Black Soldiers in Jim Crow Texas, 1899–1917.* Centennial Series of the Association of Former Students, no. 57. College Station: Texas A&M University Press, 1995.

Clendenen, Clarence C. *Blood on the Border: The United States Army and the Mexican Irregulars.* New York: Macmillan, 1969.

Conway, Elliot. *The Buffalo Soldier.* New York: State Mutual Book and Periodical Service, 1988; reprinted, Thorndike: Thorndike Press, 1990.

Cox, Clinton. *The Forgotten Heroes: The Story of the Buffalo Soldiers.* New York: Scholastic, 1993. Juvenile.

DeBarthe, Joe. *Life and Adventures of Frank Grouard*, ed. Edgar J. Stewart. Norman: University of Oklahoma Press, 1958. A scout for the U.S. army. Though Grouard claimed a Polynesian heritage, many believed he was a mulatto who was hiding his Black identity.

Department of War. *Monthly Reports of the Ninth and Tenth Cavalry Units and the Twenty-Fourth and Twenty-Fifth Infantry Units, 1866–1890.* Washington, DC: National Archives.

Downey, Fairfax. *The Buffalo Soldiers in the Indian Wars.* New York: McGraw Hill, 1969. Juvenile.

Dunlay, Thomas W. *Wolves for the Blue Soldiers: Indian Scouts and Auxiliaries with the United States Army, 1860–1890.* Lincoln: University of Nebraska Press, 1982.

Eppinga, Jane. *Henry Ossian Flipper: West Point's First Black Graduate.* Plano, TX: Republic of Texas Press, 1996.

Erwin, Sarah, ed. *The Buffalo Soldier on the American Frontier.* Tulsa: Thomas Gilcrease Museum Association, 1996.

Finley, James P. *The Buffalo Soldiers at Fort Huachuca.* Vol. 1, *Military Events in the American Southwest from 1910–1916.* Fort Huachuca Museum Society, 1993.

_____. *The Buffalo Soldiers at Fort Huachuca*. Vol. 2, *Military Lifestyles in the Southwest, 1917-1930*. Fort Huachuca Museum Society, 1996.

_____. *The Buffalo Soldiers at Fort Huachuca*. Vol. 3, *Military Life Along the Border from 1930-1939*. Fort Huachuca Museum Society, 1996.

Finley, Leighton. *Notebook and Photograph Pertaining to Service as a Lieutenant with the 10th Cavalry, U.S. Army in Texas and Arizona During the Indian War*. Tucson: University of Arizona Library, n.d.

Fletcher, Marvin E. *The Black Soldier and Officer in the United States Army, 1891-1917*. Columbia: University of Missouri Press, 1974.

Flipper, Henry. *The Colored Cadet at West Point*. New York: Homer and Lee, 1878; reprinted, Jackson, NY: Arno Press, 1968.

_____. *Negro Frontiersman: The Western Memoirs of Henry O. Flipper*, ed. Theodore D. Harris. El Paso: Texas Western College Press, 1963; reprinted, *Black Frontiersman: The Memoirs of Henry O. Flipper: First Black Graduate of West Point*, ed. Theodore D. Harris. Fort Worth: Texas Christian University Press, 1997.

_____. *The Western Memoirs of Henry O. Flipper, 1878-1916*. El Paso: Texas Western College Press, 1963.

Foraker, Joseph Benson. *The Black Battalion: They Ask No Favors Because They Are Negroes, But Only for Justice Because They Are Men, Speech of Hon. Joseph B. Foraker of Ohio in the Senate of the United States, January 12, 1909*. Washington, DC: n.p., 1909.

_____. *Notes of a Busy Life*. American Studies Series. Cincinnati: Stewart and Kidd, 1916. Autobiography of U.S. senator involved in the Brownsville Affray.

Fowler, Arlen L. *The Black Infantry in the West, 1869-1891*. Contributions in Afro-American and African Studies, no. 6. Westport, CT: Greenwood Publishing Company, 1971; reprinted, Norman: University of Oklahoma Press, 1996. Study of the 24th and 25th Infantry.

Glass, Edward L. N. *The History of the Tenth Cavalry: 1866-1921*. Tucson: Acme Printing Company, 1921; reprinted, Fort Collins, CO: The Old Army Press, 1972.

Good, Donnie D., ed. *The Buffalo Soldier*. Tulsa: Thomas Gilcrease Institute, 1970; reprinted, Thomas Gilcrease Museum Association, 1996.

Goodman, Charles R. *Buffalo Soldier*. Los Angeles: Holloway House, 1992.

Greene, Robert Ewell. *The Early Life of Col. Charles Young 1864-1889*. Washington, DC: n.p., 1973.

_____. *Who Were the Real Buffalo Soldiers?: Black Defenders of America*. Fort Washington, MD: R. E. Greene, 1994.

Hargrove, Hondon B. *Buffalo Soldiers in Italy: Black Americans in World War II*. Jefferson, NC: McFarland, 1985.

Haynes, Robert. *A Night of Violence: The Houston Riot of 1917*. Baton Rouge: Louisiana University Press, 1976.

Hewman, William. *Buffalo Soldier*. New York: Dodd Mead and Company, 1969.

Hilton, David Edmond. *Lieutenant Henry O Flipper: "Buffalo Soldier": West Point's First Black Graduate, the American Frontier's First Black Officer*. Odessa, TX: Kwik Kopy Printing, 1992.

Historical and Pictorial Review, 24ᵗʰ Infantry Regiment. Baton Rouge: Army and Navy Publishing Company, 1941. Compiled by unit members.

Hutcheson, Grote. *A Register of the Commissioned Officers Belonging to the Ninth U.S. Cavalry from its Organization, July 28, 1866 to July 28, 1893*. Fort Robinson: n.p., 1893.

_____. *History of the Ninth Cavalry*. Los Angeles: n.p., 1894.

Jackson, Jesse. *A Social History of the Tenth Cavalry, 1931–1941*. Fort Leavenworth, KS: U.S. Army Command and General Staff College, 1975.

Jackson, Sara Dunlap, ed. *The Colored Cadet at West Point*, by Henry O. Flipper. New York: Arno Press, 1968.

Johnson, Barry C. *Flipper's Dismissal: The Ruin of Lt. Henry O. Flipper, U.S.A., First Colored Graduate of West Point*. London: Privately Printed, 1980.

Johnson, Harry. *Buffalo Soldiers: The Formation of the Ninth Cavalry Regiment, July 1866–1867*. Fort Leavenworth, KS: U.S. Army Command and General Staff College, 1991.

Joseph, Harriett Denise. *The Brownsville Raid*. Brownsville: Texas Southmost College, 1976.

Kinevan, Marcos E. *Frontier Cavalryman: Lieutenant John Bigelow and the Buffalo Soldiers in Texas*. El Paso: Texas Western Press, 1998. Bigelow and the 10ᵗʰ Cavalry.

Knapp, George E., interviewer. *Buffalo Soldiers at Fort Leavenworth in the 1930s and Early 1940s*. Fort Leavenworth: Combat Studies Institute. U.S. Army Command and General Staff College, 1991.

Lamm, Alan K. *Five Black Preachers in Army Blue, 1884–1901: The Buffalo Soldier Chaplains*. Lewiston, NY: Edwin Mellen Press, 1998.

Lane, Ann J. *The Brownsville Affair: National Crisis and Black Reaction*. Port Washington, NY: Kennikat Press, 1971.

Langellier, John Phillip. *Men A-Marching: The African American Soldier in the West, 1866–1896*. Springfield, PA: Steven Wright Publishing, 1995.

_____. *Chaplain Allen Allensworth and the 24ᵗʰ Infantry, 1886–1906*. Tucson: Tucson Corral of the Westerners, 1992.

The Last Buffalo : Walter E. Potts, Oldest Documented Buffalo Soldier. Sunnyvale: Vidor Publishing, 1998.

Laughlin, David. *Buffalo Soldiers: An Illustrated 30 Year History of the 10ᵗʰ Regiment of U.S. Cavalry*. Tucson: Blue Horse Productions, 1991.

Leckie, William H. *The Buffalo Soldiers: A Narrative of the Negro Cavalry in the West, 1869–1891*. Norman: University of Oklahoma Press, 1967. Details the activities of the 9ᵗʰ and 10ᵗʰ Cavalry.

Leckie, William H., and Shirley Leckie. *Unlikely Warrior: General Benjamin H. Grierson and His Family*. Norman: University of Oklahoma Press, 1984. White officer of the 10th Cavalry.

Ledbetter, Barbara A. Neal. *Fort Belknap Frontier Saga: Indians, Negroes, and Anglo-Americans on the Texas Frontier*. Burnet, TX: Eakin Publications, 1982.

Lee, Irvin. *Negro Medal of Honor Men*. New York: Dodd, Mead and Company, 1967, reprinted, 1969. Includes chapter on winners of the 9th and 10th Cavalry.

Lee, Ulysses. *The Employment of Negro Troops*. Washington, DC: Office of the Chief of Military History, United States Army, 1966. Activities and forts in the West.

Lekson, Stephen H. *Nana's Raid: Apache Warfare in Southern New Mexico, 1881*. El Paso: Texas Western Press, 1987. 9th Cavalry.

Marshall, Otto Miller. *The Wham Paymaster Robbery*. Pima, AZ: Pima Chamber of Commerce, 1967. The unsolved $29,000 1889 army paymaster robbery, with eight escorts of the 10th Cavalry wounded.

Mauge, Clarence A. *The Buffalo Soldier*. New York: Carlton Press, 1993.

McChristian, Douglas C., ed. *Garrison Tangles in the Friendless Tenth: The Journal of First Lieutenant John Bigelow, Jr., Fort Davis, Texas*. Bryan, TX: J. M. Carroll, 1985.

————. *Roster of Non-Commissioned Officers of the Tenth U.S. Cavalry*. St. Paul: William Kennedy Printing Company, 1897; reprinted, Bryan, TX: J. M. Carroll, 1983.

McMiller, Anita Williams. *Buffalo Soldiers: The Formation of the Tenth Cavalry Regiment from September, 1866 to August, 1867*. Fort Leavenworth, KS: U.S. Army Command and General Staff College, 1990.

Medley, Jensen. *Illustrated Review, Ninth U.S. Cavalry*. Fort D. A. Russell, Wyoming, 1910.

Miller, Robert H. *Buffalo Soldiers*. Morristown, NJ: Silver Burdett Press, 1992. Juvenile.

————. *Buffalo Soldiers: Reflections of a Black Cowboy*. Morristown, NJ: Silver Burdett Press, 1991.

————. *Buffalo Soldiers: The Story of Emanuel Stance*. Morristown, NJ: Silver Burdett Press, 1995. Medal of Honor winner. Juvenile.

Muller, William G. *The Twenty Fourth Infantry: Past and Present*. The Author, 1923; reprinted, Fort Collins, CO: Old Army Press, 1972.

Nankivell, John H. *The History of the Twenty-Fifth Regiment, United States Infantry, 1869–1926*. Denver: Smith-Brooks Printing Company, 1926; reprinted, Fort Collins, CO: Old Army Press, 1972. Nankivell, a white officer who served with the 25th Infantry, details their activities in the Rocky Mountain West, the Spanish American War, the Philippines, and other places.

On the Trail of the Buffalo Soldier: Bibliographies of African-Americans in the U.S. Army, 1866–1917. Wilmington, DE: Scholarly Resources, 1994.

Pfeifer, Kathryn B. *Henry O. Flipper*. New York: TFC Books, 1993. Juvenile.

Place, Marian T. *Rifles and War Bonnets: Negro Cavalry in the West*. New York: Ives Washburn, 1968. History of the 10th Cavalry. Juvenile.

Powell, Anthony L. *The Post Civil War Army and the Black Soldier, 1866–1898*. New York: Random House, 1995.

Prebble, J. *The Buffalo Soldiers*. New York: Harcourt, Brace, 1959.

Reef, Catherine. *Buffalo Soldiers*. New York: Twenty-First Century Books, 1993.

Remington, Frederic. *Frederic Remington's Own West*, ed. Harold McCracken. New York: The Dial Press, 1960. Reflections on Buffalo Soldiers.

Richter, William L. *The Army in Texas During Reconstruction, 1865–1870*. College Station: Texas A&M University Press, 1987.

Rickey, Don. *Forty Miles a Day on Beans and Hay: The Enlisted Soldier Fighting the Indian Wars*. Norman: University of Oklahoma Press, 1963. Buffalo Soldiers included.

Robinson, Charles M. III. *The Court Martial of Lieutenant Henry Flipper*. Southwestern Studies, no. 100. El Paso: Texas Western, 1994.

Rodenbough, Theodore F. *The Army of the United Sates: Historical Sketches of the 9th and 10th Regiments of Cavalry and the 24th and 25th Regiments of Infantry*. New York: Maynard, Merrill and Company, 1896.

————. *The Tenth Regiment of Cavalry*. New York: Maynard, Merrill and Company, 1896.

Rodney, George B. *As a Cavalryman Remembers*. Caldwell, ID: Caxton Printers, 1944.

Roster of Non-Commissioned Officers of the Tenth U.S. Cavalry, with Some Regimental Reminiscences, Appendixes, etc., Connected with the Early History of the Regiment. St. Paul: William Kennedy Printing Company, 1897; reprinted, Bryan, Texas: J. M. Carroll, 1983.

Sayre, Harold Ray. *Warriors of Color*. Fort Davis, TX: Harold Ray Sayre, 1995.

Schubert, Frank N. *Black Valor: Buffalo Soldiers and the Medal of Honor, 1870–1898*. Wilmington, DE: Scholarly Resources, 1997.

————. *Buffalo Soldiers, Braves, and the Brass: The Story of Fort Robinson, Nebraska*. Shippensburg, PA: White Mane Publishing Company, 1993.

————, ed. *On the Trail of the Buffalo Soldier: Biographies of African-Americans in the U.S. Army, 1866–1917*. Wilmington, DE: Scholarly Resources, 1995.

Scipio, L. Albert II. *The Last of the Black Regulars: A History of the 24th Infantry Regiment (1869–1951)*. Silver Springs, MD: Roman Publications, 1983.

Scott, Edward Van Zile. *The Unwept: Black American Soldiers and the Spanish-American War.* Montgomery, AL: The Black Belt Press, 1996. Troops included Buffalo Soldiers.

Second Lieut. Henry Ossian Flipper. Washington, DC: n.p., 1901. Attempt to restore Flipper to duty 18 years after his court-martial. Library of Congress pamphlet.

Seraile, William. *Voice of Dissent: Theophilus Gould Steward (1843–1924) and Black America.* Brooklyn: Carlson Publishing Company, 1991. History of a chaplain of the 25th Infantry.

Singletary, Otis. *Negro Militia and Reconstruction.* Austin: University of Texas Press, 1957.

Stallard, Patricia Y. *Glittering Misery: Dependents of the Indian Fighting Army.* Fort Collins, CO: Old Army Press, 1978.

Steward, Theophilus G. *Active Service; or Gospel Work Among U.S. Soldiers.* New York: U.S. Army Association, n.d. Author was chaplain of Buffalo Soldiers.

————. *The Colored Regulars in the United States Army.* Philadelphia, PA: A.M.E. Book Concern, 1904.

————. *From 1864 to 1914, Fifty Years in the Gospel Ministry; Twenty-Seven Years in the Pastorate; Sixteen Years Active Service as Chaplain in the U.S. Army; Seven Years Professor in Wilberforce University; Two Trips to Europe; A Trip to Mexico.* Philadelphia: A.M.E. Book Concern, 1921.

Stovall, TaRessa. *The Buffalo Soldiers.* Broomall, PA: Chelsea House, 1997. Juvenile.

Taylor, Quintard. *The Colored Cadet at West Point: Autobiography of Lt. Henry Ossian Flipper, U.S.A.* Blacks in the American West Series. Lincoln: University of Nebraska Press, 1998.

Thompson, Jerry. *Sabers on the Rio Grande.* Austin: Presdial, 1974.

Thweatt, Hiram H., comp. *What the Newspapers say of the Negro Soldier in the Spanish American War and the Return of the 10th Cavalry.* Thomasville, GA: n.p., 1908.

Tillman, Benjamin R. *The Race Problem. The Brownsville Raid. Speech of Hon. Benjamin R. Tillman, of South Carolina, in the Senate of the United States, Saturday, January 12, 1907.* Washington, DC: n.p., 1918.

Tillman, Robert. *Case of the United States vs. Corporal Robert Tillman, et al., 24th U.S. Infantry: Copy of Proceedings of Trial by General Court-Martial at Fort Sam Houston, Texas, February-March, 1918.* San Antonio: Alamo Printing Company, 1918. Trial relating to Houston Riot, 1918.

Tompkins, Frank. *Chasing Villa.* Harrisburg, PA: The Military Service Publishing Company, 1934.

Troxel, O. C., et al, eds. *Narrative of Service of the Tenth U.S. Cavalry in the Punitive Expedition*. Tucson: Acme Printing Company, 1921. Pamphlet.

U.S. War Department. *Names of Enlisted Men Discharged on Account of Brownsville Affray, with Application for Reenlistment: Letter from Acting Secretary of War*. Senate Documents No. 430, 60th Cong., 1st sess. Washington, DC: Government Printing Office, 1908.

Unit Members. *Historical and Pictorial Review of the Tenth Cavalry Regiment*. Baton Rouge: Army and Navy Publishing Company, 1941.

Unit Members. *Historical and Pictorial Review, 9th Cavalry Regiment, Second Cavalry Division of the United States Army*. Baton Rouge: Army and Navy Publishing Company, 1941.

United States Army Cavalry, 10th Squadron, Unit History, 1st Squadron 10th Cavalry: Buffalo Soldiers. United States: 1st Squadron 19th Cavalry, 1970.

Utley, Robert M. *Frontier Regulars: The United States Army and the Indian, 1866–1891*. New York: Macmillan, 1973.

Vandiver, Frank E. *Black Jack: The Life and Times of John J. Pershing*, 2 vols. College Station: Texas A&M University Press, 1977.

Weaver, John D. *The Brownsville Raid*. New York: Norton and Company, 1970; reprinted, College Station: Texas A&M University Press, 1992.

Weinen, Alexander. *Buffalo Soldiers: Die Rolle der Schwarzen in den amerikanischen Streitkraften des 19. Jahrhunderts*. Wyk auf Fohr, Germany: Verlag fur Amerikanistik, 1992.

Wharfield, H. B. *Tenth Cavalry and Border Fights*. El Cajon, CA: The Author, 1964.

_____. *With Scouts and Cavalry at Fort Apache*, ed. John Alexander Carroll. Tucson: Arizona Pioneers' Historical Society, 1965. 10th Cavalry.

Whitman, Sidney E. *The Troopers: An Informal History of the Plains Cavalry, 1865–1890*. New York: Hastings House, 1962.

Willard, T. *Buffalo Soldiers*. New York: Tom Doherty Associates, 1996.

Wooster, Robert. *Fort Davis: Outpost on Texas Frontier*. Austin: Texas Historical Association, 1994.

_____. *History of Fort Davis, Texas*. Southwest Cultural Resources Center Professional Papers, no. 34. Santa Fe: National Park Service, 1990.

_____. *The Military and United States Indian Policy, 1865–1903*. New Haven: Yale University Press, 1988. Some accounts of Buffalo Soldiers and Indian policy.

_____. *Soldiers, Sutlers, and Settlers: Garrison Life on the Texas Frontier*. The Clayton Wheat Williams Texas Life Series, no. 2. College Station: Texas A&M University Press, 1987. Some accounts of Buffalo Soldiers.

Theses and Dissertations:

Adams, Thomas Richard. "The Houston Riot of 1917." Master's thesis, Texas A&M University, 1972.

Austerman, Wayne Randolph. "Black Regulars: The 41st Infantry in Texas, 1867–1869." Master's thesis, Louisiana State University, 1971.

Blassingame, John W. "The Organization and Use of Negro Troops in the Union Army, 1863–1865." Master's thesis, Howard University, 1961.

Boyd, Thomas J. "The Use of Negro Troops by Kansas during the Civil War." Master's thesis, Kansas State Teachers College, 1950.

Clark, Michael J. "A History of the Twenty-Fourth United States Infantry Regiment in Utah, 1896–1900." Ph.D. diss., University of Utah, 1979.

_____. "U.S. Army Pioneers: Black Soldiers in Nineteenth Century Utah." Ph.D. diss., University of Utah, 1981.

Cole, George D. "Brush Fire War, 1916 Style." Master's thesis, Louisiana State University, 1962.

Cook, Lawrence Hugh. "The Brownsville Affray of 1906." Master's thesis, University of Colorado, 1942.

Fain, Samuel S. "The Pershing Punitive Expedition and Its Diplomatic Battlegrounds." Master's thesis, University of Arizona, 1951.

Fletcher, Marvin E. "The Blacks in Blue: Negro Volunteers in Reconstruction." Master's thesis, University of Wisconsin, 1964.

_____. "The Negro Soldier and the United States Army, 1891–1917." Ph.D. diss., University of Wisconsin, 1968.

Fowler, Arlen L. "The Negro Infantry in the West, 1869–1891." Ph.D. diss., Washington State University, 1968.

Green, Robert E. "Colonel Charles Young, Soldier and Diplomat." Master's thesis, Howard University, 1972.

Harris, Theodore D. "Henry Ossian Flipper: The First Negro Graduate of West Point." Ph.D. diss., University of Minnesota, 1971.

Jackson, James W. "The Black Man and Military Mobilization in the United States, 1916–1919." Master's thesis, California State University-Hayward, 1970.

Johnson, Harry. "Buffalo Soldiers: The Formation of the Ninth Cavalry Regiment, July 1866–1867." Master's thesis, U.S. Army Command and General Staff College, 1991.

Johnson, Robert B. "The Punitive Expedition: A Military, Diplomatic, and Political History of Pershing's Chase after Pancho Villa, 1916–1917." Ph.D. diss., University of Southern California, 1964.

Kubela, Marguerite E. "History of Fort Concho, Texas." Master's thesis, University of Texas, 1936.

Lamm, Alan K. "Buffalo Soldier Chaplains: A Case Study of the Five Black United States Army Chaplains, 1884–1901." Ph.D. diss., University of South Carolina, 1995.

Lewis, Francis E.   "Negro Army Regulars in the Spanish-American War:
    Smoked Yankees at Santiago de Cuba." Master's thesis, U.S. Army
    Command and General Staff College, 1969. Buffalo Soldiers numbered
    among the troops.
McClung, Donald R. "Henry O. Flipper: The First Negro Officer in the United
    States Army, 1878–1882." Master's thesis, East Texas State Univer-
    sity, 1970.
McMiller, Anita Williams.   "Buffalo Soldiers: The Formation of the Tenth
    Cavalry Regiment from September, 1866 to August, 1867." Master's
    thesis, U.S. Army Command and General Staff College, 1990.
Nance, Carol Conley. "United States Army Scouts: The Southwestern Experi-
    ence, 1866–1890." Master's thesis, North Texas State University,
    1975.
Nash, Horace Daniel.   "Blacks on the Border: Columbus, New Mexico,
    1916–1922." Master's thesis, New Mexico State University, 1988.
————. "Town and Sword: Black Soldiers in Columbus, New Mexico, in
    the Early Twentieth Century." Ph.D. diss., Mississippi State Univer-
    sity, 1996.
Park, Phocion Samuel, Jr. "The Twenty-Fourth Infantry Regiment and the
    Houston Riot of 1917." Master's thesis, University of Houston, 1971.
Phillips, Thomas D. "The Black Regulars: Negro Soldiers in the United States
    Army, 1866–1891." Ph.D. diss., University of Wisconsin, 1970.
————. "The Negro Regulars: Negro Soldiers in the United States Army,
    1866–1890." Ph.D. diss., University of Wisconsin, 1966.
Salter, Krewasky.   "Sable Officers: African-American Military Officers,
    1861–1918." Master's thesis, Florida State University, 1993.
Schubert, Frank N.   "The Black Regular Army Regiments in Wyoming,
    1885–1912." Master's thesis, University of Wyoming, 1970.
————. "Fort Robinson, Nebraska: The History of a Military Community,
    1874–1916." Ph.D. diss., University of Michigan, 1977.
Shadley, Frank W.   "The American Punitive Expedition Into Mexico,
    1916–1917." Master's thesis, College of the Pacific, 1952.
Siler, Benjamin T. "The Brownsville, Texas, Affray of August 13–14, 1906,
    and Subsequent Proceedings (A Historical Interpretation)."   Master's
    thesis, North Carolina College of Durham, 1963.
Temple, Frank M.   "Colonel B. H. Grierson's Texas Commands." Master's
    thesis, Texas Tech University, 1956.
Thompson, Erwin N. "The Negro Regiments of the U.S. Army, 1866–1900."
    Master's thesis, University of California, 1966.
Tinsley, James A. "The Brownsville Affray." Master's thesis, University of
    North Carolina, 1948.
White, William Bruce. "The Military and the Melting Pot: The American
    Army and Minority Groups, 1865–1924." Ph.D. diss., University of
    Wisconsin, 1968.

Other:

The Black Soldiers of West Texas: A History of the Buffalo Soldiers. Blue Horse Productions, 1987. Videocassette.

"The Brownsville Raid" theater stills collection, compiled by Bert Andrews, Negro Ensemble Company production, 1970s. Schomburg Center.

"Buddha Sunday Series Presents the Buffalo Soldiers." Buddha Records, 1960. Soundrecording.

Buffalo Soldiers. National Black Programming Consortium. Program #3 of the "The Black Frontier" Series. Videorecording.

Colored Troops Disembarking, 1898. Newsreel of the 24th Infantry returning from the Spanish American War.

A Day With the Tenth Cavalry at Fort Huachuca. Documentary, Lincoln Motion Picture Company, 1922. The 10th in training.

"Lest We Forget...." Program, Buffalo Soldier Monument Dedication. Fort Leavenworth, Kansas, July 25, 1992.

Major General Michael S. Davidson. Address to 101st Anniversary Convention of the 9th and 10th Cavalry Regimental Association, 28 July 1967.

Mary Brent Parker papers, 1878–1907. Denver Public Library. Newspaper clippings and poems collected by the wife of Colonel Parker of the 9th Cavalry.

Steamer Mascotte Arriving at Tampa. Edison newsreel, 1898. Battalion of the 24th Infantry arriving at Tampa, Florida, aboard the Mascotte.

25th Infantry. American Mutoscope and Biograph Company. 25th Infantry returning from the Battle of Mt. Arayat, Philippines, 23 March 1900. Library of Congress Motion Picture, Broadcast and Recorded Sound division. Film.

National Archives:

Letters Received, Selected Documents Relating to the Activities of the Ninth and Tenth Cavalry in the Campaign Against Victorio, 1879–80. File No. 6058–1879.

Letters Sent, Tenth United States Cavalry, 1866-83.

Organizational Returns, Ninth Cavalry, 1866–93.

Organizational Returns, Tenth Cavalry, 1866–88.

Selected Letters Received Relating to the Ninth and Tenth Regiments, United States Cavalry.

Selected Letters Received Relating to the Tenth United States Cavalry, 1873–76.

Tenth United States Cavalry, Historical Sketch, 1866–92, Major John Bigelow, Jr.

Record Group 94, Records of the War Department.
1.   Selected Letters Received Relating to the 24th and 25th Infantry Regiments at Adjutant General's Office, 1866–1891.
2.   Regimental Returns of the 24th and 25th Infantry Regiments, 1869–1891.
Record Group 391, Records of the War Department Mobile Commands.
1.   25th Infantry Regiment Scrapbook.

Environmental Issues

Articles:

Alexander, Nick. "Fighting Toxic Racism in Northern California." [NYC] *Guardian* (26 December 1990). Richmond, California.

Broyles, Karen. "Chevron Set for Court Date to Answer Allegations of 'Environmental Racism.'" *The Oil Daily*, 13 May 1997. A suit brought by 2,500 Black residents of Kennedy Heights, Houston.

Bullard, Robert D. "Solid Waste Sites and the Black Houston Community." *Sociological Inquiry* 53 (Spring 1983).

Dolin, Eric J. "Black Americans' Attitudes toward Wildlife." *Journal of Environmental Education* 20 (1988). Survey conducted in Denver indicates that Blacks are less interested in and concerned about wildlife that whites.

Hollandsworth, Skip. "Refinery Woe." *Texas Monthly*, May 1995. Residents of Corpus Christi's "Refinery Row" blame pollution for high cancer rates and file suits.

McAdams, D. Claire. "Environmental Activism and the Intersection of Race, Class, and Gender: Patterns in Central Texas." *Sociological Abstracts* (August 1991, Supplement 167).

Norris, Bill. "LA Flats come Complete with a Teacher." *Times Educational Supplement* 4004 (26 March 1993). EEXCELL (Educational Excellence for Children with Environmental Limitations) project.

Rose, Mark. "Odessa Branch of NAAP Wins Environmental Justice Case in Texas." *Crisis* 104 (July 1997). Texas branch wins settlement against Dynagen, Rexene and Shell Oil.

Savage, J. A. "Breathing Fire: White Middle-Class Richmond Residents are Finally Joining Poor Blacks and Latinos in Their Decades-Old Battle against Chevron's Pollution." *San Francisco Bay Guardian* (East Bay Edition) 26 (11 March 1992).

Smith, Rhonda. "MOSES leads Winona, Texas, to Environmental Justice."
    Crisis 104 (July 1997). MOSES (Mothers Organized to Stop Envi-
    ronmental Sins) leads a successful fight against a polluting disposal
    service.
Sonenshein, Raphael J. "The Battle over Liquor Stores in South Central Los
    Angeles: The Management of an Interminority Conflict." *Urban Af-
    fairs Review* 31 (1996).

Estevanico and Spanish Explorations

Articles:

Allen, Anne B. "Estevanico the Moor." *American History* 32 (1 July 1997).

Browning, James B. "Negro Companions of the Spanish Explorers in the New World." *Howard University Studies in History* 11 (November 1930).

Buchanan, William J. "Legend of the Black Conquistador." *Mankind Magazine* 1 (February 1968); reprinted in *The Black Military Experience in the American West*, ed. John M. Carroll. New York: Liveright Publishing, 1971.

Burt, Olive W. "Estevanico, the Black." Section in *Negroes in the Early West*. New York: Julian Messner, 1969. Juvenile.

Chávez, Fray Angélico. "De Vargas' Negro Drummer." *El Palacio* 56 (May 1949); reprinted in *The Black Military Experience in the American West*, ed. John M. Carroll. New York: Liveright Publishing, 1971. Early Black pioneer, Sebastián Rodriguez.

_____. "Pohe-Yomo's Representative and the Pueblo Revolt of 1680." *New Mexico Historical Review* 42 (1967). Black involvement in the 1680 revolt.

Chipman, Donald E. "In Search of Cabeza de Vaca's Route Across Texas: An Historiographical Survey." *Southwestern Historical Quarterly* 91 (October 1987). Includes Estevanico.

Harris, Richard E. "Estevanico: A Worldly-Wise Slave." Appendix in *The First Hundred Years: A History of Arizona Blacks*. Apache Junction, AZ: Relmo Publishers, 1983.

Heald, Weldon F. "Black Pathfinder of the Desserts." *Crisis* 57 (December 1950).

Heard, J. Norman. "The Odyssey of Estevanico." Chapter in *The Black Frontiersmen: Adventures of Negroes Among American Indians, 1528–1918*. New York: John Day Co., 1969. Juvenile.

"Hidden Histories." *Quantum* 13 (Spring 1996). Blacks with the Conquistadors in New Mexico.

Hughes, Langston. "Esteban, Discoverer of Arizona." Chapter in *Famous Negroes of America*. New York: Dodd, Mead and Company, 1966. Juvenile.

Katz, William Loren. "Estevanico: He Opened Up the Southwest." Chapter in *Black People Who Made the Old West*. New York: Thomas Y. Crowell, 1977. Juvenile.

King, James Ferguson. "Descriptive Data on Negro Slaves in Spanish Importation Records and Bills of Sale." *Journal of Negro History* 28 (1943).

_____. "Evolution of the Free Slave Trade Principle in Spanish Colonial Administration." *Hispanic American Historical Review* 22 (1942).

_____. "Negro History in Continental Spanish America." *Journal of Negro History* 29 (1944).

Laughlin, Florence. "Estevanico and the Cities of Gold." *Black World* 12 (August 1963).

_____. "A Negro Pioneer in New Mexico: Estevanico and the Cities of Gold." *Negro Digest* 12 (August 1963). Romanticized account.

Logan, Rayford Whittingham. "Estevanico, Negro Discoverer of the Southwest: A Critical Reexamination" *Phylon* 1 (Fourth Quarter 1940).

_____. "Notes on R. R. Wright's 'Negro Companions of the Spanish Explorers.'" *Phylon* 2 (1941).

Mirsky, Jeannette. "Zeroing In on a Fugitive Figure: The First Negro in America." *Midway* 8 (June 1967).

Riley, Carroll. "Blacks in the Early Southwest. *Ethnohistory* 19 (Summer 1972). Blacks on early Spanish expeditions.

Rippy, J. Fred. "The Negro and the Spanish Pioneer in the New World." *Journal of Negro History* 6 (April 1921).

Wright, Richard R. "Negro Companions of the Spanish Explorers." *American Anthropologist* 4 (April-June 1902); reprinted in *Phylon* 2 (1941); reprinted in *The Making of Black America*, Vol. 1, *The Origins of Black Americans*, ed. August Meier and Elliott Rudwick. New York: Atheneum, 1969.

_____. "A Negro Discovered New Mexico." *AME Review* 13 (July 1896).

Zimmerman, Karl H. "Drummer for De Vargas." *New Mexico Magazine* 45 (August 1967).

Books:

Abdul-Jabbar, Kareem. *Black Profiles in Courage*. New York: Avon Books, 1997. Profiles of Estevanico and Bass Reeves.

Alegria, Ricardo E. *Juan Guarrido, el conquistador negro en las Antillas, Florida, Mexico y California c. 1503–1540*. San Juan de Puerto Rico: Centro de Estudios Avanzados de Puerto Rico y el Caribe, 1990.

Arrington, Carolyn. *Estevanico: Black Explorer in Spanish Texas*. Austin: Eakin Press, 1986. Juvenile.

Browning, James B. *Negro Companions of the Spanish Pioneers in the New World*. Washington, DC: Howard University Studies in History, 1931.

Cabeza de Vaca, Alvar Núñez. *The Journey of Alvar Núñez Cabeza de Vaca and his companions from Florida to the Pacific, 1528–1536: translated from his own narrative by Fanny Bandelier, together with the report of Father Marcos of Nizza and a letter from the Viceroy Mendoza*. New York: A. S. Barnes and Company, 1905. Estevanico included in this account.

Hodge, Frederick W., ed. *Spanish Explorers in the Southern United States*. New York: 1907.

Miller, Robert H. *The Story of Jean Baptiste Du Sable*. Englewood Cliffs, NJ: Silver Burdett Press, 1994.

Mumford, Donald. *From Africa to the Arctic: Five Explorers*. The African Diaspora Series. Seattle: Ananse Press, 1992. Includes York, Estevanico, and James Beckwourth.

Shepherd, Elizabeth. *The Discoveries of Esteban the Black*. New York: Dodd, Mead, 1970. Juvenile.

Terrell, John Upton. *Estevanico the Black*. Los Angeles: Westernlore Press, 1968.

Thesis:

Ibrahim, Shirley Diane. "Estevan, the Moor of New Mexico: An Experiment in Point of View." Ed.D. thesis, East Texas State University, 1978.

Exodus and Migration

Articles:

Athearn, Robert G. "Black Exodus: The Migration of 1879." *Prairie Scout* 3 (1975).

———. "The Promised Land: A Black View." *Record* 34 (1973). Blacks move out of the South to Kansas.

Barry, Louise. "The Emigrant Aid Company Parties of 1854–5." *Kansas Historical Quarterly* 12 (May 1943).

Bingham, Anne E. "Sixteen Years of a Kansas Farm, 1870–1886." *Kansas State Historical Society Collections* 15 (1919). Tells of Black Exodusters.

"Blacks in California Move Down South in Reverse Migration." *Jet*, 26 January 1998. From 1990–1995, 103,494 Black Californians migrated to the South.

"Chief Sam and the Negro Exodus." *Literary Digest* 48 (21 March 1914).

Deusen, John G. Wan. "The Exodus of 1879." *Journal of Negro History* 21 (April 1936).

Donald, Henderson H. "The Negro Migration of 1916–1918." *Journal of Negro History* 6 (October 1921).

Douglass, Frederick. "The Negro Exodus from the Gulf States." *Journal of Social Science* 11 (May 1880).

Fleming, Walter L. "'Pap' Singleton, Father of the Exodus." *American Journal of Sociology* 15 (July 1909).

———. "Pap Singleton, the Moses of the Colored Exodus." *American Journal of Sociology* 15 (July 1909).

Grenz, Suzanna M. "The Exodusters of 1879: St. Louis and Kansas City Responses." *Missouri Historical Review* 73 (October 1978).

Hamilton, Kenneth Marvin. "The Origins and Early Promotion of Nicodemus: A Pre-Exodus, All-Black Town." *Kansas History* 5 (1982).

Harlow, R. V. "Rise and Fall of Emigrant Aid Movement in Kansas." *American Historical Review* 41 (October 1935).

Hawkins, Homer C. "Trends in Black Migration from 1863 to 1960." *Phylon* 34 (June 1973). Black migration to southwestern U.S., then to Oklahoma Territory, then north.

Herbert, Solomon J. "Blacks Who Migrated West Between 1915 and 1945." *Crisis* 97 (February 1990). Migration from the South to Los Angeles.

Higgins, Billy D. "Negro Thought and the Exodus of 1879." *Phylon* 32 (1971).

Hill, James L. "Migration of Blacks to Iowa, 1820–1960." *Journal of Negro History* 66 (Winter 1981–1982).

King, Henry. "A Year of the Exodus in Kansas." *Scribner's Monthly* 20 (June 1880).

Lightfoot, Billy Bob. "The Negro Exodus from Comanche County, Texas." *Southwestern Historical Quarterly* 56 (January 1953).

Linsin, Christopher E. "Point of Conflict: Twentieth-Century Black Migration and Urbanization." *Journal of Urban History* 21 (1995).

Painter, Nell Irvin. "Millenarian Aspects of the Exodus to Kansas." *Journal of Social History* 9 (1976). Argues new factors behind the Kansas Exodus movement.

Roseman, Curtis C. , and Seong Woo. "Linked and Independent African American Migration from Los Angeles." *Professional Geographer* 50 (May 1998).

Salisbury, Robert S. "William Windom and the Exodus Movement of 1879–1880." *Southern Studies* 26 (1987).

Schwendemann, Glen. "The Exodusters of 1879." *Kansas Historical Quarterly* 29 (1963).

_____. "The 'Exodusters' on the Missouri." *Kansas Historical Quarterly* 29 (Spring 1963). The 1879–1880 migration.

_____. "Nicodemus: Negro Haven on the Solomon." *Kansas Historical Quarterly* 34 (Spring 1968). Includes biographies of early settlers.

_____. "St. Louis and the Exodusters of 1879." *Journal of Negro History* 46 (January 1961). What the city did with immigrants moving through to Kansas.

_____. "Wyandotte and the First 'Exodusters' of 1879." *Kansas Historical Quarterly* 26 (Autumn 1960).

Sherman, Joan R. "James Monroe Whitfield, Poet and Emigrationist: A Voice of Protest and Despair." *Journal of Negro History* 57 (1972).

Strickland, Arvarh E. "Toward the Promised Land: The Exodus to Kansas and Afterward." *Missouri Historical Review* 69 (July 1975).

Toll, William. "Black Families and Migration to a Multiracial Society: Portland, Oregon, 1900–1924." *Journal of American Ethnic History* 17 (Spring 1998).

Van Deusen, John. "The Exodus of 1879." *Journal of Negro History* 21 (April 1936).

Williams, Nudie E. "Black Newspapers and the Exodusters of 1879." *Kansas History* 8 (Winter 1985/1986).

Woods, Randall B. "After the Exodus: John Lewis Waller and the Black Elite, 1878–1900." *Kansas Historical Quarterly* 43 (Summer 1977).

Woods, Randall B., and David A. Sloan. "Kansas Quakers and the 'Great Exodus': Conflicting Perceptions of Responsibility with a Nineteenth Century Reform Community." *Historian* 48 (November 1985). The Kansas Freedmen's Relief Association.

Woodson, Carter G. "The Exodus to the West." Chapter in *A Century of Negro Migration*. Washington, DC: Association for the Study of Negro Life and History, 1918; reprinted, New York: AMS Press, 1970.

Woolfolk, George Ruble. "Turner's Safety-Valve and Free Negro Westward Migration." *Journal of Negro History* 50 (July 1965).

————. "Turner's Safety Valve and Free Negro Westward Migration." *Pacific Northwest Quarterly* 56 (July 1965).

Books:

Chambers, W. L. *Niles of Nicodemus: Exploiter of Kansas Exodusters, Negro Indemnity and Equality of Blacks with Whites His Obsession, Beats Bankers, Bench, and Barrister; Courter League to Post-War K.K.K. Riots and Finally Prison.* Los Angeles: Los Angeles Washington High School, Vocational Training Press, 1925. Exposé on John W. Niles, president of the town's self-governing organization.

Fleming, Walter L. *"Pap" Singleton, the Moses of the Colored Exodus.* Baton Rouge, LA: Ortlieb's Printing House, 1909. Reprinted from the *American Journal of Sociology* 15 (July 1909).

Fletcher, Frank H. *Negro Exodus: Report of Col. Frank H. Fletcher, Agent Appointed by the St. Louis Commission to Visit Kansas for the Purpose of Obtaining Information in Regard to Colored Emigration.* n.p., 188?

Gordon, Jacob U. *Narratives of African Americans in Kansas, 1870–1992: Beyond the Exodust Movement.* Lewiston, NY: Edwin Mellen Press, 1993.

Painter, Nell Irvin. *Exodusters: Black Migration to Kansas After Reconstruction.* New York: Knopf, 1977; reprinted, Lawrence: University Press of Kansas, 1986.

Redkey, Edwin S. *Black Exodus.* New Haven: Yale University Press, 1969.

Thayer, Eli. *A History of the Kansas Crusade.* Black Heritage Library Collection Series. Freeport, NY: Books for Libraries Press, 1971. Reprint of 1889 edition. Aid for Exodusters through New England Emigrant Aid Company.

Theses:

Blake, Ella Lee. "The Great Exodus to Kansas, 1878–1880." Master's thesis, Kansas State College, 1942.

Chartrand, Robert Lee. "The Negro Exodus from the Southern States to Kansas: 1869–1886." Master's thesis, University of Kansas City, 1949.

Gedge, Charles H. "Westward migration of Blacks in the Nineteenth Century with Special Reference to the Kansas Exodus." Master's thesis, Roosevelt University, 1976.

Gift, Elmer Birdell. "Causes and History of the Negro Exodus into Kansas, 1879–1880." Master's thesis, University of Kansas, 1915.

Grant, Truett King. "The Negro Exodus of 1879–1880." Master's thesis, Baylor University, 1952.

Schwendemann, Glen. "Negro Exodus to Kansas: The First Phase, March-July, 1879." Master's thesis, University of Oklahoma, 1957.

Williams, Corinne Hare. "The Migration of Negroes to the West, 1877–1900, with Special Reference to Kansas." Master's thesis, Howard University, 1944.

Williams, Nudie E. "Black Newspapers and the Exodusters of 1879." Master's thesis, Oklahoma State University, 1977.

Health

Articles:

Asinof, E. "Ghetto Doctor; Multipurpose Medical Center in Compton, California." *Today's Health* 50 (April 1972).

Baker, F. M., et al. "Black, Middle-Class Women in San Antonio, Texas." *Journal of the National Medical Association* 84 (June 1992). Mechanisms through which women handled stress.

Bergin, A. "The Black Side of Health Care." *Arizona* (August 1976).

Bishop, Jennifer, Carl A. Huether, Claudine Torfs, Frederick Lorey, and James Deddens. "Epidemiologic Study of Down Syndrome in a Racially Diverse California Population, 1989–1991." *American Journal of Epidemiology* 145 (15 January 1997).

"Black Women in Colorado: Two Early Portraits." *Frontiers: A Journal of Women's Studies* 7 (1984). Biographies of nurse Daisy Jones and cowgirl Beatrice Boyer Jones.

Borrud, Lori G., Patricia C. Pillow, and Pamela K. Allen. "Food Group Contributors to Nutrient intake in Whites, Blacks, and Mexican American in Texas." *Journal of the American Dietetic Association* 89 (August 1989). Targeted dietary planning.

Boskin, Joseph, and Victor Pilson, M.D. "The Los Angeles Riot of 1965: A Medical Profile of an Urban Crisis." *Pacific Historical Review* 39 (August 1970). Analyzes emergency room records and finds the number of wounded was inflated.

Braveman, P., S. Egerter, F. Edmonston, and M. Verdon. "Racial/Ethnic Differences in the Likelihood of Cesarean Delivery, California." *American Journal of Public Health* 85 (1995).

Breslaw, L., et al. "Health and Race in California." *American Journal of Public Health* 61 (April 1971).

Browne, H. A. "Tuberculosis in the Negro Child in Arkansas: Thomas C. McRae Memorial Sanatorium, Alexander, Arkansas." *Journal of School Health* 33 (March 1968).

Bullington, Bruce. "Concerning Heroin Use and Official Records (Police of Federal Bureau of Narcotics; Commenting on a 1967 Article by Lee Robins and George E. Murphy, Concerning Drug Use in the Normal Population of Young Negroes in St. Louis, Mo.)." *American Journal of Public Health* 59 (October 1969).

Buzi, Ruth S., Weinman, Maxine L., and Smith, Peggy B. "Ethnic Differences in STD Rates Among Female Adolescents." *Adolescence* 33 (Summer 1998). Sampling conducted at two family planning clinics in Houston.

Carney, Tom. "A Pair Deals Seven of a Kind: Educational Preparation and Poise Result in Historic Delivery." *Black Issues in Higher Education* 14 (11 December 1997). Black perinatologists Paula Renee Mahone, MD, and Karen Lynn Drake, MD, are the two physicians who delivered the McCaughey septuplets.

Catania, J. A. et al. "Changes in Condom Use among Black, Hispanic, and White Heterosexuals in San Francisco: The AMEN Cohort Survey." *Journal of Sex Research* 119 (1993).

_____. "Correlates of Condom Use among Black, Hispanic, and White Heterosexuals in San Francisco: The AMEN Longitudinal Survey." *AIDS Education and Prevention* 6 (1994).

_____. "Condom Use in Multi-Ethnic Neighborhoods of San Francisco: The Population-Based AMEN (AIDS in Multi-Ethnic Neighborhoods Study." *American Journal of Public Health* 82 (1992).

Cayer, N. Joseph, and Deborah L. Roepke. *Health Care in Arizona: A Black Perspective*. Tempe: School of Public Affairs, Arizona State University, 1986.

Cowie, M. R., C. E. Fahrenbruch, L. A. Cobb, and A. P. Hallstrom. "Out-of-Hospital Cardiac Arrest: Racial Differences in Outcome in Seattle." *American Journal of Public Health* 83 (1993).

Cramer, James C. "Trends in Infant Mortality among Racial and Ethnic Groups in California." *Social Science Research* 17 (1988).

Danley, K. L., J. L. Richardson, L. Bernstein, B. Langholz, and R. K. Ross. "Prostate Cancer: Trends in Mortality and Stage-Specific Incidence Rates by Racial/Ethnic Group in Los Angeles County, California." *Cancer Causes and Control* 6 (1995).

Ellen, J. M., R. P. Kohn, G. A. Bolan, S. Shiboski, and N. Krieger. "Socioeconomic Differences in Sexually Transmitted Disease Rates Among Black and White Adolescents, San Francisco, 1990 to 1992." *American Journal of Public Health* 85 (November 1995).

Evenson, Richard C., and Dong W. Cho. "Norms for the Missouri Impatient Behavior Scale: Sex, Race and Age Differences in Psychiatric Symptoms." *Journal of Clinical Psychology* 43 (1987).

Ewing, Nadia et al. "Newborn Diagnosis of Abnormal Hemoglobins from a Large Municipal Hospital in Los Angeles." *American Journal of Health* 71 (June 1981).

"Factors Associated with Self-Perceived Excellent and Very Good Health among Blacks—Kansas, 1995." *Morbidity and Mortality Weekly Report* 45 (25 October 1996). Satisfaction of Black's with health and raising Black mortality age will require public health initiatives.

Feigelman, William, and Julia Lee. "Probing the Paradoxical Pattern of Cigarette Smoking among African-Americans: Low Teenage Consumption and High Adult Use." *Journal of Drug Education* 25 (1995). Based on the 1990 California Tobacco Survey.

Fischer, Waller A., and Dwight E. Breed. "Negro Health Week in Texas." *Survey* 45 (16 October 1920)."

Fraser, Gare E., et al. "Association Among Health Habits, Risk Factors, and All-Cause Mortality in a Black California Population." *Epidemiology* 8 (1997).

Fullilove, Mindy T., et al. "Black Women and AIDS Prevention: A View towards Understanding the Gender Rules." *Journal of Sex Research* 27 (1990). Examines patterns of sexual behavior.

_____. "Crack Cocaine Use and High-Risk Behaviors among Sexually Active Black Adolescents." *Journal of Adolescent Health* 14 (1993). Indicates that crack users are more likely to engage in high-risk sexual behavior.

_____. "Is 'Black Achievement' an Oxymoron?" *Thought and Action* 4 (Fall 1988). Examines underrepresentation of Blacks in medicine and medical education, plus an effective California program.

Fullilove, R. E., et al. "Risk of Sexually Transmitted Disease among Black Adolescent Crack Users in Oakland and San Francisco, Calif." *JAMA* 263 (9 February 1990).

Gilliand, Frank D., Thomas M. Becker, and Charles R. Key. "Contrasting Trends of Prostate Cancer Incidence and Mortality in New Mexico's Hispanics, Non-Hispanic Whites, American Indians, and Blacks." *Cancer: Diagnosis, Treatment, Research* 73 (15 April 1994).

Hankin, Janet R. "FAS Prevention Strategies: Passive and Active Measures." *Alcohol Health and Research World* 18 (1994). Research on alcohol beverage warning labels and prevention methods conducted in Tuba City, Arizona and King County, Washington.

Hargrave, Rita, et al. "Defining Mental Health Needs for Black Patients with AIDS in Alameda County." *Journal of the National Medical Association* 83 (1991). Role of psychiatric diagnosis and treatment for Blacks with AIDS.

Hart, Vicki R., et al. "Strategies for Increasing Participation of Ethnic Minorities in Alzheimer's Disease Diagnostic Centers: A Multifaceted Approach in California." *Gerontologist* 36 (April 1996).

Hutson, H. Range, Deidre Anglin, Demetrios N. Kyriacou, Joel Hart and Kelvin
      Spears. "The Epidemic of Gang-Related Homicides in Los Angeles
      County from 1979 through 1984." *JAMA, The Journal of the Ameri-
      can Medical Association* 274 (4 October 1995). Epidemic numbers of
      Black homicides in Los Angeles city and county.
Jackson, Jacquelyne Johnson. "Suzanne J. Terrell: This Other Kind of Doctors:
      Traditional Medical Systems in Black Neighborhoods in Austin,
      Texas." *Contemporary Sociology* 20 (September 1991).
Klitsch, M. "Prenatal Exposure to Tobacco, Alcohol or other Drugs Found for
      More than One in Ten California Newborns." *Family Planning Per-
      spectives* 26 (March/April 1994). Urine samples of 30,000 women in-
      dicate Black women and those receiving no prenatal care used drugs or
      alcohol during pregnancy.
Klonoff-Cohen, Hillary Sandra, and Sharon Leigh Edelstein. "A Case-Control
      Study of Routine and Death Scene Sleep Position and Sudden Infant
      Death Syndrome in Southern California." *Journal of the American
      Medical Association* 273 (8 March 1995). Study participants included
      Black, white, Latino, and Asian parents of infants who died of SIDS.
Land, G. H., and J. W. Stockbauer. "Smoking and Pregnancy Outcome: Trends
      among Black Teenage Mothers in Missouri." *American Journal of
      Public Health* 83 (August 1993). Research indicates a drop in smoking
      among Black teenagers.
Lindan, C. P., et al. "Underreporting of Minority AIDS Deaths in San Fran-
      cisco Bay Area, 1985–86." *Public Health Reports* 105 (July-August
      1990).
Logue, Barbara J. "Race Differences in Long-Term Disability: Middle-Aged and
      Older American Indians, Blacks, and Whites in Oklahoma." *Social Sci-
      ence Journal* 27 (1990).
Luckman, R., and P. Davis. "The Epidemiology of Acute Appendicitis in Cali-
      fornia: Racial, Gender, and Seasonal Variation." *Epidemiology* 2
      (1991).
Mathis, Annie Maie. "Negro Public Health Nursing in Texas." *Southern
      Workman* 56 (July 1927).
Maynard, C. "Characteristics of Black Patients Admitted to Coronary Care
      Units in Metropolitan Seattle: Results from the Myocardial Infarction
      Triage and Intervention Registry." *American Journal of Cardiology* 67
      (1 January 1991).
McAuley, William J. "History, Race, and Attachment to Place Among Elders
      in the Rural All-Black Towns of Oklahoma." *Journals of Gerontology-
      Series B* 53 (January 1998).
McEwen, Melanie, Pauline Johnson, and Jacque Neatherlin. "School-Based
      Management of Chronic Asthma Among Inner-City African-American
      Schoolchildren in Dallas, Texas." *Journal of School Health* 68 (May
      1998).

Mitchell, Mark A. "Benefits of Violence Prevention for African-American Youth." *Journal of Health Care for the Poor and Undeserved* 2 (Spring 1992). Kansas City research.

Montesano, Philip M. "The Amazing Dr. Ezra Johnson." *Urban West* 1 (January/February 1968). Profile of Black medical doctor in San Francisco.

Moses, V., et al. "A Thirty-Year Review of Maternal Mortality in Oklahoma, 1950 through 1979." *American Journal of Obstetrics and Gynecology* 157 (November 1987).

Newell, Guy R., Lori G. Borrud, and R. Sue McPherson. "Nutrient Intakes of Whites, Blacks and Mexican Americans in Southeast Texas." *Preventive Medicine* 17 (September 1988). Targeted dietary planning.

"No Black Applicants Accepted for Fall at University of California, San Diego's Medical School." *Jet*, 18 August 1997.

"Noted Neurosurgeon Keith Black to Head Brain Cancer Institute at Cedars-Sinai in L.A." *Jet*, June 1997. Specialist in malignant tumors will head the new unit.

Peterson, John L., O. A. Grinstead, E. Golden, J. A. Catania, S. Kegles, and T. J. Coates. "Correlates of HIV Risk Behaviors in Black and White San Francisco Heterosexuals: The Population-based AIDS in Multiethnic Neighborhoods (AMEN) Study." *Ethnicity and Disease* 2 (1992).

Peterson, John L., et al. "High-Risk Sexual Behavior and Condom Use among Gay and Bisexual African-American Men." *American Journal of Public Health* 82 (November 1992). Survey of 250 men in San Francisco Bay area.

Pihoker, Catherine, Carla R. Scott, and Juneal Smith. "Non-Insulin Dependent Diabetes Mellitus in African-American Youths in Arkansas." *Clinical Pediatrics* 37 (February 1998). Black children may be at increased risk of non-insulin dependent diabetes mellitus.

"Programs That Work: Young Adults for Positive Achievement." *Essence* 26 (October 1995). California school fights teen pregnancy through education.

"Project Hi Blood: A Door-to-Door Fight Against Hypertension: Kansas City Ghetto Program." *Ebony,* February 1975.

Reed, T. Edward. "Research on Blood Groups and Selection from the Child Health and Development Studies, Oakland, California." *American Journal of Human Genetics* 19 (November 1967).

Roemer, M. I. "Health Resources and Services in the Watts Area of Los Angeles." *California's Health* 23 (February-March 1966).

Rose, Jerome C. "Biological Consequences of Segregation and Economic Deprivation: A Post-Slavery Population from Southwest Arkansas." *Journal of Economic History* 49 (June 1989).

Rosenblatt, Abram, and C. Clifford Attkisson. "Integrating Systems of Care in California for Youth with Severe Emotional Disturbance: I. A. Descriptive Overview of the California AB377 Evaluation Project." *Journal of Child and Family Studies* 1 (1992).

Ruffin, Orolee. "'Jim-Crowing' Nurses." *Crisis* 37 (April 1930).

Rumberger, Russell W., and J. Douglas Willms. "The Impact of Racial and Ethnic Segregation on the Achievement Gap in California High Schools." *Educational Evaluation and Policy Analysis* 14 (1992).

Samson, Jacques, and Magdeleine Yerlès. "Racial Differences in Sports Performance." 18th Annual Meeting of the Canadian Association of Sport Sciences (1985, Quebec, Canada). *Canadian Journal of Sport Sciences* 13 (1988).

Schaffer, Ruth C. "The Health and Social Functions of Black Midwives on the Texas Brazos Bottom, 1920–1985." *Rural Sociology* 56 (Spring 1991).

"Self-Perceived Excellent and Very Good Health Among Blacks—Kansas, 1995." *Morbidity and Mortality* 45 (1996).

Silverman, B. G. "Black Adolescent Crack Users in Oakland: No Quick Fix." *JAMA* 264 (18 July 1990). Comment on Fullilove article (above).

Smith, C. Calvin. "Serving the Poorest of the Poor: Black Medical Practitioners in the Arkansas Delta, 1880–1960." *Arkansas Historical Quarterly* 57 (Fall 1998).

Sutocky, J. W., J. M. Shultz, and K. W. Kizer. "Alcohol-Related Mortality in California, 1980 to 1989." *American Journal of Public Health* 83 (1993). Examines ethnicity.

Takeuchi, David T., Stanley Sue, and May Yeh. "Return Rates and Outcomes from Ethnicity-Specific Mental Health Programs in Los Angeles." *American Journal of Public Health* 85 (1995).

Taylor, Ronald L. "The *Larry P.* Decision a Decade Later: Problems and Future Directions." *Mental Retardation* 28 (1990). Focus on Black children from San Francisco who were classified as educably mentally retarded.

Terry, Dorothy Givens. "From ABCs to EKGs." *Black Issues in Higher Education* 12 (16 November 1995). Special programs for aspiring minority doctors at the Charles R. Drew University of Medicine, Los Angeles.

Vadheim, C. M., D. P. Greenberg, N. Bordenave, L. Ziontz, and P. Christenson. "Risk Factors for Invasive Haemophilus Influenza Type B in Los Angeles County Children 18–60 Months of Age." *American Journal of Epidemiology* 136 (15 July 1992). Due to various factors, Black children are more at risk.

Wilson, S. R., et al. "The Fresno Asthma Project: A Model Intervention to Control Asthma in Multiethnic, Low Income, Inner-City Communities." *Health Education and Behavior* 25 (February 1998).

Zolopa, Andrew R., Judith A. Hahn, Robert Gorter, Jeanne Miranda, and Dan Wlodarczyk. "HIV and Tuberculosis Infection in San Francisco Homeless Adults." *Journal of the American Medical Association* 272 (10 August 1994). Sample of 1,226 adults included 49% Blacks.

Books:

Arkansas Department of Education, Division of Negro Education. *Problems of Negro Health in Arkansas: Preliminary Study Bulletin*. Little Rock: State Department of Education, 1939. Public health concerns.

A Baseline Survey of AIDS Risk Behaviors and Attitudes in San Francisco's Black Communities. San Francisco: Polaris Research and Development, 1987.

Bernstein, Leslie. *Cancer in Los Angeles County: A Portrait of Incidence and Mortality, 1972–1987*. Los Angeles: Kenneth Norris Jr. Comprehensive Cancer Center, University of Southern California and the California Tumor Registry, Dept. of Health Services, State of California, 1991. Includes Black statistics.

Black Infant Health Improvement Project. *Report on Infant Health in San Francisco, 1991*. San Francisco: San Francisco Department of Public Health, 1993.

California. African American Task Force. *African American Task Force Report on the Year 2000: Health Promotion Objectives and Recommendations for California*. Sacramento: California Department of Health Services, Health Promotion Section, 1992.

Estrada, Antonio L. *AIDS Knowledge, Attitudes and Beliefs among Blacks, Hispanics and Native Americans in Arizona*. Tucson: Southwestern Border Rural Health Research Center, College of Medicine, University of Arizona, 1990.

Excess Mortality among California's Minority Populations. Sacramento: State of California, Department of Health Services, Health Data and Statistics Branch, 1986.

Ferguson, Ronald F. *The Drug Problem in Black Communities. Working Paper 87–01–01*. October 1987. Information analysis. ERIC. ED 347 218. Interviews conducted in Washington, DC, Cleveland and San Francisco.

HIV Risk and Oregon People of Color: A Data Source Book. Portland, OR: Oregon Health Division, Center for Disease Prevention and Epidemiology, HIV Program, 1993.

Hendricks, Leo E. *Unmarried Adolescent Fathers: Problems They Encounter and the Ways They Cope With Them: The Tulsa, Oklahoma Sample, Final Report*. Washington, DC: Mental Health Research and Development Center, Institute for Urban Affairs and Research, Howard University, 1979.

Hernández, Santos H. *Patterns of Utilization of Services by Hispanics and Blacks in the Colorado State Mental Health System: Executive Summary*. Denver: Colorado Department of Institutions, Division of Mental Health, 1985.

Lipscomb, Wendell R. *Ghetto Youth: A One Year Follow-Up Study of a Work Training Project*. Berkeley: Bureau of Adult Health and Chronic Diseases, California Department of Public Health, 1970.

Mackey, Anita J. *My Life: An Autobiographical Account of the Life of Harvey A. Mackey, Including the Diary Saga: Around the World on a Needle*. Santa Barbara: The Author, 1992. California biography written to inspire others with diabetes.

Martinez, Luciano S. *Report on the Ethnic Minority at the University of Utah with a Specific Look at the Health Sciences*. Salt Lake City: University of Utah, 1978. ERIC. ED 149 940. Student recruitment, enrollment, etc.

Multicultural Health: Mortality Patterns by Race and Ethnicity, Oregon, 1986–1994. Portland, OR: Oregon Department of Human Resources, Health Division, Center for Disease Prevention and Epidemiology, Center for Health Statistics, 1997. Mortality and race statistics.

Murray, Betty. *A National Study of Minority Group Barriers to Allied Health Professions Education in the Southwest. Final Report*. San Antonio: Southwest Program Development Corporation, 1975. ERIC. ED 118 297. A two year study conducted in California, Colorado, New Mexico, Oklahoma and Texas.

National Urban League. Community Relations Project. *Report of the Health Consultant for Oklahoma City, Oklahoma*. Oklahoma City: Council of Social Welfare, 1946.

_____. *Report on the Field Services of the Specialist in Health*. Houston: Council of Social Agencies, 1945. Public health of Houston Blacks.

_____. *Report on the Field Services of the Specialist in Social Group Work and Recreation in Houston, Texas, November 3–December 20, 1945*. Houston: Community Relations Project, National Urban League, 1945.

_____. *A Review of the Economic and Cultural Problems of Houston, Texas; as They Relate to Conditions in the Negro Population*. New York: National Urban League, 1945.

Perry, Michael. *Health Risk Behaviors of African-American Kansans, 1995*. Topeka: Kansas Department of Health and Environment, Bureau for Disease Prevention and Health Promotion, 1997.

Prescription for Neglect: Experiences of Older Blacks and Mexican Americans with the American Health Care System. Los Angeles: Andrus Gerontology Center, University of Southern California, 1979. Medical care in Los Angels.

Stanford, E. Percil, et al. *The Elder Black*. San Diego: Center on Aging, San Diego State University, 1978. Black aged in San Diego.

Sutton, Donald, and Ralph F. Baker. *Oakland Crack Task Force: A Portrait of Community Mobilization*. Oregon: Western Center for Drug-Free Schools and Communities, 1990. ERIC. ED 322 270. Task force

created by citizens to fight problems of crack cocaine, with focus on the
Black family.

Terrell, Suzanne J. *The Other Kind of Doctors: Traditional Medical Systems in Black Neighborhoods in Austin, Texas.* Immigrant Communities and Ethnic Minorities in the U.S. and Canada Series. New York: AMS Press, 1990.

United States Commission on Civil Rights. Colorado Advisory Committee. *Access to the Medical Profession in Colorado by Minorities and Women: A Report.* Washington, DC: The Commission, 1976.

Urban League of Denver. *Urban League-Sachs Foundation Health Project: A Tuberculosis Case-Finding Program in a Selected Area in Denver, Colorado, 1955.* Denver: n.p., 1955.

Valdez, R. Burciaga, and G. Dallek. *Does the Health Care System Serve Black and Latino Communities in Los Angeles County?* Claremont, CA: Tomas Rivera Center, 1991.

Vyas, Avni P. *1987–1992 Fort Worth Health Statistics: With Emphasis on the African-American Community in Forth Worth.* Fort Worth: Health Statistics and Information Services, 1994.

Workshop: Alcoholism, How it Relates to the Black Family and Community: Summary, October 21–22, 1976, Phoenix Civic Plaza, Phoenix, Arizona. Phoenix: The Division of Behavioral Health, City of Phoenix, 1976.

Theses and Dissertations:

Allen, Juna S. "The Communication Channels used by Blacks and Hispanics to Obtain Health Information." Master's thesis, Texas Southern University, 1987. Health attitudes in Houston.

Bailey, Eric J. *Urban African American Health Care.* Lanham, MD: University Press of America, 1991. Urban Health case studies in Michigan and Texas.

Bruton, Joseph. "Evaluation of Des Moines, Iowa 'Blacks' Knowledge of HIV/AIDS." Master's thesis, University of Wisconsin-Stout, 1989.

Chandler-Smith, Ruby. "Blacks and the Utilization of Mental Health Services." M.S.W. thesis, California State University, 1982. Sacramento community mental health services.

Connole, Ellen Marie. "Racial Differences in Neonatal Mortality." M.S.P.H. thesis, University of Colorado, 1996.

Curry, Mitchell Lee. "The Role of Religious Experience in Psychotherapy and Mental Illness of Black People in a South Central Los Angeles Community." Min.D. thesis, School of Theology of Claremont, 1979.

Finley, Jarvis M. "Fertility Trends and Differentials in Seattle." Ph.D. diss., University of Washington, 1958. Analyzed by economic class, race, and education.

Franklin, Ruth. "Study of the Services Needed and/or Available to Negro New-
    comer Families: A Study of Perception of Eleven Health and Welfare
    Agencies Serving the Community of Watts." Master's thesis, Univer-
    sity of Southern California, Los Angeles, 1962.
Fuller, William. "The Definition, Etiology and Treatment of Mental Illness
    Among Adult Black Males with Middle and Low Socioeconomic Back-
    grounds." Ed.D. thesis, University of Northern Colorado, 1982. Black
    mental health in Texas study.
Hardman, Peggy Jane. "The Anti-Tuberculosis Crusade and the Texas African-
    American Community, 1900–1950." Ph.D. diss., Texas Tech Univer-
    sity, 1997. The first study on efforts to control TB in the Black com-
    munity.
Hewitt, David John. "The Association of Race and Hypertension: A Cross-
    Sectional Study of Whites, Blacks, and Mexican-Americans in San Di-
    ego." M.P.H. thesis, San Diego State University, 1991.
Hollinger, William H. "Health of the Negro in San Francisco, California."
    Master's thesis, Stanford University, 1948.
Houston, Faye Ruff. "A Process Evaluation of an American Heart Association
    Hypertension Program for Black Churches Entitled 'Hypertension: Life
    or Death, It's Your Choice.'" M.P.H. thesis, University of Texas
    Health Science Center at Houston, School of Public Health, 1992.
Huling, William Edward. "Aging Blacks in Suburbia: Patterns of Culture Re-
    flected in the Social Organization of a California Community." Thesis,
    University of Southern California, 1978.
Hutchinson, Janis Faye. "Understanding Condom Use among Young Adult Af-
    rican-American Women in Houston, Texas." M.P.H. thesis, Univer-
    sity of Texas Health Science Center at Houston, School of Public
    Health, 1997.
Idleburg, Dorothy Ann. "An Exploratory Study of Treatment Outcomes in a 12-
    Year Follow-Up of Black and White Female Alcoholics." Ph.D. diss.,
    Washington University, 1982.
Johnson, Kenneth L. "A Study of the Health Problems of Negro Senior-High-
    School Youth in Arkansas." Ph.D. diss., Boston University, School of
    Education, 1959.
Keck, Canada Kristine. "The Initiation and Duration of Breastfeeding among
    Employed Women in the United States." Ph.D. diss., Ohio State Uni-
    versity, 1997. Race and region included in factors analyzed.
Kerr, George R. "An Investigation of the Pica Practices of Pregnant Women in
    Houston and Prairie View, Texas." Ph.D. diss., University of Texas
    Health Science Center at Houston, 1996. A study of pica or craving for
    nonnutritive substances such as starch (Subjects were 88.6% Black).
Lancaster, Lucila. "The Effectiveness of School-Based Prenatal Care for the Pre-
    vention of Low Birthweight." M.P.H. thesis, University of Texas
    Health Science Center at Houston, School of Public Health, 1996.

Landrine, Hope, Elizabeth A. Klonoff and Roxana Alcaraz. "Racial Discrimination in Minors' Access to Tobacco." *Journal of Black Psychology* 23 (May 1997). Black children sold cigarettes more often than whites in California where purchases by minors are illegal.

Lavine, Margaret Singleton. "The Distribution of Organ Donors and Organ Recipients among Caucasians, Blacks, and Hispanics." M.S.N. thesis, University of Texas, 1992.

Mopkins, Patricia Ann. "Lifestyles and Socio-Economic Status of Los Angeles Aged Blacks in Retirement Homes." Master's thesis, California State University, Dominguez Hills, 1981.

Rainville, Alice Johannah. "An Investigation of the Pica Practices of Pregnant Women in Houston and Prairie View, Texas." Ph.D. diss, University of Texas Health Science Center at Houston, 1997. Study of craving of nonnutritive substances among pregnant Black women.

Roberts, Faye E. Campbell. "A Proposal for a Case Control Study of Risk Factors for Unintended Childbearing among African-American Teens in Houston, Texas, 1995." M.P.H. thesis, University of Texas Health Science Center at Houston, School of Public Health, 1995.

Robinson, Louie. "Death Threatens Western Town." *Ebony*, June 1967. Arsenic in the water supply at Allensworth.

Serlin, Carla G. Jacobs. "A Study of Black Health Behavior in a Neighborhood Health Center." Ph.D. diss., University of Northern Colorado, 1980. Denver center.

Snow, Loudell Marie Fromme. "The Medical System of a Group of Urban Blacks." Ph.D. diss., University of Arizona, 1971.

Sovyanhadi, Marta Lukas. "The Influence of Prepregnancy Weight and Maternal Weight Gain: On Birth Weight among Black WIC Participants in San Bernardino County." Dr.P.H. thesis, Loma Linda University, 1994.

Sumbureru, Dale. "The Influence of Lifestyle on Longevity among Black Seventh-Day Adventists in California: An Epidemiologic Approach." Dr.P.H. thesis, Loma Linda University, 1988.

Tang, Rosa A. "Development of an Interviewer-Administered Survey of Adherence Related to Glaucoma Regimen among African-American Patients in Houston." M.P.H. thesis, University of Texas Health Science Center at Houston, School of Public Health, 1995.

Tanner, Lenora Russell. "Attitudes of Elderly Blacks toward the Aged and Aging." Master's thesis, San Diego State University, 1979. Focus on San Diego.

Yousuf, Hasan Mohammed. "The Prevalence and Risks of Human Immunodeficiency Virus (HIV) Infection among High Risk African American Persons in Houston, Texas." M.P.H. thesis, University of Texas Health Science Center at Houston, School of Public Health, 1995.

Other:

Death in the Hood. Lanita Duke, producer, 1997. Documentary focusing on the drug trade and homicides among Black youth.

Kansas-Nebraska Act

Articles:

Bierbaum, Milton E. "Frederick Starr. A Missouri Border Abolitionist: The Making of a Martyr." *Missouri Historical Review* 58 (1964). Portrait of an abolitionist.

Blue, Frederick J. "The Ohio Free Soilers and the Problems of Factionalism." *Ohio History* 76 (1967). The Ohio party and the effects of the Kansas-Nebraska Act.

Hart, Charles Desmond. "The Natural Limits of Slavery Expansion: Kansas-Nebraska, 1854." *Kansas Historical Quarterly* 34 (Spring 1968). Congressional debate on the slavery issue.

Hodder, Frank H. "Genesis of the Kansas-Nebraska Act." *Wisconsin State Historical Society Proceedings* 60 (1913).

_____. "The Railroad Background of the Kansas-Nebraska Act." *Mississippi Valley Historical Review* 12 (June 1925).

Howard, Victor B. "Presbyterians, the Kansas-Nebraska Act, and the Election of 1856." *Journal of Presbyterian History* 49 (1971).

Johannsen, Robert W. "The Kansas-Nebraska Act and the Pacific Northwest Frontier." *Pacific Northwest Review* 21 (May 1953).

Klem, Mary J. "The Kansas-Nebraska Slavery Bill and Missouri's Part in the Conflict." *Mississippi Valley Historical Association Proceedings* 9 (1919).

Nichols, Roy F. "The Kansas-Nebraska Act: A Century of Historiography." *Mississippi Valley Historical Review* 43 (September 1956).

Osborne, D. F. "The Sectional Struggle over Rights of Slavery in New Territory added to the U.S." *Georgia Historical Quarterly* 15 (September 1931). Missouri Compromise.

Parks, J. H. "The Tennessee Whigs and the Kansas-Nebraska Bill, 1854." *Journal of Southern History* 10 (August 1944).

Plummer, Mark A. "Lincoln's First Direct Reply to Douglas on Squatter Sovereignty Recalled." *Lincoln Herald* 7 (1969). The issue was the Kansas-Nebraska Act.

Rosenberg, Norman L. "Personal Liberty Laws and Sectional Crisis: 1850–1861." *Civil War History* 17 (1971). Second swell of such laws came after the enactment of the Act.

Russell, Robert Royal. "The Issues in the Congressional Struggle over the Kansas-Nebraska Bill, 1854." *Journal of Southern History* 29 (1963).

Wilson, Major L. "Of Time and the Union: Kansas-Nebraska and the Appeal from Prescription to Principle." *Midwest Quarterly* 10 (1968).

Wolff, Gerald W. "Party and Section: The Senate and the Kansas-Nebraska Bill." *Civil War History* 18 (1972).

_____. "A Scalogram Analysis of the Kansas-Nebraska Bill of 1854 and Related Roll Calls in the House of Representatives." *Computers and the Humanities* 8 (1974).

_____. "The Senate and the Kansas-Nebraska Bill." *Civil War History: A Journal of the Middle Period* 18 (December 1972).

Books:

American Abolition Society. *The Kansas Struggle, of 1865, in Congress, and in the Presidential Campaign: With Suggestions for the Future.* New York: American Abolition Society, 1857.

Benjamin, Judah Philip. *Kansas Bill.* Washington, DC: Gideon and Company, 1858. Speeches.

Chase, Salmon P. *Maintain Plighted Faith. Speech of Hon. S. P. Chase, of Ohio, in the Senate, February 3, 1854, Against the Repeal of the Missouri Prohibition of Slavery North of 36°, 30´.* Washington, DC: J. T. and L. Towers, 1854. Kansas-Nebraska Bill and Missouri Compromise.

The Constitution of the United States: With the Acts of Congress, Relating to Slavery, Embracing the Constitution, the Fugitive Slave Act of 1793, the Missouri Compromise Act of 1820, the Fugitive Slave Law of 1850, and the Nebraska and Kansas Bill, Carefully Compiled. Rochester, NY: D. M. Dewey, 1854.

Harris, Wiley Pope. *Speech of Hon. W. P. Harris, of Mississippi, on the Nebraska and Kansas Bill, Delivered in the House of Representatives, April 24, and 26, 1854.* Washington, DC: Congressional Globe Office, 1854.

[Marsh, Leonard]. *A Bake-Pan for the Dough-Faces: Try It/By One of Them.* Burlington, VT: C. Goodrich, 1854. Kansas-Nebraska Bill and slavery.

The Nebraska Question: Comprising Speeches in the United States Senate by Mr. Douglas, Mr. Chase, Mr. Smith, Mr. Everett, Mr. Wade, Mr. Badger, Mr. Seward and Mr. Sumner, Together with the History of the

Missouri Compromise: Daniel Webster's Memorial in Regard to It—History of the Annexation of Texas—The Organization of the Oregon Territory—and the Compromises of 1850. New York: Redfield and Company, 1854.

Nelson, John. *A Discourse on the Proposed Repeal of the Missouri Compromise: Delivered on Fast Day, April 6, 1854, in the First Congregational Church, in Leicester, Mass., by J. Nelson.* Worcester, MA: E. R. Fiske, 1854.

Parker, Theodore. *The Nebraska Question. Some Thought on the New Assault upon Freedom in America, and the General State of the Country in Relation Thereunto, Set Forth in a Discourse Preached at the Music Hall in Boston, on Monday, Feb. 12, 1854.* Boston: B. B. Mussey and Company, 1854.

Right of Petition, New England Clergymen: Remarks of Messrs. Everett, Mason, Pettit, Messrs. Douglas, Butler, Seward, Messrs. Houston, Adams, Badger. On the Memorial from Some 3,050 Clergymen of All Denominations and Sects in the Different States in New England, Remonstrating Against the Passage of the Nebraska Bill. Senate of the United States, March 14, 1854. Washington, DC: Buell and Blanchard, Printers, 1854. Slavery and the church.

Seward, William Henry. *Freedom and Public Faith: Speech of William H. Seward, on the Abrogation of the Missouri Compromise, in the Kansas and Nebraska Bills.* Washington, DC: Buell and Blanchard, Printers, 1854.

Stephens, Alexander Hamilton. *Speech of the Hon. A. H. Stephens of Georgia in the House of Representatives, February 17, 1854, on Nebraska and Kansas.* Washington, DC: Sentinel Office, 1854.

Sumner, Charles. *Final Protest for Himself and the Clergy on New England Against Slavery in Kansas and Nebraska. Speech of Hon. Charles Sumner, on the Night of the Passage of the Kansas and Nebraska Bill. In the Senate of the United States, May 25, 1854.* Washington, DC: Buell and Blanchard, Printers, 1854.

————. *The Landmark of Freedom. Speech of Hon. Charles Sumner, Against the Repeal of the Missouri Prohibition of Slavery North of 36° 30. In the Senate, February 21, 1854.* Washington, DC: Buell and Blanchard, Printers, 1854.

Toombs, Robert Augustus. *Speech of the Hon. Robert Toombs, of Georgia, in the United States Senate, February 23, 1854.* Washington, DC: Sentinel Office, 1854.

United States. Congress. House. Committee to Investigate The Troubles in Kansas. *Subduing Freedom in Kansas: Report of the Congressional Committee, Presented in the House of Representatives on Tuesday, July 1, 1856.* New York: Greeley and McElrath, 1856.

Washburne, Elihu Benjamin. *Nebraska and Kansas—Rights of the North. Speech of Mr. Washburne, of Illinois, in the House of Representatives,*

April 5, 1854. Delivered in the Committee of the Whole on the State of the Union. Washington, DC: Congressional Globe Office, 1854.

Yates, Richard. *Speech of Hon. Richard Yates of Illinois, on the State of Parties, the Condition of the Union, and a Public Policy.* Delivered in the House of Representatives, February 28, 1855. Washington, DC: Congressional Globe Office, 1855.

Ku Klux Klan and Lynching

Articles:

Abbey, Sue W. "The Ku Klux Klan in Arizona, 1921–1925." *Journal of Arizona History* 14 (Spring 1973).

"Activities of the Ku Klux Klan in Saskatchewan." *Queen's Quarterly* 35 (Autumn 1928).

"Aftermaths." *Crises* 6 (August 1913). Two 1899 lynchings in Arkansas.

Alexander, Charles C. "Defeat, Decline, Disintegration: The Ku Klux Klan in Arkansas." *Arkansas Historical Quarterly* 22 (Winter 1963).

————. "Secrecy Bids for Power: The Ku Klux Klan in Texas Politics in the 1920s." *Mid-America* 46 (January 1964).

————. "White Robed Reformers: The Ku Klux Klan Comes to Arkansas, 1921-22." *Arkansas Historical Quarterly* 22 (Spring 1963).

————. "White Robes in Politics: The Ku Klux Klan in Arkansas, 1921–1924." *Arkansas Historical Quarterly* 22 (Fall 1963).

Allen, Lee N. "The Democratic Presidential Primary Election of 1924 in Texas." *Southwestern Historical Quarterly* 61 (April 1958).

"An American Atrocity." *Independent* 87 (31 July 1916). Black teenager is lynched in Waco.

Anon. "Activities of Ku Klux Klan in Saskatchewan." *Queen's Quarterly* 35 (Autumn 1928).

"Another Victim at the Stake." *Voice of The Negro* 1 (April 1904). Black man Glenco Bays burned at the stake in Crossett, Arkansas.

"Anti-Klan Group Wrecks Frisco Theater Showing 1915 *Birth of a Nation*." *Variety*, 18 June 1980.

"Auto-da-fe in Tyler, Texas." *Crisis* 4 (September 1912). The burning of a Black man. "Auto-da-fé" means the burning of a heretic.

"Background on the Ku Klux Klan." Nova Scotia Human Rights Commission. n.d.

Bagnall, Robert. "An Oklahoma Lynching." *Crisis* 37 (August 1930). Mob attacks jail in Chickasha, Oklahoma, and kill Black teenager Henry Argo in May 1930.

Bentley, Max. "The Ku Klux Klan in Texas." *McClure's* 57 (May 1924).

————. "A Texan Challenges the Klan." *Collier's*, 3 November 1923.

"Black Lawyers in Calif. Urge Outlawing of KKK." *Jet*, 13 November 1980.

"Black Marines Battle Ku Klux Klan at Camp Pendleton Base." *Black Scholar* 8 (April 1977).

Blagden, Willie Sue. "Arkansas Flogging." *The New Republic*, 1 July 1936. Southern woman whipped by white men for inquiring into the possible lynching of a Black man.

Blake, Aldrich. "Oklahoma's Klan-Fighting Governor." *Nation*, 3 October 1923.

Bliss, David. "Antiwar Movement Attacks Links of Houston Police to Ku Klux Klan." *Militant* 34 (27 November 1970).

Bliven, Bruce. "From the Oklahoma Front." *The New Republic*, 17 October 1923. Spotlight on the Klan.

Bracken, Lil. "The Lynching of Emmett Till." *New Odyssey* 1 (Spring 1992). Emmett Till, murdered in Mississippi in 1955, is memorialized in the Dr. Martin Luther King statue in Denver.

Buecker, Thomas R. "Confrontation at Sturgis: An Episode in Civil-Military Race Relations, 1885." *South Dakota History* 14 (Fall 1984). Includes account of the lynching of a Black soldier in Sturgis, South Dakota, on August 25, 1885.

Burbank, Garin. "Agrarian Radicals and their Opponents: Political Conflict in Southern Oklahoma, 1910–1924." *Journal of American History* 58 (June 1971). Klan activities.

"The Burden." *Crisis* 11 (January 1916). Article and photographs of the burning of Will Stanley at Temple, Texas.

Butler, Charles C. "Lynching." *Report: Colorado Bar Association, Twelfth Annual Meeting, at Colorado Springs, September 3 and 4, 1909*. Vol. 12.

Byrne, Kevin, and Oliver Houghton. "Texas Klan Rally: Cow Pasture Politics." *Space City* 3 (31 August 1971).

Calbreath, D. "Kovering the Klan." *Columbia Journalism Review* (March/April 1981).

Calderwood, William. "The Decline of the Progressive Party in Saskatchewan, 1925–1930." *Saskatchewan History* 21 (Autumn 1968).

————. "Religious Reactions to the Ku Klux Klan in Saskatchewan." *Saskatchewan History* 26 (Autumn 1973).

————. "Pulpit, Press, and Political Reactions to the Ku Klux Klan in Saskatchewan." Chapter in *Prophecy and Protest*, eds. S. Clark, J. Grayson and L. Grayson. Toronto: Gage, 1975.

"Calif. Senate OKs Bill to Reduce KKK Violence." *Jet*, 6 August 1981.

Calvin, Floyd J. "The Present South." *The Messenger* 5 (January 1923). Black worker taken from a train in Kansas and shot by a lynch mob in Texarkana, Arkansas.

"Canada's 'Keep-Out' to Klanism." *Literary Digest* 76 (3 February 1923).

Cantrell, Gregg. "Racial Violence and Reconstruction Politics in Texas, 1867–1868." *Southwestern Historical Quarterly* 93 (1990).

Capeci, Dominic J. "The Lynching of Cleo Wright: Federal Protection of Constitutional Rights during World War II." *Journal of American History* 72 (October 1985). Lynching in Missouri.

Chalmers, David M. "Twisting the Klan's Shirttail in Kansas." Chapter in *Hooded Americanism: The History of the Ku Klux Klan.* Chicago: Quadrangle Books, 1968.

Chamberlain, C. W. "Last of the Badmen." *Negro Digest* 5 (November 1946). Vigilantes hang seven men but spare the life of notorious Black man Ben Hodges, severing his heel tendons instead.

Clark, Malcolm, Jr. "The Bigot Disclosed: 90 Years of Nativism." *Oregon Historical Quarterly* 75 (1974). About half of the article focuses on the Ku Klux Klan.

Cobb, Ronald Lee. "Guthrie Mound and the Hanging of John Guthrie." *Kansas History* 5 (Autumn 1982). Antislavery sympathizer lynched by proslavery mob in 1860.

Coleman, Frank. "Freedom from Fear on the Home Front: Federal Prosecution of 'Village Tyrants' and Lynch-Mobs." *Iowa Law Review* 29 (March 1944). Includes lynching of Cleo Wright, a Black man, in Missouri.

"Constitution Week in Oklahoma." *Literary Digest* 79 (13 October 1923). Klan activities.

Cosner, B. "When the Klan Came to Arizona." *Arizona* (May 1975).

Crabb, Beth. "May 1930: White Man's Justice for a Black Man's Crime." *Journal of Negro History* 75 (Winter-Spring 1990). Lynchings of George Hughes in Sherman, Texas; Sam Johnson in Honey Grove, Texas; and Henry Argo at Chickasha, Oklahoma.

"Crime." *Crisis* 2 (May 1911). Information on twenty Blacks murdered by mobs in Palestine, Texas, during July 1910.

"Crime." *Crisis* 11 (February 1916). Contains account of armed Blacks rescuing two others from a lynching in Muskogee, Oklahoma.

Crowell, Evelyn Miller. "My Father and the Klan." *The New Republic*, 1 July 1946. The Klan in Texas.

Curriden, Mark. "In Defense of KKK: Texas Lawyer Anthony Griffin Fights for KKK's First Amendment Right." *Barrister* 21, 1994 Annual. "Profiles of the Profession 1994" features Black attorney.

Davis, James H. "Colorado Under the Klan." *Colorado Magazine* 42 (Spring 1965).

_____. "The Ku Klux Klan in Denver and Colorado Springs." Chapter in *The 1967 Denver Westerners Brand Book.* Boulder: Johnson Publishing Company, 1968.

"Democracy or Invisible Empire?" *Current Opinion* 75 (November 1923). The Klan in Oklahoma.

Devine, Edward T. "The Klan in Texas." *Survey* 48 (1 April and 13 May 1922).

_____. "More About the Klan." *Survey* 48 (8 April 1922).

Dew, Charles B. "Black Ironworkers and the Slave Insurrection Panic of 1856." *Journal of Southern History* 41 (August 1975). Lynchings, including those in Texas.

Dew, Lee A. "The Lynching of 'Boll Weevil.'" *Midwest Quarterly* 12 (Winter 1971). Ringleaders of a lynching in Jonesboro, Arkansas, of Wade Thomas.

Douglas, W. A. S. "Ku Klux." *American Mercury* 13 (March 1928). The Klan in Oklahoma.

Du Bois, W. E. B. "Postscript: Coffeeville, Kansas." *Crisis* 34 (July 1927). Attempted lynching of a Black man leads to a riot.

Dyer, Thomas G. "A Most Unexampled Exhibition of Madness and Brutality': Judge Lynch in Saline County, Missouri, 1859. Part I." *Missouri Historical Review* 89 (April 1995). Four lynchings of slaves.

_____. "A Most Unexampled Exhibition of Madness and Brutality': Judge Lynch in Saline County, Missouri, 1859. Part II." *Missouri Historical Review* 89 (July 1995).

Fanning, Jerry, and Andy Bustin. "KKK Grand Dragon Indicted in Houston." *Militant* 35 (17 September 1971).

"The Fight in Texas Against Lynching." *World's Work* 37 (April 1919).

Ford, E. C. "A Horrible Blot on the Fair Name of Kansas." *Negro History Bulletin* 19 (November 1955). Eyewitness account of the Leavenworth, Kansas, lynching of an innocent Black man. It might have been Fred Alexander, burned in 1901.

"468th & 469th; 248th." *Time*, 11 May 1936. Lynchings in Georgia and Arkansas.

"Frank." *Crisis* 10 (October 1915). Included in the article is a report of the burning of a Black man in Temple, Texas, in front of a crowd of 10,000.

Frost, Stanley. "Behind the White Hoods: The Regeneration of Oklahoma." *Outlook* 135 (21 November 1923).

_____. "The Klan, the King, and a Revolution: The Regeneration of Oklahoma. *Outlook* 135 (28 November 1923).

_____. "Night Riding Reformers: The Regeneration of Oklahoma." *Outlook* 135 (14 November 1923).

_____. "The Oklahoma Regicides Act." *Outlook* 135 (7 November 1923).

"General Race News." *Half-Century Magazine*, December 1919. White Pine Bluff, Arkansas, preacher who supported lynching in his sermon was told by congregation to leave town.

Gilfert, Shirley. "Nebraska City Mobocracy." *Old West* 26 (Summer 1990). Black men Henry Jackson and Henry Martin lynched in 1878.

Goldberg, Robert A. "Beneath the Hood and Robe: A Socioeconomic Analysis of Ku Klux Klan Membership in Denver, Colorado, 1921–1925." *Western Historical Quarterly* 11 (April 1980).

Grann, David. "Firestarters." *New Republic*, 20 July 1998. Visit to Jasper, Texas, following the dragging to death of James Byrd, Jr.

Griffith, Charles B., and Donald W. Stewart. "Has a Court of Equity Power to Enjoin Parading by the Ku Klux Klan in Mask?" *Central Law Journal* 96 (November 1923). The Klan in Kansas.

Hamil, Harold. "When the Klan Visited Sterling High." *Denver Post Empire Magazine*, 27 October 1974. Klan in Colorado.

Henson, T. "Ku Klux Klan in Western Canada." *Alberta History* 25, no. 4 (1977).

Holsinger, M. Paul. "The Oregon School Bill Controversy, 1922–1925." *Pacific History Review* 37 (August 1968). KKK influences state legislature.

"The Horizon. Ghetto" *Crisis* 13 (January 1917). Includes item on the $1,000 compensation obtained by a Black man in Arkansas for a mob beating.

"The Horizon. Ghetto" *Crisis* 13 (April 1917). Lawsuit against the Black Paul Quinn College by the husband of a murdered woman whose attacker was lynched. The student newspaper reported the husband was a murder suspect.

Horowitz, David A. "The Klansman as Outsider: Ethnocultural Solidarity and Antielitism in the Oregon Ku Klux Klan of the 1920's." *Pacific Northwest Quarterly* 80 (January 1989).

_____. "Social Morality and Personal Revitalization: Oregon's Ku Klux Klan in the 1920's." *Oregon Historical Quarterly* 90 (1989).

"Houston Socialist Candidate Debates Klan Leader." *Militant* 35 (18 June 1971).

"I.L.D. Calls for Texas Investigation." *Equal Justice* 13 (May 1939). A Black teenager is whipped.

"Jack, the Klan-Fighter in Oklahoma." *Literary Digest* 79 (20 October 1923).

Jackson, Kenneth. "Dallas: Dynamo of the Southwest." Chapter in *The Ku Klux Klan in the City, 1915–1930*. New York: Oxford University Press, 1967.

Jones, Lila Lee. "The Ku Klux Klan in Eastern Kansas during the 1920's" *Emporia State Research Studies* 23 (Winter 1975).

"Judge Lynch and the Pole Cat." *Newsweek*, 9 February 1942. Lynching at Sikeston, Missouri, was filmed.

"'Judicial Lynching at Brownsville': November 9, 1906." *Crisis* 80 (January 1973).

"KKK in Oregon." *Survey* 49 (1922).

"Kansas versus New Jersey." *Colored American Magazine*, February 1901. Includes item about Black man Fred Alexander, lynched in Leavenworth, Kansas.

Keith, Adam. "K.K.K....Klose Kall in Kolorado." *Denver* 1 (August 1965).

"KKK Offers Jobs to All in Sheet-Sewing Drive." *Jet*, 19 June 1980. The Klan in Arizona.

Khan, Israel. "Two Weeks of Hostility: The Klan is Back!" *Contrast* 4 (1972).

"Klan Victories in Oregon and Texas." *Literary Digest* 75 (25 November 1922).

"The Klandidate." *Nation* 231 (5 July 1980). Klansman runs for office.

Knox, Peter. "The Campus and the Klan: A Classic Lesson in Civility." *Colorado: Views From CU-Boulder* (December 1997). University president George Norlin (1919–1939) stands up to the Klan.

Kouris, Diana Allen. "The Lynching: Calamity in Brown's Park." *True West* 42 (September 1995). The lynching of John Bennett.

"Ku Klux Kanada." *Maclean's*, 4 April 1977. The Klan in Canada.

"Ku Klux Klan: Attempts to Establish Ku Klux Klan in Canada." *Canadian Forum* 10 (April 1930).

"Ku Klux Klan in Politics." *Literary Digest* 73 (10 June 1922). The Klan in Oregon.

"Ku Klux Klan." *Oregon Voter* 31 (11 November 1922).

"Ku Klux Klan in Oklahoma." *Current Opinion* 75 (November 1923).

"The Ku Klux Klan in Saskatchewan." *Queen's Quarterly* 35 (August 1928).

"The Ku Klux Klan Victory in Texas." *Literary Digest* 74 (5 August 1922).

"Ku Klux Violence to Teachers in the South." *American Missionary Magazine* 18 (September 1874). Includes Texas.

Lawson, Michael. "Omaha, a City in Ferment: Summer of 1919." *Nebraska History* 58 (Fall 1977). Information about the September race riot.

"The Leavenworth Lynching." *American Review of Reviews* 23 (March 1901). The lynching of Fred Alexander in Leavenworth, Kansas.

"Legal Lynching Disapproved." *International Juridical Association Monthly Bulletin* 1 (October 1932). Reversal of convictions of Blacks in Oklahoma and Missouri.

"Lesson Learned." *Time*, 11 December 1933. The lynching of Lloyd Warner, a Black man, of St. Joseph, Missouri.

Lindsey, Benjamin Barr. "The Beast in a New Form." *The New Republic*, 24 December 1924. The Klan in Colorado.

————. "My Fight with the Ku Klux Klan." *Survey Graphic* 54 (1 June 1925). The Klan in Colorado.

"The Looking Glass. As to Lynching in Texas." *Crisis* 16 (October 1918).

"The Looking Glass. Contrasts." *Crisis* 20 (June 1920). Includes the murder of a Black man named Price in St. Augustine, Texas.

Loveless, Dawn. "Lynch Law in Oregon." *Labor Defender* 10 (April 1934). Oregon Supreme Court grants a rehearing for a Black person sentenced to hang.

"Lynched." *Crisis* 41 [sic 39] (June 1932). Black man, Dave Tillus, lynched in Crockett, Texas, for frightening a white woman.

"Lynching." Chapter in *Races Riots in Black and White*, ed. J. Paul Mitchell. Englewood Cliffs, NJ: Prentice-Hall, 1970. Includes the lynching of Fred Alexander at Leavenworth, Kansas.

"Lynching." *Newsweek*, 2 February 1942. Black man Cleo Wright dragged to death behind a car at Sikeston, Missouri.

"A Lynching in Arkansas." *Colored American Magazine*, August 1905. Joseph Woodman, a Black man, lynched for running away with a white girl.

"The Lynching Horror." *Nation*, 29 August 1901. Blacks lynched, homes burned, and driven out in Pierce City, Missouri and Grayson County, Texas.

"Lynching in Omaha." Chapter in *Racial Violence in the United States*, ed. Allen D. Grimshaw. Chicago: Aldine, 1969. Originally published in the *New York Times*, 30 September 1919, titled "700 Federal Troops Quiet Omaha; Mayor Recovering; Omaha Mob Rule Defended by Most of the Population."

"A Lynching? We're Too Busy." *New Masses* 10 (20 February 1934). Reaction of former governor Ferguson to the lynching of Black man David Gregory in Kountze, Texas.

"The Lynching at Wewoka." *Crisis* 7 (January 1914). In November 1913, John Cudjo lynched in Seminole County, Oklahoma.

Marriner, Gerald Lynn. "Klan Politics in Colorado." *Journal of the West* 15 (January 1976).

"Martial Law in Oklahoma." *Outlook* 135 (26 September 1923). Klan activity.

"Masked Floggers of Tulsa." *Literary Digest* 78 (22 September 1923). Klan activity.

"Mass Murder in America." *The New Republic*, 13 December 1933. Lynchings in California, Missouri and elsewhere.

"Mass Murders or Civilized Society?" *The Sign* 13 (January 1934). Lynchings in California, Missouri and elsewhere.

"Massachusetts as an Example." *American Monthly Review of Reviews* 23 (March 1901). Looks at the lynching of Fred Alexander in Leavenworth, Kansas.

Mazzulla, Fred, and Jo Mazzulla. "A Klan Album." *Colorado Magazine* 42 (Spring 1965). Photographs of the Klan and its women's' auxiliary.

McAllister, Henry. "What Can Be Done to Stop Lynching?" *American Law Review* 39 (January-February 1905). The 1904 speech to the Colorado Bar Association.

————. "What Can Be Done to Stop Lynching?" *Report of the Seventh Annual Meeting of the Colorado Bar Association*. n.p., n.d.

McGraw, Dan. "Justice Delayed." *U.S. News and World Report*, 1 March 1999. Jasper County, Texas, district attorney Guy James Gray to prosecute John William King for the murder of James Byrd, Jr. When a child, Gray's father told him of the murder of a Black man in the town square during the 1930s who was also dragged behind a truck.

McKemy, Al. "Negro Murderer Lynched." *Missouri State Genealogical Association Journal* 13 (Summer 1993). The lynching of Arthur McNeal at Richmond, Missouri, in 1901.

McLoughlin, William G. "The Choctaw Slave Burning: A Crisis in Mission Work Among the Indians." *Journal of the West* 13 (January 1974). Black slave commits suicide over a murder and mistress is burned at the stake.

Melching, Richard. "The Activities of the Ku Klux Klan in Anaheim, California, 1923–1925." *Southern California Quarterly* 56 (Summer 1974).

"Missouri Heads 1931 Lynching Parade." *Literary Digest* 108 (31 January 1931). Article includes photograph.

"Missouri Lynching." *International Juridical Association Monthly Bulletin* 10 (March 1942). Black man Cleo Wright lynched at Sikeston.

"Missouri Mob Murder." *Outlook and Independent* 157 (28 January 1931). Lynching of Black man at Maryville.

"More Texas Klansmen Indicted." *Militant* 35 (25 June 1971).

"Mr. White Challenges the Klan." *Outlook* 138 (October 1924). Anti-Klan platform of governor candidate.

"Negro is Lynched by Missouri Crowd." *Interracial Review* 15 (February 1942).

Nelson, Llewellyn. "The K.K.K. for Boredom." *The New Republic*, 14 January 1925. Oklahoma and the Klan.

Neuringer, Sheldon. "Governor Walton's War on the Ku Klux Klan: An Episode in Oklahoma History, 1923–1924." *Chronicles of Oklahoma* 45 (Summer 1967). Examines why the popular governor eventually turned against the Klan.

"No Lynching in Texas, State Uses New Method." *Southern Frontier* 3 (January 1942). Using new tactics, an individual will kill a Black person or a gang might mutilate Black persons, but not kill them.

Nova Scotia Human Rights Commission. "Background on the Ku Klux Klan." n.d.

O'Brien, Patrick G. "'I Want Everyone to Know the Shame of the State': Henry J. Allen Confronts the Ku Klux Klan, 1921–1923." *Kansas History* 19 (1996).

"Okla. Youth Buried, KKK Recruiting Mission Fails." *Jet*, 21 February 1980.

"Oklahoma Kingless, Not Klanless." *Literary Digest* 79 (8 December 1923).

"The Oklahoma Lynching." *Crisis* 2 (August 1911). Governor's letter about the lynching of a Black woman and her child in Okemah.

"One of the Advocates of 'The League of Nations.'" *Crusader* 2 (November 1919). Mississippi senator Williams approves of the Omaha lynchings.

Papanikolas, Helen Zeese. "The Greeks of Carbon County." *Utah Historical Quarterly* 22 (April 1954). Klan Activities in Utah and the lynching of a Black man.

_____. "Tragedy and Hate." *Utah Historical Quarterly* 38 (Spring 1970). Klan activities plus description and photo of a lynching.

_____. "Utah's Ethnic Legacy." *Dialogue* 19 (1986).

Parker, George Wells. "The Omaha Mob." *Crusader* 2 (November 1919). Mob lynches Black accused rapist Will Brown and attempted to lynch the mayor during attack on the jail.

Parker, Paula. "The Ku Klux Klan Congressman." *Black Enterprise*, October 1980.

Paul, Justus F. "The Ku Klux Klan in the Midwest: A Note on the 1936 Nebraska Elections." *North Dakota Quarterly* 39 (Autumn 1971). Ties the Nebraska Protective Association (the Klan) to the Republican campaign of 1936.

Peterson, Joe. "The Great Ku Klux Klan Rally in Issaquah, Washington." *Pacific Northwest Forum* 2, no. 4 (1977).

Petrie, John Clarence. "Flogging Arouses Various Opinions." *Christian Century* 51 (22 July 1936). Reverend Claude Williams and Miss Willie Sue Blagden beaten in Earle, Arkansas.

Pfeifer, Michael J. "The Ritual of Lynching: Extralegal Justice in Missouri, 1890–1942." *Gateway Heritage* 13 (Winter 1993).

Preece, Harold. "Texas Holiday." *Crisis* 43 (January 1936). In 1935, two Black teenagers are lynched in Columbus, Texas.

"Protests From Georgia and Arkansas." *Crisis* 19 (January 1920). Topic of lynching.

Rambow, Charles. "The Ku Klux Klan in the 1920's: A Concentration on the Black Hills." *South Dakota History* 4 (Winter 1973). The Klan in South Dakota.

"Rampages of Ku Klux Klan on Pacific Coast." *Messenger* 4 (June 1922). Activity in Bakersfield and Oregon.

"The Real Causes of Two Race Riots." *Crisis* 19 (December 1919). Riots in Phillips County, Arkansas and in Omaha, Nebraska. A man named Brown was lynched in Omaha.

"Report Card: KKK Makes the Grade." *New West* 6 (January 1981).

"A Reversion to Savagery." *Outlook* 110 (11 August 1915). The burning of Will Stanley in Temple, Texas.

Rhomberg, Chris. "White Nativism and Urban Politics: The 1920s Ku Klux Klan in Oakland, California." *Journal of American Ethnic History* 17 (Winter 1998).

Ring, Harry. "Houston Election Campaign puts Socialists on the Map." *Militant* 35 (24 December 1971). The Klan in Texas.

"The Riots at Charleston, Longview, Omaha and Knoxville." Section in *Negro Year Book...1921–1922*, ed. Monroe N. Work. Tuskegee Institute: Negro Year Book Publishing Company, 1922.

Roberts, Waldo. "The Ku Kluxing of Oregon." *Outlook* 133 (14 March 1923).

"San Jose Protestors Thwart KKK Rally." *Jet*, 7 May 1981.

Schuyler, Michael W. "The Ku Klux Klan in Nebraska, 1920–1930." *Nebraska History* 66 (Fall 1985).

"Sikeston Lynching—Continued and Closed." *Southern Frontier* 3 (August 1942). Murder of Cleo Wright in Missouri.

Singer, Stu. "Armed Clansmen Threaten Socialists." *Militant* 39 (7 March 1975). The Klan in Texas.

"Six Women." *Crisis* 8 (May 1914). Includes a Black woman lynched in Wagoner, Oklahoma.

Sloan, Charles William, Jr. "Kansas Battles the Invisible Empire: The Legal Ouster of the KKK from Kansas, 1922–1927." *Kansas Historical Quarterly* 57 (Autumn 1974).

Smallwood, James M. "When the Klan Rode: White Terror in Reconstruction Texas." *Journal of the West* 25 (October 1986).

"Somewhere in America, 1942." *Colliers,* 28 March 1942. Lynching of Cleo Wright in Sikeston, Missouri.

Sonnichsen, C. L., and M. G. McKinney. "El Paso—From War to Depression." *Southwestern Historical Quarterly* 74 (January 1971). The Klan in Texas.

Stiff, Cary. "Black Colorado." Black Colorado Series. *Denver Post Empire Magazine,* July 13–Nov. 16, 1969. Twelve installments. Barney Ford, Isom Dart, the Ku Klux Klan, Dearfield, etc.

"Suffering Natural Consequences of Its Actions." *Christian Advocate* 75 (31 May 1900). Colorado abolished capital punishment and a lynching ensued. In addition, a Black man named Calvin Kunblern was lynched in Pueblo on May 22.

Sullivan, Mark. "Midsummer Politics and Primaries." *World's Work* 44 (July 1922). The Klan in Texas.

"The Supremacy of the Mob." *Voice of the Negro* 3 (May 1906). Black man lynched in Tennessee, and three in Springfield, Missouri.

Swain, John D. "A Warning To the South." *Voice of the Negro* 3 (June 1906). Three Black men lynched at Springfield, Missouri.

Swallow, Craig F. "The Ku Klux Klan in Nevada during the 1920s." *Nevada Historical Society Quarterly* 24 (Fall 1981).

Sweetman, Alice M. "Mondak: Planned City of Hope Astride Montana-Dakota Border." *Montana, The Magazine of Western History* 15 (June 1965). Information on lynching of Black man, J. C. Collins.

"Talking Points." *Crusader* 4 (July 1921). Notes Black attack on whites in Mulberry, Kansas, where a Black man was lynched for allegedly attacking a white girl.

"A Texas Horror." *Crisis* 24 (July 1932). Blacks lynched—three burned alive—following the murder of a white girl in Kirwin, Texas.

"The Texas Horror." *Public Opinion* 14 (11 February 1893). The lynching of Henry Smith.

"Texas Officials Approve Lynching of Negroes Too Young for Capital Punishment." *International Juridical Association Monthly Bulletin* 4 (November 1935). Victims Ernest Collins and Bennie Mitchell.

"Thirteen Lynched in Arkansas." *Voice of the Negro* 5 (May 1904). Blacks shot and killed.

"This Week." *The New Republic*, 4 October 1933. Police in Dallas prevent a double lynching.

Thompson, Helen. "Freedom fighter." *Texas Monthly*, March 1995. Profile of Black Galveston attorney Anthony Griffin, who represented the Ku Klux Klan at the same time he was pro bono counsel for the NAACP.

"Three Important Cases." *Crisis* 30 (May 1925). One case reveals the attempts to collect damages for the 1922 lynching of John Harrison, a Black man.

"Three White Men Discharged from Air Force for Racial Incident, Other Problems." *Jet*, 13 April 1998. Whites parade in building on Offutt Air Force Base (Nebraska) with pillowcases over their heads, imitating Klansmen.

Toll, William. "Progress and Piety: The Ku Klux Klan and Social Change in Tillamook, Oregon." *Pacific Northwest Quarterly* 69 (April 1978).

"Torture and Lynching." *Outlook* 71 (28 June 1902). Black man burned at Lansing, Texas.

Toy, Eckard V. "The Ku Klux Klan in Oregon." Chapter in *Experiences in a Promised land: Essays in Pacific Northwest History*, eds. G. Thomas Edwards and Carlos A. Schwantes. Seattle: University of Washington Press, 1986.

_____. "The Ku Klux Klan in Tillamook, Oregon." *Pacific Northwest Quarterly* 2 (March-December 1981).

_____. "The Ku Klux Klan in Tillamook, Oregon." Chapter in *The Northwest Mosaic*, eds. James A. Halseth and Bruce Alden Glasrud. Boulder: Pruett Publishing, 1977.

Twain, Mark. "The United States of Lynchdom." Chapter in *Europe and Elsewhere*, ed. Albert Bigelow Paine. New York: Harper and Brothers, 1923. Twain wrote this article in 1901 after the lynching of three Missouri Blacks.

"Two Lynchings." *The Independent*, 52 (31 May 1900). Report of the lynching of a Black person in Georgia, and another in Colorado.

"Two Lynchings in April." *International Juridical Association Monthly Bulletin* 4 (May 1936). Two Black men lynched, one at Lepanto, Arkansas.

Tyack, David B. "Perils of Pluralism: The Background of the Pierce Case." *American Historical Review* 74 (October 1968). Oregon and the Klan.

"University of Oklahoma and the Ku Klux Klan." *School and Society* 16 (7 October 1922).

Valentine, C. "The Man Whom They Lynched." *Crusader* 2 (November 1919). Lynching of Will Brown in Omaha.

"The Week." *The New Republic*, 4 October 1933. Column reported police in Dallas prevent a double lynching.

"What Ku Klux Klan Stands For." *News Advocate*. 16 July 1922, 16 November 1922, and August 1923. The Klan in Utah.

"When Men Become Beasts." *Frontier Times* 11 (June 1914). The lynching of Henry Smith in Paris, Texas.

"When the Klan Rode in Portland." *Portland Observer* (15 February 1973).

"Why Kansas Bans the Klan." *Literary Digest* 75 (11 November 1922).

"William Allen White's War on the Klan." *Literary Digest* 83 (11 October 1924). The Klan in Kansas.

Williams, Charleea H. "Recent Developments in 'the Land of the Free.'" *Colored American Magazine*, August 1902. Lynchings of Louis F. Wright at New Madrid, Missouri, and William H. Wallace at La Junta, Colorado.

Williams, Dennis A., and William J. Cook. "Mistaken Identity: Causing Racial Harassment at Camp Pendleton Marine Base." *Newsweek*, 13 December 1976.

"Wiping Out Oregon's School Law." *Literary Digest* 81 (26 April 1924). Oregon and the Klan.

Wood, W. D. "The Ku Klux Klan." *Quarterly of the Texas State Historical Association* 9 (April 1906).

"Worries and Concerns." *Colorado Heritage* (Winter 1991). Describes the lynching of Black youth Preston Porter in Colorado.

Wyllie, Irvin G. "Race and Class Conflict on Missouri's Cotton Frontier." *Journal of Southern History* 20 (May 1954). Anti-Black violence in Pemiscot County, and the lynching of A. B. Richardson.

Zylstra, Don. "When the Ku Klux Klan Ran Denver." *Denver Post Roundup*, 5 January 1958.

Books:

Alexander, Charles C. *Crusade for Conformity: The Ku Klux Klan in Texas, 1920–1930.* Houston: Texas Gulf Coast Historical Association, 1962.

_____. *The Ku Klux Klan in the Southwest.* Lexington: University of Kentucky Press, 1965.

Benjamin, R. C. O. *Southern Outrages: A Statistical Record of Lawless Doings.* Los Angeles: The Author, 1894. Black author details deaths in Paris, Texas, Texarkana, Arkansas, and other places.

Chalmers, David M. *Hooded Americanism: The History of the Ku Klux Klan.* Chicago: Quadrangle Books, 1968.

Clough, Frank C. *William Allen White of Emporia.* New York: McGraw-Hill, 1941. White ran for governor of Kansas on an anti-Klan platform.

The Englewood Raiders: A Story of the Celebrated Ku Klux Klan Case at Los Angeles, and Speeches to the Jury. Los Angeles: L. L. Bryson, 1923.

Gerlach, Larry R. *Blazing Crosses in Zion: The Ku Klux Klan in Utah.* Logan: Utah State University Press, 1982.

Goldberg, Robert A. *Hooded Empire: The Ku Klux Klan in Colorado.* Urbana: University of Illinois Press, 1981.

Graves, John W. *Town and Country: Race Relations in an Urban-Rural Context, Arkansas, 1865–1905.* Fayetteville: University of Arkansas Press, 1990. Includes violence and lynchings.

Haldeman-Julius, Marcet. *The Story of a Lynching: An Exploration of Southern Psychology*. Girard, KS: Haldeman-Julius Publications, 1927. Two incidents in Little Rock involving lynching.

Hinshaw, David. *A Man from Kansas: The Story of William Allen White*. New York: G;. P. Putnam's Sons, 1945. White ran for governor on an anti-Klan platform.

Jackson, Kenneth. *The Ku Klux Klan in the City, 1915–1930*. New York: Oxford University Press, 1967.

Johnson, Walter. *William Allen White's America*. New York: Henry Holt and Company, 1947. White ran for governor on an anti-Klan platform.

Ku-Klux Klan. *Constitution and Laws of the Women of the Ku Klux Klan. Adopted by First Imperial Klonvocation at St. Louis, Missouri, on the Sixth Day of January, 1927*. St. Louis: Ku Klux Klan, 1927.

Ku Klux Klan, California Knights. *The Klan in Action: A Manual of Leadership and Organization for Officers of Local Klan Committee*. n.p, 192?. Mimeo located at the University of California, Berkeley.

Lacy, Steve. *The Lynching of Robert Marshall*. Prince, UT: Castle Press, 1978. Marshall, a Black man, lynched near Price, Utah.

Lay, Shawn. *The Invisible Empire in the West: Toward a New Historical Appraisal of the Ku Klux Klan of the 1920s*. Urbana: University of Illinois Press, 1992.

———. *War, Revolution, and the Ku Klux Klan: A Study of Intolerance in a Border City*. El Paso: Texas Western Press, 1985.

Lief, Alfred. *Democracy's (George W.) Norris: The Biography of A Lonely Crusade*. New York: Stackpole Sons, 1939. U.S. Senator fights the Klan.

Lindsey, Benjamin Barr. *My Fight with the Ku Klux Klan*. n.p.: n.d. Reprinted from *Survey Graphic*, June 1925.

Lowitt, Richard. *George W. Norris: The Triumph of A Progressive, 1933–1944*. Urbana: University of Illinois Press, 1978. U.S. Senator fights the Klan.

Maier, Howard. *Undertow*. Garden City, NY: Doubleday, Doran and Company, 1945. White soldiers who failed to prevent the lynching of a Black soldier develop mental problems.

McAlpine, J. *Report Arising out of the Activities of the Ku Klux Klan in British Columbia*. Presented to the Honourable Minister of Labour for the Province of British Columbia, 1981.

McBee, William D. *The Oklahoma Revolution*. Oklahoma City: Modern Publishers, 1956. Governor John Walton and the Klan.

Monks, William. *A History of Southern Missouri and Northern Arkansas; Being an Account of the Early Settlements, the Civil War, the Ku-Klux, and the Times of Peace*. West Plain, MO: West Plains Journal Company, 1907.

NAACP 1940–55. General Office File. Lynching. Sikeston, Missouri, 1942. Frederick, MD: University Publications of America, 1986.

NAACP 1940–55. General Office File. Lynching. Willie Vinson, Texarkana, Texas, 1942. Frederick, MD: University Publications of America, 1986.

NAACP Administrative File. Subject File. Lynching—Boise, Idaho, 1924. Frederick, MD: University Publications of America, 1986.

NAACP Administrative File. Subject File. Lynching—Colorado, 1919–1920, 1930. Frederick, MD: University Publications of America, 1986.

NAACP Administrative File. Subject File. Lynching—Green River, Wyoming, 1918. Frederick, MD: University Publications of America, 1986.

NAACP Administrative File. Subject File. Lynching—Nebraska, 1919, 1929. Frederick, MD: University Publications of America, 1986.

NAACP Administrative File. Subject File. Lynching—New Mexico, 1926, 1928. Frederick, MD: University Publications of America, 1986.

NAACP Administrative File. Subject File. Lynching—North Dakota, 1926. Frederick, MD: University Publications of America, 1986.

NAACP Administrative File. Subject File. Lynching—Oklahoma, 1914–1936. Frederick, MD: University Publications of America, 1986.

NAACP Administrative File. Subject File. Lynching—South Dakota, 1930, 1933. Frederick, MD: University Publications of America, 1986.

NAACP Administrative File. Subject File. Lynching—Texas, 1916–1939. Frederick, MD: University Publications of America, 1986.

NAACP Administrative File. Subject File. Lynching—Utah, 1925. Frederick, MD: University Publications of America, 1986.

National Association for the Advancement of Colored People. *An American Lynching. Being the Burning at the Stake of Henry Lowry at Nodena, Arkansas, January 26, 1921, as Told in American Newspapers.* New York: NAACP, 1921.

————. *Burning at Stake in the United States. A Record of the Public Burning by Mobs of Five Men, During the First Five Months of 1919, in the States of Arkansas, Florida, Georgia, Mississippi, and Texas.* New York: NAACP, 1919; reprinted, Baltimore: Black Classic Press, 1986.

Norris, George W. *Fighting Liberal, The Autobiography of George W. Norris.* New York: Macmillan Company, 1945. U.S. Senator fights the Klan.

Omaha's Riot in Story and Picture. Omaha: Educational Publishing Company, 192? Omaha riot of 1919.

Palmer, Irenas J. *The Black Man's Burden; or, The Horrors of Southern Lynchings. The Most Thrilling Expos of Southern Lawlessness Ever Presented to the American People...the Methods of the Lynchers. The Frightful Experience of Julius Gardner, of Arkansas, a Man Who was Actually Lynched. Mr. Gardner is the Only Colored Man Who, Having Been Accused of Crime and Arrested by a Southern Mob, Has Lived to*

Relate His Experience. Olean, NY: Oleana Evening Herald Print, 1902.

Rice, Lawrence D. *The Negro in Texas 1874–1900.* Baton Rouge: Louisiana State University Press, 1971. Discusses violence and lynching.

The Rocky Mountain American. Boulder: Rocky Mountain American Printing and Publishing Company, 1925. Colorado Ku Klux Klan.

Sawyer, Reuben H. *The Truth About The Invisible Empire, Knights of the Ku Klux Klan.* Portland, OR: Northwest Domain, 1922. Klan pamphlet.

Sher, J. *White Hoods: Canada's Ku Klux Klan.* Vancouver: New Star Books, 1983.

Shufeldt, Robert W. *The Negro: A Menace to American Civilization.* Boston: Richard G. Badger, 1907. Includes photographs of the lynching of Henry Smith at Paris, Texas.

Texas. Governor. *Message of Governor J. S. Hogg, of Texas, to the Twenty-Third Legislature, on the Subject of Lynch Law.* Austin: Governor's Office, 1893.

Trelease, Allen W. *White Terror: The Ku Klux Klan Conspiracy and Southern Reconstruction.* New York: 1971.

Tucker, Howard A. *History of Governor Walton's War on Ku Klux Klan, the Invisible Empire.* Oklahoma City: Southwest Publishing, 1923.

Turnbull, George H. *An Oregon Crusader.* Portland, OR: Binfords and Mort, Publishers, 1955. Newspaper reporter George Putnam opposes the Klan.

Uchill, Ida L. *Pioneers, Peddlers, and Tsadikim.* Denver: Sage Books, 1957. Jews and the Klan in Colorado.

United States Commission on Civil Rights. Montana Advisory Committee. *White Supremacist Activity in Montana.* Denver, CO: The Commission, Rocky Mountain Regional Office, 1994.

Witcher, Walter C. *The Reign of Terror in Oklahoma, a Detailed Account of the Klan's Barbarous Practices and Brutal Outrages Against Individuals; its Control Over Judges and Juries and Governor Walton's Heroic Fight, Including a General Exposure of Klan Secrets, Sham and Hypocrisy.* Fort Worth: Witcher, 1923.

Theses and Dissertations:

Alexander, Charles C. "Invisible Empire in the Southwest: The Ku Klux Klan in Texas, Louisiana, Oklahoma, and Arkansas, 1920–1930." Ph.D. diss., University of Texas, 1962.

Atchison, Carla Joan. "Nativism in Colorado Politics: The American Protective Association and the Ku Klux Klan." Master's thesis, University of Colorado, 1972.

Bryant, Janet. "The Ku Klux Klan and the Oregon Compulsory School Bill of 1922." Master's thesis, Reed College, 1970.

Calderwood, William. "The Rise and Fall of the Ku Klux Klan in Saskatche-
    wan." Master's thesis, University of Saskatchewan, 1968.
Chapman, David L. "Lynching in Texas." Master's thesis, Texas Tech Univer-
    sity, 1973.
Clark, Carter Blue. "A History of the Ku Klux Klan in Oklahoma." Ph.D.
    diss., University of Oklahoma, 1976.
Clubb, Inez. "A History of the Ku Klux Klan in Oklahoma from 1920 to the
    Present." Master's thesis, Oklahoma State University, 1941.
Cocoltchos, Christopher Nickolas. "The Invisible Government and the Viable
    Community: Ku Klux Klan in Orange County, California, during the
    1920's." Ph.D. diss., University of California, Los Angeles, 1979.
Davis, James H. "The Rise of the Ku Klux Klan in Colorado, 1921–1925."
    Master's thesis, University of Denver, 1963.
Estes, Mary Elizabeth. "An Historical Survey of Lynchings in Oklahoma and
    Texas." Master's thesis, University of Oklahoma, 1942.
Findley, James Lee, Jr. "Lynching and the Texas Anti-Lynching Law of 1897."
    Master's thesis, Baylor University, 1974.
Ginn, Duane E. "Racial Violence in Texas, 1884–1900." Master's thesis, Uni-
    versity of Houston, 1974.
Goldberg, Robert A. "Hooded Empire: The Ku Klux Klan in Colorado,
    1921–1932." Ph.D. diss., University of Wisconsin-Madison, 1977.
Harwood, William L. "The Ku Klux Klan in Grand Forks." Honors thesis,
    University of North Dakota, 1968.
Jones, Lila Lee. "The Ku Klux Klan in Eastern Kansas during the 1920's."
    Master's thesis, Emporia Kansas State College, 1972.
Keener, Charles Virgil. "Racial Turmoil in Texas, 1865–1874." Master's the-
    sis, North Texas State University, 1971.
Kilgore, Linda Elaine. "The Ku Klux Klan and the Press in
    Texas—1920–1927." Master's thesis, University of Texas, 1964.
Kremm, Thomas Wesley. "Race Relations in Texas, 1865 to 1870." Master's
    thesis, University of Houston, 1970.
Kroutter, Thomas E., Jr. "The Ku Klux Klan in Jefferson County, Texas,
    1921–1924." Master's thesis, Lamar University, 1972.
Large, John J., Jr. "The 'Invisible Empire' and Missouri Politics: The Influ-
    ence of the revived Ku Klux Klan in the Election Campaign of 1924 as
    Reported in Missouri Newspapers." Master's thesis, University of
    Missouri-Columbia, 1957.
Livingston, David W. "The Lynching of Negroes in Texas, 1900–1925." Mas-
    ter's thesis, East Texas State University, 1972.
Rice, Lawrence D. "The Negro in Texas, 1874–1900." Ph.D. diss., Texas Tech
    University, 1967.
Rothwell, Charles Easton. "The Ku Klux Klan in the State of Oregon." Bache-
    lor's thesis, Reed College, 1924.
Saalfield, Lawrence J. "Forces of Prejudice in Oregon, 1920–1925." Master's
    thesis, Reed College, 1924. Ku Klux Klan in Oregon.

Salley, Robert Lee. "Activities of the Knights of the Ku Klux Klan in Southern California: 1921–1925." Master's thesis, University of Southern California, Los Angeles, 1963.

Steers, Nina A. "The Ku Klux Klan in Oklahoma during the 1920's." Master's thesis, Columbia University, 1965.

Torrance, Lois F. "The Ku Klux Klan in Dallas, 1915–1928: An American Paradox." Master's thesis, Southern Methodist University, 1948.

Toy, Eckard V. "The Ku Klux Klan in Oregon." Master's thesis, University of Oregon, 1959.

Von Brauchitsch, Dennis M. "The Ku Klux Klan in California, 1921 to 1924." Master's thesis, California State University, 1967.

Walrod, Stephen T. "The Ku Klux Klan in Colorado, 1921–1926." Bachelor's thesis, Princeton University, 1970.

Webb, Warren Franklin. "A History of Lynching in California Since 1875." Master's thesis, University of California, Berkeley, 1935.

Legal Affairs

Articles:

"Accolades for Cochran." *Jet*, 24 March 1997. Johnnie Cochran, Jr. honored at LA's Living Legends Series.

"African American Lawyers: A Voice for Unification." *Texas Bar Journal* 57 (September 1994). Black attorneys in Texas.

"African American Lawyers Organize." *Texas Bar Journal* 55 (October 1992). Interview of Sheila Jackson Lee, chair of the African American Section of the Texas State Bar.

Allen, Peter. "Judicial Unrestraint." *California Lawyer* 10 (July 1990). Race discrimination and Black judges.

Andrews, Irving P. "Robert Rhone, Jr. (Six of the Greatest: A Tribute to Outstanding Lawyers in Colorado History)." *Colorado Lawyer* 25 (July 1996). Biography.

Aubry, Erin J. "The L.A. Reality." *Black Enterprise*, November 1995. Special section on the affirmative action "war" in California and Black activity in Los Angeles.

Barrier, W. Christopher. "Members of the Club." *Arkansas Quarterly* 14 (July 1980). Employment discrimination against both female and Black attorneys.

Baxter, Michael St. Patrick. "Black Bay Street Lawyers and Other Oxymora." *Canadian Business Law Journal* 30 (July 1988). Prestigious Bay Street law firms tend not to hire Blacks.

Beck, Deborah E. "School Choice as a Method for Desegregating an Inner-City School District." *California Law Review* 81 (July 1993). Highlights problems in Kansas City, Missouri.

Berg, Martin. "Of Pride and History." *California Lawyer* 12 (February 1992). Interview of LeGrand Clegg III, Compton city attorney.

Brown, Robert L., and Sheila Campbell. "How the Public Views Female and Black Attorneys." *Arkansas Lawyer* 32 (Fall 1997). Public opinion.

Burke, John Francis. "A Twist in Houston." *Commonweal* 124 (5 December 1997). Houston voters defeat an anti-affirmation action initiative.

Carter, Phyllis Harden. "Has the Color Barrier Fallen?" *Arkansas Lawyer* 22 (January 1988). Race discrimination and Black attorneys in Arkansas.

_____. "Judge George Howard, Jr." *Arkansas Lawyer* 21 (July 1987). Biography of Judge Howard of the Arkansas Supreme Court.

Chambers, Marcia. "At 95, He's a Model for All Lawyers." *National Law Journal* 11 (24 April 1989). Interview with Nathan B. Young, Jr., of St. Louis.

Chaplin, Heather. "Affirmative Reaction: UC Law Schools Struggle with Declining Minority Enrollment." *California Lawyer* 17 (September 1997). Social aspects of legal education.

"Charles M. Stokes, Pioneering Judge, Dies at 93." *Jet*, 13 January 1997. Obituary of Seattle judge.

Chenoweth, Karin. "Texas Twister." *Black Issues in Higher Education* 13 (11 July 1996). The successful Graduate Opportunities Program (GOP) at he University of Texas at Austin and the *Hopwood* v. *Texas* decision.

Cleaver, Kathleen Neal. "Mobilizing for Mumia Abu-Jamal in Paris." *Yale Journal of Law and the Humanities* 10 (Summer 1998). International public opinion regarding Black Panther Party member convicted of the murder of a policeman.

Cray, Ed. "Blacks and Browns in Blue-Chip Firms." *California Lawyer* 4 (October 1984). Employment of minority attorneys in California.

Curriden, Mark. "In Defense of KKK: Texas Lawyer Anthony Griffin Fights for KKK's First Amendment Right." *Barrister* 21, 1994 Annual. "Profiles of the Profession 1994" features Black attorney.

Davidson, Idelle. "The Wright Legacy." *California Lawyer* 18 (April 1998). Biography of Crispus Attucks Wright.

Eastland, Terry. "The Yellow Pose of Texas: Hopwood Upheld Dooms Affirmative Action Admissions." *American Spectator* 29 (September 1996). The Supreme Court refuses to review the 5th Circuit Court of Appeals ruling that the University of Texas Law School can not use race in admissions.

Egan, Timothy, Sara Mosle and Linda Greenhouse. "Type-A Gandhi." *New York Times Magazine*, 4 January 1998. Spokane civil rights attorney Carl Maxey.

"Family of 1991 Hate Slaying Victim Receives $900,000 Settlement." *Jet*, 28 August 1995. Settlement paid by company owning the convenience store where the three skinhead killers purchased beer.

Feinsilber, Pamela. "Righting an Old Wrong." *California Lawyer* 10 (August 1990). History of litigation regarding the Port Chicago Mutiny at California's Concord Naval Weapons Station.

Gergen, David. "Becoming 'Race' Savvy." *U.S. News and World Report*, 2 June 1997. Proposal to emulate U.S. Army's success in promoting racial equality in light of decreased Black admissions in the UCLA and University of Texas law schools.

Ginsburg, Loren R. "Sam Cary (Six of the Greatest: A Tribute to Outstanding Lawyers in Colorado History)." *Colorado Lawyer* 23 (July 1994). Biography.

Gite, Lloyd. "Vanessa Gilmore: Stating Her Case in Texas." *Essence*, January 1995. The youngest federal judge in the country and the only Black woman on the federal bench in Texas.

Glover, David M. "Opportunities." *Arkansas Lawyer* 24 (January 1990). Employment discrimination and its prevention is Arkansas.

Goode, Victor. "The Possibility of Afro-Texan Unity." *Texas Bar Journal* 54 (October 1991). Planning by the Texas Association of African American Lawyers.

Graves, Earl G. "Repelling the Siege." *Black Enterprise* , August 1996. Caveats concerning the California Civil Rights Initiative.

Griffen, Wendell L. "Reflections on Rodney Slater." *Arkansas Lawyer* 32 (Spring 1997). Biography of Rodney E. Slater, President Clinton's Federal Highway Administrator.

Gwynne, S. C. "Back to the Future." *Time*, 2 June 1997. Effects of ending affirmative action to law schools in Texas and California.

_____. "The Second Coming of a Nightmare." *Time*, 1 March 1999. Murder of James Byrd, Jr., in Jasper, Texas and conviction of John William King.

Higginbotham, A. Leon, Jr. "Breaking Thurgood Marshall's Promise." *Black Issues in Higher Education* 14 (5 February 1998). Former judge discusses *Hopwood* v. *Texas*.

Holitik, Diane Schratz. "Time for Change." *Arkansas Lawyer* 32 (Fall 1997). Biography of Arkansas' Judge Joyce Williams Warren.

Hornblower, Margot. "Taking It All Back: At Pete Wilson's Urging, the University of California Says No to Racial Preferences." *Time*, 31 July 1995.

"Institutionalized Racism." *National Review*, 12 September 1992. Suit won by whites against the University of Texas School of Law.

Ivins, Molly. "In Memoriam: A Great Spirit (and Voice) Has Left Us." *Texas Tech Law Review* 27 (Fall 1996). Appreciation of Barbara Jordan.

"Janice Brown Appointed by Governor to Become First Black Woman on California Supreme Court." *Jet*, 29 April 1996.

"Judge Ronnie White of Missouri is Picked for Federal Bench." *Jet*, 21 July 1997. White awaits confirmation.

Keaton, Diane. "The Presiding Judge." *California Lawyer* 8 (September 1988). Candace Cooper of the Los Angeles Superior Court is elected president of the California Judges Association.

"L.A. Attorney Crispus Attucks Wright Gives USC Law School $2 Million."
    Jet, 11 August 1997." Retired civil attorney donates money to the
    Wright Scholarship Endowment, the largest gift ever from a Black per-
    son.

Leo, John. "Finally, the People Vote on a Taboo." U.S. News and World Re-
    port, 4 March 1996. Predictions and comments on the November Cali-
    fornia Civil Rights Initiative.

"Los Angeles Jury Awards Three Black Men $611,000 in Brutality Case Against
    Sheriff's Dept." Jet, 14 August 1995.

"Michael Douglas Elected Nevada District Court Judge." Jet, 23 December
    1996.

Morrow, Lance. "Something We Cannot Accept." Time, 8 March 1999. Im-
    plications of death sentence imposed on John William King for the
    murder of James Byrd, Jr., in Jasper, Texas.

Pearson, Martin. "From Gambia to Los Angeles." New Law Journal 6657 (22
    July 1994). Edi Faal, born in Gambia, wins acquittal for accused man
    charged with beating Reginald Denny.

Petersilia, Joan. "Racial Disparities in the Criminal Justice System: A Sum-
    mary." Crime and Delinquency 31 (January 1985). Study of discrimi-
    nation in the criminal justice system in California, Michigan and
    Texas.

Peterson, Edwin J. "The Oregon Supreme Court Task Force on Racial Issues in
    the Courts: A Call for Self-Determination." Willamette Law Review
    32 (Summer 1996). Black law students and discrimination in justice
    administration in Oregon.

Porter, Lindbergh, Jr. "Great Necessities Call Out Great Virtues." San Fran-
    cisco Attorney 24 (February-March 1998). Black attorneys and legal
    etiquette.

Pressman, Steven. "On Her Own: Like Many Black Attorneys, Solo Practitio-
    ner Adrienne Beasley Makes Her Living with a Gritty Brand of Law."
    California Lawyer 10 (February 1990). Interview with California law-
    yer.

_____. "Willie Brown, Esquire: The Assembly Speaker's Law Practice is
    Actually Pretty simple. When He Talks, People Usually Listen."
    California Lawyer 10 (January 1990). Interview of California legislator
    Brown.

Rappaport, Michael D. "Placement Patterns of University of California-Los
    Angeles Law School Minority Graduates." Black Law Journal 7 (Fall
    1981). Address of Rappaport concerning career patterns of minority at-
    torneys.

Richardson, Susan. "Smaller Institutions Expect Increased Minority Presence as
    a Result of Hopwood Decision." Black Issues in Higher Education 14
    (1 May 1997). Affirmative action in Texas education.

Roaf, Andree. "W. Harold Flowers: Mentor, Advisor and Inspiration." Arkan-
    sas Lawyer 19 (June 1985). Biography of Flowers.

Rosen, Jeffrey. "Sandramandered." *New Republic*, 8 July 1996. Supreme Court justice O'Connor strikes down majority-Black congressional districts in Texas and North Carolina.

Silas, Faye A. "Black, White St. Louis Lawyers Moving Closer." *Bar Leader* 10 (July-August 1984). Blacks, the Mound City Bar Association and the Bar Association of Metropolitan St. Louis.

Silverman, Robert A., Marc Riedel and Leslie W. Kennedy. "Murdered Children: A Comparison of Racial Differences Across Two Jurisdictions." *Journal of Criminal Justice* 18 (September-October 1990). Comparative demographics for Illinois and Ontario.

Simon, Paul. "White Hood, Black Robes." *Black Issues in Higher Education* 13 (13 June 1996). Possible effects of *Hopwood* v. *Texas* at the University of Texas at Austin.

Simons, Ted. "Derrick Bell: Civil Rights Attorney Impresses State Bar Members." *Arizona Attorney* 30 (August-September 1993). Address by Bell to the Arizona State Bar.

Slind-Flor, Victoria. "Firm Firsts. *National Law Journal* 13 (27 May 1991). David R. Andrews becomes manager partner in California's McCutchen, Doyle, Brown and Enersen law firm.

Smith, Eric L., Deborrah M. Wilkinson and Marjorie Whigham-Desir. "A Disturbing Proposition." *Black Enterprise*, January 1998. Anti-affirmative action bills are being proposed around the country, including some western states.

Steinhardt, Anne E. "Will She Appeal? To Pete Wilson, That Is. Santa Clara's Judge LaDoris Cordell is in the Running for a Higher Court." *California Lawyer* 11 (September 1991). Black judges and judicial selection.

Tepperman, Jean. "Black and Blue: African American Activists Tackle Cultural Issues Surrounding Domestic Violence." *California Lawyer* 16 (May 1996). Family violence in California.

Traub, James. "Testing Texas." *New Republic*, 6 April 1998. The *Hopwood* v. *Texas* decision and the University of Texas Law School.

Ware, Leland. "Contributions of Missouri's Black Lawyers to Securing Equal Justice." *Journal of the Missouri Bar* 45 (June 1989). History of race discrimination.

Welch, Susan, and John Gruhl. "Does Bakke Matter? Affirmative Action and Minority Enrollments in Medical and Law Schools. *Ohio State Law Journal* 59 (June 1998). Social aspects of the Bakke decision twenty years after.

Zeldis, Nancy. "U.S.-Canada Group Meet on Judicial Minority Issues." *New York Law Journal* 200 (13 December 1988). Black judges and social aspects of the legal profession.

Zirkel, Perry A. "Rights of Passage?" *Phi Delta Kappan* 80 (February 1999). Law suit filed by parents against a Livingstone, Texas, middle school on behalf of fifth-grader Charles Ryan.

Books:

Fry, Susan and Vincent Schiraldi. *Young African American Men and the Criminal Justice System in California.* San Francisco: Center on Juvenile and Criminal Justice, 1990.

Ginger, Ann Fagan, ed. *Minimizing Racism in Jury Trials: The voir dire Conducted by Charles R. Garry in People of California v. Huey P. Newton.* Berkeley, CA: National Lawyers Guild, 1970.

Oregon. Supreme Court. Task Force on Racial/Ethnic Issues in the Judicial System. *Report of the Oregon Supreme Court Task Force on Racial/Ethnic Issues in the Judicial System.* Salem, OR: Office of the State Court Administrator, Oregon Judicial Department, 1994.

Schiraldi, Vincent, Sue Kuyper and Sharon Hewitt. *Young African Americans and the Criminal Justice System in California: Five Years Later.* San Francisco: Center on Juvenile and Criminal Justice, 1996.

State Government Affirmative Action in Mid-America: An Update: A Report. Prepared by the Iowa, Kansas, Missouri, and Nebraska Advisory Committees to the United States Commission on Civil Rights. Washington, DC: The Commission, 1982.

United States Commission on Civil Rights. Montana Advisory Committee. *Access to the Legal Profession in Montana: A Report.* Washington, DC: The Commission, 1981. Law schools and admissions.

_____. Nebraska Advisory Committee. *Private Sector Affirmative Action, Omaha: A Report.* Washington, DC: The Commission, 1979.

Walker, W. James St. G. *"Race," Rights and the Law in the Supreme Court of Canada: Historical Case Studies.* Waterloo, ON: Osgoode Society for Canadian Legal History: Wilfrid Laurier University Press, 1997.

George McJunkin

Articles:

Agogino, George. "The McJunkin Controversy: A Search for Answers at Wild Horse Arroyo." *New Mexico Magazine* 49 (May-June 1971).

Hewett, Jaxon. "The Bookish Black at Wild Horse Arroyo: How the Folsom Man Came to Light." *New Mexico Magazine* 49 (January-February 1971).

Preston, Douglas. "Fossils and the Folsom Cowboy." *Natural History* 106 (February 1997).

Books:

Folsom, Franklin. *Black Cowboy: The Life and Legend of George McJunkin*, 3[d] ed. Niwot, CO: Roberts Rinehart Publishers, 1992. Juvenile.

_____. *The Life and Legend of George McJunkin: Black Cowboy*. Nashville: T. Nelson, 1973. Juvenile.

Music

Articles:

Allen, William Duncan. "An Overview of Black Concert Music and Musicians in Northern California from the 1940s to the 1980s." *Black Music Research Journal* 9 (Spring 1989).

Bales, Mary Virginia. "Some Negro Folk-Songs of Texas." Chapter in *Follow de Drinkin' Gou'd*, ed. Frank Dobie. Dallas: Southern Methodist University Press, 1965.

"Big Break for Crystal Joy." *Ebony*, October 1959. The musical career of Canadian-born singer Crystal Joy, and her sponsorship by Steve Allen.

"Billie Berg's: Hollywood Jazz Temple Draws Stars and Hoi Polloi." *Ebony*, April 1948. Article featuring a nightclub that showcased famous Black jazz artists.

"Boss of the Blues." *Ebony*, March 1954. Biography of jump blues, rock and jazz singer Big Joe Turner, "The Singing Bartender from Kansas City."

Bowen, Elbert R. "Negro Minstrels in Early Rural Missouri." *Missouri Historical Review* 47 (January 1953).

Brennan, Tim. "Off the Gansta Tip: A Rap Appreciation, or Forgetting about Los Angeles." *Critical Inquiry* 20 (Summer 1994). Appreciation of rap for its own aesthetics.

Brokow, John W. "The Minstrel Show in the Hoblitzelle Theatre Arts Library." *Library Chronicle of the University of Texas* 4 (1972). Describes the collection.

Brooks, Christopher. "Coming Home: An Interview with Sippie Wallace." *Texas Humanist* (July/August 1985). Blues singer of the 1920s restarts her career.

Caldwell, Hansonia L. "Music in the Lives of Blacks in California: The Beginnings." *Black Music Research Bulletin* 10 (Spring 1988).

Cochran, Alfred W. "Jazz in Kansas City, the Midwest, and the Southwest, 1920–1940." *Journal of the West* 22 (July 1983).

Creighton, Helen. "Collecting Songs of Nova Scotia Blacks." *Folklore Studies in Honour of Herbert Halpert: A Festschrift.* Published by St. John's Memorial University of Newfoundland, 1980.

Dingus, Anne. "Mance Lipscomb." *Texas Monthly*, April 1998. Profile of the Texas "songster."

Djedje, Jacqueline Cogdell. "Gospel Music in the Los Angeles Black Community: A Historical Overview." *Black Music Research Journal* 9 (Spring 1989).

_____. "Los Angeles Composers of African-American Gospel Music: Composer Bibliography, the First Generation." *American Music* (Winter 1993).

Eastman, Ralph. "Central Avenue Blues: The Making of Los Angeles Rhythm and Blues, 1942–1947." *Black Music Research Journal* 9 (Spring 1989).

"Fatha Hines Settles Down." *Ebony*, October 1957. Profile of big band leader and pianist Earl "Fatha" Hines who decides to quit the road and settle in the Bay Area.

Feid, Jan. "Milligan's Island." *Texas Monthly*, April 1997. Profile of blue-eyed Black albino Malford Milligan, Texas soul singer.

Floyd, Samuel A., Jr. "A Black Composer in Nineteenth-Century St. Louis." *19th Century Music* 4/2 (1980). Profile of Joseph W. Postlewaite.

_____. "J. W. Postlewaite of St. Louis: A Search for His Identity." *Black Perspective in Music, USA* 6/2 (Fall 1978). Profile of composer and band leader.

Floyd, Samuel A., Jr., and Marsha J. Reisser. "On Researching Black Music in California: A Preliminary Report About Sources and Resources." *Black Music Research Journal* 9 (Spring 1989).

Fried, Michael. "W. Elmer Keeton and His WPA Chorus: Oakland's Musical Civil Rights Pioneers of the New Deal Era." *California History* 75 (1996).

"Gateway Singers." *Ebony*, September 1957. West Coast folk group features four white men and Black female, Elmorlee Thomas.

Govenar, Alan B. "Cowboy Blues: Early Black Music in the West." *Studies in Popular Cuiture* 16 (1994).

_____. "Snuff Johnson: Black Cowboy Blues." *Living Blues* 25 (1 July 1994).

Guida, Louis. "Musical Traditions of Twentieth-Century African-American Cowboys." Chapter in *Juneteenth Texas: Essays in African American Folklore, eds.* Francis Edward Abernethy, Carolyn Fiedler Satterwhite, Patrick B. Mullen, and Alan B. Govenar. Texas Folklore Society Publication, no. 54. Denton, TX: University of North Texas Press, 1996. Black social life and customs.

"Hadda Brooks." *Ebony*, April 1951. Focus on singer Brooks and her West Coast television show.

"Jo Baker Goes to Hollywood." *Ebony*, August 1952. Performer Josephine Baker's opening night at L.A.'s Criss, and the star-studded audience.

Johnston, Thomas F. "Blacks in Art Music in Western Canada." *Canadian Journal of Anthropology* 19/2 (1981). Blacks in classical and jazz music.

_____. "Music and Blacks in 18th- and 19th-Century Canada." *Anthropological Journal of Canada* 18/4 (1980).

"K.C. in Swingtime and Now." *International Review of African American Art* 14 (1997). Blues music in Kansas City during the 1930s and its depiction in Black art.

"King Cole Decorates His New Home." *Ebony*, April 1949. Nat "King" Cole's new house and negative reactions from L.A. neighbors.

"Little Gary Ferguson." *Ebony*, May 1966. Feature on the six-year-old singer and composer from Dallas.

"Lou Rawls at Home: He Feels Like a Natural Man." *Ebony*, September 1985. Singer Rawls interviewed at his home in the Hancock Park section of Los Angeles.

Marmorstein, Gary. "Central Avenue Jazz: Los Angeles Black Music of the Forties." *Southern California Quarterly* 70 (Winter 1988).

"Miss Gabby Lee." *Ebony*, April 1955. Torch singer Lee performs in L.A.

Moore, Shirley Ann. "'Her Husband Didn't Have a Word to Say.': Black Women and Blues Clubs in Richmond, California, during World War II." Chapter in *American Labor in the Era of World War II*, eds. Sally M. Miller and Daniel A. Cornford. Westport, CT: Praeger, 1995.

Morthland, John. "True Blues." *Texas Monthly*, May 1994. Houston blues scene.

"Mr. B Finds His Dream House." *Ebony*, October 1952. The remodeling of singer Billy Eckstine's house in Encino.

Mullen, Patrick B. _____. "A Negro Street Performer: Tradition and Innovation." *Western Folklore* 29, no. 2 (1970). Study of Galveston street entertainer George "Bongo Joe" Coleman.

_____. "The Prism of Race: Two Texas Folk Performers." *Southern Folklore* 54 (Spring 1997). Music of Lightnin' Hopkins and George Coleman (Bongo Joe).

Nash, Horace Daniel. "Community Building on the Border: The Role of the 24th Infantry Band at Columbus, New Mexico, 1916–1922." *Fort Concho and the South Plains Journal* 22 (Summer 1990).

O'Connor, Patrick Joseph. "The Black Experience and the Blues in 1950s Wichita." *Mid-America Folklore* 21 (1993).

Parrish, William E. "Blind Boone's Ragtime." *Missouri Life* (November-December 1979). John William Boone, classical and ragtime composer.

Pierce, Kingston. "Amazing Grace: The Gospel According to Seattle's Black Churches." *Washington: The Evergreen State Magazine* 4 (March—April 1988).

"Rap With Strings." *Black Issues in Higher Education* 12 (9 January 1996). Feature on Gregory T. S. Walker, University of Colorado music professor.

Rice, Marc. "Frompin' in the Great Plains: Listening and Dancing to the Jazz Orchestra of Alphonso Trent, 1925–44." *Great Plains Quarterly* 16 (Spring 1966).

Rinne, Henry Q. "A Short History of the Alphonso Trent Orchestra." *Arkansas Historical Quarterly* 45 (Autumn 1986).

Robinson, Louie. "Las Vegas: Entertainment Capital of the World." *Ebony*, April 1972. Article about Black entertainers and their opportunities in Las Vegas.

_____. "Lola Falana." *Ebony*, October 1979. Las Vegas entertainer recalls her path to stardom.

Rosenberg, Neil V. "Ethnicity and Class: Black Country Musicians in the Maritimes." *Journal of Canadian Studies* 23 (1988).

Savage, W. Sherman. "Jazz and the American Frontier: Turner Webb, and the Oklahoma City Blue Devils." *Journal of the West* 28 (July 1989).

Sawyer, Eugene T. "Old Time Minstrels of San Francisco, Recollections of a Pioneer." *Overland Monthly* 81 (1923).

Schwarz, K. Robert. "Black Maestros on the Podium, But No Pedestal." *New York Times* (11 October 1992). Includes Michael Morgan, musical director of the Oakland East Bay Symphony and James DePriest, music director of the Oregon Symphony.

Still, William Grant. "My Arkansas Boyhood." *Arkansas Historical Quarterly* 26 (1967). The great composer recounts his youth in Little Rock.

Stowe, David W. "Jazz in the West: Cultural Frontier and Region during the Swing Era." *Western Historical Quarterly* 23 (February 1992).

Thomas, Gates. "South Texas Negro Work-Songs: Collected and Uncollected." Chapter in *Rainbow in the Morning*, ed. J. Frank Dobie. Hatboro, PA: Folklore Association, 1965.

Van Biema, David. "What Goes 'Round…." *Time*, 23 September 1996. Death of rapper Tupac Shakur.

"The Womenfolk." *Ebony*, June 1964. Profile of West Coast racially mixed, all-female quintet.

Books:

Bagley, Julian. *Welcome to the San Francisco Opera House*. Berkeley: Bancroft Library, University of California/Berkeley, Regional Oral History, 1973. Interview of Bagley, concierge and tour conductor of the opera house.

Barlow, William. *Looking Up at Down: The Emergence of Blues Culture.* Philadelphia: Temple University Press, 1989. Blues in Kansas City and St. Louis.

California Soul: Music of African Americans in the West. Berkeley: University of California Press, 1998.

Cox, Bette Yarbrough. *Central Avenue—Its Rise and Fall, 1890–c. 1955: Including the Musical Renaissance of Black Los Angeles.* BEEM Publishers, 1996. History and musician interviews.

Cross, Brian. *It's Not About a Salary—: Rap, Race and Resistance in Los Angeles.* New York: Verso, 1993.

Debarros, Paul. *Jackson Street After Hours: The Roots of Jazz in Seattle.* Seattle: Sasquatch Books, 1993.

Djedje, Jacqueline Cogdell, and Eddie S. Meadows, eds. *The Soul of California: Music of African Americans.* Berkeley: University of California Press, 1998.

Dobie, J. Frank, ed. *Rainbow in the Morning.* Hatboro, PA: Folklore Associates, 1926; reprinted, Southern Methodist University Press, 1965. Black folk songs, work songs, social life, and customs.

Gilmore, John. *Swinging in Paradise: The Story of Jazz in Montreal.* Montreal: Vehicule Press, 1988.

Govenar, Alan B. *The Early Years of Rhythm and Blues: Focus on Houston.* Houston: Rice University Press, 1990.

————. *Meeting the Blues: The Rise of the Texas Sound.* Dallas: Taylor, 1988.

Guida, Louis, Lorenzo Thomas, and Cheryl Cohen. *Blues Music in Arkansas.* Philadelphia, PA: Portfolio Associates, 1982. History and criticism.

Hildebrand, Lee. *Bay Area Blues.* Rohnert Park, CA: Pomegranate Artbooks, 1993. San Francisco Bay blues. Photography by Michelle Vignes.

Jackson, Bruce, ed. *Wake up Dead Man: Afro-American Worksongs from Texas Prisons.* Cambridge: Harvard University Press, 1972.

Lomax, John A., and Alan Lomax, eds. *Negro Folksongs as Sung by Lead Belly.* New York: New York: 1936.

McIntyre, Paul. *Black Pentecostal Music in Windsor.* Ottawa: National Museums of Canada, 1976.

Newcomb, Bobby. *Bobby Newcomb's San Francisco Minstrel's Songster.* New York: 1868.

Parks, H. B. *Follow de Drinkin' Gou'd.* Publications of the Texas Folk Lore Society, ed. J. Frank Dobie, no. 7. Austin: Texas Folk Lore Society, 1928; reprinted, Austin: Proceedings of the Texas Folk-Lore Society, 1965. Discussion of the song and its origins.

Reed, Tom. *The Black Music History of Los Angeles—Its Roots: 50 Years in Black Music.* Los Angeles: Black Accent on L.A. Press, 1992.

Russell, Ross. *Jazz Style in Kansas City and the Southwest.* Berkeley: University of California Press, 1971.

Scarborough, Dorothy. *On the Trail of the Negro Folksong*. Cambridge: Harvard University, 1925; reprinted, Hatboro, PA: Folklore Associates, 1963.

Songs Sung by the Famous Canadian Jubilee Singers, the Royal Paragon Male Quartette and Imperial Orchestra: Five Years' Tour of Great Britain, Three Years' Tour of United States. Hamilton, ON: Duncan Lithograph Company, 189? Black spirituals and plantation melodies.

Turner, Martha Anne. *The Yellow Rose of Texas: Her Saga and Her Song*. Austin: Shoal Creek Publishers, 1976.

_____. *The Yellow Rose of Texas: The Story of a Song*. El Paso: Texas Western Press, 1971. Recounts the story of Emily, a slave woman captured by Mexican general Santa Ana, and how she inspired the song.

Young, William H., and Nathan B. Young. *Your Kansas and Mine*. Kansas City: Young and Young, 1950. Jazz Age, includes Missouri.

Theses and Dissertations:

Anderson, Edison H., Sr. "The Historical Development of Music in the Negro Secondary Schools of Oklahoma and at Langston University." Ph.D. diss., State University of Iowa, 1957. From 1878 to 1954.

Bales, Mary Virginia. "Negro Folk-Songs in Texas, Their Definition and Origin." Master's thesis, Texas Christian University, 1927.

Batterson, Jack A. "Life and Career of Blind Boone." Master's thesis, University of Missouri-Columbia, 1986. John William Boone, classical and ragtime composer.

Buckner, Reginald Tyrone. "A History of Music Education in the Black Community of Kansas City, Kansas, 1905–1954." Ph.D. diss., University of Minnesota, 1974.

Dunlap, James Edward, Jr. "The Relationship of Musical Achievement as Measured by the Cowell Music Achievement Test to Socio-Economic Status, Race, Community Size, and the Presence of the Father in the Home in Seventh-Grade General Music Classes in Arkansas and Mississippi." D.M.E. diss., Indiana University, 1975.

Houser, Steven. "O. Anderson Fuller, the First Black Doctor of Philosophy in Music in America and His Development of the Music Education Curriculum at Lincoln-University." Ph.D. diss., University of Missouri-Columbia, 1982.

Smith, La Clede. "The Status and Problem of Music Appreciation in the Negro High School of Texas, and Remedial Measures." Master's degree, 1938.

Trantham, Carrie P. "An Investigation of the Unpublished Negro Folk-Songs of Dorothy Scarborough." Master's thesis, Baylor University, 1941.

Other:

"Duke Ellington at Fargo, 1940." Book-of-the-Month Records, 1978. Ellington and orchestra play a 1940 dance in Fargo. Soundrecording.

In the Key of Oscar. National Film Board of Canada, William R. Cunningham and Sylvia Sweeney, 1992. Biography of musician Oscar Peterson. Videorecording.

"Mance Lipscomb: Texas Sharecropper and Songster." Soundrecording.

"Ragtime Texas." Henry Thomas [Complete Recorded Works, 1927–1929]. Sound recording.

Bill Pickett

Articles:

"Bill 'Dusky Demon' Pickett: December 5, 1870." *Jet*, 9 December 1996. Brief article for "This Week in Black History" column.

"Black Cowboy Stamp Worth Million After Postal Service Goof." *Jet*, 14 February 1994.

"Mistaken Identity Prompts Postal Service to Recall Legends of the West Stamps Series." *Jet*, 7 February 1994.

Mundis, Jerrold J. "He Took the Bull by the Horns." *American Heritage* 19 (December 1967).

Roth, Barbara Williams. "The 101 Ranch Wild West Show, 1904–1932." *Chronicles of Oklahoma* 43 (1966). The Miller Brothers show that featured Pickett.

Tyler, Ronnie C. "The Greatest Show in Mexico: A Wild West Spectacular in the Bull Ring." *American West* 9 (1972). The climax of the 101 Wild West Show in 1908 and Bill Pickett.

Welch, Edward M., Jr. "Bill Pickett and the Ponca City Press, 1908–1916: A Tale of Partisan Reporting and a Cowpoke Done Wrong." Paper presented at the Association for Education in Journalism and Mass Communication conference, Anaheim, California, August 1996.

Books:

Hancock, Sibyl. *Bill Pickett: First Rodeo Star*. New York: Harcourt Brace Jovanovich, 1977. Juvenile.

Hanes, Bailey C. *Bill Pickett, Bulldogger: The Biography of a Black Cowboy*. Norman: University of Oklahoma Press, 1977.

Johnson, Cecil. *Guts: Legendary Black Rodeo Cowboy Bill Pickett*. Fort Worth: Summit Group, 1994.

Pinkney, Andrea Davis. *Bill Pickett, Rodeo Ridin' Cowboy*. San Diego: Harcourt Brace and Company, 1996.

Sanford, William R., and Carl R. Green. *Bill Pickett: African-American Rodeo Star*. Legendary Heroes of the Wild West Series. Springfield, NJ: Enslow Publishers, 1997. Juvenile.

Wallis, Michael. *The Real Wild West: The 101 Ranch and the Creation of the American West*. New York: St. Martin's Press, 1999.

Other:

Bill Pickett: Willie M. Piclett, 1870–1932. "Legends of the West": A collection of U.S. commemorative stamps. Kansas City, MO: U.S. Postal Service, 1993.

"The Bull-Dogger" motion picture stills collection. Photograph of poster from the 1923 film. Schomburg Center.

York

Articles:

Curtis, K. D. "York, The Slave Explorer." *Negro Digest* 11 (May 1962).

Heard, J. Norman. "A Giant with Lewis and Clark." Chapter in *The Black Frontiersmen: Adventures of Negroes Among American Indians, 1528–1918.*

Pollard, Lancaster. "Indians Consider Negro Slave Accompanying Lewis and Clark Expedition 'Big Medicine.'" *The Oregonian* (7 April 1963).

Polos, Nicholas C. "Explorer with Lewis and Clark." *Negro History Bulletin* 45 (October-November 1982).

Zochert, Donald. "This Nation Never saw a Black Man Before." *American Heritage* 22 (February 1971).

Books:

Betts, Robert B. *In Search of York: The Slave Who Went to the Pacific with Lewis and Clark.* Boulder: Colorado Associated University Press, 1985.

Arizona

Articles:

Abbey, Sue W. "The Ku Klux Klan in Arizona, 1921–1925." *Journal of Arizona History* 14 (Spring 1973).

Alozie, Nicholas O. "Political Tolerance Hypotheses and White Opposition to a Martin Luther King Holiday in Arizona." *Social Science Journal* 32 (1995). Arizona voters reject the holiday in 1990, but approved it in 1992 after national condemnation.

"Arizona State's Minority Faculty Cite Frustration, Difficulties." *Black Issues in Higher Education* 9 (31 December 1992).

Baumler, Mark F., and Richard V. N. Ahlstrom. "The Garfield Monument: An 1886 Memorial of the Buffalo Soldiers in Arizona." *Cochise County Quarterly* 18 (Spring 1988).

Bergin, A. "The Black Side of Health Care." *Arizona* (August 1976).

Booth, Peter MacMillan. "Cactizonians: The Civilian Conservation Corps in Pima County, 1933–1942." *Journal of Arizona History* 32 (Autumn 1991). One Black profiled.

Boulay, P. C. "Black and White in Arizona Schools." *Arizona Teacher* 57 (September 1968).

Boyles, L. "A Look at the Problem through the Eyes of Negroes." *Arizona* (June 1968). Blacks in Phoenix speak out.

Bradford, Viola. "Letter From Arizona." *Southern Courier* (24 June 1967). Black student and her first year at the University of Arizona.

Bradley, John Ed. "Buffalo Soldier: In His Quest to become a Coach in the NBA, Kareem Abdul-Jabbar will go Anywhere to gain Experience—Even to an Apache Reservation in Arizona." *Sports Illustrated* 89 (30 November 1998).

"Brief History of Troop 'K,' Tenth U.S. Cavalry." *Colored American Magazine* 7 (December 1904). The 10th in Arizona and Montana.

Coleman, Anita Scott. "Arizona and New Mexico—The Land of Esperanza." *Messenger* 8 (September 1926). The status of Blacks.

Cook, J. E. "Black Capitalism—By the Time It Gets to Phoenix the Hard Core will be Softer." *Arizona* (30 March 1969).

Cosner, B. "When the Klan Came to Arizona." *Arizona* (May 1975).

Daniels, Hayzel Burton. "A Black Magistrate's Struggles." Chapter in *Arizona Memories*, eds. Anne Hodges Morgan and Rennard Stickland. Tucson: University of Arizona Press, 1984.

Eppinga, Jane. "Henry O. Flipper in the Court of Private Land Claims: The Career of West Point's First Black Graduate." *Journal of Arizona History* 36 (Spring 1995).

Flipper, Henry O. "Did a Negro Discover Arizona and New Mexico?" n.p., 1896; reprinted, Chapter in *Black Frontiersman: The Memoirs of Henry O. Flipper: First Black Graduate of West Point*, ed. Theodore D. Harris. Fort Worth: Texas Christian University Press, 1997.

Gill, Mary E., and John S. Goff. "Joseph H. Kibbey and School Segregation in Arizona." *Journal of Arizona History* 21 (1980). Governor Joseph H. Kibbey and his fight for equal education.

Glass, Edward L. N. "The Buffalo Soldiers in Arizona." Chapter in *The History of the Tenth Cavalry, 1866–1921*. Tucson: Edward L. N. Glass, 1921.

Gordon, Leonard. "College Student Stereotypes of Blacks and Jews on Two Campuses: Four Studies Spanning 50 Years." *Sociology and Social Research* 7 (April 1986). Arizona State and Princeton.

Hankin, Janet R. "FAS Prevention Strategies: Passive and Active Measures." *Alcohol Health and Research World* 18 (1994). Research on alcohol beverage warning labels and prevention methods conducted in Tuba City, Arizona and King County, Washington.

Hardaway, Roger D. "Unlawful Love: A History of Arizona's Miscegenation Law." *Journal of Arizona History* 27 (1986). The 1865 miscegenation law remained in effect until 1962.

Hindman, Jane E. "Quilt Talk: Verbal Performance Among a Group of African-American Quilters." *Uncoverings* 13 (1992).

Hoffman, Paul Dennis. "Minorities and Ethnics in the Arizona Press: Arizona Newspaper Portrayals During American Involvement in World War I" *Locus* 1 (1989).

Holmes, Edward, Jr. "A Brief Review of Black Cowboys in the Territory of Arizona." Phoenix: University of Arizona, Arizona Historical Foundation, 1984. Manuscript.

"KKK Offers Jobs to All in Sheet-Sewing Drive." *Jet*, 19 June 1980. The Klan in Arizona.

Landin, E. C. "Recognition and Honor." *Arizona* (September 1967).

Luckingham, Bradford. "The African Americans." Chapter in *Minorities in Phoenix: A Profile of Mexican American, Chinese American and African American Communities, 1860–1992*. Tucson: University of Arizona Press, 1994.

Maur, Geoffrey. "Blacks of Phoenix, 1890–1930." Phoenix: University of Arizona, Arizona Historical Society. Manuscript.

Mayer, Martin. "The Good Slum Schools." *Harper's Magazine* 222 (April 1961). Various school teaching programs, including ones in Kansas City and Tucson.

Melcher, Mary. "Blacks and Whites Together: Interracial Leadership in the Phoenix Civil Rights Movement." *Journal of Arizona History* 32 (Summer 1991).

Muller, Carol Ann. "Nigger Ben McLendon and His Lost Gold Mine." *Journal of Arizona History* 14 (Winter 1973).

Newhall, R. "The Negro in Phoenix." *Phoenix Point West* 6 (September 1965).

———. "We Shall Overcome." *Phoenix Point West* 6 (June 1965).

North, George E., and O. Lee Buchanan. "Maternal Attitudes in a Poverty Era." *Journal of Negro Education* 37 (Fall 1968). Survey conducted in Phoenix using the Parental Attitude Research Instrument and the Illinois Test of Psycholingual Ability tests.

Roberts, Shirley J. "Minority-Group Poverty in Phoenix: A Socio-Economic Survey." *Journal of Arizona History* 14 (Winter 1973).

Rodriguez, Roberto. "Mapping a Course for Success." *Black Issues in Higher Education* 13 (21 March 1996). MAP program and minorities.

Romano, Patrick S., et al. "Smoking, Social Support, and Hassles in an Urban African-American Community." *American Journal of Public Health* 81 (November 1991). California household survey conducted in Oakland and San Francisco.

Schulberg, Budd. "Black Phoenix: An Introduction." *Antioch Review* 27 (Fall 1967).

Simons, Ted. "Derrick Bell: Civil Rights Attorney Impresses State Bar Members." *Arizona Attorney* 30 (August-September 1993). Address by Bell to the Arizona State Bar.

Stocker, J. "Segregation's Last Stand: The Prospective Victory Over Discrimination in Arizona's Schools." *Frontier* 2 (April 1957).

Thomas, A. "Discrimination in Employment." *Arizona Frontier* 1 (August 1961).

"Three Negroes Say the Black Man's Middle-Class Haven is a Figment of the White Man's Imagination." *Arizona* (1971).

Ward, C. H. "A Trip to the Cavalry Camp in Southern Arizona." *Cosmopolitan* 2 (October 1886).

Warren, Renee E. "No Promised Land in AZ." *Black Enterprise*, February 1991.

Warren, Renee E., and Alfred Edmond, Jr. "A King Day in Arizona." *Black Enterprise*, July 1990.

Wharfield, H. B. "A Fight with the Yaquis at Bear Valley, 1918." *Arizoniana* 4 (1963). Skirmish of January 9, 1918, involving the 10th Cavalry.

Whitaker, Matthew C. "Phoenix: Civic, Literary, and Mutual Aid Associa-
     tions." Chapter in *Encyclopedia of African-American Associations*, ed.
     Nina Mjagkij. New York: Garland Publishing.
_____. "The Rise of Black Phoenix: African-American Migration, Settle-
     ment and Community Development in Maricopa County, Arizona,
     1868–1930." *Journal of Negro History* 83

Books:

*African Art in Cultural Context: An Exhibition From the Collections of the
     Heard Museum and Arizona State University Art Collections, June 9
     through August 11, 1980, Memorial Union, Arizona State University*.
     Tempe: Arizona State University, 1980. Exhibit catalogue.
Arizona Black Directory Committee (NAACP). *Arizona Black Directory*. n.p.:
     Arizona Black Directory Committee and the NAACP Southwest Area
     Conference, 1979. Black business enterprises directory.
Arizona Council for Civic Unity. *Close the Breach*. Phoenix: The Council,
     1949. A study of school segregation in Phoenix.
Arizona Town Hall. *Harmonizing Arizona's Ethnic and Cultural Diversity:
     Sixtieth Arizona Town Hall*. Phoenix: Arizona Town Hall, 1992.
Artists of the Black Community of Arizona ("Exhibition of Works at the Ari-
     zona Bank Galleria by Artists of the Black Community of Arizona,"
     September 30–Octobr 30, 1981). Phoenix: Arizona Bank, 1981, cata-
     log.
Banner, Warren M., and Theodora M. Dyer. *Economic and Cultural Progress of
     the Negro, Phoenix, Arizona*. New York: National Urban League,
     1965. Black economic and social conditions.
Black Board of Directors Project. Phoenix: The Project, 1984–1987. Blacks in
     business.
Black Commerce Directory. Phoenix: TNT Enterprises, 1986–current? Ari-
     zona's Black commerce directory.
Blacks in Public Education: Report of 1988 Black Town Hall, October, 1988.
     Tempe: Morrison Institute for Public Policy, 1988. Blacks and educa-
     tion in Arizona.
Bockman, John F. *Ten Studies Pertaining to Residence, Mobility, and School
     Attendance Patterns of Discrete Black and Mexican American Popula-
     tions in Tucson, Arizona, Between 1918 and 1976*, Vol. I. Tucson:
     Tucson Unified School District, 1978. ERIC. ED 219 167.
_____. *Ten Studies Pertaining to Residence, Mobility, and School Atten-
     dance Patterns of Discrete Black and Mexican American Populations in
     Tucson, Arizona, Between 1918 and 1976*, Vol. II. Tucson: Tucson
     Unified School District, 1978. ERIC. ED 219 168.
Bortner, M. A. *Black Adolescents and Juvenile Justice: Background Report to
     the 1990 Arizona Black Town Hall*. Tempe: Arizona Board of Re-
     gents, 1990.

Brown, Anthony V., et al. *African-American Architectural Presence in Arizona*, 2^d ed. Tempe: Arizona State University Herberger Center for Design Excellence, 1993.

Brown, Charles C. , and Damaris Bradish. *If You're Young and Black...A Report of a Summer Program with Black Male Youth in Tucson, Arizona, with Recommendations for Program Development.* Tucson: Arizona University, 1970. ERIC. ED 079 445. Proposal for development of a project for Black youth in the South Park area.

Cayer, N. Joseph, and Deborah L. Roepke. *Health Care in Arizona: A Black Perspective.* Tempe: School of Public Affairs, Arizona State University, 1986.

Christopherson, Victor A. *Rural Blacks in Southern Arizona.* Paper presented at the Annual Meeting of the Rural Sociological Society, San Francisco, August 1975. ERIC. ED 128 471. Investigates family patterns and value orientations of rural Blacks.

Colton, Ray Charles. *The American Civil War in the Western Territories of New Mexico, Arizona, Colorado and Utah.* Norman: University of Oklahoma Press, 1959.

Conrad, Clifton, and Mary Talbott. *The Demographic Transformation of Arizona: Implications for Minority Participants in Higher Education.* Topical Paper no. 21. Tucson: Arizona University, 1983. ERIC. ED 236 993. Higher education for changing state demographics.

Critical Issues in Educating the Disadvantaged: Symposium Proceedings, 1970. Tempe: College of Education, Arizona State University, 1970. Blacks and Latino disadvantaged.

Crow, John E. *Discrimination, Poverty, and the Negro: Arizona in the National Context.* Tucson: University of Arizona Press, 1968.

Davis, James P. *Success Story: Negro Farmers.* Little Rock: U.S. Department of Agriculture, 1952. U. S. Production and Marketing Administration booklet covering seventeen states.

Directory and a Brief Outline of the Negro in Flagstaff. Flagstaff: n.p., 1958.

Dolman, Geoffrey, Jr., and Norman S. Kaufman. *Minorities in Higher Education: The Changing Southwest—Arizona.* Princeton, NJ: College Entrance Examination Board; and Boulder, CO: Western Interstate Commission for Higher Education, 1984. ERIC. ED 275 558. Academic persistence, educational attainment, etc.

Estrada, Antonio L. *AIDS Knowledge, Attitudes and Beliefs among Blacks, Hispanics and Native Americans in Arizona.* Tucson: Southwest Border Rural Health Research Center, College of Medicine, University of Arizona, 1990.

Freemasons. Grand Lodge of Arizona. *Proceedings of the First and Second Annual Communication...and Masonic Grand Chapter of the Eastern Star...Held at Yuma, 1920; and at Tucson, April 19, 20, 21, 1921.* Tucson: Masonic Grand Lodge of Arizona, 1921.

Gordon, Leonard, and Albert J. Mayer. *The Cost and Quality of Housing by Income Level of Anglos, Blacks, and Hispanics.* Phoenix: n.p., 1980.

Greene, George M. *Arizona Black Leadership Journal: Motivating and Leading a New Generation.* Phoenix: Omega Psi Phi Fraternity, Phi Iota Chapter, 1991.

Haggerson, Nelson L. *Oh Yes I Can!: A Biography of Arlena E. Seneca.* n.p.: Nornel Associates, 1994. Biography of an educator.

Harris, Richard E. *Black Heritage in Arizona.* Phoenix: Phoenix Urban League, 1977.

_____. *The First Hundred Years: A History of Arizona Blacks.* Apache Junction, AZ: Relmo Publishers, 1983.

Hernández, Maria. *Typewritten Transcript of Oral History Interview: Madge E. Copeland.* With two cassettes, description of Phoenix life. Hayden Library, ASU.

_____. *Typewritten Transcript of Oral History Interview with Irene McClellan King, 1981, July 29 and August 3.* With five cassettes, description of Laveen and Phoenix life. Hayden Library, ASU.

_____. *Typewritten Transcript of Oral History Interview with Veora E. Johnson, 1981.* With cassette, experiences of one of the first Black women in Mesa. Hayden Library, ASU.

Interracial Committee, Tucson. *A Study of the Negroes of Tucson.* Tucson: The Committee, 1946.

James, Franklin J., et al. *Discrimination, Segregation, and Minority Housing Conditions in Sunbelt Cities: A Study of Denver, Houston, and Phoenix.* Denver: Center for Public-Private Sector Cooperation, University of Colorado-Denver, 1983.

Jeffrey, Ruby P., and Carl E. Craig. *Distribution of Indians, Negroes, and Spanish-Americans in Arizona.* Phoenix: Arizona State Employment Service, 1965.

Ku Klux Klan California Knights. *The Klan in Action: A Manual of Leadership and Organization for Officers of Local Klan Committees.* n.p., 192?

Lawson, Harry, ed. *African American Churches in Tucson: A Report of the African American History Internship Project.* n.p., 1990.

_____. *African Americans in Aviation in Arizona: A Report of the African American History Intern Project.* Tucson: Arizona Historical Society, 1989.

_____. *The History of African Americans in Tucson.* Vol. 1, *From 1860 to 1960: An Afrocentric Perspective.* Tucson: Lawson's Psychological Services, 1997.

Luckingham, Bradford. *Minorities in Phoenix: A Profile of Mexican American, Chinese American and African American Communities, 1860–1992.* Tucson: University of Arizona Press, 1994.

Meals and Memoirs: Recipes and Recollections of African Americans in Tucson. Tucson: African American Historical and Genealogical Society, Tucson Chapter, 1993. Pre-1960s recipes and interviews.

Racial-Ethnic Distribution of Public Schools: Pupils and Employees. Racial-Ethnic Survey, Division of Equal Educational Opportunities, Arizona Department of Education, 1970–71. Phoenix: Arizona State Department of Education, 1971. ERIC. ED 071 822. Study of K-12 students and employees.

Racial-Ethnic Survey: Pupils and Employees. Division of Equal Educational Opportunities, Arizona Department of Education. Spring 1972. Phoenix: Arizona State Department of Education, 1972. ERIC. ED 071 809. Study of K-12 students and employees.

Rawick, George P. *The American Slave: A Composite Autobiography: Supplement, Series 2.* Contributions in Afro-American and African Studies, no. 49. Westport, CT: Greenwood Press, 1979. Profiles of slaves in Arizona.

Reschly, Daniel J., and Jane Ross-Reynolds. *An Investigation of WISC-R Item Bias with Black, Chicano, Native American Papago, and White Children: Implications for Nondiscriminatory Assessment.* Iowa, 1982. ERIC. ED 222 529. Item bias in testing, drawn from sample of 950 students from Pima County.

Robbins, Carolyn C. *Lew Davis: "The Negro in America's Wars" and Other Major Paintings: Scottsdale Center for the Arts, Scottsdale, Arizona, September 13, 1990–November 11, 1990.* Scottsdale: Scottsdale Center for the Arts, 1990. Art exhibition catalogue.

Rochlin, Jay. *Race and Class on Campus: Conversations with Ricardo's Daughter.* Tucson: University of Arizona Press, 1997. Encounters with racism.

Ruby, Jeffrey P., and Carl E. Craig. *Arizona State Employment Service Information Prepared for the Centennial Celebration of the Emancipation Proclamation.* Phoenix: Arizona State Employment Service, 1963. Discrimination in employment.

Sanchez, Tani D. , comp. *Meals and Memoirs: Recipes and Recollections of African Americans in Tucson, Arizona.* Tucson: African American Historical and Genealogical Society Tucson Chapter, 1993.

School Desegregation in Tempe, Arizona: A Staff Report of the U.S. Commission on Civil Rights. Washington, DC: U.S. Commission on Civil Rights, 1977.

Smith, Gloria Lawsha. *African Americans and Arizona's Three C's: Cotton, Copper, Cattle.* Tucson: Gloria L. Smith, 1992. Supplement to *Black Heritage Trails and Tales of Tucson and Old Fort Huachuca.*

————. *Arizona's Black Americana.* Tucson: Gloria L. Smith, 1977.

————. *Arizona's Slice of Black Americana: A Regional Survey of History for Teachers or Students of History and Literature.* Tucson: Gloria L. Smith, 1977.

_____. *Black Americana in Arizona.* Tucson: Gloria L. Smith, 1977.

_____. *Black Americana in Arizona: With 1992 Supplement: African-Americana in Arizona.* Tucson: Gloria L. Smith, 1992.

_____. *Black Heritage Trails and Tales of Tucson and Old Fort Huachuca near Sierra Vista, Arizona: A Tourist Guide, A Research Guide.* Tucson: Gloria L. Smith, 1985.

_____. *The Spirit of the Buffalo Soldier: In Celebration of Buffalo Soldier Days in Arizona.* Tucson: Gloria L. Smith, 1993.

Swanson, Mark T. *An Archeological Investigation of the Historic Black Settlement at Mobile, Arizona.* Statistical Research Technical Series No. 34. Tucson: Statistical Research, 1992.

Tucson/Pima County Community Profile, African American Task Force. *African American Task Force Report.* Tucson: Tucson/Pima County Community Profile, 1993.

Twenty Years After Brown: The Shadows of the Past.: A Report of the U.S. Commission on Civil Rights. Washington, DC: The U.S. Commission on Civil Rights, 1974.

Valencia, Richard R. *Understanding School Closures: Discriminating Impact on Chicano and Black Students.* Stanford: Stanford Center for Chicano Research, Stanford University, 1984. Public school closings in Phoenix, Arizona.

Workshop: Alcoholism, How it Relates to the Black Family and Community: Summary, October 21–22, 1976, Phoenix Civic Plaza, Phoenix, Arizona. Phoenix: The Division of Behavioral Health, City of Phoenix, 1976.

Theses and Dissertation:

Breit, Amelia. "Problems of Negro Youth in Tucson." Master's thesis, University of Arizona, 1947.

Carrillo, Carol Adams. "'Cognitive Impulsivity' in Mexican American, Negro, and Anglo-American School Children." Master's thesis, University of Arizona, 1969. Ethno-psychology.

Chavez, Gene T. "Chicano, Black, and Anglo Students' Satisfaction with Their University Experiences." Ph.D. diss., Arizona State University, 1985.

Daniels, Hayzel Burton. "Negro High School in Tucson." Master's thesis, University of Arizona, 1941.

Dickey, Lloyd Duquesne. "Adult Education in Phoenix, Arizona, with Special Reference to Negro Adults." MA Ed. thesis, Arizona State University, 1943.

Favors-Curtis, Juanita G. "A Study of the Conditions of the Negro Rural Schools in Maricopa County." MA Ed. thesis, Arizona State University, 1944.

Gwynn, Douglas Bruce. "Communalism: A Study of its Effects on Job Success." Master's thesis, Arizona State University, 1971. Employment, Blacks and Latinos.

Hackett, Mattie Nance. "A Survey of the Living Conditions of Girls in the Negro Schools of Phoenix, Arizona." MA Ed. thesis, Arizona State University, 1939.

Hale, Georgia Marie Mitchell. "Factors and Strategies Affecting the Career Patterns of Black Managers." Ph.D. diss., Arizona State University, 1985.

Hall, Mary Anne. "Factors Related to Occupational Success Among Primary and Secondary Minority Groups in a Job Program." Master's thesis, Arizona State University, 1973. Employment, Blacks and Latinos.

Hammel, Genie Teague. "The Association between Socio-Economic Status and Family Life for Negroes and Mexican-Americans in Tucson, Arizona." Master's thesis, University of Arizona, 1970.

Herbert, Elizabeth J. "Proxemic Patterns of Blacks and Whites from Flagstaff, Arizona." Master's thesis, Northern Arizona University, 1974.

Hristofi, Anastasia. "Value Orientations for Achievement and Occupational Success." Master's thesis, Arizona State University, 1973. Blacks, Latinos, and employment.

Hunt, Walter E. "The Nonwhite Population of Phoenix: Changes Between 1950 and 1960." Master's thesis, Arizona State University, 1966.

Jackson, Thomas Conrad. "Negro Education in Arizona." Master's thesis, University of Arizona, 1941.

Johnson-Parrott, Katie J. "Personal Comfort Experienced by Black Students in a Rural Community College: Implications for Retention." Ed.D. thesis, Arizona State University, 1988.

King, Ira Clinton. "A Comparison of the Role Expectation by Parents by Racial Group and Selected Socio-Economic Factors of Elementary Principals." Thesis, Arizona State University, 1975. Study conducted in Phoenix.

Landrum, Leah Nicole. "The Martin Luther King, Jr. Holiday Controversy in Arizona." Master's thesis, Arizona Sate University, 1991.

Lewis, Eddie J. "A Study of the Distinctiveness of Black Attitudes Toward Education in the Roosevelt School District." Ed.D. thesis, Arizona State University, 1992.

Lorenzini, August Peter. "A Study of the Patterns of Communication Used by Fifty Negro and Fifty Spanish-Named Residents of Phoenix, Arizona." Ph.D. diss., University of Denver, 1962.

McClellan, William Circe. "The Status and Function of Negro Men Teachers in the Public Elementary Schools in Tucson." MA Ed. thesis, Arizona State University, 1948.

Nimmons, Robert Kim. "Arizona's Forgotten Past: The Negro in Arizona, 1539–1965." Master's thesis, Northern Arizona University, 1971.

Parham, Joseph. "Relationships Between Academic Achievement, Attitudes and Attrition of Black Athletes at Arizona Sate University." Thesis, Arizona State University, 1973.

Popov, Boris Jakob. "Black and Mexican-American Enrollees' Perceptions of the Concentrated Employment Program in Phoenix." Master's thesis, Arizona State University, 1972.

Ragsdale, Lincoln Johnson. "Minority Entrepreneurship: Profiling an African-American Entrepreneur." Ph.D. diss., Union Graduate School, 1989.

Searfoss, Linda Rae. "An Examination of Negro Success and Failure in Job Training Programs." Master's thesis, Arizona State University, 1972.

Smith, E. Jim. "A Comparison of Transfer and Non-Transfer Students in an Open Enrollment District." Thesis, Arizona State University, 1977. School integration.

Snow, Loudell Marie Fromme. "The Medical System of a Group of Urban Blacks." Ph.D. diss., University of Arizona, 1971.

Tavares, Mahalia. "Black High School Dropouts: Categorization and Variables in Education that Affect Minority Students." Ph.D. diss., University of Arizona, 1992.

Thompson, Amelia Ellen Brown. "Home Environment and School Achievement." MA Ed. thesis, Arizona State University, 1939. Blacks and ability testing.

Thul, Lynn Byrd. "African-American School Segregation in Arizona from 1863–1954." Master's thesis, Arizona State University, 1993.

Whitaker, Matthew C. "In Search of Black Phoenicians: African-American Culture and Community in Phoenix, Arizona, 1868–1940." Master's thesis, Arizona State University, 1997.

Wienker, Curtis Wakefield. "The Influence of Culture and Demography on the Population Biology of a Non-Isolate: The Colored People of McNary, Arizona." Thesis, University of Arizona, 1975.

Yancy, James Walter. "The Negro of Tucson, Past and Present." Master's thesis, University of Arizona, 1933.

Zanders, Ida O. Williams. "Negro Education in Tucson, Arizona." Master's thesis, University of Arizona, 1946.

Black Newspapers:

PHOENIX

Arizona Gleam. Phoenix. 1935–1946.

Arizona Informant #1. Phoenix. 1958–1961.

Arizona Informant #2. Phoenix. 1971–current.

Arizona Sun. Phoenix. 1940–1965.

Arizona Tribune. Phoenix. 1958–1979.

Bessie Coleman Aero News. Phoenix. 1930.

Index. Phoenix. 1936–1942.

Phoenix Now Magazine. Phoenix. 1972–1973.

Phoenix Now News-Magazine. Phoenix. 1974.

Arizona Now Newspaper. Phoenix.

1974–? Continues *Phoenix Now News-Magazine.*
Phoenix Press Weekly. Phoenix. 1981–1982.
Phoenix Western Dispatch. Phoenix. 1924–1929.
Tribune. Phoenix. 1918–1941.
Western Dispatch. Phoenix. 1927–1929.

TUCSON

Arizona Times. Tucson. 1930–1934.
Arizona's Negro Journal. Tucson. 1941–1946.

Balance Sheet. Tucson. 1980–?
Inter-State Review. Tucson. 1920–1935.
Tucson Spokesman. Tucson. 192?

VARIOUS COMMUNITIES

Fact Sheets. Publication of the Arizona Council for Civic Unity. 1950.
93^d Blue Helmet. Fort Huachuca. 1942–1943.
Nogales Bullet. Nogales. 1921–? Published by the 25th Infantry.

Other:

Almost Free. William McCune Productions for Television, Phoenix, 1990. Westward immigration to Arizona.

Cultural Heritage Awareness for New Goals in Education (CHANGE), Phoenix Union High School District #210. Curriculum units on Arizona ethnic groups.

Heritage. KOOL-TV, Phoenix, 1978. History of Blacks in Phoenix. Videorecording.

Rediscovering America: Buffalo Soldiers. Discovery Communications, Bethesda, MD, 1997. Videorecording.

Robert Colescott. University of Colorado-Boulder Department of Fine Arts interview of Tucson artist. Videorecording.

Arkansas

Articles:

"Aftermaths." *Crises* 6 (August 1913). Two 1899 lynchings in Arkansas.

Alexander, Charles C. "Defeat, Decline, Disintegration: The Ku Klux Klan in Arkansas." *Arkansas Historical Quarterly* 22 (Winter 1963).

_____. "White Robed Reformers: The Ku Klux Klan Comes to Arkansas, 1921-22." *Arkansas Historical Quarterly* 22 (Spring 1963).

_____. "White Robes in Politics: The Ku Klux Klan in Arkansas, 1921–1924." *Arkansas Historical Quarterly* 22 (Fall 1963).

"Another Victim at the Stake." *Voice of The Negro* 1 (April 1904). Black man Glenco Bays burned at the stake in Crossett, Arkansas.

"Arkansas Justice." *Crisis* 21 (February 1921). Race riots.

"Arkansas Moves Toward Freedom." *Christian Century* 53 (22 July 1936). Race problems.

Barrier, W. Christopher. "Members of the Club." *Arkansas Quarterly* 14 (July 1980). Employment discrimination against both female and Black attorneys.

Bayless, Garland E. "The State Penitentiary Under Democratic Control, 1874–1896." *Arkansas Historical Quarterly* 34 (Autumn 1975). Mentions Black involvement.

Beatty-Brown, Florence. "Legal Status of Arkansas Negroes Before Emancipation." *Arkansas Historical Quarterly* 28 (1969).

Benjamin, R. C. O. *Southern Outrages: A Statistical Record of Lawless Doings*. Los Angeles: The Author, 1894. Black author details deaths in Paris, Texas, Texarkana, Arkansas, and other places.

Biegert, M. Langley. "Legacy of Resistance: Uncovering the History of Collective Action by Black Agricultural Workers in Central East Arkansas from the 1860s to the 1930s." *Journal of Social History* 32 (Fall 1998).

Blagden, Willie Sue. "Arkansas Flogging." *The New Republic*, 1 July 1936. Southern woman whipped by white men for inquiring into the possible lynching of a Black man.

Blount, Carolyne S. "Arkansas Public Health Director M. Joycelyn Elders, M.D.: A Caring Crusader." *Time*, 19 April 1991.

Bogle, Lori. "Black Arkansas." *Chronicles of Oklahoma* 72 (Summer 1994). As civil rights in late 1880s Arkansas deteriorated, Blacks looked to Oklahoma.

Boyett, Gene W. "The Black Experience in the First Decade of Reconstruction in Pope County, Arkansas." *Arkansas Historical Quarterly* 51 (Summer 1992).

Brown, Robert L., and Sheila Campbell. "How the Public Views Female and Black Attorneys." *Arkansas Lawyer* 32 (Fall 1997). Public opinion.

Brown, Roxanne. "Thirty-Four Years at the Governor's Mansion." *Ebony*, July 1989. Profile of Eliza Jane Ashley.

Calvin, Floyd J. "The Present South." *The Messenger* 5 (January 1923). Black worker taken from a train in Kansas and shot by a lynch mob in Texarkana, Arkansas.

Carmichael, Maude. "Federal Experiments with Negro Labor on Abandoned Plantations in Arkansas: 1862–1865." *Arkansas Historical Quarterly* 20 (June 1942).

Carter, Phyllis Harden. "Has the Color Barrier Fallen?" *Arkansas Lawyer* 22 (January 1988). Race discrimination and Black attorneys in Arkansas.

_____. "Judge George Howard, Jr." *Arkansas Lawyer* 21 (July 1987). Biography of Judge Howard of the Arkansas Supreme Court.

Cathey, Clyde W. "Slavery in Arkansas." *Journal of Negro History* 3 (1944).

Chester, S. H. "African Slavery as I Knew It in Southern Arkansas." *Tennessee Historical Magazine* 9 (October 1925).

Cothran, Tilman C., and William M. Phillips, Jr. "Expansion of Negro Suffrage in Arkansas." *Journal of Negro Education* 26 (Summer 1957).

Dew, Lee A. "The Lynching of 'Boll Weevil.'" *Midwest Quarterly* 12 (Winter 1971). Ringleaders of a lynching in Jonesboro.

Dillard, Tom W. "'Golden Prospects and Fraternal Amenities': Mifflin W. Gibbs's Arkansas Years." *Arkansas Historical Quarterly* 35 (1976).

_____. "Scipio A. Jones." *Arkansas Historical Quarterly* 31 (1972). Black politico of the Republican Party.

_____. "To the Back of the Elephant: Racial Conflict in the Arkansas Republican Party." *Arkansas Historical Quarterly* 33 (Spring 1974). Recounts struggles of Blacks to gain power in the Party before 1928.

Dillon, Andrew. "Arkansas as a Negro Republic." *New Mexico Humanities Review* 33 (1990).

Dougan, Michael B. "Life in Confederate Arkansas." *Arkansas Historical Quarterly* 31 (Spring 1972). Includes slavery issue.

Driggs, O. T., Jr. "Arkansas Politics" The Essence of the Powell Clayton Regime, 1868–1871." *Arkansas Historical Quarterly* 8 (Spring 1949).

"Due Process of Law in Arkansas." *The New Republic*, 14 March 1923.

Dyson, Lowell K. "The Southern Tenant Farmers Union and Depression Politics." *Political Science Quarterly* 88 (1973). An interracial union started in Arkansas.

Feistman, Eugene G. "Racial Disfranchisement in Arkansas 1867–1868." *Arkansas Historical Quarterly* 9 (1950).

Finley, Randy. "Black Arkansas and World War One." *Arkansas Historical Quarterly* 49 (Fall 1990).

Fisher, Mike. "The First Kansas Colored: Massacre at Poison Springs." *Kansas History* 2 (1979).

————. "Remember Poison Spring." *Missouri Historical Review* 74 (1980).

"468th & 469th; 248th." *Time*, 11 May 1936. Lynchings in Georgia and Arkansas.

Frank, Kenny A. "The California Overland Express Through Indian Territory and Western Arkansas." *Arkansas Historical Quarterly* 33 (Spring 1974). A traveler observes surroundings, including slavery.

French, A. "Plantation Life in Arkansas." *Atlantic* 68 (1891).

Froelich, Jacqueline. "Eureka Springs in Black and White: The lost History of an African-American Neighborhood." *Arkansas Historical Quarterly* 56 (Summer 1997).

"From Hope, Ark., With New Hope for a New America." *Ebony*, November 1995. President Clinton discusses civil rights.

Galonska, Juliet L. "African-American Deputy Marshals in Arkansas." *Crm: Cultural Resource Management* 20 (1997). Profile of lawmen.

Gatewood, Willard B., Jr. "Arkansas Negroes in the 1890's: Documents." *Arkansas Historical Quarterly* 33 (Winter 1974).

————. "John Hanks Alexander of Arkansas: Second Black Graduate of West Point." *Arkansas Historical Quarterly* 41 (1982).

————. "Negro Legislators in Arkansas, 1891: A Document." *Arkansas Historical Quarterly* 31 (Autumn 1972).

————. "Sunnyside: The Evolution of an Arkansas Plantation, 1840–1945." *Arkansas Historical Quarterly* 50 (Spring 1991). Includes Black experience to Sunnyside demonstrating how plantation life helped to shape the Southern economy.

Gay, Faith. "Power in the Delta." *Southern Exposure* 17 (Winter 1989). Attempts to disfranchise Blacks.

"General Race News." *Half-Century Magazine*, December 1919. White Pine Bluff, Arkansas, preacher who supported lynching in his sermon was told by congregation to leave town.

Glover, David M. "Opportunities." *Arkansas Lawyer* 24 (January 1990). Employment discrimination and its prevention is Arkansas.

Graves, John W. "Arkansas Separate Coach Law of 1891." *Arkansas Historical Quarterly* 32 (Summer 1973).

_____. "Arkansas Separate Coach Law of 1891." *Journal of the West* 7 (October 1968).

_____. "Jim Crow in Arkansas: A Reconsideration of Urban Races Relations in the Post-Reconstruction South." *Journal of Southern History* 55 (August 1989).

_____. "Negro Disfranchisement in Arkansas." *Arkansas Historical Quarterly* 26 (Autumn 1967). Jim Crow and Blacks in Arkansas during the Late 1800s.

_____. "Sunnyside: The Evolution of an Arkansas Plantation, 1840–1945." *Arkansas Historical Quarterly* 50 (Spring 1991). Operation of Sunnyside, including Black experiences, shows how plantation life helped to shape the Southern economy.

Green, Bernal L. "Comment on Poverty, Race, and Culture in a Rural Arkansas Community." *Human Organization* 35 (1976).

Griffen, Wendell L. "Reflections on Rodney Slater." *Arkansas Lawyer* 32 (Spring 1997). Biography of Rodney E. Slater, President Clinton's Federal Highway Administrator.

Grinstead, Mary Jo, and Sandra Scholtz. "Poverty, Race, and Culture in a Rural Arkansas Community." *Human Organization* 35 (1976).

Griswold, Nat. "Arkansans Organize for Public Schools." *New South* 14 (June 1959). Article by the executive director of the Arkansas Council on Human Relations.

Higgins, Billy D. "The Origins and Fate of the Marion County Free Black Community." *Arkansas Historical Quarterly* 54 (Winter 1995).

Holitik, Diane Schratz. "Time for Change." *Arkansas Lawyer* 32 (Fall 1997). Biography of Arkansas' Judge Joyce Williams Warren.

Holmes, William F. "The Arkansas Cotton Pickers Strike of 1891 and the Demise of the Colored Farmers' Alliance." *Arkansas Historical Quarterly* 32 (Summer 1973).

_____. "The Demise of the Colored Farmers' Alliance." *Journal of Southern History* 41 (1975).

"The Horizon. Ghetto" *Crisis* 13 (January 1917). Includes item on the $1,000 compensation obtained by a Black man in Arkansas for a mob beating.

Hughes, Michael A. "Wartime Gristmill Destruction in Northwest Arkansas and Military Farm Colonies." *Arkansas Historical Quarterly* 46 (Summer 1987). Black involvement.

Hume, Richard L. "The Arkansas Constitutional Convention of 1868: A Case Study in the Politics of Reconstruction." *Journal of Southern History* 39 (1973). Blacks and "outside" whites were outnumbered by Southern whites in the convention, and made the decisions.

Johnson, William R. "Prelude to the Missouri Compromise." *New York Historical Society Quarterly* 48 (1964). Effects of the proposed bill to create the Territory of Arkansas.

_____. "Prelude to the Missouri Compromise." *Arkansas Historical Quarterly* 24 (1965). Effects of Congressional debates over Missouri and Arkansas.

Kennedy, Thomas C. "The Rise and Decline of a Black Monthly Meeting: Southland, Arkansas, 1864–1925." *Southern Friend* 19 (Fall 1997). Black Quakers.

Kerlin, Robert T. "Open Letter to the Governor of Arkansas." *Nation* 112 (15 June 1921). Racial conditions in the state.

Kousser, J. Morgan. "A Black Protest in the 'Era of Accommodation.'" *Arkansas Historical Quarterly* 34 (1975). Arkansas Blacks oppose Jim Crow laws.

Ledbetter, Cal, Jr. "The Constitution of 1868: Conqueror's Constitution or Constitutional Continuity?" *Arkansas Historical Quarterly* 44 (Spring 1985). Black involvement.

Lisenby, Foy. "A Survey of Arkansas' Image Problem." *Arkansas Historical Quarterly* 30 (Spring-Winter 1971). Black treatment an image problem.

Littlefield, Daniel F., Jr., and Patricia Washington McGraw. "Arkansas *Freeman*, 1869–1870—The Birth of the Black Press in Arkansas." *Phylon* 40 (March 1979). Republican newspaper was also the first of 100 newspapers owned and operated by Blacks in Arkansas.

Lovett, B. L. "African Americans, Civil War, and the Aftermath in Arkansas." *Arkansas Historical Quarterly* 54 (Fall 1995).

"A Lynching in Arkansas." *Colored American Magazine*, August 1905. Joseph Woodman, a Black man, lynched for running away with a white girl.

MacMillen, Neil R. "White Citizen's Council and Resistance to School Desegregation in Arkansas." *Arkansas Historical Quarterly* 30 (Summer 1971).

"Massacring Whites in Arkansas." *Nation* 109 (6 December 1919. Whites killing Blacks.

Mitchell, J. B. "An Analysis of Population by Race, Nativity and Residence." *Arkansas Historical Quarterly* 8 (Summer 1949).

Moneyhon, Carl H. "Black Politics in Arkansas During the Gilded Age, 1876–1900." *Arkansas Historical Quarterly* 44 (Autumn 1985).

Morgan, Gordon, and Peter Kunkel. "Arkansas' Ozark Mountain Blacks: An Introduction." *Phylon* 34 (September 1973). Blacks living in Batesville, Arkansas.

Morgan, Joan. "Former Surgeon General, Back on Campus, Confronts Opposition: University Voices Support." *Black Issues in Higher Education* 11 (26 January 1995).

Mühlen, Norbert. "Im Süden der USA: Eine Reise durch Mississippi und Arkansas." *Monat* 18 (1966). Views of race problems in Mississippi and Arkansas.

Nam, Tae Y. "A Manifesto of the Black Student Activists in a Southern Black College Under the Integration Order." *Journal of Negro Education* 46 (1977).

Nash, Horace Daniel. "Blacks in Arkansas during Reconstruction: The Ex-Slave Narratives." *Arkansas Historical Quarterly* 48 (Fall 1989).

Nichols, Guerdon D. "Breaking the Color Barrier at the University of Arkansas." *Arkansas Historical Quarterly* 27 (1968). The admission of the first Black student to the university since Reconstruction.

Palmer, Paul C. "Miscegenation as an Issue in the Arkansas Constitutional Convention of 1868." *Arkansas Historical Quarterly* 24 (1965). Proposed state constitutional amendment against interracial marriages.

Patton, Adell, Jr. "The 'Back to Africa' Movement in Arkansas." *Arkansas Historical Quarterly* 51 (Summer 1992).

Pearce, Larry Wesley. "The American Missionary Association and the Freedman's Bureau in Arkansas, 1866–1868." *Arkansas Historical Quarterly* 30 (1971).

_____. "Enoch K. Miller and the Freedman's Schools." *Arkansas Historical Quarterly* 31 (1972). The superintendent of the American Missionary Association and his work with the Bureau.

Petrie, John Clarence. "Flogging Arouses Various Opinions." *Christian Century* 51 (22 July 1936). Reverend Claude Williams and Miss Willie Sue Blagden beaten in Earle, Arkansas.

Phillips, W. M., Jr. "The Boycott: A Negro Community in Conflict (Pine Bluff, Ark.)." *Phylon* 22 (Spring 1961).

Pihoker, Catherine, Carla R. Scott, and Juneal Smith. "Non-Insulin Dependent Diabetes Mellitus in African-American Youths in Arkansas." *Clinical Pediatrics* 37 (February 1998).

"Protests From Georgia and Arkansas." *Crisis* 19 (January 1920). Topic of lynching.

"Race Conflicts in Arkansas." *Survey* 42 (13 December 1919).

"The Real Causes of Two Race Riots." *Crisis* 19 (December 1919). Riots in Phillips County, Arkansas and in Omaha, Nebraska. A man named Brown was lynched in Omaha.

Reynolds, John H. "Presidential Reconstruction in Arkansas." *Arkansas Historical Association* 1 (1906).

Richter, William L. "'A Dear Little Job': Second Lieutenant Hiram F. Willis, Freedmen's Bureau in Southwestern Arkansas, 1866–1868." *Arkansas Historical Quarterly* 50 (Summer 1991). Includes Black experiences during Reconstruction.

Rinne, Henry Q. "A Short History of the Alphonso Trent Orchestra." *Arkansas Historical Quarterly* 45 (Autumn 1986).

Roaf, Andree. "W. Harold Flowers: Mentor, Advisor and Inspiration." *Arkansas Lawyer* 19 (June 1985). Biography of Flowers.

Robinson, J. T. "History of Suffrage in Arkansas." *Arkansas Historical Association* 3 (1911).

Robotham, Rosemarie. "Broken Promises." *Essence* 27 (May 1996). Continued poverty in a Black and poor Tri-State Delta area.

Rogers, William Warren. "Negro Knights of Labor in Arkansas: A Case Study on the 'Miscellaneous' Strike." *Labor History* 10 (Summer 1969). Assesses a strike in Pulaski County.

Rose, Jerome C. "Biological Consequences of Segregation and Economic Deprivation: A Post-Slavery Population from Southwest Arkansas." *Journal of Economic History* 49 (June 1989).

Rothrock, Thomas. "Joseph Carter Corbin and Negro Education in the University of Arkansas." *Arkansas Historical Quarterly* 30 (Winter 1971). Corbin's role in developing the university.

Roy, Jesse H. "Negro Judges in the United States." *Negro History Bulletin* 28 (1965). Account of Philadelphia-born Mifflin Wister Gibbs, a gold prospector in California and British Columbia, and the first Black judge in Arkansas (1873).

"Samuel C. Coleman, November 10, 1980." *Jet*, 13 November 1995. Coleman honored on that date as the oldest Black war veteran, was also a physician in Pine Bluff, Hot Springs, Fordyce and Arkansas City.

Santi, Lawrence. "Black-White Differences in Household Income in the State of Arkansas, 1989: Results of a Regression Analysis." *Arkansas Business and Economic Review* 31 (Spring 1998).

"School Desegregation is Entering a New Phase: Analysis of Houston and New Orleans." *New South* 15 (October 1960).

"Second Man Convicted of Killing Black Transvestite in Arkansas." *Jet*, 28 July 1997.

Shafer, Robert S. "White Persons Held to Racial Slavery in Antebellum Arkansas." *Arkansas Historical Quarterly* 44 (Summer 1985).

Silas, Faye A. "Black, White St. Louis Lawyers Moving Closer." *Bar Leader* 10 (July-August 1984). Blacks, the Mound City Bar Association and the Bar Association of Metropolitan St. Louis.

Smith, C. Calvin. "Serving the Poorest of the Poor: Black Medical Practitioners in the Arkansas Delta, 1880–1960." *Arkansas Historical Quarterly* 57 (Fall 1998).

Smith, Lauren A. "Saints in the Basement." *Christian Century* 75 (17 September 1958). Blacks and clergy in Arkansas.

"Sorry: Desegregation 40 Years On." *The Economist* 344 (27 September 1997). Anniversary of desegregation.

Spencer, Annie Laurie. "The Blacks of Union County." *Arkansas Historical Quarterly* 12 (1953).

St. Hillaire, Joseph M. "The Negro Delegates in the Arkansas Constitutional Convention." *Arkansas Historical Quarterly* 33 (Spring 1974). Profiles the eight Black delegates at the convention.

Stephan, A. Stephen. "Changes in the Status of Negroes in Arkansas, 1948–50." *Arkansas Historical Quarterly* 9 (1950).

_____. "Desegregation of Higher Education in Arkansas." *Journal of Negro Education* 27 (Summer 1958).

_____. "Negro Public College in Arkansas." *Journal of Negro Education* 31 (Summer 1962).

Stewart, D. D. "Posthospital Social Adjustment of Former Mental Patients from Two Arkansas Counties." *Southwestern Social Sciences* Quarterly 35 (March 1955).

Tedford, Harold C. "Circuses in Northwest Arkansas, 1865–1889." *Arkansas Historical Quarterly* 32 (Summer 1973). Mentions Black performers.

"Thirteen Lynched in Arkansas." *Voice of the Negro* 5 (May 1904). Blacks shot and killed.

"Three Important Cases." *Crisis* 30 (May 1925). One case reveals the attempts to collect damages for the 1922 lynching of John Harrison, a Black man.

Trieber, J. "Legal Status of Negroes in Arkansas before the Civil War." *Arkansas Historical Association* 3 (1911).

Trotter-Worsley, Maggie Binns. *Brief Reports from Some of the Many African American Families Who Dared to Help Make Drew County Great.* Washington, DC: The author, 1995.

"Two Lynchings in April." *International Juridical Association Monthly Bulletin* 4 (May 1936). Two Black men lynched, one at Lepanto, Arkansas.

Van Deburg, William L. "The Slave Drivers of Arkansas: A New View From the Narratives." *Arkansas Historical Quarterly* 34 (Autumn 1975).

Vogler, Myrtle Clarine. "Negroes of Area Joined Back to Africa Movement in 1892." *Independence County Chronicle* 16 (1975).

Walz, Robert B. "Arkansas Slaveholdings and Slaveholders in 1850." *Arkansas Historical Quarterly* 12 (1953).

"White Landlords, Robbing Negro Tenants, Let Loose Arkansas Reign of Terror." *Appeal to Reason* (14 February 1920). Murder of Black tenant farmers in Elaine, Arkansas, 1919.

White, Walter F. "Massacring Whites in Arkansas." *Nation* 109 (6 December 1919). Race riots.

_____. "Race Conflict in Arkansas." *Survey* 42 (13 December 1919).

Williams, Nudie E. "Black Political Patronage in the Western District of Arkansas, 1871–1892." *Journal of the Fort Smith Historical Society* 11 (September 1987).

Wise, Leah. "The Elaine Massacre." *Southern Exposure* 1 (1974). Black sharecroppers and tenant farmers in 1919.

Woodruff, Nan Elizabeth. "African-American Struggles for Citizenship in the Arkansas and Mississippi Deltas in the Age of Jim Crow." *Radical History Review* 55 (Winter 1993).

Zellar, Gary. "H. C. Ray and Racial Politics in the African American Extension Service Program in Arkansas, 1915–1929." *Agricultural History* 72 (Spring 1998).

Little Rock

Anthony, Mary. "Dean of the School Marms." *Negro Digest* (May 1951). Profile of Mrs. Charlotte Stephens, the first Black teacher in Little Rock, plus the first woman of Little Rock to have a school named for her (1951).

Armstrong, Liz S. "Court Reinstates Desegregation Plan for Little Rock." *Education Week* (9 January 1991).

Barnes, Julian E. "Segregation, Now: Forty Years After the Forced Integration of Little Rock's Central High School." *U.S. News and World Report* 123 (22 September 1997).

Bartley, Numan. "Looking Back at Little Rock." *Arkansas Historical Quarterly* 25 (Summer 1966). Desegregation comes to Little Rock.

Bennett, Lerone, Jr. "Chronicles of Black Courage: The Little Rock 10." *Ebony*, December 1997.

Calloway-Thomas, C., and T. Garner. "Daisy Bates and the Little Rock School Crisis: Forging the Way." *Journal of Black Studies* 26 (May 1996).

Campbell, Ernest Q., and Thomas F. Pettigrew. "Racial and Moral Crisis: The Role of the Little Rock Ministers." *American Journal of Sociology* 64 (March 1959).

Cartwright, Colbert S. "Band Together for Genuine Unity." *New South* 16 (February 1958). Little Rock minister's talk at the Fourth Conference on Community Unity.

Christophe, LeRoy Matthew. *The Arkansas African American Hall of Fame*, eds. Erma Glasco Davis and Faustine Childress Wilson. Little Rock: National Dunbar Alumni Association of Little Rock, 1993. Biography.

"Clinton Opens School Doors for Little Rock Nine on 40th Anniversary." *Jet*, 13 October 1997.

Copeland, Larry. "Integration of Little Rock Central High School Mark 40th Anniversary." *Tribune News Service* (20 August 1997).

Diamond, Raymond T. "Confrontation as Rejoinder to Compromise: Reflections on the Little Rock Desegregation Crisis." *National Black Law Journal* 11 (Spring 1989).

"Drive for Gold Medals Begins in Congress for Little Rock Nine." *Jet*, 27 October 1997.

Eckford, Elizabeth. "The First Day: Little Rock, 1957." Chapter in *Growing Up Southern*, ed. Chris Mayfield. New York: Pantheon Books, 1981. One of the "Little Rock Nine."

Edna, Jodi. "President Clinton Calls for Racial Understanding During Commemoration of 40th Anniversary of Little Rock Nine. *Tribune News Service* (25 September 1997).

Gates, L. "Power From the Pedestal: The Women's Emergency Committee and the Little Rock Nine." *Arkansas Historical Quarterly* 55 (Spring 1996).

Haiken, Elizabeth. "'The Lord Helps Those Who Help Themselves': Black Laundresses in Little Rock, Arkansas, 1917–1921." *Arkansas Historical Quarterly* 49 (Spring 1990).

Hunter, Maclean. "Recalling Little Rock's Trauma." *Maclean's*, 6 October 1997.

Kennan, Clara B. "The First Negro Teacher in Little Rock." *Arkansas Historical Quarterly* 9 (1950).

Kirk, John A. "The Little Rock Crisis and Postwar Black Activism in Arkansas." *Arkansas Historical Quarterly* 56 (Fall 1997).

Leland, John, and Vern E. Smith. "Echoes of Little Rock." *Newsweek,* 29 September 1997.

"Little Rock Nine: September 25, 1957." *Jet*, 29 September 1997.

Malveaux, Julianne. "Required Reading: A Lesson on Integration." *Black Issues in Higher Education* 11 (22 September 1994). Little Rock desegregation.

McConnellogue, Ken. "Feature Alum: Carlotta Walls Lanier." *Spectrum Magazine*, May 1999. Little Rock Nine student recalls the past.

Newson, Moses. "The Little Rock Nine." *Crisis* 94 (November 1987).

Phillip, Mary-Christine. "Central High Redux." *Black Issues in Higher Education* 10 (13 January 1994).

Richards, Ira Don. "Little Rock on the Road to Reunion, 1865–1880." *Arkansas Historical Quarterly* 25 (1966). Little Rock following the Civil War.

Samuels, Gertrude. "Little Rock Revisited—Tokenism Plus." *New York Times Magazine* (2 June 1963).

Stern, M. "Eisenhower and Kennedy: A Comparison of Confrontations at Little Rock and Ole Miss." *Policy Studies Journal* (Autumn 1993).

Still, William Grant. "My Arkansas Boyhood." *Arkansas Historical Quarterly* 26 (1967). The great composer recounts his youth in Little Rock.

Trescott, Jacqueline. "Daisy Bates: Before and After Little Rock." *Crisis* 88 (1981).

Valentine, Victoria. "Integration's Rocky Path: Ernest Green Stood Out at Central High." *Emerge* 5 (May 1994).

Vander Zanden, James W. "The Impact of Little Rock." *Journal of Educational Sociology* 35 (April 1962).

"Where Are They Now?" *Time*, 24 June 1996. Profile of Elizabeth Eckford.

Woods, Henry, and Beth Deere. "Reflections on the Little Rock School Case." *Arkansas Law Review* 44 (Fall 1991).

Books:

Adams, Julianne Lewis, and Thomas A. DeBlack. *Civil Obedience: An Oral History of School Desegregation in Fayetteville, Arkansas, 1954–1965.* Fayetteville: University of Arkansas Press, 1994.

Adams-Middleton, Peggy. *Clow: A Traditional African American Community since 1860, Ozan, Arkansas.* n.p.: The author, 1992. Clow and Ozan histories.

African Methodist Episcopal Church. Arkansas Conference. *Second Session of the Arkansas Annual Conference of the African M. E. Church: Convened in Campbell's Chapel, Little Rock, Ark., Sept. 15, 1869.* Little Rock: Woodruff and Blocher, 1869.

Arkansas Department of Education, Division of Negro Education. *Four Years with the Public Schools in Arkansas, 1937–1927.* Little Rock: Arkansas Department of Education, 192? Report by A. B. Hill, state superintendent of education.

_____. *Problems of Negro Health in Arkansas: Preliminary Study Bulletin.* Little Rock: State Department of Education, 1939. Public health concerns.

Bailey, Minnie Thomas. *Reconstruction in Indian Territory: A Story of Avarice, Discrimination, and Opportunism.* Port Washington, NY: Kennikat Press, 1972.

Baskett, Tom, ed. *Persistence of the Spirit: The Black Experience in Arkansas.* Arkansas: Resource Center, Arkansas Endowment for the Humanities, 1986.

Bell, Minnie Burton. *Journeying Through Mirrors: The Burtons.* Baltimore: Gateway Press, 1994. Biography of Burton family of Earle, Arkansas.

Bell, Rose S. *Beyond the Strawberry Patch.* Nashville: Winston-Dereck Publishers, 1985. Blacks and country life.

Benton, Corrine. *The Return to the Promised Land.* Pittsburgh, PA: Dorrance, 1995. Biography of Powell and Brewer families.

Bush, A. E., and P. L. Dorman, eds. *History of the Mosaic Templars of America: Its Founders and Officials.* Black Biographical Dictionaries, 1790–1950 Series, no. 50. Little Rock: Central Printing Company, 1924. John E. Bush and the Mosaic Templars.

Cortner, Richard C. *A Mob Intent on Death: The NAACP and the Arkansas Riot Cases.* Middletown, CT: Wesleyan University Press, 1988. Riot, Phillips County, AR.

Creger, Ralph. *This is What We Found.* New York: L. Stuart, 1960. A white father and son champion equal rights in Little Rock.

Davis, James P. *Success Story: Negro Farmers.* Little Rock: U.S. Department of Agriculture, 1952. U.S. Production and Marketing Administration booklet covering seventeen states.

Dorson, J. L. *Negro Tales from Pine Bluff, Arkansas, and Calvin, Michigan.* Bloomington: Indiana University Press, 1958.

Dorson, Richard Mercer, ed. *Negro Tales from Pine Bluff, Arkansas, and Calvin, Michigan.* Bloomington, IN: Indiana University Press, 1968; reprinted, *American Negro Folktales.* Greenwich, CT: Fawcett Publications, 1967. Tales from Calvin, Michigan and Pine Bluff, Arkansas.

Federal Writers' Project, Work Projects Administration. *Slave Narratives: A Folk History of Slavery in the United States from Interviews with Former Slaves.* Vol. 3, *Arkansas.* Washington, DC: Work Projects Administration, 1941.

Finley, Randy. *From Slavery to Uncertain Freedom: The Freedmen's Bureau in Arkansas, 1865–1869.* Fayetteville: University of Arkansas Press, 1996.

The First Annual Report of the Executive Committee of Colored Evangelization to the General Assembly Sitting at Hot Springs, Arkansas, May 19, 1892. Birmingham, AL: Roberts and Son, 1892. Focus on establishment of Presbyterian Churches among Blacks in the South. Library of Congress.

Fletcher, John Gould. *Arkansas.* Chapel Hill: University of North Carolina Press, 1947. Has some information on Blacks in Arkansas history.

Gordon, Fon Louise. *Caste and Class: The Black Experience in Arkansas, 1880–1920.* Athens, GA: University of Georgia Press, 1995.

Graves, John W. *Town and Country: Race Relations in an Urban-Rural Context: Arkansas, 1865–1905.* Fayetteville, AR: University of Arkansas Press, 1990. 19th century.

Griffin, Marie Jones. *Dr. Fred Thomas Jones, Sr.: A Black Trailblazer: Outstanding Physician and Surgeon: Dedicated Civic and Religious Leader, 1877–1938.* Chicago: National Publishing House, 1995.

Guida, Louis, Lorenzo Thomas, and Cheryl Cohen. *Blues Music in Arkansas.* Philadelphia, PA: Portfolio Associates, 1982. History and criticism.

Iroquois Research Institute. *George Berry Washington, Black Plantation Owner.* Fairfax, VA: The Institute, 1981. Biography.

Kester, Howard. *Revolt Among the Sharecroppers.* New York: Arno Press, 1969. Southern Tenant Farmers' Union.

Lohse, Stefanie. *"God Spared a Few to Tell the Tale.": Eine Analyse von Interviews mit Ex-Sklaven aur Arkansas, USA.* Würzburg: Königshausen & Neumann, 1991.

Maruoka, Emily Franklin. *Success, in Spite of Adversities: An Autobiography.* n.p., 1988.

McCool, B. Boren. *Union, Reaction, and Riot: A Biography of a Rural Race Riot.* Memphis: Memphis State University, 1970. Riot, Phillips County, AR.

Moneyhon, Carl H. *The Impact of the Civil War and Reconstruction on Arkansas: Persistence in the Midst of Ruin.* Baton Rouge: Louisiana State University Press, 1994.

Monks, William. *A History of Southern Missouri and Northern Arkansas; Being an Account of the Early Settlements, the Civil War, the Ku-Klux, and the Times of Peace.* West Plain, MO: West Plains Journal Company, 1907.

Morgan, Gordon, and Izola Preston. *The Edge of Campus. A Journal of the Black Experience at the University of Arkansas.* Fayetteville: University of Arkansas Press, 1990.

Morgan, Gordon. *Marianna: A Sociological Essay on an Eastern Arkansas Town.* Jefferson City, MO: New Scholars Press, 1973.

Morgan, Marian B., and Izola Preston. *The Arkansas African-American Quizbook.* Cane Hill, AR: ARC Press, 1993.

NAACP 1940–1955. Legal File. Transportation—Royal v. Arkansas. Frederick, MD: University Publications of America, 1992.

NAACP 1940–55. Legal File. Crime—Bone Brothers, 1938–39. Frederick, MD: University Publications of America, 1988. Criminal justice.

NAACP 1940–55. Legal File. Voting—Arkansas, 1943–47. Frederick, MD: University Publications of America, 1986.

NAACP Administrative File. Subject File. New York Foundation, Dec. 7, 1919–Dec. 12, 1921. Frederick, MD: University Publications of America, 1990. Phillips County.

NAACP Administrative File. Subject File. Politics—Judge J. O. Livesay, June 11–June 23, 1932. Frederick, MD: University Publications of America, 1990. Selection and appointment of judges.

NAACP Branch Files. Camden, Arkansas, 1928–1934. Frederick, MD: University Publications of America, 1991.

NAACP Legal File. Cases Supported. Callie Henry, 1924–1926. Frederick, MD: University Publications of America, 1988.

NAACP Legal File. Cases Supported—Arkansas Primary Case, 1928–1930, 1932, Undated. Frederick, MD: University Publications of America, 1986.

National Association for the Advancement of Colored People. *An American Lynching. Being the Burning at the Stake of Henry Lowry at Nodena, Arkansas, January 26, 1921, as Told in American Newspapers.* New York: NAACP, 1921.

National Association for the Advancement of Colored People. *Burning at Stake in the United States. A Record of the Public Burning by Mobs of Five Men, During the First Five Months of 1919, in the States of Arkansas, Florida, Georgia, Mississippi, and Texas.* New York: NAACP, 1919.

————. *Burning at Stake in the United States. A Record of the Public Burning by Mobs of Six Men During the First Six Months of 1919 in the States of Arkansas, Florida, Georgia, Mississippi and Texas.* New York: NAACP, 1919.

Neighborhood Arts Program of the Arkansas Arts Center Presents a Week of American Experiences: Black History Week, Feb. 23–27, 1981. Little Rock: Arkansas Arts Center, Neighborhood Arts Program, 1981. Exhibits and entertainers.

Order of the Eastern Star. Grand Chapter of Arkansas. *Proceedings...Annual Communication.* Pine Bluff: The Order, 1929.

Palmer, Irenas J. *The Black Man's Burden; or, The Horrors of Southern Lynchings. The Most Thrilling Expos of Southern Lawlessness Ever Presented to the American People...the Methods of the Lynchers. The Frightful Experience of Julius Gardner, of Arkansas, a Man Who was Actually Lynched. Mr. Gardner is the Only Colored Man Who, Having Been Accused of Crime and Arrested by a Southern Mob, Has Lived to Relate His Experience.* Olean, NY: Oleana Evening Herald Print, 1902.

Patterson, Ruth Polk. *The Seed of Sally Good'n: A Black Family of Arkansas, 1833–1953.* Lexington, KY: University Press of Kentucky, 1985.

Powell, Clayton. *The Aftermath of the Civil War, in Arkansas.* New York: Negro Universities Press, 1969.

Preston, Izola. *Arkansas Black Heritage: A Tour of Historical Sites.* Cane Hill, AR: Arc Press, 1993.

_____. *The Arkansas African-American Quizbook.* Cane Hill, AR: Arc Press, 1993.

Proceedings of the Ninth Annual Communication of the Grand Chapter Order Eastern Star, State of Arkansas: Held in the City of Arkadelphia, Commencing June 12, 1894. Pine Bluff: Graphic Printing Company, 1894. Library of Congress pamphlet.

Rawick, George P., ed. *The American Slave: A Composite Autobiography.* Westport, CT: Greenwood Publishing Company, 1972. Transcriptions of narratives for the 1936–1938 Federal Writers' Project. Vol. 9, parts 1 and 2; and Vol. 10, parts 3 and 4.

Redkey, Edwin S. *Black Exodus.* New Haven: Yale University Press, 1969.

Reed, Roy. *Faubus: The Life and Times of an American Prodigal.* Fayetteville: University of Arkansas Press, 1997.

Richard, Eugene Scott. *Few Comforts or Surprises: The Arkansas Delta.* Cambridge, MA: MIT Press, 1973. Blacks in rural Arkansas.

Rose, Jerome C., ed. *Gone to a Better Land: A Biohistory of a Rural Black Cemetery in the Post-Reconstruction South.* Fayetteville, AR: Arkansas Archeological Survey, 1985.

Sanders, Ellaraino, and Bernice A. Sanders. *Another Kind of Treasure: A Story of Dreams Fulfilled.* Los Angeles: Dream Time Publishers, 1997. Biography of former slave Silvia Mack Gardner, who lived to the age of 110.

Staples, Thomas Starling. *Reconstruction in Arkansas, 1862–1874.* New York: Columbia University, 1923; reprinted, Gloucester, MA: P. Smith, 1964.

Strong-Eldridge, Thelma. *Funeral Programs, Columbia County, Arkansas, Connections.* Chicago: The author, 1995. Genealogy material.

Student Nonviolent Coordinating Committee (SNCC). *The General Condition of the Arkansas Negro.* Atlanta: SNCC, 1965.

Tanner, Hiram L. *Malvern Negro Public School Prior to WWII: The Black Legacy of Malvern.* New York: Vantage Press, 1992. Malvern, AK.

Taylor, Orville W. *Negro Slavery in Arkansas*. Durham: Duke University Press, 1958.

Thompson, George. *Arkansas and Reconstruction: The Influence of Geography, Economics, and Personality*. Port Washington, NY: Kennikat Press, 1976.

Trotter-Worsley, Maggie Binns. *Brief Reports from Some of the Many African American Families Who Dared to Help Make Drew County Great*. Washington, DC: The author, 1995.

United States Army. Dept. of the Tennessee. General Superintendent of Freedmen. *Report of the General Superintendent of Freedmen Department of the Tennessee and State of Arkansas for 1864*. Memphis, TN: Adjutant General's Office: Dept. of the Tennessee, 1865.

United States, Bureau of Refugees, Freedmen and Abandoned Lands. *Records of the Superintendent of Education for the State of Arkansas, Bureau of Refugees, Freedmen, and Abandoned Lands, 1865–1871*. n.p.: The Bureau, 1865–1871.

Wiley, Electa Campbell. *Human Resources and Elitism in Hope, Arkansas, 1900–1935*. Hope, AR: The author, 1981. Buildings and history of Hope.

Williams, Lee E., and Lee E. Williams III. *Anatomy of Four Race Riots: Racial Conflict in Knoxville, Elaine (Ark.), Tulsa, and Chicago*. Jackson, MI: University and College Press of Mississippi, 1972. Riots following W.W.I.

Little Rock

Alford, Dale, ands L'Moore Alford. *The Case of the Sleeping People (Finally Awakened by Little Rock School Frustrations)*. Little Rock, AR: n.p., 1959.

Arkansas Gazette. *Crisis in the South: The Little Rock Story; a Selection of Editorials*. Little Rock: Arkansas Gazette, 1959. Segregation in education.

Bates, Daisy. *The Long Shadow of Little Rock: A Memoir*. New York: David McKay, 1962; reprinted, Fayetteville: University of Arkansas Press, 1987. Bates led the effort to enroll the "Little Rock Nine."

Beals, Melba Pattillo. *Warriors Don't Cry: A Searing Memoir of the Battle to Integrate Little Rock's Central High*. Pocket Books, 1994.

Blossom, Virgil T. *It Has Happened Here*. New York: Harper, 1959. Little Rock school desegregation account by the superintendent of schools.

Brown, Robert Raymond. *Bigger Than Little Rock*. Greenwich, CT: Seabury Press, 1958. Episcopal bishop of Little Rock talks of segregation and race relations.

Bumbarger, Chester, et al. *A Report to the Board of Directors of the Little Rock School District, Little Rock, Arkansas. An Evaluation of the Progress toward the Achievement of a Racially Integrated Educational System and a Projection of a Plan for Further Action.* Eugene: University of Oregon, 1967. ERIC. ED 012 959. Assessment of the school district's progress in moving for a dual to an integrated system.

Campbell, Ernest Q., and Thomas F. Pettigrew. *Christians in Racial Crisis: A Study of Little Rock's Ministry, Including Statements on Desegregation and Race Relations by the Leading Religious Denominations of the United States.* Washington, DC: Public Affairs Press, 1959.

Edwards, Audrey, and Craig K. Polite. *Children of the Dream: The Psychology of Black Success.* New York: Doubleday, 1992. The Little Rock Nine.

Freyer, Tony Allen. *The Little Rock Crisis: A Constitutional Interpretation.* Contributions in Legal Studies, no. 30. Westport, CT: Greenwood Press, 1984.

Haldeman-Julius, Marcet. *The Story of a Lynching: An Exploration of Southern Psychology.* Girard, KS: Haldeman-Julius Publications, 1927. Two incidents in Little Rock involving lynching.

Hays, Brooks. *The Eisenhower Administration.* n.p., 1973. Little Rock integration.

_____. *A Southern Moderate Speaks.* Chapel Hill: University of North Carolina Press, 1959. Topics of segregation and education by a moderate defeated by a segregationist following the Little Rock school desegregation.

Huckaby, Elizabeth. *Crisis at Central High: Little Rock, 1958–58.* Baton Rouge: Louisiana State University Press, 1980.

Jones, Faustine Childress. *A Traditional Model of Educational Excellence: Dunbar High School of Little Rock, Arkansas.* Washington, DC: Howard University Press, 1981.

Kelso, Richard. *Days of Courage: The Little Rock Story.* Austin: Raintree Steck-Vaughn, 1993.

Lucas, Eileen, and Mark Anthony. *Cracking the Wall: The Struggles of the Little Rock Nine.* Minneapolis: Lerner Publishing, 1997.

Metcalf, George R. *From Little Rock to Boston: The History of School Desegregation.* Westport, CT: Greenwood Press, 1983.

Murphy, Sara, and Patrick Murphy. *Breaking the Silences: Little Rock's Women's Emergency Committee to Open Our Schools, 1958–1963.* Fayetteville, University of Arkansas Press, 1997.

NAACP Branch Files. Little Rock, Arkansas, 1918–1940. Frederick, MD: University Publications of America, 1991.

O'Neill, Laurie A. *Little Rock: The Desegregation of Central High.* Brookfield, CT: Millbrook, 1994. Race relations for juveniles.

Pattillo, Lois. *Little Rock Roots: Biographies in Arkansas Black History: The Lives of Blacks Who Have Made History in Arkansas Since 1900.* Little Rock: Lois Pattillo Books, 1981.

Proceedings of the Eighth Annual Convocation of the Most Excellent Royal Arch Chapter of Free Masons for the State and Jurisdiction of Arkansas, and of a Meeting Preliminary to the Same, Held in the City of Little Rock, Ark., Dec. 16th, and 17th, Anno Inventionis 2428, A.D. 1898. Pine Bluff: Courier Printing Company, 1899. Library of Congress pamphlet.

Record, C. Wilson, and Jane Cassels Record, eds. *Little Rock, U.S.A.: Materials for Analysis.* San Francisco: Chandler, 1960.

Silverman, Corinne. *The Little Rock Story.* Inter-University Case Program Series. Tuscaloosa: University of Alabama Press, 1959.

Spitzberg, Irving J., Jr. *Racial Politics in Little Rock, 1954–1964.* New York: Garland, 1989.

Survey of Negroes in Little Rock and North Little Rock. Little Rock: Writers' Program of the Work Projects Administration in the State of Arkansas, 1941.

Teitelbaum, Dora. *Ballade de Little-Rock; Traduit du Yiddish par Chalres Dobzynski; Bois Gravé de Frans Masereel.* Lyon: A. Henneuse, 1959. Protest poetry.

_____. *Di Balade fun Lit-Rak (La ballade de Little-Rock); He-lah Oon sha'ar bild fon Ollie Harrington.* Paris: Vogue, 1959. Little Rock public schools.

Terry, Adolphine. *Charlotte Stephens: Little Rock's First Black Teacher.* Little Rock: Academic Press of Arkansas, 1973.

Thomas, Charles E. *Jelly Roll: A Black Neighborhood in a Southern Mill Town.* Little Rock: Rose, 1986.

Women's Emergency Committee for Public Schools. *Little Rock Report: The City, Its People, Its Business, 1957–1959.* Little Rock: Women's Emergency Committee to Open Our Schools, 1959.

Writers' Program of the Work Projects Administration in the State of Arkansas. *Survey of Negroes in Little Rock and North Little Rock.* Little Rock: Urban League of Greater Little Rock, 1941.

Theses and Dissertations:

Alexander, Charles C. "Invisible Empire in the Southwest: The Ku Klux Klan in Texas, Louisiana, Oklahoma, and Arkansas, 1920–1930." Ph.D. diss., University of Texas, 1962.

Bayless, Garland E. "Public Affairs in Arkansas, 1874–1896." Thesis, University of Texas, 1972. Arkansas politics, government, and Blacks.

Belcher, Leon Harold. "An Experimental Investigative Study of Certain Personality Characteristics and Academic Achievements of Negro Children from Broken Homes of Townsend Park School, Pine Bluff, Arkansas." Ed.D. thesis, Colorado State University, 1961.

Christophe, Leroy M., Sr. "A Study of the Provisions for the Pre-Service and In-Service Education of Secondary-School Principals in Arkansas Negro Colleges with Recommendations for Improvement." Ph.D. diss., New York University, 1954.

Claye, Clifton M. "A Study of the Relationship between Self-Concepts and Attitudes toward the Negro among Secondary School Pupils in Three Schools of Arkansas." Ph.D. diss., University of Arkansas, 1958.

Coker, Donald R. "The Relationship of Readiness Test Scores to Selected Socio-Economic Factors of Lower Class families." Ph.D. diss., University of Arkansas, 1966. Study of participants and non-participants in Fayetteville Head Start program.

Davis, Lawrence A. "A Comparison of the Philosophies, Purposes and Functions of the Negro Land-Grant Colleges and Universities with Emphasis upon the Program of the Agricultural, Mechanical, and Normal College, Pine Bluff, Arkansas." Ph.D. diss., University of Arkansas, 1960.

Dunlap, James Edward, Jr. "The Relationship of Musical Achievement as Measured by the Cowell Music Achievement Test to Socio-Economic Status, Race, Community Size, and the Presence of the Father in the Home in Seventh-Grade General Music Classes in Arkansas and Mississippi." D.M.E. diss., Indiana University, 1975.

Facen, Geneva Z. "The Determination of the Degree of Tensions Produced in Selected White Students when presented with Certain Beliefs and Factual Materials pertaining to Negroes." Ph.D. diss., University of Arkansas, 1959. Study conducted at the University of Arkansas.

Finley, Randy. "The Freedmen's Bureau in Arkansas." Ph.D. diss., University of Arkansas-Fayetteville, 1992.

Gestaut, Joseph P. "Survey of Student Participation in Extracurricular Activities in Integrated High Schools of Arkansas as Depicted by Yearbooks." Thesis, University of Arkansas, 1974.

Gibson, De Lois. "A Historical Study of Philander Smith College, 1877 to 1969." Thesis, University of Arkansas, 1972.

Gordon, Fon Louise. "The Black Experience in Arkansas, 1880–1920." Ph.D. diss., University of Arkansas, 1989.

Graves, John W. "The Arkansas Negro and Segregation, 1890–1903." Master's thesis, University of Arkansas-Fayetteville, 1967.

Handy, Norman W. "A Descriptive Study of the Perceptions of Crossover Teachers in Little Rock, Arkansas and Jackson, Mississippi." Thesis, University of Arkansas, 1974. Faculty integration.

Hanners, LaVerne. "The Written and Spoken Dialect of the Southeast Arkansas Black College Student." Ed.D. thesis, Ball State University, 1979. Black English.

Hobby, Selma Ann Plowman. "The Little Rock Public Schools During Reconstruction, 1865–1874." Thesis, University of Arkansas, 1967.

Holtzclaw, Thelbert E. "An Analysis of the Vocational Preferences of Seniors in the Negro Secondary Schools of Arkansas with Implications for Possible Curriculum Modification." Ph.D. diss., University of Arkansas, 1955. Interest inventory.

Johnson, Autrey B. "A Comparative Study of White and Negro Guidance Programs and the Administrators' Attitudes toward These Programs in Selected School Districts of Arkansas." Ph.D. diss., University of Arkansas, 1962.

Johnson, Kenneth L. "A Study of the Health Problems of Negro Senior-High-School Youth in Arkansas." Ph.D. diss., Boston University, 1959.

Jones, Katherine L. S. "The Language Development of Head Start Children." Ph.D. diss., University of Arkansas, 1966. Study of language development of Head Start and non-Head Start children of Little Rock.

Lee, Lurline M. "The Origin, Development, and Present Status of Arkansas' Program of Higher Education for Negroes." Ph.D. diss., Michigan State University, 1955.

Lewis, Todd Everett. "Race Relations in Arkansas, 1910–1929." Ph.D. diss., University of Arkansas, 1995.

London, Arcenia Phillips. "Determinants of Self-Acceptance of Black Female School Teachers Selected from the Syracuse Public School System and from Little Rock, Arkansas Public School System." Thesis, Syracuse University, 1976.

Lovell, Linda Jeanne. "African-American Narratives from Arkansas: A Study from the 1936–1938 Federal Writers' Project. A Folk History of Slavery in the United States." Ph.D. diss., University of Arkansas, Fayetteville, 1991.

Merrill, Pierce K. "Race as a Factor in Achievement in Plantation Areas of Arkansas." Ph.D. diss., Vanderbilt University, 1951. Study of discrimination against Black sharecroppers.

Mitchell, Fred Tom. "Proposed Plan for Training Negro Teachers of Vocational Agriculture: A Study Based on Conditions in the State of Arkansas." Ph.D. diss., Cornell University, 1931.

Patterson, Ruth Polk. "Developing an Afro-American Studies Program in the Integrated Public Schools: Problems and Procedures." Ph.D. diss., Emory University, 1977. Focus on Little Rock.

Reynolds, Jack Q. "Historical and Current Issues in Racial Integration in the Public Schools of Arkansas." Ph.D. diss., University of Arkansas, 1957.

Rigby, Gerald. "Little Rock and Desegregation: An Analysis of the Political Implementation of Legal Decision." Ph.D. diss., University of California, Los Angeles, 1960.

Rush, William. "Present Status and Future Prospects of the Negro High Schools in Arkansas, 1954–1969." Ed.D. thesis, University of Arkansas, 1969.

Schrock, Earl F. "A Study of the Dialect of the Blacks in Pope County, Arkansas." Ph.D. diss., University of Arkansas, 1980.

Staples, Thomas Starling. "Reconstruction in Arkansas, 1862–1874." Thesis, Columbia University, 1923.

Starlard, Victor D. "Factors Associated with Negro Voting in a Delta County of Arkansas." Ph.D. diss., University of Arkansas, 1961.

Sylvia, Michael F. "Black Populations in Arkansas." Master's thesis, University of Arkansas-Fayetteville, 1981.

Taylor, Orville W. "Negro Slavery in Arkansas." Ph.D. diss., Duke University, 1956.

Traber, Michael. "The Treatment of the Little Rock, Arkansas, School Integration Incident in the Daily Press of the Union of South Africa, West Nigeria and Ghana from September 1 to October 31, 1957." Ph.D. diss., New York University, 1960.

Wallace, David Edwin. "The Little Rock Central Desegregation Crisis of 1957." Ph.D. diss., University of Missouri, 1977.

Walz, Robert B. "Migration into Arkansas, 1834–1880." Ph.D. diss., University of Texas, 1958. Some race-related data.

Black Newspapers:[1]

ARGENTIA
Arkansas African Methodist. Argentia. 1894–1920.
Voice of the Twentieth Century. Argentia. 1901–1922.

CAMDEN
Arkansas Survey-Journal. Little Rock. 1934–1955.
Camden News. Camden. 1940.
Camden Weekly. Camden. 1961.
Courier. Camden. 1892–1893.
Express. Camden. 1939.
South Arkansas Journal. Camden. 1962.
Southern Negro. Camden. 1907–1910.

CONWAY
People's Intelligencer Conway. 1923–1931.
Watchman. Conway. 1896–1897.
Weekly Colored Tidings #1. Conway. 1927–1928.
Weekly Colored Tidings #2. Conway. 1928–1929.

DERMOTT
Advocate. Dermott. 1895–1901.
Afro-American. Dermott. 1903.
Fraternal World. Dermott. 1902–1904.
Industrial Chronicle. Dermott. 1909–1921.
South East Advocate. Dermott. 1907–1910.
South Eastern Baptist. Dermott. 1899–1906.
Southern Afro-American. Dermott. 1896–1904.

EL DORADO
Dixie Appeal. El Dorado. 1904–1906.
Washington Hi Bulletin. El Dorado. 1930.

FORDYCE
Bradley District Herald. Fordyce. 1913–1919.
Evangel. Fordyce. 1900–1902.
Negro Advocate. Fordyce. 1917–1922.

---

[1] Single-lined boxed items were published by the same publisher. Double-lined boxed items indicate changes in masthead name.

Star Messenger. Fordyce.
1900–1913.
Western Star. Fordyce. 1900–1909.

FORREST CITY
Advocate. Forrest City. 1886–1888.
Arkansas Baptist Flashlight. Forrest
City. 1939.
Enterprise. Forrest City.
1889–1890.
Herald. Forrest City. 1896–1903.
Homeland. Forrest City. 1991–199?
New Light. Forrest City.
1899–1902.
Royal Messenger. Forrest City.
1915–1922.
Southern Liberator. Forrest City.
1936.

FORT SMITH
Appreciator. Fort Smith.
1898–1900.
Appreciation-Union. Fort Smith.
1912–1922.
Arkansas Appreciator. Fort Smith.
1898–1912.
Arkansas Baptist Flashlight. Fort
Smith. 194?
Banner. Fort Smith. 1896–1897.
Fraternal Union. Fort Smith.
1907–1914.
Golden Epoch. Fort Smith.
1888–1890.
Informer. Fort Smith. 1912.
Our Eastern Star. Fort Smith.
1899–1908.
People's Protector. Fort Smith.
1889–1892.
Pythian Herald. Fort Smith.
1904–1908.

HELENA
Arkansas Mule. Helena. 1890–1891.
Arkansas Survey Journal. Little
Rock. 1934–1955.
Baptist Reporter. Helena.
1891–1907.

Colored American. Helena.
1902–1903.
Golden Epoch. Helena. 1881–1888.
Informer. Helena. 1939.
Interstate Reporter. Helena.
1891–1934.
Jacob's Friend. Helena. 1888–1890.
New Era. Helena. 1888–1891.
People's Friend. Helena.
1888–1890.
Press. Helena. 1937–1938.
Progress. Helena. 1880–1902.
Reporter. Helena. 1891–1901.
Royal Messenger. Helena.
1909–1922.
Southern Mediator Journal. Helena.
1940.
Southern Review. Helena.
1882–1890.
Times. Helena. 1886.
World Picture. Helena. 1950.

HOLLY GROVE
Arkansas Banner. Holly Grove.
1887–1890.
Star. Holly Grove. 1887–1890.

HOT SPRINGS
Arkansas Mansion. Hot Springs.
1883.
Arkansas Review. Hot Springs.
1898–1927.
Arkansas Survey-Journal. Little
Rock. 1934–1955.

Citizen. Hot Springs. 1958–1977.
Arkansas Citizen. Hot Springs.
1962–1977.

Citizen Weekly. Hot Springs.
Crusader Journal. Hot Springs.
1940–1947.
Crystal. Hot Springs. 1898–1899.
Hot Springs Echo. Hot Springs.
1898–1946.
Negro Voice. Hot Springs. 1933.
Sun. Hot Springs. 1885–1892.
W. O. U. Messenger. Hot Springs.
1930–1933.

LITTLE ROCK

American Guide. Little Rock.
   1889–1906.
Arkansas Banner. Little Rock.
   1911–1926.
Arkansas Baptist. Little Rock.
   1882–1937.
Arkansas Baptist Flashlight. Little
   Rock. 1935–1952.
Arkansas Carrier. Little Rock.
   1975–1977.

Arkansas Dispatch. Little Rock.
   1880–1897.
Arkansas Weekly Mansion. Little
   Rock. 1880–1886.
Arkansas Mansion. Little Rock.
   1886–1887.

Arkansas Flashlight. Little Rock.
   195?
Arkansas Freeman. Little Rock.
   1869–1871.
Arkansas Herald. Little Rock.
   1880–1884.
Arkansas Herald Mansion. Little
   Rock. 1884–1886.
Arkansas Journal and Advertiser.
   Little Rock. 1960.
Arkansas Monitor. Little Rock.
   1911–1912.
Arkansas Review. Little Rock.
   1883–1890.
Arkansas State Press. Little Rock.
   1941–199?

Arkansas Survey. Little Rock.
   1923–1935.
Arkansas Survey-Journal. Little
   Rock. 1934–1971. Con-
   tinues *Arkansas Survey.*
   Printed editions for Camden,
   Pine Bluff, Helena, and Hot
   Springs.

Arkansas Times. Little Rock.
   1925–1933.
Arkansas Tribune. Little Rock.
   1973.

Arkansas Vanguard. Little Rock.
   1940.
Arkansas Voice. Little Rock. 1965.
Arkansas Weekly Mansion. Little
   Rock. 1880–1886.
Arkansas Weekly Sentinel. Little
   Rock. 1978–1983.
Arkansas Wesleyan. Little Rock.
   1892–1898.
Arkansas World. Little Rock.
   1940–1957.
*Arkansas-Oklahoma African Method-
   ist.* Little Rock. 1949.
Arkansaw Dispatch. Little Rock.
   1886–1896.
Baptist College News. Little Rock.
   1912–1922.
Baptist Vanguard. Little Rock.
   1884–1976.
Black Consumer. Little Rock.
   1972–1973.
College Advocate. Little Rock.
   1910.
College Messenger. Little Rock.
   1911–1912.
College Quarterly. Little Rock.
   1913.
Colored Churchman. Little Rock.
   1930–1939.
Commercial Gazette. Little Rock.
   1902–1903.
Consumer. Little Rock. 1973–199?
Enterprise. Little Rock. 1906–1907.
Eulogizer. Little Rock. 1910–1911.
Fulcrum. Little Rock. 1906–1912.
Fulcrum's Weekly. Little Rock.
   1907.
Fulton's Sun. Little Rock.
   1884–1885.
Herald Mansion. Little Rock.
   1884–1886.
Little Rock Reporter. Little Rock.
   1901–1906.
Reporter. Little Rock. 1907–1909.
Little Rock Sun. Little Rock.
   1884–1890.
Mansion. Little Rock. 1886–1887.
Minority Business Journal. Little
   Rock. 1972–1973.

Mosaic Guide. Little Rock.
    1885–1886.
Mosaic Guide. Little Rock.
    1888–1926.
National Democrat. Little Rock.
    1890–1891.
Observer. Little Rock. 1925–1927.
Our Review. Little Rock.
    1908–1920.
Panther Journal. Little Rock (Philan-
    der Smith College)
    194?–195?
People's Herald. Little Rock.
    1900–1903.
Shorter Bugle. Little Rock. 1952.
Southern Christian Recorder. Little
    Rock. 1886–1946.
Southern Mediator Journal. Little
    Rock. 1938–1978.
Southern Mediator. Little Rock.
    1979–1987.
State Press. Little Rock.
    1941–1959.
State Weekly News. Little Rock.
    1976–199?
Stateside Mediator. Little Rock.
    1980–1983.
Sun. Little Rock. 1884–1890.
Taborian Visitor. Little Rock.
    1895–1917.
Twin City Press. Little Rock.
    1937–1940.
Visitor. Little Rock. 1898.
Voice of the Twentieth Century. Lit-
    tle Rock. 1898–1901.
Western Review. Little Rock.
    1919–1925.

MARIANNA
Elevator. Marianna. 1904–1905.
Enterprise. Marianna. 1907–1908.
Opinion-Enterprise. Marianna.
    1907–1926.

MONTROSE
Trumpet. Montrose. 1901–1906.
Union Trumpet. Montrose.
    1906–1910.

MORRILTON
Clarion. Morrilton. 1888–1890.
Conway County Clarion. Morrilton.
    1887–1888.
Tribune. Morrilton. 1905–1909.
Voice. Morrilton. 1919–1924.

NEWPORT
Arkansas Progress. Newport.
    1887–1888.
Headlight. Newport. 1909–1914.
White River Advance. Newport.
    1913–1920.
White River Advocate. Newport.
    1913–1926.

NORTH LITTLE ROCK
African Methodist. North Little
    Rock. 1919–1922.
Arkansas African Methodist. North
    Little Rock. 1921–1927.
Eastern Star. North Little Rock.
    1898–1899.
Our Eastern Star. North Little Rock.
    1899–1905.
University Herald. North Little Rock.
    1898–1906.
Voice. North Little Rock.
    1906–1907.
Voice of the Twentieth Century.
    North Little Rock.
    1898–1922.

OSCEOLA
Arkansas Advocate. Osceola.
    1895–1898.
Plaindealer. Osceola. 1895–1897.

PINE BLUFF
*Agricultural, Mechanical and Normal
    College Informer.* Pine
    Bluff. 1940–?
Arkansas American. Pine Bluff.
    1925–1926.
Arkansas Baptist Flashlight. Pine
    Bluff. 1948–1949.
Arkansas Colored Catholic. Pine
    Bluff. 1899–1902.

Arkansas Dispatch. Pine Bluff.
    1962, 1975–1976.
Arkansas Masonic Monitor. Pine
    Bluff. 1917–1923.
Arkansas Mirror. Pine Bluff.
    1967–1970.
Arkansas Survey-Journal. Little
    Rock. 1934–1955.
Arkansayer. Pine Bluff. 1928–1940.
Arkansayer. Pine Bluff. 1945–1973.
Baptist Organ. Pine Bluff.
    1882–1883.
Christian Educator. Pine Bluff.
    ?–1950.
Echo. Pine Bluff. 1889–1900.
Echo-Progress. Pine Bluff. 1900.
Five Star Final. Pine Bluff.
Pine Bluff Press. Pine Bluff.
    1868–1879.
Hornet. Pine Bluff. 1889.
Negro Spokesman. Pine Bluff.
    1938–1958.
Pine Bluff Post. Pine Bluff.
    1902–1908.
Pine Bluff Press. Pine Bluff.
    1937–1942.
Arkansas State Press. Little Rock.
    1941–1959.
Arkansas State Press. Little Rock.
    1984. Revival of 1941
    newspaper.
Pine Bluff Weekly Herald. Pine Bluff.
    1900–1907.
Pine City News. Pine Bluff. 1910.
Republican. Pine Bluff. 1887–1888.
Richard Allen Review. Pine Bluff.
    1910.
True Reformer. Pine Bluff. 1885.
Weekly Echo. Pine Bluff. 188?

STAMPS
Arkansas School News. Stamps.
    1915–1922.
Reminder. Stamps. 1913.
Times. Stamps. 1911–1913.

TEXARKANA
Arkansas Appreciator. Texarkana.
    1913–1915.
Appreciator-Union. Texarkana.
    1915–1922.
Fraternal Union. Texarkana.
    1900–1906.
Progressive Citizen. Texarkana.
    1920–1922.
Sun. Texarkana. 1885–1892.
Universal Brotherhood. Texarkana.
    1940.

WEST MEMPHIS
Arkansas World. West Memphis.
    1958–1963.
Many Voices. West Memphis.
    1970–1972.

WYNNE
Life Line. Wynne. 1906–1919.
Pilot. Wynne. 1897–1919.

VARIOUS COMMUNITIES
Arkansas Baptist Flashlight. Car-
    lisle. 1940–1946.
Baxter Vidette. Baxter. 1902.
Black Vanguard. Danville. 1968–?
Eastern Arkansas World. Earle.
    1940.
Freelance. Augusta. 1902–1903.
Headlight. Marion. 1886–1888.
Heber Springs Headlight. Heber
    Springs. 1907–1918.
Herald. Eufaula. 1893–1899.
Messenger. Dumas. 1900–1901.
Monitor. Malvern. 1902–1903.
New Era. Eudora. 1905–1912.
News. Crosett. 1906–1907.
News. Jericho. 1901–1902.
People's Protector. Van Buren.
    1888.
Progress. Kingsland. 1900–1902.
Reporting Star. Arkadelphia.
    1900–1904.

School Herald. Warren. 1912–1923.
Southern Mediator. Jacksonville.
    1978–1979.

Tri-State Defender. Arkansas-
    Mississippi-Tennessee
    Quarterly. 1994?.
Zion Trumpet. Nashville.
    1941–1946.

Other:

African-American Baptist Annual Reports, 1865–1990s: Arkansas. National Archives, microfilm. Books, pamphlets, periodicals, statistics, biographies, etc.

As We See It. Chris Pechin, producer and director. WTTW-TV, Chicago. The desegregation of Little Rock, 1980. Videorecording.

Library of Congress and National Archives. *Records of the Assistant Commissioner, Bureau of Refugees, Freedmen, and Abandoned Lands. 1865–1870*, microfilm. M979.

Library of Congress and National Archives. *Records of the Superintendent of Education, Bureau of Refugees, Freedmen, and Abandoned Lands. 1865–1871*, microfilm. M980.

Library of Congress and National Archives. *The General Education Board: The Early Southern Program*, microfilm. Nos. 98.

Records of the Assistant Commissioner, Bureau of Refugees, Freedmen, and Abandoned Lands: Arkansas, 1865–1869. National Archives, microfilm.

Records of the Superintendent of Education, Bureau of Refugees, Freedmen, and Abandoned Lands: Arkansas, 1865–1871. National Archives, microfilm.

California

Articles:

"Accused Racist Sentenced to Six Months; Must Donate $5,000 to NAACP." *Jet*, 24 February 1997. Daniel Allen Vanbogaert of Westchester, California, received a jail sentence and fine for hate crimes.

"Admission of California." *Negro History Bulletin* 14 (October 1950). Roles of Blacks.

Albin, Ray R. "The Perkins Case: The Ordeal of Three Slaves in Gold Rush California." *California History* 67 (December 1988).

Alexander, Nick. "Bay Area Gets Black-run Public TV." [NYC] *Guardian* (25 September 1991).

_____. "Fighting Toxic Racism in Northern California." [NYC] *Guardian* (26 December 1990). Richmond, California.

Allen, Peter. "Judicial Unrestraint." *California Lawyer* 10 (July 1990). Race discrimination and Black judges.

Allen, Robert L. "Final Outcome?: Fifty Years after the Port Chicago Mutiny." *American Visions,* April-May 1994. Includes article on the Navy investigation.

Allen, William Duncan. "An Overview of Black Concert Music and Musicians in Northern California from the 1940s to the 1980s." *Black Music Research Journal* 9 (Spring 1989).

"Allensworth." *Tulares* (June 1956). A description published by the Tulare County Historical Society.

Alvarez, Robert R., Jr. "The Lemon Grove Incident: The Nation's First Successful Desegregation Court Case." *Journal of San Diego History* 32 (Spring 1986).

Arvey, Verna. "Tolerance." *Opportunity* 18 (August 1944). Anti-Jewish and anti-Black propaganda.

Asinof, E. "Ghetto Doctor; Multipurpose Medical Center in Compton, California." *Today's Health* 50 (April 1972).

Aubry, Erin J. "The L.A. Reality." *Black Enterprise,* November 1995. Special section on the affirmative action "war" in California and Black activity in Los Angeles.

"Ban Outlawed: California Supreme Court Holds Union May Not Refuse Membership to Negroes." *Business Week,* 13 January 1945.

Banks, Henry A. "Black Consciousness: A Student Survey." *The Black Scholar* 2 (September 1970). High school and college student survey.

Barnett, Larry D. "Interracial Marriage in California." *Marriage and Family Living* 25 (November 1963).

Bartlett, Virginia Stivers. "Uncle Nate of Palomar: The Entertaining Story of the Carefree Life of Nathaniel Harrison, a Negro, but Known as the First White Man to Live on Palomar Mountain." *Westways* (October 1931).

Bass, Sandra. "Blacks, Browns and the Blues: Police and Minorities in California." *Public Affairs Report* 38 (November 1997).

Beasley, Delilah L. "California Colored Women Trail Blazers." Chapter in *Homespun Heroines and Other Women of Distinction,* ed. Hallie Q. Brown. Xenia, OH: Aldine Publishing Company, 1926; reprinted, New York: Oxford University Press, 1988.

Beasley, Delilah L., and M. N. Work, comps. "California Freedom Papers." *Journal of Negro History* 3 (January 1918).

Bell, Howard Holman. "Negroes in California, 1849–1858." *Phylon* 28 (Summer 1967).

Berg, Martin. "Of Pride and History." *California Lawyer* 12 (February 1992). Interview of LeGrand Clegg III, Compton city attorney.

Bergman, G. M. "Jacob Dodson: The Other Pathfinder." *Negro Digest* 14 (August 1965).

————. "The Negro Who Rode with Frémont in 1847." *Negro History Bulletin* 28 (1964). Contributions of Jacob Dodson.

Berwanger, Eugene H. "The 'Black Law' Question in Ante-Bellum California." *Journal of the West* 6 (April 1967). Attempts to restrict Black immigration.

Bibbs, Sushell. "Mary Ellen Pleasant: Mother of Civil Rights in California." *Historic Nantucket* 44 (1995).

"Billie Berg's: Hollywood Jazz Temple Draws Stars and Hoi Polloi." *Ebony,* April 1948. Article featuring a nightclub that showcased famous Black jazz artists.

"Black Higher Education in California: A Fading Dream." *The Journal of Blacks in Higher Education* 8 (Summer 1995).

"Black Law School Enrollments: A Virtual Eviction in Texas and California." *The Journal of Blacks in Higher Education* 16 (Summer 1997).

"Black Lawyers in Calif. Urge Outlawing of KKK." *Jet,* 13 November 1980.

"Black Marines Battle Ku Klux Klan at Camp Pendleton Base." *Black Scholar* 8 (April 1977).

"Blacks in California Move Down South in Reverse Migration." *Jet*, 26 January 1998. From 1990–1995, 103,494 Black Californians migrated to the South.

Bond, Marjorie H. "Teenage Attitudes and Attitude Change as Measured by the Q-Technique." *Journal of Educational Sociology* 36 (September 1962). Concerns an interracial workshop, Brotherhood, USA.

Bowers, George B. "Will Imperial Valley Become a Land of Opportunity for Negro Citizens?" *Southern Workman* 59 (July 1930).

Bragg, Susan. "Knowledge is Power: Sacramento Blacks and the Public Schools, 1854–1860." *California History* 75 (Fall 1996).

Brand, Lillian. "I Teach Colored Children." *Opportunity* 15 (February 1937). White teacher in Black primary school.

Breslaw, L., et al. "Health and Race in California." *American Journal of Public Health* 61 (April 1971).

Buckbee, Edna Bryan. "The 'Boys' Called Her 'Mammy' Pleasant." *The Pony Express* 20 (October 1953).

Bunzel, John H. "Black and White at Stanford." *Public Interest* 105 (August 1991). Racism in higher education.

Burma, John Harmon. "Research Note on the Measurement of Interracial Marriage." *American Journal of Sociology* 57 (May 1952). Study following the repeal of California's anti-miscegenation law.

Buskin, Martin. "How Schoolmen are Handling the Hot Ones: Integration, Innovation, and Negotiation." *School Management* 11 (June 1967). Inglewood and other schools.

Caesar, Clarence. "The Historical Demographics of Sacramento's Black Community, 1848–1900." *California History* 75 (Fall 1996).

Cahill, Edvina. "Keep the Kids Busy." *Crisis* 54 (March 1947). Hunters Point Junior City youth project.

Cain, Bruce. "The Contemporary Context of Ethnic and Racial Politics in California." Chapter in *Racial and Ethnic Politics in California*, eds. Bryan O. Jackson and Michael B. Preston. Berkeley: Institute of Governmental Studies, University of California, 1991.

Caldwell, Dan. "The Negroization of the Chinese Stereotype in California." *Southern California Quarterly* 53 (June 1971). Conversion of Chinese images to negative stereotypes of Blacks.

Caldwell, Hansonia L. "Music in the Lives of Blacks in California: The Beginnings." *Black Music Research Bulletin* 10 (Spring 1988).

"Calif. Senate OKs Bill to Reduce KKK Violence." *Jet*, 6 August 1981.

"California Black Artists." College of Marin Art Gallery, Kentfield, California. March 13–April 10, 1970. Catalogue.

"California Freedom Papers." *Journal of Negro History* 3 (January 1918). Copies of manumission papers, 1851–1856.

"California Law on Teaching Negro History: Document." *Integrated Education* 4 (April-May 1966).

"California Representative Maxine Waters, Always Outspoken, Sounds Off on Homophobia Among Blacks and Racism among Gays and Lesbians." *The Advocate* (26 January 1993).

"California's Law on Negro History." *Black World* 30 (February 1967).

Campbell, Leon G. "The First Californians: Presidial Society in Spanish California, 1769–1822." *Journal of the West* 11 (October 1972). Plan to use Blacks to block English and Russian colonization.

"Cardinal McIntyre: A Ramparts Special Report." *Ramparts* 3 (November 1964). The Cardinal's refusal to support racial equality in California.

Carter, Thomas P., and Nathaniel Hickerson. "A California Citizens' Committee Studies Its Schools and De Facto Segregation." *Journal of Negro Education* 37 (Spring 1968).

Casey, Ann. "Thomas Starr King and the Succession Movement." *Historical Society of Southern California Quarterly* 43 (September 1961). Civil War arguments.

Chamberland, Carol P. "The House That Bop Built." *California History* 75 (1996).

Chandler, Robert J. "Friends in Time of Need: Republicans and Black Civil Rights in California During the Civil War Era." *Arizona and the West* 24 (Winter 1982).

Chaplin, Heather. "Affirmative Reaction: UC Law Schools Struggle with Declining Minority Enrollment." *California Lawyer* 17 (September 1997). Social aspects of legal education.

Chavez, Linda. "Is Affirmative Action on the Way Out? Should It Be?" *Commentary* 105 (March 1998). Contends that double standards, quotas and preferences are in place for minorities in higher education.

Ching, Adele. "San Mateo Negroes." *Problems of American Communities* 1 (1945). Publication of Mills College.

Clark, Alice M. "De Facto Integration in Bel Air." *Saturday Review* 49 (15 January 1966).

Clark, Blake. "An Enterprising Minority: California Company, Formed to Help Blacks Become Businessmen, Sees Success in Corporate Involvement." *National Civic Review* 59 (October 1970).

Clark, Kenneth B. "Observations on Little Rock." *New South* 13 (June 1958).

Clark, William V., and Julian Ware. "Trends in Residential Integration by Socioeconomic Status in Southern California." *Urban Affairs Review* 32 (July 1997).

Coffelt, Beth. "Black: Late Drawings of Robert Arneson." *American Ceramics* 12 (1995). Source of Arneson's drawings of Black males may have stemmed from a racial dispute with a department member.

Cole, Olen, Jr. "Black Youth in the National Youth Administration in California, 1935–1943." *Southern California Quarterly* 73 (Winter 1991).

Colley, N. S., and M. L. McGhee. "The California and Washington Fair Housing Cases." *Law in Transition* 22 (Summer 1962).

Coombs, Orde. "The Necessity of Excellence: Nairobi College." *Change* 5 (1973). Focus on higher education at Nairobi College in East Palo Alto.

Cooney, Perceval J. "Southern California in Civil War Days." *Historical Society of Southern California Annual* 13 (1924).

Cooper, Robert. "Detracking Reform in an Urban California High School: Improving the Schooling Experiences of African American Students." *Journal of Negro Education* 65 (Spring 1996).

Covington, Floyd C. "Union Styles: Black Labor in White Coats." *Opportunity* 9 (July 1931). Dining car cook and waiters' union.

Crabtree, Susan. "Reform Warriors." *Insight* 11 (23 October 1995). Conservative Black women in California and Virginia, and welfare reform.

Cramer, James C. "Trends in Infant Mortality among Racial and Ethnic Groups in California." *Social Science Research* 17 (1988).

Cray, Ed. "Blacks and Browns in Blue-Chip Firms." *California Lawyer* 4 (October 1984). Employment of minority attorneys in California.

Cress, R. D., and E. A. Holly. "Incidence of Cutaneous Melanoma Among Non-Hispanic Whites, Hispanics, Asians, and Blacks: An Analysis of California Cancer Registry Data, 1988–93" *Cancer Causes and Control* 8 (1997).

Crossen, Chris. "Changing the Face of Backpacking: A Determined Band Wants to Expose More African-Americans to the Joys of Backpacking." *Backpacker*, May 1996). Plan developed in Haywood, California.

Crouchett, Lawrence P., Lonnie G. Bunch III, and Martha Kendall Winnacker. *The History of the East Bay Afro-American Community, 1851–1977.* Oakland: Northern California Center for Afro-American History and Life, 1989.

Culp, Jerome M., Jr. "Notes from California: Rodney King and the Race Question." *Denver University Law Review* 70 (1993).

Cuninggim, Merrimon. "Integration in Professional Education: The Story of Perkins, Southern Methodist University." *Annals of the American Academy of Political and Social Science* 304 (March 1956).

Davidson, Idelle. "The Wright Legacy." *California Lawyer* 18 (April 1998). Biography of Crispus Attucks Wright.

Davis, Angela Y. "The Soledad Brothers." *Black Scholar* 2 (April-May 1971).

Davis, Mike. "Behind the Orange Curtain." *Nation* (31 October 1994). Violence against Blacks and Mexican-Americans in Orange County.

————. "The Sky Falls on Compton." *Nation* (19 September 1994). Latinos and Blacks.

de Graaf, Lawrence B. "California Blacks." Chapter in *A Guide to the History of California*, eds. Gloria Ricci Lothrop and Doyce B. Junis, Jr. Westport, CT: Greenwood Press, 1989.

DeBerry, Clyde E. "Vocational (Career) Education in Black Cities." *Journal of Negro Education* 42 (1973). Cites the Riverside Opportunities Industrialization Center as a model for vocational education.

Dellums, Ronald. "Responsibility of Black Politics." *Black Scholar* 10 (January/February 1979). Insights from a California member of Congress.

Dent, Harold E., Armando M. Mendocal III, and W. D. Pierce. "Court Bans Use of I.Q. Tests for Blacks for Any Purpose in California State Schools: Press Release by Law Offices of Public Advocates, Inc., San Francisco, California." *Negro Educational Review* 38 (April/July 1987). Students with mental handicaps.

"Desegregation: 10 Blueprints for Action." *School Management* (October 1966). Includes desegregation plans for Riverside.

Drake, Cisco. "How Pico Boulevard Got Its Name." *The Message Magazine* (March/April, 1970). Biography of Pío Pico, California governor.

Du Bois, W. E. B. "Colored California." *Crisis* 6 (August 1913).

Dummet, Clifton O. "California's Pioneer Dentist." *Crisis* 80 (1973). Profile of one of California's first Black dentists.

Duncan, T. Roger. "Does California Have 'Segregated' Schools?" *California Teachers Association Journal* 61 (March 1965).

Dunn, Linda. "Finding Permanent Homes for Black Children: The California Inland Area Urban League Project." *Children Today* 10 (September-October 1981). Recruitment of Blacks to adopt Black children in foster care.

Dymally, Mervyn Malcolm. "The Struggle for the Inclusion of Negro History in Our Text-Books: A California Experience." *Negro History Bulletin* 33 (December 1970).

Earle, John J. "The Sentiment of the People of California With Respect to the Civil War." *American Historical Association Annual Report, for the Year 1907*. Washington, DC: 1908.

Eaton, Joseph W. "A California Triviality." *Crisis* 57 (May 1950). Racist mural in the state capitol building.

Edwards, Malcolm. "'The War of Complexional Distinction': Blacks in Gold Rush California and British Columbia." *California Historical Quarterly* 56 (Spring 1977). Racial discrimination against Blacks in California caused 800 to move to British Columbia, where they continued to encounter discrimination.

Ellison, Joseph. "Designs for a Pacific Republic, 1843–1862." *Oregon Historical Quarterly* 21 (December 1930). Civil War issues.

"A Federal Judge in California Revises the IQ Test Ban He Imposed Six Years Ago to Permit Some Black Children to be Tested." *APA Monitor* 23 (December 1992).

Feigelman, William, and Julia Lee. "Probing the Paradoxical Pattern of Cigarette Smoking among African-Americans: Low Teenage Consumption and High Adult Use." *Journal of Drug Education* 25 (1995). Based on the 1990 California Tobacco Survey.

Feinsilber, Pamela. "Righting an Old Wrong." *California Lawyer* 10 (August 1990). History of litigation regarding the Port Chicago Mutiny at California's Concord Naval Weapons Station.

Fields, Cheryl D. "It's Not Rocket Science." *Black Issues in Higher Education* 15 (2 April 1998). Special section on Black scientists reviews recruiting of undergraduates at Stanford, Berkeley and two other schools.

"The Fire That Time." *New South* 20 (November 1965). Watts riot.

Fisher, James A. "A History of the Political and Social Development of the Black Community in California, 1859–1950." *Journal of Negro History* 56 (September 1971).

————. "The Political Development of the Black Community in California, 1850–1950." *California Historical Quarterly* 50 (September 1971). Black struggles for political power.

————. "The Struggle for Negro Testimony in California, 1851–1863." *Southern California Quarterly* 51 (December 1969). Twelve year struggle (1851-1863) by Blacks to testify in court for or against whites.

Floyd, Samuel A., Jr., and Marsha J. Reisser. "On Researching Black Music in California: A Preliminary Report About Sources and Resources." *Black Music Research Journal* 9 (Spring 1989).

Foner, Philip S. "Reverend George Washington Woodbey: Early Twentieth Century California Black Socialist." *Journal of Negro History* 61 (April 1976).

Forbes, Jack D. "California's Black Pioneers." *Liberator* 8 (April 1968).

Foster, Michele. "As California Goes, So Goes the Nation." *Journal of Negro Education* 65 (Spring 1996). Historic and contemporary discriminatory treatment of Blacks in California schools.

Fraser, Gare E., et al. "Association Among Health Habits, Risk Factors, and All-Cause Mortality in a Black California Population." *Epidemiology* 8 (1997).

Fullilove, Mindy T., et al. "Is 'Black Achievement' an Oxymoron?" *Thought and Action* 4 (Fall 1988). Examines underrepresentation of Blacks in medicine and medical education, plus an effective California program.

Garciá, Mikel, and Jerry Wright. "Race Consciousness in Black Los Angeles, 1886–1915." *CAAS Reports* 12 (Spring-Fall 1989).

Garver, T. H. "Dimensions of Black Exhibitions at La Jolla Museum." *Artforum* (May 1970).

Gayl, Stephen. "Tom Bradley's California Quest." *Black Enterprise*, May 1982.

Gergen, David. "Becoming 'Race' Savvy." *U.S. News and World Report*, 2 June 1997. Proposal to emulate U.S. Army's success in promoting racial equality in light of decreased Black admissions in the UCLA and University of Texas law schools.

Gilbert, Benjamin F. "The Confederate Minority in California." *California Historical Society Quarterly* 20 (June 1941).

Gitelson, Alfred E. "The Power and Duty to Integrate. *Integrated Education* 8 (May-June 1970). L.A. court bans segregation.

"Good for Blacks: California." *Economist* 280 (1–7 August 1981). Opportunities in California.

Graves, Earl G. "The Ballot and the Dollar." *Black Enterprise*, November 1995. The move of the Black Enterprise/Pepsi Golf and Tennis Challenge from California to Miami is one example of Blacks leveraging their economic and political clout to achieve full freedom and economic equality.

————. "Repelling the Siege." *Black Enterprise* , August 1996. Caveats concerning the California Civil Rights Initiative.

Guimary, Donald L. "Ethnic Minorities in Newsrooms of Major Market Media in California." *Journalism Quarterly* 61 (Winter 1984).

————. "Non-Whites in Newsrooms of California Dailies." *Journalism Quarterly* 65 (Winter 1988).

Gunsky, Frederic R. "Racial and Ethnic Survey of California Public Schools." *Integrated Education* 5 (June-July 1967).

Gwynne, S. C. "Back to the Future." *Time*, 2 June 1997. Effects of ending affirmative action to law schools in Texas and California.

Haehn, James O. "Racial Minorities in Northern California." *North State Review* 1 (May 1964). Explains the low percentage of Black residents.

Halpern, Ray, and Betty Halpern. "Integration in Berkeley: The City That went to School." *Nation* 206 (13 May 1968).

Halpern, Ray. "Tactics for Integration." *Saturday Review* 51 (21 December 1968). Berkeley education plan.

Hargrave, Rita, et al. "Defining Mental Health Needs for Black Patients with AIDS in Alameda County." *Journal of the National Medical Association* 83 (1991). Role of psychiatric diagnosis and treatment for Blacks with AIDS.

Harris, Sheldon. "San Fernando"s Black Revolt." *Commonweal* 80 (31 January 1969).

Hart, Vicki R., et al. "Strategies for Increasing Participation of Ethnic Minorities in Alzheimer's Disease Diagnostic Centers: A Multifaceted Approach in California." *Gerontologist* 36 (April 1996).

Hayes-Bautista, David E., and Gregory Rodriguez. "Inglewood: A Multiethnic Utopia?" *New Republic*, 5 September 1994.

Heath, G. Louis. "Control-Identities of Negro and White Students in a California City: San Francisco Bay Area." *Journal of Secondary Education* 45 (May 1970).

Heer, David M. "Negro-White Marriages in the United States." *Journal of Marriage and The Family* 28 (August 1966). Analyzes trends in those marriages in California, Hawaii, Michigan and Nebraska.

Heizer, Robert F. "Civil Rights in California in the 1850's—A Case Study." *Anthropological Society Papers* 31 (1964). *The People* v. *Hall* and the extension of exclusionary testimony.

Hendrick, Irving G. "Approaching Equality of Educational Opportunity in California: The Successful Struggle of Black Citizens, 1880–1920." *Pacific Historian* 25 (Winter 1981).

Henry, Charles P. "The Role of Race in the Bradley-Deukmejian Campaign."
Critical Perspectives of Third World America 1 (Fall 1983).

Herberg, Will. "Who are the Guilty Ones?" *National Review*, 7 September
1965.

Hickerson, Nathaniel. "Some Aspects of School Integration in a California
High School." *Journal of Negro Education* 34 (Spring 1965). Summa-
tion of dissertation work.

Hill, Beatrice M., and Nelson S. Burke. "Some Disadvantaged Youths Look at
Their Schools." *Journal of Negro Education* 37 (Spring 1968). Views
of fifteen youth.

Hilton, Keith Orlando. "Disneyland Dumped." *Black Issues in Higher Education* 12 (24 August 1995). Black organizations boycott California because of governor Pet Wilson's anti-affirmative action stance.

"Hitch for Cleaver." *Economist* 228 (28 September 1968). The president of the
University of California comments on Eldridge Cleaver.

Hodge, Jacqueline G. "Ask, Seek, Knock—Desegregate." *Crisis* 70 (December
1963). Desegregation in Fresno.

Holmes, Bob. "A Study in Subtlety: Riverside Renewal." *Inter-racial Review*
36 (June 1963). Urban renewal and Blacks in Riverside.

Holmes, Robert. "Soledad Report: One Year Later." *Black Politician* 3 (1971).
Changes at the prison—influence of Black legislators, promotion of
Blacks, etc.

Hoover, Mary Eleanor Rhodes. "The Nairobi Day School: An African American Independent School, 1966–1984." *Journal of Negro Education* 61
(Spring 1992). Profile of a private school in East Palo Alto.

Hornblower, Margot. "Taking It All Back: At Pete Wilson's Urging, the University of California Says No to Racial Preferences." *Time*, 31 July
1995.

Hudson, Lynn M. "A New Look, or 'I'm Not Mammy to Everybody in California': Mary Ellen Pleasant, a Black Entrepreneur." *Journal of the
West* 32 (July 1993).

Hunter, Robert G. "Hollywood and the Negro." *Black World* 15 (May 1966).
Discrimination in the motion picture industry.

Inghram, Dorothy. "An Experiment in Intercultural Education." *California
Journal of Elementary Education* 22 (November 1953). Mill School,
San Bernardino.

Ise, Claudine. "'Aesthetic Interventions: Contemporary African American Artists' at CSU Dominguez Hills." *Artweek* 27 (April 1996). Review of
the exhibition.

Jackson, Sametta Wallace. "Mifflin Wistar Gibbs." *Negro History Bulletin* 4
(May 1941). Biography.

"Janice Brown Appointed by Governor to Become First Black Woman on Cali-
     fornia Supreme Court." *Jet*, 29 April 1996.
Jenkins, Velesta. "White Racism and Black Response in California History."
     Chapter in *Ethnic Conflict in California History*, ed. Charles Wollen-
     berg. Los Angeles: Tinnon-Brown, 1970.
Jensen, Joan M. "Apartheid: Pacific Coast Style." *Pacific Historical Review*
     38 (1969). Restrictive covenants in California through 1967.
"Juanita M. McDonald Wins Congressional Seat in California." *Jet*, 22 April
     1996.
Kaplan, M. "Discrimination in California Housing: The Need for Additional
     Legislation." *California Law Review* 50 (October 1962).
Kennedy, R. "Justice Murphy's Concurrence in *Oyama* v. *California*: Cussing
     Out Racism. *Texas Law Review* (May 1996).
"The Klandidate." *Nation* 231 (5 July 1980). Klansman runs for office.
Klein, Stephen P., et al. "Race and Imprisonment Decisions in California."
     Science 247 (1990).
Kolemaine, R. S. "Black Operators in Heritage Touring." *American Visions*,
     April-May 1994. Profiles Black heritage tours in California, Nova
     Scotia and Ontario.
Kossow, Henry H. "An Integration Success Story." *American School Board
     Journal* (July 1965). Del Passo Heights school system.
Krauthammer, Charles. "Lies, Damn Lies and Racial Statistics." *Time*, 20
     April 1998. Author contends the drop in minority admissions to the
     University of California has been overplayed.
Lamoreaux, Lillian A. "There's Work to be Done." *Opportunity* 19 (December
     1941). Race relations in the Santa Barbara schools.
Lampkin, Daisy E. "California Campaigns for the N.A.A.C.P." *Crisis* 41
     (July 1934).
Landrine, Hope, Elizabeth A. Klonoff and Roxana Alcaraz. "Racial Discrimina-
     tion in Minors' Access to Tobacco." *Journal of Black Psychology* 23
     (May 1997). Black children sold cigarettes more often than whites in
     California where purchases by minors are illegal.
Lapp, Rudolph M. "Jeremiah Sanderson: Early California Negro." *Journal of
     Negro History* 53 (October 1968). Educator and church member.
_____. "The Negro in Gold Rush California." *Journal of Negro History* 49
     (April 1964).
_____. "Negro Rights Activities in Gold Rush California." *California His-
     torical Society Quarterly* 45 (1966). Includes information regarding the
     Colored Conventions.
Lee, Charles S., and Lester Sloan. "'It's Our Turn Now.'" *Newsweek*, 21 No-
     vember 1994. Problems between Blacks and Latinos in Compton.
Leo, John. "Finally, the People Vote on a Taboo." *U.S. News and World Re-
     port*, 4 March 1996. Predictions and comments on the November Cali-
     fornia Civil Rights Initiative.

Leonard, Jonathan Shawn.   "The Effect of Unions on the Employment of Blacks, Hispanics, and Women."   *Industrial and Labor Relations Review* 39 (October 1985).

Liss, Andrea.   "Facing History."   *Afterimage* 23 (September/October 1995).   Author discussed "Hidden Witness: African Americans in Early Photography" and Carrie Mae Weems Reacts to "Hidden Witness" shows at the J. Paul Getty Museum in Malibu.

Loury, Gary.   "Absolute California."   *The New Republic*, 18 November 1996.   Attack on affirmative action.

Lovdjieff, Crist.   "Guru of San Quentin."   *Esquire* 67 (April 1967).   Eldridge Cleaver.

Lowery, Mark.   "The Golden State War: Californians Have Pushed Their Divisive Affirmative-Action Debate onto the National Agenda."   *Black Enterprise*, November 1995.

"Lynch Law in California."   *Green Bag* 14 (1902).

Magner, Denise K.   "Plan Aims to Raise Eligibility of Blacks for U. of Cal. System."   *Chronicle of Higher Education* 36 (4 April 1990).

"Making Leadership a Career. An Interview with Dr. Blenda J. Wilson."   *Black Issues in Higher Education* 13 (17 October 1996).   Interview with the president of the University of California-Northridge.

Malveaux, Julianne.   "Affirmative Discrimination."   *Black Issues in Higher Education* 14 (21 August 1997).   Proposition 209.

Marascuilo, Leonard A., and Kathleen Penfield.   "A Northern Urban Community's Attitudes Toward Racial Imbalance in Schools and Classrooms."   *School Review* (Winter 1966).

Marks-Forman, Lorene.   "Overground Railroad—California Junction."   *Crisis* 91 (May 1984).

Marlowe, John, and Katharyn Culler.   "How We're Adding Racial Balance to the Math Equation."   *Executive Educator* 9 (April 1987).   An Albany, California high school addresses racial imbalances through remedial math programs.

Marshall, Rachelle.   "Concrete Curtain—The East Palo Alto Story."   *Crisis* 64 (November 1957).   Problem of school integration.

"Mass Murder in America."   *The New Republic*, 13 December 1933.   Lynchings in California, Missouri and elsewhere.

"Mass Murders or Civilized Society?"   *The Sign* 13 (January 1934).   Lynchings in California, Missouri and elsewhere.

Matthews, William C.   "The Negro Bloc."   *Opportunity* 5 (February 1927).   Study of 1926 elections.

Mayer, William.   "Sacramento's Fight for Integration in Public Housing."   *Crisis* 60 (January 1953).

McBroome, Delores Nason.   "Catalyst for Change: Wartime Housing and African-Americans in California's East Bay."   Chapter in *American Labor in the Era of World War II*, eds. Sally M. Miller and Daniel A. Cornford. Westport, CT: Praeger, 1995.

McCubrey, Joanne. "Trailblazer of Black History." *Westways* 82 (1 February 1990). Profile.

McKenney, J. Wilson. "California Equalizes Opportunity: School Districts Struggle with Educational Problems." *California Teachers Association Journal* 61 (March 1965). Examines segregation.

McMillen, Liz. "Universities Are Lagging in Hiring Women and Blacks for Faculty Jobs, 2 Studies Find." *Chronicle of Higher Education* 33 (8 July 1987). Study looks at the University of Virginia and the University of California.

McWilliams, Carey. "Minorities in California." *California Librarian* 6 (December 1944).

Meckler, Zane. "De Facto Segregation in California." *California Teachers Association Journal* 58 (January 1963).

Meer, Bernard, and Edward Freedman. "The Impact of Negro Neighbors on White Home Owners." *Social Forces* 45 (September 1966).

Melching, Richard. "The Activities of the Ku Klux Klan in Anaheim, California, 1923–1925." *Southern California Quarterly* 56 (Summer 1974).

Miller, Betsey. "Common Heritage." *Artweek* 21 (21 June 1990). Six Black artists from the Bay Area and their exhibit at the Mary Porter Sesnon Gallery, University of California, Santa Cruz.

"Minority Applications Increase at University of California." *Black Issues in Higher Education* 14 (19 February 1998).

"Minority Groups in California." *Monthly Labor Review* 89 (September 1966).

Montesano, Philip M. "A Black Pioneer's Trip to California." *Pacific Historian* 13 (Winter 1969). The 1849 trip from Missouri by Alvin Aaron Coffey.

_____. "The Mystery of the San Jose Statues." *Urban West* 1 (March-April 1968). Describes three sculptures by Edmonia Lewis at the San Jose Public Library.

Moore, Jesse T. "Seeking a New Life: Blacks in Post-Civil War Colorado." *Journal of Negro History* 78 (Summer 1993).

Moore, Joe Louis. "In Our Own Image: Black Artists in California, 1880–1970." *California History* 75 (Fall 1996).

Moore, Shirley Ann. "African Americans in California: A Brief Historiography." *California History* 75 (1996).

_____. "Getting There, Being There: African-American Migration to Richmond, California, 1910–1945." Chapter in *The Great Migration in Historical Perspective: New Dimensions of Race, Class, and Gender*, ed. Joe William Trotter, Jr. Bloomington: Indiana University Press, 1991.

_____. "'Her Husband Didn't Have a Word to Say.': Black Women and Blues Clubs in Richmond, California, during World War II." Chapter in *American Labor in the Era of World War II,* eds. Sally M. Miller and Daniel A. Cornford. Westport, CT: Praeger, 1995.

_____. "'Not in Somebody's Kitchen': African American Women Workers in Richmond, California, and the Impact of World War II. Chapter in *Writing the Range: Race, Class, and Culture in the Women's West*, eds. Elizabeth Jameson and Susan Armitage. Norman: University of Oklahoma Press, 1997.

Morris, James R. "Social-Economic Background of Negro Youth in California." *Journal of Negro Education* 20 (1951).

"Mr. B Finds His Dream House." *Ebony*, October 1952. The remodeling of singer Billy Eckstine's house in Encino.

Munitz, B. "California State University System and First Amendment Rights to Free Speech." *Education* 112 (Autumn 1991).

Muraskin, William Alan. "The Social Foundations of the Black Community: The Fraternities, The California Masons as a Test Case." *Midcontinent American Studies Journal* 11 (Fall 1970).

Murphy, Larry George. "The Church and Black Californians: A Mid-Nineteenth Century Struggle for Civil Justice." *Foundations* 18 (April/June 1975).

"NAACP Sticks to Hollywood Deadline: No Set Quota for Negroes in Production Crews." *Broadcasting* 32 (16 September 1963).

"Nation's NAACP Chapters on Alert After Recent Attacks on West Coast." *Jet*, 16 August 1993. Examines situations in Sacramento and Tacoma.

"New Board Member." *Jet*, 26 April 1999. Tyrone Smith first Black named to the board of directors for the West Basin Municipal Water District (Inglewood).

"The New Racial Divide:" *World Press Review* 43 (July 1996). Reprinted from *Le Nouvel Observateur*, by Philippe Bouulet-Gercourt. Whites and Latinos against Blacks.

Newman, Lucile F. "Folklore of Pregnancy: Wives' Tales in Contra Costa County, California." *Western Folklore* 28 (1969). Examination of birth folktales in California.

Noguera, P. A. "Responding to the Crisis Confronting California's Black Male Youth: Providing Support Without Furthering Marginialization." *The Journal of Negro Education* 65 (Spring 1996). Special edition: *The Education of African Americans in California*.

"Northern California, Jim Crow or Cosmopolitan?" *Black World* 9 (February 1951).

Obesrweiser, David, Jr. "The CIO: A Vanguard for Civil Rights in Southern California, 1940–1946." Chapter in *American Labor in the Era of World War II*, eds. Sally M. Miller and Daniel A. Cornford. Westport, CT: Praeger, 1995.

Ogbu, John U. "Low School Performance as Adaptation: The Case of Blacks in Stockton, California." Chapter in *Minority Status and Schooling*, eds. Margaret A. Gibson and John U. Ogbu. New York: Garland, 1991.

Ong, Paul M., and J. R. Lawrence. "Race and Employment Dislocation in Cali-
     fornia's Aerospace Industry." *Review of Black Political Economy*
     (Winter 1995).
Orlans, Harold. "Changing Conditions: Minority Education at Oaks College."
     Thought and Action 6 (Spring 1990). The University of Califor-
     nia–Santa Cruz.
Owen, Chandler. "Dr. Eugene Curry Nelson: A Professional and Business Man
     of a New Type among Negroes." *Messenger* 6 (October 1924).
Parker, Paula. "The Ku Klux Klan Congressman." *Black Enterprise*, October
     1980.
Parsons, Edgar W. "California Faces Crucial Civil Rights Test." *Phi Delta
     Kappan* (October 1964).
"Paul R. Williams." *Opportunity* 6 (March 1928). Biography of the architect
     with images of buildings he designed.
Peck, James. "The Proof of the Pudding." *Crisis* 56 (November 1949). CORE
     fights Jim Crow at the Bimini baths.
Peshkin, Alan, and Carolyne J. White. "Four Black American Students: Com-
     ing of Age in a Multiethnic High School." *Teachers College Record*
     92 (Fall 1990). Focus on a northern California school.
Petersilia, Joan. "Racial Disparities in the Criminal Justice System: A Sum-
     mary." *Crime and Delinquency* 31 (January 1985). Study of discrimi-
     nation in the criminal justice system in California, Michigan and
     Texas.
Platt, Anthony M. "U.S. Race Relations at the Crossroads in California."
     Monthly Review, October 1996.
"The Political Magic of Willie Brown and Higher Education Opportunities for
     Blacks in California." *The Journal of Blacks in Higher Education* 8
     (Summer 1995).
Polos, Nicholas C. "Segregation and John Swett." *Southern California Quar-
     terly* 46 (March 1964). California's 4th superintendent of public in-
     struction advocated education for every child.
Porter, Lindbergh, Jr. "Great Necessities Call Out Great Virtues." *San Fran-
     cisco Attorney* 24 (February-March 1998). Black attorneys and legal
     etiquette.
Prasse, David P., and Daniel J. Reschly. "Larry P.: A Case of Segregation,
     Testing, or Program Efficacy?" *Exceptional Children* 52 (January
     1986). Mentally handicapped and Black.
Pressman, Steven. "On Her Own: Like Many Black Attorneys, Solo Practitio-
     ner Adrienne Beasley Makes Her Living with a Gritty Brand of Law."
     California Lawyer 10 (February 1990). Interview with California law-
     yer.
_____. "Willie Brown, Esquire: The Assembly Speaker's Law Practice is
     Actually Pretty simple. When He Talks, People Usually Listen."
     California Lawyer 10 (January 1990). Interview of California legislator
     Brown.

"Proclamation of the Mayor of Monterey, California, Shedo S. Russo; First Negro History Celebration Here, Initiated by the Lamplighters Study Club." *Negro History Bulletin* 25 (December 1961).

"Programs That Work: Young Adults for Positive Achievement." *Essence* 26 (October 1995). California school fights teen pregnancy through education.

Pulliam, Roger L. "Allan Bakke vs. Regents of the University of California: Analysis and Implications." *Western Journal of Black Studies* 2 (March 1978).

Rabkin, Jeremy A. "Diversity Snobs." *American Spectator*, August 1997). Admissions decrease for Black students at Berkeley and the University of Texas law schools.

"Racial Furor in Compton, CA, Over High School Gridder Who Punched Referee for Allegedly Calling Him 'Nigger.'" *Jet*, 11 December 1995.

"Rampages of Ku Klux Klan on the Pacific Coast." *Messenger* 4 (June 1922). The Klan in Bakersfield and Oregon.

Ratnesar, Romesh. "The Next Big Divide?" *Time*, 1 December 1997. Blacks and Latinos struggle for control of public schools, such as East Palo Alto.

Record, C. Wilson. "The Chico Story: A Black and White Harvest." *Crisis* 68 (1951)

_____. "Negroes in the California Agriculture Labor Force." *Social Problems* 6 (Spring 1959).

_____. "Promised Land: School Board and Negro Teacher in California." *The Teacher* (March 1962); reprinted, *Integrated Education* 1 (April 1963).

_____. "Racial Diversity in California Public Schools." *Journal of Negro Education* 29 (Winter 1959).

_____. "Racial Integration in California Schools." *Journal of Negro Education* 27 (Winter 1958).

_____. "Willie Stokes at the Golden Gate." *Crisis* 56 (June 1949).

Reed, Bernice Anita. "Accommodation between Negro and White Employees in a West Coast Aircraft Industry, 1942–1944." *Social Forces* 26 (October 1947).

"Report Card: KKK Makes the Grade." *New West* 6 (January 1981).

Richard, Eugene Scott. "Culture Change due to Migration: Study of Negro Migration to California." *Sociology and Social Research* 26 (March 1942).

Ridout, Lionel Utley. "The Church, the Chinese, and the Negroes in California, 1849–1893." *Historical Magazine of the Protestant Episcopal Church* 28 (June 1959). Recalls Peter William Cassey and his Phoenixonian Institute.

Riley, L. H. "Miscegenation Statutes: A Re-Evaluation of their Constitutionality in Light of Changing Social and Political Conditions." *Southern California Law Review* 32 (Fall 1958).

"Riot and Premise Protection." *Security World* 2 (September 1965).

Rischin, Moses. "Immigration, Migration, and Minorities in California: A Reassessment." *Pacific Historical Review* 41 (1972).

Ritter, Earnestine. "The Negro Takes Strides." *California Sun Magazine* 11 (Fall and Winter 1959–60).

Robinson, Louie. "Death Threatens Western Town." *Ebony*, June 1967. Arsenic in the water supply at Allensworth.

"The Rodney King Trials: Civil Rights Prosecutions and Double Jeopardy." *UCLA Law Review* 41 (February 1994).

Rodriguez, Roberto. "Coalition." *Black Issues in Higher Education* 12 (21 September 1995). Blacks and Latinos unite against California's anti-affirmative action initiative.

Rogers, Ray. "Panthers and Tribesmen: Black Guns on Campus." *Nation* 208 (5 May 1969). Panthers and Ron Karenga's US at UC.

Rollins, C. "Fascism at Soledad." *Black Scholar* 2 (April-May 1971). Problems in the prison.

Rubin, Lillian. "The Racist Liberals—An Episode in a County Jail." *Transaction* 5 (1968). An analysis of the racial relations between 70 women (one Black) arrested in the Alameda County jail and the mostly Black inmates, after an anti-war demonstration.

"Ruchell McGee: Slave Rebel." *Black Scholar* 4 (1971). The sole survivor of the Marin County shoot-out at the courthouse.

Rumberger, Russell W., and J. Douglas Willms. "The Impact of Racial and Ethnic Segregation on the Achievement Gap in California High Schools." *Educational Evaluation and Policy Analysis* 14 (1992).

Rust, Ben. "Racial Discrimination and the Teacher Shortage in California." *Frontier* 8 (May 1957).

Rydall, E. H. "California for Colored Folk." *Colored American Magazine* 12 (May 1907).

"San Jose Protestors Thwart KKK Rally." *Jet*, 7 May 1981.

Sankore, Shelby. "Negro in California History." *Black World* 15 (February 1966).

Savage, J. A. "Breathing Fire: White Middle-Class Richmond Residents are Finally Joining Poor Blacks and Latinos in Their Decades-Old Battle against Chevron's Pollution." *San Francisco Bay Guardian* (East Bay Edition) 26 (11 March 1992).

Schmidt, Peter. "California District strives to mix Blacks, Hispanics." *Education Week* 14 (12 April 1995). Integration efforts in Pasadena.

"School Progress in San Bernardino—Documents." *Integrated Education* 5 (April–May 1967). Complaints by CORE, NAACP and others.

Scott, J. W., et al. "The Board of Regents of the University of California, Governance, and Affirmative Action." *Academe* (July/August 1996).

"Segregation." *Southern California Law Review* 36 (1963). *Jackson v. Pasadena School District.*

"Self-Help Program Stirs a Negro Slum: Operation Bootstrap." *Business Week*, 25 March 1967.

Sheppard, Stephanie. "Augustus F. Hawkins: Champion of the People." *Sepia* 28 (July 1979).

Siegel, Stanley. "Incident in Pasadena." *Frontier* 17 (December 1965). Reactions to speech by sheriff of Selma, Alabama.

Singer, Harry, and Irving G. Hendrick. "Total School Integration: An Experiment in Social Reconstruction. *Phi Delta Kappan* 49 (November 1967). Pasadena school system.

Slind-Flor, Victoria. "Firm Firsts. *National Law Journal* 13 (27 May 1991). David R. Andrews becomes manager partner in California's McCutchen, Doyle, Brown and Enersen law firm.

"Sketches of Inequality: Employment Situation of Hispanics, Blacks and Asians in California." *California Tomorrow* 2 (Winter 1987).

Slater, J. "Ron Dellums and the Politics of Niggers." *Ebony*, May 1972. U.S. Congressman.

Smith, Eric L., Deborrah M. Wilkinson and Marjorie Whigham-Desir. "A Disturbing Proposition." *Black Enterprise*, January 1988. The impact of Proposition 209 on Blacks.

Smith, Herman T. "Politics and Policies of the Negro Community." Chapter in *California Politics and Policies: Original Essays*, eds. Eugene P. Dvorin and Arthur J. Misner. Reading PA: Addison-Wesley, 1966.

Smith, Stan. "Compton...A Case Study in Gradual Integration." *California Sun Magazine* 12 (Fall and Winter 1960-1961).

Smith, William Thomas. "Hollywood Report." *Phylon* 6 (1945). Lists film industry employees and finds racist policies still in effect.

"Southern Pacific Jim-Crow." *Crisis* 61 (April 1954). Discrimination on Southern Pacific train runs in California.

Spaulding, Imogene. "The Attitude of California to the Civil War." *Historical Society of Southern California Annual* 12 (1912–1913).

Specht, Harry. "Community Development in Low-Income Negro Areas." *Social Work* 11 (October 1966). The Richmond Community Development Demonstration Project.

Spencer, S. "On the Front Lines: With Affirmative Action Under Attack, Many Black Business Owners in California are Fighting for their Lives." *Black Enterprise*, 1995.

Spickard, Paul R. "Work and Hope: African American Women in Southern California during World War II." *Journal of the West* 32 (July 1993).

Spoehr, L. W. "Sambo the Heathen Chinese: Californians' Racial Stereotypes in the Late 1870's." *Pacific Historical Review* 42 (May 1973).

St. James, Nicole. "Grabbing Another Slice." *Black Enterprise*, December 1997. Black company PacPizza L. L. C. becomes Pizza Hut's second largest franchiser with restaurants in northern California, southern Oregon and western Nevada.

Stanley, Gerald. "Civil War Politics in California." *Southern California Quarterly* 64 (Summer 1982).

_____. "Racism and the Early Republican Party: The 1856 Presidential Election in California." *Pacific Historical Review* 42 (1974).

Stegner, Wallace Earle. "Changes in the Black Ghetto: East Palo Alto." *Saturday Review* 53 (1 August 1970).

Steinfield, Melvin. "California Black Legislators: Leadership Roles." *Black Politician* 3 (1971). Profile of the six legislators.

Steinhardt, Anne E. "Will She Appeal? To Pete Wilson, That Is. Santa Clara's Judge LaDoris Cordell is in the Running for a Higher Court." *California Lawyer* 11 (September 1991). Black judges and judicial selection.

Stewart, J. B. "Race, Science, and 'Just-Us': Understanding Jurors' Reasonable Doubt in the O.J. Simpson Trial." *Black Scholar* 25 (1995).

Struhsaker, Virginia L. "Stockton's Black Pioneers." *Pacific Historian* 19 (Winter 1975).

Studer, Robert. "Willie Brown: California's Brash New Speaker." *Sepia* 30 (April 1981).

Tachibana, Judy. "Minority Two-Year Transfer Rates Not Making the Grade in California." *Black Issues in Higher Education* 7 (30 August 1990).

Taylor, Paul S. "Foundations of California Rural Society. *California Historical Society Quarterly* 24 (September 1945).

Tepperman, Jean. "Black and Blue: African American Activists Tackle cultural Issues Surrounding Domestic Violence." *California Lawyer* 16 (May 1996). Family violence in California.

Texeira, Mary. "Policing the Internally Colonized: Slavery, Rodney King, Mark Furman, and Beyond." *Western Journal of Black Studies* 19 (Winter 1995).

Thurman, A. Odell. "The Negro in California Before 1890." *Pacific Historian* 19 (Winter 1975); *Pacific Historian* 20 (Spring 1976); and *Pacific Historian* 20 (Summer 1976).

Tierney, William G. "Affirmative Action in California: Looking Back." *Journal of Negro Education* 65 (Spring 1996).

Tolbert, Emory J. "Outpost Garveyism and the UNIA Rank and File." *Journal of Black Studies* 5 (1975).

Tolbert, Emory J., and Lawrence B. de Graaf. "The Unseen Minority: Blacks in Orange County." *Journal of Orange County Studies* 3/4 (Fall 1989/Spring 1991).

Townsend, Chauncey. "Out of the Kitchen." *Crisis* 42 (January 1935). Biographical sketch of Louise Beavers, famous Black actor.

Truman, Ben Cummings. "The Passing of a Sierra Knight." *Overland Monthly* 42 (July 1903). Biography of George Monroe, Pony Express rider and stage driver.

Twyman, Winkfield F., Jr. "A Critique of the California Civil Rights Initiative." *National Black Law Journal* 14 (Spring 1997).

Tyler, Bruce. "Zoot-Suit Culture and the Black Press." *Journal of American Culture* 17 (Summer 1994).

"The Unsinkable Willie Brown." *Urban West* 2 (October 1968). Account of the California state legislator.

Walker, R. "California's Collision of Race and Class." *Representations* (Summer 1996).

Walter, Helen B. "Confederates in Southern California." *Historical Society of Southern California Quarterly* 25 (March 1953).

Walters, Ronald. "The Imperative of Popular Black Struggle: Three Examples from Miami, Los Angeles and Chicago." *Black Scholar* 24 (Fall 1994). Includes LA's mass disobedience following the Rodney King beating and the Simi Valley court ruling.

Weber, Francis. "California's Negro Heritage." *Black World* 16 (February 1967).

Webster, Argow. "Formula for Explosion." *Frontier* 16 (October 1965).

Weiler, Kathleen. "The School at Allensworth." *Journal of Education* 17 (1990). California all-Black town.

Welch, Susan, and John Gruhl. "Does Bakke Matter? Affirmative Action and Minority Enrollments in Medical and Law Schools. *Ohio State Law Journal* 59 (June 1998). Social aspects of the Bakke decision twenty years after.

Wellman, David. "The Wrong Way to Find Jobs for Negroes: The Case History of an Employment Program that Turned into a Fiasco." *Transaction* 5 (April 1968). California's TIDE program.

White, Milton. "Malcolm X in the Military." *The Black Scholar* 1 (May 1970). A Malcolm X organization develops at the Vandenberg Air Force Base.

Wilkerson, Margaret. "Black Theatre in California." *Drama Review* 16 (1972).

Willard, Charles, and Melvin Johnson. "'What's Wrong with the Niggers and Why Are They So Mad at the Police?: Probable Cause for Disaster in South-Central L.A., 1992.' From 'Police 187.'" *Obsidian II* 10 (Spring-Winter 1995). Interviews of gang members and their reasons for hating the police.

Williams, Dennis A., and William J. Cook. "Mistaken Identity: Causing Racial Harassment at Camp Pendleton Marine Base." *Newsweek*, 13 December 1976.

Williams, Franklin H. "California's New Civil Rights Tool." *Christian Century* 77 (15 June 1960). State Justice Department and its constitutional rights section.

Williams, Paul R. "The Rich Legacy of a Black Architect." *Ebony*, March 1994.

Williams, Rev. Cecil. "A Conversation with Angela." *Black Scholar* 3 (March–April 1973). Exclusive interview while Davis was still imprisoned for murder, kidnapping, and other charges.

Wilson, Clint, Jr. "Gilbert Lindsay: Once He Was a Lonely Janitor." *Sepia* 28 (September 1979).

Wilson, Joyce R. "Yvonne Braithwaite." *Urban West* 2 (December 1968). Profile of a member of the California state assembly.

Wilson, S. R., et al. "The Fresno Asthma Project: A Model Intervention to Control Asthma in Multiethnic, Low Income, Inner-City Communities." *Health Education and Behavior* 25 (February 1998).

Wolfinger, Raymond E., and Fred I. Greenstein. "The Repeal of Fair Housing in California: An Analysis of Referendum Voting." *American Political Science Review* 62 (1968). Californians voted against fair housing legislation in 1964.

Wollenberg, Charles. "Blacks vs. Navy Blue: The Mare Island Mutiny Court Martial." *California History* 58 (Spring 1979).

_____. "*James* v. *Marinship*: Trouble on the New Black Frontier." *California History* 60 (Fall 1981).

_____. "*Mendez* vs. *Westminster*: Race, Nationality and Segregation in California Schools." *California Historical Quarterly* 53 (Winter 1974). Concentrates on Mexican-Americans but includes Blacks.

Angela Y. Davis

Miller, Judy Ann. "The State of California vs. Angela Y. Davis and Ruchell McGee." *Black Politician* 2 (1971). Issues surrounding the case.

"The Path of Angela Davis: From Promising Childhood to Desperate Flight." *Life* 69 (11 September 1970).

Reich, Kenneth. "Angela Davis—Is She More Red than Black?" *Black Politician* 1 (January 1970).

Roberts, Myron. "The Angela Heresy." *Los Angeles* 14 (November 1969).

Rouse, Deborah L. "Rediscovering Angela Davis." *Emerge* 8 (June 1997).

"Support for Angela Davis: Letters to the Editor." *Library Journal* 96 (15 March 1971).

Williams, Rev. Cecil. "A Conversation with Angela." *Black Scholar* 3 (March–April 1973). Exclusive interview while Davis was still imprisoned for murder, kidnapping, and other charges.

Berkeley—U.C. and Community

Allen, Gary. "Black Power: American Opinion Goes to a Berkeley Rally." *American Opinion* 10 (January 1967).

Benet, James. "Busing in Berkeley Proves to be Neither Calamity nor Cure-All." *City* 4 (June-July 1970).

Billingsley, Andrew, Douglas Davidson, and Theresa Loya. "Ethnic Studies at Berkeley." *California Monthly* 80 (June–July 1970.

Blake, J. Herman. "The Agony and the Rage." *Black World* (March 1967). Racism at Berkeley.

Farrell, Charles S. "Stung by Racial Incidents and Charges of Indifference, Berkeley Trying to Become Model Integrated University." *Chronicle of Higher Education* 34 (27 January 1988).

Freudenthal, Daniel K. "How Berkeley Came to Grips with De Facto Segregation." *Phi Delta Kappan* 46 (December 1964).

Gardner, David P. "Some Marginal Notes on the Berkeley-Eldridge Cleaver Affair." *California Digest* 1 (December 1968).

Halpern, Ray. "Tactics for Integration." *Saturday Review* 51 (December 1968). Berkeley concerns.

Hamilton, Charles J., Jr. "A Black Militant Inside the System." *Wall Street Journal,* 31 July 1968. Ronald V. Dellums, Berkeley city councilman.

Johnson, Margaret. "The Negroes in West Berkeley." Chapter in *Immigration and Race Problems* (1949–1953). Publication of Mills College.

Lunemann, Alan. "Desegregation and Achievement: A Cross-Sectional and Semi-Longitudinal Look at Berkeley, California." *Journal of Negro Education* 42 (Fall 1974). Examines effects of desegregation through achievement tests.

McEntire, Sterling M. "A Study of Racial Attitudes in Neighborhoods, Infiltrated by Non-Whites, San Francisco, Oakland, and Berkeley, California." *Northern California Real Estate Report* (2^d Quarter 1955).

Miller, Karen K. "Race, Power, and the Emergence of Black Studies in Higher Education." *American Studies* 31 (Fall 1990). University of Colorado-Berkeley.

O'Brien, Eileen M. "Berkeley Model Proves Successful for Blacks', Hispanics' Calculus Performance." *Black Issues in Higher Education* 5 (2 March 1989). Describes successful remedial calculus program.

"139X." *National Review,* 8 October 1968. Eldridge Cleaver's "Social Analysis 139X" course at the University of California, Berkeley.

Pete, Gregory. "The Battle of Berkeley." *Crisis* 92 (1985). Housing in Berkeley.

Rowe, Robert N. "Is Berkeley School Integration Successful?" *American School Board Journal* (December 1965).

"School Segregation in Berkeley." *Integrated Education* 2 (April–May 1964).

Sullivan, Neil Vincent. "The Eye of the Hurricane." *Integrated Education* 3 (August-November 1965), School segregation at Berkeley.

————. "Myths and Gaps in School Integration." *Today's Education* 57 (September 1968). Berkeley school system.

Sullivan, Neil Vincent, and Thomas D. Wogaman. "Berkeley: Anatomy of Community Change." *Public Management* 51 (May 1969). Berkeley and school desegregation.

Wiggins, David K. "The Future of College Athletics Is at Stake: Black Athletes and Racial Turmoil on Three Predominantly White University Campuses, 1968–1972." *Journal of Sport History* 15 (1988). UC-Berkeley, Syracuse, and Oregon State University.

————. "Desegregation in Berkeley: Some Applicable Lessons." *Urban Review* 3 (1969). Berkeley public school system in 1969.

Wogaman, Thomas D. "The Berkeley Story: Desegregation under the Ramsey Plan." *California Education* 3 (December 1965).

Black Panther Party/Eldridge Cleaver

Abron, JoNina M. "Reflections of a Former Oakland Public School Parent." *Black Scholar* 27 (Summer 1997). Parent who was a teacher at a school founded by the Black Panthers examines education of daughter in the Oakland (California) and Kalamazoo (Michigan) school systems.

Allman, T. D. "The Rebirth of Eldridge Cleaver." *New York Times Magazine*, 16 January 1977. Interview of Cleaver following his return from exile.

Anderson, Jervis. "Race, Rage and Eldridge Cleaver. "*Commentary* 46 (December 1968).

Aust, Stefan. "An Interview with Eldridge Cleaver." *Black Panther*, 11 October 1969. Interview while in exile.

Baker, Karin. "Geronimo Pratt, Political Prisoner." *Against the Current* (July-August 1994). Black Panther leader.

Baker, Ross K. "Putting Down the Gun: Panthers Outgrow Their Rhetoric." *Nation*, 16 July 1973.

Baranski, Lynne, and Richard Lemon. "Black Panthers No More, Eldridge Cleaver and Kathleen Cleaver Now Lionize the U.S. System." *People*, 22 March 1982.

Bartlett, Laile E. "The Education of Eldridge Cleaver." *Reader's Digest*, September 1976. Interview following Cleaver's return from exile.

Bergman, Lowell, and David Weir. "Revolution on Ice: How the Black Panthers Lost the FBI's War of Dirty Tricks." *Rolling Stone*, 9 September 1976. Revelations of a Senate hearing.

"Black Panther Sisters Talk About Women's Liberation." *The Movement* (September 1969).

Brown, Angela Darlean. "Women and the Black Panther Party: An Interview with Angela Brown." *Socialist Review* 26 (1996).

Brown, Elaine. "A Taste of Power." *Essence* 23 (February 1993).

Buckley, William F., Jr. "Cleaver for President." *National Review*, 3 December 1968.

————. "Eldridge Cleaver, Come Home." *National Review*, 24 December 1976.

————. "Looking for a Home." *National Review*, 5 December 1975.

Burlingham, B. "Huey Newton's Revival Meeting in Oakland." *Ramparts Magazine* 11 (September 1972).

"Case of Clark Squire: Computer Programmer, Black Panther, Prisoner—Interim Report." *Computers and Automation* 20 (February 1971).

Cleaver, Eldridge, and K. Willenson. "Old Panther with a New Purr." *Newsweek,* 17 March 1975.

Cleaver, Kathleen Neal. "How TV Wrecked the Black Panthers." *Channels,* November-December 1982.

————. "Mobilizing for Mumia Abu-Jamal in Paris." *Yale Journal of Law and the Humanities* 10 (Summer 1998). International public opinion regarding Black Panther Party member convicted of the murder of a policeman.

————. "On Eldridge Cleaver." *Ramparts Magazine* 7 (June 1969).

"Cleaver and Berrigan." *Commonweal,* 14 June 1968. Editors assess two articles.

"Cleaver in Cuba." *Time,* 30 May 1969.

"Cleaver on Zionism." *Win,* 19 February 1976.

"Cleaver Speaks." *New York Times Magazine,* 1 November 1970. The opening of Panther headquarters in Algiers.

Cloud, Stanley. "Cleaver in Exile." *Time,* 24 October 1969. The author reported seeing Cleaver in a Moscow airport.

Coles, Robert. "Black Anger." *Atlantic,* June 1968. Review of *Soul on Ice.*

Collier, Peter. "Looking Backward: Memories of the Sixties Left." Chapter in *Political Passages,* ed. John Bunzel. New York: Free Press, 1988. Article about Cleaver.

"Contempt in Chicago." *Time,* 14 November 1969. Bobby Seale.

"Convincing Case for a Pardon." *Christianity Today,* 18 February 1977. Article about Cleaver.

Courtright, J. A. "Rhetoric of the Gun: An Analysis of the Rhetorical Mortifications of the Black Panther Party." *Journal of Black Studies* 4 (March 1974).

Cox, Craig. "Copycats: The New Black Panthers Struggle for Street Cred." *Utne Reader* 79 (January-February 1997). New groups are attempting to revive the BPP while the original members view that with disdain.

Cox, H. G. "Preventative War Against the Black Panthers." *Christianity and Crisis* 29 (5 January 1970).

Coyne, John R., Jr. "The Cleaver Compromise." *National Review,* 5 November 1968.

Cunningham, James. "The Case of the Severed Lifeline." *Negro Digest,* October 1969. Article about Cleaver.

de Gramont, Sanche. "Our Other Man in Algiers." *New York Times Magazine,* 1 November 1970. The opening of the Panther headquarters in Algiers.

"Disorder in the Court." *Time,* 7 November 1969. Bobby Seale.

Douglas, Emory. "Art in Service for the People." *Black Scholar* 9 (November 1977). Philosophy of Douglas, former artist for the Black Panther Party newspaper.

Douglass, Elaine. "Conversion of Eldridge Cleaver." *Encore,* 2 February 1976.

"Ex-FBI Agent Exposes Use of Information to Destroy BPP." *Freedom Magazine* 18 (January 1985).

"Eight Minus One is Seven." *Senior Scholastic* 95 (8 December 1969). Bobby Seale.

"Eldridge Cleaver." Chapter in *From Camelot to Kent State: The Sixties Experience in the Words of Those Who Lived* It, eds. Joan Morrison and Robert K. Morrison. New York: Times Books, 1987.

"Eldridge Cleaver Designs Pants 'for Men Only.'" *Jet*, 22 September 1978.

Epstein, Edward Jay. "The Panthers and the Police: A Pattern of Genocide?" *The New Yorker*, 13 February 1971. Panthers claim police killed 28 of their number.

Feaver, G. "Panther's Road to Suicide." *Encounter* 36 (May 1971).

Fischer, Mary A. "The Wrong Man." *GQ-Gentlemen's Quarterly*, March 1995. Geronimo ji-jaga Pratt.

Frame, Randy. "Whatever Happened to Eldridge Cleaver?" *Christianity Today*, 20 April 1984.

"Free Huey." *Newsweek,* 15 June 1970.

Fruchtman, Rob, and Carole Blue. "Eldridge Cleaver: Inside Speaking Out." *Berkeley Barb*, 30 July 1976.

Gates, Henry Louis. "Cuban Experience: Eldridge Cleaver on Ice," Part I. *Transition* 49 (1975).

_____. "Eldridge Cleaver on Ice: Algeria and After." *Ch'Indaba* 2 (1976). Part II of Gate's interview.

Gilman, Richard. "Review of *Soul on Fire*." *The New Republic*, 20 January 1979.

Giovanni, Nikki. "Leave It to Cleaver." *Encore*, 19 May 1975. Article about Cleaver.

Goldberg, A. "Changing Times Changed Cleaver." *In These Times*, 13 April 1977.

_____. "Panthers After the Trial." *Ramparts Magazine* 10 (March 1972).

Goldman, Peter. "The Panthers: Their Decline—and Fall?" *Newsweek*, 22 March 1971.

Goldsmith, Jeffrey S. "A Soul's Struggle" (review of *Soul on Fire*). *Christian Century*, May 1979.

Goodgame, Dan. "California's Crazy Primary." *Time*, 12 May 1986. Focus on Cleaver.

Henderson, William L., and Larry C. Ledebur. "Programs for the Economic Development of the American Negro Community: The Militant Approaches; the Moderate Approach." *American Journal of Economics and Sociology* 29 (October 1970). Includes Black Panther Party and the Black Muslims.

Hentoff, Nat. "*Playboy* Interview: Eldridge Cleaver." *Playboy*, December 1969. Overview of Cleaver's thoughts, reprinted in *Eldridge Cleaver: Post-Prison Writings and Speeches*.

Herve, Julia Wright. "The Black Scholar Interviews Kathleen Cleaver." *Black Scholar* 3 (December 1971).

Howard, Willie Abraham, Jr. "Black Panther (Requiem for Huey P. Newton)." *African American Review* 26 (Summer 1992). Poem.

"Huey Freed." *Newsweek,* 17 August 1970.

Jacobs, Paul. "The Return of the Native." *Mother Jones*, August 1976. Eldridge Cleaver.

Jennings, Regina B. "A Panther Remembers." *Essence* 21 (February 1991).

Johnson, Charles. "A Soul's Jagged Arc." *New York Times Magazine*, 3 January 1999.

Johnson, J. "Huey Newton in Prison: An Interview." *Ramparts Magazine* 9 (September 1970).

Johnson, Pamela. "The Last Revolutionary." *Essence*, November 1997. Interview with Geronimo ji-jaga Pratt after his release from prison.

Jones, Charles E. "The Political Repression of the Black Panther Party 1966–1971: The Case of the Oakland Bay Area." *Journal of Black Studies* 18 (June 1988).

Keerdoja, Eileen, and Pamela Abramson. "Once a Panther, Now a Crusader." *Newsweek*, 13 August 1979. Eldridge Cleaver.

Klapper, Zina. "Cleaver's a Sperm Lover." *Mother Jones*, September 1980.

Kleffner, Heike. "The Black Panthers: Interviews with Geronimo ji-jaga Pratt and Mumia Abu-Jamal." *Race and Class* 35 (July-September 1993).

Latimer, Phil. "Those Amazing Black Panthers." *Negro History Bulletin* 47 (July 1984).

Lewis, Ida. "Getting Ready for Eldridge Cleaver's New Revolutionary Tales." *Encore*, 22 September 1975.

————. "What's the Big Deal?" *Encore*, 22 December 1975. Both articles question Cleaver's politics.

Lukas, J. A. "Bobby Seale's Birthday Cake (Oh Far Out!)" *New York Times Magazine* 31 October 1971.

Marable, Manning. "Political Profiles: Eldridge Cleaver and Paul Robeson." *Alternatives* 2 (Winter 1980).

Marine, Gene. "Persecution and Assassination of the Black Panthers as Performed by the Oakland Police under the Direction of Chief Charles R. Gain, Mayor John Reading, et al." *Ramparts* 6 (29 June 1968).

Maust, John. "Cleaver: Gazing at a Different Moon." *Christianity Today*, 7 December 1979.

Mayfield, Julian. "New Mainstream." *Nation*, 13 May 1968. Eldridge Cleaver.

McClintock, David. "The Black Panthers: Negro Militants Use Free Food, Medical Aid to Promote Revolution: Anti-Capitalist Indoctrination Comes After Breakfast: Many Leaders Are Jailed." *Wall Street Journal* 29 August 1969.

McFadden, Jerome. "Eldridge Cleaver's Last Interview before Prison." *Sepia*, February 1976.

"Mistrial for Huey—II." *Newsweek,* 20 December 1971.

Montagno, Margaret. "Home, Sweet Home." *Newsweek*, 1 December 1975. Eldridge Cleaver.

Morgan, J. "Challenge of Bobby Seale." *New Statesman* 80 (31 July 1970).

Morrison, Joan, and Robert K. Morrison, eds. "Eldridge Cleaver." Chapter in *From Camelot to Kent State: The Sixties Experience in the Words of Those Who Lived It.* New York: Times Books, 1987.

Munford, Clarence J. "The Fallacy of Lumpen Ideology." *Black Scholar* 5 (July-August 1973).

Newton, Huey P. "He Won't Bleed Me: A Revolutionary Analysis of 'Sweet Sweetback's Baadasssss Song.'" *The Black Panther* 6 (19 June 1971).

Nieboer, Roger. "Guns and Huey Newton." *American Theatre* 12 (February 1995). Article about the biographical play, "Servant of the People."

Nower, Joyce. "Cleaver's Vision of America and the New White Radical: A Legacy of Malcolm X." *Negro American Literature Forum* 4 (March 1970).

"Other Voices, Other Strategies." *Time,* April 1970. Bobby Seale.

Pacion, Stanley. "Soul on Ice? The Talents and Troubles of Eldridge Cleaver." *Dissent* 16 (July-August 1969).

Parks, Gordon. "Eldridge Cleaver in Algiers: A Visit with Papa Rage." *Life,* 6 February 1970. Cleaver in exile.

_____. "What Became of the Prophets of Rage?" In "The Dream Then and Now." *Life* special issue, Spring 1988. A look at old radicals of the 1960s, including Eldridge Cleaver.

"The Party's Over." *Newsweek,* 5 September 1977. Eldridge Cleaver.

Poinsett, Alex. "Where Are the Revolutionaries?" *Ebony,* February 1976. Eldridge Cleaver.

Pratt, Geronimo ji-jaga, and Mumia Abu-Jamal. "The Black Panthers: Interviews with Geronimo Ji-jaga Pratt and Mumia Abu-Jamal." *Race and Class* 35 (July-September 1993).

Pringle, J. "Cleaver in Cuba." *Time,* 30 May 1969.

"Professor on Ice." *Time,* 27 September 1968. Eldridge Cleaver.

Rauber, Paul. "Cleaver Chases Dellums' Seat." *In These Times,* 22 February 1984.

Ritter, Bill. "Cleaver and Colson Praise the Lord." *In These Times,* 13 April 1977.

Rogers, Ray. "Panthers and Tribesmen: Black Guns on Campus." *Nation* 208 (5 May 1969). Panthers and Ron Karenga's US at UC.

Sayre, Nora. "Black Panthers Are Coming: America on the Eve of Race Revolution." *New Statesman* 77 (2 May 1969).

Schaeffer, Robert. "Wrapping Himself in the Flag." *East Bay Voice,* July 1976. Interview with Cleaver.

Schanche, Don A. "Burn the Mother Down." *Saturday Evening Post,* 16 November 1968. Interview of Cleaver.

_____. "Panthers against the Wall." *Atlantic,* May 1970. Eldridge Cleaver.

Schroth, Raymond A. "Cleage and Cleaver." *America,* 1 February 1969.

Seale, Bobby. "Selections From the Biography of Huey P. Newton: With an Introduction by Eldridge Cleaver." *Ramparts Magazine* 7 (26 October 1968).

_____. "Selections From the Biography of Huey P. Newton: With an Introduction by Eldridge Cleaver." *Ramparts Magazine* 7 (17 November 1968).

Simms, Gregory. "Cleaver Reveals Why He Didn't Surrender in His Sexy Suit." *Jet*, 18 November 1976.

Simon, Jacqueline. "Interview with Eldridge Cleaver." *Punto de Contacto/Point of Contact* 1 (1975). Interview before returning to the U.S.

Sokolov, R. A. "Inside the Panthers." *Newsweek*, 15 June 1970.

"Soul on the Lam." *Newsweek*, 9 December 1968. Eldridge Cleaver.

Stanton, Junious R. "Bobby Seale: The Last Original Panther." *About Time* 22 (October 1994).

Steel, Ronald. "Letters from Oakland: The Panthers." *New York Review of Books* 13 (11 September 1969).

Stephens, James M., Jr. "Inside Report on Transformed Black Panthers." *Jet*, 11 May 1972. Eldridge Cleaver.

"Still a Brother: Eldridge Cleaver's Overture to Huey P. Newton." *Black Male/Female Relationships* 2 (Winter 1981).

Swados, H. "Old Con, Black Panther, Brilliant Writer and Quintessential American." *New York Times Magazine*, 7 September 1969. Eldridge Cleaver.

Swaim, L. "Eldridge Cleaver." *North American Review* 5 (July 1968).

_____. "Interview With a Black Panther." *North American Review* 5 (July 1968).

"Tame Panthers? B. Seale's Oakland Mayoral Campaign." *Time*, 25 December 1972.

Taylor, Curtice. "Eldridge Cleaver: The *Rolling Stone* Interview." *Rolling Stone*, 11 September 1974. Paris interview.

"Then There Were Seven." *Newsweek*, 17 November 1969. Bobby Seale.

Thomas, Tony. "Black Nationalism and Confused Marxists." *Black Scholar* 4 (September 1972). Eldridge Cleaver.

Thompson, Cordell. "Changed Cleaver Returns to U.S." *Jet*, 4 December 1975.

_____. "Mrs. Eldridge Cleaver Returns to U.S. to Give State of Revolution Message." *Jet*, 2 December 1971.

Tinney, James S. "Views of a Regenerate Radical." *Christianity Today*, 8 June 1977. Cleaver interviewed by a Black Christian.

"Two for the Show." *Newsweek*, 10 November 1969. Bobby Seale.

Tyehimba, Cheo. "Panther Mania." *Essence* 25 (February 1995). History of activism.

Warnken, William P., Jr. "Eldridge Cleaver: From Savior to Saved." *Minority Voices* 1 (1977).

Watson, D. L. "Police and the Panther." *Crisis* 81 (January 1974).

Watts, Daniel H. "The Carmichael/Cleaver Debate." *Liberator*, September 1969.

"What Ever Happened to Eldridge Cleaver." *U.S. News and World Report* 9 June 1969.

"Whatever Happened to...Eldridge Cleaver?" *Ebony*, March 1988.

Willenson, Kim, and Jane Friedman. "Old Panther with a New Purr." *Newsweek*, 17 March 1975.

Williams, Yohuru. "American Exported Black Nationalism: The Student Coordinating Committee, the Black Panther Party, and the Worldwide Freedom Struggle, 1967–1972." *Negro History Bulletin* 60 (July–September 1997).

"Who Killed Alex Rackley?" *Newsweek,* 30 March 1970. Bobby Seale.

"A Word from the Peace and Freedom Candidate." *Newsweek*, 16 September 1968. Eldridge Cleaver.

Los Angeles, Including Watts

"Accolades for Cochran." *Jet*, 24 March 1997. Johnnie Cochran, Jr. honored at LA's Living Legends Series.

Adler, Patricia Rae. "Watts: A Legacy of Lines." *Westways* 58 (August 1966). Watts riot.

"The Affirmative Action War in California." *Black Enterprise*, November 1995.

"After the Blood Bath." *Newsweek,* 30 August 1965. Watts riot.

Alarcon, Evelina. "The Los Angeles Rebellion." *Political Affairs* (June 1992).

Allen, Gary. "The Plan to Burn Los Angeles." *American Opinion* 10 (May 1967). Watts riot. Author describes the Watts riot as a Communist conspiracy.

Allen, Gary, and Bill Richardson. "Los Angeles: Hell in the City of the Angels." *American Opinion* 8 (September 1965). The 1965 Watts riot.

Aptheker, Herbert. "The Watts Ghetto Uprising." *Political Affairs* 44 (October 1964).

Aubry, Erin J. "The L.A. Reality." *Black Enterprise*, November 1995.

"Bad Mass Transit a Factor in Watts Riot." *American City* 81 (November 1966).

Bart, Peter. "Panel on Watts Riots Warns of Further Racial Violence." *New York Times* (7 December 1965). Summary an analysis of McCone Commission report on the Los Angeles uprising of 1965.

Beck, Nicholas. "NAACP in Los Angeles." *California Sun Magazine* 11 (Fall and Winter, 1959–1960).

"Behind the Riots: Family Life Breakdown in Negro Slums Sows Seeds of Racial Violence; Husbandless Homes Spawn Young Hoodlums, Impede Reforms, Sociologists Say." *Wall Street Journal,* 16 August 1965. Los Angeles and Chicago riots of 1965.

Berkeley, Ellen P. "Workshop in Watts." *Architectural Forum* 130 (January–February 1969). The Urban Workshop, Black architectural planners.

Bianchi, Eugene C. "Los Angeles Tragedy: And Opportunity." *America* 113 (11 September 1965).

"Black Ghetto in Revolt." *Economist* 216 (21 October 1965). Watts riot.

"Blacks Losing Political Clout to Hispanics in Los Angeles." *Jet*, 19 May 1997.

Blauner, Robert. "Whitewash over Watts." *Trans-action* 3 (March–April 1966). Watts riot.

Boskin, Joseph, and Victor Pilson, M.D. "The Los Angeles Riot of 1965: A Medical Profile of an Urban Crisis." *Pacific Historical Review* 39 (August 1970). Analyzes emergency room records and finds the number of wounded was inflated.

Boskin, Joseph. "Violence in the Ghettos." *New Mexico Quarterly* 37 (Winter 1968). Partly concerns Watts riot.

Boyd, Malcolm. "Violence in Los Angeles." *Christian Century* 82 (8 September 1965).

Buggs, John A. "Report from Los Angeles." *Journal of Intergroup Relations* 5 (Autumn 1966). Watts riot.

Bullock, Paul, and Robert Singleton. "Some Problems of Minority-Group Education in the Los Angeles Public Schools." *Journal of Negro Education* 32 (Spring 1963). Focus on Blacks and Chicanos.

Bullock, Paul. "Poverty in Los Angeles: Facts and Fantasies About South and East Los Angeles." *Frontier* 17 (September 1966). Black and Mexican areas.

Bunch, Lonnie III. "A Past Not Necessarily Prologue: The African American in Los Angeles." Chapter in *20th Century Los Angeles: Power, Promotion, and Social Conflict,* eds. Norman M. Klein and Martin J. Schiesl. Claremont, CA: Regina Books, 1990.

Bunche, Ralph Johnson. "My Most Unforgettable Character." *Reader's Digest* 95 (September 1969). UN official describes Los Angeles upbringing.

Burma, John Harmon. "Interethnic Marriage in Los Angeles, 1948–1959." *Social Forces* 42 (December 1963).

Caughey, John Walton, and LaRee Caughey. "Decentrialization of the Los Angeles Schools: Front for Segregation." *Integrated Education* 41 (1969).

————. "Segregation Increases in Los Angeles." *CTA Journal* (October 1968).

Caughey, LaRee. "Los Angeles: No Birmingham West." *Frontier* 14 (July 1963).

Cervantes, Alfonso J. "To Prevent a Chain of Super-Watts." *Harvard Business Review* 45 (September 1967). Call for support of ghetto businesses.

"A Chronicle of Desegregation in Los Angeles." *Integrated Education* 20 (January-April 1982).

"Citing Bias against Minister, Blacks Picket and Close Korean Hat Shop in Los Angeles." *Jet*, 17 June 1996.

Cohen, Nathan E. "The Los Angeles Riot Study." *Social Work* 12 (October 1967).

Crabb, Riley Hansard. "Long Hot Week in Los Angeles." *Round Robin, The Journal of Borderland Studies* 21 (September 1965).

"Crime Without Punishment." *National Review*, 15 November 1993. Editorial about the failure to properly punish those who attacked Reginald Denny during the 1992 LA riots.

Crumbley, F. H. "A Los Angeles Citizen." *Colored American Magazine* 9 (September 1905).

Curtis, Lynn A. "One Year Later: The Los Angeles Riots and a New National Policy." *Denver University Law Review* 70 (1993).

Davis, Mike. "The L.A. Inferno. April 30." *Socialist Review* 22 (January-March 1992).

de Graaf, Lawrence B. "The City of Black Angels: Emergence of the Los Angeles Ghetto, 1890–1930." *Pacific Historical Review* 39 (August 1970).

DiPasquale, D., and Glaeser, E. L. "The Los Angeles Riot and the Economics of Urban Unrest." *Journal of Urban Economics* 43 (January 1989).

Djedje, Jacqueline Cogdell. "Gospel Music in the Los Angeles Black Community: A Historical Overview." *Black Music Research Journal* 9 (Spring 1989).

_____. "Los Angeles Composers of African-American Gospel Music: Composer Bibliography, the First Generation." *American Music* (Winter 1993).

"Does Anyone Really Care? Negroes Who Rioted in Los Angeles." *Christian Century* 82 (22 September 1965).

Dunne, John Gregory. "Law and Disorder in Los Angeles." *New York Review of Books* (October 10 and October 24, 1991). The L.A. police department and racism.

_____. "T.V.'s Riot Squad." *The New Republic*, 11 September 1965. Bias in television reporting of the Watts riot.

_____. "The Ugly Mood of Watts: Militant Leaders in Los Angeles' Negro Ghetto are Trying to Win Power by Threatening Whites with Violence—And Behind Their Threats Lies Hatred." *Saturday Evening Post* 239 (16 July 1966).

Eastman, Ralph. "Central Avenue Blues: The Making of Los Angeles Rhythm and Blues, 1942–1947." *Black Music Research Journal* 9 (Spring 1989).

Egly, Paul. "Los Angeles Experience." *Center Magazine* 15 (July-August 1982). Discussion on segregation.

"The 8th International Conference of Blacks in Dance and Dance in Black America II." *Talking Drums! The Journal of Black Dance* 5 (January 1995). The 1994 International Conference of Blacks in Dance, Los Angeles.

Ewing, Nadia et al. "Newborn Diagnosis of Abnormal Hemoglobins from a Large Municipal Hospital in Los Angeles." *American Journal of Health* 71 (June 1981).

"Fallen Angels." *The New Republic*, 9 June 1969. Thomas Bradley's campaign for mayor of Los Angeles.

"First Negro History Class in Los Angeles City Schools at Dorsey Adult School." *Negro History Bulletin* 25 (October 1961).

Flamming, Douglas. "African Americans and the Politics of Race in Progressive-Era Los Angeles." Chapter in *California Progressivism Revisited*, eds. William Deverall and Tom Sitton. Berkeley: University of California Press, 1994.

Fogelson, Robert M. "White on Black: A Critique of the McCone Commission Report on the Los Angeles Riots." *Political Science Quarterly* 82 (September 1967). Questions the results of the commission.

Fowler, John W. *Spreading Joy*. Los Angeles: n.p., 1937. Selections from the author's column "Spreading Joy" that appeared in various Black California newspapers.

Garciá, Mikel. "Black Women as Community Builders—Los Angeles, 1896–1920." *NWSA Perspectives* 5 (Spring-Summer 1987).

Garneau, George. "Minority Teamwork: Black, Hispanic Newspapers Team Up in Los Angeles Area." *Editor and Publisher, the Fourth Estate* 128 (14 January 1999). Merging of non-editorial operations of Urban Newspapers of Los Angeles and Central News-Wave Publications to form the Wave Community Newspapers.

Germond, Jack W. "L.A.'s About to say 'So Long, Sam'!" *The New Republic*, 24 May 1969. The mayoral campaign of Sam Yorty and Thomas Bradley.

Giles, Dari. "City of Angels: While You're in Town on Business, Find Time to Work on L.A.'s After-Work Life." *Black Enterprise*, January 1998. Tour guide for business people.

Goldstein, Michael. "The Political Careers of Fred Roberts and Tom Bradley: Political Style and Black Politics in Los Angeles." *Western Journal of Black Studies* 5 (Summer 1981).

Goodman, George W. "Watts, U.S.A.: A Post Mortem." *Crisis* 72 (October 1965). Watts riot.

Grigsby, J. Eugene III, and Mary L. Hruby. "Recent Changes in the Housing Status of Blacks in Los Angeles." *Review of Black Political Economy* 19 (Winter-Spring 1991).

Grigsby, J. Eugene III. "The Rise and Decline of Black Neighborhoods in Los Angeles." *CAAS Report* 12 (Spring-Fall 1989).

Gutierrez, Henry J. "Racial Politics in Los Angeles: Black and Mexican American Challenges to Unequal Education in the 1960s." *Southern California Quarterly* 78 (Spring 1996).

Hacker, Frederick J. "What the McCone Commission Didn't See." *Frontier* 17 (March 1966). Watts riot.

Hahn, Harlan, and Timothy Almy. "Ethnic Politics and Racial Issues: Voting in Los Angeles." *Western Political Quarterly* 24 (December 1971). Voting patterns in the 1969 mayoral election.

Haines, Aubrey. "Words...and Deeds." *Frontier* 7 (August 1956). Los Angeles restrictive housing covenants.

Hall, Martin H. "What God Hath Wrought: Experiment in Church Integration in Los Angeles." *Frontier* 8 (September 1957).

Hamamoto, Darrell Y. "Black-Korean Conflict in Los Angeles." *Z Magazine* 5 (July 1992).

Hannon, Michael. "Behind the Watts Revolt." *New Politics* 4 (Summer 1965).

Harris, Joanne. "Portfolio." *American Visions*, August–September 1996. Profiles of artists Barbara Thomas and Marita Dingus of Seattle and Kira Lynn Harris of Los Angeles.

Hayden, Delores. "Biddy Mason's Los Angeles, 1851–1891." *California History* 68 (Fall 1989).

Henehan, Anne. "On-The-Spot In Watts...Facing the Problems of Minority Ghettos in Today's Cities." *Senior Scholastic* 89 (20 January 1967).

Herbert, Solomon J. "Blacks Who Migrated West between 1915 and 1945." *Crisis* 98 (February 1990). Black migration from the South to California.

Herman, Melvin, and Flora Rheta Schreiber. "Psychiatrists Analyze the Los Angeles Riots." *Science Digest* 58 (November 1965).

Heussenstamm, F. K. "Bumper Stickers and the Cops." *Trans-action* 8 (1971). LA police give traffic citations to drivers who sport Black Panther stickers on their cars.

Hicks, Joe, Antonio Villaragosa, and Angela Oh. "Los Angeles Rebellion and Beyond." *Against the Current* 40 (September-October 1992).

"Hidden Community: The Los Angeles Negro." *Frontier* 6 (June 1955).

Hohn, F. R. "What's Happening? Council of Black Administrators." *Journal of Secondary Education* 44 (February 1969). Administrators from Los Angeles.

———. "What's Happening? Project APEX, Los Angeles." *Journal of Secondary Education* 42 (November 1967). Busing program to alleviate segregation.

Hulet, Diana. "McDaniel, 20-ish, Does Hollywood Her Way." *American Photo*, May–June 1995. Hollywood's Melodie McDaniel.

Hutson, H. Range, Deidre Anglin, Demetrios N. Kyriacou, Joel Hart and Kelvin Spears. "The Epidemic of Gang-Related Homicides in Los Angeles County from 1979 through 1984." *JAMA, The Journal of the American Medical Association* 274 (4 October 1995). Epidemic numbers of Black homicides in Los Angeles city and county.

"The Insurrection." *Frontier* 16 (September 1965). Watts riot.

Jackson, Morton B. "Second Civil War—A Closer Look at Los Angeles Riots." *U.S. News and World Report,* 20 September 1965.

Jacobs, Paul. "The Lower Depths in Los Angeles." *Midstream* 13 (May 1967). Unemployed Blacks and employment agencies.

Jeffe, Jerry. "Diversity in south Central." *California Journal* 26 (February 1995). Blacks and Korean-Americans strive for reconciliation following the 1992 riot.

Jeffries, Vincent, and H. Edward Ransford. "Interracial Social Contact and Middle-Class White Reactions to the Watts Riot." *Social Problems* 16 (Winter 1969).

"Jo Baker Goes to Hollywood." *Ebony*, August 1952. Performer Josephine Baker's opening night at L.A.'s Criss, and the star-studded audience.

Johnson, Charles. "Negro Workers in Los Angeles Industries." *Opportunity* 6 (August 1928).

Johnson, James Weldon. "Robert C. Owens, a Pacific Coast Successful Negro: Adapted from Notes Furnished by James W. Johnson." *Colored American Magazine* 9 (July 1905). Famous writer presents a Black L.A. resident.

Johnson, Paula B., Davis O. Sears, and John B. McConahay. "Black Invisibility, the Press, and the Los Angeles Riot." *American Journal of Sociology* 76 (1971). Examines Black invisibility in the press from 1892, during the riot, and afterward.

Jordan, June. "The Truth of Rodney King." *Progressive* 57 (June 1993).

Kandel, Susan. "Museum of African American Art, Los Angeles: Exhibit." *Arts Magazine* 66 (December 1991).

"Karl Fleming of *Newsweek* is Beaten Up Getting a Story in Watts." *New South* 21 (Summer 1966). Watts riot.

Keaton, Diane. "The Presiding Judge." *California Lawyer* 8 (September 1988). Candace Cooper of the Los Angeles Superior Court is elected president of the California Judges Association.

Kerby, Phil. "Minorities Oppose Los Angles School System: Persistent Desegregation." *Christian Century* 85 (4 September 1968).

_____. "Race, Television and Yorty." *Nation* 208 (31 March 1969). The Sam Yorty and Thomas Bradley mayoral campaign.

_____. "The Report on the McCone Commission Report on Watts." *Frontier* 17 (February 1966). Watts riot.

_____. "Riding Shotgun in Watts." *Nation* 207 (2 September 1968). Watts riot.

_____. "Victory for a Specter." *Nation* 208 (16 June 1969). Sam Yorty and Thomas Bradley mayoral campaign.

Kifano, Subira. "Afrocentric Education in Supplementary Schools: Paradigm and Practice at the Mary McLeod Bethune Institute." *Journal of Negro Education* 65 (Spring 1996). Report on an Afrocentric supplementary school.

"King Cole Decorates His New Home." *Ebony*, April 1949. Nat "King" Cole's new house and negative reactions from L.A. neighbors.

King, Martin Luther, and M. L. Schwartz. "Beyond the Los Angeles Riots." *Saturday Review* (13 November 1965).

Kirschman, Richard. "Actors 'On Cue' for Watts Workshop." *Urban West* 2 (February 1969). Sidney Poitier, Greg Morris, and Talmadge Sprott interviewed about Douglass House.

Kissinger, C. Clark. "L.A. Revisited: A Riot Recast as Rebellion." *National Catholic Reporter* (18 September 1992).

Kopkind, Andrew. "Lesson of Watts." *New Statesman* 70 (17 December 1965).

_____. "The Spectre of Watts Returns." *New Statesman* 71 (3 June 1966).

_____. "Watts, Waiting for D-Day." *The New Republic*, 11 June 1966.

"L.A. Attorney Crispus Attucks Wright Gives USC Law School $2 Million." Jet, 11 August 1997." Retired civil attorney donates money to the Wright Scholarship Endowment, the largest gift ever from a Black person.

Larsen, Cecil Evva. "Control Patterns in an Interracial School: The Thomas Jefferson High School in East Los Angeles." *Sociology and Social Research* 30 (May 1946).

"Learn, Baby, Learn." *Los Angeles Magazine* 10 (October 1965). Watts riot.

"Lessons of Los Angeles." *New Statesman* 70 (20 August 1965). Watts riot.

Lomax, Almena (Davis). "The Muslim Trial in Los Angeles." *Frontier* 14 (July 1963).

"Loren Miller, January 30, 1903–July 14, 1967." *Crisis* 74 (August-September 1967). Los Angeles jurist and journalist.

"Loren Miller's Contributions." *Crisis* 74 (August-September 1967). Los Angeles jurist and journalist.

"Los Angeles: A Civil Revolt." *Liberation* 10 (October 1965). Watts riot.

"Los Angeles en feu." *Paris Match* (28 August 1965). Watts riot.

"Los Angeles Jury Awards Three Black Men $611,000 in Brutality Case Against Sheriff's Dept." *Jet*, 14 August 1995.

"The Los Angeles Negro." *Frontier* 6 (June 1955).

"Los Angeles 1972: A Panorama of Black Artists." Los Angeles County Museum of Art, Los Angeles, California. February 8–March 19, 1972. Catalogue.

"Los Angeles Riot Heaps Nisei Business with $1 Million Loss." *Pacific Citizen* 61 (20 August 1965).

"Los Angeles Searches for Answer to Riots." *Business World* (21 August 1965).

"Los Angeles Riot." *Crisis* 72 (August–September 1965).

"Lou Rawls at Home: He Feels Like a Natural Man." *Ebony*, September 1985. Singer Rawls interviewed at his home in the Hancock Park section of Los Angeles.

Mallory, Maria. "'Don't Let Disappointment Dis You.'" *Business Week*, 22 November 1993. The 1st African Methodist Episcopal Church and its programs.

Marmorstein, Gary. "Central Avenue Jazz: Los Angeles Black Music of the Forties." *Southern California Quarterly* 70 (Winter 1988).

Marx, Wesley. "The Negro Community: A Better Chance." *Los Angeles* 3 (March 1962).

Mason, William M., and James Anderson. "Los Angeles Black Heritage." *Museum Alliance Quarterly* 8 (Winter 1969-70).

Mastronarde, Linda. "Watts—A Colonial Situation." *Community* 27 (September 1967).

Maxted, Julia, and Abebe Zegeye. "Race, Class and Polarization in Los Angeles." Chapter in *Exploitation and Exclusion: Race and Class in Contemporary U.S. Society*, eds. Abebe Zegeye, et al. London: Hans Zell, 1991.

McConahay, John B. "Attitudes of Negroes toward the Church following the Los Angeles Riot." *Sociological Analysis* 31 (1970).

McCord, William. "Burn, Baby, Burn." *The New Leader* 48 (August 1965).

_____. and John Howard. Negro Opinions in Three Riot Cities. *American Behavioral Scientist* 11 (March 1968). Includes Los Angeles and Oakland.

McGrory, Mary. "A New Outburst in Watts." *America* 114 (2 April 1966).

McWilliams, Carey. "Watts: The Forgotten Slum." *Nation* 201 (30 August 1965). Watts riot.

Meriwether, Louise M. "What the People of Watts Say." *Frontier* 16 (October 1965).

Merrill, R. J. "Shaping a Future." *Artweek* 23 (27 February 1992). Palmer C. Hayden exhibition.

Metcalf, Allen C. "A Negro Congressman from Los Angeles?" *Frontier* 9 (April 1958). Possible results through redrawing of election district boundaries.

Metz, William. "Negro Segregation in Los Angeles—Does it Exist?" *California Sun Magazine* 12 (Fall-Winter 1960).

Meyer, Marshall W. "Police Shootings at Minorities: The Case of Los Angeles." *Annals of the American Academy of Political and Social Science* 452 (1980).

"Miss Gabby Lee." *Ebony*, April 1955. Torch singer Lee performs in L.A.

Moore, E. T. "Library Burns in the Los Angeles Riot: Willowbrook Branch." *ALA Bulletin* 59 (December 1965).

Morris, Richard T., and Vincent Jeffries. "Violence Next Door." *Social Forces* 46 (1968). A study on six white communities after the Watts riot.

Moss, Rick. "Not Quite Paradise: The Development of the African American Community in Los Angeles through 1950." *California History* 75 (1996).

Moynihan, Daniel Patrick. "Behind Los Angeles: Jobless Negroes and the Boom." *Reporter* 33 (9 September 1965). The 1965 riot.

Muller, Gilbert H. "Double Agent: The Los Angeles Crime Cycle of Walter
       Mosley." Chapter in *Los Angeles in Fiction: A Collection of Essays*,
       ed. David Fine. Albuquerque: University of New Mexico Press, 1995.

Murty, K. S. "The Black Community's Reactions to the 1992 Los Angeles
       Riot." *Deviant Behavior* (January-March 1994). Interview of 227
       Black community members, including 26 who participated in the riot.

Myers, Chris. "View from South Central." *International Review of African
       American Art* 13 (Winter 1996). The Art Team of LA works with tal-
       ented youth.

"'Negro After Watts.' *Time* Essay." *Time,* 27 August 1965.

"Negro Police Officers in Los Angeles, by One of Los Angeles' Negro Police
       Officers, Who, for Obvious Reasons Remains Anonymous." *Crisis* 41
       (August 1934).

Nevins, Allan. "Dateline Watts: From the Ashes, A Solution." *Saturday Re-
       view* 50 (23 September 1967).

"No Busing for Watts." *Nation* 206 (18 March 1968). Watts riot.

Norman, Alex J. "Black-Korean Relations: From Desperation to Dialogue, or
       from Shouting to Shooting to Sitting and Talking." *Journal of Multi-
       cultural Social Work* 3 (1994).

Norris, Bill. "LA Flats Come Complete with a Teacher." *Times Educational
       Supplement* 4004 (26 March 1993). EEXCELL (Educational Excel-
       lence for Children with Environmental Limitations) project.

"Not Just America." *Economist* 216 (21 August 1965). Watts riot.

"Noted Neurosurgeon Keith Black to Head Brain Cancer Institute at Cedars-Sinai
       in L.A." *Jet*, 23 June 1997. Specialist in malignant tumors will head
       the new unit.

Novick, Michael. "L.A. Nazi Leader Found guilty in Cross-burning." [NYC]
       Guardian (13 November 1991). Tom Metzger and the White Aryan Re-
       sistance.

_____. "Nazi Confab Poses as Black History Event." [NYC] *Guardian* (12
       February 1992). L.A. event.

Oberschall, Anthony R. "Los Angeles Riot of August, 1965." *Social Prob-
       lems* 15 (Winter 1968).

"Objective and Dispassionate Study?" *Social Service Review* 40 (March 1966).
       McCone report of Watts riot.

Oliver, M., and J. Johnson. "Inter-Ethnic Conflict in an Urban Ghetto: The
       Case of Blacks and Latinos in Los Angeles." *Research in Social
       Movements, Conflict and Change* 6 (1984).

Oliver, M., et al. "Brown and Black in White: The Social Adjustment and Aca-
       demic Performance of Chicano and Black Students in a Predominantly
       White University." *Urban Review* 17 (1985). Experiences at UCLA.

Olson, E. "APEX, an Area Concept." *Journal of Secondary Education* 43 (No-
       vember 1968). Los Angeles voluntary desegregation plan.

Orfield, Gary. "Lessons of the Los Angeles Desegregation Case." *Education
       and Urban Society* 16 (May 1984).

Orpaz, Yitshak. "Judgment Day in Los Angeles." *Atlas* 11 (April 1966). Watts riot.

Page, Donald. "Watts—One year Later." *Employment Service Review* 3 (August 1966).

Panunzio, Constantine Marie. "Intermarriage in Los 'Angeles, 1924–33." *American Journal of Sociology* 47 (March 1942).

Parker, Michael. "Watts: The Liberal Response." *New Politics* 4 (Summer 1965).

Parrott, Wanda Sue. "Studio Watts Workshop." *Arts and Society* 5 (Fall–Winter 1968). Workshop for dropouts established in 1965.

"A Past Not Necessarily Prologue: The Afro-American in Los Angeles," In *20th Century Los Angeles: Power, Promotion, and Social Conflict*, eds. Norman M. Klein and Martin J. Schiesl. Claremont, CA: Regina Books, 1990.

Patterson, Beeman Coolidge. "Political Action of Negroes in Los Angeles: A Case Study in the Attainment of Councilmanic Representation." *Phylon* 30 (Summer 1969).

Pearson, Martin. "From Gambia to Los Angeles." *New Law Journal* 6657 (22 July 1994). Edi Faal, born in Gambia, wins acquittal for accused man charged with beating Reginald Denny.

Perry, Mary Ellen. "The Prizefighter–Professor Heads a Black Curriculum." *Urban West* 1 (August 1968). Nathan Hare at California State College-Los Angeles.

Poe, Elizabeth. "Segregation in the Los Angeles Schools." *Frontier* 13 (October 1962).

————. "Watts." *Frontier* 16 (September 1965). Watts riot.

"Prejudice Still a Big Factor in Housing." *USA Today*, April 1997. Based on the Los Angeles Survey of Urban Inequality, white hostility and institutional discrimination contribute to segregation.

Pynchon, Thomas. "A Journey into the Mind of Watts." *New York Times Magazine*, 11 June 1966.

"The Racial Disturbance in Los Angeles." *Frontier* 13 (June 1962).

Ransford, Harry Edward. "Isolation, Powerlessness, and Violence: A Study of Attitudes and Participation in the Watts Riot." *American Journal of Sociology* 73 (March 1968).

Rappaport, Michael D. "Placement Patterns of University of California-Los Angeles Law School Minority Graduates." *Black Law Journal* 7 (Fall 1981). Address of Rappaport concerning career patterns of minority attorneys.

"Report from Los Angeles, The Watts Riot of 1965." *Journal of Intergroup Relations* 5 (Autumn 1966).

Reynolds, Anthony M. "Urban Negro Toasts: A Hustler's View from L.A." *Western Folklore* 33 (1974).

Richardson, Henry J. III. "The International Implications of the Los Angeles Riots." *Denver University Law Review* 70 (1993). Exporting racism.

Roberts, Myron. "The Angela Heresy." *Los Angeles* 14 (November 1969).

_____. "If It's Bradley...." *Los Angeles* 14 (May 1969). If Thomas Bradley won the mayoral election.

_____. "The Plot to Seize Los Angeles." *Los Angeles* 14 (January 1969). The Thomas Bradley mayoral campaign.

_____. "Summertime: Will the Livin' be Easy." *Los Angeles* 13 (June 1968). Thomas Bradley and the Los Angeles community.

_____. "A Whitey's Tour of Watts." *Los Angeles* 13 (June 1968). Watts riot.

Roberts, S. V. "Russians Are Coming at UCLA: The Firing of A. Davis." *Commonweal* 91 (November 1969).

Robertson, Gil. "Inside Leimert Park: This Three-Sq.-Mile Commercial Center is an Example of a Community Recycling Its Dollars." *Black Enterprise*, June 1997. Designed by Frederick Law Olmsted and formerly restricted to whites, this LA planned community is now the home to middle-class Blacks.

Robinson, Louie. "This Would Never Have Happened...If They Hadn't Kicked that Man: Police Action Ignites Fiery L.A. Riot." *Ebony,* 20 (October 1965).

Roemer, M. I. "Health Resources and Services in the Watts Area of Los Angeles." *California's Health* 23 (February-March 1966).

Roseman, Curtis C. , and Seong Woo. "Linked and Independent African American Migration from Los Angeles." *Professional Geographer* 50 (May 1998).

Rossell, Christine H. "Is It the Busing or the Blacks?: Research Note." *Urban Affairs Quarterly* 24 (September 1988). Busing for integration in Baton Rouge and Los Angeles.

Rustin, Bayard. "Some Lessons from Watts." *Journal of Intergroup Relations* 5 (Autumn 1966). Watts riot.

_____. "The Watts' Manifesto.'" *New America* (17 September 1965). Watts riot.

_____. "The Watts 'Manifesto' and the McCone Report." *Commentary* 41 (March 1966). Watts riot.

_____. "The Watts 'Manifesto' and the McCone Report." Chapter in *Racism in California*, eds. Roger Daniels and Spencer C. Olin, Jr. New York: Macmillan, 1972.

"Sam of Watts." *Arts and Architecture* 68 (July 1951). Simon Rodia, builder of the Watts Towers.

Sanders, Stanley. "The Other Alternative." *Black World* 15 (May 1966). Watts riot.

_____. "Riot as a Weapon: The Language of Watts." *Nation* 201 (20 December 1965). Lack of understanding between Blacks and whites will lead to more riots.

Sayre, Nora. "Conversations in Watts." *New Statesman* 75 (2 February 1968). Watts riot.

Schneider, Mark, and Thomas Phelan. "Blacks and Jobs: Never the Twain Shall Meet?" *Urban Affairs Quarterly* 26 (December 1990). Data collected in New York City, Chicago and Los Angeles indicate that Blacks who move from the inner-city do no relocate to suburbs that have jobs.

Schneider, William. "Shattering an Urban Liberal Coalition." *National Journal* 29 (19 April 1997). The reelection of Richard Riodan as LA mayor.

Schreiber, Flora Rheta, and Melvin Herman. "Psychiatrists Analyze the Los Angeles riots." *Science Digest* 58 (November 1965).

Schulberg, Budd. "The Angry Voices of Watts." *Los Angeles* 11 (June 1966). Watts riot.

Scoble, Harry M. "McCone Commission and Social Science." *Phylon* 29 (Summer 1968). Watts riot.

Scott, Johnie. "How Is It—My Home is Watts." *Harpers Magazine* 233 (October 1966). School integration.

"Search for Why's." *Senior Scholastic* 87 (23 September 1965). Watts riot.

Sears, David O. "Black Attitudes Toward the Political System in the Aftermath of the Watts Insurrection." *Midwest Journal of Political Science* 13 (November 1969).

Sears, David O., and John B. McConahay. "Participation in the Los Angeles Riot." *Social Problem* 17 (Summer 1969).

Sears, David O., and Tommy Mack Tomlinson. "Riot Ideology in Los Angeles: A Study of Negro Attitudes. *Social Science Quarterly* 49 (December 1968). Watts riot.

Seidenbaum, Art. "Los Angeles: Private Integration of the Public Schools. *Integrated Education.* (November-December 1968).

Selby, Earl, and Anne Selby. "Watts: Where Welfare Bred Violence." *Reader's Digest* 88 (May 1966). Watts riot.

"A Self Help Program Stirs a Negro Slum: Some Idealistic Young Negroes, With an Assist From Business, Are Training Watts District Los Angeles, California, Residents for Jobs, Are Setting and Example That Is Helping the Hard Core Poor in Other Cities." *Business Week*, 25 March 1967.

Sepia (November 1965). Issue devoted to various aspects of the Watts riot.

Sherman, Jimmie. "From the Ashes: A Personal Reaction to the Revolt of Watts." *Antioch Review* 27 (Fall 1967). Personal account of the Watts riot.

"A Shift in the Wind in Washington: Riots, Pillage, Violence Defiance of Law and Order; There Is Worry in Washington That things Have Gone Too Far, That a Public Reaction Is Setting In: Danger Facing Big Cities; Negro Life Deteriorating, the Negro Family Structure Approaching Complete Breakdown: Equal Rights Assured By Law Are Turning Out Not to Be the Complete Answer to Negro Problems: For a Shocked Los Angeles Now the Morning After; What's It Like Trying to Pick Up the Pieces After a Negro Uprising in a Big City." *U.S. News and World Report*, 6 September 1965.

Shorr, Howard. "'Race Prejudice is Not Inborn—It is Learned': The Exhibit Controversy at the Los Angeles Museum of History, Science and Art." *California* 69 (Fall 1990). Study of 1950–1952 exhibit "Man in Our Changing World" and its impact on race relations in L.A.

Sides, Josh. "Battle on the Home Front: African American Shipyard Workers in World War II Los Angeles." *California History* 75 (1996).

_____. "'You Understand My Condition': The Civil Rights Congress in the Los Angeles African-American Community, 1946–1952." *Pacific Historical Review* 67 (May 1998). The CRC's civil rights campaign.

Simmons, Dackeyla Q. "Building Hope in Los Angeles." *Black Enterprise*, September 1989. A $50 million partnership between Chase Manhattan Mortgage Corporation, the Los Angeles Urban League, and Operation Hope to make home ownership a reality.

Singleton, Robert, and P. Bullock. "Some Problems in Minority-Group Education in Los Angeles Public Schools." *Journal of Negro Education* 32 (Spring 1963).

Skinner, Robert E. "Streets of Fear: The Los Angeles Novels of Chester Himes." Chapter in *Los Angeles in Fiction: A Collection of Essays*, ed. David Fine. Albuquerque: University of New Mexico Press, 1995.

Sollen, Robert H. "The Insurrection." *Frontier* 16 (September 1965).

"Some Problems in Minority Group Education in the Los Angeles Public Schools." *Journal of Negro Education* 32 (Spring 1963).

Sonenshein, Raphael J. "The Dynamics of Biracial Coalitions: Crossover Politics in Los Angeles." *Western Political Quarterly* 42 (June 1989).

"Statement of Representatives of Black Students Union: California State College, Los Angeles." *California Digest* 1 (December 1968).

Sun, William H., and Fay C. Fei. "The Colored Theatre of Los Angeles." *TDR* 36 (Summer 1992).

"Symposium on Watts 1965." *Law in Transition Quarterly* 3 (Summer 1966). The law and those involved in the Watts riot.

Takahashi, Dean. "The L.A. Riots and Media Preparedness." *Editor and Publisher* (23 May 1992). *L.A. Times* reporting by one of its writers.

Takeuchi, David T., Stanley Sue, and May Yeh. "Return Rates and Outcomes from Ethnicity-Specific Mental Health Programs in Los Angeles." *American Journal of Public Health* 85 (1995).

Taylor, William C. "Storm Over Los Angeles." *Political Affairs* 44 (October 1965).

"Terror in Los Angeles: Interview with a Policeman Assigned to the Watts Area." *National Review*, 7 September 1965. Watts riot.

Terry, Don. "A Multiracial Farewell to 'Mama'; Slain Korean Bridged Racial Chasm in a Section of Los Angeles." *New York Times*, 12 February 1999. Blacks and Korean-Americans honor Chung-bok Hong, slain in a robbery.

Terry, Dorothy Givens. "From ABCs to EKGs." *Black Issues in Higher Education* 12 (16 November 1995). Special programs for aspiring minority doctors at the Charles R. Drew University of Medicine.

Thompson, Noah Davis. "California: The Horn of Plenty." *Messenger* 6 (July 1924). Blacks in Los Angeles.

"Trouble from Los Angeles." *Economist* 218 (19 March 1966).

Unseem, B. "The State and Collective Disorders: The Los Angeles Riot/Protest of April 1992." *Social Forces* 75 (December 1997).

Waldinger, Roger. "Black/Immigrant Competition Re-Assessed: New Evidence from Los Angeles." *Sociological Perspectives* 40 (Fall 1997).

Waldman, Tom. "Light-Rail Run-Around?: Los Angeles Transit Line By-Passes Blacks." *California Journal* 21 (March 1990).

Walker, Olive. "Windsor Hills School Story: Black School's I.Q. Highest in Los Angeles." *Integrated Education—Race and School* 8 (May 1970).

"Watts: The Forgotten Slum." *Nation* 201 (30 August 1965).

"Watts and the 'War on Poverty.'" *Political Affairs* 44 (October 1965).

"A Watts Report: No Progress; The Plight of Los Angeles Ghettos Is, If Anything, Bleaker Than Before the Riots." *Business Week,* 14 August 1971.

"Watts Revisited." *Economist* 220 (13 August 1966). Watts riot.

Weatherwax, John M. "Los Angeles 1781." *Negro History Bulletin* 18 (1954).

Weinberg, Carl. "Educational Level and Perceptions of Los Angeles Negroes of Educational Conditions in a Riot Area." *Journal of Negro Education* 36 (Fall 1967).

Weinberg, Meyer. "Bibliography of Desegregation: Los Angeles." *Integrated Education* 20 (January-April 1982).

"What for Watts?" *Economist* 217 (11 December 1965). Watts riot.

Wheeldin, Donald. "The Situation in Watts Today." *Freedomways* 7 (Winter 1967).

Wilkinson, Frank. "And Now the Bill Comes Due." *Frontier* 16 (October 1965). Watts riot.

Williams, Robert L. "The Negro's Migration to Los Angeles, 1900–1946." *Negro History Bulletin* 19 (July 1965). Migration patterns and adjustments.

Williford, Stanley O. "Watts—Five years Later." *Black Politician* 2 (October 1970).

Wilson, Joyce R. "Why the Watts Festival Failed." *Urban West* 3 (October 1969).

Work, Lena Brown. "A Different View of Watts: Follow-Up Report." *Harper's Magazine* 234 (May 1967). Successful graduates of Jordan High School.

Oakland

Abron, JoNina M. "Reflections of a Former Oakland Public School Parent." *Black Scholar* 27 (Summer 1997). Parent who was a teacher at a school founded by the Black Panthers examines education of daughter in the Oakland (California) and Kalamazoo (Michigan) school systems.

Brown, Ann. "Oakland's Renaissance." *Black Enterprise*, June 1996. Feature article includes travel and information.

Buel, Ronald A. "Creating a Slum: Banks, City, Landlords Contribute to Decay in Ghetto in Oakland; Curbless Streets, Rundown Housing Deter Lenders; Absentee Owners Assailed." *Wall Street Journal*, 30 January 1969.

Burlingham, B. "Huey Newton's Revival Meeting in Oakland." *Ramparts Magazine* 11 (September 1972).

"California Black Craftsmen." Mills College Art Gallery, Oakland, California. February 15–March 8, 1972. Catalogue.

"A Crisis in Any Language." *U.S. News and World Report*, 13 January 1997. The Oakland School Board and Ebonics.

"'Ebonics' Not Mentioned in Oakland's Final Report." *Black Issues in Higher Education* 14 (29 May 1997).

Ekberg, Dennis, and Claude Ury. "'Education for What?' A Report on an M. D. T. A. Program." *Journal of Negro Education* 37 (Winter 1968). The MDTA program in West Oakland.

Elliott, Merle Hugh, and Alden W. Badal. "Achievement and Racial Composition of Schools." *California Journal of Educational Research* 16 (September 1965). Oakland schools.

Fields, Cheryl D. "Ebonics 101: What Have We Learned?" *Black Issues in Higher Education* 13 (23 January 1997).

Fried, Michael. "W. Elmer Keeton and His WPA Chorus: Oakland's Musical Civil Rights Pioneers of the New Deal Era." *California History* 75 (1996).

Fullilove, R. E., et al. "Risk of Sexually Transmitted Disease among Black Adolescent Crack Users in Oakland and San Francisco, Calif." *JAMA* 263 (9 February 1990).

"Furor Over Ebonics." *Black Issues in Higher Education* 13 (9 January 1997).

Gura, Mark. "Fixated on Ebonics: Let's Concentrate on the Kids." *Educational Leadership* 54 (April 1997).

Hansen, J. L. "Residential Segregation of Blacks by Income Group: Evidence From Oakland." *Population Research and Policy Review*, 1996.

Heilbron, Jacob. "Speech Therapy: Ebonics: It's Worse Than You Think." *The New Republic*, 20 January 1997.

_____. "Speech Therapy Pundits are Slamming the Oakland School Board for Calling Black English a Separate Language." *The New Republic*, 20 January 1997.

Johnson, Marilynn S. "Urban Arsenals: War Housing and Social Change in Richmond and Oakland, California, 1941–1945." *Pacific Historical Review* 60 (August 1991). Evolution of race relations.

Jones, Charles E. "The Political Repression of the Black Panther Party 1966–1971: The Case of the Oakland Bay Area." *Journal of Black Studies* 18 (June 1988).

Kirp, David L. "Race, Schooling, and Interest Politics: The Oakland Story." *School Review* 87 (August 1979). School desegregation in Oakland.

Leland, John, and Nadine Joseph. "Hooked on Ebonics." *Newsweek*, 13 January 1997. The Oakland controversy.

Les, Kathleen. "Oakland." *California Journal* 29 (June 1988). Poor economic conditions among the 44% Black population.

Malveaux, Julianne. "Sidetracked by Pundocracy: Speaking of Education." *Black Issues in Higher Education* 13 (23 January 1997). The Ebonics controversy in Oakland.

Mary, Judith V. "Two Model Cities: Negotiations in Oakland." *Politics and Society* 2 (1971). Factions within the program.

McEntire, Sterling M. "A Study of Racial Attitudes in Neighborhoods, Infiltrated by Non-Whites, San Francisco, Oakland, and Berkeley, California." *Northern California Real Estate Report* (2^d Quarter 1955).

"Oakland Amends Ebonics Resolution." *Black Issues in Higher Education* 13 (6 February 1997).

"Oakland Business Men." *Colored American Magazine* 9 (November 1905).

Pullum, Geoffrey K. "Language That Dare not Speak Its Name." *Nature* 386 (27 March 1997). The Ebonics controversy in Oakland.

Reed, T. Edward. "Research on Blood Groups and Selection from the Child Health and Development Studies, Oakland, California." *American Journal of Human Genetics* 19 (November 1967).

Rhomberg, Chris. "White Nativism and Urban Politics: The 1920s Ku Klux Klan in Oakland, California." *Journal of American Ethnic History* 17 (Winter 1998).

Romano, Patrick S., et al. "Smoking, Social Support, and Hassles in an Urban African-American Community." *American Journal of Public Health* 81 (November 1991). California household survey conducted in Oakland and San Francisco.

"Roundup Report: How Schools Meet Desegregation Challenges." *Nation's Schools* 78 (November 1966). Pasadena, San Mateo, Los Angeles, and Oakland.

Sawyer, Barbara. "Negroes in West Oakland." *Immigration and Race Problems* (1949–1953). Publication of Mills College.

Schwarz, K. Robert. "Black Maestros on the Podium, But No Pedestal" *New York Times* (11 October 1992). Includes Michael Morgan, musical director of the Oakland East Bay Symphony.

Silverman, B. G. "Black Adolescent Crack Users in Oakland: No Quick Fix." *JAMA* 264 (18 July 1990). Comment on R. E. Fullilove's medical article.

Steel, Ronald. "Letters from Oakland: The Panthers." *New York Review of Books* 13 (11 September 1969).

Taylor, Orlando L. "The Ebonics Debate: Separating Fact from Fallacy." *Black Issues in Higher Education* 13 (23 January 1997).

"Transmission and Use of an Illegal Syringe Exchange and Injection-Related Risk Behaviors among Street-Recruited Injection Drug Users in Oakland, California, 1992 to 1995." *AIDS Weekly Plus*, 5 October 1998.

Warden, Donald. "Walk in Dignity." *Congressional Record* (18 May 1964). Oakland's Afro-American Association president speaks to integration.

White, Jack. "Ebonics According to Buckwheat." *Time*, 13 January 1997. The Oakland controversy.

Williams, Robert L. "The Ebonics Controversy." *Journal of Black Psychology* 23 (August 1997). Includes the controversy over Ebonics in the Oakland Public School System.

San Diego

Blevins, Clifton, and Wallace Homitz. "What the San Diego Negro is Thinking." *San Diego Magazine* 17 (September 1965).

Carlton, Robert L. "Blacks in San Diego County: A Social Profile, 1850–1880." *Journal of San Diego History* 21 (1975).

"Economic Well-Being of Blacks in San Diego." *San Diego Economic Bulletin* 34 (August 1986).

Hocker, Cliff, and Anasa Briggs-Graves. "What to Do When You're in San Diego." *Black Enterprise*, 1975.

Howison, Victorinne Hall. "We Like Our Negro Teacher." *Opportunity* 23 (July–Septembr 1945). About Blossom Lorraine Van Lowe, San Diego's first Black teacher.

Keen, Harold. "De Facto Segregation in San Diego." *San Diego and Point Magazine* 18 (August 1966).

_____. "San Diego's Racial Powder Keg: The Fuse is None Too Long." *San Diego and Point Magazine* 16 (July 1963).

Madyun, Gail, and Larry Malone. "Black Pioneers in San Diego, 1880–1920." *Journal of San Diego History* 27 (Spring 1981).

Morgan, Joan. "SDSU Rallies Against Swastikas." *Black Issues in Higher Education* 9 (23 April 1992).

"No Black Applicants Accepted for Fall at University of California, San Diego's Medical School." *Jet*, 18 August 1997.

Roeser, Veronica A. "De Facto School Segregation and the Law: Focus San Diego." *San Diego Law Review* 5 (January 1968).

"San Diego Parents Sue to End Segregation." *Classroom Teacher* 10 (December 1967).

Schwartz, Henry. "The Mary Walker Incident: Black Prejudice in San Diego, 1866." *Journal of San Diego History* 19 (1973).

Steinfield, Melvin. "Blacks in the Appointive Process (A Case Study)." *Black Politician* 2 (1971). Politics effectively shuts out Blacks and other minorities from San Diego boards and commissions.

————. "In San Diego, New Evidence of Growing Black Power and Black Unity." *San Diego and Point Magazine* 19 (January 1967).

Tarquinio, Cherly. "Black Culture Instruction Program Lags in San Diego Schools." *Classroom Teacher* 10 (April 1968).

"UC Dan Diego Names College After Thurgood Marshall." *Black Issues in Higher Education* 10 (18 November 1993).

Weber, David J. "A Black American in Mexican San Diego: Two Recently Discovered Documents." *Journal of San Diego History* 20 (Spring 1974).

San Francisco

"Anti-Klan Group Wrecks Frisco Theater Showing 1915 *Birth of a Nation.*" *Variety*, 18 June 1980.

Babow, Irving. "Discrimination in Places of Public Accommodation: Findings of the San Francisco Civil Rights Inventory." *Journal of Intergroup Relations* 2 (Fall 1961).

————. "Restrictive Practices in Public Accommodations in a Northern Community: Emphasis on Status of the Negro." *Phylon* 24 (Spring 1963). San Francisco.

Bond, Horace Mann. "What the San Francisco Conference Means to the Negro." *Journal of Negro Education* 14 (Fall 1945). United Nations conference.

Bowser, Benjamin P. "Bayview-Hunter's Point: San Francisco's Black Ghetto Revisited." *Urban Anthropology* 17 (Winter 1988).

Broussard, Albert S. "Civil Rights Leaders in San Francisco, 1940's." Chapter in *Peoples of Color in the American West*, eds. Sucheng Chan, et al. Lexington, MA: D. C. Heath, 1994.

————. "Oral Recollections and the Historical Reconstruction of Black San Francisco, 1915–1940." *Oral History Review* 12 (1984).

————. "Organizing the Black Community in the San Francisco Bay Area, 1915–1930." *Arizona and the West* 23 (Winter 1981).

————. "The Politics of Despair: Black San Franciscans and the Political Process, 1920–1940." *Journal of Negro History* 69 (Winter 1984).

————. "Strange Territory, Familiar Leadership: The Impact of World War II on San Francisco's Black Community." *California History* 65 (March 1986).

Bunzel, John H. "Black Studies at San Francisco State." *Public Interest* 13 (Fall 1968).

Canter, Donald. "How Negro Removal Became Black Renewal: San Francisco's Western Addition." *City* 4 (October/November 1970).

Castro, Peter. "No Mere Mayor." *People Weekly*, 24 June 1996. Willie Lewis Brown, the first Black mayor of San Francisco.

Catania, J. A. et al. "Changes in Condom Use among Black, Hispanic, and White Heterosexuals in San Francisco: The AMEN Cohort Survey." *Journal of Sex Research* 119 (1993).

————. "Correlates of Condom Use among Black, Hispanic, and White Heterosexuals in San Francisco: The AMEN Longitudinal Survey." *AIDS Education and Prevention* 6 (1994).

————. "Condom Use in Multi-Ethnic Neighborhoods of San Francisco: The Population-Based AMEN (AIDS in Multi-Ethnic Neighborhoods) Study." *American Journal of Public Health* 82 (1992).

Cowan, Robert E. "The Leidesdorff Estate: A Forgotten Chapter in the Romantic History of Early San Francisco." *California Historical Society Quarterly* 7 (June 1928).

De Ford, Miriam Allen. "Who Was Leidesdorff?" *Westways* 45 (March 1953). A founder of San Francisco.

Derrick, John A. Lincoln. "Booker T. Washington Orphanage of California." *Colored American Magazine* 10 (March 1906). A San Francisco orphanage.

"Discrimination in Places of Public Accommodation: Findings of the San Francisco Civil Rights Inventory." *Journal of Intergroup Relations* 2 (Autumn 1961).

Dyke, Jeani. "San Francisco: The Negro Problem Turned on its Head." *Immigration and Race Problems*. (1961). Publication of Mills College.

Ellen, J. M., et al. "Socioeconomic Differences in Sexually Transmitted Disease Rates Among Black and White Adolescents, San Francisco, 1990 to 1992." *American Journal of Public Health* (November 1995).

"Fair California." *Economist* 219 (14 May 1966). Race discrimination in San Francisco housing.

FitzSimons, Casey. "'Alchemy' at New Langton Arts." *Artweek* 29 (March 1998). Review of exhibition by Thomas Allen Harris and Lyle Ashton Harris in San Francisco.

"Fatha Hines Settles Down." *Ebony*, October 1957. Profile of big band leader and pianist Earl "Fatha" Hines who decides to quit the road and settle in the Bay Area.

"Five Blacks Awarded 'Genius' Grants from MacArthur Foundation." *Jet*, 8 July 1996. Actress and Playwright Anna Deavere Smith of San Francisco was a recipient.

Fullilove, Mindy T., et al. "Black Women and AIDS Prevention: A View towards Understanding the Gender Rules." *Journal of Sex Research* 27 (1990). Examines patterns of sexual behavior.

————. "Crack Cocaine Use and High-Risk Behaviors among Sexually Active Black Adolescents." *Journal of Adolescent Health* 14 (1993). Indicates that crack users are more likely to engage in high-risk sexual behavior.

Fullilove, R. E., et al. "Risk of Sexually Transmitted Disease among Black Adolescent Crack Users in Oakland and San Francisco, Calif." *JAMA* 263 (9 February 1990).

Gorham, Thelma Thurston. "Negroes and Japanese Evacuees." *Crisis* 52 (November 1945). Japanese returned to homes in San Francisco to find Blacks occupying some of them.

Graves, Jacqueline M. "NetNoir, San Francisco: Afrocentric Digital Content and Services." *Fortune* 132 (10 July 1995). Afrocentric forum at America Online.

"Idle Hands." *Economist* 221 (8 October 1966). Race in San Francisco.

James, Joseph. "Race Relations on the Pacific Coast, San Francisco." *Journal of Educational Sociology* 19 (November 1945).

Johnsen, Leigh Dana. "Equal Rights and the 'Heathen Chinee': Black Activism in San Francisco, 1865–1875." *Western Historical Quarterly* 11 (1980).

Jones, Martin H., and Martin C. Jones. "The Neglected Client." *Black Scholar* 1 (March 1970). Two counselors employed at Cal State-San Francisco describe their attitudes towards counseling.

Krebs, Ottole. "The Post-War Negro in San Francisco, 1948–49." *American Communities* 2 (1948–1949). Mills College publication.

Lemke-Santangelo, Gretchen. "African American Migrant Women in the San Francisco East Bay Area." Chapter in *American Labor in the Era of World War II*, eds. Sally M. Miller and Daniel A. Cornford. Westport, CT: Praeger, 1995.

Levene, Carol. "The Negro in San Francisco." *Common Ground* 9 (Spring 1949).

Lindan, C. P., et al. "Underreporting of Minority AIDS Deaths in San Francisco Bay Area, 1985–86." *Public Health Reports* 105 (July-August 1990).

Major, Reginald. "Integration for Excellence." *Nation* (12 September 1966). San Francisco schools.

Marcus, R., et al. "San Francisco Offers Cultural Programs for All." *American School Board Journal* 153 (August 1966).

Massey, Douglas S., and E. Fong. "Segregation and Neighborhood Quality: Blacks, Hispanics, and Asians in the San Francisco Metropolitan Area." *Social Forces* 69 (September 1990).

McEntire, Davis, and Julia R. Tarnpol. "Postwar Status of Negro Workers in San Francisco." *Monthly Labor Review* 70 (June 1950).

Meister, Dick. "Black Nationalism in San Francisco Ghetto." *Frontier* 14 (January 1963).

Miller, Vincent P., and John M. Quigley. "Segregating by Racial and Demographic Group: Evidence from the San Francisco Bay Area." *Urban Studies* 27 (February 1990).

"Minority Worker Hiring and Referral in San Francisco." *Monthly Labor Review* 81 (October 1958).

Mishida, Mo. "A Revolutionary Nationalist Perspective of the San Francisco State Strike." *Amerasia Journal* 15 (1989).

Montesano, Philip M. "The Amazing Dr. Ezra Johnson." *Urban West* 1 (January/February 1968). Profile of Black medical doctor in San Francisco.

_____. "San Francisco Black Churches in the Early 1860's: Political Pressure Group." *California Historical Quarterly* 52 (Summer 1973). Political involvement of Black churches dating back to the early 1860s.

_____. "San Francisco in the Early 1860s: Social and Cultural Life of the Negro Community." *Urban West* 1 (November–December 1967).

_____. "Social and Cultural Life of the Negro Community in San Francisco in the Early 1860's." *Urban West* 1 (November-December 1967).

Peterson, John L., et al. "High-Risk Sexual Behavior and Condom Use among Gay and Bisexual African-American Men." *American Journal of Public Health* 82 (November 1992). Survey of 250 men in San Francisco Bay area.

Pierce, Joseph. "Black Business in the City." *San Francisco Business* 4 (April 1969).

Pittman, John. "Negroes Challenge the Jackboot in San Francisco." *Freedomways* 7 (Winter 1967). Repression and racism.

"Postwar Status of Negro Workers in San Francisco Area." *Monthly Labor Review* 70 (June 1950).

Romano, Patrick S., et al. "Smoking, Social Support, and Hassles in an Urban African-American Community." *American Journal of Public Health* 81 (November 1991). California household survey conducted in Oakland and San Francisco.

Rosenblatt, Abram, and C. Clifford Attkisson. "Integrating Systems of Care in California for Youth with Severe Emotional Disturbance: I. A. Descriptive Overview of the California AB377 Evaluation Project." *Journal of Child and Family Studies* 1 (1992).

"San Francisco's State." *Economist* 229 (28 December 1968). Black and white conflicts and the Panthers at California State University—San Francisco.

Savage, W. Sherman. "The Influence of William Alexander Leidesdorff on the History of California." *Journal of Negro History* 38 (July 1953).

_____. "Intrigue in California (1846). *Midwest Journal* 2 (Winter 1949). Letters to Thomas Oliver Larkin from William Leidesdorff.

_____. "Mary Ellen Pleasant." Section in *Notable American Women, 1607–1950*. Cambridge: Harvard University Press, 1971.

Sawyer, Eugene T. "Old Time Minstrels of San Francisco, Recollections of a Pioneer." *Overland Monthly* 81 (1923).

"School Busing Battle, Spreads to North and West: Now It's Places Such as San Francisco and Pontiac, Michigan, Where Integration Troubles Are Flaring: In the South Busing Continues to Grow." *U.S. News and World Report* 13 September 1971.

Scott, Jeffrey A. "The Sixties Student Movement at San Francisco State College: A New Perspective." *Wazo Weusi Journal* 1 (Fall 1992).

Sherman, Joan R. "James Monroe Whitfield, Poet and Emigrationist: A Voice of Protest and Despair." *Journal of Negro History* 57 (1972). Barber and poet who also lived in San Francisco, advocated racial separatism and racial justice.

Snorgrass, J. William. "The Black Press in the San Francisco Bay Area, 1856–1900." *California History* 60 (1981–1982).

Stanford, Darryl. "From 'Guerrilla Astronomer' to Department Chair." *Mercury* (San Francisco), May/June 1995. Autobiographical profile of the author, an astronomer and chair of the Department of Astronomy at the City College of San Francisco.

Strupp, Joe. "San Francisco Bay Area Weekly Approaches 50." *Editor and Publisher* 127 (2 July 1994). History of the *Sun-Reporter*.

Swanston, David. "How to Wreck a Campus." *Nation* 206 (8 January 1968). California State University—San Francisco.

Tarshis, Jerome. "San Francisco." *Artforum* 9 (October 1970). Works of five Bay area artists.

————. "San Francisco." *Artforum* 9 (December 1970). Notes 3rd anniversary of Black Man's Art Gallery.

Taylor, Ronald L. "The *Larry P.* Decision a Decade later: Problems and Future Directions." *Mental Retardation* 28 (1990). Focus on Black children from San Francisco who were classified as educably mentally retarded.

Telfer, John H. "Philip Alexander Bell and the *San Francisco Elevator*." *San Francisco Negro Historical and Cultural Society Monograph* 9 (August 1966).

Tompkins, E. Berkeley. "Black Ahab: William T. Shorey, Whaling Master." *California Historical Quarterly* 51 (Spring 1972). The only Black sea captain on the Pacific coast, Shorey operated out of San Francisco.

Townsend, Jonas Holland. "American Caste and Common Schools." *Anglo-African Magazine* 1 (March 1859). Attempts by residents of Grass Valley, Sacramento, and San Francisco to secure education for their children.

Webster, Staten Wentford. "The Influence of Interracial Contact on Social Acceptance in a Newly Integrated School." *Journal of Educational Psychology* 52 (December 1961). Focus on San Francisco.

White, Ted W. "The Field of Vision Narrows." *Urban West* (June 1969). San Francisco police and the Black community.

Williams, Franklin H. "Jim Crow Dies Hard." *Crisis* 60 (February 1963). Housing in San Francisco.

Woodring, P. "Struggle for Black Identity." *Saturday Review* 52 (18 January 1969). Activity at California State University—San Francisco.

Young, Richard. "The Impact of Protest Leadership on Negro Politicians in San Francisco." *Western Political Quarterly* 22 (March 1969).

Slaves and Slavery

Beasley, Delilah L. "California Freedom Papers." *Journal of Negro History* 3 (January 1918).

_____. "Slavery in California." *Journal of Negro History* 3 (January 1918).

Broussard, Albert S. "Slavery in California Revisited: The Fate of a Kentucky Slave in Gold Rush California." *Pacific Historian* 29 (Spring 1985).

Coy, Owen C. "Evidences of Slavery in California." *Grizzly Bear* 19 (October 1916).

De Ferrari, Carlo M. "Steven Spencer Hill, Fugitive from Labor." *Quarterly* (January-March 1966). Publication of Tuolumne County recounts Hill's struggles to free himself from slavery.

Dunaway, Clyde Augustus. "Slavery in California after 1848." Chapter in *American Historical Association Annual Reports for the Year 1905*, Vol. 1. Washington, DC: U.S. Government Printing Office, 1906.

Franklin, William E. "The Archy Case: The California Supreme Court Refuses to Free a Slave." *Pacific Historical Review* 32 (May 1963).

Friedman, Ralph. "They Came as Bonded." *Fortnight* (October 1955).

Gibson, Patricia. "California and the Compromise of 1850." *Journal of the West* 8 (1969). The role of California in the congressional debate, with slavery being the main issue.

Heizer, Robert F. "Civil Rights in California in the 1850's—A Case History." *Kroeber Anthropological Society Papers*, no. 31 (1965).

"How Thomas Starr King Saved California to the Union during the Slavery Discussion." *California History Nugget* 3 (October-November 1929).

Lapp, Rudolph M. "The Negro in Gold Rush California." *Journal of Negro History* 49 (April 1964). Slaves and free Blacks as miners, laborers, cooks, etc.

Parish, John C. "A Project for a California Slave Colony in 1851." *Huntington Library Bulletin* 8 (October 1935). A proposal by James Gadsden.

Stanley, Gerald. "The Politics of the Antebellum Far West: The Impact of the Slavery and Race Issues in California." *Journal of the West* 16 (October 1977).

Thacker, M. Eva. "California's Dixie Land." *California History Nugget* 5 (March 1938). James Gadsden's plan to bring Negro slaves to California to work the cotton.

Williams, David A. "California Democrats of 1860: Division, Disruption, Defeat." *Southern California Quarterly* 55 (1973). Pro-slavery and pro-Southern sentiments.

Books:

African American Resource Directory: Alcohol and other Drugs. Sacramento: California Department of Alcohol and Drug Programs, 1995.

Alexander, Charles C. *Battles and Victories of Allen Allensworth.* Boston: Sherman, French, 1914. Black chaplain.

Allen, Robert L. *The Port Chicago Mutiny.* New York: Amistad, 1993. WWII trial.

Almaguer, Tomás. *Racial Fault Lines: The Historical Origins of White Supremacy in California.* Berkeley: University of California Press, 1994.

American and Foreign Anti-Slavery Society. *Address to the Inhabitants of New Mexico and California, on the Omission by Congress to Provide Them with Territorial Governments, and on the Social and Political Evils of Slavery.* New York: The Society, 1849.

American Civil Liberties Union, Southern California Branch. *Day of Protest Night of Violence, the Century City Peace March: A Report of the American Civil Liberties Union of Southern California.* Los Angeles: Sawyer Press, 1967.

Amerson, A. Wayne. *Northern California and Its Challenges to a Negro in the Mid-1900s.* Berkeley: Regional Oral History Office, Earl Warren Oral History Project, 1974.

Andrews, Lori B. *Black Power, White Blood: The Life and Times of Johnny Spain.* New York: Pantheon Books, 1996. Story of Larry Armstrong (Jonny Spain), the only one of the "San Quentin Six" to be convicted. Utilizes "invented dialogue."

Anthony, Earl. *The Time of the Furnaces; A Case Study of Black Student Revolt.* New York: Dial Press, 1971. San Fernando State College.

Armstrong, Gregory. *The Dragon has Come: The Last Fourteen Months in the Life of George Jackson.* New York: Harper and Row, 1974. Profile of a "Soledad Brother."

Arrowhead Allied Arts Council. *Arrowhead Allied Arts Council Presents Festival of Arts, May 2–12, 1968.* San Bernardino: The Arts Council, 1968. Catalogue of African American art exhibit.

Baker, William P., and Henry C. Jensen. *Mexican American, Black and Other Graduates and Dropouts: A Follow-Up Study Covering 15 Years of Change, 1956–1971.* San Jose: East Side Union High School District, 1973. California high school.

Baltich, Frances. *Search for Safety: The Founding of Stockton's Black Community.* Stockton, CA: F. Baltich, 1982.

Barbour, W. Miller. *An Exploratory Study of Socio-Economic Problems Affecting the Negro-White Relationship in Richmond, California, a Project of United Community Defense Services, Inc.* New York: National Urban League, 1952.

Bass, Charlotta A. *Forty Years: Memoirs from the Pages of a Newspaper.* Los Angeles: Bass Publishers, 1960. Editor of the *California Eagle.*

Batty, Joseph. *Over the Wilds of California; or, Eight Years from Home.* Leeds, England: J. Parrott, 1867. Includes an account of the Englishman living with a Black miner.

Baugh, John Gordon. *Linguistic Style-Shifting in Black English.* Ph.D. diss., University of Pennsylvania, 1979. Black English in California.

Bay Area Urban League. *Annual Report.* San Francisco: The League, 1925.

Bazaar, Mona, ed. *The Trial of Huey Newton.* Los Angeles: n.p., 196?

Bean, Walton. *California: An Interpretive History.* New York: McGraw-Hill, 1968. Contains various aspects of Black history.

Beasley, Delilah L. *The Negro Trailblazers of California: A Compilation of Records from the California Archives in the Bancroft Library at the University of California, in Berkeley; and from the Diaries, Old Papers, and Conversations of Old Pioneers in the State of California.* Los Angeles: Times Mirror Printing and Binding House, 1919; reprinted San Francisco: R&E Research, 1968; reprinted, New York; Negro University Press, 1969; reprinted, New York: G. K. Hall, 1997.

Becks, Edward R. *Journey into "Z" Country.* Redwood City, CA: Gekoyo Publishing Company, 1975. Blacks in Mateo County.

Belous, Russell E. *America's Black Heritage.* Los Angeles: Los Angeles County Museum of Natural History, 1969. History of Blacks in California.

Bettencourt, John. *Black Interments, Sacramento City Cemetery, 1850–1910: A Survey and Study of Black-American Burials in the City Cemetery from 1850 Past the Turn of the Century.* Sacramento: Sacramento City Cemetery Archives, 1992.

Beyond the Rodney King Story: An Investigation of Police Conduct in Minority Communities. Boston: Northeastern University Press, 1995.

Black Alternatives Conference. *The Fairmont Papers: Black Alternatives Conference, San Francisco, December 1980.* San Francisco: Institute for Contemporary Studies, 1981. Blacks and education, suffrage, and economics.

Black Business in San Diego Directory. San Diego: W. L. Morrow, 1965.

The Black Family: Are Our Youth at Risk? Sacramento: Joint Publications Office, 1989. A report by the California legislative assembly.

Black Legislation Passed by the 1971 Session of the California Legislature: Summaries of Major Bills Affecting Blacks. Sacramento: Black Legislative Caucus, 1972.

Black Student Union, University of California, Riverside. Riverside, CA: 1969.

Blacks in Sacramento County. Sacramento: Community Services Planning Council, 1989. Statistical information.

Bonjean, Charles M., and Wyman J. Crow. *Voices that Count: Establishment, Brown and Black Influentials in San Diego County, California.* La Jolla, CA: Western Behavioral Sciences Institute, 1969.

Braden, Ann. *House Un-American Activities Committee: Bulwark of Segregation.* Los Angeles: National Committee to Abolish the House Un-American Activities Committee, 1964. Claims that the Committee was undermining integration.

Bradford, Amory. *Oakland's Not For Burning*. New York: David McKay Company, 1968. How Oakland avoided riots.

Browning, Rufus P., Dale Rogers Marshall, and David H. Tabb. *Protest is not Enough: The Struggle of Blacks and Hispanics for Equality in Urban Politics*. Berkeley: University of California Press, 1984. Political participation.

Bugliosi, Vincent. *Outrage: The Five Reasons Why O.J. Simpson Got Away with Murder*. New York: W. W. Norton, 1996.

Bullock, James, and Lanny Berry, eds. *Marin City, U.S.A.* Sausalito: Graphic Arts of Marin, Inc., 1970. Project resulting from Black students involved with the Tamalpais Union High School district.

Bunch, Lonnie G. *Black Angelenos: The Afro-American in Los Angeles 1850–1950*: [Exhibition] June 11, 1988–March 6, 1989. Los Angeles: California Afro-American Museum, 1988.

Bunzel, John H. *Race Relations on Campus: Stanford Students Speak*. Stanford, CA: Stanford Alumni Association, 1992.

California. African American Task Force. *African American Task Force Report on the Year 2000: Health Promotion Objectives and Recommendations for California*. Sacramento: California Department of Health Services, Health Promotion Section, 1992.

California. Colored Citizens. State Executive Committee. *Address of the State Executive Committee, to the Colored People of the State of California*. Sacramento: The Committee, 1859.

California. Department of Social Welfare. *Cultural Differences: Training in Nondiscrimination*. Sacramento: The Department, 1965. Includes Blacks, Asians, and Latinos.

California. Legislature. Joint Committee on the Master Plan for Higher Education. *Report of the Joint Committee on the Master Plan for Higher Education*. Sacramento: The Committee, 1973.

California. Resources Agency, Department of Parks and Recreation. *Allensworth Feasibility Study*. Sacramento: Department of Parks and Recreation, 1975.

California Afro-American Museum. *Continuity and Change: Emerging Afro-American Artists, California 1986*. Los Angeles: The Museum, 1986. Exhibition catalogue.

California Afro-American Oral History Project. *California Afro-American Oral History Project Transcripts, 1967–1979*. Berkeley: Regional Oral History Office, Bancroft Library, University of California, Berkeley. Interviews with Blacks who helped to shape California history. Eleven volumes.

California Commission on Discrimination in Teacher Employment. *Report*. Sacramento: the Commission, 1959.

California Current Review of Human Resources. *Desegregating California Schools*. San Francisco: League of Women Voters, 1969.

California Department of Education. *The Commission on Discrimination in Teacher Employment: Services, Polities, Principles, Statues.* Sacramento. The Department, 1960.

California Department of Industrial Relations, Division of Labor Statistics and Research. *Black Californians: Population, Education, Income, Employment.* San Francisco: California Department of Industrial Relations, Division of Fair Employment Practices, 1963.

_____. *Black Californians: Population, Education, Income, Employment.* San Francisco: Fair Employment Practice Commission, Division of Fair Employment Practices, Dept. of Industrial Relations, Agriculture and Services Agency, State of California, 1974. Based on 1970 census.

_____. *Negro Californians: Population, Employment, Income, Education.* San Francisco: Division of Fair Employment Practices, 1963; reprinted, 1965. Based on 1960 census.

California History Series. San Francisco: San Francisco Negro Historical and Cultural Society, 1965. Black California history.

California Librarians Black Caucus/UCLA Mentor Program Handbook. 1991. ERIC. ED 344 591. Handbook to assisting in increasing Black librarians.

California Originals: Profiles of People Who Made an Original Imprint on California. San Francisco: Pacific Gas and Electric Company, 1982. Blacks included.

California Soul: Music of African Americans in the West. Berkeley: University of California Press, 1998.

California State Fair Employment Practice Commission. *Negroes and Mexican Americans in South and East Los Angeles.* San Francisco: California State Fair Employment Practice Commission, 1968.

_____. *Supplement to Negro Californians, 1960: Population, Employment, Income, Education.* San Francisco: California State Fair Employment Practice Commission, 1965.

Chandler, Robert J., ed. *California and the Civil War, 1861–1865.* San Francisco: Book Club of California, 1992.

Chandler, Trevor L. *A Conversation with Mervyn M. Dymally, Lieutenant Governor, State of California.* Seattle: Office of Minority Affairs, University of Washington, 1975. Blacks and politics.

Chapel, Les. *The Black Man's Place in America.* New York: Vantage Press, 1991. California Biography.

Chavez, Lydia. *The Color Bind: California's Battle to End Affirmative Action.* Berkeley: University of California Press, 1998.

Chronopoulos, Themis. *Racial Turmoil at San Jose State: The Incident of the 1967 University of Texas at El Paso vs. San Jose State Football Game. April 1995.* Research paper. ERIC. ED 386 095. Black student athlete protest against discrimination, organized by Harry Edwards.

Citizens Committee for Responsible Corporate Action. *Corporate Apartheid, California, U.S.A. Style: The Exclusion of Blacks, Mexican-*

Americans and Females from Corporate Power: A Study. San Francisco: The Committee, 1971.

Clausen, Edwin G., and Jack Birmingham. *Chinese and African Professionals in California: A Case Study of Equality and Opportunity in the United States*. Washington, DC: University Press of America, 1982.

Clemens, Sydney G. *The Sun's Not Broken, Cloud's Just in the Way: On Child-Centered Teaching*. Mt. Ranier, MD: Gryphon House, 1983. Case studies of education in California and New York.

Cochran, Johnnie L., and Tim Rutten. *Journey to Justice*. New York: Ballentine, 1997.

Cole, Peter K. *Cole's War with Ignorance and Deceit, and his Lecture on Education Delivered in the St. Cyprian Church, Tuesday Evening, August 11, 1857*. San Francisco: J. H. Udell and R. P. Locke, 1857. Includes preparations for the third Convention of Colored Citizens, 1857.

Colonization of Free Blacks. Memorial of Leonard Dugged, George A. Balley, and 240 Other Free Colored Persons of California, Praying Congress to Provide Means for their Colonization to Some Country in Which Their Color will not be a Badge of Degradation. Washington, DC, 1862.

Colored Directory of the Leading Cities of Northern California, 1916–1917, comp. Charles F. Tilghman. Oakland: Tilghman Printing Company, 1916.

Colored People's Business Directory, v. 1, 1925. San Diego: City Printing Company, 1925.

Cooley, Armanda, Carrie Bass, and Marsha Rubin-Jackson. *Madam Foreman: A Rush to Judgment?* Beverly Hills: Dove Books, 1995. O.J. Simpson Trial.

Coro Foundation, San Francisco. *The Negro Community Leaders in Pasadena: A Social and Economic Survey of the Northwest Area of Pasadena*. San Francisco: Coro Foundation, 1961.

Crouchett, Lawrence P. *William Byron Rumford: The Life and Public Service of a California Legislator*. El Cerrito, CA: Downey Place Publishing House, 1984.

———, et al. *Visions Toward Tomorrow: A History of the East Bay Afro-American Community, 1852–1977*. Oakland: Northern California Center for Afro-American History and Life, 1989.

Crouchett, Lorraine Jacobs. *Delilah Leontium Beasley: Oakland's Crusading Journalist*. E. Cerrito, CA: Downey Place Publishing House, 1990.

Culver City, Administrative Office. *Racial Transition and Culver City*, ed. John Greenwood. Culver City, CA: n.p., 1968.

Davis, Angela, and Bettina Aptheker. *If They Come in the Morning: Voices of Resistance*. New York: The Third Press, 1971. Collection of letters, poetry and essays.

Davis, Angela Y. *Angela Davis, an Autobiography*. New York: Random House, 1974.

Deverell, William, and Tom Sitton, eds. *California Progressivism Revisited.* Berkeley: University of California Press, 1994. Women and Blacks in California politics.

Djedje, Jacqueline Cogdell, and Eddie S. Meadows, eds. *The Soul of California: Music of African Americans.* Berkeley: University of California Press, 1998.

Dugged, Leonard. *Colonization of Free Blacks. Memorial of Leonard Dugged, George A. Bailey, and 240 Other Free Colored Persons of California, Praying Congress to Provide Means for their Colonization to Some Country in Which Their Color will not be a Badge of Degradation.* Washington, DC: n.p., 1862.

Dwinelle, John W. *Argument of Mr. John W. Dwinelle on the Right of Colored Children to be Admitted to the Public Schools.* San Francisco: Bacon and Company, 1870. Discrimination and California supreme court.

Dymally, Mervyn Malcolm. *The Struggle for the Inclusion of Negro History in Our Text-Books...A California Experience.* San Francisco: R&E Research Associates, 1970.

Early, Laura. *The Collection History of Blacks in Tehama County: First Half-Century of the 1800's.* n.p., 1972. Originally a high school paper, actually written on the last half of the 19th century.

East Bay Colored Business Directory, 1930. Oakland: California Voice Press, 1930.

Elman, Richard M. *Ill-at-Ease in Compton.* New York: Pantheon Books, 1967. A study that includes maps.

Encarnation, Dennis J., and Craig E. Richards. *Race and Educational Employment: Public and Catholic Schools Compared. Project Report No. 84-A15.* Research report, June 1984. ERIC. ED 352 725. Examines minority employment in six San Francisco Bay area counties.

Evans, Arthur, ed. *Centennial Yearbook of the Most Worshipful Prince Hall Grand Lodge Free and Accepted Masons, California and Jurisdiction.* San Francisco: n.p., 1955.

Excess Deaths among California's Minority Populations. Sacramento: State of California, Department of Health Services, Health Data and Statistics Branch, 1986.

Fair and Open Environment? Bigotry and Violence on College Campuses in California. Washington, DC: U.S. Commission on Civil Rights, 1991.

Finke, Blythe Foote. *Angela Davis: Traitor or Martyr of the Freedom of Expression.* Charlotteville, NY: Sam Har Press, 1972. Short book based on Davis' speeches.

First African Methodist Episcopal Church, 78th Anniversary, June 2, 1936. Located in the Bancroft Library, University of California, Berkeley. Church history.

Fisher, Sethard. *Black Elected Officials in California.* San Francisco: R&E
    Research Associates, 1978.
Fitch, Robert Beck. *Mark Will Ward: A Black Family in the City.* Creative
    Education, 1972. Oakland, juvenile.
Five Views. Sacramento: State of California, Department of Parks and Recrea-
    tion, Office of Historic Preservation, 1988. Black history in California
    included.
Foner, Philip S., ed. *Black Socialist Preacher: The Teachings of Reverend
    George Washington Woodbey and His Disciple, Reverend G. W. Slater,
    Jr.* San Francisco: Synthesis Publications, 1983.
Foster, Michele, and G. A. Duncan, eds. *The Education of African Americans in
    California.* Special issue of the *Journal of Negro Education* 65 (Spring
    1996).
Frakes, George E. *Minorities in California History.* New York: Random
    House, 1971.
Frye, Hardy. *Negroes in California from 1841 to 1875.* California History Se-
    ries. San Francisco: Negro Historical and Cultural Society, 1968.
Garden City Women's Club. *History of Black Americans in Santa Clara Valley.*
    Sunnyvale, CA and Lockheed Missiles and Space Company, 1978.
Gibbs, Mifflin Wistar. *Shadow and Light: An Autobiography with Reminis-
    cences of the Last and Present Century.* Washington, DC: 1902; re-
    printed, New York: Arno Press and the New York Times, 1968; re-
    printed, Lincoln: University of Nebraska Press, 1995. Autobiography
    of public official and newspaper editor.
Gober, Dom. *Black Cop.* Los Angeles: Holloway House, 1974.
Goldner, William. *New Housing for Negroes: Recent Experience.* Berkeley:
    Real Estate Research Program, University of California, 1958. Study
    of housing in California.
Goode, Kenneth G. *California's Black Pioneers: A Brief Historical Survey.*
    Santa Barbara: McNally and Loftin, 1974.
Gooding-Williams, Robert, ed. *Reading Rodney King/Reading Urban Uprising.*
    New York: Routledge, 1993.
Hatcher, Bunny Nightwalker. *Hate Crime in Los Angeles County 1990. A
    Report to the Los Angeles County Board of Supervisors.* Technical re-
    port, February 1991. ERIC. ED 337 549. Report concludes that such
    acts have increased.
Hausler, Donald. *Blacks in Oakland, 1852–1987.* Oakland, CA: Donald
    Hausler, 1987.
Hayes, Robert Lee. *The Black American Travel Guide.* San Francisco: Straight
    Arrow Books, 1971. Guide to California cities, plus others.
Hazen, Don, ed. *Inside the L.A. Riots: What Really Happened, and Why it
    Will Happen Again: Essays and Articles.* New York: Institute for Al-
    ternative Journalism, 1992.

Heizer, Robert F., and Alan J. Almquist. *The Other Californians: Prejudice and Discrimination Under Spain, Mexico, and the United States to 1920.* Berkeley: University of California Press, 1971.

Hendrick, Irving G. *The Development of a School Integration Plan in Riverside, California: A History and Perspective.* Riverside: Riverside Unified School District and the University of California-Riverside, 1968.

Herndon, James. *The Way It Spozed to Be.* New York: Simon and Schuster, 1968. A biographical sketch of a junior high school in California.

Hewes, Lawrence I. *Intergroup Relations in San Diego: Some Aspects of Community Life in San Diego Which Particularly Affect Minority Groups.* San Francisco: American Council on Race Relations, 1946.

Hippler, Arthur E. *Hunter's Point: A Black Ghetto.* New York: Basic Books, 1974.

Holdredge, Helen. *Mammy Pleasant.* New York: Putnam Publishing, 1953.

Holisi, Clyde, and James Mtume. *The Quotable Karenga.* Los Angeles: US Organization, 1967.

Holladay, Susan C. *Bibliography of Resources for the History of Blacks in Butte County, California, during the Nineteenth Century and Early Twentieth Century.* Chico: n.p., 1979.

Home For The Aged and Infirmed Colored People of California, Constitution and By-Laws. Oakland: Jordan Print Company, 189?

Horvat, Erin McNamara. *Structure, Standpoint and Practices: The Construction and Meaning of the Boundaries of Blackness for African-American Female High School Seniors in the College Choice Process.* March 1997. ERIC. ED 407 884. The role of race in selecting a college.

Hudson, Karen E. *The Will and the Way: Paul R. Williams, Architect.* New York: Rizzoli, 1994. Paul Williams (1894–1980) biography, juvenile.

Huff, Karen. *The History of Black San Diego: 1804–1993.* Chula Vista: ICAN Press, 1995.

Improving Racial Balance and Intergroup Relations: An Advisory Report to the Board of Education, Inglewood Unified School District. Sacramento: California State Department of Education, June, 1968.

Interracial Council for Business Opportunity. *Minority Vendors Guide, Southern California.* Las Angeles: The Council, 1971.

Irvin, Dona L. *The Unsung Heart of Black America: A Middle-Class Church at Mid-century.* Columbia, MO: University of Missouri Press, 1992.

Jackson, George. *Soledad Brother.* New York: Bantam, 1970.

————. *Soledad Brother: The Prison Letters of George Jackson.* New York: Bantam Books, 1970; reprinted, Chicago: Lawrence Hill Books, 1994.

James, Joy, ed. *The Angela Y. Davis Reader.* Malden, MA: Blackwell Publishers, 1998. A collection of Davis' seminal writings.

Johanesen, Harry. *California Negro History: Black's Role in the Old West.* Washington, DC: U.S. Government Printing Office, 1968. Ten articles that appeared in the San Francisco *Examiner* during 1968.

Johnson, Ezra R. *Emancipation Oration.* San Francisco: The Elevator Office, 1867. The Emancipation Proclamation and Blacks in California.

Kanter, Martha J. *An Examination of Demographic, Institutional, and Assessment Factors Affecting Access to Higher Education for Underrepresented Students in the California Community Colleges.* Research report, April 1990. ERIC. ED 317 239.

Koon, Stacey C., and Robert Deitz. *Presumed Guilty: The Tragedy of the Rodney King Affair.* Washington, DC: Regency Gateway, 1992.

Kraus, Henry. *In the City was a Garden: A Housing Project Chronicle.* New York: Renaissance Press, 1951. Blacks and housing in San Pedro.

Ku Klux Klan, California Knights. *The Klan in Action: A Manual of Leadership and Organization for Officers of Local Klan Committee.* n.p, 192?. Mimeo located at the University of California, Berkeley.

Lamott, Kenneth Church. *Anti-California: Report from our First Parafascist State.* Boston: Little, Brown and Company, 1971. Social life and customs, including Blacks.

Landes, Ruth. *Culture in American Education: Anthropological Approaches to Minority and Dominant Groups in the Schools.* New York: Wiley, 1958. Minorities in California schools.

Lapp, Rudolph M. *Afro-Americans in California*, 2^d ed. San Francisco: Boyd and Fraser Publishing Company, 1987.

————. *Archy Lee: A California Fugitive Slave Case.* San Francisco: Book Club of California, 1969.

————. *Blacks in Gold Rush California.* New Haven: Yale University Press, 1977; reprinted, Yale Western American Series, no. 13. New Haven: Yale University Press, 1995.

Laurenti, Luigi. *Property Values and Race: Special Research Report to the Commission on Race and Housing.* Berkeley: University of California Press, 1960. California cities included in study of 20 neighborhoods.

League of Women Voters of San Diego. *Dimensions in Discrimination. A Preliminary Survey of Dan Diego's Community Problems of Discrimination.* San Diego: The League, 1965.

Lee, Warren W. *A Dream for South Central: the Autobiography of an Afro-Americanized Korean Christian Minister.* W. W. Lee, 19?

Lemke-Santangelo, Gretchen. *Abiding Courage: African American Migrant Women and the East Bay Community.* Chapel Hill: University of North Carolina Press, 1996. Rural-urban migration to the Bay area.

Liberatore, Paul. *The Road to Hell: The True Story of George Jackson, Stephen Bingham, and the San Quentin Massacre.* New York: Atlantic Monthly Press, 1996.

Limited Life Opportunities for Black and Latino Youth. Report on a Public Hearing by the Los Angeles County Commission on Human Relations. Compton, California, 26 April 1990. ERIC. ED 337 521. The effects of poverty.

Lothrop, Gloria Ricci, and Doyce B. Nunis, Jr., eds. *A Guide to the History of California.* Westport, CT: Greenwood Press, 1989.

Mann, Eric. *Comrade George: An Investigation into the Life, Political Thought, and Assassination of George Jackson.* New York: Harper and Row, 1974.

Marascuilo, Leonard A. *Attitudes Toward de facto Segregation in a Northern City, 1964–1965.* Berkeley: University of California, 1967.

Matthews, Miriam. *The Negro in California from 1781–1910.* Los Angeles: 1944. Bibliography.

Mays, Iantha (Villa). *History of California Association of Colored Women's Clubs, Inc., 1906–1955.* Oakland: n.p., 1955. East Bay Negro Historical Society collection.

McBroome, Delores Nason. *Parallel Communities: African Americans in California's East Bay, 1850–1963.* New York: Garland Publishers, 1993.

McCord, William, et al. *Life Styles in the Black Ghetto.* New York: W. W. Norton and Company, 1969. Urban life in California cities.

McEntire, Davis. *Residence and Race.* Berkeley: University of California Press, 1960.

McWilliams, Carey. *Report on Importation of Negro Labor to California, August 10, 1942.* n.p.: California Division of Immigration and Housing, 1942.

_____. *Southern California Country, an Island on the Land.* New York: Duell, Sloan and Pearce, 1946.

Meiklejohn Civil Liberties Institute. *Angela Davis Case Collection: Annotated Procedural Guide and Index.* Berkeley: the Institute, 1974.

Mikell, Robert S. *A Pictorial History of Allensworth: A Unique Black Town.* Fresno: n.p., 1985.

Milner, Christina, and Richard Milner. *Black Players: The Secret World of Black Pimps.* Boston: Little, Brown and Company, 1973.

Monographs, Blacks in the West. San Francisco African American Historical and Manuscript Series, no. 1. San Francisco: San Francisco African American Historical and Cultural Society, 1976. History of Blacks in California.

Moore, Shirley Ann. *To Place Our Deeds. The African American Community in Richmond, California, 1910–1963.* Berkeley: University of California Press, 1999.

Moses, H. Vincent, and Celena Turney, eds. *Our Families/Our Stories: From the African American Community, Riverside California.* Ormond Beach, FL: Riverside Museum Press, 1997.

Murray, Betty. *A National Study of Minority Group Barriers to Allied Health Professions Education in the Southwest. Final Report.* San Antonio: Southwest Program Development Corporation, 1975. ERIC. ED 118 297. A two year study conducted in California, Colorado, New Mexico, Oklahoma and Texas.

Myrdal, Gunner. *An American Dilemma.* New York: Harper Row, 1944.

NAACP 1940–55. Crime—Mitchell, Willie, 1939. Frederick, MD: University Publications of America, 1988. Murder trial.

NAACP Branch Files. California State Conference, 1932–1938. Frederick, MD: University Publications of America, 1991. Civil rights.

NAACP Branch Files. Northern Branch, California, 1916–1918, 1920–1934. Frederick, MD: University Publications of America, 1991.

NAACP Branch Files. San Diego, California, 1914–1939. Frederick, MD: University Publications of America, 1991.

Nairobi Research Institute. *Blacks in Public Higher Education in California.* Sacramento: Joint Committee on the Master Plan for Higher Education, 1973.

National Association for the Advancement of Colored People. *Yearbook of the Northern California Branch of the National Association for the Advancement of Colored People.* Oakland, 1919.

————. West Coast Region. *NAACP Civil Rights Program, Including NAACP Legislative Score Board.* Oakland: Tilghman Press, 1960.

————. *West Coast Regional Annual Conference, September 19, 20, 21, 1969, Pacific Grove, California.* Oakland: Tilghman Press, 1969.

National Committee to Free Angela Davis, Los Angeles. *A Political Biography of Angela Davis.* Los Angeles: The Committee, 1970.

The Negro in American Art. Los Angeles: California University Art Galleries, 1966. A catalogue of an exhibition.

Negro Californians. State of California, Division of Fair Employment Practices, June 1963. Biographies.

Negro Who's Who in California. Los Angeles: Negro Who's Who in California, 1948.

New Age Publishing Company. *The Official California Negro Directory and Classified Buyers' Guide: A West Coast Directory.* Los Angeles: New Age Publishing Company, 1939.

O'Meara, James. *Broderick and Gwin.* San Francisco: Bacon and Company, 1881. Proslavery and antislavery advocates.

Ogbu, John U. *The Next Generation: An Ethnography of Education in an Urban Neighborhood.* New York: Academic Press, 1974.

Ogden, Diane. *History of Blacks in Bakersfield.* Bakersfield: The Author, 1973.

Payne, J. Gregory, and Scott C. Ratzan. *Tom Bradley, The Impossible Dream: A Biography.* Santa Monica: Roundtable Publications, 1986.

Payne, J. Gregory. *Public Libraries Face California Ethnic and Racial Diversity Report.* Rand Corporation, 1988.

Perry, Pettis. *The War and the Negro People: Report by Pettis Perry, Member State Committee, to Northern California Conference on Negro Work.* San Francisco: 1941.

Pettigrew, Thomas, and Dennis A. Alston. *Tom Bradley's Campaign for Governor: The Dilemma of Race and Political Strategies.* Washington,

DC: Joint Center for Political and Economic Studies, 1988.   Blacks, politics and government in California.

Poston, Marvin. *Making Opportunities in Vision Care*. Berkeley: Regional Oral History Office, University of California, 1985.   Biography about optometrists.

Praetzellis, Mary, and Adrian Praetzellis.   *"We Were There Too": Archaeology of and African-American Family in Sacramento, California*.   Rohnert Park, CA: Cultural Resources Facility, Sonoma State University, 1992.   Excavations of Cook family property.

A Preliminary Report on the Status of African-American Males in California. Opportunity or Chaos: A Generation in Peril.   31 July 1992.   ERIC. ED 351 415. A study mandated by the state legislature.

Putnam, Carleton. *Framework for Love: A Study in Racial Realities: Address at the University of California at Davis with Subsequent Questions and Answers*.   Washington, DC: National Putnam Letters Committee, 1964.

Racial or Ethnic Distribution of Staff and Students in California Public Schools. 1988–89.   General report, 1989.   ERIC.   ED 315 477.

Ransford, Harry Edward.   *Race and Class in American Society: Black, Latino, Anglo*.   Rochester, VT: Schenkman Books, 1994.

Richard, Eugene Scott.   *A Census Study of the Negro in California*.   Los Angeles: University of California, 1940.   Statistics from 1850 to 1930.

Richardson, James.   *Willie Brown: Style, Power, and a Passion for Politics*. Berkeley: University of California Press, 1996.

Richmond Unified School District.   *Black History: Supplement to U.S. History Program, Grades 8 and 11*.   Richmond: Richmond Unified School District, 1969.   Sources to integrate with the standard history program.

Riles, Wilson C.   *Racial and Ethnic Survey of California Public Schools.   Part II, Distribution of Employees*.   Sacramento: California Department of Education, 1967.

Riles, Wilson C., and Frederick R. Gunsky.   *Racial and Ethnic Survey of California Public Schools.   Part I, Distribution of Pupils*.   Sacramento: California State Department of Education, 1967.

Riverside Political Prisoners Defense Committee.   *The Frame-Up: Outrage in The Desert: The Political Trial of Gary Lawton, Nehemiah Jackson, and Larrie Gardner*.   San Bernardino: The Committee, 1973.   Black political prisoners.

Robinson, Clarence.   *The Impossible Dream: One Man's Drive to End Racial Oppression: An Autobiography*.   Vallejo: Amper Publishing, 1998.

Ross, John Stewart.   *Compilation of Approved Decisions and Regulations of Free and Accepted Masons of California*.   San Francisco: Published by Order of Grand Lodge, 1932.

Sacramento Observer.   *Who's Who in the Negro Community of Sacramento, California: The People in Business, the Institutions, and Organizations*.   Sacramento: Sacramento Negro Directory, 1965.

Satterwhite, Frank J., and Betty S. Satterwhite. *California Directory of Afro-American Educators*. Los Angeles: n.p., 1970.

Schatzman, Dennis C. *The Simpson Trial in Black and White*. Santa Monica: General Publishing Group, 1996. Justice administration and the OJ trial.

Shippey, Mervyn G. *A Short History of the Visalia Colored School*. San Francisco: R&E Research Associates, 1970. Review of California supreme court case of *Wysinger* v. *Cruikshank* that ended segregation in that school system in 1890.

Shover, Michele. *Blacks in Chico, 1860–1935: Climbing the Slippery Rope*. Chico: Association for Northern California Records and Research, 1991. Race relations.

Skinner, Byron Richard. *Black Origins in the Inland Empire*. San Bernardino: Book Attic Press, 1983. Blacks in San Bernardino.

Smith, J. Alfred. *Thus Far by Faith: A Study of Historical Backgrounds and the First Fifty Years of the Allen Temple Baptist Church*. Oakland: Color Art Press, 1973.

Snyder, David L. *Negro Civil Rights in California: 1850*. Sacramento: Sacramento Book Collectors Club. 1969. Only 300 copies printed.

Somerville, John Alexander. *Man of Color, an Autobiography. A Factual Report on the Status of the American Negro Today*. Los Angeles: L. L. Morrison, 1949. Race relations by the first Black person to receive a degree in dentistry from the University of Southern California.

Southern California Black Pages. Corona, CA: Southern California Black Pages, 1991. Black business directory.

Stanford, E. Percil, et al. *The Elder Black*. San Diego: Center on Aging, San Diego State University, 1978. Black aged in San Diego.

Staples, Robert. *The World of Black Singles: Changing Patterns of Male/Female Relations*. Westport, CT: Greenwood Press, 1981.

State Convention of the Colored Citizens of the State of California. *Proceedings of the California State Convention of Colored Citizens held in Sacramento the 25th, 26th, 27th, and 28th of October 1865*. San Francisco: Printed at the Office of *The Elevator*, 1865. Proceedings of the 4th state convention.

State Convention of the Colored Citizens of the State of California. *Proceedings of the First State Convention of the Colored Citizens of the State of California*. Sacramento: Democratic State Journal, 1855; reprinted, San Francisco: R&E Research Associates, 1969. First convention.

State Convention of the Colored Citizens of the State of California. *Proceedings of the first State Conventions of the Colored Citizens of the State of California, 1855, 1856, and 1865*, Adam S. Etervich, ed. San Francisco: R&E Research Associates, 1969. Collection of original proceedings.

State Convention of the Colored Citizens of the State of California. *Proceedings of the Second Annual Convention of the Colored Citizens of the*

State of California. San Francisco: J. H. Udell and W. Randall, Printers, 1856.

Supplement to Negro Californians, 1960. San Francisco: Fair Employment Practice Commission, 1965.

Sutton, Donald, and Ralph F. Baker. *Oakland Crack Task Force: A Portrait of Community Mobilization.* Oregon: Western Center for Drug-Free Schools and Communities, 1990. ERIC. ED 322 270. Task force created by citizens to fight problems of crack cocaine, with focus on the Black family.

Tate, Will D. *The New Black Urban Elites.* San Francisco: R & E Research Associates, 1976. Race relations and civil rights in California.

Taylor-Gibbs, Jewelle. *Race and Justice: Rodney King and O.J. Simpson in a House Divided.* New York: Simon and Schuster, 1996.

Templeton, John. *Our Roots Run Deep: The Black Experience in California.* San Jose: Aspire Books, 1991.

The Thirteenth Armored Division: A History of the Blacks Cats from Texas to France, Germany, and Austria and Back to California. Baton Rouge: Army and Navy Publishing Company, 1946. Regimental history.

Thurman, A. Odell. *The Negro in California before 1890.* San Francisco: R&E Research Associates, 1973. Reprint of 1945 thesis.

Thurman, Sue Bailey. *Pioneers of Negro Origin in California.* San Francisco: Acme Publishing Company, 1949; reprinted 1971.

Uhlenberg, Peter. *Minorities in California's Population.* n.p., 1969. Work based on the 1960 census.

United States. Commission on Civil Rights, California State Advisory Committee. *Police- Community relations in East Los Angeles, California: A Report to the United States Commission on Civil Rights.* Washington, DC: United States Commission on Civil Rights, 1970.

Vallejo Unified School District. *The Findings of a Survey to Develop an Inventory of Problems and Practices Regarding Ethnic Imbalances in California Schools.* Vallejo: Vallejo Unified School District, 1965.

Walton, Sidney F. *The Black Curriculum: Developing a Program in Afro-American Studies.* Palo Alto: Black Liberation Publications, 1969.

————. *Excerpts from the Book The Black Curriculum: Developing a Program in Afro-American Studies.* Oakland: Black Liberation Publications, 1968.

Watkins, Ben, ed. *We Also Serve: 10 Per Cent of a Nation Working and Fighting for Victory.* Oakland: Charles F. Tilghman, 1944. Oakland Blacks in WWII.

Watkins, Walter F. *The Cry of the West: The Story of the Mighty Struggle for Religious Freedom in California.* Berkeley: Oakland, Bridges Printing Company, 1932; reprinted, San Francisco: R&E Research Associates, 1969. Reverend Gordon C. Coleman and the struggle for autonomy for the Negro Baptist Association.

Weiss, Myra Tanner. *Vigilante Terror in Fontana: The Tragic Story of O'Day H. Short and His Family*. Los Angeles: Socialist Workers Party, 1946. Vigilance committees in Fontana.

Wenkert, Robert, John Magney, and Ann Neel. *Two Weeks of Racial Crisis in Richmond, California*. Berkeley: Survey Research Center, University of California, 1967.

Wenkert, Robert, John Magney, and Fred Templeton. *An Historical Digest of Negro-White Relations in Richmond, California*. Berkeley: Survey Research Center, University of California, 1967.

Wesley, Charles H. *History of the Improved Benevolent and Protective Order of the Elks of the World*. Washington, DC: Association for the Study of Negro Life and History, 1955.

West Coast 74, Black Image: 1974 Invitational Exhibition: [Exhibition Dates, E. B. Crocker Art Gallery, Sacramento, California, September 13–13 October, 1974, Los Angeles Municipal Art Gallery, Barnsdall Park, Los Angeles, California, January 22–16 February, 1975]. Sacramento: Crocker Art Gallery, 1974. 20th century Black art.

Wheeler, B. Gordon. *Black California: The History of African-Americans in the Golden State*. New York: Hippocrene Books, 1992.

Who's Who Among Black Women in California. Inglewood: Who's Who Among Black Women in California, 1982.

Williams, Cecil. *No Hiding Place: Empowerment and Recovery for Our Troubled Communities*. San Francisco: HarperSanFrancisco, 1992. Black church involvement.

Williams, David. *David C. Broderick, A Political Portrait*. San Marino: The Huntington Library, 1969. Antislavery advocate.

Williams, Franklin H. *Keepers of the Wall: A Survey Reveals the Methods by Which Some Real Estate Dealers Help Create and Maintain California's Modern Ghettos*. n.p., 1960.

Williams, Harry Wheaton. *Reflections of a Longtime Black Family in Richmond*. Berkeley: Regional Oral History Office, the Bancroft Library, University of California, 1990.

Williams, Robin, et al. *Strangers Next Door: Ethnic Relations in American Communities*. Englewood Cliffs, NJ: Prentice-Hall, 1964. Interracial relationships in four communities (Elmira, New York; Savannah, Georgia; and Steubenville, Ohio), plus Bakersfield.

Williams, Solomon. *The Lily White Marina*. New York: Vantage Press, 1993. Blacks in California.

Williamson, Alfred E. *California Black Business Directory*. San Francisco: Williamson and Associates Advertising Agency, 1985.

Wilson, Alan Bond. *The Consequences of Segregation: Academic Achievement in a Northern Community*. Berkeley: University of California, 1966. Segregation in the Richmond school system.

_____. *Education of Disadvantaged Children in California, a Report to the California State Committee on Public Education.* Berkeley: University of California, 1966.

Wollenberg, Charles. *All Deliberate Speed: Segregation and Exclusion in California Schools, 1855–1975.* Berkeley: University of California Press, 1975.

_____. *Ethnic Conflict in California History.* Los Angeles: Tinnon-Brown, 1970. Race discrimination.

_____. *Marinship at War: Shipbuilding and Social Change in Wartime Sausalito.* Berkeley: Western Heritage of California, 1990.Blacks and shipbuilding in WWII.

XETV. *The Racial Issue in San Diego: A Report of a Television Program and the Reaction to it from the San Diego Community.* San Diego: XETV: 1965.

Berkeley

Berkeley Board of Education. *Integration: A Plan for Berkeley.* Berkeley: Berkeley Board of Education, 1967.

_____. *Committee to Study Certain Interracial Problems in the Berkeley Schools and Their Effect Upon Education.* Berkeley: Berkeley Board of Education, 1959.

_____. *De Facto Segregation Study Committee. Report.* Berkeley: Berkeley Board of Education, 1963.

_____. *Desegregation of the Berkeley Public Schools, Its Feasibility and Implementation.* Berkeley: Berkeley Board of Education, 1964.

_____. *Integration of the Berkeley Elementary Schools: A Report to the Superintendent, by the Summer Staff Task Force.* Berkeley Board of Education, 1967.

Berkeley Interracial Committee. *Achievements of the Negro in California: A Supplement to be used with Achievements of the Negro in Chicago Published by Board of Education, City of Chicago.* Berkeley: Berkeley Interracial Committee, 1945. Uses material found in *The Negro Trail Blazers* book by Beasley.

Casstwens, Thomas W. *Politics, Housing and Race Relations: The Defeat of Berkeley's Fair Housing Ordinance.* Berkeley: University of California Institute of Government Studies, 1965.

Citizens Commission of the Berkeley Unified School District. *De Facto Segregation in Berkeley Public Schools.* Berkeley: The Commission, 1963.

De Facto Desegregation in Berkeley Public Schools. Berkeley: Board of Education, 1963.

Desegregation of the Berkeley Public Schools, Its Feasibility and Implementation. Berkeley: Board of Education, 1964.

Farber, Thomas. *Tales for the Son of my Unborn Child: Berkeley, 1966–1969.* New York: Dutton, 1971. Social conditions.

Hart-Nibbrig, Nand Engie. *The Attitudes of Black Political Leaders Toward Regional Governance in the San Francisco Bay Area: A Case Study of Black Activists in Berkeley, California.* Seattle: Distributed by the Institute of Governmental Research, 1974.

Rorabaugh, W. J. *Berkeley at War: The 1960s.* New York: Oxford University Press, 1989.

Sullivan, Neil Vincent. *Integration: A Plan for Berkeley. A Report to the Berkeley Board of Education.* Berkeley: Berkeley Board of Education, 1967.

————. *Now is the Time: Integration in the Berkeley Schools.* Bloomington: Indiana University Press, 1969.

Sullivan, Neil Vincent, and Evelyn S. Stewart. *Now is the Time: Integration in the Berkeley Schools.* Bloomington: Indiana University Press, 1970.

United States Commission on Civil Rights. *School Desegregation in Berkeley, California: A Staff Report.* Washington, DC: The Commission, 1977.

Wennerberg, C. H. *Desegregation of the Berkeley Public Schools: Its Feasibility and Implementation.* Berkeley: Berkeley Unified School District, 1964.

Black Panther Party/Eldridge Cleaver

Anthony, Earl. *Picking Up the Gun: A Report on the Black Panthers.* New York: Dial Press, 1970.

————. *Spitting in the Wind: The True Story Behind the Violent Legacy of the Black Panther Party.* Santa Monica: Roundtable Publications, 1990.

Baruch, Rugh-Marion, and Pirkle Jones. *The Vanguard: A Photographic Essay on the Black Panthers.* Boston: Beacon Press, 1970.

The Black Panther Leaders Speak: Huey P. Newton, Bobby Seale, Eldridge Cleaver and Company Speak Out through the Black Panther Party's Official Newspaper. Metuchen, NJ: Scarecrow Press, 1976.

The Black Panther Party. New York: Merit, 1966. Booklet.

Black Panther Party Investigations. Washington, DC: U.S. Government Printing Office, 1970. House Un-American Activities Committee report.

Bond, Julian. *The Trial of Bobby Seale: With Special Contributions of Julian Bond and Dorsen, Charles Rembar and a Personal Statement by Bobby Seale.* New York: Priam Books, 1970.

Boone, Pat. *Pray to Win: God Wants You to Succeed.* New York: G. P. Putnam's Sons, 1980. Included is an account of a dinner with Cleaver.

Boyd, Herb. *Black Panthers for Beginners.* New York: Writers and Readers Publishing, 1995. Documentary comic book.

Brent, William Lee. *Long Time Gone: A Black Panther's True-Life Story of His Hijacking and Twenty-Five Years in Cuba.* New York: Random

House, 1996. Brent's flight after a 1969 shootout with San Francisco police.

Brown, Elaine. *A Taste of Power: A Black Woman's Story.* New York: Pantheon Books, 1993. The head of the Black Panther Party.

Cannon, Terry. *All Power to the People: The Story of the Black Panther Party.* San Francisco: People's Press, 1970.

Churchill, Ward, and Jim vander Wall. *Agents of Repression: The FBI's Secret Wars Against the Black Panther Party and the American Indian Movement.* Boston: South End Press, 1990.

Cleaver, Eldridge. *On the Ideology of the Black Panther Party*, pt. 1. San Francisco: Ministry of Information, Black Panther Party, 1970. BPP platform and program.

_____. *Post-Prison Writings and Speeches*, ed. Robert Scheer. New York: Random House, 1969.

_____. *Revolution in the Congo, by Eldridge Cleaver and Members of the Black Panther Party Delegation to the People's Republic of the Congo, May 1971.* London: Stage 1 for the Revolutionary Peoples' Communications Network, 1971.

_____. *Zur Klassenanalyse der Black Panther Partei. Erziehung und Revolution.* Frankfort am Main: Verlag Roter Stern, 1970.

Cohen, Jerry, and William S. Murphy. *Burn, Baby Burn!* New York: Dutton, 1966.

Cole, Lewis. *This Side of Glory: The Autobiography of David Hilliard and the Story of the Black Panthers.* New York: Little, Brown and Company, 1993.

Commission of Inquiry into the Black Panthers and the Police. *Search and Destroy: A Report*, 1st ed. New York: Metropolitan Applied Research Center, 1973.

Demny, Oliver. *Die Wut des Panthers: Schwarzer Widerstand in den USA.* Münster: Unrast, 1994.

Erikson, Erik Homburger. *In Search of Common Ground: Conversations with Erik H. Erikson and Huey P. Newton.* New York: Norton, 1973.

Foner, Philip S., ed. *The Black Panthers Speak.* Philadelphia: Lippincott, 1970.

Forman, James. *The Making of Black Revolutionaries.* New York: Macmillan, 1972. Forman's account.

Freed, Donald. *Agony in New Haven: The Trial of Bobby Seale, Erika Huggins, and the Black Panther Party.* New York: Simon and Schuster, 1973.

Genet, Jean. *Here and Now for Bobby Seale: Essays.* New York: Committee to Defend the Panthers, 1970.

Ginger, Ann Fagan, ed. *Minimizing Racism in Jury Trials: The voir dire Conducted by Charles R. Garry in People of California v. Huey P. Newton.* Berkeley, CA: National Lawyers Guild, 1970.

Haskins, James S. *Power to the People: The Rise and Fall of the Black Panther Party.* New York: Simon and Schuster Children's Publishing, 1996. Juvenile literature.

Heath, G. Louis. *The Black Panther Leaders Speak.* Metuchen, NJ: Scarecrow Press, 1976. Anthology of writings.

————. *Off the Pigs: The History and Literature of the Black Panther Party.* Metuchen, NJ: Scarecrow Press, 1976. Anthology of writings.

Hill, Norman. *The Black Panther Menace: America's Neo-Nazis.* New York: Popular Library, 1971.

Hilliard, David, and Lewis Cole. *This Side of Glory: The Autobiography of David Hilliard and the Story of the Black Panther Party.* Boston: Little, Brown and Company, 1993.

Keating, Edward M. *Free Huey!* Berkeley: Ramparts Press, 1971.

Kennebeck, Edwin. *Juror Number Four: The Trial of Thirteen Black Panthers As Seen From the Jury Box.* New York: Norton, 1973.

Kugelmass, J. Alvin. *The Black Panthers.* New York: Universal Publishing and Distributing Corporation, 1969.

Lipscomb, Wendell R. *Ghetto Youth: A One Year Follow-Up Study of a Work Training Project.* Berkeley: Bureau of Adult Health and Chronic Diseases, California Department of Public Health, 1970.

Lockwood, Lee. *Conversation with Eldridge Cleaver: Algiers.* New York: McGraw-Hill, 1970. Interview of Cleaver in Algiers.

Major, Reginald. *A Panther is a Black Cat.* New York: W. W. Morrow, 1971.

Marine, Gene. *The Black Panthers.* New York: New American Library, 1969. The first study of California Black Panther leadership.

Marshall, C. Alan. *What Ever Happened to the Black Panthers?* Baltimore: Marshall Publishing, 1993.

McKnight, Gerald. *The Terrorist Mind.* Indianapolis: Bobbs-Merrill, 1974.

Milstein, Tom. *A Perspective on the Panthers: A Commentary Report.* New York: Commentary, 1970.

Ministry of Information Black Paper. Oakland, CA: Black Panther Party for Self-Defense, 1968. Pamphlet.

Moore, Gilbert. *A Special Rage.* New York: Harper and Row, 1971. Huey P. Newton.

Newton, Huey P. *Essays from the Minister of Defense.* n.p., 1968.

————. *The Genius of Huey P. Newton, Minister of Defense, Black Panther Party.* San Francisco: Ministry of Information, Black Panther Party, 1970.

————. *Huey Newton Talks to the Movement about the Black Panther Party, Cultural Nationalism, SNCC, Liberals and White Revolutionaries.* Chicago: Students for a Democratic Society (SDS), 1968.

————. *Selbstverteidigung!* Frankfort am Main: Roter Stern, 1971.

————. *To Die for the People: The Writings of Huey P. Newton.* New York: Random House, 1972.

_____. *War Against the Panthers: A Study of Repression in America*. Baltimore: Black Classic Press, 1995; reprinted, New York: Writers and Readers Publishing, 1998.

Newton, Michael. *Bitter Grain: Huey Newton and the Black Panther Party*. Los Angeles: Holloway House Publishing, 1991.

Oliver, John A. *Eldridge Cleaver Reborn*. Plainfield, NJ: Logos, 1977. Cleaver as a born again Christian.

On the Ideology of the Black Panther Party. San Francisco: Black Panther Party, 1970. Pamphlet.

Otis, George. *Eldridge Cleaver: Ice and Fire!* Van Nuys, CA: Bible Voice, 1977. Television evangelist presents Cleaver as a born again Christian.

Pearson, Hugh. *The Shadow of the Panther: Huey Newton and the Price of Black Power in America*. Reading, MA: Addison-Wesley Publishing Company, 1994.

Pratt, Elmer. "Geronimo". *The New Urban Guerrilla*. Oakland: Black Panther Party, 1971. Book of essays.

Revolution in the Congo. London: Stage 1, 1971. Pamphlet.

Rosebury, Celia. *Black Liberation on Trial: The Case of Huey Newton*. Berkeley: Bay Area Committee to; Defend Political Freedom, 1968.

Rout, Kathleen. *Eldridge Cleaver*. New York: Macmillan, 1991.

Schanche, Don A. *The Panther Paradox: A Liberal's Dilemma*. New York: D. McKay Company, 1970.

Schuler, Conrad. *Black Panther: Zur Konsolidierung des Klassenkampfes in den USA*. Munchen: Trikont-Verl, 1969.

Seale, Bobby. *A Lonely Rage: The Autobiography of Bobby Seale*. New York: Times Books, 1978.

_____. *Seize the Time: The Story of the Black Panther Party and Huey P. Newton*. New York: Vintage Books, 1968.

Shakur, Assata. *Assata, an Autobiography*. Westport, CT: L. Hill, 1987. Woman BPP member.

Sheehy, Gail. *Panthermania: The Clash of Black Against Black in One American City*. New York: Harper and Row, 1971.

Spichal, Dieter. *Die Black Panther Party: Ihre Revolutionre Ideologie und Strategie in Beziehung zur Geschichte und Situation der Afro-Amerikaner, zur Dritten Welt und zum Marximus-Leninismus*. Osnabrück: Biblio-Verlag, 1974.

U.S. Congress, 92^d, 1st session, House of Representatives, Committee on Internal Security. *Gun Barrel Politics: The Black Panther Party, 1966–1971*. Washington, DC: Government Printing Office, 1971.

United States. Congress. House. Committee on Internal Security. *The Black Panther Party, Its Origin and Development as Reflected in Its Official Weekly Newspaper, the Black Panther, Black Community News Service: Staff Study, Ninety-First Congress, Second Session*. Washington, DC: U.S. Government Printing Office, 1970.

Van Peebles, Mario, and J. Tarika Lewis. *Panther: A Pictorial History of the Black Panthers and the Story behind the Film*. New York: Newmarket Press, 1995.

Williams, Julian E. *The Black Panthers are not Black, They are Red*. Tulsa: Christian Crusade Publications, 1970.

Los Angeles, Including Watts

American Civil Liberties Union, Southern California Branch *Police Malpractice and the Watts Riot: A Report*. Los Angeles: ACLU, 1966.

Anderson, E. Frederick. *The Development of Leadership and Organization Building in the Black Community of Los Angeles from 1900 Through World War II*. San Francisco: R&E Research Associates, 1980.

Bakeer, Donald. *Crips: The Story of a South Central L.A. Street Gang*. Inglewood: Precocious Publishing, 1992. History of Black street gang, the largest in L.A.

Baldassare, Mark, ed. *The Los Angeles Riots: Lessons for the Urban Future*. Boulder: Westview Press, 1994. Riots, race relations, and urban policy.

Baruch, Dorothy (Walter). *Glass House of Prejudice*. New York: Morrow and Company, 1946. Race problems in Los Angeles.

Black Business Directory 1, no. 1. Los Angeles: E. M. Cavin, John L. Hathman, F. J. Brown, and R. H. Ferguson, 1969.

Black-Korean Encounter: Toward Understanding and Alliance: Dialogue Between Black and Korean Americans in the Aftermath of the 1992 Los Angeles Riots: A Two-Day Symposium, May 22–23, 1992. Los Angeles: Institute for Asian American and Pacific Asian Studies, California State University, Los Angeles: Claremont, CA: Distributed by Regina Books, 1994.

Bond, J. Max. *The Negro in Los Angeles*. San Francisco: R&E Associates, 1972.

Bullock, Paul. *Aspiration vs. Opportunity: "Careers" in the Inner City*. Policy Papers in Human Resources and Industrial Relations no. 20. Ann Arbor: University of Michigan-Wayne State University, 1973. Black and Latino youth employment in the Los Angeles metropolitan area.

————. *Watts: The Aftermath: An Inside View of the Ghetto, by the People of Watts, California*. New York: Grove Press, 1969. Social conditions and 1965 riot.

Bunch, Lonnie III. *Black Angelenos: The Afro-American in Los Angeles, 1850–1950*. Los Angeles: California Afro-American Museum, 1988.

Burby, Liza N. *The Watts Riot*. San Diego: Lucent Books, 1997. Describes the 1965 Watts riot.

California Bureau of Criminal Statistics. *Watts Riot Arrests, Los Angeles, August 1965: Final Disposition: A Statistical Accounting as of June 30, 1966, of the Procedures followed in Completing Actions Initiated by the Arrest of Participants in the Watts Riots of August 1965.* Sacramento: Bureau of Criminal Statistics, 1966.

California Department of Education. Office of Compensatory Education. *An Analysis of Comparative Data from Schools in Predominantly Negro, Mexican-American, and Privileged Sections of Los Angeles: Final Report of Research Project Sponsored by Compensatory Education Commission Under Grant M-522 and M-622.* Sacramento: The Department, 1967.

California Department of Industrial Relations, Division of Labor Statistics and Research *Negroes and Mexican Americans in South and East Los Angeles: Changes Between 1960 and 1965 in Population, Employment, Income, and Family Status. An Analysis of a U.S. Census Survey of November 1965.* San Francisco: The Department, 1966.

California Division of Fair Employment Practices. *Negroes and Mexican Americans in South and East Los Angeles: Changes between 1960 and 1965 in Population, Employment, Income, and Family Status.* San Francisco: Division of Fair Employment Practices, 1966.

California Governor's Commission on the Los Angeles Riot. *Transcripts, Depositions, Consultants Reports, and Selected Documents of the Governor's Commission on the Los Angeles Riots.* Los Angeles: California Governor's Commission on the Watts riot, 1965.

_____ *Violence in the City: An end or a Beginning? A Report.* Los Angeles: California Governor's Commission on the Los Angeles Riot, 1965. Watts riot, 1965.

Cannon, Lou. *Official Negligence: How Rodney King and the Riots Changed Los Angeles and the L.A.P.D.* New York: Times Books, 1997.

Case, Frederick E. *Black Capitalism: Problems in Development; A Case Study of Los Angeles.* New York: Praeger, 1972.

Case, Frederick E., and James H. Kirk. *The Housing Status of Minority Families, Los Angeles, 1956.* Los Angeles: Los Angeles Urban League, 1958.

Caughey, John Walton, and LaRee Caughey. *School Segregation on Our Doorstep: The Los Angeles Story.* Los Angeles: Quail Books, 1966.

_____. *Segregation Blights Our Schools: An Analysis Based on the 1966 Official Report on Racial and Ethnic Distribution School by Schools Throughout the Los Angeles System.* Los Angeles: Quail Books, 1967.

Chang, Edward T., and Russell C. Leong. *Los Angeles—Struggles Toward Multiethnic Community: Asian American, African American, and Latino Perspectives.* Seattle: University of Washington Press, 1994.

Charles, Roland, and Toyomi Igus, eds. *Life in a Day of Black L.A.: The Way We See It: L.A.'s Black Photographers Present a New Perspective on Their City.* Los Angeles: CAAS Publications, University of California, Los Angeles, 1992. Catalog of exhibit organized by the UCLA

Center for Afro-American Studies and Black Photographers of California.

Cohen, Jerry, and William S. Murphy. *Burn, Baby, Burn! The Los Angeles Race Riot, August, 1965*. New York: E. P. Dutton, 1966.

Cohen, Nathan E., ed. *The Context of the Curfew Area*. Los Angeles: Institute of Government and Public Affairs, University of California, 1967.

_____. *The Los Angeles Riots: A Socio-Psychological Study*. New York: Praeger, 1970. Watts riot.

_____. *Summary and Implications for Policy*. Los Angeles: Institute of Government Affairs, University of California, 1967. Watts riot, 1965.

Collins, Keith Edison. *Black Los Angeles: The Maturing of the Ghetto, 1940–1950*. Saratoga, CA: Century Twenty-One Publishers, 1980.

Community Welfare Federation of Los Angeles, Social Welfare Department. *The Facilities for the Care of Dependent, Semi-Delinquent and Delinquent Negro Children in Los Angeles*. Los Angeles: Social Welfare Department, 1925.

Congress of Racial Equality, Los Angeles. *Segregated Schools in Los Angeles*. Los Angeles: CORE, 1963. Prepared by the Los Angeles CORE education committee.

Conot, Robert E. *Rivers of Blood, Years of Darkness: The Unforgettable Classic Account of the Watts Riot*. New York: Morrow, 1968.

Coonradt, Frederic C. *The Negro News Media and the Los Angles Riots*. Los Angeles: School of Journalism, University of Southern California, Los Angeles, 1965.

Cox, Bette Yarbrough. *Central Avenue—Its Rise and Fall, 1890–c. 1955: Including the Musical Renaissance of Black Los Angeles*. BEEM Publishers, 1996. History and musician interviews.

Cross, Brian. *It's Not About a Salary—: Rap, Race and Resistance in Los Angeles*. New York: Verso, 1993.

Crump, Spencer. *Black Riot in Los Angeles: The Story of the Watts Tragedy*. Los Angeles: Trans-Anglo Books, 1966.

Davis, Mike. *City of Quartz: Excavating the Future in Los Angeles*. New York: Verso, 1990. Rodney King and the 1992 riots.

de Graaf, Lawrence B. *Negro Migration to Los Angeles, 1930 to 1950: A Dissertation, University of California, Los Angeles, 1962*. San Francisco: R&E Research Associates, 1974.

The Decline and the Fall of the "Spectacular" Commodity-Economy. Los Angeles: Frontier Press, 1965. Watts riot essay.

Delk, James D. *Fires and Furies: The Los Angeles Riots of 1992: What Really Happened*. Palm Springs, CA: ETC Publications, 1995.

Draper, Hal. *Jim Crow in Los Angeles*. Los Angeles: Workers Party, 1946.

Dreams on Fire, Embers of Hope: From the Pulpits of Los Angeles After the Riots. St. Louis, MO: Chalice Press, 1992. Church sermons.

Dunitz, Robin J. *Los Angeles Murals by African-American Artists: A Book of Postcards*. Los Angeles: RJD Enterprise, 1995.

The Englewood Raiders: A Story of the Celebrated Ku Klux Klan Case at Los Angeles, and Speeches to the Jury. Los Angeles: L. L. Bryson, 1923.

_____, comp. *The Los Angeles Riots.* Mass Violence in America Series. New York: Arno Press, 1969.

Ervin, James McFarline. *The Participation of the Negro in the Community Life of Los Angeles.* San Francisco: R&E Research Associates, 1973.

Federal Writers Project. "History of the Negro of Los Angeles County." Manuscript in Sacramento State Library, 1936.

Fisher, Lloyd Horace. *The Problem of Violence: Observations on Race Conflict in Los Angeles.* Chicago: American Council on Race Relations, 1947. Discrimination.

Fogelson, Robert M. *The Fragmented Metropolis: Los Angeles, 1850–1930.* Cambridge: Harvard University Press, 1967. Migration and segregation of Blacks.

Folb, Edith A. *Black Vernacular Vocabulary: A Study of Intra/Intercultural Concerns and Usage.* Afro-American Studies Monograph Series no. 5. Los Angeles: University of California Los Angeles, 1973. Black English in Los Angeles.

Fraser, George C., and Margaret Thoren, eds. *SuccessGuide.* Vol. 4: *The Guide to Black Resources in Los Angeles.* Cleveland, OH: SuccessSource, 1993.

George, Lynell. *No Crystal Stair: African-Americans in the City of Angels.* New York: Verso Press, 1992.

Georges, Kathi, and Jennifer Joseph, eds. *The Verdict Is In.* Manic D. Press, 1993. The Rodney King case.

The Greater Los Angeles Blackbook. Los Angeles: The Blackbook, 1984. Black business directory.

Grodzins, Morton. *The Metropolitan Area as a Racial Problem, 1958.* Pittsburgh: University of Pittsburgh Press, 1959. Describes conditions in Los Angeles.

Hamilton, Sue L., and John Hamilton, eds. *The Los Angeles Riots.* Abdo and Daughters, 1992. Juvenile.

Hill, George H. *Black Radio in Los Angeles, Chicago, New York.* Carson, CA: Daystar Publishing Company, 1987.

Horne, Gerald. *Fire This Time: The Watts Uprising and the 1960s.* Carter G. Woodson Institute Series in Black Studies. Charlottesville, VA: University Press of Virginia, 1965; reprinted, New York: De Capo Press, 1997. Blacks, race relations and the 1965 Watts riot.

Ijere, Martin O. *An Overview of Black Entrepreneurship*: Los Angeles. Los Angeles: Center for Afro-American Studies, University of California, 1975.

Jackson, Morton B. *The Second Civil War Commentary as Broadcast on KMPC Radio and KTLA Channel 5.* Hollywood: Golden West Broadcasters, 1965. Watts riot.

Jacobs, Paul. *Prelude to a Riot: A View of Urban America from the Bottom.* New York: Random House, 1967. Study of federal services in Watts.

Jones, Richard O. *When Mama's Gone.* Los Angeles: Milligan Books, 1998. Single parents.

Kendall, Robert. *Never Say Nigger.* London: Library 33, 1966. Blacks and education in Los Angeles. Originally published as *White Teacher in a Black School.*

————. *White Teacher in a Black School.* New York: Devin-Adair, 1964. Blacks and education in Los Angeles.

Khalifah, H. Khalif, ed. *Rodney King and the L.A. Rebellion: A 1992 Black Rebellion in the United States: Analysis and Commentary.* Hampton, VA: U.B and U.S. Communications Systems, 1992.

Kimtex Corporation. *Anarchy Los Angeles.* Los Angeles: Kimtex Corporation, 1965. "Shocking photos" of the Watts riot.

Kogan, Susan, and Robert Rueda. *Comparing the Effects of Teacher-Directed Homework and Student-Centered Homework on Return Rate and Homework Attitudes of Minority Learning Disabled Students.* Roundtable Paper presented at the Annual Meeting of the American Educational Research Association, Chicago, 24–28 March 1997. ERIC. ED 406 804. Study conducted at LA high school consisting of 87% Blacks and 10% Latinos.

League of California Cities, Los Angeles County Division, Social Issues Committee. *Report and Recommendations on Poverty and Race.* Berkeley: The League, 1969.

Los Angeles City Board of Education, Emergency Education Program. *Historical Background of the Negro in Los Angeles.* Los Angeles: The Board, 1935.

Los Angeles Co., Calif. District Attorney's Office. *Report by District Attorney of Los Angeles to the Governor's Commission on the Los Angeles Riots.* Los Angeles: The District Attorney's Office, 1965.

Los Angeles County Board of Supervisors. *Hate Crime in Los Angeles County 1988.* Los Angeles: The Board, 1989.

Los Angeles County Museum of Natural History. *An Exhibition of America's Black Heritage: Held at the Los Angeles County Museum of Natural History, December 3, 1969 through February 15, 1970.* Los Angeles: The Los Angeles County Museum of Natural History, 1969. Exhibition bulletin #5.

Los Angeles County Probation Department. *Riot Participant Study: Juvenile Offenders.* Los Angeles: The Office, 1965. Study following the Watts riot.

Los Angeles County Public Library Ethnic Resource Center: The American Indian Resource Center, Asian Pacific Resource Center, Black Resource Center, and Chicano Resource Center. Program description, 1988. ERIC. ED 298 962. Information on the resources of the centers.

Los Angeles County. Commission on Human Relations. *The Urban Reality: A Comparative Study of the Socio-Economic Situation of Mexican-Americans, Negroes, and Anglo-Caucasians in Los Angeles County.* Los Angeles: The Commission, 1965.

Los Angeles Negro City Directory and Who's Who, 1930–1931. Los Angeles: 1930.

Los Angeles Negro City Directory and Who's Who. Los Angeles: California Eagle, 1900.

The Los Angeles Riots: A Socio-Psychological Study. New York: Praeger, 1970.

Los Angeles Urban League, Health and Welfare Department. *Minority Housing in Metropolitan Los Angeles: A Summary Report.* Los Angeles: Los Angeles Urban League, 1959.

Lynell, George. No Crystal Stair: *African-Americans in the City of Angels.* New York: Verso, 1992. Social conditions in LA.

Madhubuti, Haki R., ed. *Why L.A. Happened: Implications of the '92 Los Angeles Rebellion.* Chicago: Third World Press, 1993.

Manes, Hugh R. *A Report on law Enforcement and the Negro Citizen in Los Angeles.* Hollywood: Hugh R. Manes, 1963.

Mason, Felicia Lendonia. *The Black Newspaper's Editorial Viewpoint on Brown Versus Board of Education: An Analysis of Four Papers from 1954–1984.* 1988. ERIC CS 211 461. The *Los Angeles Sentinel* is one of Four Black papers that analyzed the decision over thirty years.

McQuiston, John Mark. *Negro Residential Invasion in Los Angeles County.* Los Angeles: McQuiston Associates, 1969.

Murphy, Raymond John. *The Structure of Discontent: The Relationship Between Social Structure, Grievance, and Support for the Los Angeles Riot.* Los Angeles: Institute of Government and Public Affairs, University of California, 1967.

National Association for the Advancement of Colored People. *Nineteenth Annual Conference, The National Association for the Advancement of Colored People at Los Angeles, California, June 27–July 3, 1928.* New York: Herald-Nathan Press, 1928.

Negro Culinary Art Club of Los Angeles: Eliza's Cook Book, Favorite Recipes. Los Angeles: Wetzel Publishing Company, 1936.

Negro Who's Who in California. Los Angeles: Negro Who's Who in California, 1948. Included in *Black Biographical Dictionaries, 1790–1950,* no. 297, 1987.

O'Toole, James. *Watts and Woodstock: Identity and Culture in the United States and South Africa.* New York: Holt, Rinehart and Winston, 1973. Case studies of Black social conditions in Watts and South Africa.

Official Central Avenue District Directory. Los Angeles: New Age Publishers, 1940. Black business district.

"One Day We're Going to Rise Up": Voices from the 1992 Los Angeles Rebellion and the Reunification. Chicago: People's Tribune, 1992.

Ong, Paul M. *The Effects of Race and Life-Cycle on Home Ownership: A Study of Blacks and Whites in Los Angeles 1970 to 1980.* Los Angeles: University of California, Los Angeles, 1986.

Prescription for Neglect: Experiences of Older Blacks and Mexican Americans with the American Health Care System. Los Angeles: Andrus Gerontology Center, University of Southern California, 1979. Health care in Los Angeles.

Pynchon, Thomas. *A Journey into the Mind of Watts.* Westminster, England: 1983. Blacks and police shootings in Los Angeles.

Rabey, Steve. "Palette of Forgiveness." *Christianity Today,* 7 October 1996. Profile of painter Thomas Blackshear II of Blackshear Gallery, Colorado Springs.

Rabinovitz, Francine F. *Minorities in Suburbs: The Los Angeles Experience.* Lexington, MA: Lexington Books, 1977. Blacks and housing discrimination in Los Angeles.

Raine, Walter Jerome. *Los Angeles Riot Study: The Ghetto Merchant Survey.* Los Angeles: UCLA Institute of Government and Public Affairs, 1967.

―――――. *The Perception of Police Brutality in South Central Los Angeles.* Los Angeles, Institute of Government and Public Affairs, University of California, 1967.

Ransford, H. Edward. *Race and Class in American Society: Black, Latino, Anglo,* 2nd ed. Rochester, VT: Schenkman Books, 1994. Social conditions in the LA area.

Ray, MaryEllen Bell. *The City of Watts, California: 1907 to 1926.* Los Angeles: Rising Publishing, 1985.

Reed, Tom. *The Black Music History of Los Angeles—Its Roots: 50 Years in Black Music.* Los Angeles: Black Accent on L.A. Press, 1992.

The Rising Negro. Los Angeles: Principals' Club, 1928. Series—*Los Angeles School Journal* 11 (June 4, 1928).

Robinson, Duane Morris. *Chance to Belong: Story of the Los Angeles Youth Project, 1943–1949.* New York: Woman's Press, 1949. L.A. youth project.

Rossa, Delia. *Why Watts Exploded: How the Ghetto Fought Back.* Los Angeles: Socialist Workers Party, L.A. Local, 1966. Watts riot.

Rustin, Bayard. *The Watts "Manifesto" and the McCone Report. A Commentary Report With Study Guide and Letters.* New York: Commentary, 1966. Watts riot.

Salak, John. *The Los Angeles Riots: America's Cities in Crisis.* Brookfield, CT: Millbrook Press, 1993.

Schulberg, Budd, ed. *From the Ashes: Voices of Watts.* New York: New American Library, 1969.

Scoble, Harry M. *Negro Politics in Los Angeles: The Quest for Power.* Los Angeles: Institute of Government and Public Affairs, University of California, 1967.

Scruggs, Baxter S. *A Man in Our Community: The Biography of L. G. Robinson of Los Angeles, California.* Gardenia: The Institute Press, 1937.

Sears, David O. *Political Attitudes of Los Angeles Negroes.* Los Angeles: Institute of Government and Public Affairs, University of California, 1967.

Sears, David O., and John B. McConahay. *The Los Angeles Riot Study; The Politics of Discontent: Blocked Mechanisms of Grievance Redress and the Psychology of the New Urban Black Man.* Los Angeles: University of California, Institute of Public Affairs, 1967. Office of Economic Opportunity-sponsored research.

_____. *Political Attitude of Los Angeles Negroes.* Los Angeles: UCLA Institute of Government and Public Affairs, 1967.

_____. *The Politics of Discontent: Blocked Mechanisms of Grievance Redress and the Psychology of the New Urban Black Man.* Los Angeles: University of California Institute of Government and Public Affairs, 1967. Watts riot.

_____. *The Politics of Violence: The New Urban Blacks and the Watts Riot.* Boston: Houghton Mifflin, 1973; reprinted, Washington, DC: University Press of America, 1981. Watts riot.

_____. *Riot Participation.* Los Angeles: University of California Institute of Government and Public Affairs, 1967. Watts riot.

Selected 1970 Census Population and Housing Characteristics for Blacks and Spanish Americans in Los Angeles County. Los Angeles: Los Angeles County Department of Regional Planning, Population and Human Resources Section, 1980. Statistical information.

Shakur, Sanjika [Monster Kody Scott]. *Monster: The Autobiography of an L.A. Gang Member.* New York: Atlantic Monthly Press, 1993.

Sherwood, Frank P. *The Mayor and the Fire Chief: The Fight over Integrating the Los Angeles Fire Department.* New York: Inter-University Case Program, 1959.

Shevky, Eshref, and Marilyn Williams. *The Social Areas of Los Angeles, Analysis and Typology.* Berkeley: University of California Press, 1949.

Singleton, Robert, and Paul Bullock. *Some Problems in Minority Group Education in the Los Angeles Public Schools.* Washington, DC: Howard University Press, 1963.

Sonenshein, Raphael J. *Politics in Black and White: Race and Power in Los Angeles.* Princeton: Princeton University Press, 1993.

Tolbert, Emory J. *The UNIA and Black Los Angeles: Ideology and Community in the American Garvey Movement.* Los Angeles: Center for Afro-American Studies, University of California, 1980.

Tomlinson, Tommy M. *Ideological Foundations for Negro Action: A Comparative Analysis of Militant and Non-Militant Views of the Los Angeles Riot.* Los Angeles: University of California Institute of Government and Public Affairs, 1967.

Tomlinson, Tommy M., and David O. Sears. *Negro Attitudes Toward the Riot.* Los Angeles: University of California Institute of Government and Public Affairs, 1967.

Tomlinson, Tommy M., and Diana L. Ten Houten. *Method: Negro Reaction Survey.* Los Angeles: University of California Institute of Government and Public Affairs, 1967. Watts riot.

United States Commission on Civil Rights, California Advisory Committee *An Analysis of the McCone Commission Report.* Washington, DC: United States Commission on Civil Rights, 1966. Watts riot.

University of California, Los Angeles. Institute of Government and Public Affairs. *Los Angeles Riot Study.* Los Angeles: UCLA, 1967.

Valdez, R. Burciaga, and G. Dallek. *Does the Health Care System Serve Black and Latino Communities in Los Angeles County?* Claremont, CA: Tomas Rivera Center, 1991.

Vernon, Robert, and George Novack. *Watts and Harlem The Rising Revolt in the Black Ghettos.* New York: Pioneer Publishers, 1965.

Violence in the City—An End or a Beginning?: A Report by the Governor's Commission on the Los Angeles Riots. Los Angeles: The Commission, 2 December 1965. Warning that other riots will occur if problems not corrected.

Vivian, Octavia B. *The Story of the Negro in Los Angeles County.* San Francisco: R&E Research Associates, 1970. Compiled by WPA Federal Writers Project, 1936.

Watts Writers' Workshop. *From the Ashes: Voices of Watts,* ed. Budd Schulberg. New York: New American Library, 1967.

Weatherwax, John M. *The Founders of Los Angeles.* Los Angeles: Bryant Foundation, 1954. Ethnicity of the founders.

Williams, Greg Alan. *A Gathering of Heroes: Reflections on Rage and Responsibility: A Memoir of the Los Angeles Riots.* Chicago: Academy Chicago, 1996. *Baywatch* African American actor Alan Williams and his eyewitness account.

Wilson, Wayne. *Racial Hiring Practices of Los Angeles Area Sports Organizations.* Los Angeles: Amateur Athletic Foundation of Los Angeles, 1992.

Yu, Eui-Young. *Black-Korean Encounter: Toward Understanding and Alliance: Dialogue Between Black and Korean Americans in the Aftermath of the 1992 Los Angeles Riots: A Two-Day Symposium, May 22–23, 1992.* Los Angeles: Regina Books [Distributor], 1994.

San Francisco

Babow, Irving, and Edward Howden. *A Civil Rights Inventory of San Francisco*. San Francisco: Council for Civic Unity of San Francisco,
1958.

Bagley, Julian. *Welcome to the San Francisco Opera House*. Berkeley: Bancroft Library, University of California/Berkeley, Regional Oral History,
1973. Interview of Bagley, concierge and tour conductor of the opera
house.

*A Baseline Survey of AIDS Risk Behaviors and Attitudes in San Francisco's
Black Communities*. San Francisco: Polaris Research and Development, 1987.

Black Infant Health Improvement Project. *Report on Infant Health in San Francisco, 1991*. San Francisco: San Francisco Department of Public
Health, 1993.

Blackman's Art Gallery, San Francisco. *Blackman's Art Gallery: Dedicated to
Black Culture*. San Francisco: S. F. Golden Printers, 1970. Brochure.

Booker T. Washington Foundation. Cablecommunications Resource Center-
West. *How Blacks use Television for Entertainment and Information:
A Survey Research Project*. Washington, DC: National Science Foun-
dation, 1978. Television viewing habits of Blacks in San Francisco.

Broussard, Albert S. *Black San Francisco: The Struggle for Racial Equality in
the West, 1900–1954*. Lawrence, KS: University Press of Kansas,
1993.

California Department of Employment, San Francisco Office. *The Economic
Status of Negroes in the San Francisco-Oakland Bay Area: A Report
Based on the 1960 Census Population*. San Francisco: The Depart-
ment, 1963.

California Employment Service, Research and Statistics Section. *The Economic
Status of Negroes in the San Francisco-Oakland Bay Area: A Report
Based on the 1960 Census of Population*. San Francisco: n.p., 1963.

Daniels, Douglas. *Pioneer Urbanites: A Social and Cultural History of Black
San Francisco*. Philadelphia: Temple University Press, 1980; reprinted, Berkeley: University of California Press, 1991.

Far West Surveys. *The Negro Consumer in the San Francisco Bay Area: A
Survey of Product Use and Brand Preference*. San Francisco: KSAN
radio, 1958.

Feldman, Harvey, et al. *Preparing for Prison: Life in San Francisco's Inner-
City Neighborhoods. Draft*. January 1992. ERIC. ED 360 439. Ideology formerly associated with gangs have been incorporated by inner-
city youth generally.

Ferguson, Ronald F. *The Drug Problem in Black Communities. Working Paper 87–01–01*. October 1987. Information analysis. ERIC. ED 347
218. Interviews conducted in Washington, DC, Cleveland and San
Francisco.

Fine, Doris R. *When Leadership Fails: Desegregation and Demoralization in the San Francisco Schools*. New Brunswick, NJ: Transaction Books, 1986.

France, Edward E. *Some Aspects of the Migration of the Negro to the San Francisco Bay Area Since 1940*. San Francisco: R&E Research Associates, 1974.

Hart-Nibbrig, Nand Engie. *The Attitudes of Black Political Leaders Toward Regional Governance in the San Francisco Bay Area: A Case Study of Black Activists in Berkeley, California*. Seattle: Distributed by the Institute of Governmental Research, 1974.

Hildebrand, Lee. *Bay Area Blues*. Rohnert Park, CA: Pomegranate Artbooks, 1993. San Francisco Bay blues.

Holdredge, Helen. *Mammy Pleasant: San Francisco's Powerful and Sinister Ruler, 1815–1904*. New York: Ballantine, 1953.

————. *Mammy Pleasant's Cookbook*. San Francisco: 101 Productions, 1970. Includes biographical information. Sensationalized account.

————. *Mammy Pleasant's Partner*. New York: Putnam, 1954. Mrs. Pleasant's business partner Thomas Bell.

Johnson, Charles, Herman H. Long, and Grace Jones. *The Negro War Worker in San Francisco, a Local Self Survey*. San Francisco: YWCA, 1944. The Negro family and adjustment.

Jones, Jack. *The View from Watts*. n.p., 1965. Collection of *LA Times* articles.

Karagueuzian, Dikran. *Blow It Up! The Black Student Revolt at San Francisco State College and the Emergence of Dr. Hayakawa*. Boston: Gambit, 1971.

Lortie, Francis N., Jr. *San Francisco's Black Community, 1870–1890: Dilemmas in the Struggle for Equality*. San Francisco: R&E Associates, 1973.

Marshall, Joseph, and Lonnie Wheeler. *Street Soldier: One Man's Struggle to Save a Generation, One Life at a Time*. New York: Delacorte Press, 1996. San Francisco's Omega Boys Club, rehabilitation, and gang members.

Minutes of a Baptist Convention. San Francisco: n.p., 1860.

Montesano, Philip M. *Some Aspects of the Free Negro Question in San Francisco, 1849–1870*. San Francisco: R&E Research Associates, 1973.

NAACP Branch Files. San Francisco, California, 1917–1939. Frederick, MD: University Publications of America, 1991.

Newcomb, Bobby. *Bobby Newcomb's San Francisco Minstrel's Songster*. New York: 1868.

Orrick, William H. *College in Crisis, a Report to the National Commission on the Causes and Prevention of Violence by William H. Orrick, Jr., Director, San Francisco State College Study Team*. Nashville: Aurora Publishers, 1970. The campus strike, the Black community, the Black Student Union, and the Black Studies program.

Parker, Elizabeth L., and James Abajian. *A Walking Tour of the Black Presence in San Francisco During the Nineteenth Century*. San Francisco: San Francisco African American Historical and Cultural Society, 1974.

Plan of Action for Challenging Times. *Directory of Black Businesses in San Francisco*. San Francisco: 1969.

Platt, William J., et al. *Racial Balance in the San Francisco Unified School District—Phase I*. Menlo Park: Stanford Research Institute, 1966.

Proceedings of the California Baptist State Convention. San Francisco: n.p., 1867.

Rainey, Douglas L., and David J. Venediger. *Directory of Minority Contractors and Black Businesses in the Bay Area*. San Francisco: Core Foundation, 1970.

Record, C. Wilson. *Minority Groups and Intergroup Relations in the San Francisco Bay Area*. Berkeley: Institute of Governmental Studies, University of California, 1963.

Reller, Theodore L. *Problems of Public Education in the San Francisco Bay Area*. Berkeley: Institute of Governmental Studies, 1963. Inner-city Oakland schools.

Rose, Tom and John W. Kinch. *The San Francisco Non-White Population, 1950–1960*. San Francisco: Council for Civic Unity, 1961.

Third Anniversary of the San Francisco Baptist Association. San Francisco: n.p., 1853.

United States Civil Service Commission. *Hearings, May 4–6, 1967*. Washington, DC: U.S. Government Printing Office, 1967. Concerns of housing and employment for Blacks and other minorities in the San Francisco-Oakland area.

Vignes, Michelle. *Bay Area Blues*. San Francisco: Pomegranate, 1993. Photos by Vignes, text by Lee Hildebrand.

Weaver, Robert C. *The Negro War Worker in San Francisco*. San Francisco: 1944.

Slaves and Slavery

Bell, John. *The Compromise Bill: Speech of Hon. John Bell, of Tennessee, in the Senate of the United States, July 3 and 5, 1850, on the Bill for the Admission of California into the Union, the Establishment of Territorial Governments for Utah and New Mexico, and Making Proposals to Texas for the Settlement of Her Northern and Western Boundaries*. Washington, DC: Congressional Globe Office, 1850. Extension of slavery.

Blue, Daniel. *Petition of Daniel Blue for Guardianship of the Girl, Edith, Being Held as a Slave in Sacramento County, 1864*. Manuscript in the California state archives.

Cleveland, Chauncey Fitch. *The California Question. Speech of Hon. Chauncey F. Cleveland, of Connecticut, in the House of Representa-*

tives, April 19, 1850, in Committee of the Whole on the State of the Union, on the President's Message transmitting the Constitution of California. Washington, DC: Congressional Globe Office, 1850. Discussion of the extension of slavery to California.

Cole, Cornelius. *Speech of Hon. Cornelius Cole, of California, on Arming the Slaves.* Washington, DC: McGill and Witherow, 1864.

Fowler, Orin. *Slavery in California and New Mexico. Speech of Mr. Orin Fowler, of Massachusetts, in the House of Representatives, March 11, 1850.* Washington, DC: Buell and Blanchard, Printers, 1850.

Gartner, Vallejo. *Slavery in California.* San Francisco, 1932. Manuscript in California Historical Society library.

Lapp, Rudolph M. *Archy Lee: A California Fugitive Slave Case.* San Francisco: Book Club of California, 1969.

Mann, Horace. *Horace Mann's Letters on the Extension of Slavery into California and New Mexico; and on the Duty of Congress to Provide the Trial by Jury for Alleged Fugitive Slaves.* Washington, DC: Buell and Blanchard, 1850.

Mungen, Donna. *Life and Times of Biddy Mason: From Slavery to Wealthy California Laundress.* n.p., 1976.

Reynolds, Marion Hobart. *Instances of Negro Slavery in California.* Cambridge, MA: The Author, 1914.

Seward, William Henry. *California, Union and Freedom.* Washington, DC: Buell and Blanchard, 1971. Slavery.

Smith, Truman. *Speech of Mr. Smith, of Conn.: On the Bill "To Admit California into the Union, to Establish Territorial Governments for Utah and New Mexico, Making Proposals to Texas for the Establishment of the Western and Northern Boundaries"...Delivered in the Senate of the United States, July 8, 1850.* Washington, DC: Gideon and Company, Printers, 1850. Extension of slavery.

Williams, James. *Life and Adventures of James Williams, a Fugitive Slave.* San Francisco: Women's Union Print, 1873.

Zabriskie, James C. *Speech of Col. Jas. Zabriskie, on the Subject of Slavery, and in Reply to the Address of the Pittsburgh Convention, and Geo. C. Bates, Esq. Delivered at Sacramento, Cal., on the 10th Day of May, A.D. 1856.* Sacramento: Democratic State Journal Office, 1856.

Theses and Dissertations:

Adair, Harriet Elaine. "Trends in School Desegregation: A Historical Case Study of Dayton, Denver, Los Angeles and Seattle." Ed.D. diss., Brigham Young University, 1986.

Adler, Patricia Rae. "Watts: From Suburb to Black Ghetto." Ph.D. diss., University of Southern California, 1977.

Alancraig, Helen Smith. "Codornices Village: A Study of Nonsegregated Public Housing in the San Francisco Bay Area." Master's thesis, University of California, Berkeley, 1953.

Alexander, Ruth. "Racial Characteristics and Conditions of the Student Population at Watsonville Union High School." Master's thesis, Stanford University, 1940.

Almaguer, Tomás. "Class, Race, and Capitalist Development: The Social Transformation of a Southern California County, 1848-1903." Ph.D. diss., University of California, Berkeley, 1979.

Ament, Emily Ann. "Delinquency in Oakland: Comparison of Juvenile Delinquents in High and Low Rate Areas, 1944. MSW thesis, University of California, Berkeley, 1946.

Anderson, Dorothy June. "A Museum Folklife Program in a Multi-Cultural Urban Community: A Study at the California Academy of Sciences, San Francisco." Master's thesis, University of California, Berkeley, 1985.

Anderson, E. Frederick. "The Development of Leadership and Organization Building in the Black Community of Los Angeles from 1900 through World War II." Ph.D. diss., University of Southern California, 1976.

Anton, Kristin Palmquist. "Eligibility and Enrollment in California Public Higher Education." Ph.D. diss., University of California, Berkeley, 1980.

Arrington, John Nathan. "A Comparison of Language, Communicative Styles and Speech Patterns of Blacks and Non-Blacks." Ph.D. diss., United States International University, 1976. Study of San Diego teens.

Austin, Michael. "Harlem of the West: The Douglas Hotel and Creole Palace Nite Club." Master's thesis, University of San Diego, 1994.

Barnett, Wilhelmina Irene. "The American Negro, 1878–1900, as Portrayed in the *San Francisco Examiner*." Master's thesis, Howard University, 1948.

Barnhill, Donna. "The *Sun Reporter*: Its Role as a Negro Weekly in the San Francisco Bay Area Negro Community." Master's thesis, California State University, San Francisco, 1965.

Beck, Patrick Nicholas. "The Other Children: Minority Education in California Public Schools from Statehood to 1890." Ph.D. diss., University of California, Los Angeles, 1975.

Becker, Natalie. "The Struggle for Power in the Anti-Poverty Program in San Francisco." M.C.P. thesis, University of California, Berkeley, 1968.

Bond, J. Max. "The Negro in Los Angeles." Ph.D. diss., University of Southern California, Los Angeles, 1936.

Branham, Ethel. "A Study of Independent Adoptions by Negro Parents in Metropolitan Los Angeles." Master's thesis, University of Southern California, Los Angeles, 1949.

Brent, John Etta. "The American Negro, 1901–1907, as Portrayed in the *San Francisco Examiner*." Master's thesis, Howard University, 1951.

Brigham, Robert. "Land Ownership and Occupancy by Negroes in Manhattan Beach, California." Master's thesis, California State University, Fresno, 1965.

Broussard, Albert S. "The New Racial Frontier: San Francisco's Black Community, 1900–1940." Ph.D. diss., Duke University, 1977.

Brown, Angela Darlean. "Servants of the People: A History of Women in the Black Panther Party." AB thesis, Harvard University, 1992.

Brown, William Henry, Jr. "Class Aspects of Residential Development and Choice in the Oakland Black Community." Ph.D. diss., University of California, Berkeley, 1970.

Burch, Edward Alexander. "Attitudes of Employers Engaged in Manufacturing in the Los Angeles Area Relative to the Employment of Negroes." Master's thesis, University of Southern California, Los Angeles, 1948

Caesar, Clarence. "An Historical Overview of the Development of the Black Community of Sacramento, California, 1850–1983." Master's thesis, California State University, Sacramento, 1985.

Captain, Gwendolyn. "Social, Religious, and Leisure Pursuits of Northern California's African American Population: The Discovery of Gold Through World War II." Master's thesis, University of California, Berkeley, 1995.

Carlton, Robert L. "Blacks in San Diego County, 1850–1900." Master's thesis, San Diego State University, 1977.

Carlyle, John Dorotha. "A Comparative Study of Internal-External Control in Black Professional Educators and Black Semiskilled Workers in Los Angeles and San Diego." Ph.D. diss., United States International University, 1972.

Carmichael, Benjamin Green. "Hunters Point: A Participant Observer's View." M. Crim. thesis, University of California, Berkeley, 1968.

Carmichael, Gwenn Waline. "Social and Demographic Correlates of Racial Desegregation in California Public Schools." Ph.D. diss., University of California, Berkeley, 1975.

Carpenter-Stevenson, Sandy. "A Descriptive Study of Administrators of Afro-American Descent in the Oakland Unified School District, 1970–1985." Ph.D. diss., University of San Francisco, 1988.

Cartland, Earl Fernando. "A Study of Negroes Living in Pasadena." Master's thesis, Whittier College, 1948.

Casey, John A. "Effects of Desegregation: Relationship among Human Modifiable/Nonmodifiable Attributes and Frequency of Interracial Interactions of Blacks, Hispanics, Asians and Whites in Grades 1–12." Ed.D. thesis, University of San Francisco, 1984.

Casimere, Gerald Lee. "Ethnicity: As an Element in the Socio-Economic Development of Minority Communities." Master's thesis, Stanford University, 1970. Community development.

Chandler-Smith, Ruby. "Blacks and the Utilization of Mental Health Services." M.S.W. thesis, California State University, 1982. Sacramento community mental health services.

Chang, Edward T. "New Urban Crisis: Korean-Black Conflicts in Los Angeles." Ph.D. diss., University of California, Berkeley, 1990.

Cockerham, William Carl. "The Black Athlete and the Bay Area Press, 1968." M. Journalism thesis, University of California, Berkeley, 1968.

Cocoltchos, Christopher Nickolas. "The Invisible Government and the Viable Community: Ku Klux Klan in Orange County, California, during the 1920's." Ph.D. diss., University of California, Los Angeles, 1979.

Cole, Olen, Jr. "Black Youth in the Program of the Civilian Conservation Corps for California, 1933–1942." Ph.D. diss., University of North Carolina, Chapel Hill, 1986.

Coley, Geraldine Jones. "Black News in the Leading San Diego Daily Newspapers." Ph.D. diss., United States International University, 1976.

Collins, Keith Edison. "Black Los Angeles: The Maturing of the Ghetto, 1940–1950." Thesis, University of California, San Diego, 1975.

Cook, Daisy Louise. "Afro-Americans' Self-Perceptions of their Verbal Ability to Communicate." Ph.D. diss., United States International University, 1993. California study if self-perception and verbal ability.

Cooper, Donald G. "The Controversy over Desegregation in the Los Angeles Unified School District, 1963–1981." Ph.D. diss., University of Southern California, Los Angeles, 1991.

Couchman, Iain Spencer Balfour. "Self-Concept of Low-Income Blacks: A Descriptive Evaluation." Thesis, University of Oregon, 1969. Case studies in Oakland.

Crigler, William Robert. "The Employment Status of Blacks in Los Angeles: Ten Years After the Kerner Commission Report." Ph.D. diss., Claremont Graduate School, 1979.

Crimi, James E. "The Social Status of the Negro in Pasadena, California." Master's thesis, University of Southern California, Los Angeles, 1941.

Crossley, Lucy C. "Use of Services by A[id to] F[amilies with] D[ependent] C[hildren] Negro Mothers: A Study of Cultural Influences on the Attitudes of AFDC Mothers of Fresno County, California." Master's thesis, California State University, 1968.

Curry, Mitchell Lee. "The Role of Religious Experience in Psychotherapy and Mental Illness of Black People in a South Central Los Angeles Community." Min.D. thesis, School of Theology of Claremont, 1979.

Curtis, Austin. "The Black Panther Party in Oakland, California, 1966–1972." Master's thesis, University of Southern Mississippi, 1993.

Curtoys, Charles Jeremy. "The Paradox of Equality: A Study of the California Fair Employment Practice Commission." Ph.D. diss., University of California, Berkeley, 1976.

Dailey-Wilson, Virginia Lee. "A Study for the Development of Recruitment Strategies for Underrepresented Minority Students to a Metropolitan

Community College." Ph.D. diss., Pepperdine University, 1989. Recruitment model for West Los Angeles.

Daniels, Douglas. "Afro-San Franciscans: A Social History of Pioneer Urbanites 1860-1930." Ph.D. diss., University of California, Berkeley, 1975.

Davis, Clifford Linden, Jr. "Black Student Movements and Their Influence in the High Schools in the Los Angeles City Unified School District." Ed.D. thesis, University of California, Los Angeles, 1971.

Davison, Belinda. "Educational Status of the Negro in the San Francisco Bay Region." Master's thesis, University of California, Berkeley, 1921.

de Graaf, Lawrence B. "Negro Migration to Los Angeles, 1930–1950." Ph.D. diss, University of California, Los Angeles, 1962.

De Kam, Elizabeth J. "A Home to Call One's Own: A Textual Analysis of the Story of Residential Racial-Restrictive Covenants in the California *Eagle* and Los Angeles *Sentinel*." Master's thesis, California Sate University, 1993.

Detre, Les S. "Revolutionary Millenarianism and the Black Panther Party." Master's thesis, McGill University, 1973.

Dillard, Tom W. "The Black Moses of the West: A Biography of Mifflin Wistar Gibbs, 1823–1915." Master's thesis, University of Arkansas, 1974.

Drake, E. Maylon. "Employment of Negro Teachers." Ph.D. diss., University of Southern California, Los Angeles, 1963. Analyzes impact of 1959 Fair Employment Practices Act on Los Angeles teachers.

Eason, Charles Lewis. "An Analysis of the Social Attitudes and Casual Factors of Negro Problem Boys of the Los Angeles City Schools." Master's thesis, University of Southern California, Los Angeles, 1936.

Eddington, Neil Arthur. "The Urban Plantation: The Ethnography of an Oral Tradition in a Negro Community." Ph.D. diss., University of California, Berkeley, 1967. Research in Hunters Point.

Edwards, Patricia Bowman. "The Rhetorical Strategies and Tactics of the Black Panther Party as a Social-Change Movement, 1966–1973." Master's thesis, North Texas State University, 1974.

Elioff, Ione Hill. "Reactions of Parents from Diverse Social Backgrounds to their Experience in a Parent Participation Preschool Program." Master's thesis, California State University, San Francisco, 1968. Research project involving 22 Berkeley schools.

Embry, Robert Carlton. "Differences in School-Community Related Administrative Functions Among Racially Contrasted Secondary Schools in the Los Angeles Metropolitan Area." Thesis, Brigham Young University, 1976.

Erikkson, Elberta, Alan Mills, and Barbara Phillips. "A Study of Interracial Marriage (Black-White) in the Bay Area." Master's thesis (joint), California State University, Sacramento, 1962.

Ervin, James McFarline. "The Participation of the Negro in the Community Life of Los Angeles." Master's thesis, University of Southern California, Los Angeles, 1931.

Ficocelli-Lepore, Sandra. "Desegregation in Los Angeles: A Critical Assessment for Metropolitan Planning." Master's thesis, California State University, Dominguez Hills, 1980.

Fine, Doris R. "Civil Rights, Uncivil Schools: Disarray and Demoralization in the Public Schools of San Francisco (California)." Ph.D. diss., Education and Sociology, University of California, Berkeley, 1983.

Fisher, James A. "A History of the Political and Social Development of the Black Community in California, 1871–1876." Ph.D. diss., State University of New York at Stony Brook, 1971.

_____. "A Social History of Negroes in California, 1860–1900." Master's thesis, California State University, Sacramento, 1966.

Fort, Edward Bernard. "A Case Study of the Struggle to Secure an Administrative Plan for Eliminating de facto Segregation in the Junior High Schools in Sacramento, California." Ed.D. thesis, University of California, Berkeley, 1964.

France, Edward E. "Some Aspects of the Migration of the Negro to the San Francisco Bay Area since 1940." Ph.D. diss., University of California, Berkeley, 1962.

Francis, Robert Coleman. "A Survey of Negro Business in the San Francisco Bay Area." Master's thesis, University of California, Berkeley, 1928.

Franklin, Ruth. "Study of the Services Needed and/or Available to Negro Newcomer Families: A Study of Perception of Eleven Health and Welfare Agencies Serving the Community of Watts." Master's thesis, University of Southern California, Los Angeles, 1962.

Frelow, Robert Dean. "Intergroup Associations at an East Bay Junior High School." Master's thesis, California State University, San Francisco, 1964.

Garciá, Mikel. "Adaption Strategies of the Los Angeles Black Community, 1883–1919." Ph.D. diss., University of California, Irvine, 1985.

Gitchoff, George Thomas. "Community Response to Racial Tensions: An Exploratory Study of the Street Gang Program in Richmond." Master's thesis, University of California, Berkeley, 1966.

Godfrey, Brian John. "Inner-city Neighborhoods in Transitions: The Morphogenesis of San Francisco's Ethnic and Nonconformist Communities." Ph.D. diss., University of California, Berkeley, 1984.

Goggin, Daniel James. "Situational vs. Structural Causes of Homelessness Among Single Black Men in Orange County, California." MSW thesis, California State University, Long Beach, 1994.

Goldsmith, Renee Lois. "Negro Youth Culture and Identity: The Case of Hunters Point." M. Crim. thesis, University of California, Berkeley, 1967.

Graham, Luelva Broussard. "A Survey of Counseling Needs as Reported by Negro Female Students in the Twelfth Grade of the Los Angeles Area." Master's thesis, University of California, 1967.

Grant, Bradford Curtis. "Affordable Home Wanted Please: Black Family Wants to Cooperatively Own and Live in House in East Palo Alto." Master's thesis, University of California, Berkeley, 1980.

Grant, Doris. "A Comparison of the Self-Concept of Two Groups of Culturally Disadvantaged Kindergarten Children." Master's thesis, California State University, 1966. Effectiveness of a Palo Alto Head Start program.

Gray, Pamela Lee. "Yvonne Brathwaite Burke: The Congressional Career of California's First Black Congresswoman, 1972–1978." Ph.D. diss., University of Southern California, 1987.

Gray, Renata Ena. "Museum Design for the East Bay Negro Historical Society." Master's thesis, University of California, Berkeley, 1981.

Gray, Willa Bowser. "Residential Patterns and Associated Socio-Economic Characteristics of Black Populations of Varying City-Suburban Locations within the San Francisco Area: A Census-Based Analysis with Emphasis on Black Suburbanized Populations of 1970." D.S.W. diss., University of California, Berkeley, 1975.

Gruber, John Peter. "Comprehensive Plan for Corrections: City and County of San Francisco." Ph.D. diss., University of California, Berkeley, 1975.

Grunwald, Joan H. "A Study of the Play Patterns of a Certain Class of Low Income Four Year Old Children." Master's thesis, California State University, San Francisco, 1968. A study of 25 pre-schoolers, mostly Black, in East Menlo Park.

Guerra, Fernando J. "Ethnic Politics in Los Angeles: The Emergence of Black, Jewish, Latino and Asian Officeholders, 1900–1989." Ph.D. diss., University of Michigan, 1990.

Guillow, Lawrence Edward. "The Origins of Race Relations in Los Angeles, 1820–1880: A Multi-Ethnic Study." Ph.D. diss., Arizona State University, 1996.

Harper, Helena Hester. "A Study of Colored Unmarried Mothers in Los Angeles." Master's thesis, University of Southern California, Los Angeles, 1932.

Harris, Florence. "The Adjustment of the Negro in a California Junior High School." Master's thesis, Stanford University, 1949.

Harris, LeRoy E. "The Other Side of the Freeway: A Study of Settlement Patterns of Negroes and Mexican Americans in San Diego, California." Ph.D. diss., Carnegie-Mellon University, 1974.

Harris, Theresa Ella. "Family Planning Practices of a Selected Group of Black Married Women of Child-Bearing Age from the Western Addition of San Francisco." Master's thesis, California State University, 1971.

Harrison, Gloria. "The National Association for the Advancement of Colored People in California." Master's thesis, Stanford University, 1949.

Hart-Nibbrig, Nand Engie. "The Attitudes of Black Political Leaders toward Regional Governance in the San Francisco Bay Area: A Case Study of Black Activists in Berkeley, California." Ph.D. diss., University of California, Berkeley, 1974.

Hayes, Edward C. "Power Structure and the Urban Crisis: Oakland, California." Ph.D. diss., University of California, Berkeley, 1968.

Hekymara, Kuregiy. "The Third World Movement and its History in the San Francisco State College Strike of 1968-1969." Ph.D. diss., University of California, Berkeley, 1972.

Henderson, Wesley Howard. "Two Case Studies of African-American Architects' Careers in Los Angeles 1890–1945: Paul R. Williams, FAIA and James H. Garrot, AIA." Ph.D. diss, UCLA, 1992.

Henry, Curtis Charles. "The Spatial Interaction of Black Families in Suburban Cities in the Bay Area: A Study of Black Subsystem Linkages." Ph.D. diss., University of California, Berkeley, 1978.

Henry, Helen Elizabeth. "A Study of Attitudes and Social Values of the Youth of Four Selected Negro Churches of Los Angeles." Master's thesis, University of Southern California, Los Angeles, 1945.

Herman, David George. "Neighbors on the Golden Mountain: The Americanization of Immigrants in California. Public Instruction as an Agency of Ethnic Assimilation, 1850–1933." Ph.D. diss., University of California, Berkeley, 1981.

Hewitt, David John. "The Association of Race and Hypertension: A Cross-Sectional Study of Whites, Blacks, and Mexican-Americans in San Diego." M.P.H. thesis, San Diego State University, 1991.

Hickerson, Nathaniel. "Comparisons Between Negro and Non-Negro Students in Participation in the Formal and Informal Activities of a California High School." Ed.D., University of California, Berkeley, 1963.

Ho, Christine G. T. "The Caribbean Connection: Transnational Social Networks, Non-Assimilation and the Structure of Group Life among Afro-Trinidadian Immigrants in Los Angeles." Ph.D. diss., University of California, Los Angeles, 1985.

Hobbs, Thaddeus Henry. "The Dynamics of Negroes in Politics in the Los Angeles Metropolitan Area: 1945–1956." Master's thesis, University of Southern California, Los Angeles, 1960.

Holder, Kit Kim. "The History of the Black Panther Party, 1966–1971: A Curriculum Tool for Afrikan-American Studies." Ph.D. diss., University of Massachusetts, 1990.

Hollinger, William H. "Health of the Negro in San Francisco, California." Master's thesis, Stanford University, 1948.

Hopkins, Charles W. "The Deradicalization of the Black Panther Party, 1967–1973." Ph.D. diss., University of North Carolina at Chapel Hill, 1978.

Hudson, Lynn M. "When 'Mammy' Becomes a Millionaire: Mary Ellen Pleasant, an African American Entrepreneur." Ph.D. diss., Indiana University, 1996.

Hughes, William Edward. "Lower Socio-Economic Class Negro Children's Perceptions of their Teachers' Feeling Toward Them Related to Self-Perception, School Achievement, and Behavior." Master's thesis, California State University, San Francisco, 1968. Research conducted on a small Northern California school system.

Huling, William Edward. "Aging Blacks in Suburbia: Patterns of Culture Reflected in the Social Organization of a California Community." Thesis, University of Southern California, 1978.

Jacobs, Barbara D. "The Los Angeles Unified School District's Desegregation Case: A Legal History." Ph.D. diss., Pepperdine University, 1989.

Jernagin, Howard Eugene. "The American Negro, 1908–1912, as Portrayed in the *San Francisco Examiner*." Master's thesis, Howard University, 1957.

Johnson, Milo Perry. "The Trade and Industrial Education of Negroes in the Los Angeles Area." Master's thesis, University of California, Los Angeles, 1945.

Jones, Charles E. "An Analysis of the Political Repression of the Black Panther Party." Master's thesis, University of Idaho, 1979.

Jordan, Kenneth Allen. "The Geography of Consumer Economics among Black Americans in Oakland: A Cultural-Behavioral Perspective." Ph.D. diss., University of California, Berkeley, 1977.

Joseph, Eric Anthony. "Mandate for Diversity: A Comparative Analysis of the Black Studies Movement at San Francisco State University and the African-American Experience at Biola University." Ed.D. thesis, Biola University, 1994.

Kahl, Sue Ann. "An Evaluation of the Interdepartmental African Studies Unit at Lowell Junior High School in Oakland." Master's thesis, California State University, San Francisco, 1968.

Kaiser, Evelyn Lois. "The Unattached Negro Woman on Relief: A Study of Fifty Unattached Women on Relief in the Compton district office of the State Relief Administration of California in Los Angeles." Master's thesis, University of Southern California, Los Angeles, 1939.

Kassebaum, Peter Arthur. "Making Out in Del Paso Heights." Master's thesis, California State University, 1966. Survey of Blacks in Del Paso Heights.

Keeler, Kathleen F. R. "Post-School Adjustment of Educable Mentally Retarded Youth Educated in San Francisco." Ph.D. diss., Colorado State College, Greeley, 1963. Homemaking skills recommended as important for the "Negro and the Mexican-American group."

Kurth, Myrtle. "A Study of Four Racial Groups in a Pasadena Junior High School." Master's thesis, University of Southern California, Los Angeles, 1941.

Laurenti, Luigi Mario. "Effects of Nonwhite Purchase and Occupancy on Market Prices of Residents in San Francisco, Oakland, and Philadelphia." Ph.D. diss., University of California, Berkeley, 1957.

Lawrence, Paul Frederick. "The Vocational Aspirations of Negro Youth in Secondary Schools of California." Ph.D. diss., Stanford University, 1948.

Lemke-Santangelo, Gretchen. "A Long Road to Freedom: African American Migrant Women and Social Change in the San Francisco East Bay Area, 1940–1950." Ph.D. diss., Duke University, 1993.

Leon, Wilmer Joseph. "The Negro Contractor in Oakland, California and Adjacent Cities." Master's thesis, University of California, Berkeley, 1954.

Leonard, Kevin Allen. "Years of Hope, Days of Fear: The Impact of World War II on Race Relations in Los Angeles." Ph.D. diss., University of California-Davis, 1992.

Levenson, Rosaline. "The Negro Vote in California in 1952." Master's thesis, University of California, Berkeley, 1953.

Lewis, Edna. "Black Men in Watts, 1967: An Exploratory Study of Negro Males' Willingness to Accept Social Workers in a Ghetto Area." Master's thesis, California State University-Fresno, 1968.

Long, John Cornelius. "The Disciples of Christ and Negro Education." Ph.D. diss., University of Southern California, Los Angeles, 1960. Study of the ten schools.

Lortie, Francis N., Jr. "San Francisco's Black Community, 1870–1890: Dilemmas in the Struggle for Equality." Master's thesis, California State University, 1970.

Lukas, Henry J. "California—1850's and the Slavery Question." Master's thesis, University of Wisconsin, Madison, 1968.

Mabson, Berlinda (Davison). "Educational Status of the Negro in the San Francisco Bay Region." Master's thesis, University of California, Berkeley, 1921.

Manning, Jane Francis. "William A. Leidesdorff's Career in California." Master's thesis, University of California, Berkeley, 1941.

McBroome, Delores Nason. "Parallel Communities: African Americans in California's East Bay, 1850–1963." Ph.D. diss., University of Oregon, 1991.

McChesney, Robert W. "The Korean-Black Conflicts: A Critical Communication Approach." Ph.D. diss., University of Wisconsin-Madison, 1993.

McCorry, Jesse James. "The Political Economy of Leadership Innovation in the Oakland Public Schools." Ph.D. diss., University of California, Berkeley, 1974.

McPherson, Hallie M. "William McKendree Gwin, Expansionist." Ph.D. diss., University of California, Berkeley, 1931. Proslavery leader.

McQuiston, John Mark. "Patterns of Negro Residential Invasion in Los Angeles County." Master's thesis, University of Southern California, Los Angeles, 1968.

McSpadden, Hiltrude. "Sutter and Leidesdorff in the International Competition for California." Master's thesis, Stanford University, 1935.

Meldrum, George Weston. "The History and the Treatment of Foreign and Minority Groups in California, 1830–1860." Ph.D. diss., Stanford University, 1949.

Miller, Karen K. "Black Studies in California Higher Education, 1965–1980." Ph.D. diss., University of California, Santa Barbara, 1986.

Milner, Christina. "Black Pimps and Their Prostitutes: Social Organizations and Value System of a Ghetto Occupational Subculture." Ph.D. diss., University of California, Berkeley, 1970.

Mingori, Lynn Bosley. "The History of Negro Education in California, 1850–1890." Master's thesis, University of Southern California, Los Angeles, 1971.

Mitchell-Kernan, Claudia. "Language Behavior in a Black Urban Community." Ph.D. diss., University of California, Berkeley, 1969.

Montesano, Philip M. "The San Francisco Black Community, 1849–1890: The Quest for 'Equality Before the Law.'" Ph.D. diss., University of California, Santa Barbara, 1974.

_____. "Some Aspects of the Free Negro Question in San Francisco, 1849–1870." Master's thesis, University of San Francisco, 1967.

Montgomery, Winifred. "College Persistence among Black Undergraduate Attending the University of California at Berkeley." Ph.D. diss., University of California, Berkeley, 1989.

Moody, William P. "The Civil War and Reconstruction in California Politics." Ph.D. diss., University of California, Los Angeles, 1950.

Moore, Shirley Ann. "The Community in Richmond, California, 1910-1963." Ph.D. diss., University of California, Berkeley, 1989.

Mopkins, Patricia Ann. "Lifestyles and Socio-Economic Status of Los Angeles Aged Blacks in Retirement Homes." Master's thesis, California State University, Dominguez Hills, 1981.

Morgan, Elizabeth Pryor. "The Process of Parenting Among Twenty-four Black Families in Berkeley, California." Ph.D. diss., University of California, Berkeley, 1981.

Morris, James R. "The Social-Economic Background of Negro Youth in California." Ph.D. diss., Stanford University, 1947.

Mosley, Ruth J. Edwards. "A Study of the Negro Families in Los Angeles." Master's thesis, University of Southern California, Los Angeles, 1938.

Murphy, Larry George. "Equality Before the Law: The Struggle of Nineteenth-Century Black Californians for Social and Political Justice." Ph.D. diss., Graduate Theological Union, 1973.

Myhill, Marjorie Baum. "The Anti-Poverty Program in the Western Addition." M.C.P. thesis, University of California, Berkeley, 1968.

Nakamura, K. F. "Case Study of a Housing Redevelopment Project in a Four-Block Area of the Western Addition, San Francisco, California." Master's thesis, University of California, Berkeley, 1955.

Newton, Huey P. "War Against the Panthers: A Study of Repression in America." Ph.D. diss., University of California-Santa Cruz, 1980.

O'Connor, George M. "The Negro and the Police in Los Angeles." Master's thesis, University of Southern California, Los Angeles, 1955.

Okelo, Arnethia Wright. "A Comparative Study of the Recommended Art Education curricula of Kenya and California in terms of Achieving the Perceived Goals/Needs of Kenyans and Afro-Americans." Ph.D., University of California, Berkeley, 1976.

Ostrov, Gordon I. "Family Solidarity and School Dropouts: A Comparative Study of Adolescents from Negro Ethnic Group Families, City of Fresno, California, Dichotomized by Drop[outs and Graduates from High School." Master's thesis, California State University, Fresno, 1968.

Parker, Heather Rose. "African-American and Chicano Political Organization and Interaction in Los Angeles, 1960–1973." Ph.D. diss., University of California, Los Angeles, 1996.

Patterson, Beeman Coolidge. "The Politics of Recognition: Negro Politics in Los Angeles, 1960–1963." Ph.D. diss., University of California, Los Angeles, 1967.

Penn, Nolan. "Occupational Choices of Tenth Grade Students and the Influences of Racial and Socio-Economic Factors Upon Them." Master's thesis, University of Southern California, Los Angeles, 1952. Students at a Compton junior high school.

Persoff, Jessica Williams. "Racial Integration and Scholastic Achievement in Berkeley, California, Elementary Public Schools." M.C.P. thesis, University of California, Berkeley, 1969.

Pitts, J. C. "The Organization and Administration of School Clubs in the Jefferson High School of Los Angeles, California." Master's thesis, University of Southern California, Los Angeles, 1941.

Price, Thomas Aubrey. "Negro Storefront Churches in San Francisco: A Study of Their Spatial Characteristics in Two Selected Neighborhoods." Master's thesis, California State University, 1969.

Prince, Virginia Ann. "A Sociological Analysis of the Negro Press in Los Angeles." Master's thesis, University of Southern California, Los Angeles, 1946.

Rader, Tonja Evetts. "A Creative Dance and Body Movement Experience and its Effect Upon the Self-Concept of Disadvantaged Nursery School Children." Master's thesis, California State University, San Francisco, 1968. Research involving Black children in a San Francisco school.

Ragan, Roger L. "Attitudes of White Methodist Church Members in Selected Los Angeles Metropolitan Area Churches toward Residential Segregation of the Negro." Ph.D. diss., Southern California School of Theology, 1963. Tolerance and intolerance.

Ramey, Earl. "The Political Career of William McKendree Gwin." Master's thesis, Stanford University, 1930. Proslavery leader.

Ramsey, Eleanor Mason. "Allensworth: A Study in Social Change." Ph.D. diss., University of California, Berkeley, 1977.

Ratterman, Breen. "Guidance Practices for Negro Youth in Selected California Secondary Schools." Master's thesis, Stanford University, 1948.

Reynolds, Harry James. "A Study of Factors Affecting the Implementation of a Dropout Prevention Project in West Oakland." Ed.D. thesis, University of California, Berkeley, 1974.

Rice, Bobbylyne. "High School Teachers' Perceptions of African-American Male High School Students in San Francisco." Ph.D. diss., University of San Francisco, 1988.

Richards, Eugene Scott. "The Effects of the Negro's Migration to Southern California Since 1920 Upon His Sociocultural Patterns." Ph.D. diss., University of Southern California, Los Angeles, 1941.

Richards, Lenora Alexander. "A Study of the Social Welfare Activities of the Los Angeles Urban League." Master's thesis, University of Southern California, Los Angeles, Los Angeles, 1941.

Richardson, Adeline Claff. "A Follow-Up Study of Negro Girl Graduates of a Los Angeles High School." Master's thesis, University of Southern California, Los Angeles, 1941.

Riddick, Larry Eugen. "Race and School Finance in California." Ph.D. diss., University of California, Berkeley, 1973.

Riggle, William Henry. "The White, the Black and the Gray: A Study of Student Subcultures in a Suburban California High School." Ed.D. thesis, University of California, Berkeley.

Riker, Samuel. "The Effects of Training in Test Taking Techniques on Minority Group Job Applicants." Master's thesis, California State University, San Francisco, 1966. Spanish-American and Negro subjects from San Francisco used to research test-taking abilities and their relationship to job abilities.

Robertson, Florence (Keeney). "Problems in Training Adult Negroes in Los Angeles." Master's thesis, University of Southern California, Los Angeles, 1929. Racial attitudes of Blacks in Los Angeles.

Robinson, Effie Marie. "Social Problems of Dependent and Neglected Negro Children of Oakland, California." MSW, University of California, Berkeley, 1945.

Robinson, James Lee. "Tom Bradley: Los Angeles's First Black Mayor." Ph.D. diss., University of California at Los Angeles, 1976.

Rothstein, Mignon E. "A Study of the Growth of Negro Population in Los Angeles and Available Housing Facilities Between 1940 and 1946." Master's thesis, University of Southern California, Los Angeles, 1950.

Rouzan, Joseph T. "Attitudinal Factors Affecting Recruitment of Blacks into the Los Angeles Police Department." Master's thesis, Pepperdine University, 1973.

Salley, Robert Lee. "Activities of the Knights of the Ku Klux Klan in Southern California: 1921–1925." Master's thesis, University of Southern California, Los Angeles, 1963.

Sandoval, Sally Jane. "Ghetto Growing Pains: The Impact of Negro Migration on the City of Los Angeles, 1940–1960." Master's thesis, California State University, Fullerton, 1974.

Schmidt, Donald Ray. "Responses of Non-Negro Renters and Owners in Los Angeles and Orange Counties to the Prospect of Ethnic Change." Master's thesis, University of Southern California, Los Angeles, 1965.

Schuerman, Leo Anthony. "Assimilation of Minority Subpopulations in Los Angeles County." Master's thesis, University of Southern California, Los Angeles, 1969.

Sherer, Harry. "Antecedent Conditions and Academic Achievement of Ethnically Different Students in Junior College." Thesis, University of California, Los Angeles, 1967.

Shim, Jae Chul. "Impersonal Influence and the Growth of an Ethnic Community: The Origin and Consequence of Korean-Black Conflicts in Southern California." Ph.D. diss., University of Wisconsin-Madison, 1992.

Siller, Betty Dyberg. "The Fugitive Slave in California." Master's thesis, Sacramento State College, 1966.

Silverman, Max. "Urban Redevelopment and Community Response: African Americans in San Francisco's Western Addition." Master's thesis, San Francisco State University, 1994.

Skjeie, Sheila M. "California and the Fifteenth Amendment: A Study of Racism." Ph.D. diss., Sacramento State University, Sacramento, 1973.

Sloan, Jesse Lee. "Blacks in Construction: A Case Study of Oakland, California, and the Oakland Public Schools Construction Program 1960–1978." Master's thesis, San Francisco State University, 1979.

Smith, Alonzo N. "Black Employment in the Los Angeles Area, 1938–1948." Ph.D. diss., University of California, Los Angeles, 1978.

Smith, Paul Alan. "Negro Settlement and Railway Growth in Los Angeles, California, 1890–1930." Master's thesis, California State University, Northridge, 1973.

Smith, William Reid. "Police Control and the Black Community in Richmond, California." Ph.D. diss., University of California, Berkeley, 1971.

Soderstrom, Mary McGowan. "The Dissemination of Information in the Berkeley School Desegregation Decision." M. Journalism thesis, University of California, Berkeley, 1969.

Sovyanhadi, Marta Lukas. "The Influence of Prepregnancy Weight and Maternal Weight Gain: On Birth Weight among Black WIC Participants in San Bernardino County." Dr.P.H. thesis, Loma Linda University, 1994.

Stewart, Helen L. "Buffering: The Leadership Style of Huey P. Newton, Co-Founder of the Black Panther Party." Ph.D. diss., Brandeis University, 1980.

Stripp, Fred S. "The Relationship of the San Francisco Bay Area Negro-American Work with the Labor Unions Affiliated with the A.F.L. and the C.I.O." Ph.D. diss., Pacific School of Religion, Berkeley, 1948.

Strohm, Susan Mary. "Black Community Organization and the Role of the Black Press in Resource Mobilization in Los Angeles from 1940–1980." Ph.D. diss., University of Minnesota, 1989.

Sumbureru, Dale. "The Influence of Lifestyle on Longevity among Black Seventh-Day Adventists in California: An Epidemiologic Approach." Dr.P.H. thesis, Loma Linda University, 1988.

Sweeting, Anthony. "The Dunbar Hotel and Central Avenue Renaissance, 1781–1950." Ph.D. diss., University of California, Los Angeles, 1992.

Tanner, Lenora Russell. "Attitudes of Elderly Blacks toward the Aged and Aging." Master's thesis, San Diego State University, 1979. Focus on San Diego.

Tatum, Beverly Daniel. "Life in Isolation: Black Families Living in a Predominantly White Community." Ph.D. diss., University of Michigan, 1984.

Taylor, Dora Jones. "Broken Homes as a Factor in the Maladjustment of Delinquent Negro Boys in Los Angeles." Master's thesis, University of Southern California, Los Angeles, 1936.

Thurman, A. Odell. "The Negro in California Before 1890." Master's thesis, University of the Pacific, Stockton, 1945.

Tisdale, James Douglass. "A Study of the Attitudes of Outstanding Teachers in Black Educationally Disadvantaged, Inner City Elementary Schools in the Los Angeles Unified School District." Ed.D. thesis, Brigham Young University, 1971.

Tolbert, Emory J. "The UNIA in Los Angeles: A Study of Western Garveyism." Ph.D. diss., University of California, Los Angeles, 1975.

Treisman, Philip Michael. "A Study of the Mathematics Performance of Black Students at the University of California, Berkeley." Ph.D. diss., University of California, Berkeley, 1985.

Tyler, Bruce. "Black Radicalism in Southern California, 1950–1982." Ph.D. diss., University of California, Los Angeles, 1983.

Unrau, Harlan D. "The Double V Movement in Los Angeles During the Second World War: A Study in Negro Protest." Master's thesis, California State College, Fullerton, 1971. Fight against both racism here and Nazism abroad.

Von Brauchitsch, Dennis M. "The Ku Klux Klan in California, 1921 to 1924." Master's thesis, California State University, 1967.

Watson, Homer K. "Causes of Delinquency Among Fifty Negro Boys Assigned to Special Schools in Los Angeles." Master's thesis, University of Southern California, Los Angeles, 1923.

Webb, Warren Franklin. "A History of Lynching in California since 1875." Master's thesis, University of California, Berkeley, 1935.

Wellman, David Thomas. "Negro Leadership in San Francisco." Master's thesis, University of California, Berkeley, 1966.

Whitaker, Hazel Gottschalk. "A Study of Gifted Negro Children in the Los Angeles City Schools." Master's thesis, University of Southern California, Los Angeles, 1931.

White, Vivian Elizabeth. "The Social Contributions of a Welfare Center for Negro Girls in the City of Los Angeles, California." MA thesis, University of Southern California, Los Angeles, 1947.

Wilkerson, Margaret. "Black Theatre in the San Francisco Bay Area and in the Los Angeles Area: A Report and Analysis." Ph.D. diss., University of California, Berkeley, 1972.

Williams, Dorothy S. "Ecology of Negro Communities in Los Angeles County: 1940–1959." Ph.D. diss., University of Southern California, 1961.

Williams, Eddie Paul. "Occupational Decision-Making of Twelfth-Grade Black and White Male Students in California and North Carolina in 1969." Ph.D. diss., University of California, Berkeley, 1977.

Williams, Jan Gates. "Folk Medical Beliefs and Maternal Behavior: A Study Based on a Group of East Oakland Afro-American Women." Master's thesis, University of California, Berkeley, 1982.

Williams, Mildred. "An Historical Sketch of the Development of the Black Church in America and in Oakland, California." Master's thesis, Bay City Bible College, 1990.

Williams, Valena Minor. "The Black Press in Oakland: Will It Survive?" M.Journalism, University of California, Berkeley, 1981.

Williams, William James. "Attacking Poverty in the Watts Area: Small Business Development Under the Economic Opportunity Act of 1964." Ph.D. diss., University of Southern California, Los Angeles, 1966.

Wilson, Don J. "An Historical Analysis of the Black Administrator in the Los Angeles Unified School District." Thesis, University of California, Los Angeles, 1972.

Wong, Harold H. "The Relative Economic Status of Chinese, Japanese, Black, and White Men in California." Ph.D. diss., University of California, Berkeley, 1974.

Yoo, Hyunsuk. "Korean-Americans and African-Americans in the Los Angeles Riots: A Study of the Rhetoric of Conflict." Ph.D. diss., University of Pittsburgh, 1996. The 1992 Los Angeles riots and the role of the media.

Zhou, Jing. "Earnings of Chinese, Black, Hispanic, and Non-Hispanic White Men in the South and California: A Comparative Study." Ph.D. diss., Vanderbilt University, 1995.

Zubrinski, Camille Leslie. "'I Have Always Wanted to Have a Neighbor, Just Like You': Race and Residential Segregation in the City of Angels." Ph.D. diss., University of California, Los Angeles.

Black Newspapers:[1]

BAKERSFIELD

Antelope Valley Metro Star.
Bakersfield. 1975–1981.

Bakersfield Advocate. Bakersfield.
197?–1979.
Bakersfield News Observer.
Bakersfield. 1977–current.
Bakersfield News. Bakersfield.
1955–1975.
The News Publication. Bakersfield.
195?–1961. Continued by
Outlook: The News Publica-
tion.
Outlook: The News Publication.
Bakersfield. 1961–1964.
Outlook. Bakersfield. 1966–1970.
Outlook News. Bakersfield.
1966–1970.

Bakersfield Outlook. Bakersfield.
196?
Challenger. Bakersfield. 1970–19??
Colored Citizen. Bakersfield.
1913–1915.
Echo. Berkeley. 1881.
Metro Star. Bakersfield.
1975–1981.
San Fernando News Observer.
Bakersfield. 1981–current.

BERKELEY

Alameda Publishing Com-
pany
Berkeley Tri City Post. For Berkeley,
Oakland, Richmond, and
San Francisco.
1963–current.
Oakland Sea-Side Post.
Richmond Post. Richmond. 1963.

San Francisco Post. San Francisco.
1963.

Bay Viewer. Berkeley. 1969–1979.
Berkeley Post. Berkeley.
1963–current.
Black Panther. Berkeley. 1968–?
California Voice. Berkeley.
1919–current.
Peace and Freedom National Orga-
nizer. Berkeley. 1968–?

Voices From Within.
Arm the Spirit. Berkeley. 1979.

Seaside Post. Berkeley. 1963–1972.

COMPTON

Rapid Publishing
Carson Bulletin. Compton.
1974–current.
Compton Bulletin. Compton.
1975–current.
(Continued)
Lynwood Journal. Compton. 199?
Wilmington Beacon. Wilmington.

Compton Metropolitan Gazette.
Compton. 1966.
Compton Tri-City News. Compton.
1959–?
Herald American. Compton.
1935–1952.
Inglewood Tribune. Inglewood and
Compton. 1990–current.
Metropolitan Gazette. Compton.
1966–current.
Western Advocate. Compton.
1966–1970.
Wilmington Beacon. Compton.
199?

---

[1] Single-lined boxed items were published by the same publishers. Double-lined boxed items indicate change in masthead names.

CULVER CITY

Crenshaw News. Culver City.
1975–1987.
Culver City Star. Culver City.
1980–current.
Culver City Wave. Culver City. ?
L.A. Focus. Culver City. 1995–?

EAST PALO ALTO

Exploratory Globe. East Palo Alto.
19??–19??

Peninsula Bulletin. East Palo Alto.
1967–1969.
Peninsula Bulletin Weekly. East Palo
Alto. 1968–1971.
Peninsula Bulletin. East Palo Alto.
1971–1979.

**Firestone Park
News/Southwest
News Press**
Culver City Star. Culver City. 1980.
*Firestone Park News/Southwest News
Press.* Firestone Park.
1924.
Watts Star Review. Watts. 1875.

FRESNO

California Advocate. Fresno.
1967–current.
Fresno County Banner. Fresno.
189–190?
*Fresno People's Paper [Black Free
Press].* Fresno. 1970–?
Grapevine. Fresno. 1969–1979.
La Voz de Aztlan. Fresno.
1974–1982.
Uhuru Na Umoja. Fresno.
1974–1983.

HOLLYWOOD

National Record. Hollywood.
1944–current.
Record. Hollywood. 1944–1983.

INGLEWOOD

Impact. Inglewood. 198?–1989.
Ofari's Bi-Monthly. 1984–199?

Inglewood Tribune. Inglewood and
Compton. 1990–current.
LA Bay News Observer. Inglewood.
1981–current.
Minority Business Enterprise.
Inglewood. 1984–current.
News Advertiser. Inglewood. 1970.

LOS ANGELES

Afro-Tempo. Los Angeles.
1940–1945.

Angeles Mesa News Advertiser-Press.
19??–1978.
Angeles Mesa Wave. Los Angeles.
1978-19??

Black Lace. Los Angeles.
1993–current.
Black Progress Review. Los Angeles.
1989–?
Bronze Tattler. Los Angeles.
1939–1941?
Bronzeville News. Los Angeles.
1943–1944.
California Cactus. Los Angeles.
1912.
California Eagle. Los Angeles.
1879–1981.
California News. Los Angeles.
1926–1944.
California Tribune. Los Angeles.
1947–1950.

**Central News-Wave Publica-
tions:**
Angeles Mesa Wave. Los Angeles.
1925.
Central News. Los Angeles.
1919–current.

Central News Wave. Los Angeles. 1919–1975.

Central Star/Journal Wave. Los Angeles. 1919–current.

Compton/Carson Wave. Los Angeles.

Culver City/Marina del Rey Wave. Los Angeles. 1980–current.

Inglewood Hawthorne Gardena Wave. Los Angeles. 19??–1976.

Hawthorne Wave. Los Angeles. 1978–current.

Inglewood Wave. Los Angeles. 1976–19??

Inglewood Hawthorne Wave. Los Angeles. 1978–current.

Inglewood Wave. Los Angeles. 1981–199?

Los Angeles Sentinel. Los Angeles. 1934.

Lynwood Wave. Lynwood. 1919.

Mesa Tribune Wave. Los Angeles. 1919–current.

Southeast Wave-Star. Los Angeles. 1918–current.

Southside Journal. 1919–?

Southside Journal Wave. Los Angeles. 1972–current.

(Continued)

Southwest News #1. Los Angeles. 1891–1897.

Southwest News #2. Los Angeles. 1953–current.

Southwest News Wave. Los Angeles. 1919–current.

Southwest Sun. Los Angeles.

Southwest Topics. 1919–1941.

Southwest Topic-Wave. Los Angeles. 1941–current?

Southwest Wave. Los Angeles. 1919–current.

Southwest Wave Star. Los Angeles.

Southwestern Sun. Los Angeles. 1948–1972.

Southwestern Sun Wave. Los Angeles. 1972–current.

Topic-Wave Southwest. Los Angeles. 1918–current.

Tribune News Advertiser-Press. Los Angeles. 19??–1978.

Tribune News Wave. Los Angeles. 1919–19??

Westchester Star Weekly. Westchester.

Westchester Wave. Westchester. 1980.

Central Southwest News. Los Angeles. 1970.

Citizens Advocate. Los Angeles. 1916–1923.

Citizens' Voice. Los Angeles. 1964–1975.

City: Issues of African-American Urban Space. Los Angeles. 1994–?

Courier. Los Angeles. 1954–1971.

Craftsman Aero News. Los Angeles. 1939–1940.

Criterion. Los Angeles. 1942–1951.

Defender. Los Angeles. 1916–1919.

Eastside News. Los Angeles. 1936.

Los Angeles Sentinel. Los Angeles. 1934–current.

El Mundo. Los Angeles. 1993–current.

Enterprise. Los Angeles. 1907–1915.

Firestone Park News and Southeast News Press. Los Angeles. 1916–current.

First Word. Los Angeles. 1943–1946.

Free Angela and All Political Prisoners: The Newsletter of the United Committee to Free Angela. Los Angeles. 1970–197?

Gazette Publications:
The Gazette. For Los Angeles, Pasa-
    dena, and San Fernando Val-
    ley.

Happenings. Los Angeles.
    1962–1977.
Harambee #1. Los Angeles. 1967.
Harambee #2. Los Angeles. 1975.
Hard Line. Los Angeles. 1967.

**Herald-Dispatch Publica-
    tions.**
Herald Dispatch. Los Angeles.
    1952–current. L.A. edition
    and national edition.
Weekend Herald Dispatch. Los Ange-
    les. 1977–1981.

Holoman's Black Achievers. Los
    Angeles. 1991–?
IBA Magazine: Inside Black America.
    Los Angeles. 1990–?

Illustrated Reflector. Los Angeles.
    1939.
Graphic. Los Angeles. 1939.

Liberator. Los Angeles. 1900–1922.
Lomax Poll. Los Angeles. 1967–?
Los Angeles Advocate. Los Angeles.
    1888–?
Los Angeles Afro-American. Los
    Angeles. 191?
Los Angeles Beam. Los Angeles.
    194?
Los Angeles Central Avenues News.
    Los Angeles. 1910–1911.
Los Angeles Evening Express. Los
    Angeles. 1913–1925.
Los Angeles First Word. Los Ange-
    les. 1943–1946.
Los Angeles Guardian. Los Angeles.
Los Angeles Herald American. Los
    Angeles. 193?–?
Los Angeles Illustrated Journal. Los
    Angeles. 1956–?

Los Angeles Metropolitan Gazette.
    Los Angeles. 1966–?
Los Angeles New Era. Los Angeles.
    1939–?
Los Angeles News Press. Los Ange-
    les. 1962–1976.
Los Angeles News. Los Angeles.
    1959–1980.
Los Angeles Observer. Los Angeles.
    1888–?
Los Angeles Open City. Los Ange-
    les. 196?–?

Los Angeles Owl. Los Angeles.
    1879–1892.
California Eagle. Los Angeles.
    1891–1966 (*L.A. Eagle* be-
    fore 1913; *L.A. California
    Eagle* 1913–1951; *L.A. New
    California Eagle*
    1951–1966).
Los Angeles Pacific Defender. Los
    Angeles. 1923–1937.
    Merged with the *News*,
    1936.
Los Angeles California News. Los
    Angeles. 1929–1936.
    Merged with *Eagle*, 1936.

Los Angeles Pacific Enterprise. Los
    Angeles. 1927–?
Los Angeles Post. Los Angeles.
    1915–?
Los Angeles Postage Stamp. Los
    Angeles. 191?
Los Angeles Record. Los Angeles.
    1944–current.
Los Angeles Reflector. Los Angeles.
    193?
Los Angeles Sentinel. Los Angeles.
    1934–current.
Los Angeles Spark. Los Angeles.
    196?

Los Angeles Star Review and the Advertiser Review. Los Angeles. 19??–1951.
Star Review. Los Angeles. 195?

Los Angeles Tattler. Los Angeles. 1944–1946.
Los Angeles Teller. Los Angeles. 1944–1946.
Los Angeles Town Talk. Los Angeles. 1930–?
Los Angeles Tribune [Founded as *Los Angeles Interfaith Churchman*]. Los Angeles. 1940–1963.
Los Angeles United Pictorial Review. Los Angeles. 1965–?
Los Angeles Valvardian. Los Angeles. 1940–?

Los Angeles War Worker. Los Angeles. 1943–?
Los Angeles Now. Los Angeles. 1944–1946.
Los Angeles Watts Advertiser-Review. Los Angeles. 1908–1940.
Los Angeles Watts Advertiser. Los Angeles. 1908–1928.
Los Angeles Watts Review. Los Angeles. 1915–1929.

Los Angeles Watts Herald. Los Angeles. 1923–192?

Los Angeles Watts News. Los Angeles. 1906–1918.
Merged with:
Suburban Home. Los Angeles. 1918.
Los Angeles Suburban Home. Los Angeles. 1914–1918.
Los Angeles Suburban Home and Watts News. Los Angeles. 1914–1925.

Los Angeles Watts Observer. Los Angeles. 1913–1920. White-owned?

Los Angeles Watts Review. Los Angeles. 1915–1929. White-owned?
Los Angeles Western Clarion. Los Angeles. 1926–?
Los Angeles Western Record. Los Angeles. 1936–?
Los Angeles WLCAC News. Los Angeles. 1967–?
Militant. Los Angeles. 1944–1946.
National African American News. Van Nuys. 1996–current.
National Herald. Los Angeles. 1976–1977.

Neighborhood News. Los Angeles. 1930–1956.
American News. Los Angeles. 1956–1960.

New Watts Awakening. Los Angeles. 1972–?

New Age. Los Angeles. 1907–1926. Acquired:
Los Angeles Western Dispatch. Los Angeles. 1921–1922.
New Age Dispatch. Los Angeles. 1925–1948.

New Age Negro. Los Angeles. 1904–1925.
News Advertiser. Inglewood.
News. Los Angeles. 1944–1946.
News-Guardian. Los Angeles. 1937–1944.
Newsletter/Los Angeles Chapter, Western Christian Leadership Conference. Los Angeles. 1965–?

Open Sesame. Los Angeles. 1893–1895.
Searchlight. Los Angeles. 1896–1908.

Orange Star Review. Los Angeles. 1975–1976.
Outlet. Los Angeles. ?–1925.

Pacific Defender. Los Angeles.
    1923–1938.
Players. Los Angeles. 1973–current.
Respect. Los Angeles. 1969–?
Scoop. Los Angeles. 1966–1977.
Scoop. San Francisco. 196?
Searchlight and Open Sesame. Los
    Angeles. 1893–1908.

Southeast News Press Pub-
    lishers:
Firestone Park News. Los Angeles.
Spokesman #2. San Francisco.
    1965–1967. Also pub-
    lished as the *Hunter's Point*
    Spokesman. Hunter's
    Point.
Herald-Dispatch. Los Angeles.
    1981–?

Southern California Guide. Los Ange-
    les. 1891–1895.
Southwest News #2. Los Angeles.
    1953–current.
Spoken Word. Los Angeles.
    1934–1937.
Spotlight. Los Angeles.
    1944–1951.
Teller. Los Angeles. 1944–1946.
Truth Messenger. Los Angeles.
    1899–?
Turning Point: Of, By and For the
    L.A. County African Ameri-
    can Community. Los Ange-
    les. 1993–?
United Pictorial Review. Los Ange-
    les. 1965–1975.
Voice of BETHRUM. Los Angeles.
    1971.
Watts Times. Los Angeles.
    197?–1980.
WCLC Newsletter. Los Angeles.
    1965–1970.
Weekly Observer. Los Angeles.
    1888.

Western Christian Recorder. Los
    Angeles. 1900–1947.
    AME Church.
Western Dispatch. Los Angeles.
    1921–1922.
Western Informant. Los Angeles.
    1936–?
Western News. Los Angeles. 1889.
What's Going On. Los Angeles.
    1975–1987.

MENLO PARK
Belmont Courier Bulletin. Menlo
    Park. 1978.
Black Times Voices of the National
    Community. Menlo Park.
    1971–1986.
Menlo Atherton Recorder. Menlo
    Park. 1978.
Ravenswood Post. Menlo Park.
    1953–1981.
San Carlos Enquirer. Menlo Park.
    1978.

OAKLAND
Auto Workers Focus: The Rank and
    File Newsletter of the Black
    Panther Caucus. Oakland.
    1969–1970.
Beacon. Oakland. 1945–1947.
Berkeley Tri-City Post. Oakland.
    1963–current.
Black Nation. Oakland. 1981.
Black Panther. Oakland.
    1965–1980.
Burning Spear. Oakland.
    1968–1987.
California Voice. Oakland.
    1919–1989.
California World. Oakland. 1919.
Commemorator. Black Panther Party,
    Oakland. 199?–1993.
Flatlands. Oakland. 1966–1967.
Herald. Oakland. 1943–1951.

I Am We: Newsletter of the Committee for Justice for Huey P. Newton and the Black Panther Party. Oakland. 1975–1978.

Illustrated Guide. Oakland. 1892–1900.

Independent. Oakland. 1929–1931.

Justice for Huey Newsletter. Oakland. 1974.

Kemet. Oakland. 1979–?

Light. Oakland. 1944–1946.

Newark Forum. Oakland. 1977.

Night Edition News. Oakland. 1972–1978.

Oakland Golden State. Oakland. 192?

Oakland Independent. Oakland. 1929–1935.

Oakland New Day Informer. Oakland. ?–1944.

Oakland Post. Oakland. 1963–current.

Oakland Times-Journal. Oakland. 1952–1987.

Pacific Times. Oakland. 1912.

Richmond Post. Oakland. 1963–current.

San Francisco Mundo Hispano. Oakland. 1975.

San Francisco Post. Oakland. 1963–current.

Seaside Post. Oakland. 1963–current.

Stand on the Forward Side: Quarterly Newsletter of the Committee in Solidarity with African Independence. Oakland. 1982–?

Sunshine. Oakland. 1907–1922. Also published as *Oakland Sunshine*, 194?

California Voice. Oakland. 1919–1971.

South End News. 1930?

Florence Messenger. Florence. 1930–?

Compton Westside Bee. 1930–?

Times. Oakland. 1923–1924.

Uhuru. Oakland. 1970.

Unity. Oakland. 1970–current.

Voice. Oakland. 1962–1970.

Western American. Oakland. 1926–1929.

Western Outlook. Oakland. 1894–1907.

PACOIMA

Black World. Pacoima. 1970–1971.

San Fernando Gazette Express. Pacoima. 1966–current.

PALO ALTO

Black Times Voices of the National Community. Palo Alto. 1971–1978.

Palo Alto Community Bulletin. Palo Alto. 1968–?

Palo Alto Explanatory Globe. Palo Alto. 196?

Palo Alto Peninsula Bulletin Weekly. Palo Alto. 1967–?

Palo Alto Ravenswood Post. Palo Alto. 1953–?

Pamoja Venceremos. Palo Alto. 1971–1973.

Peninsula Bulletin. Palo Alto. 1966–1981.

PASADENA

Crown City Press. Pasadena. 1956–19??

Los Angeles Metropolitan Gazette. Pasadena. 1962–199?

Pasadena Crown City Press. Pasadena. 1956–196?

Pasadena Eagle. Pasadena. 1968–1973.

> *The Eagle.* Altadena. 1973–?

Pasadena Equalizer. Pasadena. 1968.
Pasadena Gazette. Pasadena.
　1966–current.
Pasadena Informer. Pasadena.
　1930–?
Pasadena Journal News. Pasadena.
　1989–1994.
Pasadena/San Gabriel Valley Journal.
　1994–?
Plain Truth. Pasadena. 1934.

POMONA
Pomona Clarion. Pomona.
　1970–1979.
Pomona Freewalk Gazette. Pomona.
　1962–?
Pomona Inlands Report. Pomona.
　1961–?

QUARTZ HILL
Antelope Valley Metro Star. Quartz
　Hill. 1980–199?
Bakersfield Metro Star. Quartz Hill.
　1980–199?
Los Angeles Metro Star. Quartz Hill.
　1980–199?

RIVERSIDE

> *Black Voice News.* Riverside.
> 　1972–current.
> *Voice.* Riverside. 1984–1990.
> *Black Voice News.* Riverside.
> 　1990–?

Observer. Riverside. 1962–1976.
Riverside Reporter. Riverside.
　1969–?

SACRAMENTO
American. Sacramento. 1944–1947.
California Times. Sacramento.
　1856–1857.
Forum. Sacramento. 1906.

Hollywood Happenings. Sacramento.
　1994.
Los Angeles Happenings. Sacra-
　mento. 1981–1983.
Outlook. Sacramento. 1942–1967.
Request Line. Sacramento. 1994–?
Sacramento Observer. Sacramento.
　1962–current.
Settlers and Miners Tribune. Sacra-
　mento. 1850.
Western Outlook. Sacramento.
　1981–1983.
Western Review. Sacramento.
　1914–1926.

SAN BERNARDINO
Precinct Reporter. San Bernardino.
　1965–current.
San Bernardino American. San
　Bernardino. 1969–current.
San Bernardino Tri-County Bulletin.
　San Bernardino.
　1945–1952.

SAN DIEGO
Comet. San Diego. 1946–1953.
Eagle. San Diego. 1922–1925.
Informer. San Diego. 1937–1947.
Light House. San Diego.
　1939–1975.
New Idea. San Diego. 1921–1926.
San Diego Black Pages. San Diego.
San Diego Ledger. San Diego.
　192?–?
San Diego Monitor. San Diego.
　1988–current.
San Diego Plaindealer. San Diego.
　194?–19??
*San Diego Southeast [San Diego Re-
　porter and Shopper].* San
　Diego. 1969.
South California Informant. San Di-
　ego. 1889.

San Diego Voice. San Diego.
1964–1974.
San Diego Union. San Diego.
1963–1968.
San Diego Viewpoint. San Diego.
1969.
San Diego Voice and Viewpoint. San
Diego. 1960–current.

SAN FERNANDO

San Fernando Gazette Express. San
Fernando. 1966–current.
San Fernando Valley African Ameri-
can Chronicle News. San
Fernando Valley.
199?–current.

SAN FRANCISCO

Alto California. San Francisco.
1851.
Bay Area Report. San Francisco
1987.
Bay Guardian. San Francisco.
1975–1976.
Black Dialogue. San Francisco.
1965–1979.

Black Panther. San Francisco.
1967–1980.
Black Panther Party Intercommunal
News Service. San Fran-
cisco. Formerly, Black Panther.

Black Power. San Francisco.
1972–1974.
Bulletin/Ministry of Information.
San Francisco. 196?–?
California Voice. San Francisco.
1919–current.
Call. San Francisco. 1894–1904.
Citizen. San Francisco. 1888–1890.
Free Lance. San Francisco.
191?–19??
Independent. San Francisco. 1903–?

Insurgent. San Francisco. 1965.
Labor Herald. San Francisco.
1948–1951.

Mirror of the Times. San Francisco.
1855–1862.
Elevator. San Francisco.
1862–1898.
Pacific Coast Appeal. San Francisco.
1898–1925.
Pacific Coast Appeal and San Francisco Elevator.
1904–1905.
New Bay Review. San Francisco.
1976–current.
San Francisco Bay Review. San Francisco. 1996–current.

Observer. San Francisco.
1962–1981.
Pacific Appeal. San Francisco.
1862–1879.
People's Advocate. San Francisco.
1944.

San Francisco Fillmore Shopping
Guide. San Francisco.
1950–?
San Francisco Independent. San
Francisco. 195?

San Francisco Free Lance. San Fran-
cisco. 191?–?
San Francisco Golden State News.
San Francisco. 194?–?
San Francisco Graphic. San Fran-
cisco. 1949.
San Francisco Hunter's Point Beacon.
Hunter's Point.
1943–1945.
San Francisco Pacific Times. San
Francisco, Bakersfield, San
Jose, and North Yakima,
WA. 1944–?
San Francisco People's Advocate.
San Francisco. 1944–?

San Francisco Post. San Francisco. 1963–current.

San Francisco Reporter. San Francisco. 1900–?

┌─────────────────────────────────────┐
San Francisco Reporter. San Francisco. 1943–1949.

San Francisco Sun Reporter. San Francisco. 1945–current.

Sun. San Francisco. 1942–1949.
└─────────────────────────────────────┘

San Francisco Sun. San Francisco. 1910.

San Francisco Tribune. San Francisco. 194?

San Francisco West Coast Star. San Francisco. 194?

┌─────────────────────────────────────┐
San Francisco Western Appeal. San Francisco. 1918–1927.

Western American. Oakland. 1926–1929.

Oakland Independent. Oakland. 1929–1936.

San Francisco Spokesman #1. San Francisco. 1935–1938.
└─────────────────────────────────────┘

Scoop. San Francisco. 196?

Sentinel. San Francisco. 1880–1890.

Spokesman #2. San Francisco. 1965–1967.

Urban West. San Francisco. 1967–1973.

Vindicator. San Francisco. 1884–1906.

Western Outlook. San Francisco. 1894–1928.

SAN JOSE

Forum. San Jose. 1908.

Journal. San Jose. 197?–19??

La Voz Latina. San Jose. 1993–1994.

San Jose Forum. San Jose, Marysville, Pacific Grove, Hollister, and Goldfield, NV. 1908–?

SAN JOAQUIN

Bakersfield Colored Citizen. San Joaquin Valley industrial edition. 1914.

San Joaquin Progressor. San Joaquin. 1969–1972.

SANTA ANA

Orange County Star Review. Santa Anna.

Tri-County Bulletin. Santa Ana. 198?–current.

SANTA MONICA

Bay Cities Informer. Santa Monica. ?–1946.

Santa Monica Bay Cities Informer. Santa Monica. 194?

STOCKTON

Guide. Stockton. 1944–1947.

Observer. Stockton. 1979–1984.

Press. Stockton. 1944.

San Joaquin Progressor. Stockton. 1969–1972.

Stockton California Echo. Stockton. 1962–?

Stockton California Negro Press. Stockton. 194?

Stockton Progressor [a.k.a.: *San Joaquin Progressor*] Stockton. 1969–?

VARIOUS COMMUNITIES

Afro-American Speaks. San Pedro. 1971.

Bayou Talk. Moreno Valley. 1992–?

Black Echo. Milpitas. 1969–1974.

Black Times. Albany. 1971–1973.

Black Unity. Oceanside. 1970.

Black Vibrations. Santa Barbara. 19??–1975.

Call. Bell Gardens. 1972–1976.

Carson Courier. Carson. 1980.
Colored Citizen. Red Lands. 1905–?
Ethiopian Mirror. Beverly Hills.
    1988–current.
Feeling Good. Manhattan Beach.
    1988–current.
Hambone. Stanford. 1974. Annual.
Heritage Newsletter: California African American Genealogical Society. Monthly heritage newsletter. 1988–1991?
Long Beach Express. Long Beach.
    1966–current.
Lynwood Journal.
    Lynwood/Compton.
    1919–current.

Metro Reporter Publications.

Newspapers for Berkeley, Oakland, Peninsula, Richmond, San Francisco, San Joaquin, San Jose, and Vallejo/Fairfield.
Berkeley Metro Reporter. San Francisco. 1975–current.

Oakland Metro Reporter. San Francisco. 1974–current.
    (Continued)
Peninsula Metro Reporter. San Francisco. 1975–current.
Richmond Metro Reporter. San Francisco. 1975–current.
San Francisco Metro Reporter. San Francisco. 1973–current.
San Joaquin Metro Reporter. San Francisco. 1973–current.
San Jose/Peninsula Metro Reporter. San Francisco. 1975–current.
Vallejo Metro Reporter. San Francisco. 1975–current.

News. Richmond. 1945–1946.
Post News Sentinel. Seaside.
    1947–current.
Pamoja. Emeryville. 1980.
Pasadena Eagle. Altadena.
    1968–1976.
Star News-The Voice. Chula Vista.
    1970–1979.
Wilmington Beacon. Wilmington.
    1990–current.

Black Periodicals and Journals:

A. M. E. Guide. Los Angeles.
Accent/L.A. "News, Entertainment & the Arts." Monthly magazine, 1987–1990.
African Arts/Arts D'Afrique. Los Angeles. 1967–current?
Africana Newsletter. Stanford.
    1962–1964.
Alameda County Human Relations Commission Newsletter. Oakland. 1966.
Aldebaran Review. Berkeley. 1968. Interracial literacy magazine.

Ante. Los Angeles. 1964–1968. Interracial literary magazine.
Antinarcissus: Surrealist Conquest. San Francisco. 1969. Interracial literary magazine.
Archon. Oakland. 1931. Zeta Phi Beta sorority bi-annual.
Ball and Chain Review. Berkeley and Albany. 1969–1970. Published by the organization—Black Journalists.
Baptist Herald. Oakland.
    1915–1916. Publication of the Beth Eden Baptist Church.

Bay Area Scoop. San Francisco.
    1969–? San Francisco edi-
    tion of *Scoop.*
Scoop. Los Angeles. 1967. Enter-
    tainment industry news.

Bayviewer. Berkeley. 1967–?
Black Business Review. Oakland.
    1969.
Black Cobra. Sacramento.
    1967–1969.
Black Dialogue. San Francisco.
    1965–1969.
Black Economic Community Maga-
    zine. San Diego.
Black Family. Berkeley. 1971–? By
    the Black Studies Student
    Association, UC-Berkeley.
Black Fire. San Francisco. 1968–?
    California State University,
    Black Students Union.
Black Graphics International. San
    Francisco. 1969–?
Black Guards Organ. San Francisco.
    1970–? By the African De-
    scendants Peoples Republic
    Provisional Government.
Black Lace. Los Angeles.
    1991–current. Quarterly.
    Black lesbian audience.
Black Law Journal. Los Angeles.
    Current. UCLA.
Black Orange Magazine. Orange
    County.
Black Panther Community Newslet-
    ter. 1969–?
Black Politician: A Journal of Cur-
    rent Political Thought. Los
    Angeles. 1969–1974.
Black Politics: A Journal of Libera-
    tion. Berkeley.
    1968–1969.
Black Power. San Francisco. 1967–?
    By House of Umoja.

Black Scholar. Oakland.
    1969–current.
Black Student Union News Service.
    Hayward. 1969–? Black
    Student Union, California
    State University, Haywood.
Black Thoughts Journal. Berkeley.
    1973–1983.
Black Unity. Berkeley. 1969–?
    Muslim-oriented.
Black Voice. Los Angeles. 1968–?
Breakthrough. San Francisco.
    1969–?
Broadway. Los Angeles. 194?
Bronze America. Hollywood.
    1963–1974.
Bronze California. Los Angeles.
    1963–1965.
Bronze Tattler. Los Angeles. 194?
Budget. San Francisco. 1894–?
    Typewritten and for mem-
    bers of the Assembly Club.

CAAS Newsletter/UCLA Center for
    Afro-American Studies. Los
    Angeles. 1977–1988.
CAAS Report/UCLA Center for Afro-
    American Studies. Los An-
    geles. 1989–?

California Cactus. Los Angeles.
    1909–1911.
California History Series. San Fran-
    cisco. 1965–? San Fran-
    cisco African American His-
    torical and Cultural Society
    monographs.
Campus CORE-lator. Berkeley.
    1964–1967. Berkeley cam-
    pus CORE.
Change! Oakland. 1967–? Unitar-
    ian-Universalist Project
    East Bay.
Choice Magazine. San Francisco.
    1981–1987.

Christian Register. Oakland. 1923–1925. First African Methodist Episcopal Church.

Chronicle. Oakland. 1925. Beth Eden Baptist Church.

Clarion. Los Angeles. 192?

Cloud's Children's Pictorial. Los Angeles. 1936–? Free publication of Cloud's Photographic Studios.

Coastlines. Los Angeles and Santa Monica. 1955–1964. Interracial literary magazine.

Colleague. Los Angeles. 1954–? Los Angeles branch, National Urban League.

Combination. Oakland. 1963–1968. The Bay Area Studio/Printing Company.

Community Reporter. Los Angeles. 1949–1951. Los Angeles County Conference on Community Relations.

Compassionate Review and World Youth Crusader. San Francisco. 1966–? United African Appeal, Inc. and World Youth.

Contact. Sausalito. 1958–1965. Interracial literary magazine.

Craftsmen Aero-News. Los Angeles. 1937–1938. Black Wings, Inc.

Criterion. Oakland. 1941.

Cure: Citizens United for Racial Equality. San Diego. 1969.

Dare. Los Angeles. 1965–?

Deserted Times. San Francisco. 1968–? Literary magazine.

Dust. El Cerrito. 1964–? Interracial literary magazine.

Ebon. San Francisco. 1970–? San Francisco Comic Book Company.

Echo. Pasadena. 192?–? First AME Church, Pasadena.

Education Corps Newsletter. Greenbrae. 1969.

Elegant. Los Angeles. 1964–1968. Fashion magazine.

Equalizer. Los Angeles. 1968–1969. National Equalizer Enterprises.

Exclusive Magazine. Los Angeles. 198?–?

Fair Lady Magazine. Oakland. ?

Fair Practices News. San Francisco. 1960–1963. California State Fair Employment Practices Commission.

Falcon. Oakland. 1960–?

Family Savings and Loan Association Community Newsletter. Los Angeles. 1967–?

Femme [a.k.a. *Femne*]. Los Angeles. 1954–1962. For "Negro women."

Flash. Los Angeles. 1929–1930. News magazine.

Golden Pen. Los Angeles. 1970–? Monthly by the public relations office of the Golden State Mutual Life Insurance Company.

Golden State Mutual Messenger. Los Angeles. 1930–1950. By the Golden State Mutual Life Insurance Company. [a.k.a. *Golden State Mutual Insurance Company Bulletin, Golden State News,* etc.]

Grok. San Francisco. 1967-? Interracial literary magazine.

Guiding Star. Los Angeles, San Diego, Berkeley, etc. 1930–1963. Golden State

Grand Chapter, Order of the
Eastern Star, Prince Hall
Rite of Adoption, California
and its Jurisdiction.

Hamitic Review. Los Angeles. 1935.

*Hollywood-Wilshire Fair Housing
Council News.* Los Ange-
les. 1969–?

*Hunters Point-Bayview Community
Health Service News.* San
Francisco. 1969–?

*International Review of African
American Art.* Los Angeles.
1991.

Ivy Leaf. Berkeley. 1922–?. Sorority monthly periodical.

Journal Advocate. Berkeley. 1956–?
East Bay Cities Business
League.

Journal of Black Poetry. San Francisco. 1966–1969.

Journal of Black Psychology. Thousand Oaks. Quarterly.

Journal of Black Studies. Thousand
Oaks. 1970–current.

*Journal of New African Literature and
the Arts.* Stanford. 1966–?

Journal of Pan African Studies.
Fresno. 1987–current.

*Journal of the African Methodist
Episcopal Convention.* San
Francisco. 1863.

Lamppost. San Francisco.
1899–191? Youth for Serv-
ice.

Liberator. Los Angeles. 191?;
1959–?

Lou Jones Newsletter. San Mateo
1959–? Intergroup Rela-
tions Association of Northern California.

Lunar Visitor. San Francisco.
1862–? Literary magazine
edited by pastor of the First

AME Zion Church, John
Jamison Moore.

Mafundi Potential. Los Angeles.
1970–? Mafundi Institute.

Marin City Memo. Marin City.
1966–? Southern Marin
Economic Opportunity
Council.

Messenger. Los Angeles.
1940–1951. Golden State
Mutual Life Insurance Company.

*Mid-Peninsula Citizens for Fair Hous-
ing Newsletter.* Palo Alto.
1965–?

Minaret. San Francisco. 1970–?
Muhammad's Mosque No.
26.

Minority Business Entrepreneur.
Torrence,. 1984. Maga-
zine.

Movement. San Francisco.
1965–1970. SNCC Com-
mittee of California.

NAACP Bulletin. Oakland 194?–?
Alemeda County branch of
the NAACP.

NAACP Freedom Journal. Stanford.
1953–1969. Stanford Uni-
versity branch.

National Baptist Extension Advocate.
Los Angeles. 1925–? Na-
tional Baptist Extension
Board of America, the California Baptist State Con-
vention, and the Masonic
Brotherhood.

National Lever. Los Angeles.
1915–?

Neighborhood Legal News. San Francisco. 1968–? Western Ad-
dition Law Office Commu-
nity Education Project.

New Day Informer. Oakland.
1924–1929.

New Lady Magazine. Hayward.
    1969–1974.

New Tide. Los Angeles. 1934–?

News Edition. Los Angeles. 1934–?

*News From Bay Area Council Against
    Discrimination.* San Fran-
    cisco. 194?–1944.

News Letter. San Francisco. 196?–?
    Plan of Action for Challeng-
    ing Times, Inc.

*Nommo: African Student Newsmaga-
    zine at UCLA.* Los Angeles.
    1968–?

Now, Inc. Los Angeles. 19431946.

O.E.D.C. Reporter. Oakland.
    1965–1968. Oakland Eco-
    nomic Development Coun-
    cil.

Outlet. Los Angeles. 1924–1925.

Pastime. San Francisco. 1967–?

Peace Guide. Los Angeles.

*Phase II: Journal of Black Art Ren-
    aissance.* Berkeley.
    1970–? Black Heritage
    Class, University of Cali-
    fornia.

Plain Talking. Los Angeles. 1931–?

Players. Los Angeles. 1973.
    Monthly.

Praisesinger Annual. San Francisco.
    Newsletter of the African
    American Historical and
    Cultural Society of San
    Francisco, 1974–1977?.

*Quarterly Bibliography on Cultural
    Differences.* Sacramento.
    1964–? California State Li-
    brary.

Quotable Karenga. Los Angeles.
    1972–1974.

Railroad Men's Guide. 191?

Richmond Neighborhood Courier.
    Richmond. 196?–?

Roots in Revolt. San Francisco.
    1968–? Black Community

Research and Communica-
    tion Project.

Sepia Hollywood. Los Angeles.
    1944–1950. Monthly en-
    tertainment magazine.

Shrewd. Los Angeles. 1968. Bi-
    monthly.

Silhouette Pictorial. Los Angeles.
    1940–1950.

Skills Center News Letter. Oakland.
    1969–? East Bay Skills
    Center.

Soledad Brothers News Letter. San
    Francisco. 1970–?

Soul Illustrated. Los Angeles.
    1968–1973. Entertainment
    magazine.

Soul. Los Angeles. 1965–1982.

*Soulbook: The Quarterly Journal of
    Revolutionary Afroamerica.*
    Berkeley. 1964–?

*Stanford Research Institute Research
    Memorandum.* Menlo Park.
    1967–? For the San Fran-
    cisco Unified School Dis-
    trict to study the alleviation
    of racial imbalance.

Syndrome. Oakland. 1967–? Cul-
    tural Motivation Publica-
    tions, Inc.

The Grapevine. San Mateo. 196?–?
    San Mateo Community
    Service Center.

The Integrator. Los Angeles. 1968–?
    Crenshaw Neighbors, Inc.

*This is L.A.: L.A.'s Only Sepia
    Magazine.* Los Angeles.
    1960–?

*Tribune: A Magazine of Report and
    Opinion.* Los Angeles.
    1964–1965.

Uhuru. Oakland. 1968–? Political
    and literary publication.

Uprising. Pasadena. 1967–1968.
 Continued by *Nigger Upris-*
 ing.
Nigger Uprising. Los Angeles.
 1968.

Urban Light. Los Angeles.
 1931–1935. L.A. branch of
 the National Urban League.
Urban West. San Francisco. 1967–?
Val Verde News. Los Angeles.
 1954–? Val Verde Im-
 provement Association.
Voice of Watts. Los Angeles.
 1968–?
WACO Organizer. San Francisco.
 1967–? Western Addition
 Community Organization.
Watts Summer Festival. Los Angeles.
 1966–1975 (Annual).
We Not They. San Rafael. 1968–?
 Marin County Human
 Rights Commission.
We: A Monthly Calendar of Bay Area
 Events. Oakland.
 1958–1959.

Western Informant: The Modern
 Magazine. Los Angeles.
 1936–1938.
 Followed by:

Los Angeles AFRO-TEMPO, newspaper. 19391943.

Western Light. Santa Monica.
 1939–? Most Worshipful
 Sovereign Grand Lodge of
 Free and Accepted Masons
 of California and its Jurisdiction.
Prince Hall Masonic Digest. Oakland. 1951–1966. Prince
 Hall Grand Lodge of Free and
 Accepted Masons of Cali-
 fornia and Its Jurisdiction.

Western Star of Zion. Redding.
 1902–? African Methodist
 Episcopal Church on the Pacific Coast.
Western States Review. Los Angeles.
 1928–? "A magazine de-
 voted to the advancement of
 the colored people."
Wildcat. San Francisco. 1970–?
 Revolutionary interracial
 publication.
Woman's Journal. Oakland, Los Angeles. 194?–? California
 Association of Colored
 Women's Clubs.

Other:

African-American Baptist Annual Reports, 1865–1990s: California. National
 Archives, microfilm. Books, pamphlets, periodicals, statistics, biogra-
 phies, etc.
Angela Davis Case Collection, Meiklejohn Civil Liberties Institute, Berkeley,
 California. Edited by Ann Fagan Ginger. Dobbs Ferry, NY: Trans-
 Media Publishing Company, 1974.
Bathing Beauty Parade at Pacific Beach, 1925. Newsreel film of Black beauty
 contest at California's Pacific Beach.

Berkeley in the Sixties. Mark Kitchell, producer, 1990. Documentary includes highlights of Huey P. Newton and Dr. Martin Luther King, Jr. Video-recording.

Birth of a Nation: 4*29*1992. Matthew McDaniel, producer, 1993. Community expresses views following the Rodney King verdict. Videorecording.

Black Panther. Third World Newsreel. 1968. Originally released as *Off the Pig*, the short film examines the Panther leadership in 1967. Videocassette.

Black Persons as a Percent of the Total Population in the Los Angeles Five County Area by Census Tracts—1980 Census. Sherman Oaks, CA: Western Economics Research Company, 1981. Map.

Bobby Seale. Third World Newsreel. 1971. Videocassette. The Black Panther Party chairman talks about treatment as a political Prisoner.

Clement, Don. *Los Angeles County: The Census Story*. Los Angeles: Los Angeles Times, 1991. Ethnographic maps of Los Angeles County from 1980 and 1990.

Down For the Hood: Five Unfinished Stories. Terry Halberg and Lisa Pendl, producers, 1994. Documentary focuses on five former LA gang members who were shot, and now are in wheelchairs. Videorecording.

Dreams of a City: Creating East Palo Alto. Michael Levin, producer, 1997. Documentary about the largely African American community south of San Francisco.

Equal Protection of the Laws. Paul Burnford Film Productions, 1967. Film. Explores integration efforts in Riverside.

Frontline: L.A. is Burning, Five Reports from a Divided City. PBS Video, 1993.

Hands on the Verdict: The 1992 L.A. Uprising. Crips, Bloods, and Racism. Videorecording.

In Search of a Common Destiny: Blacks and American Society. Listening to America with Bill Moyers, 1994. Includes interviews related to Rodney King verdict. Videorecording.

Lincoln Pictorial. Lincoln Motion Picture Company newsreel, 1918. Los Angeles Black community.

Long Train Running: The Story of the Oakland Blues. Marlon Riggs, producer, 1983. Documentary.

May Day Panther. Third World Newsreel. 1969. Short film on a Panther rally in San Francisco with Panther leaders. Videocassette.

Merchandising Murder. Josh Freed, 1994. Documentary, the O.J. Simpson Case. Videorecording.

The Nation Erupts (Part 1 & 2). Caryn Rogoff, producer, 1992. Aftermath of the Rodney King verdict. Videorecording.

Negroes as a Percent of the Total Population in the Bay Area and Vicinity, by Census Tracts—1970 Census. Sherman Oaks, CA: Western Economics Research Company, 1973. Map.

Negroes as a Percent of the Total Population in the Los Angeles Five County Area by Census Tracts—1970 Census. Sherman Oaks, CA: Western Economics Research Company, 1971. Map.

No Loans Today: South Central Los Angeles. Videorecording. 1995. Daily life of the Black community centering on economic services (pawnshop, check cashing, etc.).

Pizza Pizza Daddy-O. Bess Lomax Hawes, producer, 1969. Study of eight jump rope and singing games performed by Black children on a Los Angeles playground.

The Rodney King Case: What the Jury Saw in "California v. Powell." Court TV, 1992. Videorecording.

San Francisco State: On Strike. San Francisco Newsreel, 1969.

Scarborough's Faire. KGTV, San Diego. Danny L. Scarborough and the San Diego State University Black Repertory Total Theatrical Experience, a dance troupe. 1980. Videorecording.

School Colors. PBS Video, 1994. Berkeley High School students and race issues from 1968–1994. Videorecording.

The Spirit of Allensworth. KTEH-TV with Spirit Productions. 1980. All-Black town. Videorecording.

State of Emergency: Inside the Los Angeles Police Department. Julia Meltzer and Elizabeth Canner. 1993. Videorecording. Investigative documentary of the L.A. Police Department following the beating of Rodney King.

William A. Leidesdorff papers. Portfolio of 20 items, dated 1843–1848.

Colorado

Articles:

Andrews, Irving P. "Robert Rhone, Jr. (Six of the Greatest: A Tribute to Outstanding Lawyers in Colorado History)." *Colorado Lawyer* 25 (July 1996). Biography.

Armitage, Susan, Theresa Banfield, and Sarah Jacobson. "Black Women and Their Communities in Colorado." *Frontiers: A Journal of Women's Studies* 2 (Summer 1977).

Barker, Gordon H., and W. Thomas Adams. "Negro Delinquents in Public Training Schools in the West." *Journal of Negro Education* 32 (Summer 1963). A study of boys at the Lookout Mountain School for Boys in Golden.

Barnes, Medill McCormick. "The Neighborhood School Comes to Denver." *Integrator* 2 (Fall 1969).

Bernard, William S. "Education for Tolerance." *Crisis* 46 (August 1939). Description of his course in race problems at the University of Colorado-Boulder.

Berwanger, Eugene H. "Hardin and Langston: Western Spokesmen of the Reconstruction Era." *Journal of Negro History* 64 (Spring 1979). William J. Hardin in Colorado and Charles H. Langston in Kansas struggle for civil rights.

_____. "Reconstruction on the Frontier: The Equal Rights Struggle in Colorado: 1865–1867." *Pacific Historical Review* 44 (1975). Black organized opposition to the territory's proposed constitution that would deny them the right to vote.

_____. "Three Against Johnson: Colorado Republican Editors React to Reconstruction." *Social Science Journal* 12 (1976).

_____. "William J. Hardin: Colorado Spokesman for Racial Justice, 1863–1873." *Colorado Magazine* 52 (Winter 1975).

Block, Augusta Hauck. "Old Lige." *Colorado Magazine* 19, no. 4 (1942). Denver's unofficial town crier, Elijah Wentworth.

Bowie, Nolan A. "Blacks and the Mass Media." *Crisis* 92 (1985).

Bracken, Lil. "The Lynching of Emmett Till." *New Odyssey* 1 (Spring 1992). Emmett Till, murdered in Mississippi in 1955, is memorialized in the Dr. Martin Luther King statue in Denver.

Butler, Charles C. "Lynching." *Report: Colorado Bar Association, Twelfth Annual Meeting, at Colorado Springs, September 3 and 4, 1909.* Vol. 12.

Clarke, Caroline Veronica. "Denver: The Mile-High City Gains Altitude." *Black Enterprise*, May 1994. Business opportunities for Blacks.

Cochran, Elizabeth. "Black Women in Colorado: Two Early Portraits." *Frontiers* 7, no. 3 (1984).

"Colorado Schools to Lose Funding Over Minority Graduation Rates." *Black Issues in Higher Education* 8 (13 February 1992).

"Colorado State King Day Observance Shows Logistical Dilemma Faced by Many Campuses." *Black Issues in Higher Education* 7 (20 December 1990).

"CSU Employee Loses Discrimination Claim." *Black Issues in Higher Education* 7 (3 January 1991).

Davis, James H. "Colorado Under the Klan." *Colorado Magazine* 42 (Spring 1965).

_____. "The Ku Klux Klan in Denver and Colorado Springs." Chapter in *The 1967 Denver Westerners Brand Book.* Boulder: Johnson Publishing Company, 1968.

"Denver, the City Beautiful—Denver, The City of Lights." *Colored American Magazine* (12 May, 1907).

Dickson, Lynda Faye. "African-American Women's Clubs in Denver, 1890s–1920s." Chapter in *Peoples of Color in the American West.* Lexington, MA: D. C. Heath and Company, 1994.

_____. "Towards a Broader Angle of Vision in Uncovering Women's History: Black Women's Clubs Revisited." *Frontiers: A Journal of Women's Studies* 9, no. 2 (1987).

Dolin, Eric J. "Black Americans' Attitudes toward Wildlife." *Journal of Environmental Education* 20 (1988). Survey conducted in Denver indicates that Blacks are less interested in and concerned about wildlife that whites.

"Ed J. Sanderlin." *The Trail* 1 (May 1909). Obit.

Fauset, Jessie Redmon. "Out of the West." *Crisis* 27 (November 1923). Description of Denver.

Giles, Dari. "Getting Down in Denver." *Essence* 28 (September 1997). Black contributions and points of interest.

Gill, Gerald R. "'Win or Lose—We Win': The 1952 Vice-Presidential Campaign of Charlotta Bass." Chapter in *The Afro-American Woman:*

Struggles and Images, eds. Sharon Harley and Rosalyn Terborg-Penn. Port Washington, NY: Kennikat Press, 1978.

Ginsburg, Loren R. "Sam Cary (Six of the Greatest: A Tribute to Outstanding Lawyers in Colorado History)." *Colorado Lawyer* 23 (July 1994). Biography.

Goldberg, Robert A. "Beneath the Hood and Robe: A Socioeconomic Analysis of Ku Klux Klan Membership in Denver, Colorado, 1921–1925." *Western Historical Quarterly* 11 (April 1980).

Grant, Billie Arlene. "Growing Up Black in Denver." *Odyssey West* 9 (March 1990).

Gwaltney, William W., and Thomas Welle. "By Force of Arms: The Buffalo Soldiers of Colorado." *Colorado Heritage* (Spring 1996).

Hamil, Harold. "When the Klan Visited Sterling High." *Denver Post Empire Magazine*, 27 October 1974. Klan in Colorado.

Hansen, Moya. "Entitled to Full and Equal Enjoyment and Entertainment in the Denver Black Community, 1900 to 1930." *University of Colorado at Denver Historical Studies Journal* 10 (Spring 1993).

Harris, Andrew. "Deerfield [sic], A Negro Ghost Town in Weld County, Colorado." *Negro History Bulletin* 27 (1963).

Harvey, James R. "Negroes in Colorado." *Colorado Magazine* 26 (July 1949). Condensed from master's thesis, with four interviews.

"Henry Oscar Wagoner: 'The Douglass of the West.'" *Colored American Magazine* 5 (July 1905).

Hill, Daniel Grafton. "The Negro in the Early History of the West." *Iliff Review* 3 (1946). Focus on Colorado.

Jackson, Harold E. "Discrimination and Busing: The Denver School Board Election of May 1969." *Rocky Mountain Social Science Journal* 8 (1971). Analysis of the 1969 election and voter attitudes.

Johnson, Frederick. "Agricultural Negro Colony in Eastern Colorado." *Western Farm Life Journal* (11 May 1915). Dearfield.

Keith, Adam. "K.K.K....Klose Kall in Kolorado." *Denver* 1 (August 1965).

King, William M. "Black Children, White Law: Black Efforts to Secure Public Education in Central City, Colorado, 1864–1869." *Essays and Monographs in Colorado History* 3 (1984). Black parents in Central City fight for the education of their children.

_____. "The End of an Era: Denver's Last Legal Public Execution, July 27, 1886." *Journal of Negro History* 68 (Winter 1983). The botched legal hanging of Andrew Green led future hangings to be conducted in private.

Knox, Peter. "The Campus and the Klan: A Classic Lesson in Civility." *Colorado: Views From CU-Boulder* (December 1997). University president George Norlin (1919–1939) stands up to the Klan.

Kouris, Diana Allen. "The Lynching: Calamity in Brown's Park." *True West* 42 (September 1995). The lynching of John Bennett.

Lanza, Ruth Willett. "Aunt Clara Brown: Black Angel of Central City." *True West* 38 (April 1991). Former slave becomes renowned citizen.

Leonard, Stephen J. "Black-White Relations in Denver, 1930's–1970's." *Midwest Review* 12 (1990).

Lindsey, Benjamin Barr. "The Beast in a New Form." *The New Republic*, 24 December 1924. The Klan in Colorado.

————. "My Fight with the Ku Klux Klan." *Survey Graphic* 54 (1 June 1925). The Klan in Colorado.

Lovrich, Nicholas P. "Differing Priorities in an Urban Electorate: Service Preferences among Anglo, Black, and Mexican American Voters." Satisfaction of various groups with Denver city services.

Lovrich, Nicholas P., and Otwin Marenin. "A Comparison of Black and Mexican American Voters in Denver: Assertive Versus Acquiescent Political Orientations and Voting Behavior in an Urban Electorate." *Western Political Quarterly* 29 (1976).

Margolis, Eric. "Black Miners." Section in "Western Coal Mining as a Way of Life: An Oral History of the Colorado Coal Miner to 1914." *Journal of the West* 24 (July 1985).

Marriner, Gerald Lynn. "Klan Politics in Colorado." *Journal of the West* 15 (January 1976).

Mazzulla, Fred, and Jo Mazzulla. "A Klan Album." *Colorado Magazine* 42 (Spring 1965). Photographs of the Klan and its women's auxiliary.

McAllister, Henry. "What Can Be Done to Stop Lynching?" *American Law Review* 39 (January-February 1905). The 1904 speech to the Colorado Bar Association.

————. "What Can Be Done to Stop Lynching?" *Report of the Seventh Annual Meeting of the Colorado Bar Association.* n.p., n.d.

McBride, Conrad L. "The 1964 Election in Colorado." *Western Political Quarterly* 18 (1965). Analysis of groups on color and voting patterns in the national election.

McGue, D. B. "John Taylor—Slave-Born Colorado Pioneer." *Colorado Magazine* 18 (September 1941). Portrait of former slave and buffalo soldier Taylor, who lived among and fought with various Indian tribes and who lived on the Ute reservation.

McNair, Wallace Yvonne. "Black Leaders Featured in Colorado Publication." *Odyssey West* 9 (November 1990). How the McNairs created *Colorado Black Leadership Profiles.*

Mergen, Bernard. "Denver and the War on Unemployment." *Colorado Magazine* 47 (Fall 1970). Includes Black involvement with the Unemployed Citizen's League of Denver.

Monnett, John H., and Michael McCarthy. "Lewis Price." Chapter in *Colorado Profiles: Men and Women Who Shaped the Centennial State.* Evergreen, CO: Cordillera Press, 1987. Price, a former slave, freight hauler, activist, founder of the *Denver Star*, died penniless in 1913 though he made $400,000 in 1891.

_____. "Preston Porter." Chapter in *Colorado Profiles: Men and Women Who Shaped the Centennial State*. Evergreen, CO: Cordillera Press, 1987. The Lincoln County burning-alive of Porter, only suspected of the rape of a white teenager.

Moore, Jesse T., Jr. "Seeking a New Life: Blacks in Post-Civil War Colorado." *Journal of Negro History* 78 (Summer 1993).

Morgan, Joan. "Colorado State King Day Observance Shows Logistical Dilemma Faced by Many Campuses." *Black Issues in Higher Education* 7 (20 December 1990). Colorado State University.

_____. "University of Colorado Suspends Blacks Charged with Assault." *Black Issues in Higher Education* 9 (9 April 1992).

Mothershead, Harmon. "Negro Rights in Colorado Territory (1859–1876)." *Colorado Magazine* 40 (July 1963). Legal discrimination against Blacks.

Norman, Mary Anne. "Civil Rights in Colorado: An Examination and Analysis of Five Cases." *Journal of the West* 25 (October 1986).

Norment, Lynn. "Conquering the Slopes." *Ebony*, May 1989. National Brotherhood of Skiers in Colorado.

Odyssey West Magazine. Denver. Begun in 1982 as *Colorado Lifestyle*, a bimonthly magazine highlighting Denver and Colorado Black communities.

"On to Denver." *Crisis* 30 (June 1925). Describes the annual NAACP meeting site.

Owens, M. Lilliana. "Julia Greeley, 'Colored Angel of Charity.'" *Colorado Magazine* 20 (September 1943). Ex-slave of the Gilpin family.

"Panel Members Say Racism Still Problem at University. *Black Issues in Higher Education* 7 (21 June 1990). University of Colorado.

Parker, Guy. "Pioneer Range Riders of Colorado." *Colorado Springs Advertiser* (15 March 1940).

Paynter, John H. "Joseph D. D. Rivers." *Journal of Negro History* 22 (1937). Obituary of Denver newspaper publisher of *The Colorado Statesman*.

Peck, Robert M. "Negro Slaves in Colorado." Unpublished manuscript, State Historical Society of Colorado.

Pierson, M. D. "All Southern Society is Assailed by the Foulest Charges: Charles Sumner's Crime Against Kansas and the Escalation of Republican Antislavery Rhetoric." *New England Quarterly* (December 1995).

Poinsett, Alex. "Newest Black Mayors: Emanuel Cleaver Wins in Kansas City and Wellington Webb Walks to Victory in Denver." *Ebony*, September 1991.

"Rap With Strings." *Black Issues in Higher Education* 12 (9 January 1996). Feature on Gregory T. S. Walker, University of Colorado music professor.

"Requiem For A High School Martyr." *Ebony*, July 1999. Death of Isaiah Shoels of Denver's Columbine High School.

Reese, Joan. "Two Enemies to Fight: Blacks Battle for Equality in Two World Wars." *Colorado Heritage* (1990).

Reid, Ira De Augustine. "Negro Life on the Western Front. *Opportunity* 7 (September 1929). The Interracial Commission of Denver.

Riordan, Maguerite. "Tolerance Goes to School in Denver—'With Liberty and Justice for All.'" *Opportunity* 25 (January-March 1947).

Rodriguez, Roberto. "Colorado State's Albert Yates: Bringing New Vision to Fort Collins." *Black Issues in Higher Education* 8 (25 April 1991). Black president.

"Roundup Report: How Schools Meet Desegregation Challenges." *Nation's Schools* 78 (November 1966). Includes Denver.

Sanford, Jay. "African-American Baseballists and the Denver Post Tournament." *Colorado Heritage* (Spring 1995).

Santillan, Richard A. "El Partido La Raza Unida [The Raza Unida Party]." *Black Politician* 3 (1971).

Schrum, Keith. "Of Myth and Men: The Trail of the Black Cowboy." *Colorado Heritage* (Autumn 1998). Profiles George McJunkin, Daniel Webster (80 John) Wallace, Bill Pickett, and Nat Love, plus provides a good overview of cowboy life.

Singleton, Janet. "Colorado's Black Business Community Emerges." *Colorado Business Magazine* 16 (December 1989).

Smith, Duane. "The Confederate Cause in the Colorado Territory, 1861–1865." *Civil War History* 7 (1961). Federal and Confederate issues, including slavery, affect Colorado.

Stiff, Cary. "Black Colorado." Black Colorado Series. *Denver Post Empire Magazine*, July 13–Nov. 16, 1969. Twelve installments. Barney Ford, Isom Dart, the Ku Klux Klan, Dearfield, etc.

Strubel, D. B. "Dearfield, Colorado: Population 1." *Denver Post Empire Magazine*, 8 August 1955.

"Suffering Natural Consequences of Its Actions." *Christian Advocate* 75 (31 May 1900). Colorado abolished capital punishment and a lynching ensued. In addition, a Black man named Calvin Kunblern was lynched in Pueblo on May 22.

Tank, Robert M. "Mobility and Occupational Structure on the Late Nineteenth-Century Urban Frontier: The Case of Denver, Colorado." *Pacific Historical Review* 47 (1978).

"Two Lynchings." *The Independent*, 52 (31 May 1900). Report of the lynching of a Black person in Georgia, and another in Colorado.

Waddell, Karen. "Dearfield...A Dream Deferred." *Colorado Heritage* (1988). Story of O. T. Jackson and the community he founded.

Waller, Reuben. "History of a Slave Written by Himself at the Age of 89 Years." *The Beecher Island Battle Memorial Association Annual*, 1961.

Watkins, Mark Hanna. "Racial Situation in Denver." *Crisis* 52 (May 1945).

Wayne, George H. "Negro Migration and Colonization in Colorado: 1870–1920." *Journal of the West* 15 (January 1976). Dearfield and other enterprises in Colorado.

"Webb Wins Second Term as Mayor of Denver." *Jet*, 26 June 1995.

"Where Negroes Keep Out Negroes: Negro Leaders Are Alarmed at What's Happening in One of Denver's Better Neighborhoods, Which Welcomed Integration Not Long Ago, They Urge Other Negroes to Stay Out: Reason, Fear That a Once White Area Now Mixed, Will Turn Into a Black Ghetto." *U.S. News and World Report* 59 (18 October 1965).

White, Evelyn C. "How Paul Stewart Mines Lost 'Gold' With a Tape Recorder." *Smithsonian* 20 (August 1989). Black American West Museum and Heritage Center.

_____. "Paul Stewart's Romance with the West." *Smithsonian* 20 (August 1989).

White, Lonnie J. "The Battle of Beecher Island: The Scouts Hold Fast on the Arickaree." *Journal of the West* 5 (January 1966). Mentions the 10th Cavalry.

White, Paula M. "G&C Equipment Corporation Cleans Up." *Black Enterprise*, August 1996. LA firm awarded contract for Colorado nuclear clean-up.

Williams, Charleea H. "Recent Developments in 'the Land of the Free.'" *Colored American Magazine*, August 1902. Lynchings of Louis F. Wright at New Madrid, Missouri, and William H. Wallace at La Junta, Colorado.

"Worries and Concerns." *Colorado Heritage* (Winter 1991). Describes the lynching of Black youth Preston Porter in Colorado.

Wyman, Walker D., and John D. Hart. "The Legend of Charlie Glass." *Colorado Magazine* 46 (Winter 1969); reprinted as a pamphlet *The Legend of Charlie Glass, Negro Cowboy on the Colorado-Utah Range*. River Falls, WI: River Falls State University Press, 1970. Top foreman of Oscar L. Turner's Lazy Y Cross Ranch.

Zollo, Richard P. "General Francis S. Dodge and His Brave Black Soldiers." *Essex Institute Historical Collections* 122 (July 1986).

Zylstra, Don. "When the Ku Klux Klan Ran Denver." *Denver Post Roundup*, 5 January 1958.

Books:

African Methodist Episcopal Church, Colorado Conference. *Minutes of the Eighth Annual Session of the Colorado Conference of the African M.E. Church. Held in Helena, Montana, October 11, 1894.* Albuquerque: J. W. Sanders, 1894.

Anderson, Robert Ball. *From Slavery to Affluence: Memoirs of Robert Anderson, Ex-slave.* Hemingford, NE: Hemingford Ledger, 1927; reprinted, Steamboat Springs, CO: Steamboat Pilot, 1967.

Atkins, James A. *The Age of Jim Crow*. New York: Vintage Press, 1964. Blacks in Denver.

_____. *Human Relations in Colorado: A Historical Record*. Denver: Colorado Department of Education, 1968.

Ball, Wilbur P. *Black Pioneers of the Prairie*, 2^d ed. Fort Morgan: Commercial-PWS Printers, 1988: reprinted, Eaton, CO: W. P. Ball, 1992. The Albert and Belle Gaines family, homesteaders of Weld County.

Bardwell, George E. *Characteristics of Negro Residences in Park Hill Area of Denver, Colorado, 1966*. Denver: Commission on Community Relations, City and County of Denver, 1966.

Bayley, David H., and Harold A. Mendelsohn. *Minorities and the Police: Confrontation in America*. New York: Free Press, 1968. Minorities in Colorado.

Black Organizations, A Directory. Denver: Western Images Publications, 1990. Civic and social organizations.

Black Settlers of the Pikes Peak Region, 1850–1899. Colorado Springs: Negro Historical Association of Colorado Springs, 1986.

Bruÿn, Kathleen. *"Aunt" Clara Brown: Story of a Black Pioneer*. Boulder: Pruett Publishing Company, 1970.

Chrisman, Harry E. *The Ladder of Rivers: The Story of I. P. (Print) Olive*. Denver: Sage Books, 1962. Also discusses Black cowhand Jim Kelly.

Coakley, Jay, and Lynda Faye Dickson. *The Perceptions and Experiences of Minority Students at the University of Colorado, Colorado Springs*. Colorado Springs: University of Colorado, Colorado Springs, 1988.

Colorado. Anti-Discrimination Commission. *Report*. Denver: The Commission, 1951/52–1954/55.

Colorado. State Historical Society. *A Calendar of the Papers of Junius R. Lewis, 1842–1938: A Holding of the Library of the State Historical Society of Colorado*. Denver: The Society, 1970. Black businessman Lewis and Colorado history.

Colorado Black Roundtable. *Building a Black Agenda: 1989 and Beyond*, eds. Gwendolyn Thomas and Sharon Bailey. Denver: The Black Roundtable, 1989.

Colorado Committee for Equal Employment Opportunities. *Taking Stock: A Final Report on the Campaign for a Fair Employment Practices Law for Colorado*. Denver: The Committee, 1951.

Colton, Ray Charles. *The American Civil War in the Western Territories of New Mexico, Arizona, Colorado and Utah*. Norman: University of Oklahoma Press, 1959.

Cortese, Charles F. *The Park Hill Experience*. Denver: Colorado Civil Rights Commission, 1974. Blacks and employment.

Denver Area Welfare Council. *A Study of Recreation in the Manual-Five Points Area, Made by Recreation and Leisure Time Division, Denver Area Welfare Council, Inc.* Denver: Denver Area Welfare Council, 1948.

Denver Gray Book, July 1921: A Complete Directory Published in the Interest of Race People and Those who Cater to their Trade. Denver: Denver Gray Book Publishing, 1921.

The Denver Independent Presents Dr. W. E. Burghardt Du Bois upon "The History of the Negro Race" at the Peoples Tabernacle, Monday, May 22, 1911. Denver: Denver Independent Publishing Company, 1911.

Denver Superintendent of Schools. *Planning Quality Education: A Proposal for Integrating the Denver Public Schools.* Denver: Superintendent of Schools, 1968.

Denver University Opinion Research Center. *Public Attitudes Toward Minorities in Denver.* Denver: Opinion Research Center, 1947; 1948.

Directory of Civic and Social Organizations in Denver's Black Communities. Denver: The Council for Self Development in association with The Denver Center for the Performing Arts, 1985.

Dorsett, Lyle W. *The Queen City: A History of Denver.* Boulder: Pruett Publishing Company, 1977.

Dr. Justina L. Ford House, Grand Opening and Dedication Ceremony. Denver: Black American West Museum and Heritage Center, 1988.

Eberhart, Perry. *Ghosts of the Colorado Plains.* Athens, OH: Swallow Press, 1986.

Federal Writers' Project, Colorado. *Colorado Negroes.* Denver, 1940. Manuscript at the Colorado History Museum.

Gehres, Eleanor M. *Barney Ford, Governor Alexander Cummings, Negro Suffrage, and the Colorado Statehood Bill of 1866.* Denver: University of Denver, 1971.

Goldberg, Robert A. *Hooded Empire: The Ku Klux Klan in Colorado.* Urbana: University of Illinois Press, 1981.

Grant, Billie Arlene. *Black Women of the West: Success in the Workplace.* Denver: Billie Arlene Grant, 1982.

————. *Liggins, Tower of Enthusiasm: A Biography of W. T. Liggins.* n.p., 1981.

Grant, Billie Arlene, Ernestine Smith, and Gladys Smith. *Growing up Black in Denver.* Denver: Billie Arlene Grant, 1988. Race relations.

Gray, Juanita R. *Denver Negro Leaders, 1973–1975.* Denver: Juanita R. Gray, 1975.

Hernández, Santos H. *Patterns of Utilization of Services by Hispanics and Blacks in the Colorado State Mental Health System: Executive Summary.* Denver: Colorado Department of Institutions, Division of Mental Health, 1985.

High Avenue to Pride: Black Achievement in Colorado. Denver: High Street Parish Community Center, 1977. Role models for community youth.

Holley, John Stokes. *The Invisible People of the Pikes Peak Region: An Afro-American Chronicle.* Colorado Springs: The Friends of the Colorado Springs Pioneer Museum: The Friends of Pikes Peak Library District, 1990.

Hunt, Inez. *Adventures of Barney Ford, A Runaway Slave.* Colorado Springs:
Colorado Springs Public Schools, 1969. Juvenile.

Jackson, Carlton. *Hattie: The Life of Hattie McDaniel.* Lanham, MD: Madison Books, 1989. McDaniel attended high school and entertained in Denver.

James, Franklin J., et al. *Discrimination, Segregation, and Minority Housing Conditions in Sunbelt Cities: A Study of Denver, Houston, and Phoenix.* Denver: Center for Public-Private Sector Cooperation, University of Colorado-Denver, 1983.

King, William M. *Going to Meet a Man: Denver's Last Legal Public Execution.* Niwot, CO: University Press of Colorado, 1990.

Lindsey, Benjamin Barr. *My Fight with the Ku Klux Klan.* n.p.: n.d. Reprinted from *Survey Graphic*, June 1925.

Mayor's Interim Survey Committee on Human Relations. *A Report of Minorities in Denver, with Recommendations by the Mayor's Interim Survey Committee on Human Relations*, Paul Roberts, chair. Denver: Mayor's Committee, 1947.

McNair, Doug, and Wallace Yvonne McNair. *Colorado Black Leadership Profiles.* Denver: Western Images Publication, 1989. Biography.

Monnett, John H. "Relief and Retribution." Chapter in *The Battle of Beecher Island and the Indian War of 1867–1869.* Niwot, CO: University Press of Colorado, 1992.

Monnett, John H., and Michael McCarthy. *Colorado Profiles: Men and Women Who Shaped the Centennial State.* Evergreen, CO: Cordillera Press, 1987. Chapters on Lewis Price and Preston Porter.

Murray, Betty. *A National Study of Minority Group Barriers to Allied Health Professions Education in the Southwest. Final Report.* San Antonio: Southwest Program Development Corporation, 1975. ERIC. ED 118 297. A two year study conducted in California, Colorado, New Mexico, Oklahoma and Texas.

NAACP Administrative File. Subject File. Civil Rights—Colorado, 1918–1920. Frederick, MD: University Publications of America, 1990.

NAACP Administrative File. Subject File. Lynching—Colorado, 1919–1920, 1930. Frederick, MD: University Publications of America, 1986.

NAACP Branch Files. Colorado Springs, Colo., 1914–1939. Frederick, MD: University Publications of America, 1991.

NAACP Branch Files. Denver, Colo., 1915–1918, 1921–1939. Frederick, MD: University Publications of America, 1991.

National Urban League. Department of Research and Investigations. *The Negro Population of Denver, Colorado: A Survey of Its Economic and Social Status, by Ira De Augustine Reid, Directory, Department of Research and Investigations...for the Denver Inter-Racial Committee.* Denver: Lincoln Press, 1929; reprinted, New York: n.p., 1939.

1970 Census of Total Population, Negro Population, Spanish-American Population: for Colorado, Regional 11: Garfield County, Mesa county, Moffat County, Rio Blanco County. Denver, Colorado: Colorado Division of Planning, 1974. African American statistics.

Parkhill, Forbes. *Mister Barney Ford; a Portrait in Bistre*. Denver: Sage Books, 1963.

Purdue, Fray Marcos, and Paul W. Stewart. *Westward Soul*. Denver: Black American West Foundation, 1976.

Rawick, George P., ed. *The American Slave: A Complete Autobiography*. Westport, CT: Greenwood Publishing Company, 1972. Transcriptions of narratives for the 1936–1938 Federal Writers' Project. Vol. 2.

Rhym, Shelly. *Through My Eyes: The Denver Negro Community, March 1934–January 1968*. Denver: Core City Ministries, 1968.

The Rocky Mountain American. Boulder: Rocky Mountain American Printing and Publishing Company, 1925, microfilm. Colorado Ku Klux Klan.

Salerno, Dan, Kim Hooper, and Ellen Baxter. *Hardship in the Heartland: Homelessness in Eight U.S. Cities*. New York: Community Service Society of New York, Institute for Social Welfare Research, 1984. Denver is one of the cities.

Shorter Community African Methodist Episcopal Church. *Centennial Celebration: 100 Years of Progress, 1868–1968*. Denver: Shorter AME, 1968.

Smith, Ernestine McClain. *Cherished Colorado Black Families*. Denver: Smith-Grant Publishers, 1989.

Spann, Dorothy Bass. *Black Pioneers. A History of a Pioneer Family in Colorado Springs*. Colorado Springs: Little London Press, 1978; reprinted, Friends of the Colorado Springs Pioneer Museum, 1990.

Talmadge, Marian, and Iris Gilmore. *Barney Ford, Black Baron*. New York: Dodd, Mead, 1973. Juvenile.

Three Resource Units for Minority Group Study. Denver: Cherry Creek Schools, 1969. Curriculum development series includes Blacks.

Tucker, Deborah L. *To Make a Mayor*. Lanham, MD: University Press of America, 1995.

Uchill, Ida L. *Pioneers, Peddlers, and Tsadikim*. Denver: Sage Books, 1957. Jews and the Klan in Colorado.

United States Commission on Civil Rights. Colorado Advisory Committee. *Access to the Medical Profession in Colorado by Minorities and Women: A Report*. Washington, DC: The Commission, 1976.

_____. *Hearing Before the United States Commission on Civil Rights: Hearing Held in Denver, Colorado, February 17–19, 1976*. Washington, DC: The Commission, 1977.

_____. *School Desegregation in Colorado Springs, Colorado: A Staff Report of the U.S. Commission on Civil Rights*. Washington, DC: U.S. Government Printing Office, 1977. Discrimination and segregation in education.

Updated Race and Ethnic Estimates by Zip Codes: Denver Metro Area. Pano-
	rama City, CA: Western Economic Research Company, 1989. Black
	and Latino population statistics.
Urban League of Denver. *Urban League-Sachs Foundation Health Project: A
	Tuberculosis Case-Finding Program in a Selected Area in Denver,
	Colorado, 1955.* Denver: n.p., 1955.
Yearbook of the Negro Historical Association of Colorado Springs. Colorado
	Springs: NHACS, 1983.

Theses and Dissertations:

Adair, Harriet Elaine. "Trends in School Desegregation: A Historical Case
	Study of Dayton, Denver, Los Angeles and Seattle." Ed.D. diss.,
	Brigham Young University, 1986.
Atchison, Carla Joan. "Nativism in Colorado Politics: The American Protec-
	tive Association and the Ku Klux Klan." Master's thesis, University of
	Colorado, 1972.
Baumunk, Susan B. "The Problem of Racism: An Attitudinal Study of South-
	west Denver Residents." MSW, University of Denver, 1970.
Benn, Mark S. "The Role of Similar Beliefs in Prejudice Reduction of White
	Male College Students to Black Male College Students in an Interracial
	Contact Setting." Psy.D. thesis, University of Northern Colorado,
	1986. Campus attitudes at UNC.
Campbell, Lula Lowe. "A Study of the Relations of Negro Churches in Denver
	to One Hundred Families in the Community." Master's thesis, Univer-
	sity of Denver, 1951.
Collymore, Raymond Quintin. "A Survey of the Educational Aspirations and
	Cultural Needs of the Negro and Mexican-American Students at Two
	Community Colleges in the State of Colorado." Ph.D. diss., Univer-
	sity of Colorado, 1971.
Connole, Ellen Marie. "Racial Differences in Neonatal Mortality." M.S.P.H.
	thesis, University of Colorado, 1996. Racial statistics.
Davis, James H. "The Rise of the Ku Klux Klan in Colorado, 1921–1925."
	Master's thesis, University of Denver, 1963.
Dickson, Lynda Faye. "The Early Club Movement Among Black Women in
	Denver, 1890–1925." Ph.D. diss., University of Colorado, 1982.
Gaskin, James Clyde. "A Survey of the Occupational Opportunities of Negroes
	in Denver." Master's thesis, University of Denver, 1940.
Gaston, John Coy. "The Denver, Colorado Area Black Profes-
	sional/Businesswoman's Perception of Her Communication with the
	Black Male." Ph.D. diss., University of Colorado, 1979.
Goering, Samuel Joseph. "A Study of Race Prejudice with Special Reference to
	Colorado Springs, Colorado." Master's thesis, Colorado College,
	1936.

Goldberg, Robert A. "Hooded Empire: The Ku Klux Klan in Colorado, 1921–1932." Ph.D. diss., University of Wisconsin-Madison, 1977.

Gunn, Gerald P. "Economic Aspects of Desegregation: A Case Study of the Greater Fort Collins Area." Ph.D. diss., Colorado State University, 1973. School integration.

Hanley, Glenn Roy. "The Perceptions of Black and White Undergraduate Resident Hall Students Toward the Campus Environment at the University of Northern Colorado." Ph.D. diss., University of Northern Colorado, 1979. Race relations and student attitudes.

Harvey, James R. "Negroes in Colorado." Master's thesis, University of Denver, 1941.

Hill, Daniel Grafton. "The Sociological and Economic Implications of Negro Church Leadership in Colorado." D.T. diss., Iliff School of Theology, 1946.

Holmes, Stevenson T. "An Analysis of the Factors that Influence Career Development of Selected Blacks." Ed.D. thesis, University of Northern Colorado, 1983. Black graduates in Colorado.

Koplin, Carolyn Rand. "Colorado's First Struggle for Statehood: Its Relationship to Prevailing Racial Attitudes and Reconstruction Policies." Master's thesis, Fairleigh Dickinson University, 1972.

Lyles, Lionel Dean. "An Historical-Urban Geographical Analysis of Black Neighborhood Development in Denver, 1860–1970." Ph.D. diss., University of Colorado at Boulder, 1977.

Norris, Melvin Edward, Jr. "Dearfield, Colorado—The Evolution of a Rural Black Settlement: An Historical Geography of Black Colonization on the Great Plains." Ph.D. diss., University of Colorado, 1980.

Owens, Cecil O'Brian. "The Socio-Historical Impact of Discrimination Practices on Recruiting Blacks as Police Officers." Ph.D. diss., University of Colorado, 1981.

Picher, Margaret. "Dearfield, Colorado: A Story from the Black West." Master's thesis, University of Denver, 1976.

Serlin, Carla G. Jacobs. "A Study of Black Health Behavior in a Neighborhood Health Center." Ph.D. diss., University of Northern Colorado, 1980. Denver center.

Smith, Glenn Ray. "The Black Studies Program at the University of Colorado (Boulder and Denver Campuses) 1968–1973: Development, Change and Assessments." Thesis, University of Colorado, 1974.

Taylor, Mary J. "Leadership Responses to Desegregation in the Denver Public Schools, a Historical Study: 1959–1977." Ph.D. diss., University of Denver, 1990.

Thogmorton, James Pleasant. "The Urban League of Denver, a Study in Techniques of Accommodation." Master's thesis, University of Denver, 1951.

Thornton, Lee Richard. "Is Denver Television Programming Meeting the Needs of the Black Community?" Master's thesis, University of Colorado, 1970.

Trotman, Patricia Curry. "Patterns of Interactions Among Black Organizations." Master's thesis, University of Colorado-Denver, 1987. Black societies in the Denver area.

Walrod, Stephen T. "The Ku Klux Klan in Colorado, 1921–1926." Bachelor's thesis, Princeton University, 1970.

Washington, Herman A. "The Negro Delinquent Child in the City of Denver, from September 1931 to June 1932." Master's thesis, University of Denver, 1933.

Washington, Theodore. "Urban Blacks and Wildlife: Professional Paper." Master's thesis, Colorado State University, 1976. Denver Blacks and opinions on recreation.

Watson, Frederick D. "Removing the Barricades from the Northern Schoolhouse Door: School Desegregation in Denver." Ph.D. diss., University of Colorado, 1993.

Werner, Brian R. "Colorado's Pioneer Blacks: Migration, Occupations and Race Relations in the Centennial State." Master's thesis, University of Northern Colorado, 1979.

Black Newspapers/Periodicals:[1]

COLORADO SPRINGS

African American Voice. Colorado Springs. 1991–current.

Cobbler's Digest. Colorado Springs. 1937–19?? "Distributed free for the benefit of the National Sanatorium for Tuberculous Negroes."

Colorado Advance. Colorado Springs. 1914–1917.

Colorado Advocate #1. Colorado Springs, 1892–1898.
Western Enterprise #1. Colorado Springs, 1872–1893.
Western Enterprise #2. Colorado Springs, 1896–1912.

Colorado Dispatch. Colorado Springs. 1909–1912.

Colorado Springs Advocate #2. Colorado Springs, 1919–1926.

Colorado Springs Eagle. Colorado Springs. 1910–1913.

Colorado Springs Gazette. Colorado Springs. ?–1915.

Colorado Springs Light. Colorado Springs. 1897–1912.

Colorado Springs Sun. Colorado Springs. 1897–1905. Manitou Springs edition, 1900.

Colorado Voice. Colorado Springs, 1948–1951.

Colored Dispatch. Colorado Springs, 1900–1906.

Dispatch. Colorado Springs. 1906–1913.

Sun. Colorado Springs. 1893–1894.

---

[1] Single-lined boxed items were published by the same publishers. Double-lined boxed items indicate change in masthead names.

Voice of Colorado #1. Colorado
    Springs. 1912–1914.
Voice of Colorado #2. Colorado
    Springs. 1936.

DENVER

Advocate. Denver. 1920–1922.
African Advocate. Denver.
    1890–1891.
Afro-American Weekly. Denver,
    1889–1890.
American Woodmen Bulletin. Den-
    ver. 194? Monthly.
Body of Christ. Denver. 1943–?
The Call. Denver.
Challenge. Denver. 1946–1947.
Colorado Argus and Weekly Times.
    Denver, 1889–1891.
Colorado Black Lifestyle Magazine.
    Denver. 1982–1987.
Colorado Journal. Denver, 1948.
Cosmopolitan. Denver. ?–1913.

There were numerous temporary
    name changes, mergers,
    and renamings among this
    group of newspapers.
    Therefore, they are listed
    from the first year that a
    name was used.
Daily Denver Times #2. Denver.
    1872–1873.
Denver Daily Times #1. Denver.
    1872–1886.
Evening Times. Denver.
    1872–1887.
Denver Evening Times. Denver.
    1872–1888.
Weekly Denver Times. Denver.
    1873–1882.
Colorado Argus and Denver Weekly
    Times. 1873–1891.
Denver Weekly Times. Denver.
    1873–1893.
Denver Times. Denver. 1873–1894.

Denver Times Sun. Denver.
    1873–1894.
Denver Weekly Times-Sun. Denver.
    1873–1900.
Colorado Weekly Times. Denver.
    1873–1902.
Rocky Mountain News and Colorado
    Weekly Times. Denver.
    1873–1910.
Weekly Times. Denver. 1873–1920.
Colorado Sun. Denver, 1891–1893.
Colorado Evening Sun. Denver.
    1891–1894.
Colorado Weekly Sun. Denver.
    1893–1894.

Denver Argus #1. Denver,
    1880–1881.
Denver Argus #2. Denver,
    1886–1888.
Denver Blade. Denver, 1961–1970.
Denver Challenge #1. Denver.
    1884–1891.
Denver Challenge #2. Denver.
    1946–1948.
Denver Chronicle. Denver,
    1968–1970.
Denver Inquirer. Denver.
    1952–1954.
Denver Dispatch. Denver, 1957.

The *Denver Star* survived several
    mergers and name changes.
Denver Star. Denver. 1880–1883;
    1887–1892; 1905–1912;
    1912–1974.
Colorado Statesman.   1889.
Statesman. Denver. 1889–1912.
Colorado Exponent. Denver.
    1892–1895.
Statesman-Exponent. Denver.
    1889–1896.
Independent. Denver. 1902–1913.
Other temporary name changes of the
    previous papers:

Franklin's Paper the Statesman.
           Denver.   1906–1912.
Franklin's Paper the Denver Star.
           Denver.   1889–1913.

Denver Sun. Denver.   1884–1889.
Denver Times Speaker. Denver. 190?
Denver Weekly News. Denver,
           1971–current.
Drum. Denver. 1971–1976.

Evening Post. Denver. 1892–1895.
Denver Evening Post. Denver.
           1892–1900.
Denver Post. Denver. 1901–?

Five Pointer. Denver. 1944–1946.
Militant. Denver. 1937–1966.
New American Weekly. Denver.
           1921–1922.
Observer. Denver. 1975–1976.

Odyssey West. Denver.
New Odyssey Magazine. Denver.
           1992.

Rage Magazine. Denver. 1970–?
Service Record. Denver.
Woodman Banner. Denver. Weekly
           of the Supreme Camp of the
           American Woodmen. 1925.

PUEBLO

Colorado Methodist. Pueblo.
           1882–1888.
Rocky Mountain Methodist. Pueblo.
           1881–1889.

Colorado Times. Pueblo.
           1904–1912.
Colorado Times-Eagle. Pueblo.
           1904–1914.
Colorado Eagle. Pueblo.
           1910–1914.

Pueblo Times. Pueblo. 1894–1896.
Religious World. Pueblo.
           1897–1908.

Rising Sun. Pueblo. 1911–1921.
Western Ideal #1. Pueblo.
           1911–1923.
Western Ideal #2. Pueblo.
           1919–1960.

Times. Pueblo. 1894–1896.
Tribune. Pueblo. 1898–1901.
Tribune-Press. Pueblo. 1896–1905.

Western Statesman Pueblo.
           1897–1902.
Religion World. Pueblo.
           1897–1908.

VARIOUS COMMUNITIES
Harambee. Ft. Carson. 1971–1972.
Leader. Trinidad. 1911–1915.
Megaphone. La Junta. 1913–1915.
Umoja. University of Colorado-
           Boulder. 1973–1982.
Urban Spectrum. Aurora.
           1987–current.

Other:

Afro-American News Review, 1916. Newsreel: Fifth Meeting of the American
           Woodsmen at Denver. C. M. White, Supreme Commander, appears
           along with views of interior offices.
Artie Taylor for Colorado Reflections. University of Colorado-Denver. 1983 or
           1984.   Colorado's first Black woman legislator speaks on issues.
           Sound recording.

Black Economy: And How It Affects the Black Community in Denver. Denver, 197? Panel discussion. Videorecording.

Black Employment: And How It Affects the Black Community in Denver. Denver, 197? Panel discussion. Videorecording.

Black Genealogy Search Group. Ford-Warren Library, 2828 High Street, Denver. (303) 294–0907. Meets 4th Saturday of the month.

Cedric Page for Colorado Reflections. University of Colorado-Denver. 1983 or 1984. Geography professor talks about Denver and Dearfield. Sound recording.

Dearfield, The Road Less Traveled. HomeFolks Creative Works and Northeast Denver Women's Center, 1995. Donnie L. Betts, producer and director; Reynelda Muse, producer and writer; John Amos, narrator. The history of Dearfield. Videorecording.

Family History Center. Colorado Springs. (719) 634–0572.

Happy Birthday, Mrs. Craig. A 102 year old woman, the daughter of slaves, recalls her family's journey to Nicodemus and then on to Colorado in 1915. She taught school for fifty-five years. Videorecording.

Historic Survey of the Townsite of Dearfield, Colorado: A Report. Denver: State Historical Society of Colorado, 1985.

The Need, The Dream, The Reality: Colorado Black Settlements. KOA-TV, Denver, 1989. Narrator–Reynelda Muse. Videorecording. Dearfield, Colorado.

"Oral History Interview of Willie and Clara Sims." Colorado Historical Society, 1981. The Sims talk about experiences in Oklahoma, New Mexico, and Colorado.

Rachel Noel for Colorado Reflections. University of Colorado-Denver. 1983 or 1984. Noted educator tells of discrimination of 1950s and 1960s. Sound recording.

Idaho

Articles:

Bird, Annie Laurie. "Portrait of a Frontier Politician II-Live Further West." *Idaho Yesterdays: The Quarterly Journal of the Idaho Historical Society* 1 (Fall 1967).

_____. "Portrait of a Frontier Politician IV-The Delegate from Washington Territory. *Idaho Yesterdays: The Quarterly Journal of the Idaho Historical Society* II (Fall 1958).

_____. "Portrait of a Frontier Politician- Parts V and VI: Idaho's Territorial Governor and Delegate." *Idaho Yesterdays: The Quarterly Journal of the Idaho Historical Society* 3 (Spring 1959).

Blackburn, George M., and Sherman L. Richards. "Unequal Opportunity on a Mining Frontier: The Role of Gender, Race, and Birthplace." *Pacific Historical Review* 62 (1993).

Davis, France A. "The Black Church Experience in Boise." Chapter in *The Black Church and Kinship Networks*, ed. Mamie O. Oliver. Boise: Idaho State Historical Society, 1982.

Hale, Shelley. "The Black Population and Pocatello, Idaho History." *Western Journal of Black Studies* 9 (1985).

"Lionel Hampton Gives Collection to University of Idaho." *Black Issues in Higher Education* 15 (5 March 1998). Hampton donates 1,160 pounds of memorabilia to school that named its department and its jazz festival after him.

Mercier, Laurie, and Carole Simon-Smolinski. "Idaho's African Americans." Chapter in *Idaho's Ethnic Heritage: A Resource Guide*. Boise: Idaho State Historical Society, 1990.

Newall, R. J. "40 Years of O & M." *Idaho Yesterdays: The Quarterly Journal of the Idaho Historical Society* II (Fall 1958).

Oliver, Mamie O. "Boise's Black Baptists: Heritage, Hope, and Struggle."
    Idaho Yesterdays: The Quarterly Journal of the Idaho Historical Society
    40 (Fall 1996).
Owens, Kenneth. "Pierce City Incident." *Idaho Yesterdays: The Quarterly
    Journal of the Idaho Historical Society* 3 (Fall 1959).

Books:

Aho, James Alfred. *The Politics of Righteousness: Idaho Christian Patriotism.*
    Seattle: University of Washington Press, 1990. Racism and white su-
    premacy in Idaho.
*Black Studies: A Collection of Films and Videos Pertaining to the Study of
    Black Culture and History Available from the Idaho State Library.*
    Boise: Idaho State Library, 1992.
Lane, Joan. *The Status of Minority Children in Idaho*, Vol. 3. Boise: Idaho
    State Office of Child Development,1975.
NAACP Administrative File.   Subject File.   Lynching—Boise, Idaho, 1924.
    Frederick, MD: University Publications of America, 1986.
Oliver, Mamie O., ed. *The Black Church and Kinship Networks*. Boise: Idaho
    State Historical Society, 1982.
_____. *Idaho Ebony: The Afro-American Presence in Idaho State History.*
    Boise: Idaho State Historical Society, 1990.
Salzman, Stephanie A.   *Casual Attributions as Predictors of Academic
    Achievement in Father-Absent Children.* Paper presented at the Annual
    Meeting of the American Educational Research Association, San Fran-
    cisco, 27–31 March 1989. FRIC, ED 307 314. Sample drawn from a
    metropolitan area of southeastern Idaho includes Blacks.
United States Commission on Civil Rights. Idaho Advisory Committee. *Big-
    otry and Violence in Idaho: A Report. Prepared by the Idaho Advisory
    Committee to the United States Commission on Civil Rights.* Wash-
    ington, DC: The Commission, 1986.

Other:

Pocatello's African Americans: A Community Within a Community. Produced
    by the Education Committee of the Pocatello chapter of the NAACP.
    Videorecording.

Iowa

Articles:

"An Iowa Emancipator." *Annals of Iowa* 30 (April 1950). Major General Granville Dodge.

"An Iowa Fugitive Slave Case." *Annals of Iowa* 2 (1896).

Anderson, Ruth B. "Then and Now: Black Boycott in Waterloo." *Integrateducation* 21 (January/December 1983). Student demonstrations and desegregation.

Arena, Frank C. "Southern Sympathizers in Iowa During Civil War Period." *Annals of Iowa* 30 (1951).

Beran, Janice A. "Diamonds in Iowa: Blacks, Buxton, and Baseball." *Journal of Negro History* 75 (Summer, Fall 1990).

Bergmann, Leola Nelson. "The Negro in Iowa: Before the Civil War to World War II." *Iowa Journal of History and Politics* 46 (January 1948).

Berrier, G. Gail. "The Negro Suffrage Issue in Iowa, 1865–1868." *Annals of Iowa* 39 (Spring 1968).

Black, Paul D. "Lynchings in Iowa." *Iowa Journal of History and Politics* 10 (April 1912).

Carney, Tom. "A Pair Deals Seven of a Kind: Educational Preparation and Poise Result in Historic Delivery." *Black Issues in Higher Education* 14 (11 December 1997). Black perinatologists Paula Renee Mahone, MD, and Karen Lynn Drake, MD, are the two physicians who delivered the McCaughey septuplets.

Chase, Hal J. "Struggle for Equality: Fort Des Moines Training Camp for Colored Officers, 1917." *Phylon* 39 (1978).

Coffin, Nathan E. "The Case of Archie P. Webb, a Free Negro." *Annals of Iowa* 11 (July-October 1913).

Connor, James. "The Antislavery Movement in Iowa." *Annals of Iowa* 40 (Summer 1970).

Doty, Franklin. "Florida, Iowa, and the National 'Balance of Power.'" *Florida Historical Quarterly* 35 (1956). How sectionalism and slavery impacted on the admission of those two states, one slave and the other, free.

Dykstra, Robert R., and Harlan Hahn. "Northern Voters and Negro Suffrage: The Case of Iowa, 1868." *Public Opinion Quarterly* 32 (Summer 1968).

Eck, Jacob Van. "Underground Railroad in Iowa." *Palimpsest* 2 (May 1921).

Ellis, Richard N. "The Civil War Letters of an Iowa Family." *Annals of Iowa* 39 (Spring 1969). Seventeen letters, twelve of which were written by a son (white) who became an officer in the all-Black regiment, 48th USCI.

Frazer, George. "The Iowa Fugitive Slave Case." *Annals of Iowa* 4 (July 1899).

————. "An Iowa Fugitive Slave Case—1850." *Annals of Iowa* 6 (April 1903).

Gallaher, Ruth. "Slavery in Iowa." *Palimpsest* 28 (May 1947).

Garretson, O. A. "Traveling on the Underground Railroad in Iowa." *Iowa Journal of History and Politics* 22 (July 1924).

Gue, B. F. "Iowa Men in John Brown's Raid." *American Historical Magazine* 1 (March 1906).

Hahn, Harlan. "Civil Liberties in Iowa." *Annals of Iowa* 38 (Summer 1965). Iowa's unique record in the protection of civil liberties.

Harlan, A. W. "Slavery in Iowa Territory." *Annals of Iowa* 2 (January 1897). Recollections by white man of Iowa slavery in 1830s and 1840s.

Hawley, C. A. "Whittier and Iowa." *Iowa Journal of History and Politics* 34 (April 1936). Abolitionist John Greenleaf Whittier and Iowa concerns.

Hewitt, William L. "Blackface in the White Mind: Racial Stereotypes in Sioux City, Iowa, 1874–1910." *Palimpsest* 71 (Summer 1990).

————. "So Few Undesirables: Race, Residence, and Occupation in Sioux City, 1890–1925." *Annals of Iowa* 50 (Fall 1989/Winter 1990).

Hill, James L. "Migration of Blacks to Iowa, 1820–1960." *Journal of Negro History* 66 (Winter 1981–1982).

Howard, Lawrence C. "The Des Moines Negro and His Contribution to American Life." *Annals of Iowa* 30 (January 1950).

Hull, Jon D. "A White Person's Town?" *Time,* 23 December 1991. Focus on Dubuque.

"Iowa Lynching." *Independent* 62 (31 January 1907).

"Iowa Schoolteacher Demonstrates Racism as Learned Behavior." *The Journal of Blacks in Higher Education* 8 (Summer 1995).

Jones, Mrs. Laurence C. "The Desire for Freedom." *Palimpsest* 7 (May 1927). Black abolitionist woman Charlotta Pyles.

Kachel, Douglas. "Fort Des Moines and Its African-American Troops in 1903/1904." *Palimpsest* 74 (Spring 1993).

La Brie, Henry G. III. "James B. Morris, Sr. and the *Iowa Bystander.*" *Annals of Iowa* 42 (1974). Examines the Black press in Iowa, including the *Bystander.*

Love, Rose Leary. "George Washington Carver—The Boy Who Wanted to Know Why?" *Negro History Bulletin* 30 (1967). The life of Carver in Kansas and Iowa before age twenty-five.

Lufkin, Jack. "Patten's Neighborhood: The Center Street Community and the African-American Printer Who Preserved It." *Iowa Heritage Illustrated* 77 (Fall 1996). Printer Robert Patten and his Des Moines neighborhood.

McNutt, George L. "Race Question Solved in Buxton." *Independent* 62 (30 May 1907).

"Memorial to African American Officers Planned for Fort Des Moines." *Negro History Bulletin* 61 (January–March 1998).

Ohrn, Deborah Gore, ed. "Iowa Women of Achievement." *Goldfinch: Iowa History for Young People* 15 (Winter 1993). At least two Black women are included.

"Only Trace Left of Negro Colony." *Argus Leader* (Sioux Falls), 8 August 1932.

Pelzer, Louis. "The Negro and Slavery in Early Iowa." *Iowa Journal of History and Politics* II (October 1904).

Reed, Charles D. "George Washington Carver, Mystic Scientist." *Annals of Iowa* 24 (1943). Biographical sketch of the famous scientist, the first Black to graduate from Iowa State, by white man who was his student friend.

Russell, Charles Edward. *A Pioneer in Early Iowa: A Sketch of the Life of Edward Russell.* Washington, DC: Ransdell Incorporated, 1941. Editor and antislavery activist.

Rutland, Robert. "Iowans and the Fourteenth Amendment." *Iowa Journal of History and Politics* 51 (1953).

Rye, Stephen H. "Buxton: Black Metropolis of Iowa." *Annals of Iowa* 41 (Spring 1972).

Shiffer, Beverly. "The Story of Buxton." *Annals of Iowa* 37 (Summer 1964).

Silbey, Joel H. "Proslavery Sentiment in Iowa." *Iowa Journal of History and Politics* 55 (October 1957).

"Slave-Catching in Iowa." *Annals of Iowa* 4 (July 1899). Editorial comment.

Smetak, Jacqueline. "Race on Campus." *Z Magazine* 5 (July-August 1992). The University of Iowa–Ames.

Stocum, Susan. "Rediscovering the Road to Freedom." *Black Issues in Higher Education* 16 (5 August 1999). Iowa's role in the Underground Railroad.

Teakle, T. "Rendition of Barclay Coppoc." *Iowa Journal of History and Politics* 10 (October 1912).

"Two Methods." *Crisis* 20 (July 1920). Vigilance committee in Des Moines proposes program for the betterment of Black children in racially mixed schools.

Van Eck, Jacob. "The Underground Railroad in Iowa." *Palimpsest* 2 (May 1921).

White, Maury. "The Legend of Jack Trice." *The Iowan* 46 (Fall 1997). First Black football player at Iowa State.

Wick, B. L. "Delia Webster." *Annals of Iowa* 18 (January 1932). Ardent abolitionist and her role in the Iowa Underground Railroad.

Williams, Ora. "Iowa, My Iowa, Free Iowa." *Annals of Iowa* 27 (July 1945). Iowa as a free state.

_____. "Story of Underground Railroad Signals." *Annals of Iowa* 27 (April 1946).

Books:

Baumgartner, David. *Racism on the Iowa Campus: A Presentation on the Student Affairs Administrator and Black Student Perspectives.* 1989. ERIC. ED 363 199. Study conducted on public college and university campuses.

Bergmann, Leola Nelson. *The Negro in Iowa.* Iowa City: State Historical Society of Iowa, 1969. Reprinted from *Iowa Journal of History and Politics* 46 (January 1948).

_____. *The Negro in Iowa, With an Editorial Addendum Twenty Years After, by William J. Peterson.* Iowa City: State Historical Society, 1969.

Briggs, John E. *History of Social Legislation in Iowa.* Iowa City: State Historical Society, 1915. Some history of Black-white relations.

Cantor, Gordon N. *Sex and Race Effects in the Conformity Behavior of Upper-Elementary-School-Aged Children*, Iowa Testing Programs Occasional Papers No. 16. Iowa City: Iowa Testing Programs, 1975. ERIC. ED 115 658. Studies of white and Black children in Iowa City.

Cook, Robert J. *Baptism of Fire: The Republican Party in Iowa, 1838–1878.* Ames: Iowa State University Press, 1994. Includes antislavery movements.

Dykstra, Robert R. *Black Freedom and White Supremacy in Iowa.*

_____. *Bright Radical Star: Black Freedom and White Supremacy on the Hawkeye Frontier.* Cambridge, MA: Harvard University Press, 1993, reprinted, Ames: Iowa State University, 1997. Includes years 1833 to 1880.

Gradwohl, David M., and Nancy M. Osborn. *Exploring Buried Buxton: Archaeology of an Abandoned Iowa Coal Mining Town with a Large Black Population.* Ames: Iowa State University Press, 1984; reprinted, 1990.

Hawthorne, Frances E. *African Americans in Iowa: A Chronicle of Contribu-
    tions, 1830–1992*. Des Moines: F. E. Hawthorne, 1992; reprinted,
    African American History Project, 1993.

Iowa Commission on the Status of African-Americans. *Annual Report/Iowa
    Commission on the Status of African-Americans*. Des Moines: The
    Commission, 1991.

Iowa Commission on the Status of Blacks. *Report of the Iowa Commission on
    the Status of Blacks to the Governor of Iowa and the State Legislature*.
    Des Moines: The Commission, 1990.

Iowa Commission on the Status of Blacks. *Report of the Iowa Commission on
    the Status of Blacks to the Governor of Iowa and the State Legislature*.
    Des Moines: The Commission, 1989.

Iowa State Colored Convention. *Proceedings of the Iowa State Colored Conven-
    tion: Held in the City of Des Moines; Wednesday and Thursday, Feb-
    ruary 12th and 13th, 1868*. Muscatine, IA: Daily Journal, 1868.

Lane, Timothy A. J. *The Sun and Its Shadow: A Study of Blacks in Iowa*.
    Cedar Falls: University of Northern Iowa, 1972.

Minard, Ralph Day. *Race Attitudes of Iowa Children*. University of Iowa Stud-
    ies Series. Iowa City: University of Iowa Press, 1931. Publication of
    dissertation.

NAACP Branch Files. Des Moines, Iowa, 1916–1939. Frederick, MD: Uni-
    versity Publications of America, 1991.

Negro Business and Information Directory. Fiscal Period, July 1, 1939–June 3,
    1940. Des Moines: Negro Chamber of Commerce of Des Moines,
    1940.

Order of the Eastern Star. Electa Grand Chapter. *Proceedings...Annual Com-
    munication*. Des Moines: The Order. Annual publication.

Reed, Cecil, and Priscilla Donovan. *Fly in the Buttermilk: The Life Story of
    Cecil Reed*. Iowa City: University of Iowa Press, 1993. Biography of
    Black Iowa legislator.

Rosenberg, Morton M. *Iowa on the Eve of the Civil War: A Decade of Fron-
    tier Politics*. Norman: University of Oklahoma Press, 1972.

Roy, Christopher D. *African Art from Iowa Private Collections*. Iowa City:
    University of Iowa Museum of Art, 1981. Exhibit catalogue.

Saenz, Rogelio et al. *Minority Groups in Iowa*. Ames: Iowa State University
    of Science and Technology, 1987. ERIC, ED 297 049. Data from
    1850 to 1980 census reports.

Schweider, Dorothy, Joseph Hraba, and Elmer Schweider. *Buxton, Works, and
    Racial Equity in a Coal Mining Community*. Ames: Iowa State Uni-
    versity Press, 1987.

Selected Civil Rights Issues in Iowa's Public Education. Washington, DC:
    U.S. Commission on Civil Rights, 1990.

State Government Affirmative Action in Mid-America: An Update: A Report.
    Prepared by the Iowa, Kansas, Missouri, and Nebraska Advisory Com-

mittees to the United States Commission on Civil Rights.   Washington, DC: The Commission, 1982.

Thompson, Era Bell. *American Daughter*. St. Paul, MN: Minnesota Historical Society Press, 1946; reprinted, 1986. Social life and customs in North Dakota and Iowa from a future editor at *Ebony*.

Thompson, John. *History and Views of Colored Officers Training Camp for 1917 at Fort Des Moines, Iowa*. Des Moines: The Bystander, 1917.

U.S. Department of Justice. *The Potentiality for Racial Conflict in the Des Moines Police Department*. Washington, DC: The Department, 1989.

United States Commission on Civil Rights. Iowa Advisory Committee. *Race Relations in Tama County: A Report. Prepared by the Iowa Advisory Committee to the U.S. Commission on Civil Rights*. Washington, DC: The Commission, 1981.

United States Commission on Civil Rights. *Report on Urban Renewal Programs and their Effects on Racial Minority Group Housing in Three Iowa Cities*. Washington, DC: U.S. Government Printing Office, 1964.

"Walk Together Children." A Report of the Iowa State Committee to the U.S. Commission on Civil Rights on Housing and Education in Waterloo, Iowa. Des Moines: Iowa State Committee to the U.S. Commission on Civil Rights, 1971. ERIC, ED 078 114. Minority groups, housing and school discrimination, etc.

Waterloo Commission on Human Rights. *Waterloo's Unfinished Business*. Waterloo: The Commission, 1967.

Theses and Dissertations:

Barnes, Ward Robert. "Anti-Slavery Politics in Iowa, 1840–1856." Master's thesis, University of Iowa, 1968.

Bruton, Joseph.   "Evaluation of Des Moines, Iowa 'Blacks' Knowledge of HIV/AIDS." Master's thesis, University of Wisconsin-Stout, 1989.

Minard, Ralph Day. "Race Attitudes of Iowa Children." Ph.D. diss., University of Iowa, 1930.

Stone, Robert B.   "The Legislative Struggle for Civil Rights in Iowa: 1947–1965." Master's thesis, Iowa State University, 1990.

Black Newspapers:[1]

BUXTON

Buxton Advocate. Buxton.
    1911–1912.
Buxton Eagle. Buxton.
    1903–1905?

Buxton Gazette. Buxton.
    1903–1909.
Buxton Leader. Buxton.
    1912–1913.
Iowa Colored Worker. Buxton.
    1907–1910.

---

[1] Double-lined boxed items indicate change in masthead names.

DAVENPORT

Cash Register. Davenport-Quad
 Cities. 1987.
Tri-City Advocate. Davenport.
 1907.
Tri-City Observer. Davenport.
 1940.

DES MOINES

Afro-Citizen. Des Moines.
 1976–1978.
Afro Des Moines Communicator.
 Des Moines. 1978.
Black Des Moines. Des Moines.
 1972–1973?
Black Revolutionary. Des Moines.
 1971.
Communicator. Des Moines.
 1986–199?
Des Moines Register and Leader.
 Des Moines. 1908–1915.

Challenger. Des Moines.
 1982–1983.
Inner City Challenger. Des
 Moines. 1981–1982.
New Challenger. Des Moines.
 1984.

Iowa Afro-Citizen. Des Moines.
 1976–1977.
Iowa Baptist Standard. Des
 Moines. 1897–1899.
Iowa Colored Woman. Des
 Moines. 1907–1909.
Iowa Observer. Des Moines.
 1936–?
Iowa Sepia News. Des Moines.
 1951–1954.

Iowa State Bystander. Des Moines.
 1894–1916.
Bystander. Des Moines.
 1916–1920.
Iowa Bystander. Des Moines.
 1920–1951.

New Iowa Bystander. Des Moines.
 1972.
Iowa Bystander. Des Moines.
 1985–?

Monitor. Des Moines. 1910.
Rising Son. Des Moines.
 1883–1885.
Weekly Advocate. Des Moines.
 1891–1894.
Weekly Avalanche. Des Moines.
 1891–1894.
Western Ledger. Des Moines.
 1908–1909. Monthly
 publication of the Colored
 Co-operative League.

KEOKUK

Baptist Herald. Keokuk. ?–1901.
Baptist Missionary. Keokuk.
 1917.
Iowa State Citizen. Keokuk.
 1897.
Western Baptist Herald. Keokuk.
 1881–1885.

OSKALOOSA

Buxton Eagle. Oskaloosa.
 1904–1906.
Gazette. Oskaloosa. 1896.
Iowa District News. Oskaloosa.
 1890–1891.
Negro Solicitor. Oskaloosa.
 1893–1889.

SIOUX CITY

Afro-American Advance. Sioux
 City. 1908–1912.
Enterprise. Sioux City.
 1936–1938.
Searchlight. Sioux City.
 1899–1902.
Silent Messenger. Sioux City.
 1937–1938.

Weekly Review. Sioux City.
    1928–1930.

WATERLOO
Observer. Waterloo. 1941.
Parker Tribune. Waterloo-Cedar
    Falls. 1980?
Post. Waterloo. 1952.
Special Delivery. Waterloo. 1987.
Star. Waterloo. 1956.
Waterloo Defender. Waterloo.
    1963–1975.

VARIOUS COMMUNITIES
Access: The Newsletter for Re-
    cruiting and Retaining

Students of Color. Cedar
    Rapids. 1992–current.
Britt Tribune. Mason City. 1911.
Colored Advance. Corning. 1882.
    Iowa's first Black newspa-
    per.
Daily Evening Journal. Washing-
    ton. 1895–1911.
Eyes: The Negroes' Own Picture
    Magazine. Iowa City.
    1947–1952.
Mwendo. Cedar Rapids. 197?
    Black literary magazine of
    Coe College.
Negro Solicitor. Oskaloosa.
    1893–1900.
New Era. Ottumwa. 1901.

Other:
African-American Baptist Annual Reports, 1865–1990s: Iowa. National Ar-
    chives, microfilm. Books, pamphlets, periodicals, statistics, biogra-
    phies, etc.
A Class Divided. WGBH Boston, 1986. Videorecording. Documents a reunion
    of students who participated in 1970 "Eye of the Storm" exercise.
The Eye of the Storm. ABC News, 1985. Videorecording. Award-winning
    "blue-eyes brown-eyes" classroom exercise on racism.

Kansas

Articles:

"A Colored Man's Letter." *The Plain Dealer*. 16 April 1880.

Athearn, Robert G. "Black Exodus: The Migration of 1879." *Prairie Scout* 3 (1975).

_____. "The Promised Land: A Black View." *Record* 34 (1973). Blacks move out of the South to Kansas.

Barry, Louise. "The Emigrant Aid Company Parties of 1854–5." *Kansas Historical Quarterly* 12 (May 1943).

Bates, Angela. "New Promise for Nicodemus." *National Parks* 66 (July 1992).

Bentz, Donald N. "Nicodemus—the Promised Land?" *Golden West* 5 (November 1968).

Berwanger, Eugene H. "Hardin and Langston: Western Spokesmen of the Reconstruction Era." *Journal of Negro History* 64 (Spring 1979). William J. Hardin in Colorado and Charles H. Langston in Kansas struggle for civil rights.

Bingham, Anne E. "Sixteen Years of a Kansas Farm, 1870–1886." *Kansas State Historical Society Collections* 15 (1919). Tells of Black Exodusters.

Blakely, Allison. "The John L. Waller Affair, 1895–1896." *Negro History Bulletin* 37 (1974).

Bontemps, Arna, and Jack Conroy. "'Leave a Summer Land Behind.'" Chapter in *Anyplace but Here*. New York: Hill and Wang, 1966.

Brady, Marilyn Dell. "Kansas Federation of Colored Women's Clubs, 1900–1930." *Kansas History* 9 (Spring 1986).

_____. "Organizing Afro-American Girls Clubs in Kansas in the 1920's." *Frontiers* 9 (1987).

Breckenridge, Jodi. "The Effects of the Kansas Governor's Academy on the Attitudes of At-Risk Students During the Summer 1991." *Negro Educational Review* 45 (April 1994).

Brill, Tom. "Henry W. Sewing: Kansas City, Kansas, Pioneer Negro Banker." *Missouri Historical Review* 62 (April 1973).

Brown, A. Theodore. "Business "Neutralism" on the Kansas Border: Kansas City, 1854–1857." *Journal of Southern History* 29 (1963). Business interests attempt to maintain neutrality between slavery and antislavery contingents.

Brown, S. "John Brown and Sons in Kansas Territory." *Indiana Magazine of History* 31 (June 1935).

Butters, Gerald R., Jr. "*The Birth of a Nation* and the Kansas Board of Review of Motion Pictures: A Censorship Struggle." *Kansas History* 14 (Spring 1991).

Carle, Glenn L. "The First Kansas Colored." *American Heritage* 43 (February 1992). The first Black men to fight and die in the Civil War.

Carper, James C. "The Popular Ideology of Segregated Schooling: Attitudes toward the Education of Blacks in Kansas, 1854–1900." *Kansas History* 1 (Winter 1978).

Castel, Albert. "Bleeding Kansas." *American History Illustrated* 10 (1975).

_____. "Civil War Kansas and the Negro." *Journal of Negro History* 51 (April 1966). Kansas supported national policies of the Radical Republicans but did not support Black rights.

Cecil-Fronsman, Bill. "'Advocate the Freedom of White Men, as Well as That of Negroes': The Kansas Free State and Antislavery Westerners in Territorial Kansas." *Kansas History* 20 (1997).

_____. "'Death to All Yankees and Traitors in Kansas': The *Squatter Sovereign* and the Defense of Slavery in Kansas." *Kansas History* 16 (1993).

"Celebration of John Brown's Day." *Americana* 5 (September-October 1910). Celebration in Osawatmie.

Chafe, William H. "The Negro and Populism: A Kansas Case Study." *Journal of Southern History* 34 (August 1968). Study of the failure of biracial populism.

Chalmers, David M. "Twisting the Klan's Shirttail in Kansas." Chapter in *Hooded Americanism: The History of the Ku Klux Klan*. Chicago: Quadrangle Books, 1968.

Chamberlain, C. W. "Last of the Badmen." *Negro Digest* 5 (November 1946). Vigilantes hang seven men but spare the life of notorious Black man Ben Hodges, severing his heel tendons instead.

Chaudhuri, Nupur. "We All Seem Like Brothers and Sisters: The African American Community in Manhattan, Kansas, 1865–1940." *Kansas History* 14 (Winter 1991).

Cobb, Ronald Lee. "Guthrie Mound and the Hanging of John Guthrie." *Kansas History* 5 (Autumn 1982). Antislavery sympathizer lynched by proslavery mob in 1860.

Cochran, Alfred W. "Jazz in Kansas City, the Midwest, and the Southwest, 1920–1940." *Journal of the West* 22 (July 1983).

Connelley, W. E., and A. Morrall. "Proslavery Activity in Kansas." *Kansas State Historical Society Transactions* 14 (1915–1918).

Cooper, Arnold. "'Protection to All, Discrimination to None': *The Parsons Weekly Blade*, 1892–1900." *Kansas History* 9 (Summer 1986). Examines Black newspaper.

Cornish, Dudley Taylor. "Kansas Negro Regiments in the Civil War." *Kansas Historical Quarterly* 20 (May 1953).

Curtis, William J. "Emily Fisher, First Independence Black Business Woman." *The Kansas City Genealogist* 36 (Fall 1995).

Dann, Martin. "From Sodom to the Promised Land: E. P. McCabe and the Movement for Oklahoma Colonization." *Kansas City Quarterly* 40 (Autumn 1974).

Davis, Kenneth S. "Eli Thayer and the Kansas Crusade." *New England Galaxy* 5 (1963). Organizer of the New England Emigrant Aid Company of Massachusetts planned to make Kansas a laboratory to show the inferiority of slave labor.

Dilliard, Irving. "James Milton Turner: A Little Known Benefactor of His People." *Journal of Negro History* 19 (October 1934).

Dobak, William A. "Civil War on the Kansas-Missouri Border: The Narrative of Former Slave Andrew Williams." *Kansas History* 6 (Winter 1983).

Donald, Henderson H. "The Negro Migration of 1916–1918." *Journal of Negro History* 6 (October 1921).

Douglass, Frederick. "The Negro Exodus from the Gulf States." *Journal of Social Science* 11 (May 1880).

Du Bois, W. E. B. "Postscript: Coffeeville, Kansas." *Crisis* 34 (July 1927). Attempted lynching of a Black man leads to a riot.

Dudziak, Mary L. "The Limits of a Good Faith: Desegregation in Topeka, Kansas, 1950–1956." *Law and History Review* 5 (Fall 1987).

Early, Gerald, ed. "Contemporary Black Writers: Celebrating 125 Years of Kansas Statehood." *Cottonwood* 38/39 (Summer/Fall 1986).

Eastin, L. J. "Notes on a Proslavery March Against Lawrence, Kan." *Kansas Historical Quarterly* 11 (February 1942).

Entz, Gary R. "Image and Reality on the Kansas Prairie: 'Pap' Singleton's Cherokee County Colony." *Kansas History* 19 (Summer 1966).

Ewy, Marvin. "The United States Army in the Kansas Border Troubles, 1855–1856." *Kansas Historical Quarterly* 32 (1966). Why the military took a neutral stance in Kansas on the eve of the Civil War.

"Factors Associated with Self-Perceived Excellent and Very Good Health among Blacks—Kansas, 1995." *Morbidity and Mortality Weekly Report* 45

(25 October 1996). Satisfaction of Black's with health and raising Black mortality age will require public health initiatives.

Fisher, Mike. "The First Kansas Colored: Massacre at Poison Springs." *Kansas History* 2 (1979).

_____. "Remember Poison Spring." *Missouri Historical Review* 74 (1980).

Fleming, Walter L. "Kansas Territory and the Buford Expedition of 1856." *Alabama Historical Society* 4 (1904).

_____. "'Pap' Singleton, Father of the Exodus." *American Journal of Sociology* 15 (July 1909).

Ford, E. C. "A Horrible Blot on the Fair Name of Kansas." *Negro History Bulletin* 19 (November 1955). Eyewitness account of the Leavenworth, Kansas, lynching of an innocent Black man. It might have been Fred Alexander, burned in 1901.

Freeman, Ruges R. "Educational Desegregation in St. Louis." *"Negro History Bulletin* 38 (1975). Focuses on desegregation between 1954 and 1955.

Frehill-Rowe, Lisa M. "Postbellum Race Relations and Rural Land Tenure: Migration of Blacks and Whites to Kansas and Nebraska, 1870–1890." *Social Forces* 72 (September 1993).

Garvin, Roy. "Benjamin, or 'Pap,' Singleton and His Followers." *Journal of Negro History* 33 (January 1948).

Gatewood, Willard B., Jr. "Kansas Negroes and the Spanish-American War." *Kansas Historical Quarterly* 37 (Autumn 1971). The all-Black 23[d] regiment.

Gibbons, V. E., ed. "Letters on the War in Kansas in 1856." *Kansas Historical Quarterly* 10 (November 1941).

Greene, James "Joe," and John Holway. "I Was Satchel's Catcher." *Journal of Popular Culture* 6 (1972).

Greener, Richard T. "The Emigration of Colored Citizens from the Southern States." *Journal of Social Science* 11 (May 1880).

Grenz, Suzanna M. "The Exodusters of 1879: St. Louis and Kansas City Responses." *Missouri Historical Review* 73 (October 1978).

Griffith, Charles B., and Donald W. Stewart. "Has a Court of Equity Power to Enjoin Parading by the Ku Klux Klan in Mask?" *Central Law Journal* 96 (November 1923). The Klan in Kansas.

Hamilton, Kenneth Marvin. "The Origins and Early Promotion of Nicodemus: A Pre-Exodus, All-Black Town." *Kansas History* 5 (Winter 1982).

Harlow, R. V. "Rise and Fall of Emigrant Aid Movement in Kansas." *American Historical Review* 41 (October 1935).

Harmon, G. D. "Buchanan's Attitude toward the Admission of Kansas on the Slavery Question." *Pennsylvania Magazine of History and Biography* 51 (January 1929).

Hart, Charles Desmond. "The Natural Limits of Slavery Expansion: Kansas-Nebraska, 1854." *Kansas Historical Quarterly* 34 (1968). Congressional debate on the expansion of slavery into Kansas.

Haven, R., ed. "John Brown and Heman Humphrey: An Unpublished Letter." *Journal of Negro History* 52 (1967). Letter of 18 April 1857 to Reverend Humphrey on plans to organize antislavery resistance in Kansas.

Haywood, C. Robert. "The Hodgeman County Colony;" *Kansas History* 12 (1989/90).

_____. "'No Less a Man': Blacks in Cow Town Dodge City, 1876–1886." *Western Historical Quarterly* 19 (May 1988).

Henderson, Cheryl Brown. "Landmark Decision: Remembering the Struggle for Equal Education." *Land and People* 6 (Spring 1994).

Henderson, Cheryl Brown, and Shariba Rivers. "The Legacy of Brown 40 Years Later." Chapter in *Forty Years After the Brown Decision: Implications of School Desegregation for U.S. Education*, Vol. 14, eds. Charles Teddlie and Kofi Lomotey. New York: AMS Press, 1996.

Hickey, Joseph V. "'Pap' Singleton's Dunlop Colony: Relief Agencies and the Failure of a Black Settlement in Eastern Kansas." *Great Plains Quarterly* 11 (Winter 1991).

Hickman, Russell K. "The Reeder Administration: Inaugurated." *Kansas Historical Quarterly* 36 (Autumn 1970). Governor Andrew H. Reeder also looked at the slavery question.

_____. "The Reeder Administration: Inaugurated, Part II—The Census of Early 1855." *Kansas Historical Quarterly* 36 (Winter 1970). Free Blacks and slaves revealed in the census.

Higgins, Billy D. "Negro Thought and the Exodus of 1879." *Phylon* 32 (Spring 1971).

Hoole, W. S., ed. "A Southerner's Viewpoint of the Kansas Situation, 1856–7." *Kansas Historical Quarterly* 3 (February 1934). Continues in following issues.

Hughey, Jeff. "Black Jack: 1856." *Civil War Times Illustrated* 14 (1976). First encounter between pro-slavery and anti-slavery forces.

Hulston, Nancy J. "'Our Schools Must Be Open to All Classes of Citizens': The Desegregation of the University of Kansas School of Medicine, 1938." *Kansas History* 19 (1966).

Johnson, S. A. "The Emigrant Aid Company in Kansas." *Kansas Historical Quarterly* 1 (November 1932).

_____. "The Emigrant Aid Company in the Kansas Conflict." *Kansas Historical Quarterly* 6 (February 1937).

Jones, Lila Lee. "The Ku Klux Klan in Eastern Kansas during the 1920's" *Emporia State Research Studies* 23 (Winter 1975).

"The Kansas Fight Against Slavery." *Kansas State Historical Society* 10 (1908).

"Kansas versus New Jersey." *Colored American Magazine*, February 1901. Includes item about Black man Fred Alexander, lynched in Leavenworth, Kansas.

Katz, Milton S., and Susan B. Tucker. "A Pioneer in Civil Rights: Esther Brown and the South Park Desegregation Case of 1948." *Kansas History* 18 (1995–1996).

King, Henry. "A Year of the Exodus in Kansas." *Scribner's Monthly* 20 (June 1880).

Klassen, Teresa C., and Owen V. Johnson. "Sharpening of the *Blade*: Black Consciousness in Kansas, 1892–97." *Journalism Quarterly* 63 (Summer 1986). Kansas Black newspaper.

Klem, Mary J. "The Kansas-Nebraska Slavery Bill and Missouri's Part in the Conflict." *Mississippi Valley Historical Association Proceedings* 9 (May 1919).

Kousser, J. Morgan. "Before Plessy, Before Brown: The Development of the Law of Racial Integration in Louisiana and Kansas." Chapter in *Toward a Usable Past*, eds. Paul Finkelman and Stephen E. Gottlieb. Athens, GA: University of Georgia Press, 1991.

Langsdorf, Edgar. "Samuel Clarke Pomeroy and the New England Emigrant Aid Company, 1854-8." *Kansas Historical Quarterly* 7 (August 1938).

"The Leavenworth Lynching." *American Review of Reviews* 23 (March 1901). The lynching of Fred Alexander in Leavenworth, Kansas.

Leiker, James N. "Black Soldiers at Fort Hayes, Kansas, 1867–1869: A Study in Civilian and Military Violence." *Great Plains Quarterly* 17 (Winter 1997).

Lewallen, Kenneth A. "'Chief' Alfred C. Sam: Black Nationalist on the Great Plains, 1913–1914." *Journal of the West* 16 (January 1977).

Love, Rose Leary. "George Washington Carver—The Boy Who Wanted to Know Why?" *Negro History Bulletin* 30 (1967). The life of Carver in Kansas and Iowa before age 25.

Lyman, W. A. "Jayhawkers—Origin of Name and Activity." *Kansas State Historical Society Transactions* 14 (1915–1918).

Lynch, William O. "Colonization of Kansas, 1854–1860." *Mississippi Valley Historical Association Proceedings* 9 (1919).

"Lynching." Chapter in *Races Riots in Black and White*, ed. J. Paul Mitchell. Englewood Cliffs, NJ: Prentice-Hall, 1970. Includes the lynching of Fred Alexander at Leavenworth, Kansas.

Malin, James C. "Identification of the Stranger at the Pottawatomie Massacre." *Kansas Historical Quarterly* 9 (February 1940). Information into John Brown's massacre.

———. "The John Brown Legend in Pictures: Kissing the Negro Baby." *Kansas Historical Quarterly* 8 (1939).

———. "The Proslavery Background of the Kansas Struggle." *Mississippi Valley Historical Review* 10 (December 1923).

Martin, Patricia. "Teaching in a Segregated School." *Mennonite Life* 22 (1967). Experiences in two sub-standard schools.

"Massachusetts as an Example." *American Monthly Review of Reviews* 23 (March 1901). Looks at the lynching of Fred Alexander in Leavenworth, Kansas.

McConnell, Judith Lynne. "Kindergarten in Kansas: A View from the Beginning." *Journal of Education* 177 (1995). The first Black kindergarten west of the Mississippi, established in 1893.

McCoy, Sondra Van Meter. "A Spirited Tradition: Black Newspapers in Kansas." Kansas State Historical Society, 1984.

McKenna, Jeanne. "With the help of God and Lucy Stone." *Kansas Historical Quarterly* 36 (1970). Unsuccessful effort in 1867 to enfranchise Blacks and women.

McKusker, Kristine M. "'The Forgotten Years' of America's Civil Rights Movement: Wartime Protests at the University of Kansas, 1939–1945." *Kansas History* 17 (Spring 1994).

Mechem, K. "The Mythical Jawhawk." *Kansas Historical Quarterly* 13 (February 1944).

Miller, Susan, and Antonia Quintana Pigno. "Claude McKay: The Kansas State College Interlude, 1912–1914." *Minorities Resources and Research Center Newsletter (KSU)* (November 1982).

Monhollon, Rusty L. "Taking the Plunge: Race, Rights, and the Politics of Desegregation in Lawrence, Kansas, 1960." *Kansas History* 20 (Autumn 1997).

Moore, N. Webster. "James Milton Turner: Diplomat, Educator, and Defender of Rights." *Missouri Historical Society Bulletin* 27 (April 1971).

"Mr. White Challenges the Klan." *Outlook* 138 (October 1924). Anti-Klan platform of governor candidate.

Neet, Sharon E. "Black Newspapers Published in Pittsburgh, Kansas, 1895–1915." Kansas State Historical Society (Papers in History) 9, no. 1 (Spring 1978).

"Notes on the Proslavery March Against Lawrence." *Kansas Historical Quarterly* 11 (1942).

Oates, Stephen B. "To Wash This Land in Blood...John Brown in Kansas, Part I. *American West* 6 (1969). Brown's involvement with antislavery.

————. "To Wash This Land in Blood...John Brown in Kansas, part II. *American West* 6 (1969). Continuation of the previous article.

O'Brien, Claire. "'With One Mighty Pull': Interracial Town Boosting in Nicodemus, Kansas." *Great Plains Quarterly* 16 (Spring 1996).

O'Brien, Patrick G. "'I Want Everyone to Know the Shame of the State': Henry J. Allen Confronts the Ku Klux Klan, 1921–1923." *Kansas History* 19 (1996).

O'Connor, Patrick Joseph. "The Black Experience and the Blues in 1950s Wichita." *Mid-America Folklore* 21 (1993).

"Only All Negro Village in Kansas, Nicodemus, is Fading into History." *Kansas City Times* (May 28, 1959).

Overturf, Wayne. "John Brown's Cabin at Nebraska City." *Nebraska Historical Magazine* 21 (1940).

Painter, Nell Irvin. "Millenarian Aspects of the Exodus to Kansas." *Journal of Social History* 9 (Spring 1976). Argues new factors behind the Kansas Exodus movement.

Pantle, Alberta, ed. "The Story of a Kansas Freedman." *Kansas Historical Quarterly* 11 (November 1942).

Pendleton, Jason. "Jim Crow Strikes Out: Interracial Baseball in Wichita, Kansas, 1920–1935." *Kansas History* 20 (Summer 1997).

Peoples, Morgan D. "'Kansas Fever' in North Louisiana." *Louisiana History* 11 (Spring 1970). Describes the emigration of Blacks from the lower Mississippi Valley and a U.S. Senate investigation.

Phillip, Mary-Christine. "Supreme Court Casts Doubt on Kansas City School Desegregation Plan." *Black Issues in Higher Education* 12 (29 June 1995).

Porter, Kenneth Wiggins. "Racism in Children's Rhymes and Sayings, Central Kansas, 1910–1918." *Western Folklore* 24 (1965). Sayings and rhymes using the word "nigger" heard as a child.

Quantic, Diane Dufva. "Black Authors in Kansas." *Kansas English* 55 (December 1969).

"Records from the Provost Marshal's File Naming Black Persons." *The Kansas City Genealogist* 37 (Fall 1996).

Rickey, Don. "An Indian Wars Combat Record." *By Valor and Arms* 2 (1975).

Savage, W. Sherman. "The Negro in the Westward Movement." *Journal of Negro History* 25 (October 1940).

Schultz, Elizabeth. "Dreams Deferred: The Personal Narratives of Four Black Kansans." *American Studies* 34 (Fall 1993). Use of three autobiographies and an interview to capture the difficult life of Black Kansas youth (Langston Hughes, Frank Marshall Davis, Gordon Parks and Grant Cushinberry).

Schwendemann, Glen. "The Exodusters of 1879." *Kansas Historical Quarterly* 29 (1963).

_____. "The 'Exodusters' on the Missouri." *Kansas Historical Quarterly* 29 (Spring 1963). The 1879–1880 migration.

_____. "Nicodemus: Negro Haven on the Solomon." *Kansas Historical Quarterly* 34 (Spring 1968). Includes biographies of early settlers.

_____. "St. Louis and the Exodusters of 1879." *Journal of Negro History* 46 (January 1961). What the city did with immigrants moving through to Kansas.

_____. "Wyandotte and the First 'Exodusters' of 1879." *Kansas Historical Quarterly* 26 (Autumn 1960).

Scott, Mark. "Langston Hughes of Kansas." *Kansas History* 3 (Spring 1980). How Hughes' Kansas childhood shaped his life.

"Self-Perceived Excellent and Very Good Health Among Blacks—Kansas, 1995." *Morbidity and Mortality* 45 (1996).

SenGupta, Gunja. "Servants for Freedom: Christian Abolitionists in Territorial Kansas, 1854–1858." *Kansas History* 16 (Autumn 1993).

Sheridan, Richard B. "From Slavery in Missouri to Freedom in Kansas: The Influx of Black Fugitives and Contrabands into Kansas, 1854–1864." *Kansas History* 12 (Spring 1989).

Shoemaker, Floyd C. "Missouri's Proslavery Fight for Kansas, 1854–1855." *Missouri Historical Review* 48 (1954).

Sloan, Charles William, Jr. "Kansas Battles the Invisible Empire: The Legal Ouster of the KKK from Kansas, 1922–1927." *Kansas Historical Quarterly* 57 (Autumn 1974).

Socolofsky, Homer, and Virgil Dean, comps. "Blacks." Chapter in *Kansas History: An Annotated Bibliography*. Westport, CT: Greenwood Press, 1992.

Spring, Leverett W. "Kansas and the Abolition of Slavery." *Magazine of Western History* 9 (1888–1889).

Steinberg, Stephen. "My Day in Nicodemus: Notes from a Field Trip to Black Kansas." *Phylon* 37 (September 1976). White New York sociologist takes a car trip to Nicodemus and goes to a service in the Black church.

Stotts, Gene. "The Negro Paul Revere of Quantrill's Raid." *Negro History Bulletin* 26 (1963). An 18-year-old Black youth's attempt to warn Lawrence.

Strickland, Arvarh E. "Toward the Promised Land: The Exodus to Kansas and Afterward." *Missouri Historical Review* 69 (July 1975).

Sutherland, Keith. "Congress and the Kansas Issue in 1860." *Kansas Historical Quarterly* 35 (1969). Arguments over the admission of Kansas as a state.

"Talking Points." *Crusader* 4 (July 1921). Notes Black attack on whites in Mulberry, Kansas, where a Black man was lynched for allegedly attacking a white girl.

Templar, George. "The Federal Judiciary of Kansas." *Kansas Historical Quarterly* 37 (Spring 1971). Includes proslavery—antislavery issues.

Tidwell, John Edgar. "*Ad Astra per Aspera*: Frank Marshall Davis." *Kansas History* 18 (1995–1996). Davis equated to the motto of Kansas.

_____. "An Interview with Frank Marshall Davis." *Black American Literature Forum* 19 (1985).

_____. "Reliving the Blues: Frank Marshall Davis and the Crafting of Self." Chapter in *Livin' the Blues: Memoirs of a Black Journalist and Poet*, ed. John Edgar Tidwell. Madison, University of Wisconsin Press, 1992.

Treadwell, William E. "The Gilded Age in Kansas." *Kansas Historical Quarterly* 40 (Spring 1974). Proslavery and antislavery controversy.

Turner, Renee D. "Round Two in Topeka: The Browns Fight For Desegregation—Again." *Emerge* 5 (May 1994).

Tuttle, William M., Jr., and Surendra Bhana. "Black Newspapers in Kansas." *American Studies* 13 (1972).

United States. Congress. House. Select Committee on Alleged Corruptions in
    Government. "The Lecompton Constitution, etc." In *The Covode In-
    vestigation. Report.* [Washington, DC 1860] 36th Cong., 1st sess.
    House. Rept. 648. Kansas and slavery.

Uzee, Philip D. "Midwestern Attitudes on the 'Kansas Fever.'" *Kansas Histori-
    cal Quarterly* 20 (1953).

Van Deusen, John. "The Exodus of 1879." *Journal of Negro History* 21 (April
    1936).

Van Meeter, Sondra. "Black Resistance to Segregation in the Wichita Public
    Schools, 1870–1912." *Midwest Quarterly* 20 (Autumn 1978).

Walters, Ronald. "The Great Plains Sit-In Movement, 1958–60." *Great Plains
    Quarterly* 16 (Spring 1996). History of Great Plains sit-ins and rela-
    tionship to others.

_____. "Standing Up in America's Heartland: Sitting in Before Greens-
    boro." *American Visions*, February 1993. History of Great Plains sit-
    ins and relationship to others.

Washington, Booker T. "A New Negro Potato King." *Outlook* 77 (14 May
    1904).

Waters, J. G. Kansas and the Wyandotte Convention." *Kansas State Historical
    Society Transactions 11* (1910).

"Why Kansas Bans the Klan." *Literary Digest* 75 (11 November 1922).

Wiggins, William H., Jr. "The Emancipation of Nicodemus." *Natural History*
    107 (July/August 1998). The August 1 emancipation celebration
    homecoming event.

Wilkins, Roger. "Dream Deferred but Not Defeated." Teachers College Record
    96 (Summer 1995). Effects of the *Brown* vs. *Board of Education* deci-
    sion.

"William Allen White's War on the Klan." *Literary Digest* 83 (11 October
    1924). The Klan in Kansas.

Williams, Nudie E. "Black Newspapers and the Exodusters of 1879." *Kansas
    History* 8 (Winter 1985/1986).

Wintz, Cary D. "Langston Hughes: A Kansas Poet in the Harlem Renais-
    sance." *Kansas Quarterly* 7 (1975).

Woods, Randall B. "After the Exodus: John Lewis Waller and the Black Elite,
    1878–1900." *Kansas Historical Quarterly* 43 (Summer 1977).

_____. "The Black American Press and the New Manifest Destiny: The
    Waller Affair." *Phylon* 38 (1977).

_____. "C. H. J. Taylor and the Movement for Black Political Independ-
    ence, 1882–1896." *Journal of Negro History* 67 (1982).

_____. "Integration, Exclusion, or Segregation? The 'Color Line' in Kan-
    sas, 1878–1900." *Western Historical Quarterly* 14 (April 1983).

Woods, Randall B., and David A. Sloan. "Kansas Quakers and the 'Great Exo-
    dus': Conflicting Perceptions of Responsibility with a Nineteenth
    Century Reform Community." *Historian* 48 (November 1985). The
    Kansas Freedmen's Relief Association.

Woodson, Carter G. "The Exodus to the West." Chapter in *A Century of Negro Migration*. Washington, DC: Association for the Study of Negro Life and History, 1918; reprinted, New York: AMS Press, 1970.

Yost, Genevieve. "History of Lynchings in Kansas." *Kansas Historical Quarterly* 2 (May 1933).

Books:

African Studies at Kansas, 1965–75: A Selection of Doctoral Dissertations on Black History, Africa, and the African Diaspora. Lawrence: Department of African Studies, University of Kansas, 1977.

Athearn, Robert G. *In Search of Canaan: Black Migration to Kansas, 1879–80*. Lawrence: Regents Press of Kansas, 1978.

Atkinson, Pansye. *Brown vs. Topeka: Segregation and Miseducation: An African American's View*. Chicago: African American Images, 1993.

Bennett, Henry. *Kansas and Slavery. Speech of Hon. Henry Bennett, of New York. Delivered in the U.S. House of Representatives, March 29, 1858*. Washington, DC: Buell and Blanchard, Printers, 1858.

————. *Speech on the Admission of Kansas and the Political Aspects of Slavery*. Washington, DC: Buell and Blanchard, 1856.

Black Historical Sites, A Beginning Point. The Society. Historical buildings.

Brown, George Washington. *Reminiscences of Gov. R. J. Walker: With the True Story of the Rescue of Kansas from Slavery*. Rockford, IL: George Washington Brown, 1902. Extension of slavery.

Bruce, Henry Clay. *The New Man: Twenty-Nine Years a Slave, Twenty-Nine Years a Free Man*. York, PA: P. Anstadt and Sons, 1895; reprinted, New York: Negro Universities Press, 1969; reprinted, Lincoln: University of Nebraska Press, 1996. Bruce's recollections.

Bruce, Janet. *The Kansas City Monarchs: Champions of Black Baseball*. Lawrence: University Press of Kansas, 1985.

Buffington, James. *Position of Massachusetts on the Slavery Question*. Washington, DC: Buell and Blanchard, Printers, 1858.

Butler, A. P., Josiah J. Evans and R. M. T. Hunter. *The Massachusetts Resolutions on the Sumner Assault, and the Slavery Issue*. Washington, DC: Congressional Globe Office, 1856. Senator Sumner's antislavery speech and its implications in Kansas.

Carper, James C. *The Popular Ideology of Segregated Schooling: Attitudes toward the Education of Blacks in Kansas, 1854–1900*. Topeka: Kansas State Historical Society, 1978.

Castel, Albert E. *A Frontier State at War: Kansas, 1861–1865*. Ithaca, NY: The American History Association, 1958.

Cemetery Register in Single Graves of Paupers, Blacks and Suicides, Mt. Calvary Cemetery, Leavenworth, Kansas. n.p., 1987. Cemetery maintained by the Catholic Diocese of Kansas City.

Chaffee, Calvin C. *The Lecompton Constitution: A Measure to Africanize the Territories of the United States. Speech of Hon. Calvin C. Chaffee, of Massachusetts. Delivered in the House of Representatives, February 24th, 1858.* Washington, DC: Buell and Blanchard, Printers, 1858.

Chambers, W. L. *Niles of Nicodemus: Exploiter of Kansas Exodusters, Negro Indemnity and Equality of Blacks with Whites His Obsession, Beats Bankers, Bench, and Barrister; Courter League to Post-War K.K.K. Riots and Finally Prison.* Los Angeles: Los Angeles Washington High School, Vocational Training Press, 1925. Exposé on John W. Niles, president of the town's self-governing organization.

Chu, Daniel, and Bill Shaw. *Going Home to Nicodemus: The Story of an African American Frontier Town and the Pioneers Who Settled It.* Morristown, NJ: J. Messner, 1994; reprinted, Englewood Cliffs: Silver Burdett Press, 1995. Juvenile.

Clay, C. C. *Speech of Mr. Clement C. Clay, Jr., of Alabama, on the Contest in Kansas, and the Plan and Purpose of Black Republicanism. Delivered in the United States Senate, on Monday, 21st April, 1856.* Washington, DC: C. Alexander, 1856.

_____. *Speech on the Bill to Admit Kansas: Southern Rights, How Menaced by Northern Republicans.* N.p., 1858.

Clough, Frank C. *William Allen White of Emporia.* New York: McGraw-Hill, 1941. White ran for governor of Kansas on an anti-Klan platform.

Cohen, William. *At Freedom's Edge: Black Mobility and the Southern White Quest for Racial Control, 1861–1915.* Baton Rouge: Louisiana State University Press, 1991.

Cordley, Richard. *A History of Lawrence, Kansas from the First Settlement to the Close of the Rebellion.* Lawrence: E. F. Caldwell, 1895.

Cornish, Dudley Taylor. *Kansas Negro Regiments in the Civil War.* Topeka: State of Kansas Commission on Civil Rights, 1969. Reprinted from *Kansas Historical Quarterly* 20 (May 1953).

Cory, Charles Estabrook. *Slavery in Kansas.* Topeka, 1902.

Cox, Thomas C. *Blacks in Topeka, Kansas, 1865–1915: A Social History.* Baton Rouge: Louisiana State University Press, 1982.

Crockett, Norman L. *The Black Towns.* Lawrence: Regents Press of Kansas, 1979. Nicodemus is one of five towns featured.

Dandridge, Deborah, et al. *Brown vs. Board of Education: In Pursuit of Freedom and Equality: Kansas and the African American Public School Experience, 1855–1955.* Topeka: Brown Foundation for Educational Equity, Excellence and Research, 1993.

Davis, Frank Marshall. *Livin' the Blues: Memoirs of a Black Journalist and Poet*, ed. John Edgar Tidwell. Madison: University of Wisconsin Press, 1992.

Democratic National Committee. *The Issue Fairly Presented. The Senate Bill for the Admission of Kansas as a State. Democracy, Law, Order, and the Will of the Majority of the Whole People of the Territory, Against Black Republicanism, Usurpation, Revolution, Anarchy, and the Will of a Meagre Minority.* Washington, DC: Printed at the Union Office, 1856. Democratic campaign literature of 1856.

Diven, Alexander S. *No More Slave States. Congress Has Full Power Over Slavery in the Territories: The Great Wrong of the Decision in the Dred Scott Case: The Duty of the Government Owes to Kansas. Speech of Alexander S. Diven, of the Twenty-Seventh District, on the Kansas Resolutions.* n.p.: 1858. Extension of slavery.

Doherty, Joseph P. *Civil Rights in Kansas: Past, Present, and Future.* Topeka: State of Kansas, Commission on Civil Rights, 1972.

Douglas, Stephen A. *Remarks of the Hon. Stephen A. Douglas, on Kansas, Utah, and the Dred Scott Decision; Delivered at Springfield, Illinois, June 12, 1857.* Chicago: Daily Times Book & Job Office, 1857.

Fauver, Bill, and Jim Ruderman. *Stride Toward Freedom: The Aftermath of Brown v. Board of Education of Topeka: A Unit of Study for Grades 9–12.* Los Angeles: National Center for History in Schools, 1991. Exercise in integration and segregation. Contains letters from teachers.

Federal Writers' Project, Work Projects Administration. *Slaves Narratives: A Folk History of Slavery in the United States from Interviews with Former Slaves.* Vol. 7, *Kansas.* Washington, DC: Work Projects Administration, 1941.

Fireside, Harvey, and Sarah B. Fuller. *Brown vs. Board of Education: Equal Schooling for All.* Springfield, NJ: Enslow Publishers Library, 1994.

Fleming, Walter L. *"Pap" Singleton, the Moses of the Colored Exodus.* Baton Rouge, LA: Ortlieb's Printing House, 1909. Reprinted from the *American Journal of Sociology* 15 (July 1909).

Fletcher, Frank H. *Negro Exodus: Report of Col. Frank H. Fletcher, Agent Appointed by the St. Louis Commission to Visit Kansas for the Purpose of Obtaining Information in Regard to Colored Emigration.* n.p., 188?

Gordon, Jacob U. *Narratives of African Americans in Kansas, 1870–1992: Beyond the Exodust Movement.* Lewiston, NY: Edwin Mellen Press, 1993.

Greenbaum, Susan G. *The Afro-American Community in Kansas City, Kansas: A History.* Kansas City, KS: City of Kansas City, 1982.

Guidelines for Integrating Minority Group Studies Into the Curriculum of Kansas Schools. Topeka: Kansas State Department of Education, 1969.

Hale, Edward Everett. *Kansas and Nebraska.* Black Heritage Library Collection Series. Freeport, NY: Books for Libraries Press, 1972.

Hallett, Benjamin Franklin. *The Remedy for Kansas—Equality of all the States in all the Territories. Address of Hon. B. F. Hallett to the Democrats of Cheshire County, at Keene, New Hampshire, Fourth of July, 1856.* Boston: Office of Boston Post, 1856.

Hamilton, Kenneth Marvin. *Black Towns and Profit: Promotion and Development in the Trans-Appalachian West, 1877–1915*. Blacks in the New World Series. Urbana: University of Illinois Press, 1991. Nicodemus included.

Higginson, Thomas Wentworth. *A Ride Through Kanzas* (sic). New York: American Anti-Slavery Society, 1856.

Hinshaw, David. *A Man from Kansas: The Story of William Allen White*. New York: G;. P. Putnam's Sons, 1945. White ran for governor on an anti-Klan platform.

In Search of the American Dream" The Experiences of Blacks in Kansas: Resource Booklet for Teachers. Topeka: Kansas State Historical Society, 1978.

The Issue Fairly Presented. The Senate Bill for the Admission of Kansas as a State. Democracy, Law, Order, and the Will of the Majority of the Whole People of the Territory, Against Black Republicanism, Usurpation, Revolution, Anarchy, and the Will of a Meager Minority. Washington, DC: Union Office, 1856.

Johnson, Walter. *William Allen White's America*. New York: Henry Holt and Company, 1947. White ran for governor on an anti-Klan platform.

Kansas State Historical Society, Historic Sites Survey. *Historic Preservation in Kansas. Black Historic Sites, A Beginning Point*. Topeka: The Society, 1977.

Kansas. Commission on Civil Rights. *Report of Progress*. Topeka: Kansas Commission on Civil Rights, 1961/62.

Kluger, Richard. *Simple Justice: The History of Brown vs. Board of Education and Black America's Struggle for Equality*. New York: Vintage Books, 1975; reprinted, Alfred A. Knopf, 1978.

Lacey, Eugene G. *Facts Concerning the Masonic Delinquency of the Grand Master of the Prince Hall Grand Lodge of Kansas. From the Records of Eugene G. Lacey*. n.p.: ca. 1929.

Learnard, O. E. *John Brown's Career in Kansas: Paper Prepared for the Veterans of '56*. n.p.: ?

Marshall, Marguerite Mitchell, et al. *An Account of Afro-Americans in Southeast Kansas, 1844–1984*, Manhattan, KS: Sunflower University Press, 1986.

Martin, Waldo E., Jr. *Brown v. Board of Education: A Brief History with Documents*. Boston: St. Martin's Press, 1998.

Maxwell, Augustus Emmett. *Slavery—Kansas—Parties Thereon. Speech of Hon. A. E. Maxwell, of Florida, Delivered in the House of Representatives, May 1, 1856*. Washington, DC: Congressional Globe Office, 1856.

Morrill, Justin S. *Admission of Kansas: Speech of Hon. J. S. Morrill of Vermont on the Admission of Kansas as a Free State into the Union: Delivered in the House of Representatives, June 28, 1856*. Washington, DC: n.p., 1856.

NAACP Administrative File. Subject File. Civil Rights—Kansas, 1920–1939. Frederick, MD: University Publications of America, 1990.

NAACP Branch Files. Fort Scott, Kansas, 1917–1924, 1928–1935. Frederick, MD: University Publications of America, 1991.

NAACP Branch Files. Kansas State Conference. Frederick, MD: University Publications of America, 1991. Civil Rights.

NAACP Branch Files. Topeka, Kansas, 1913–1939. Frederick, MD: University Publications of America, 1991.

New England Emigrant Aid Company. *Two Tracts for the Times. The One Entitled "Negro-Slavery, No Evil": by B. F. Stringfellow, of Missouri. The Other, An Answer to the Inquiry "Is It Expedient to Introduce Slavery Into Kansas?" by D. R. Goodloe, of North Carolina.* Boston: A. Mudge and Son, 1855.

Nichols, Alice. *Bleeding Kansas.* New York: Oxford University Press, 1954.

Nicodemus: Kansas Special Resources Study. Kansas: National Park Service, U.S. Department of Interior, 1993.

Painter, Nell Irvin. *Exodusters: Black Migration to Kansas After Reconstruction.* New York: Knopf, 1977; reprinted, Lawrence: University Press of Kansas, 1986.

Parks, Gordon. *The Learning Tree.* New York: Harper and Row, 1963. Famous photographer tells of growing up in Kansas.

Perry, Michael. *Health Risk Behaviors of African-American Kansans, 1995.* Topeka: Kansas Department of Health and Environment, Bureau for Disease Prevention and Health Promotion, 1997.

Phillips, William Addison. *The Conquest of Kansas.* Black Heritage Library Collection Series. Freeport, NY: Books for Libraries Press, 1971. Reprint of 1856 edition.

Portraits and Biographical Sketches of the Representative Negro Men and Women of Missouri and Kansas, for Distribution at the Cotton States and International Exposition, to be held at Atlanta, Georgia, September 18th to December 31st, 1895. Kansas City: Charles W. Lee, 1895. The venue where Booker T. Washington gave his "Atlanta Compromise" speech.

Promised Land on the Solomon: Black Settlement at Nicodemus, Kansas. Washington, DC: U.S. Government Printing Office, 1986. Frontier life and historic buildings and restoration.

Ragle, Harold E. *The Blacks of Casey and Pulaski Counties, Kentucky and of Kansas.* Liberty, KY: Casey County News, 1969. Study of the Black family.

Rawick, George P., ed. *The American Slave: A Complete Autobiography.* Westport, CT: Greenwood Publishing Company, 1972. Transcriptions of narratives for the 1936–1938 Federal Writers' Project. Vol. 17.

Rawley, James A. *Race and Politics: "Bleeding Kansas" and the Coming of the Civil War*. Philadelphia: J. B. Lippincott, 1969.

Read, John M. *Speech of Hon. John M. Read in Favor of Free Kansas, Free White Labor, and of Fremont and Dayton: At the Eighth Ward Mass Meeting, held in the Assembly Buildings, on Tuesday Evening, September 30, 1856*. Philadelphia: n.p., 1856.

Report and Testimony of the Select Committee of the United States Senate to Investigate the Causes of the Removal of the Negroes from the Southern States to the Northern States: in Three Parts. Washington, DC: U.S. Government Printing Office, 1880. Reconstruction and migration to Kansas and Indiana. 46th Congress 2[d] session, Senate Report 693.

Rich, Everett. *The Heritage of Kansas: Selected Commentaries on Past Times*. Lawrence: University of Kansas Press, 1960. Extension of slavery.

Robb, John M. *The Black Coal Miner of Southeast Kansas*. Topeka: State of Kansas Commission on Civil Rights, 1969.

Robinson, Charles. *Organization of the Free State Government in Kansas: And the Inaugural Address of Governor Robinson*. Washington, DC: Buell and Blanchard, Printers, 1856.

Ropes, Hannah Anderson. *Six Months in Kansas, By a Lady*. Freeport, NY: Books for Libraries Press, 1972. Black woman writes about her life.

Russell, Ross. *Jazz Style in Kansas City and the Southwest*. Berkeley: University of California Press, 1971.

Sanborn, F. B., ed. *The Life and Letters of John Brown, Liberator of Kansas, and Martyr of Virginia*. Boston: Roberts Brothers, 1885.

SenGupta, Gunja. *For God and Mammon: Evangelicals and Entrepreneurs, Masters and Slaves in Territorial Kansas, 1854–1860*. Athens: University of Georgia Press, 1996. Extension of slavery to the territories.

Spring, Leverett W. *Kansas: The Prelude to the War for the Union*. New York: AMS Press, 1973. Reprint of *American Commonwealths* 6 (1907).

State Government Affirmative Action in Mid-America: An Update: A Report. Prepared by the Iowa, Kansas, Missouri, and Nebraska Advisory Committees to the United States Commission on Civil Rights. Washington, DC: The Commission, 1982.

Stephenson, Wendell Holmes. *Recruiting of Negroes in Kansas*. n.p., 1930. General James H. Lane and Civil War recruitment.

Sumner, Charles. *The Barbarism of Slavery: Speech of Hon. Charles Sumner, on the Bill for the Admission of Kansas as a Free State, in the United States Senate, June 4, 1860*. Washington, DC: Buell and Blanchard, Printers; reprinted, Washington, DC: T. Hyatt, 1860; reprinted, New York: The Young Men's Republican Union, 1863.

————. *The Crime Against Kansas*. New York: Arno Press, 1969. Slavery.

_____. *The Crime Against Kansas. Speech of Hon. Charles Sumner, of Massachusetts. In the Senate of the United States, May 19, 1856.* New York: Greeley and McElrath, 1856.

_____. *The Crime Against Kansas. The Apologies for the Crime. The True Remedy. Speech of Hon. Charles Sumner. In the Senate of the United States, 19th and 20th May, 1856.* Buell and Blanchard, Printers, 1856.

_____. *The Slave Oligarchy and Its Usurpations. Outrages in Kansas. The Different Political Parties. Position of the Republican Party. Speech of Charles Sumner, November 2, 1855, in Faneuil Hall, Boston.* Boston: n.p., 1856.

Thayer, Eli. *A History of the Kansas Crusade.* Black Heritage Library Collection Series. Freeport, NY: Books for Libraries Press, 1971. Reprint of 1889 edition. Aid for Exodusters through New England Emigrant Aid Company.

United States. Commission on Civil Rights. Kansas Advisory Committee. *Prevention of Discrimination in Selected Federal Block Grant Programs—Kansas: A Report.* Washington, DC: The Commission, 1983.

United States. Commission on Civil Rights, Kansas Advisory Committee. *Racial and Religious Tensions on Selected College Campuses.* Washington, DC: The Commission, 1992.

United States. Congress. *Collection of Speeches in Congress on Slavery in Kansas, 1858–1859.* Washington, DC: n.p., 1859.

United States. Congress. House. Select Committee of Fifteen. *The Kansas Question. The Minority Report of the Select Committee of Fifteen.* Washington, DC: Buell, 1858. Slavery in Kansas.

United States. Congress. Senate. Select Committee to Investigate the Causes of the Removal of the Negroes from the Southern States to the Northern Sates. *Report and Testimony of the Select Committee of the United States Senate to Investigate the Causes of the Removal of the Negroes from the Southern States to the Northern States: In Three Parts.* Washington, DC: U.S. Government Printing Office, 1880. Includes Black migration to Kansas.

United States. National Park Service. Denver Service Center. *Draft General Management Plan, Development Concept Plan, Environmental Assessment: Brown v. Board of Education National Site, Kansas.* Denver: U.S. Department of the Interior, National Park Service, Denver Service Center, 1996.

United States. National Park Service. *Nicodemus, Kansas: Special Resource Study.* Washington, DC: National Park Service, U.S. Department of the Interior, 1993. Conservation, restoration and history of Nicodemus.

Wilson, Paul E. *A Time to Lose: Representing Kansas in Brown v. Board of Education.* Lawrence: University Press of Kansas, 1995.

Woodling, Chuck. *Against All Odds: How Kansas Won the 1988 NCAA Championship*. Lawrence: Lawrence Journal-World, 1988. Blacks and basketball.

Woods, Randall B. *A Black Odyssey: John Lewis Waller and the Promise of American Life, 1878–1900*. Lawrence: Regents Press of Kansas, 1981.

Theses and Dissertations:

Aiken, Earl Howard. "Kansas Fever." Master's thesis, Louisiana State University, 1939.

Baker, Laverne L. "Speech and Voice Characteristics of Aging Afro-American Female and Male Speakers Based on Listener Perceived Age Estimates." Ph.D. diss., Wichita State University, 1981.

Bell, J. D. "A Study of a Negro City." Master's thesis, University of Kansas, 1930.

Belleau, William J. "The Nicodemus Colony of Graham County Kansas." Master's thesis, Kansas State College, Fort Hays, 1943.

Blake, Ella Lee. "The Great Exodus to Kansas, 1878–1880." Master's thesis, Kansas State College, 1942.

Boyd, Thomas J. "The Use of Negro Troops by Kansas during the Civil War." Master's thesis, Kansas State Teachers College, 1950.

Buckner, Reginald Tyrone. "A History of Music Education in the Black Community of Kansas City, Kansas, 1905–1954." Ph.D. diss., University of Minnesota, 1974.

Caldwell, Martha B. "The Attitude of Kansas toward Reconstruction of the South." Ph.D. diss., University of Kansas, 1933. Contains attitudes toward Blacks going to Kansas following the Civil War.

Castel, Albert E. "A Frontier State at War: Kansas, 1861–1865." Thesis, University of Chicago, 1955.

Chartrand, Robert Lee. "The Negro Exodus from the Southern States to Kansas: 1869–1886." Master's thesis, University of Kansas City, 1949.

Cox, Thomas C. "Blacks in Topeka, Kansas, 1865–1915: A Social History." Ph.D. diss., Princeton University, 1980.

Davis, Nathan Tate. "Charlie Parker's Kansas City environment and its Effect on His Later Life." Ph.D. diss., Wesleyan University, 1974.

Deacon, Marie. "Kansas as the Promised Land: the View of the Black Press, 1890–1900." Master's thesis, University of Arkansas, 1973.

Gedge, Charles H. "Westward migration of Blacks in the Nineteenth Century with Special Reference to the Kansas Exodus." Master's thesis, Roosevelt University, 1976.

Gibson, Gail Maria. "Gender Differences in the Patterns of Criminal Homicide Committed by Blacks in the Metropolitan Kansas City Area between 1983 and 1986." Master's thesis, University of Missouri-Kansas City, 1987.

Gift, Elmer Birdell. "Causes and History of the Negro Exodus into Kansas, 1879–1880." Master's thesis, University of Kansas, 1915.

Grant, Truett King. "The Negro Exodus of 1879–1880." Master's thesis, Baylor University, 1952.

Hall, Ella. "The Development of the Kansas City, Kansas, Young Women's Christian Association." Master's thesis, University of Kansas, 1945.

Holman, Tom LeRoy. "James Montgomery, 1813–1871." Ph.D. diss., Oklahoma State University, 1973.

Honesty, Phyllis Wheatley. "An Analysis of Expenditures by Forty-Nine Selected Negro Families in Kansas City, Kansas." Master's thesis, Kansas State College, 1939.

Jones, Lila Lee. "The Ku Klux Klan in Eastern Kansas during the 1920's." Master's thesis, Emporia Kansas State College, 1972.

Klyman, Fred Irwin. "An Analysis of Citizen's Perceptions of Police-Community Relations Programs and Services and Relationship of Both Dogmatism and Race to Those Perceptions." Thesis, Oklahoma State University, 1973. Focus on Wichita.

Lawless, Richard M. "To do Right to God and Man: Northern Protestants and the Kansas Struggle, 1854–1859." Thesis, Graduate Theological Union, 1974. The church and race relations.

Lewallen, Sterling B. "Attitudes and Perceptions of Blacks toward Vocational Education." Ph.D. diss., Colorado State University, 1978. Vocational education in Wichita, Kansas.

Masters, Isabell. "The Life and Legacy of Oliver Brown, the First Listed Plaintiff of Brown vs. Board of Education, Topeka, Kansas." Ph.D. diss., University of Oklahoma, 1980.

McDaniel, Orval L. "A History of Nicodemus, Graham County, Kansas." Master's thesis, Kansas State College, Fort Hays, 1950.

Moten, Rashley B. "The Negro Press in Kansas." Master's thesis, University of Kansas, 1938.

Peoples, Morgan D. "Negro Migration from the Lower Mississippi Valley to Kansas: 1879–1880." Master's thesis, Louisiana State University, 1950.

Rankin, Charles Inman. "The Achievement, Personal Adjustment, and Social Adjustment of Black Elementary School Students Undergoing Forced Busing in Wichita, Kansas." Thesis, Kansas State University, 1973.

Schwendemann, Glen. "Negro Exodus to Kansas: The First Phase, March-July, 1879." Master's thesis, University of Oklahoma, 1957.

Shaw, Van B. "Nicodemus, Kansas: A Study in Isolation." Ph.D. diss., University of Missouri, 1951.

Smith, Leland George. "The Early Negroes in Kansas." Master's thesis, University of Wichita, 1932.

Smith, Thaddeus. "Western University: A ghost College in Kansas." Master's thesis, Pittsburg State College, 1966.

Vandever, Elizabeth J. "Brown v. Board of Education of Topeka: Anatomy of a Decision." Ph.D. diss., University of Kansas, 1971.

Waldron, Nell Blythe. "Colonization in Kansas from 1861 to 1890." Ph.D. diss., Northwestern University, 1925.

Williams, Corinne Hare. "The Migration of Negroes to the West, 1877–1900, with Special Reference to Kansas." Master's thesis, Howard University, 1944.

Williams, Nudie E. "Black newspapers and the Exodusters of 1879." Master's thesis, Oklahoma State University, 1977.

Wilson, Noel. "The Kansas City Call: An Inside View of the Negro Market." Ph.D. diss., University of Illinois, 1968.

Wynia, Elly M. "The Church of God and Saints of Christ: 'A Black Judeo-Christian Movement Founded in Lawrence, Kansas in 1896.'"

Zavelo, Donald. "The Black Entrepreneur in Lawrence, Kansas, 1900–1915." Master's thesis, University of Kansas, 1975.

Black Newspapers:[1]

BOGUE

Nicodemus Historical News Review. Bogue.

Nicodemus News Review. Bogue. 19??—Current? Quarterly.

COFFEYVILLE

Advocate. Coffeyville. 1894.

Afro-American Advocate. Coffeyville. 1891–1893.

American. Coffeyville. 1890–1899.

Coffeyville Globe. Coffeyville. 1918–1925.

> *Kansas Blackman.* Topeka. 1894–1896.
> *Kansas Blackman.* Coffeyville. 1894–1896.

Vindicator. Coffeyville. 1906.

FORT SCOTT

> *Colored Citizen* #1. Fort Scott. 1878. Moved to Topeka, 1878.

> *Kansas Weekly Herald.* Topeka. 1880.
> *Herald of Kansas.* Topeka. 1880.

Fair Play. Fort Scott. 1889–1900.

Freedman's Lance. Fort Scott. 1891.

Radical. Fort Scott. 1876–1879.

Southern Argus. Fort Scott. 1891–1893.

HUTCHINSON

Blade. Hutchinson. 1947–1952.

Hutchinson Blade. Hutchinson. 1914–1923.

KANSAS CITY

> *American Citizen.* Kansas City. 1888–1912.
> *Daily American Citizen.* Kansas City. 1898–1900.

Black Progress Shopper-News. Kansas City. 1968–1973.

Christian Spiritual Voice. Kansas City. 1940–1942.

---

[1] Double-lined boxed items indicate change in masthead names.

Community Challenger. Kansas
    City. 1974–1987.
Daily Citizen. Kansas City.
    1898–1900.

Daily Gazette. Kansas City.
    1887–1909.
Kansas Globe. Kansas City.
    1905–1909.
Gazette-Globe. Kansas City.
    1909–1917.
Kansas City Globe #1. Kansas City.
    1917–1918.
Kansas City Gazette-Globe. Kansas
    City. 1909–1917.

Daily Plaindealer. Kansas City.
    1907.
Golden Eaglet. Kansas City.
    1940–1944.

Independent. Kansas City.
    1914–1927.
Kansas City Advocate. Kansas City.
    1914–1932.

Kansas City Globe #2. Kansas City.
    1972–1980.
Kansas City Independent Negro.
    Kansas City. 1915–1916.
Kansas City Independent. Kansas
    City. 1891.
Kansas City News. Kansas City.
    ?–1927.
Kansas City Voice. Kansas City.
    1979–current.

Kansas City and Topeka Plaindealer.
    Kansas City. 1932–1933.
Plaindealer. Kansas City.
    1933–1958. Moved from
    Topeka in 1932.

Kansas Daily State Ledger. Kansas
    City. 1893.
Kansas Elevator. Kansas City.
    1916–1920.
Kansas Record. Kansas City.
    1902–1905.

Kansas State Globe. Kansas City.
    1983–1985.
Liberator. Kansas City. 1900–1901.
Missouri State Post. Kansas City.
    1896–1900.
National Review. Kansas City.
    1913.
People's Elevator. Kansas City.
    1892–1950.
Plaindealer. Kansas City.
    1899–1970. Editions for
    Topeka, Wichita, and na-
    tional.
Southern Argus. Kansas City.
    1891–1893.
Western Christian Recorder #1. Kan-
    sas City. 1892–1900.
Western Christian Recorder #2. Kan-
    sas City. 1920–1922.
Wyandot Echo. Kansas City.
    1928–195?

LAWRENCE

Afro-Asian Theatre Bulletin. Law-
    rence. 1965–1970.
Colored Radical. Lawrence and
    Leavenworth. 1876. First
    Black Kansas newspaper.
Ethnicity and Disease. Lawrence.
    1991–current.
Harambee. Lawrence. 1984.
Historic Times. Lawrence. 1891.
Kansas Herald and Freeman. Law-
    rence. 1914–1927.
Kansas Herald of Freedom. Lawrence.
    1855–1859.
Lawrence Vindicator. Lawrence.
    1878–1880.

LEAVENWORTH

Advocate. Leavenworth.
    1888–1891.
Leavenworth Advocate.
    Leavenworth. 1889–1891.

> *Historic Times.* Lawrence. 1891.
> *Times-Observer.* Topeka.
>   1891–1892.

Colored Radical. Lawrence and
          Leavenworth. 1876.
Democratic Standard. Leavenworth.
          1870–1888.
Leavenworth Advocate.
          Leavenworth. 1889–1891.
Leavenworth Herald. Leavenworth.
          1894–1899.

NICODEMUS
Nicodemus Historical News Review.
          Nicodemus. 1989–1992.
Nicodemus News Review. Nicodemus.
          1992. Quarterly.

> *Western Cyclone.* Nicodemus.
>   1886–1888. White-owned.
> *Nicodemus Enterprise.* Nicodemus.
>   1887. White-owned.
> *Nicodemus Cyclone.* Nicodemus.
>   1887–1889. White-owned.

PAOLA
Miami Republican. Paola.
          1866–199?
Western Spirit. Paola. 1871–199?

PARSONS
Baptist Globe. Parsons.
          1895–1897.

> *Weekly Blade.* Parson. 1892–1904.
> *Parsons Evening Herald.* Parsons.
>   1902–1904.

PERU
Freeman's Lance. Peru. 1891–1892.
Sedan Lance. Peru. 1892–1909.

PITTSBURGH

> *Afro-American.* Pittsburgh.
>   1903–1904.
> *Free Press.* Pittsburgh.
> *Afro-American.* Pittsburgh. 1903.
> *Free Press.* Pittsburgh. 1904.

Afro-American Review. Pittsburgh.
          1915–1916.
Eclipse. Pittsburgh. 1974.
Pittsburgh Plain Dealer. Pittsburgh.
          1899–1900.

> *Pittsburgh Plain Dealer.* Wichita.
>   1899–1900.
> *Wichita Searchlight.* Wichita.
>   1900–1912.
> *National Reflector.* Wichita. 1912.

Uplift. Pittsburgh. 1914.

SALINA
Afro-American. Salina. 1915–1916.
Black World Is. Salina. 1971–1976.
Salina Enterprise. Salina.
          1908–1912.

TOPEKA
American Citizen. Topeka.
          1888–1909.

> *Baptist Highlight.* Topeka.
>   1893–1894.
> *Afro-American Baptist.* Topeka.
>   1892–1894.
> *National Baptist World.* Wichita.
>   1894.

Capital Plaindealer. Topeka.
          1936–1938.

> *Colored Citizen #1.* Topeka.
>   1878–1890.
> *Tribune.* Topeka. 1880–1881.
> *Kansas State Tribune.* Topeka. 1881.
> *Colored Citizen #2.* Topeka.
>   1897–1900.

Colored Patriot. Topeka. 1882.

Colored Woman's Magazine.
Topeka. 1907–1909.
Monthly.

Ebony Times. Topeka. 1973–1978.

Evening Call. Topeka. 1893.

Topeka Call. Topeka. 1890–1898.

Weekly Call. Topeka. 1893–1899.

Helper. Topeka. 1912–1919.

Herald of Kansas. Topeka. 1880.

Kansas American. Topeka.
1933–1960.

Kansas Eagle. Topeka. 1934–1935.

Kansas Baptist Herald. Topeka.
1911–1913.

Kansas Blackman. Topeka.
1894–1896.

Kansas Blackman. Coffeyville.
1894–1896.

Kansas Daily Commonwealth.
Topeka.

Commonwealth. Topeka.
1874–1880.

Daily Commonwealth. Topeka.
1880–?

Kansas Herald. Topeka. 1880.

Kansas Sentinel. Topeka. 1960.

Kansas State Leader. Topeka. 191?

Kansas State Ledger. Topeka.
1892–1894.

State Ledger. Topeka. 1894–1912.

Kansas Tradesman. Topeka. 1922.

Kansas Watchman. Topeka.
1905–1912.

Little Weekly. Topeka. 1936–1944.

Messenger. Topeka. 1969–1970.

Kansas Messenger. Topeka. 1970.

National Watchman. Topeka.
1914–1915.

Paul Jones Monthly Magazine.
Topeka. 1907–1938.

People's Friend. Topeka.
1896–1898.

Topeka Call. Topeka. 1891–1898.

Plaindealer. Kansas City.
1899–1900.

Topeka Plaindealer. Topeka.
1900–1932.

Kansas City and Topeka Plaindealer.
Kansas City. 1932–1933.

Plaindealer. Kansas City.
1933–1958.

Third Baptist Church Herald. Topeka.
1911–1913.

Times-Observer. Topeka.
1891–1892.

Topeka Tribune #1. Topeka. 1880.

Kansas State Tribune. Topeka. 1881.

Topeka Tribune #2. Topeka.
1883–1885.

Western Recorder. Topeka.
1883–1885.

Western Index. Topeka. 1908–1921.
Moved to Houston, Texas.

Western Trumpet. Topeka. 1908.

WICHITA

Afro-American Baptist. Topeka.
1892–1894.

Baptist Highlight. Topeka.
1893–1894.

National Baptist World. Wichita.
1894.

Broad Ax. Wichita. ?–1970.

Colored Citizen. Wichita.
1902–1904.

Community Voice. Wichita.
1995–current.

Enlightener. Wichita. 1962–1970.

Factorian. Wichita. 1913–1914.

Heart of the City. Wichita.
    1991–199?
Kansas Black Journal. Wichita.
    1983–1985.
Kansas Globe. Wichita. 1887–1889.
Kansas Headlight. Wichita.
    1894–1895.
Kansas Journal. Wichita.
    1940–1944.
Kansas Weekly Journal. Topeka.
    1970–1987.
National Reflector #1. Wichita.
    1895–1900.
Negro Star. Wichita. 1908–1954.
News Hawk. Wichita. 1965–1979.
People's Elevator. Wichita-
    Independence. 1924–1930,
    1937–1943. Moved from
    Oklahoma in 1924.
People's Friend. Wichita. 1894.

Post Observer. Wichita.
    1908–1955.
Times. Wichita. 1912–1958.
Wichita Globe. Wichita.
    1887–1889.
Wichita Protest. Wichita.
    1918–1931.
Wichita Times. Wichita.
    1970–1978.
Wichita Tribune. Wichita.
    1896–1900.

VARIOUS COMMUNITIES

American Freeman. Girard.
    1929–1951.
Atchison Blade. Atchison.
    1892–1894.
Benevolent Banner. North Topeka.
    1887.
People's Elevator. Independence.
    1926–1930.

Pittsburgh Plain Dealer. Wichita.
    1899–1900.
Wichita Searchlight. Wichita.
    1899–1914.
National Reflector #2. Wichita.
    1912–1913.

Southern Argus. Baxter Springs.
    1891.
Southern Argus. Fort Scott.
    1891–1892.

Plaindealer. Kansas City.
    1945–1950.

UNIQUE. Prairie Village.
    1971–1976.

Other:

African-American Baptist Annual Reports, 1865–1990s: Kansas. National Archives, microfilm. Books, pamphlets, periodicals, statistics, biographies, etc.

Happy Birthday, Mrs. Craig. Richard Kaplan producer and director. The 102 year-old daughter of slaves tells of homesteading in "black colony" in Kansas. Videocassette.

"Interview with Gordon Parks," 1966. Audiotape. Discusses his Kansas childhood.

Schools. Kansas, Parsons, 1942–47. Papers of the NAACP. Part 3, Campaign for Educational Equality. Series B, Legal Department and Central Office Records, 1940–1950; Reel 18, FR. 0316–0322. Frederick, MD: University Publications of America, 1986. Microform.

Schools. Kansas, Wichita Schools, 1945–49. Papers of the NAACP. Part 3, Campaign for Educational Equality. Series B, Legal Department and Central Office Records, 1940–1950; Reel 2, FR. 0751–0899. Frederick, MD: University Publications of America, 1986. Microform.

Seeing Kansas City in Action. Newsreel sponsored by the St. Paul Presbyterian Church, 1921. Black professional and business life.

Missouri

Articles:

"Admission of a Negro Student to the University of Missouri." *School and Society* 43 (6 June 1936). The Lloyd Gaines case.

Allen, Ernest, Jr. "Waiting for Tojo: The Pro-Japan Vigil of Black Missourians, 1932–1943." *Gateway Heritage* 16 (Fall 1995).

Armor, David. "The Achievement Gap." *Education Week* 12 (2 August 1995). Author examines differences in Black and white test scores relative to Kansas City court case.

Barksdale, Norval P. "Gaines Case and its Effect on Negro Education in Missouri." *School and Society* 51 (9 March 1940).

Beck, Deborah E. "School Choice as a Method for Desegregating an Inner-City School District." *California Law Review* 81 (July 1993). Highlights problems in Kansas City, Missouri.

Bellamy, Donnie D. "The Education of Blacks in Missouri Prior to 1861." *Journal of Negro History* 59 (April 1974). Private efforts to educate free children.

————. "Free Blacks in Antebellum Missouri 1820–1860." *Missouri Historical Review* 67 (January 1973).

————. "The Persistence of Colonization in Missouri." *Missouri Historical Review* 72 (October 1977).

Bennett, Rob. "*Missouri* v. *Jenkins*: A Case of Legislative Underreaching." *Tax Notes* 48 (2 July 1990). School desegregation in Kansas City.

Billington, Monroe Lee. "Public School Integration in Missouri, 1954–1964." *Journal of Negro Education* 35 (Summer 1966).

"Black Family Research-Missouri Archives." *Ash Tree Echo* 28 (September 1993).

"Black Genealogy: More Data From Missouri Newspapers." *Family Records Today* 15 (April 1994).

Blassingame, John W. "Recruitment of Negro Troops in Missouri During the Civil War." *Missouri Historical Review* 58 (1964). Changing policies.

_____. "Recruitment of Colored Troops in Kentucky, Maryland and Missouri, 1863–1865." *Historian* 29 (August 1967). Issues in the recruitment of Black soldiers.

Bluford, Lucile H. "The Lloyd Gaines Story." *Journal of Educational Sociology* 32 (February 1959). Supreme Court integration case of 1939.

Bogle, Lori. "Desegregation in a Border State: The Example of Joplin, Missouri." *Missouri Historical Review* 85 (July 1991).

"Boss of the Blues." *Ebony*, March 1954. Biography of jump blues, rock and jazz singer Big Joe Turner, "The Singing Bartender from Kansas City."

Bowen, Elbert R. "Negro Minstrels in Early Rural Missouri." *Missouri Historical Review* 47 (January 1953).

Brady, A. "Federal Relations to Higher Education: New Criteria of Equality of Opportunity in Higher Education Established by United States Supreme Court Decision in the Lloyd Gaines Case." *School and Society* 49 (4 March 1939).

Brenner, Scott C. "Judicial Taxation as a Means of Remedying Public School Segregation under *Missouri* v. *Jenkins*: Boldly Going Where No Federal Court has Gone Before." *Whittier Law Review* 12 (Winter 1991). School desegregation in Kansas City.

Bringham, Robert. "Negro Education in Ante-Bellum Missouri." *Journal of Negro History* 30 (1945).

Brown, Elbert R. "Negro Minstrels in Early Rural Missouri." *Missouri Historical Review* 47 (1953).

Bruce, Nathaniel C., Patrick J. Huber, and Gary R. Kremer. "Black Education and the 'Tuskegee of the Midwest.'" *Missouri Historical Review* 86 (October 1991). Adopting Booker T. Washington's ideas on education in Missouri.

Cantor, Louis. "A Prologue to the Protest Movement: The Missouri Sharecroppers Roadside Demonstration of 1939." *Journal of American History* 55 (March 1969).

Capeci, Dominic J. "The Lynching of Cleo Wright: Federal Protection of Constitutional Rights during World War II." *Journal of American History* 72 (October 1985).

Christensen, Lawrence O. "J. Milton Turner: An Appraisal." *Missouri Historical Review* 70 (1975). White advocate of Black education and equal rights.

_____. "The Popular Image of Blacks vs. the Birthrights." *Missouri Historical Review* 81 (October 1986). History of a Black family, the Birthrights.

_____. "Schools for Blacks: J. Milton Turner in Reconstruction Missouri." *Missouri Historical Review* 76 (January 1982).

Clough, Dick B. "Teachers' Institutes: A Missouri Tradition." *Missouri Historical Review* 67 (July 1973). Also refers to the Negro Teachers' Institute.

Coleman, Frank. "Freedom from Fear on the Home Front: Federal Prosecution of 'Village Tyrants' and Lynch-Mobs." *Iowa Law Review* 29 (March 1944). Includes lynching of Cleo Wright, a Black man, in Missouri.

Corbett, Katherine T. "Missouri's Black Heritage: From Colonial Time to 1970." *Gateway Heritage* 4 (1983).

Corbett, Katherine T., and Mary E. Seematter. "A Strong Seed Planted: Black History Programming at the Missouri Historical Society." *OAH Magazine of History* 4 (Summer 1989).

Curtis, L. S. "Negro Publicly-Supported Colleges in Missouri." *Journal of Negro Education* 31 (Summer 1962).

Daniel, Walter C. W. E. B. Du Bois at Lincoln University: Founders' Day Address, 1941." *Missouri Historical Review* 74 (1980).

Davis, John Russell. "The Genesis of the Variety Theatre: The Black Crook Comes to Saint Louis." *Missouri Historical Review* 64 (1970).

Dyer, Thomas G. "A Most Unexampled Exhibition of Madness and Brutality': Judge Lynch in Saline County, Missouri, 1859. Part I." *Missouri Historical Review* 89 (April 1995). Four lynchings of slaves.

_____. "A Most Unexampled Exhibition of Madness and Brutality': Judge Lynch in Saline County, Missouri, 1859. Part II." *Missouri Historical Review* 89 (July 1995).

Elley, Christyn. "Tracing African American Ancestors." *Missouri Library World* 3 (Winter 1998). Using the archives at Missouri State.

Evenson, Richard C., and Dong W. Cho. "Norms for the Missouri Impatient Behavior Scale: Sex, Race and Age Differences in Psychiatric Symptoms." *Journal of Clinical Psychology* 43 (1987).

Farley, John E. "Race Still Matters: The Minimal Role of Income and Housing Cost as Causes of Housing Segregation in St. Louis, 1990." *Urban Affairs Review* 31 (November 1995).

Fellman, Michael. "Emancipation in Missouri." *Missouri Historical Review* 83 (October 1988).

Finley, Stephanie A. "Eradicating Dual Educational Systems through Desegregation: *Missouri v. Jenkins*." *Southern University Law Review* 17 (Spring 1990). Segregation in Missouri.

Foley, William E. "Antebellum Missouri in Historical Perspective." *Missouri Historical Review* 82 (January 1988).

Fox, Jeanne Allyson. "In Kansas City, Missouri, Economic Development Plays Catch Up to Political Clout." *Black Enterprise*, March 1978. Black economic and political status.

"Gaines Decision." *Commonweal* 29 (6 January 1939).

Giancaterino, Randy. "A Pitch for History." *American Visions*, June 1993. Negro Leagues Museum.

Gilbert, Judith A. "Esther and Her Sisters: Free Women of Color as Property Owners in Colonial St. Louis, 1765–1803." *Gateway Heritage* 17 (Summer 1996).

Glastris, Paul. "Black and Blue: A Top Cop's Painful Rethinking of Race-Based Preferences." *U.S. News and World Report*, 13 February 1995.

Goodrich, James W. "The Civil War Letters of Bethiah Pyatt McKnown," Part I. *Missouri Historical Review* 67 (January 1973). Includes aspects of Black Life.

Greene, Lorenzo J. "Lincoln University's Involvement with the Sharecropper Demonstration in Southeast Missouri, 1939–1940." *Missouri Historical Review* 82 (October 1987).

_____. "Negro Sharecroppers." *Negro History Bulletin* 3 (1968). Black sharecroppers protest by leaving the plantations.

_____. "Self Purchase by Negroes in Cole County, Missouri." *Midwest Journal* 1 (Winter 1948).

Grenz, Suzanna M. "The Exodusters of 1879: St. Louis and Kansas City Responded." *Missouri Historical Review* 73 (October 1978).

Grothaus, Larry. "The Inevitable Mr. Gaines." *Arizona and the West* 26 (Spring 1984).

_____. "Kansas City Blacks, Harry Truman, and the Pendergast Machine." *Missouri Historical Review* 69 (October 1974). Blacks and Truman had to fight against the "machine" to advance their politics.

Holland, Antonio F., and Gary R. Kremer, eds. "Some Aspects of Black Education in Reconstruction Missouri: An Address by Richard B. Foster." *Missouri Historical Review* 70 (January 1976). Foster, a white man, went South to aid in educating Blacks and helped to establish Lincoln University in Jefferson City.

Huber, Patrick J. "The Lynching of James T. Scott: The Underside of a College Town." *Gateway Heritage* 12 (Summer 1991). The 1923 lynching of Scott in Columbia.

Huber, Patrick J., and Gary R. Kremer. "Nathaniel C. Bruce, Black Education and the 'Tuskegee of the Midwest.'" *Missouri Historical Review* 86 (October 1991). History of the Bartlett Agricultural and Industrial School for Negroes (Dalton Vocational School).

"Integration by Computer." *Education Week* 13 (8 September 1993). Federal judge overseeing Kansas City desegregation plan approves integration through computer.

Jones, L. W. "Southern Higher Education Since the Gaines Decision: A Twenty Year Review." *Journal of Educational Sociology* 32 (February 1959).

"Judge Lynch and the Pole Cat." *Newsweek*, 9 February 1942. Lynching at Sikeston, Missouri, was filmed.

"Judge Ronnie White of Missouri is Picked for Federal Bench." *Jet*, 21 July 1997. White awaits confirmation.

"K.C. in Swingtime and Now." *International Review of African American Art* 14 (1997). Blues music in Kansas City during the 1930s and its depiction in Black art.

Kelleher, Daniel T. "The Case of Lloyd Lionel Gaines: The Demise of the Separate But Equal Doctrine." *Journal of Negro History* 56 (September 1971).

Kremer, Gary R., and Linda R. Gibbens. "The Missouri Industrial Home for Negro Girls: The 1930s." *American Studies* (Fall 1983).

Kremer, Gary R., and Ann Jenkins. "The Town with Black Roots." *Missouri Life* (July-August 1983). Black town of Eldridge, Missouri.

Kremer, Gary R., and Lynn Morrow. "Pennytown: A Freedmen's Hamlet, 1871–1945." *Missouri Folklore Society Journal* 11 and 12 (1989–1990). Missouri community.

"Ku Klux Klans of the Reconstruction Period in Missouri." *Missouri Historical Review* 37 (July 1943).

Land, G. H., and J. W. Stockbauer. "Smoking and Pregnancy Outcome: Trends among Black Teenage Mothers in Missouri." *American Journal of Public Health* 83 (August 1993).

Learned, H. B. "Reaction of Philip Phillips to the Repeal of the Missouri Compromise." *Mississippi Valley Historical Review* 8 (March 1922).

Ledbetter, Billy D. "White Over Black in Texas: Racial Attitudes in the Ante-Bellum Period." *Phylon* 34 (1973). Examines 1823 to 1860.

Lee, Bill R. "Missouri's Fight over Emancipation in 1863." *Missouri Historical Review* 45 (1951).

"Legal Lynching Disapproved." *International Juridical Association Monthly Bulletin* 1 (October 1932). Reversal of convictions of Blacks in Oklahoma and Missouri.

"Lesson Learned." *Time*, 11 December 1933. The lynching of Lloyd Warner, a Black man, of St. Joseph, Missouri.

Levine, Daniel U. "Negro Population Growth and Enrollment in the Public Schools: A Case Study and Its Implications." *Education and Urban Society* 1 (November 1968). Kansas City.

Lightfoot, Billy Bob. "Nobody's Nominee: Sample Orr and the Election of 1860." *Missouri Historical Review* 60 (1966). Implications of the slim loss of a Missouri Republican gubernatorial candidate in 1860.

Lingg, MaryAnn. "Preemployment Training for African American Youth." *Journal of Career Development* 22 (Fall 1995). Kmart Employment for Youth (KEY) program.

Lloyd, Fonda M. "Knocking at the Political Door." *Black Enterprise*, November 1994. Alan Wheat of Kansas City as possible Senator.

Lowe, Richard, and Randolph B. Campbell. "Wealthholding and Political Power in Antebellum Texas." *Southwestern Historical Quarterly* 79 (1975).

"Lynching." *Newsweek*, 2 February 1942. Black man Cleo Wright dragged to death behind a car at Sikeston, Missouri.

"The Lynching Horror." *Nation*, 29 August 1901. Blacks lynched, homes burned, and driven out in Pierce City, Missouri and Grayson County, Texas.

Lyons, Nancee L. "Missouri: A Black Hub in the Heartland." *American Visions,* October-November 1996. Black travel information.

"Malone, Ann Turnbo—Missouri Women in History." *Missouri Historical Review* 67 (July 1973). Biographical sketch of Black business woman.

March, David D. "The Admission of Missouri." *Missouri Historical Review* 65 (July 1971). The "Negro Question" included.

"Mass Murder in America." *The New Republic*, 13 December 1933. Lynchings in California, Missouri and elsewhere.

"Mass Murders or Civilized Society?" *The Sign* 13 (January 1934). Lynchings in California, Missouri and elsewhere.

McKemy, Al. "Negro Murderer Lynched." *Missouri State Genealogical Association Journal* 13 (Summer 1993). The lynching of Arthur McNeal at Richmond, Missouri, in 1901.

"Missouri Black Marriage Registers." *Ash Tree Echo* 28 (September 1993).

"Missouri Heads 1931 Lynching Parade." *Literary Digest* 108 (31 January 1931). Article includes photograph.

"Missouri Lynching." *International Juridical Association Monthly Bulletin* 10 (March 1942). Black man Cleo Wright lynched at Sikeston.

"Missouri Mob Murder." *Outlook and Independent* 157 (28 January 1931). Lynching of Black man at Maryville.

Mitchell, Mark A. "Benefits of Violence Prevention for African-American Youth." *Journal of Health Care for the Poor and Underserved* 2 (Spring 1992). Kansas City research.

Moore, N. Webster. "James Milton Turner: Diplomat, Educator, and Defender of Rights, 1840–1915." *Bulletin of the Missouri Historical Society* 27 (April 1971).

Morgan, Joan. "Students Lobby Administration for Mandatory Black History Curriculum at SMSU." *Black Issues in Higher Education* 9 (21 May 1992).

Murarah, Thabit. "The Black Archives of Mid-America: A Hidden Treasure." *Missouri Library World* 3 (Spring 1998).

"Negro is Lynched by Missouri Crowd." *Interracial Review* 15 (February 1942).

Nuell, Tim. "Blacks Turn to Black Press for Credibility." *St. Louis Journalism Review* 28 (March 1998). Highlights Black-owned press in St. Louis.

Nyberg, Norma. "Boone County, Missouri, Records: Register of Colored Apprentices." *Reporter Quarterly* 11 (Summer 1992).

"Old Benjamin Banneker Parkville First Black School." *Platte County, Missouri, Historical and Genealogical Society* 42 (Winter 1989).

Padget, Tania. "Tenacity: The Mother of Invention." *Black Enterprise*, April 1996. Profile of Anthony Drew and Centurion Electronics of Kansas City.

Pantle, Alberta, ed. "Larry Lapsley, 1840–97. Story of a Kansas Freedman." *Kansas Historical Quarterly* 11 (November 1942).

Parrish, William E. "Blind Boone's Ragtime." *Missouri Life* (November-December 1979). John William Boone, classical and ragtime composer.

Perkins, Drew A. "Constitutional Law-When the Prohibition on Judicial Taxation Interferes with an Equitable Remedy in a School Desegregation Case (*Missouri* v. *Jenkins*, 110 S.Ct. 1651 [1990]). *Land and Water Law Review* 26 (Winter 1991).

Pfeifer, Michael J. "The Ritual of Lynching: Extralegal Justice in Missouri, 1890–1942." *Gateway Heritage* 13 (Winter 1993).

Piety, Harold R. "Revolution Comes to East St. Louis." *FOCUS/Midwest* 6 (1968). The creation of the Black Economic Union and other activities.

Poinsett, Alex. "Newest Black Mayors: Emanuel Cleaver Wins in Kansas City and Wellington Webb Walks to Victory in Denver." *Ebony*, September 1991.

Presser, Arlynn L. "Broken Dreams: A Federal Judge in Kansas City Had a Utopian Vision for Desegregating the City's Schools." *ABA Journal* 77 (May 1991).

Reedy, Sidney J. "Higher Education and Desegregation in Missouri." *Journal of Negro Education* 27 (Summer 1958).

Richardson, Joe M. "The American Missionary Association and Black Education in Civil War Missouri." *Missouri Historical Review* 69 (July 1975).

Robertson, William E. "Housing for Blacks: A Challenge for Kansas City." *The Review of Black Political Economy* 19 (Winter-Spring 1991).

Savage, W. Sherman. "The Legal Provisions for Negro Schools in Missouri, 1865–1890." *Journal of Negro History* 16 (1931).

_____. "The Legal Provisions for Negro Schools in Missouri, 1865–1890." *Journal of Negro History* 22 (1937).

Sawyer, R. M. "The Gaines Case: The Human Side." *Negro Educational Review* 38 (January 1987). Supreme Court decision.

Schwendemann, Glen. "Thriving With the Lowest Caste: The Financial Activities of James R. Thomas in the Nineteenth-Century South." *Journal of Negro History* 63 (1978).

Sheridan, Richard B. "From Slavery in Missouri to Freedom in Kansas: The Influx of Black Fugitives and Contrabands into Kansas, 1854–1864." *Kansas History* 12 (Spring 1989).

"Sikeston Lynching—Continued and Closed." *Southern Frontier* 3 (August 1942). Murder of Cleo Wright in Missouri.

Slavens, George E. "The Missouri Negro Press, 1875–1920." *Missouri Historical Review* 64 (July 1970). Looks at the 64 newspapers published since Reconstruction.

"Somewhere in America, 1942." *Colliers*, 28 March 1942. Lynching of Cleo Wright in Sikeston, Missouri.

Sorensen, Jonathan R., and Donald H. Wallace. "Capital Punishment in Missouri: Examining the Issue of Racial Disparity." *Behavioral Sciences and the Law* 13 (1995).

Stokes, Richard L. "Decision of the Missouri Supreme Court on the Admission of Negroes to State Universities." *School and Society* 48 (3 December 1938). Supreme Court case.

Strickland, Arvarh E. "Aspects of Slavery in Missouri, 1821." *Missouri Historical Review* 65 (July 1971).

_____. "The Plight of the People in the Sharecroppers' Demonstration in Southeast Missouri." *Missouri Historical Review* 81 (October 1987).

"The Supremacy of the Mob." *Voice of the Negro* 3 (May 1906). Black man lynched in Tennessee, and three in Springfield, Missouri.

"Supreme Court Decision on Equality of Educational Privileges for White and Negro Law Students." *School and Society* 48 (17 December 1938).

"Supreme Court Gives Negroes Equal Educational Rights in Upholding Right of Admission to Missouri University's Law School." *Scholastic* 33 (7 January 1939). Lloyd Gaines case.

"Supreme Court Supports Negro School Rights." *Christian Century* 55 (28 December 1938).

Swain, John D. "A Warning To the South." *Voice of the Negro* 3 (June 1906). Three Black men lynched at Springfield, Missouri.

Swomley, John M. "Anatomy of a Stealth Candidate." *The Humanist* 55 (May/June 1995). Profile of Ron Freeman, Black fundamentalist Congressional candidate from Kansas City.

Thomas, J. C., and D. H. Hoxworth. "The Limits of Judicial Desegregation Remedies after *Missouri* v. *Jenkins*." *Publius* 21 (Summer 1991).

"Tripling Black Enrollment." *The Chronicle of Higher Education* 40 (13 July 1994). University of Missouri and its recruitment efforts.

Twain, Mark. "The United States of Lynchdom." Chapter in *Europe and Elsewhere*, ed. Albert Bigelow Paine. New York: Harper and Brothers, 1923. Twain wrote this article in 1901 after the lynching of three Missouri Blacks.

"Union Aid Benevolent Society of the Cape Girardeau Colored Citizens." *Missouri State Genealogical Association Journal* 17 (Spring 1997). Missouri society.

Villard, Oswald Garrison. "Issues and Men: Missouri Law School Case." *Nation* 147 (24 December 1938). Lloyd Gaines case.

Violette, E. M. "Black Code in Missouri." *Missouri Valley Historical Association* 6 (1913).

Wamble, Gaston Hugh. "Negroes and Missouri Protestant Churches before and after the Civil War." *Missouri Historical Review* 61 (April 1967).

Ware, Leland. "Contributions of Missouri's Black Lawyers to Securing Equal Justice." *Journal of the Missouri Bar* 45 (June 1989). History of race discrimination.

Welek, Mary. "Jordan Chambers: Black Politician and Boss." *Journal of Negro History* 57 (October 1972). Story of St. Louis Democrat.

Williams, Charleea H. "Recent Developments in 'the Land of the Free.'" *Colored American Magazine*, August 1902. Lynchings of Louis F. Wright at New Madrid, Missouri, and William H. Wallace at La Junta, Colorado.

Williams, Michael Patrick. "The Black Evangelical Ministry in the Antebellum Border States: Profiles of Elders John Berry Meachum and Noah Davis." *Foundations* 21 (1970).

"Work of the Negro Industrial Commission of Missouri." *Monthly Labor Review* 25 (November 1927). Blacks and employment.

Wyllie, Irvin G. "Race and Class Conflict on Missouri's Cotton Frontier." *Journal of Southern History* 20 (May 1954). Anti-Black violence in Pemiscot County, and the lynching of A. B. Richardson.

St. Louis

Adams, Patricia L. "Fighting for Democracy in St. Louis: Civil Rights during World War II." *Missouri Historical Review* 80 (October 1985).

Balch, Jack. "Democracy at Work: The People's Art Service Center in St. Louis." *Magazine of Art*, February 1943. A WPA program for Blacks.

Baldwin, Roger N. "Negro Segregation by Initiative Election in St. Louis." *American City* 14 (April 1916).

Bourgois, Philippe. "If You're Not Black You're White: A History of Ethnic Relations in St. Louis." *City and Society* 3 (1989).

Brodine, Virginia. "The Strange Case of the Jefferson Bank vs. CORE." *St. Louis Journalism Review* 23 (December-January 1993). Discrimination against Blacks and miscarriage of justice.

Buel, Ronald A. "Race, Welfare, and Housing in St. Louis." *Interplay* 3 (1969).

Bullington, Bruce. "Concerning Heroin Use and Official Records (Police of Federal Bureau of Narcotics; Commenting on a 1967 Article by Lee Robins and George E. Murphy, Concerning Drug Use in the Normal Population of Young Negroes in St. Louis, Mo.)." *American Journal of Public Health* 59 (October 1969).

"Ch. 2's Donn Johnson talks about TV News, Politics, Management and Racial Bias." *St. Louis Journalism Review* 26 (July-August 1996). Interview.

Chambers, Marcia. "At 95, He's a Model for All Lawyers." *National Law Journal* 11 (24 April 1989). Interview with Nathan B. Young, Jr., of St. Louis.

Christensen, Lawrence O. "Cyprian Clamorgan, the Colored Aristocracy of St. Louis." *Missouri Historical Society Bulletin* 31 (October 1974). Reprint of Clamorgan's 1858 publication about free Blacks.

_____. "Race Relations in St. Louis, 1865–1916." *Missouri Historical Review* 78 (January 1984).

_____. "The Racial Views of John W. Wheeler." *Missouri Historical Review* 67 (July 1973). St. Louis civil rights leader.

Corbett, Katherine T., and Mary E. Seematter. "Black St. Louis at the Turn of the Century." *Gateway Heritage* 71 (Summer 1986).

_____. "No Crystal Stair: Black St. Louis, 1920–1940." *Garteway Heritage* 8 (Fall 1987).

Crockett, H. J., Jr. "Study of Some Factors Affecting the Decision of Negro High School Students to Enroll in Previously All-White High Schools, St. Louis." *Social Forces* 35 (May 1957).

Cross, Joseph W. "Segregation in Reverse: St. Louis, 1873." *Journal of Negro History* 54 (1969). Catholic Archdiocese orders certain churches to be used exclusively by Blacks.

Day, Judy, and M. James Kedro. "Free Blacks in St. Louis: Antebellum Conditions, Emancipation, and the Postwar Era." *Missouri Historical Society Bulletin* 30 (January 1974). Examines racism against free Blacks in those time periods.

"Does Desegregation Help Close the Gap? Testimony of Gary Orfield, March 22, 1996." *Journal of Negro Education* 66 (Summer 1997). Excerpts from Harvard professor Gary Orfield's testimony as an expert witness against discrimination.

Dulaney, W. Marvin. "Sergeant Ira L. Cooper's Letter to the St. Louis Police Relief Association, May 25, 1924." *Journal of Negro History* 72 (1987).

Farley, John E. "Black-White Housing Segregation in the City of St. Louis: A 1988 Update." *Urban Affairs Quarterly* 26 (March 1991). Persistent patterns of segregation.

_____. "Race Still Matters: The Minimal Role of Income and Housing Cost as Causes of Housing Segregation in St. Louis, 1990." *Urban Affairs Review* (November 1995).

_____. "Racial Housing Segregation in St. Louis, 1980–1990: Comparing Block and Census Tract Levels." *Journal of Urban Affairs* 15 (1993).

Floyd, Samuel A., Jr. "A Black Composer in Nineteenth-Century St. Louis." *19th Century Music* 4/2 (1980). Profile of Joseph W. Postlewaite.

_____. "J. W. Postlewaite of St. Louis: A Search for His Identity." *Black Perspective in Music, USA* 6/2 (Fall 1978). Profile of composer and band leader.

Freeman, Gregory. "St. Louis: Bringing Minorities into the Mainstream." *Black Enterprise*, May 1994. City's first Black mayor, Freeman R. Bosley, has pushed to positively change the economic climate for Blacks.

Gersman, Elinor Mondale. "The Development of Public Education for Blacks in Nineteenth Century St. Louis, Missouri." *Journal of Negro Education*

4 (1972). Recounts struggles for equal education in substandard schools to the building of a nationally-ranked Black high school in 1910.

Glastris, Paul. "Black and Blue." *U.S. News and World Report*, 13 February 1995. Controversy over a sergeant's exam in St. Louis erupts into a debate on affirmative action.

Glover, Samuel T. "Speech at the Ratification of Emancipation in Missouri, St. Louis, July 22, 1863." *St. Louis Missouri Republican* (July 1863).

Grenz, Suzanna M. "The Exodusters of 1879: St. Louis and Kansas City Responded." *Missouri Historical Review* 73 (October 1978).

Hayakawa, S. I. "The Semantics of Being Negro." *Review of General Semantics* 10 (1953). Address to the St. Louis Urban League on February 12, 1953.

Hendron, Mary. "A Tourist in My Own Town." *U.S. News and World Report*, 30 November 1998. A Black native of St. Louis tours historical and cultural sites she or her family could not tour because of segregation.

Herman, Janet S. "The McIntosh Affair." *Missouri Historical Society Bulletin* 26 (January 1970).

Higginbotham, A. Leon, Jr. "Race, Sex, Education and Missouri Jurisprudence: *Shelly* v. *Kraemer* in a Historical Perspective." *Washington University Law Quarterly* 67 (Fall 1989). The 1948 Supreme Court case, in a suit by a St. Louis couple, held racially restrictive property deeds unenforceable.

Hunter, Lloyd A. "Slavery in St. Louis, 1804–1860." *Bulletin of the Missouri Historical Society* 30 (July 1974).

Judd, Dennis R. "The Role of Governmental Policies in Promoting Residential Segregation in the St. Louis Metropolitan Area." *Journal of Negro Education* 66 (Summer 1997). Analysis of continued housing discrimination.

Kelleher, Daniel T. "St. Louis' 1916 Residential Segregation Ordinance." *Bulletin of the Missouri Historical Society* 26 (1970).

Kempker, Donald J. "Catholic Integration in St. Louis, 1935–1947." Missouri Historical Review 73 (October 1989).

Klamer, Keith. "Minority Leader." *Vocational Education Journal* 70 (May 1995). Profile of Ranken Technical College.

Klotzer, Charles L. "An Epochal Event Misinterpreted." *St. Louis Journalism Review* 22 (September 1993). Response to article by Bill McClennan in the *St. Louis Post-Dispatch*, who wrote the celebration marking the 30th anniversary of the Jefferson Bank Protest was hollow.

Kouwenhoven, John A. "Eads Bridge: The Celebration." *Bulletin of the Missouri Historical Society* 33 (April 1974). The history of the development of Eads Bridge and the relationship to slavery.

Kremer, Gary R., and Donald H. Ewalt, Jr. "The Historian as Preservationist: A Missouri Case Study." *The Public Historian* 3 (Fall 1981). Focus on Black St. Louis neighborhood, the Ville.

Mollenkamp, Becky. "St. Louis TV Stations Lack Black Management." *St. Louis Journalism Review*, September 1996.

Moore, N. Webster. "John Berry Meachum (1789–1854): St. Louis Pioneer, Black Abolitionist, Educator, and Preacher." *Missouri Historical Society Bulletin* 29 (January 1973).

"Negro Segregation Adopted by St. Louis." *Survey* 35 (11 March 1916).

"Negro Segregation in St. Louis." *Literary Digest* 52 (18 March 1916).

"Negro-Owned Outlet Due for St. Louis." *Broadcasting* 24 (23 June 1969).

Niedowski, Erika. "Bus Battle." *New Republic*, 3 August 1998. Missouri Democrats divided over busing.

Rankine, R. M. "St. Louis Blues." *Commentary* (September 1959). Discrimination against Blacks.

Reichard, Maximilian. "Black and White on the Urban Frontier: The St. Louis Community in Transition, 1800–1830." *Missouri Historical Society Bulletin* 33 (October 1976).

Rose, Alvin W. "The Influence of a Border City Union on the Race Attitudes of Its Members." *Journal of Social Issues* 9 (Winter 1953). Based on a study of St. Louis Teamsters Local 688 that was published in *Union Solidarity: The Internal Cohesion of a Labor Union*. Minneapolis: University of Minnesota Press, 1952.

Ross, M. "They Did It in St. Louis: One Man Against Folklore." *Commentary* 4 (July 1947).

Rudwick, Elliot M. "Fifty Years of Race Relations in East St. Louis: The Breaking Down of White Supremacy." *Midcontinent American Studies Journal* 6 (1965). Looks at the evolving civil rights movement from the 1917 riots to the 1960s.

"St. Louis." *Black Enterprise*, August 1971. Black economic life.

"St. Louis: The Gateway to the West." *Ebony West* 10 (September 1995). Travel guide.

Schoenberg, Sandra, and Charles Bailey. "The Symbolic Meaning of an Elite Black Community: The Ville in St. Louis." *Missouri Historical Society Bulletin* 33 (January 1977). Area originally occupied by Germans and Irish in 1900, Blacks began to replace them about 1911.

Schwendemann, Glen. "St. Louis and the Exodusters of 1879." *Journal of Negro History* 46 (1961). What the city did with immigrants moving through to Kansas.

Seematter, Mary E. "Trials and Confessions: Race and Justice in Antebellum St. Louis." *Gateway Heritage* 12 (Fall 1991).

Smelser, M. "Housing in Creole St. Louis, 1764–1821: An Example of Cultural Change." *Louisiana Historical Quarterly* 21 (April 1938).

Smith, Eric L. "Caught Red-Handed?" *Black Enterprise*, May 1996. Wal-Mart sued for $150 million after turning down a proposal to build a store in Pine Lawn, a largely Black suburb of St. Louis.

Streifford, William M. "Racial Economic Dualism in St. Louis." *The Review of Black Political Economy* 4 (Spring 1974).

Trent, William T. "Outcomes of School Desegregation: Findings from Longitudinal Research." *Journal of Negro Education* 66 (Summer 1997).

Tushnet, Mark V. "Shelly v. Kraemer and Theories of Equality." *New York Law School Law Review* 33 (Fall 1988). Landmark housing covenant case.

Usher, Robert G. "Negro Segregation in St. Louis." *The New Republic*, 18 March 1916.

Watts, Eugene. "Black and Blue: Afro-American Police Officers in Twentieth Century St. Louis." *Journal of Urban History* 7 (February 1981).

Wells, Amy Stuart. "When School Desegregation Fuels Educational Reform: Lessons From Suburban St. Louis." *Educational Policy* (March 1994).

Slaves and Slavery

Baltimore, Lester B. "Benjamin F. Stringfellow: The Fight for Slavery on the Missouri Border." *Missouri Historical Review* 62 (1967). Proslavery advocate.

Bierbaum, Milton E. "Frederick Starr. A Missouri Border Abolitionist: The Making of a Martyr." *Missouri Historical Review* 58 (1964). Minister and antislavery activist.

Brown, Richard H. "The Missouri Crisis, Slavery, and the Politics of Jacksonianism." *South Atlantic Quarterly* 65 (1966). The rise of the Republican Party and its impacts on Southern-controlled national politics.

Dorsett, Lyle W. "Slaveholding in Jackson County, Missouri." *Missouri Historical Society Bulletin* 20 (October 1963).

Dunson, A. A. "Notes on the Missouri Germans on Slavery." *Missouri Historical Review* 59 (1965). German opposition to slavery.

Farrison, W. Edward. "A Theologian's Missouri Compromise." *Journal of Negro History* 48 (1963). Controversy in escaped slave William W. Brown's book, *Narrative of William W. Brown, Written by Himself*, and an incident in St. Louis.

Fellman, Michael. "Emancipation in Missouri." *Missouri Historical Review* 83 (October 1988).

Glover, Samuel T. "Speech at the Ratification of Emancipation in Missouri, St. Louis, July 22, 1863." *St. Louis Missouri Republican* (July 1863).

Green, Barbara L. "Slave Labor at the Maramec Iron Works, 1820–1850." *Missouri Historical Review* 73 (January 1979).

Hughes, John Starrett. "Lafayette County and the Aftermath of Slavery, 1861–1870." *Missouri Historical Review* 75 (October 1980).

Hunter, Lloyd A. "Slavery in St. Louis, 1804–1860." *Missouri Historical Society Bulletin* 30 (July 1974). Unique aspects of slavery in that city.

Klem, Mary J. "The Kansas-Nebraska Slavery Bill and Missouri's Part in the Conflict." *Mississippi Valley Historical Association Proceedings* 9 (1919).

Lee, George R. "Slavery and Emancipation in Lewis County, Missouri." *Missouri Historical Review* 65 (April 1971).

Magnaghi, Russel. "The Role of Indian Slavery in Colonial St. Louis." *Missouri Historical Society Bulletin* 31 (July 1975).

McGettigan, James William, Jr. "Boone County Slaves: Sales, Estate Divisions and Families, 1820–1865," pts. 1 and 2. *Missouri Historical Review* 72 (January and April, 1978).

Merkel, Benjamin G. "The Abolition Aspects of Missouri's Antislavery Controversy 1819–1865." *Missouri Historical Review* 44 (1950).

————. "The Underground Railroad and the Missouri Borders, 1840–1860." *Missouri Historical Review* 37 (April 1943).

Nelson, E. J. "Missouri Slavery, 1861–5." *Missouri Historical Review* 28 (July 1934).

Osborne, D. F. "The Sectional Struggle over Rights of Slavery in New Territory added to the U.S." *Georgia Historical Quarterly* 15 (September 1931). Missouri Compromise.

Ryle, Walter H. "Slavery and Party Realignment in Missouri in the State Election of 1856." *Missouri Historical Review* 39 (1945).

Sampson, F. A., and W. C. Breckenridge. "Bibliography of Slavery in Missouri." *Missouri Historical Review* 2 (April 1908).

Savage, W. Sherman. "The Contest over Slavery between Illinois and Missouri." *Journal of Negro History* 28 (1943).

Scarpino, Philip V. "Slavery in Callaway County, Missouri: 1845–1855," pts. 1 and 2. *Missouri Historical Review* 71 (October 1976 and April 1977).

Shoemaker, Floyd C. "Missouri's Proslavery Fight for Kansas, 1854–1855." *Missouri Historical Review* 48 (1954).

Strickland, Arvarh E. "Aspects of Slavery in Missouri, 1821." *Missouri Historical Review* 65 (July 1971).

Trexler, Harrison A. "Slavery in Missouri, 1804–1865." *Johns Hopkins University Studies in Historical and Political Science*, Series 32 (1914).

————. "Slavery in Missouri Territory." *Missouri Historical Review* 3 (1908–1909).

————. "The Value and the Sale of the Missouri Slave." *Missouri Historical Review* 8 (January 1914).

Winter, H. "Early Methodism and Slavery in Missouri, 1819–44: The Division of Methodism in 1845." *Missouri Historical Review* 37 (October 1942).

Books:

Address to the People of the United States, Together with the Proceedings and Resolutions of the Pro-Slavery Convention of Missouri, Held at Lexington, July, 1855. St. Louis: Republican Book and Job Office, 1855.

Alexander, H. McGee. *An Address by the Colored People of Missouri to the Friends of Equal Rights*. St. Louis: Missouri Democrat Print, 1865. State Executive Committee for Equal Political Rights in Missouri.

Baker, Thomas E., and Rex R. Campbell. *Race and Residence in Missouri Cities*. Jefferson City: Missouri Commission on Human Rights, 1971. Discrimination in ten cities.

Benton, Thomas Hart. *Historical and Legal Examination of that Part of the Decision of the supreme Court of the United States in the Dred Scott Case, Which Declares the Unconstitutionality of the Missouri Compromise Act, and the Self-Extension of the Constitution to Territories, Carrying Slavery Along with It*. New York: Johnson Reprint Corporation, 1970.

Bigotry and Violence on Missouri's College Campuses. Washington, DC: U.S. Commission on Civil Rights, 1990.

Black Pages. Saint Louis: Black Pages, Inc., 1985-current. Black business enterprises.

Black Perspectives: University of Missouri-Columbia. Columbia: The University of Missouri-Columbia, 1988. Black college students at the university.

Blattner, Teresa. *People of Color: Black Genealogical Records and Abstracts from Missouri Sources*. Bowie, MD: Heritage Books, 1993; reprinted, 1988.

Blunt, Joseph. *An Examination of the Expediency and Constitutionality of Prohibiting Slavery in the State of Missouri*. New York: C. Wiley, 1819.

Brown, B. Gratz. *Freedom and Franchise Inseparable. Letter of the Hon. B. Gratz Brown*. Washington: n.p., 1864. Letter to the Missouri *Democrat*.

_____. *Immediate Abolition of Slavery by Act of Congress. Speech of Hon. B. Gratz Brown, of Missouri, Delivered in the U.S. Senate, March 8, 1864*. Washington, DC: H. Polkinhorn, 1864.

_____. *Slavery in Its National Aspects as Related to Peace and War. An Address by B. Gratz Brown, Delivered Before the General Emancipation society of the State of Missouri, at St. Louis, on Wednesday Evening, September 17, 1862*. St. Louis: n.p., 1862.

_____. *Speech on the Subject of Gradual Emancipation in Missouri; Delivered in the Missouri House of Representatives, February 12, 1857*. St. Louis, 1857.

Brown, Josephine. *Biography of an American Bondman, by his Daughter*. Boston: R. F. Wallcut, 1855. Biography of William Wells Brown.

Brown, William Wells. *Levensgeschiedenis van den Amerikaanschen Slaaf, William Wells Brown, Amerikaansch Afgevaardigde bij het Vredescongres to Parijs, 1849, Door hem Zelven Beschreven*. Zwolle, Netherlands: W. E. J. Tjeenk Willink, 1850. Brown's experiences as a slave in St. Louis and other places.

_____. *Narrative of William W. Brown: A Fugitive Slave. Written by Himself.* Boston: Anti-Slavery Office, 1847. Covers enslavement in Missouri.

Bruce, Henry Clay. *The New Man: Twenty-Nine Years a Slave, Twenty-Nine Years a Free Man.* York, PA: P. Anstadt and Sons, 1895; reprinted, Lincoln: University of Nebraska Press, 1996. Autobiography, Missouri and slavery.

Campbell, Azzio L. *Guidance Practices in the Four Year Accredited Negro High Schools of Missouri*, Occasional Papers no. 1. Jefferson City: Lincoln University, 1950.

Campbell, Rex R., and Thomas E. Baker. *The Negro in Missouri—1970.* Jefferson City: Missouri Commission on Human Rights, 1971. Profile based on 1970 census.

Campbell, Rex R., and Peter C. Robinson. *Negroes in Missouri.* Columbia: Missouri Commission of Human Rights, 1960. Statistics on Blacks.

_____. *Negroes in Missouri: A Compilation of Statistical Data from the 1960 United States Census of Population.* Jefferson City: Missouri Commission on Human Rights, 1967. Statistics on Blacks.

Cantor, Louis. *A Prologue to the Protest Movement: The Missouri Sharecropper Roadside Demonstration of 1939.* Durham, NC: Duke University Press, 1969.

Carpenter, L. P., and Dinah Bank. *The Treatment of Minorities: A Survey of Textbooks Used in Missouri High Schools.* Jefferson City: Missouri Commission on Human Rights, December, 1971.

A Caveat; or Considerations Against the Admission of Missouri, with Slavery into the Union. New Haven: A. H. Maltby, 1820.

Cobb, Robert S. *Semi-Annual Report of the Missouri Negro Industrial Commission: Compiled by Robert S. Cobb, Secretary. January 1st–July 1st, Nineteen Twenty-One.* Jefferson City: Missouri Negro Industrial Commission, 1921.

Colored Paths: Historic Community Research for the Accurate Identification and Documentation of Historically Significant Information Pertaining to African Slaves and Their Descendants: Burial Places of African Slaves and Their Descendants Including Traditional Recollections, Census Reports, Photos: Documented in the County of Warren, 1989 and 1991 at Wesley-Smith United Methodist Church, Old and New Cemetery Grounds, 201 Highway J, Wright City, Missouri 63390. Wright City, MO: The Church, 1992.

Crossland, William A. *Industrial Conditions among Negroes in St. Louis.* St. Louis: Press of Mendle Printing Company, 1914.

Curtis, Susan. *Dancing to a Black Man's Tune: A Life of Scott Joplin.* Columbia: University of Missouri Press, 1994. Biography of premier ragtime pianist.

Curtis, William J. *A Rich Heritage: A Black History of Independence, Missouri.* Atlanta: Traco Enterprises, 1985.

Delaney, Lucy A. *From the Darkness Cometh the Light: Or, Struggles for Freedom*. St. Louis: n.d. Slave autobiography.

Dewey, Orville. *A Discourse on Slavery and the Annexation of Texas*. New York: Charles S. Francis, 1844.

Distribution of Student Population as Discussed at the Board of Education Meeting on June 19, 1969. Report of the Advisory Committee on Distribution of Student Population. interim Statement of the Advisory Committee on Distribution of Student Population. University City: University City Board of Education, 1969. Segregation in education.

Dixon, Susan. *History of Missouri Compromise and Slavery in American Politics: A True History of the Missouri Compromise and Its Repeal, and of African Slavery as a Factor in American Politics*, 2^d ed. New York: Johnson Reprint Corporation, 1970. First published as *The True History of the Missouri Compromise and Its Repeal*, 1898.

Downey, Bill. *Tom Bass, Black Horseman*. St. Louis: Saddle and Bridle, 1975. Biography of horse trainer from Mexico, Missouri.

Eliot, William Greenleaf. *The Story of Archer Alexander From Slavery to Freedom, March 30, 1863*. Boston: Cupples, Upham and Company, 1885.

Elwang, William Wilson. *The Negroes of Columbia, Missouri: A Concrete Study of the Race Problem*. Columbia, MO: University of Missouri, 1904.

Federal Writers' Project. Works Projects Administration. *Slaves Narratives: A Folk History of Slavery in the United States from Interviews with Former Slaves*. Vol. 11, *Missouri*. Washington, DC: Work Projects Administration, 1941.

Freemasons. Missouri. Grand Comandery of Knights Templars. *Proceedings...Annual Grand Conclave*. Nashville, TN: Freemasons. Annual.

Greene, Lorenzo J. *Desegregation of Schools in Missouri*. Jefferson City: Missouri Advisory Committee on Civil Rights, 1959.

Greene, Lorenzo J., Gary R. Kremer, and Antonio F. Holland. *Missouri's Black Heritage*. St. Louis: Forum Press, 1980; reprinted, Columbia, MO: University of Missouri Press, 1993.

Henderson, David. *Integration in Missouri Public Schools*. Jefferson City: Missouri Commission on Human Rights, 1974. Problems in achieving integration.

_____. *A Study of Urban-Metropolitan Education in Missouri*. Jefferson City: Missouri Department of elementary and Secondary Education, 1978. Problems in achieving integration.

Henderson, John Brooks. *Reconstruction. Speech of Hon. J. B. Henderson, of Missouri, Delivered in the Senate of the United States, June 8, 1866. Treating of American Citizenship, the True Basis of Representation, the Right of Suffrage, the Disfranchisement of Rebel Leaders, the Character of the Rebel Debt, Etc*. Washington, DC: Chronicle Printers, 1866. Black suffrage.

_____. *Speech of Hon. J. B. Henderson, of Missouri: On the Abolition of Slavery, Delivered in the Senate of the United States, March 27, 1862.* Washington, DC: L. Towers and Company, 1862.

Holland, Antonio F., et al. *The Soldiers' Dream Continued: A Pictorial History of Lincoln University of Missouri.* Jefferson City: Lincoln University, 1991.

Hopkins, Vincent Charles. *Dred Scott's Case.* New York: Fordham University Press, 1951.

Humphrey, Herman. *The Missouri Compromise: An Address Delivered before the Citizens of Pittsfield, by Rev. Herman Humphrey, D.D., in the Baptist Church, on Sabbath evening, Feb. 26, 1854.* Pittsfield, MA: Reed, Hull and Peirson, 1854.

Hurt, R. Douglas. *Agriculture and Slavery in Missouri's Little Dixie.* Columbia: University of Missouri Press, 1992.

Interdisciplinary Faculty Development in Gerontology in HBCUs: Final Report. Houston: Texas Southern University, 1991. Study and teaching gerontology in HBCUs.

Kaufman, Kenneth C. *Dred Scott's Advocate: A Biography of Roswell M. Field.* Columbia, MO: University of Missouri Press, 1996.

Ker, Rev. Leander. *Slavery Consistent with Christianity, with an Introduction, Embracing a Notice of Uncle Tom's Cabin Movement in England*, 3rd ed. Weston, MO: n.p., 1853.

Krater, Joan, et al. *Mirror Images: Teaching Writing in Black and White: Webster Groves Action Research Project*, 1994. ERIC, ED 376 463. Teachers and students in Webster Groves, Missouri explain their writing project.

Kremer, Gary R. *James Milton Turner and the Promise of America: The Public Life of a Post-Civil War Black Leader.* Columbia, MO: University of Missouri Press, 1991.

Kremer, Gary R., and Antonio F. Holland. *Missouri's Black Heritage.* Columbia: MO: University of Missouri Press, 1993.

Ku-Klux Klan. *Constitution and Laws of the Women of the Ku Klux Klan. Adopted by First Imperial Klonvocation at St. Louis, Missouri, on the Sixth Day of January, 1927.* St. Louis: Ku Klux Klan, 1927.

Lederer, Katherine. *Many Thousand Gone: Springfield's Lost Black History.* Springfield: Katherine Lederer, 1986. Blacks leave Springfield following a lynching.

Leigh, Edwin. *Bird's-Eye Views of Slavery in Missouri.* St. Louis: 1862.

Levine, Daniel U., and Robert P. Fain. *Public Reactions to a Brochure Aimed at Maintaining Confidence in the Schools of a Racially Changing urban Community.* Kansas City, MO: Center for the Study of Metropolitan Problems in Education, School of Education, University of Missouri, 1970.

[Lundy, Benjamin]. *The War in Texas; a Review of the Facts and Circumstances, Showing that this Contest is a Crusade against Mexico, Set on Foot and Supported by Slaveholders, Land Speculators, etc., in Order to Reestablish, Extend and Perpetuate the System of Slavery and the Slave Trade.* Philadelphia: Merridew and Gunn, 1837.

Lyon, James A. *An Address on the Missouri Aspect of African Colonization.* St. Louis, MO: n.p., 1850.

Marshall, Albert Prince. *Soldier's Dream: A Centennial History of Lincoln University of Missouri.* Jefferson City, MO: Lincoln University, 1966.

Meigs, Henry. *Speech of Mr. Meigs, of New York, on the Restriction of Slavery in Missouri, Delivered in the House of Representatives, January 25, 1820.* Washington, DC: 1820.

Missouri Advisory Committee to the United States Commission on Civil Rights. *Race Relations in the "Kingdom of Callaway."* Jefferson City: The Committee, 1979.

_____. *Race Relations in Cooper County, Missouri—1978.* Jefferson City: The Committee, 1979.

Missouri Association for Social Welfare, Human Rights Committee. *Missouri's Two State Universities (University of Missouri and Lincoln University): A Comparative Study of Educational Offerings.* Jefferson City: Missouri Association for Social Welfare, Human Rights Committee, 1949. Discrimination in education.

_____. *Segregated Schools in Missouri. A Study of Comparative Costs in Public Schools.* Jefferson City: Missouri Association for Social Welfare, Human Rights Committee, 1953.

Missouri Commission on Human Rights. *Study of Human Rights in Missouri.* Jefferson City: The Commission, 1960. Documents lack of progress.

Missouri Negro Industrial Commission, Second Report. Jefferson City: The Commission, 1921.

Monks, William. *A History of Southern Missouri and Northern Arkansas; Being an Account of the Early Settlements, the Civil War, the Ku-Klux, and the Times of Peace.* West Plain, MO: West Plains Journal Company, 1907.

Monti, Daniel J. *Race, Redevelopment, and the New Company Town.* SUNY Series in Urban Public Policy. Albany: State University of New York Press, 1990. Case studies, urban renewal and social conditions, St. Louis.

Moore, Glover. *The Missouri Controversy, 1819–1821.* Lexington: University of Kentucky Press, 1953.

Morris, Ann, and Henrietta Ambrose. *North Webster: A Photographic History of a Black Community.* Bloomington: Indiana University Press, 1993. Missouri Black community.

NAACP 1940–55. General Office File. Lynching. Sikeston, Missouri, 1942. Frederick, MD: University Publications of America, 1986.

1990 Pictorial Directory: Mound City Bar Association. St. Louis: Mound
    City Bar Association, 1990. Black attorneys.
Order of the Eastern Star. United Grand Chapter of Missouri. *Proceed-
    ings...Annual Communication.* Palmyra, MO: The Order. Annual.
Owen, Mary Alicia. *Voodoo Tales, as Told Among the Negroes of the South-
    west.* Freeport, NY: Books for Libraries Press, 1971. Folklore tales
    and Missouri.
Parrish, William E. *Missouri Under Radical Rule 1865–1870.* Columbia:
    University of Missouri Press, 1965.
Perry, Robert T. *Black Legislators.* San Francisco: R&E Research Associates,
    1976. Missouri politics.
Poole, Stafford, and Douglas J. Slawson. *Church and Slave in Perry County,
    Missouri, 1818–1865.* Lewiston, PA: E. Mellen Press, 1986.
*Portraits and Biographical Sketches of the Representative Negro Men and
    Women of Missouri and Kansas, for Distribution at the Cotton States
    and International Exposition, to be held at Atlanta, Georgia, September
    18th to December 31st, 1895.* Kansas City: Charles W. Lee, 1895.
    The venue where Booker T. Washington gave his "Atlanta Compro-
    mise" speech.
Rawick, George P., ed. *The American Slave: A Composite Autobiography,*
    Vol. 11. *Missouri Slave Narratives.* Westport, CT: Greenwood Pub-
    lishing Company, 1972. Transcriptions of narratives for the
    1936–1938 Federal Writers' Project.
Robertson, Peter C. *The Negro in Missouri, 1960.* Jefferson City: Missouri
    Commission on Human Rights, 1967. Data taken from 1960 census.
Robertson, William E. *The Black Elderly: A Baseline Survey in Mid-Missouri.*
    Columbia: University of Missouri-Columbia Extension Division,
    College of Community and Public Services, 1981. Black aged in
    Boone County.
Savage, W. Sherman. *The History of Lincoln University.* Jefferson City: The
    New Day Press, 1939.
Schweninger, Loren, ed. *From Tennessee Slave to St. Louis Entrepreneur: The
    Autobiography of James Thomas.* Columbia: University of Missouri
    Press, 1984.
Selby, Mark. *Agriculture Census Tables Relevant to Race.* Columbia: Uni-
    versity of Missouri-Columbia, Cooperative Extension Service, 1982.
    Black farmers' statistics.
Shipley, Alberta D., and David O. Shipley. *The History of Black Baptists in
    Missouri: National Baptist Convention, U.S.A., Inc.* Kansas City,
    MO: Missionary Baptist State Convention of Missouri, 1976.
Smith, JoAnn Adams. *Selected Neighbors and Neighborhoods of North Saint
    Louis and Selected Related Events.* St. Louis, MO: Friends of Vaughn
    Cultural Center, 1988.

State Executive Committee for Equal Political Rights in Missouri. *An Address by the Colored People of Missouri to the Friends of Equal Rights*. St. Louis: Missouri Democrat Print, 1865.

State Government Affirmative Action in Mid-America: An Update: A Report. Prepared by the Iowa, Kansas, Missouri, and Nebraska Advisory Committees to the United States Commission on Civil Rights. Washington, DC: The Commission, 1982.

Sumner, Charles. *Immediate Emancipation A War Measure! Speech of Hon. Charles Sumner, of Massachusetts, on the Bill Providing for Emancipation in Missouri. In the Senate of the United States, February 12th, 1863*. Washington, DC: H. Polkinhorn, 1863. Speech.

Taulbert, Clifton L. *The Last Train North*. Tulsa, OK: Council Oak Books, 1992; reprinted, New York: Penguin Books, 1995. Black social life and customs in St. Louis and Glen Allen, Mississippi.

Thompson, George. *The Prison Bard: or, Poems on Various Subjects. By George Thompson, for Four Years and Eleven Months a Prisoner in Missouri, for Attempting to Aid Some Slaves to Liberty. Written in Prison*. Hartford, CT: W. H. Burleigh, 1848.

_____. *Prison Life and Reflections: or, a Narrative of the Arrest, Trial, Conviction, Imprisonment, Treatment, Observations, Reflections, and Deliverance of Work, Burr, and Thompson, Who Suffered an Unjust and Cruel Imprisonment in Missouri Penitentiary, for Attempting to Aid Some Slaves to Liberty*. Hartford, CT: A. Work, 1851.

Trexler, Harrison A. *Slavery in Missouri, 1804–1865*. Baltimore: Johns Hopkins Press, 1914.

Trials and Confessions of Madison Henderson, alias Blanchard, Alfred Amos Warrick and Others, Murderers of Jesse Baker and Jacob Weaver. St. Louis: Chambers and Knapp, 1841. Four slaves tried and executed for robbery and murder.

Triplett, Robert J. *History of Missouri Black Legislators*. n.p., 1983. Black legislators and politics.

Tri-State Industrial Exposition and Fair. *Program. August 4 to 10th, Inclusive, 1907*. St. Joseph: Tri-State Industrial Exposition and Fair, 1907. Black fair.

United States Army, Military Division of the Missouri. *Correspondence Between General Pope*. St. Louis: R. P. Studley and Company, 1865. Reconstruction and Missouri.

United States Commission on Civil Rights. Missouri Advisory Committee. *Race Relations in Cooper County, Missouri, 1978: A Report*. Washington, DC: The Commission, 1979.

_____. *Race Relations in the "Kingdom" of Callaway: A Report*. Washington, DC: The Commission, 1979. Callaway County.

Van Dyke, Nicholas. *Speech of Mr. Van Dyke, on the Amendment Offered to a Bill for the Admission of Missouri into the Union, Prescribing the Re-*

striction of Slavery as an Irrevocable Principle of the State Constitution. Washington, DC: 1820.

Woods, E. M. *The Negro in Etiquette: A Novelty.* St. Louis: 1899. Negro tells college students about proper etiquette.

Writers' Program of the Work Projects Administration in the State of Missouri. *Missouri, a Guide to the "Show Me" State.* New York: Duell, Sloan and Pearce, 1941.

Young, William H., and Nathan B. Young. *Your Kansas and Mine.* Kansas City: Young and Young, 1950. Jazz Age, including Missouri.

Kansas City

Barlow, William. *Looking Up at Down: The Emergence of Blues Culture.* Philadelphia: Temple University Press, 1989. Blues in Kansas City and St. Louis.

Gorham, Thelma Thurston, ed. *Meeting the Challenge of Change: A Sixty-Year History of the St. Stephen Baptist Church.* Kansas City, MO: Grimes-Joyce Printing Company, 1963.

Greater Kansas City Director of Minority Businesses. Kansas City: Greater Kansas City Regional Economic Union. Minority businesses.

Institute for Community Studies. *Fair Housing: An Overview with Special Reference to Kansas City, Missouri.* Kansas City, MO: n.p., 1968.

Kansas City, Mo. Office of Housing and Community Development. *The Spirit of Freedom: A Profile of the History of Blacks in Kansas City, Missouri.* Kansas City, MO: Office of Housing and Community Development, 1978.

Kansas City Negro City Directory. Kansas City: Negro Chamber of Commerce, 1943.

Levine, Daniel U., and Kenneth R. Mares. *Problems and Perceptions in a Desegregated Urban High School: A Case Description and its Implications.* Kansas City, MO: Center for the Study of Metropolitan Problems in Education, School of Education, University of Missouri, 1970. Southeast High School.

Martin, Asa E. *Our Negro Population, a Sociological Study of the Negroes of Kansas City, Missouri.* Kansas City, MO: F. Hudson Publishing Company, 1913; reprinted, New York: Negro Universities Press, 1969.

National Urban League, Community Relations Project. *Report of the Health Specialist for Kansas City, Missouri, April, 1946.* n.p.: National Urban League, 1946.

_____. *Report on the Field Services of the Case Work Specialist in Kansas City, Missouri, April 15–May 4, 1946.* n.p.: National Urban League, 1946.

_____. *Report on the Field Services of the Social Group Work and Recreation Specialist in Kansas City, Missouri, April 16–May 3, 1946.* n.p.: National Urban League, 1946.

_____. *Report on the Field Services of the Specialist in Employment and industrial Relations in Kansas City, Missouri, April 13 to May 3, 1946.* n.p.: National Urban League, 1946.

National Urban League, Department of Research and Community Projects. *A Study of the Social and Economic Conditions of the Negro Population of Kansas City, Missouri.* Kansas City: National Urban League, 1946.

Russell, Ross. *Jazz Styles in Kansas City and the Southwest.* Berkeley: University of California Press, 1971.

Speer, Hugh W. *A Short History of the University of Kansas City.* 1997. Manuscript in the University of Missouri library on segregation.

A Survey of Housing Discrimination in Kansas City, Missouri. Kansas City: Kansas City Human Relations Department, 1988.

United States Commission on Civil Rights. Missouri Advisory Committee. *School Desegregation in the St. Louis and Kansas City Areas: Metropolitan Interdistrict Options: A Report.* Washington, DC: The Commission, 1981.

Young, William H., and Nathan B. Young. *Your Kansas City and Mine—1850–1950.* Kansas City, MO: William H. Young, 1950.

St. Louis

Barlow, William. *Looking Up at Down: The Emergence of Blues Culture.* Philadelphia: Temple University Press, 1989. Blues in Kansas City and St. Louis.

Board of Education of the City of St. Louis, MO. *Desegregation Report and Policy Statement, Board of Education of the City of St. Louis.* St. Louis: Board of Education, 1995.

Clamorgan, Cyprian. *The Colored Aristocracy of St. Louis.* St. Louis, MO: n.p., 1858.

Clayton, Sheryl H. *Black Men Role Models of Greater St. Louis.* East St. Louis: Essai Seay Publications, 1983. Biographies.

_____. *Black Women Role Models of Greater St. Louis.* East St. Louis, IL: Essai Seay Publications, 1982. Biographies.

Craton Liddell, A Minor, et al., Plaintiff: and Earline Caldwell, et al., and The National Association for Advancement of Colored People, and City of St. Louis, and Janice Adams, et al., and Mary Puleo, et al., Representing the Involved Citizens Committee, and United States of America, Plaintiffs-Interventors, v. The Board of Education of the City of St. Louis, State of Missouri, and Daniel Schafly et al., and the State of Missouri, et al., Defendants. U.S. Court of Appeals (8th Circuit) school integration case, 1979–1982.

Crossland, William A. *Industrial Conditions Among Negroes in St. Louis*. St. Louis: Press of Mendle Printing Company, 1914.

Douglass, Harlan P. *The St. Louis Church Survey: a Religious Investigation with a Social Background*. New York: Doran, 1924. Also deals with Negro population.

Employees Loan Company. *Negroes: Their Gift to St. Louis*. St. Louis: 1964.

Faherty, William Barnaby, and Madeline Barni Oliver. *The Religious Roots of Black Catholics of Saint Louis*. St. Louis: Saint Louis University, 1977.

Farley, John E. *Black-White Housing Segregation in the City of St. Louis: a 1988 Update*. Edwardsville, IL: Regional Research and Development Services, Southern Illinois University at Edwardsville, 1989.

Greer, Scott, et al. *The New Urbanization*. New York: St. Martin's Press, 1968. Social conditions, Accra, Ghana, and St. Louis.

Harris, Ruth Miriam. *Teachers' Social Knowledge and Its Relation to Pupils' Responses: A Study of Four St. Louis Negro Elementary Schools*. New York: Teachers College, Columbia University, 1941. Originally author's thesis at Columbia.

Kessler, John J. *The Negro and Washington University, 1948–1952*. St. Louis: 1952.

————. *Racial Discrimination in St. Louis Hotels, 1951*. St. Louis: 1951.

————. *The St. Louis Public Schools: A Survey of Race Inequalities; with a Review of Educational Opportunities for White and Negro Students in Missouri*. St. Louis: 1950.

Kremer, Gary R. *James Milton Turner and the Promise of America*. Columbia: University of Missouri Press, 1991. Famous Black Missourian.

Ledé, Naomi W. *De Facto School Segregation in St. Louis*. St. Louis: Urban League of St. Louis, 1966.

Lipsitz, George. *A Life in the Struggle: Ivory Perry and the Culture of Opposition*. Philadelphia: Temple University Press, 1995. Race relations and civil rights in St. Louis.

————. *The Sidewalks of St. Louis: Places, People, and Politics in an American City*. Columbia: University of Missouri Press, 1991. Contains information of Black performers.

Minority Business Development: Opportunities and Challenges Facing the St. Louis Region: A Report of the Confluence St. Louis Minority Business Task Force. St. Louis: The Confluence St. Louis Minority Business Task Force, 1994. Blacks in business.

Monti, Daniel J. *A Semblance of Justice: St. Louis School Desegregation and Order in Urban America*. Columbia: University of Missouri Press, 1985.

NAACP Branch Files. St. Louis, Mo., 1914–1939. Frederick, MD: University Publications of America, 1991.

Osburn, Donald D. *Negro Employment in St. Louis, 1966*. Carbondale, IL: Southern Illinois University Press, 1968.

Patterson, Ernest. *Black City Politics*. New York: Dodd, Mead, 1974. Blacks in St. Louis.

Pruitt-Igoe: The Story of a Public Housing Development: A National Prototype as Seen in the St. Louis Post-Dispatch, 1951–1975. St. Louis: St. Louis Post-Dispatch, 1975.

The Quality of Education in the Non-Integrated Schools of the St. Louis Public Schools, Presented by the Committee on Quality Education to the District Court of the Eastern District of Missouri. St. Louis: The Committee on Quality Education to the District Court of the Eastern District of Missouri, 1983.

Rainwater, Lee. *Behind Ghetto Walls: Black Families in a Federal Slum*. Chicago: Aldine Publishing Company, 1970. Lives of 10,000 St. Louis Blacks in the Pruitt-Igoe housing project.

Reichard, Maximilian. *The Black Man in St. Louis: A Preliminary Bibliography*. Monticello, IL: Council of Planning Librarians, 1974.

Rudwick, Elliot M. *Race Riot at East St. Louis*, July 2, 1917. Blacks in the New World Series. Carbondale: Southern Illinois University Press, 1964.

Schmandt, Henry J., Paul G. Steinbicker, and George D. Wendel. *Metropolitan Reform in St. Louis: A Case Study*. New York: Holt, Rinehart and Winston, 1961. Blacks in the St. Louis metropolitan area.

Schweninger, Loren, ed. *From Tennessee Slave to St. Louis Entrepreneur: The Autobiography of James Thomas*. Columbia: University of Missouri Press, 1984.

Smith, JoAnn Adams. *Selected Neighbors and Neighborhoods of North Saint Louis and Selected Related Events*. St. Louis: Friends of Vaughn Cultural Center, 1988.

Social Planning Council of St. Louis and St. Louis County. *Negro Attitude Survey of St. Louis: An Opinion and Attitude Study of a Cross Section of 167 St. Louis Negroes with Respect to the Social and Community Problems Which They Considered Most important in October 1948*. St. Louis: Research Bureau, Social Planning Council of St. Louis and St. Louis County, 1949.

St. Louis. Board of Education. *Desegregation of the St. Louis Public Schools: A Summary of Measures Taken by the Board of Education of the City of St. Louis to Implement the Supreme Court Decision of May 17, 1954*. St. Louis: 1956.

Study of Crime in the Black Community: Task Force on Crime in the Black Community. St. Louis: The Task Force on Crime in the Black Community, 1990. St. Louis.

Sutker, Solomon, and Sara Smith Sutker. *Racial Transition in the Inner Suburb: Studies of the St. Louis Area*. New York: Praeger, 1974.

Thomas, James P. *From Tennessee Slave to St. Louis Entrepreneur: The Autobiography of James Thomas*, ed. Loren Schweninger. Columbia: University of Missouri Press, 1984.

United States Commission on Civil Rights. Missouri Advisory Committee. *School Desegregation in the St. Louis and Kansas City Areas: Metropolitan Interdistrict Options: A Report*. Washington, DC: The Commission, 1981.

Urban League (St. Louis, MO), Dept. of Industrial Relations. *The Negro in the St. Louis Economy, 1954*. St. Louis: Urban League of St. Louis, 1954.

Valien, Bonita H. *The St. Louis Story: A Study of Desegregation*. New York: Anti-Defamation League of B'nai B'rith, 1956.

Wells, Amy Stuart, and Robert L. Crain. *Stepping Over the Color Line: African-American Students in White Suburban Schools*. New Haven: Yale University Press, 1997. Case studies of school integration in the St. Louis metropolitan area.

Wright, John A. *Discovering African-American St. Louis: A Guide to Historic Sites*. St. Louis: Missouri Historical Society Press, 1994.

_____. *St. Louis Black Heritage Trail*. Florissant, MO: Ferguson-Florissant School District, 1990. Text and photographs by John A. Wright.

Wright, John A., Jean E. Meeh Gosebrink, and Candace O'Connor. *Discovering African-American St. Louis: A Guide to Historic Sites*. St. Louis: Missouri Historical Society Press, 1994.

Theses and Dissertations:

Arndt, Hilda Christine. "The Adjustment of the Colored Feebleminded Child in St. Louis: A Case Study of Thirty-Four Colored Feebleminded Children." Master's thesis, Washington University, 1934.

Baker, Thomas E. "Human Rights in Missouri." Ph.D. diss., University of Missouri-Columbia, 1975.

Batterson, Jack A. "Life and Career of Blind Boone." Master's thesis, University of Missouri-Columbia, 1986. John William Boone, classical and ragtime composer.

Beatty-Brown, Florence R. "The Negro as Portrayed by the St. Louis Post-Dispatch from 1920–1950." Ph.D. diss., University of Illinois, 1951.

Bellamy, Donnie D. "Slavery, Emancipation, and Racism in Missouri, 1850–1865." Ph.D. diss., University of Missouri-Columbia, 1970.

Berry, Wilbert Lee. "The Effectiveness of Teaching Art in the Negro Elementary Schools in Missouri." Master's thesis, Colorado State College of Education, 1941.

Brand, Elaine S. "Psychological Correlates of Ethnic Esteem Among Anglo, Black, and Chicano Second-Grade and Fifth-Grade Children." thesis, University of Missouri, 1973. Missouri Children.

Brigham, Robert I. "The Education of the Negro in Missouri." Ph.D. diss., University of Missouri, 1946. Study on schools for Blacks.

Brunn, Paul Dennis. "Black Workers and Social Movements of the 1930s in St. Louis." Thesis, Washington University, 1975.

Carter, Proctor N., Jr. "Lynch-Law and the Press of Missouri." Master's thesis, University of Missouri-Columbia, 1933.

Chasteen, Edgar R. "Public Accommodations: Social Movements in Conflict or the Race is On." Ph.D. diss., University of Missouri, 1966. Study of the Public Accommodations Movement in Missouri.

Christensen, Lawrence O. "Black St. Louis: A Study in Race Relations, 1865–1916." Ph.D. diss., University of Missouri-Columbia, 1972.

Cohnberg, Pauline Techla. "A Study of Ninety Negro Tuberculosis Patients and Their Families Known to the St. Louis Provident Association, with Reference to Medical Care." Master's thesis, Washington University, 1933.

Collins, William. "Attitudes of Undergraduate Black Students at Saint Louis University." Master's thesis, St. Louis University, 1974.

Congehl, Irene Helen. "Withdrawal from High School Before Graduation by Negro Girls in Saint Louis City." MSW thesis, Washington University, 1946.

Cotton, George R. "Collegiate Technical Education for Negroes in Missouri with Proposed Plans for Development." Ph.D. diss., Ohio State University, 1944.

Crossland, William A. "The Occupations of Negroes in St. Louis." Master's thesis, Washington University, 1913.

David, John Russell. "Tragedy in Ragtime: Black Folktales from St. Louis." Ph.D. diss., St. Louis University, 1976.

Dreer, Herman. "Negro Leadership in Saint Louis: A Study in Race Relations." Ph.D. diss, University of Chicago, 1956.

Duffner, Robert William. "Slavery in Missouri River Counties, 1820–1865." Ph.D. diss., University of Missouri-Columbia, 1974.

Dwight, Margaret L. "Black Suffrage in Missouri, 1865–1877." Ph.D. diss., University of Missouri, 1978.

Dwyer, Robert J. "A Study of Desegregation and Integration in Selected School Districts of Central Missouri." Ph.D. diss., University of Missouri, 1957.

Elwang, William Wilson. "The Negroes of Columbia, Missouri: A Concrete Study of the Race Problem." Master's thesis, University of Missouri, 1902.

Everett, Syble E. "A Program for Community Enrichment for Negroes in Saint Louis, Missouri." Master's thesis, Kansas State Teachers College, 1949.

Freeman, James N. "A Program of Education in Agriculture for Negroes of Missouri Based on an Analysis of Economic Factors and of Social Activities of Negroes in Selected Communities in Southeast Missouri." Ph.D. diss., Cornell University, 1946.

Getzlow, Judith Bernice. "Effect of an Early Intervention Program on Three and Four Year Old Culturally Disadvantaged Black Children in a Small Suburban School District Over a Three Year Period (1975–1978)." Ed.D. thesis, St. Louis University, 1979.

Godown, Lois F. "Social and Economic Changes that Occur When Negroes Invade White Areas." MSW thesis, Washington University, 1946.

Grady, Michael K. "Confronting the Presumption of Unconstitutionality: An Assessment of the Implementation of Milliken II Relief for the All-Black Schools of St. Louis, Missouri." Ph.D. diss., Harvard University, 1988.

Grant, Elizabeth C. "Some Colored Working Mothers in Columbia." Master's thesis, University of Missouri-Columbia, 1938.

Grenz, Suzanna M. "The Black Community in Boone County, Missouri, 1850–1900." Ph.D. diss., University of Missouri-Columbia, 1979.

Grothaus, Larry H. "The Negro in Missouri Politics, 1890–1941." Ph.D. diss., University of Missouri-Columbia, 1970.

Gubbles, Thomas Joseph. "School Desegregation in Kansas City, Missouri, 1954–1974." Master's thesis, University of Missouri-Columbia, 1992.

Guenther, John Edward. "Negro History in the Public High Schools of Missouri." Ed.D. thesis, University of Missouri-Columbia, 1970.

Hailman, David William. "Social Factors in Syphilitic Families Known to the St. Louis Provident Association." Master's thesis, Washington University, 1932.

Harris, Ruth Miriam. "Teachers' Social Knowledge and its Relation to Pupils' Responses: A Study of Four St. Louis Negro Elementary Schools." Ph.D. diss., Columbia University, 1941.

Harrison, William Jefferson. "The New Deal in Black St. Louis: 1932–1940." Ph.D. diss., St. Louis University, 1976.

Haynes, Ross Alan. "The Importance of the Black Press in the Desegregation of the University of Missouri." Master's thesis, University of Missouri-Kansas City, 1994.

Hoard, Charles M. "A Survey of the Guidance Programs in the Missouri Negro High Schools." Ph.D. diss., Indiana University, 1953.

Holland, Antonio F. "Nathan B. Young: The Development of Black Higher Education." Ph.D. diss., University of Missouri-Columbia, 1984.

Houser, Steven. "O. Anderson Fuller, the First Black Doctor of Philosophy in Music in America and His Development of the Music Education Curriculum at Lincoln-University." Ph.D. diss., University of Missouri-Columbia, 1982.

Hurst, Robert L. "Consumer Buying Habits in Selected Areas of St. Louis, Missouri." Ph.D. diss., University of Missouri, 1954.

Idleburg, Dorothy Ann. "An Exploratory Study of Treatment Outcomes in a 12-
     Year Follow-Up of Black and White Female Alcoholics." Ph.D. diss.,
     Washington University, 1982.

Iwu, Longinus Anele. "The Financing of Minority-Owned Businesses in St.
     Louis, Missouri." Ph.D. diss., St. Louis University, 1972.

Jason, Carl E. "Integrating a Major Public High School." Ph.D. diss., St.
     Louis University, 1989. McCluer North High School, Ferguson-
     Florissant School District.

Jones, Buck. "The Role of the Black Church as a Facilitator of Political Par-
     ticipation in Metropolitan St. Louis." Master's thesis, University of
     Missouri-St. Louis, 1987.

Jones, Daisy Marie. "A Retrospective Study of the Voluntary Desegregation
     Order and Its Effects on the Vocational Technical Schools in St. Louis
     City and County." Ph.D. diss, Saint Louis University, 1987.

Jones, Mary Dixon. "A Study of the Need for a Day Care Center for Negroes in
     Saint Louis: An Analysis of the Need for Day Cary Centers of Sixty
     Families in One Negro Neighborhood in Saint Louis, Missouri." Mas-
     ter's thesis, St. Louis University 1948.

Jones-Sneed, Frances Maryanne. "The Bottom of Heaven: A Social and Cul-
     tural History of African Americans in Three Creeks, Boone County,
     Missouri." Ph.D. diss., University of Missouri-Columbia, 1991.

Judd, Charles H., and H. C. Morrison. "Survey of the St. Louis Public
     Schools." St. Louis: St. Louis Board of Education, 1917.

Kingsley, David E. "Racial Attitudes in Liberty, Missouri: Implications for
     School Desegregation." Ph.D. diss., Kansas State University, 1989.
     White suburb of Kansas City.

Kirk, James H. "Kinloch, Missouri: A Study of an All-Negro Community."
     Ph.D. diss., St. Louis University, 1951.

Kittell, Audrey Nell. "The Negro Community of Columbia, Missouri." Mas-
     ter's thesis, University of Missouri-Columbia, 1938.

Large, John J., Jr. "The 'Invisible Empire' and Missouri Politics: The Influ-
     ence of the revived Ku Klux Klan in the Election Campaign of 1924 as
     Reported in Missouri Newspapers." Master's thesis, University of
     Missouri-Columbia, 1957.

Linsin, Jimmie. "An Analysis of the Treatment of Religion, the Black-
     American, and Women in the American History Textbooks Used by the
     Public, Private, and Parochial High Schools of the City and County of
     Saint Louis, Missouri, 1972–73." Thesis, St. Louis University, 1974.

Mann, George L. "The Historical Development of Public Education in St.
     Louis, Missouri, for Negroes." Ph.D. diss., Indiana University, 1949.

Martin, Asa E. "Our Negro Population: A Sociological Study of the Negroes
     of Kansas City, Missouri." Master's thesis, William Jewell College,
     1913.

Maupin-Long, Suzanna. "'I Made It Mine Tho the Queen was Always Fair':
     The St. Louis Black Clubwoman Movement, 1931–1946." Master's

thesis, University of Missouri-St. Louis, 1988.   Black clubwoman
        movement, 1931–1946.

Meggerson-Moore, Joyce. "A Survey of a Sample of Black Families' Views of
        the Counseling Profession." Ph.D. diss., St. Louis University, 1979.
        Missouri families.

Merkel, Benjamin G. "The Antislavery Controversy in Missouri, 1819–1865."
        Ph.D. diss., Washington State University, 1939.

Mitchell, Edna Steiner. "College Attendance Plans and College Enrollment of
        Black and White Seniors in Working Class High Schools in the Kansas
        City Metropolitan Area." Ph.D. diss, University of Missouri, Kansas
        City, 1971.

Moore, William, Jr. "A Portrait: The Culturally Disadvantaged Pre-School
        Negro Child." Ph.D. diss., St. Louis University, 1964.   Study based
        on St. Louis Black children.

Mosby, Reba S.   "The Evolution of Constitutional, Legislative and Judicial
        Protection of Civil and Human Rights in Missouri: A Critical and In-
        terpretative Analysis." Ph.D. diss., St. Louis University, 1960.

Neary, Arlene Meske. "DSM-III and Psychopathy Checklist Assessment of An-
        tisocial Personality Disorder in Black and White Female Felons."
        Ed.D. diss., University of Missouri-St. Louis, 1990.   Study of 60
        Black and 60 white female felons in the state correctional facility.

Nelson, Constance Burkhardt. "An Exploratory Study of Change in Teachers'
        Attitudes Toward Intergroup Relations in the Classroom during the
        First Year of Desegregation in the Kansas City, Missouri, Public
        Schools." Ph.D. diss., University of Kansas City, 1957.   Segregation
        and psychological attitudes.

Newsom, Lionel Hodge. "Court Treatment of Intra and Inter-racial Homicide in
        St. Louis." Ph.D. diss., Washington University, 1956.   Differential
        treatment.

Onwuachi, Patrick Chike. "Religious Concepts and Socio-Cultural Dynamics
        of Afro-American Religious Cults in Saint Louis, Missouri." Ph.D.
        diss., St. Louis University, 1963. Study includes the Nation of Islam.

Patterson, Ernestine. "The Impact of the Black Struggle on Representative Gov-
        ernment in St. Louis, Missouri." Ph.D. diss., St. Louis University,
        1969.

Perry, Floyd. "Selected Variables Related to Academic Success of Black Fresh-
        men Students at the University of Missouri-Columbia." Thesis, Uni-
        versity of Missouri, 1972.

Pohlman, Vernon C.   "An Analysis of Types of Protestant Negro Churches in
        St. Louis Based Upon Internal Characteristics of the Churches and the
        Relationship to Socio-Economic Factors of Their Communities."
        Master's thesis, Washington University, 1948.

Reese, De Anna J. "Intertwining Paths: Respectability, Character, Beauty and
        the Making of Community among St. Louis Black Women
        1900–1920." Master's thesis, University of Missouri-Columbia, 1996.

Rice, Robert Ray. "The Effects of Project Head Start and Differential Housing Environment upon Child Development." Thesis, Cornell University, 1967. Child development in Kansas City, Missouri.

Sawyer, R. M. "The Gaines Case: Its Background and Influence on the University of Missouri and Lincoln University, 1936–1950." Ph.D. diss., University of Missouri, 1966. Segregation in higher education.

Schreck, Kimberly A. "Their Place in Freedom: African American Women in Transition from Slavery to Freedom, Cooper County, Missouri, 1865–1900." Master's thesis, University of Missouri-Columbia, 1993.

Simpson, Robert Bruce. "A Black Church: Ecstasy in a World of Trouble." Ph.D. diss., Washington University, 1970. Study of St. Louis Baptists.

Slavens, George E. "A History of the Missouri Negro Press." Ph.D. diss., University of Missouri-Columbia, 1969.

Smart, Alice M. "Geographic Factors in the Education of Negroes in Six Selected Areas of Missouri." Ph.D. diss., Washington University, 1952.

Smith, Gladys E. "Defining Organizational Mission: The St. Louis Desegregation Monitoring Committee." Ph.D. diss., St. Louis University, 1993.

Tompkins, Gay M. "An Historical Study of Voluntary Interdistrict School Desegregation in St. Louis County, Missouri: 1980–1986." Ph.D. diss., St. Louis University, 1991.

Black Newspapers and Periodicals:[1]

COLUMBIA

LBC Newsletter. University of Missouri-Columbia Legion of Black Collegians tri-weekly. 1979–1983.

Perspectives in Black. UMC Legion of Black Collegians annual. 1981–1987.

Professional World. Columbia. 1901–1921.

UMOJA: Legion of Black Collegians. UMC. 1977–1978.

HANNIBAL

Hannibal Register. Hannibal. 1926–1944.

Home Protective Record. Hannibal. 1908–1919.

Missouri State Register. Hannibal. 1919–1942.

JEFFERSON CITY

Campus Magazine. Jefferson City. 1949–1951.

Lincoln Clarion. Jefferson City. 1932–1954. Lincoln University.

Lincoln University Journalism Newsletter. Jefferson City. 1946. Lincoln University.

Midwest Journal. Jefferson City. 1948–1956.

---

[1] Double-lined boxed items indicate change in masthead names.

Missouri Baptist Together. Jefferson
City. 1987.
Reporters News. Jefferson City.
?–1927.
Weekly Herald. Jefferson City.
1913–1916.
Western Messenger. Jefferson City.
1899–1922.

JOPLIN
Afro-American Leader. Joplin.
1915–1918.
Joplin Advance. Joplin. 1895.

> *Joplin Uplift.* Joplin. 1926–1928.
> *Joplin-Springfield Uplift.* Joplin.
> 1926–1935.

Reminder. Joplin. 1916–1917.

KANSAS CITY
Advocate. Kansas City. 1914–1927.
Baptist Record. Kansas City.
1921–1926.

> *Call.* Kansas City. 1919–1922.
> *Kansas City Call.* Kansas City.
> 1919–1933.
> *Call.* Kansas City. 1933–current.
> *Call.* Kansas City (Tulsa edition).
> 1933–?

Career Focus. Kansas City.
1988–current.
Christian Advocate. Kansas City.
?–1946.
Colored Messenger. Kansas City.
1900–1902.
Dispatch. Kansas City. 1886–1892.
Free Press. Kansas City.
1880–1889.
*Future State: A Monthly Journal of
Negro Progress.* Kansas
City. 1891–1898.
Gate City Press. Kansas City.
1880–1889.

*Greater Kansas City Community
Challenger.* Kansas City.
197?–19??
Herald of Holiness. Kansas City.
1912–?
Inter-State Herald. Kansas City.
1903-19??
Kansas City American. Kansas City.
1927–1940.
Kansas City Globe. Kansas City.
1972–current.
Kansas City Observer. Kansas City.
1896–1902.
Kansas-Missouri Enterprise. Kansas
City. 1881–1886.
Liberator. Kansas City. 1901–1911.
Missouri Messenger. Kansas City.
1894–1900.
Missouri State Post. Kansas City.
1900.
National Mirror. Kansas City.
1885–1922.
National Notes. Kansas City.
1899–1930. National As-
sociation of Colored
Women.
New Dawn. Kansas City.
1949–1953.
New Day: The People's Magazine.
Kansas City. 1947–1949.
New Missouri. Kansas City.
1894–1898.
News Quarterly. Kansas City.
1980–current? Scottish
Rite (Masonic order) of
Kansas City.
NHSA Newsletter. Kansas City.
1964–1967.
Record Searchlight. Kansas City.
1908–1927.
Rising Son. Kansas City.
1896–1920.
Signal. Kansas City. 1908–1912.
*Silhouettes: The Official Newsletter
of the Negro League Base-*

ball *Museum*. Kansas City.
    1992–current.
Son. Kansas City. 1908–1917.
Southern Argus. Kansas City.
    1892–1893.
Sun. Kansas City. 1908–1925.
Times-Observer. Kansas City.
    1891–1892.
UNIQUE. Kansas City. 1975.
Weekly Journal. Kansas City.
    1980–1981.
Western Argus. Kansas City.
    1891–1893.
Western Christian Recorder. Kansas
    City. 1896–1921.
Western Messenger. Kansas City.
    1919–1922.
Western Recorder. Kansas City.
    1882–1885.
Western Sentinel. Kansas City.
    1879–1887.
World. Kansas City. 1885–1888.

MACON
Missouri Messenger. Macon.
    1894–1900.
Western Christian Recorder. Macon.
    1896–1921.
Western Messenger. Macon.
    1901–1922.

MOBERLY
Brother's Optic. Moberly.
    1888–1895.
Western Optic. Moberly.
    1895–1897.

ST. LOUIS
Afro-American News. St. Louis.
    1873–1893.
Afro-American. St. Louis.
    1906–1910.
Ajax: International Monthly Maga-
    zine of Poetry, Literature
    and Arts. St. Louis. 1916.

America Eagle. St. Louis.
    1894–1907.
Appeal. St. Louis. 1913–1921.
Call. St. Louis. 1935–1942.
Central Afro-American. St. Louis.
    1909–1915.
Chronicle. St. Louis. 1929–1932.
Clarion. St. Louis. 1914–1926.
Contributor. St. Louis. 1883–1886.
Daily Christian Index. St. Louis.
    1914.
Evening Whirl. St. Louis.
    1938–current.
Flashes of Negro Life. St. Louis.
    1944–1950.
Freeman's Journal. St. Louis.
    1877–1882.
Intelligencer. St. Louis.
    1902–1903.
Liberia Advocate. St. Louis.
    1846–18??
Metro-Sentinel. St. Louis.
    1971–current.
Missouri Citizen. St. Louis.
    1880–1890.
Missouri Illinois Advance Citizen.
    St. Louis. 1892–1922.
National Bar Journal. St. Louis.
    1941–current. Journal of
    the National Bar Associa-
    tion.
National Convention Voice. St.
    Louis. ?
National Protest. St. Louis.
    1897–1929.
National Tribune. St. Louis.
    1876–1882.
Negro World. St. Louis. 1875–1890.
Negro: A Journal of Essential Facts
    about the Negro. St. Louis.
    1942–1950.
New Citizen. St. Louis. 1966–1970.
New Crusader. St. Louis.
Missouri State Register.

News. St. Louis. 195?

Palladium. Saint Louis. 1884–1903.
St. Louis Palladium. St. Louis.
     1903–1912.

People's Guide. St. Louis.
     1968–current.
Pine Torch. St. Louis. 1940–1951.
Postal Alliance. St. Louis.
     1914–1940. National Alli-
     ance of Postal employees.
Proud. St. Louis. 1970–current.
Race Problem. St. Louis.
     1891–1893.
Recorder. St. Louis. 1943–1948.
Show Down. St. Louis. 1993.
St. Elizabeth Chronicle. St. Louis.
     1928–1929.
St. Louis Advance. St. Louis.
     1881–1908.
St. Louis American. St. Louis.
     1928–?
St. Louis Argus. St. Louis.
     1912–current.
St. Louis Chronicle. St. Louis.
     1890–1905.

St. Louis Crusader. St. Louis.
     1962–current.
St. Louis New Crusader. St. Louis.
     1966–1974.

St. Louis Defender. St. Louis.
     1966–1967.
St. Louis Globe-Democrat. St. Louis.
     ?–1950.
St. Louis Independent News. St.
     Louis. 1919–1922.
St. Louis Independent-Clarion. St.
     Louis. 1914–1922.
St. Louis Mirror #1. St. Louis.
     1885–1904.
St. Louis Mirror #2. St. Louis.
     1955–1973.
St. Louis Monitor. St. Louis.
     ?–1901.

St. Louis Post Dispatch. St. Louis.
     ?–1950.

St. Louis Sentinel. St. Louis.
     1968–current.
St. Louis Metro Sentinel. St. Louis.
     1971–current.

St. Louis Star Sayings. St. Louis.
     1902–1906.
St. Louis Star Tribune. St. Louis.
     1877–1880.
St. Louis Star-Times. St. Louis.
     ?–1950.
St. Louis Tribune. St. Louis.
     1877–1880.
Standard. St. Louis. 1923–1925.
Tri-State Tribune. St. Louis.
     1936–1938.
United World. St. Louis.
     1930–1938.
Vanguard. St. Louis. 1881–1911.
Welcome Friend. St. Louis.
     1870–1880.
Western Christian Recorder. St.
     Louis. 1909–1952.
Western Messenger. St. Louis.
     1901–1922.
Whirl-Examiner. St. Louis.
     1994–current.
World. St. Louis. 1936–1938.

SEDALIA
Review. Sedalia. 1903–1924.
Searchlight. Sedalia. 1908–1924.
Sedalia Sun. Sedalia. 1882–188?
Sedalia Weekly Conservator. Sedalia.
     1903–1909.
Times. Sedalia. 1893–1905.

SIKESTON
Southeast Missouri World. Sikeston.
     1939.
Southern Sun. Sikeston. 1954.

SPRINGFIELD

Afro American. Springfield.
    1896–1898.
American Negro. Springfield.
    1890–1891.
Headlight #1. Springfield.
    1888–1889.
Headlight #2. Springfield.
    1898–1900.
Tribune #1. Springfield.
    1884–1888.
Tribune #2. Springfield.
    1888–1890.

OTHER

Anchor. Caruthersville. 1911–1923.
Central Missouri Star. California.
    1900–1902.
Charleston Spokesman. Charleston.
    1934.
Critic. Richmond. 1889.
People's Elevator. Independence.
    1935.
St. Joseph Appeal. St. Joseph
    191?

Other:

African-American Baptist Annual Reports, 1865–1990s: Missouri. National Archives, microfilm. Books, pamphlets, periodicals, statistics, biographies, etc.

I Am Somebody. KMBC-TV, Claude Dorsey, producer, 1978. Profile of Project Excel at Kansas City's Central High School. Videorecording.

Life of Today. Documentary of Black citizens of Kansas City, Missouri, 1937.

Pythian Parade and 19th Biannual Encampment. Newsreel of the 19th encampment of the Pythias in St. Louis, 1920.

Schools. Missouri, 1944–47. Papers of the NAACP. Part 3, Campaign for Educational Equality. Series B, Legal Department and Central Office Records, 1940–1950; Reel 2, FR. 1160–1166. Frederick, MD: University Publications of America, 1986. Microform.

Schools. Missouri, Kansas City Art Institute, 1946. Papers of the NAACP. Part 3, Campaign for Educational Equality. Series B, Legal Department and Central Office Records, 1940–1950; Reel 2, FR. 1161–1199. Frederick, MD: University Publications of America, 1986. Microfilm.

Schools. Missouri, St. Louis, Harris Teachers College, 8–50. Papers of the NAACP. Part 3, Campaign for Educational Equality. Series B, Legal Department and Central Office Records, 1940–1950; Reel 2, FR. 1200–1221. Frederick, MD: University Publications of America, 1986. Microfilm.

Teachers' Salaries. Missouri, Festus, 1943. Papers of the NAACP. Part 3, Campaign for Educational Equality. Series B, Legal Department and Central Office Records, 1940–1950; Reel 9, FR. 0212–0300. Frederick, MD: University Publications of America, 1986. Microfilm.

Turpin's Real Reels. Turpin Film Company, Charles H. Turpin, producer, 1916. St. Louis scenes include Black church schools, Missouri's first Black constable (Charles H. Turpin), and a session of the Colored Business League, among others.

Montana

Articles:

Albright, R. E. "The American Civil War as a Factor in Montana Territorial Politics." *Pacific Historical Review* (March 1937).

"Brief History of Troop 'K', Tenth U.S. Cavalry." *Colored American Magazine* 7 (December 1904). The 10th in Arizona and Montana.

"Captain Dodge's Colored Troops to the Rescue." *Century Magazine*, October 1891. The 9th Cavalry.

Castles, Jean I. "The West: Crucible of the Negro." *Montana: The Magazine of Western History* 19 (Winter 1969).

Chaffin, Glenn. "Aunt Tish: Beloved Gourmet of the Bitter Root." *Montana: The Magazine of Western History* 21 (Autumn 1971). Former slave Tish Nevins of Hamilton.

Cooper, Gary. "Stage Coach Mary." *Ebony*, October 1959. Academy Award actor remembers Mary Fields of Montana.

Davison, Stanley R., and Dale Tash. "Confederate Backwash in Montana Territory." *Montana: The Magazine of Western History* 17 (Autumn 1967). Pro-Southern and anti-Black Democrat leanings following the Civil War.

Denyssey, Hugh A. "Terry Patts: Plainsman." *Montana: The Magazine of Western History* 12 (October 1967).

Ege, Robert J. "Braves of all Colors: The Story of Isaiah Dorman, Killed at the Little Big Horn." *Montana: The Magazine of Western History* 16 (Winter 1966); reprinted in *The Black Military Experience in the American West*, ed. John M. Carroll. New York: Liveright Press, 1971.

_____. "Custer's Negro Interpreter." *Negro Digest* 14 (February 1965). Biography of Isaiah Dorman.

_____. "Isaiah Dorman: Negro Casualty with Reno." *Montana: The Magazine of Western History* 16 (January 1966). Dorman, a.k.a. Azimpa, a runaway slave.

Everett, George. "Westerners." *Wild West* 8 (February 1996). Includes profile of Mary Fields.

Fletcher, Marvin E. "The Black Bicycle Corps." *Arizona and the West* 16 (Autumn 1974). The 25th Infantry at Fort Missoula and the bicycle test for military transport.

Frisch, Paul A. "'Gibraltar of Unionism': Women, Blacks and the Anti-Chinese Movement in Butte, Montana, 1880–1900." *Southwest Economy and Society* 6 (1984).

"The Great Bicycle Ride." *Montana Sports Outdoors*, August 1960. Military experiment.

Harris, Mark. "The Legend of Black Mary." *Negro Digest* (August 1950).

Hay, Kenneth W. "I Remember Old Yogo and the Weatherwax: A Boyhood Idyll about Glory Holes and Bonanza Dreams." *Montana: The Magazine of Western History* 25 (Spring 1975). Includes Millie Ringgold, a Black miner.

Hardeman, Nicholas P. "Brick Stronghold of the Border: Fort Assinniboine, 1879–1911." *Montana: The Magazine of Western History* 29 (Spring 1979). The 10th Cavalry in the 1980s.

"Henry W. Blake: Proper Bostonian, Purposeful Pioneer." *Montana Magazine of Western History* 14 (Autumn 1964). Blake recalls some incidents involving Blacks.

Howell, Edgar M. "A Special Artist in the Indian Wars." *Montana: The Magazine of Western History* 15 (Spring 1965). Includes T. R. Davis' drawing of Buffalo Soldiers.

Lang, William L. "The Nearly Forgotten Blacks On Last Chance Gulch, 1900–1912." Chapter in *Montana Vistas*, ed. Robert R. Swartout, Jr. Washington, DC: University Press of America, 1981.

_____. "The Nearly Forgotten Blacks On Last Chance Gulch, 1900–1912." *Pacific Northwest Quarterly* 70 (April 1979). Helena's Black community.

_____. "Tempest on Clore Street: Race and Politics in Helena, Montana, 1906." *Scratchgravel Hills* 3 (Summer 1980). Political controversy surrounding the Zanzibar Club, a Black-owned saloon.

"Lynch Law and Treason: Lynching of Frank Little in Butte." *Literary Digest* 55 (13 August 1917).

McConnell, Roland C. "Isaiah Dorman and the Custer Expedition." *Journal of Negro History* 33 (July 1948).

McFarland, Carl. "Abraham Lincoln and Montana Territory." *Montana* 5 (Autumn 1955). The slavery question in the creation of the Territory of Montana.

McMillan, Christian. "Border State Terror and the Genesis of the African American Community in Deer Lodge and Chateau Counties, Montana, 1870–1890." *Journal of Negro History* 79 (Spring 1994).

Moss, James M. "Recent Experiments in Infantry Bicycling Corps." *Outings* (February 1897). The 25th Infantry Bicycle Corps at Fort Missoula, Montana.

Myers, Rex C. "Montana's Negro Newspapers, 1894–1911." *Montana Journalism Review* 16 (1973). Profile of three newspapers.

Reynolds, George W. "Nature Sets the Stage as Defeated Men Pray for Quenching Rains." *Montana: The Magazine of Western History* 10 (Autumn 1960). Role of Black troops near Wallace, Montana, aid in fire fighting.

Richards, Paul. "Martin Luther King Day: 48 down, 2 To Go." *In These Times* (20 February 1991). Endeavor to recognize Martin Luther King Day.

Rosenblatt, Roger. "Their Finest Minute." *New York Times Magazine* (3 July 1994). Billings fights racism.

Seraile, William. "Fort Missoula, 1891–1998." Chapter in *Voice of Dissent: Theophilus Gould Steward (1843–1924) and Black America*. Brooklyn, NY: Carlson Publishing, 1991.

_____. "Saving Souls on the Frontier: A Chaplain's Labor." *Montana, the Magazine of Western History* 42 (Winter 1992).

_____. "Theophilus G. Steward, Intellectual Chaplain, 25th U.S. Colored Infantry." *Nebraska History* 66 (Fall 1985).

Smurr, J. W. "Jim Crow Out West." Chapter in *Historical Essays on Montana and the Northwest*, eds. J. W. Smurr and Ross Coole. Helena, MT: The Western Press, 1957.

Smythe, Donald. "John J. Pershing at Fort Assiniboine." *Montana, the Magazine of Western History* 18 (January 1969). Pershing was lieutenant with the 10th Cavalry.

_____. "John J. Pershing: Frontier Cavalryman." *New Mexico Historical Review* 38 (1963). Pershing with the 10th Cavalry at Fort Assiniboine.

"Stagecoach Mary." *Catholic Digest* (December 1959). Mary Fields, taken from the Gary Cooper article.

Sweetman, Alice M. "Mondak: Planned City of Hope Astride Montana-Dakota Border." *Montana: The Magazine of Western History* 11 (October 1965). Includes the lynching of a Black man, J. C. Collins.

Books:

African Methodist Episcopal Church, Colorado Conference. *Minutes of the Eighth Annual Session of the Colorado Conference of the African M.E. Church. Held in Helena, Montana, October 11, 1894*. Albuquerque: J. W. Sanders, 1894.

Bailey, Linda C. *Fort Missoula's Military Cyclists: The Story of the 25th U.S. Infantry Bicycle Corps.* Missoula: The Friends of the Historical Museum at Fort Missoula, 1997. Monograph.

Fowler, Arlen L. *The Black Infantry in the West, 1869–1891.* Contributions in Afro-American and African Studies, no. 6. Westport, CT: Greenwood Publishing Company, 1971; reprinted, Norman: University of Oklahoma Press, 1996. Includes Black soldiers in Montana.

Gordon, Taylor. *Born to Be.* Blacks in the American West Series. New York: Civici, Friede, 1929; reprinted, Lincoln: University of Nebraska Press, 1995. Growing up in a Black community in White Sulphur Springs.

Miller, Robert H. *The Story of "Stagecoach" Mary Fields.* Englewood Cliffs, NJ: Silver Burdett Press, 1995.

Minutes of the Eighth Annual Session of the Colorado Conference of the African M. E. Church—Held in Helena, Montana, October 11, 1894. Albuquerque: Edmund G. Rose, Book and Job Printer, n.d.

Montana Federation of Negro Women's Clubs, State Journal. Butte: Oates and Roberts, 1921. Proceedings of the first session of the Montana State Federation of Negro Women's Clubs held at Schaffer A.M.E. Chapel, Butte, Montana.

NAACP Administrative File. Subject File. Civil Rights—Montana, 1936–1939. Frederick, MD: University Publications of America, 1990.

Thompson, Lucille Smith, and Alma Smith Jacobs. *The Negro in Montana 1800–1945: A Selective Bibliography.* Helena: Montana State Library, 1970.

United States Commission on Civil Rights. Montana Advisory Committee. *Access to the Legal Profession in Montana: A Report.* Washington, DC: The Commission, 1981. Law schools and admissions.

————. Montana Advisory Committee. *White Supremacist Activity in Montana.* Denver, CO: The Commission, Rocky Mountain Regional Office, 1994.

————. *The Media in Montana: Its Effects on Minorities and Women: A Report.* Washington, DC: The Commission, 1976.

Black Newspapers:

Colored Citizen. Helena. 1894.

Everybody. Missoula. 1959–1987.

Fort Harrison Knocker. Fort Harrison. 1902–? Activities of Black troops.

Montana Plaindealer. Helena. 1906–1911.

New Age. Butte. 1902–1903.

Northwest Enterprise. Seattle. 1920–1962. Carried a column of Montana news.

Reporter. Helena. 1899–1901.

Nebraska

Articles:

Bitzes, John G. "The Anti-Greek Riot of 1909—South Omaha." *Nebraska History* 51 (Summer 1970). Mentions Blacks and lynching.

Brands, William Joseph. "Nebraska College, the Episcopal School at Nebraska City, 1868–1885." *Nebraska History* 52 (Summer 1971). Brief descriptions of Black experiences there.

Broussard, Albert S. "George Albert Flippin and Race Relations in a Western Rural Community." *Midwest Review* 12 (1990).

Buecker, Thomas R. "Fort Niobrara, 1880–1906: Guardian of the Rosebud Sioux." *Nebraska History* 65 (Fall 1984).

_____. "One Soldier's Service: Caleb Benson in the Ninth and Tenth Cavalry, 1875–1908." *Nebraska History* 74 (Summer 1973).

_____. "Prelude to Brownsville: The Twenty-Fifth Infantry at Fort Niobrara, Nebraska, 1902–66." *Great Plains Quarterly* 16 (Spring 1996).

_____. "The Tenth Cavalry at Fort Robinson: Black Troops in the West, 1902–1907." *Military Images* 12 (May-June 1991).

Burns, Robert H. "The Newman Ranches: Pioneer Cattle Ranches of the West." *Nebraska History* 34 (1953).

Chudacoff, Howard P. "Where Rolls the Dark Missouri Down." *Nebraska History* 52 (Spring 1971). Includes rise of Blacks in Omaha population.

"A Colored Man's Experience on a Nebraska Homestead." *Omaha World Herald* (11 February 1899).

"Conservatives Contest Florida, Nebraska Scholarship Plans for Blacks." *Black Issues in Higher Education* 7 (7 June 1990).

Dales, David G. "North Platte Racial Incident: Black-White Confrontation, 1929." *Nebraska History* 60 (1979).

Frehill-Rowe, Lisa M. "Postbellum Race Relations and Rural Land Tenure: Migration of Blacks and Whites to Kansas and Nebraska, 1870–1890." *Social Forces* 72 (September 1993).

Gatewood, Willard B., Jr. "The Perils of Passing: The McCarys of Omaha." *Nebraska History* 71 (1990).

Gilfert, Shirley. "Nebraska City Mobocracy." *Old West* 26 (Summer 1990). Black men Henry Jackson and Henry Martin lynched in 1878.

Hart, Charles Desmond. "The Natural Limits of Slavery Expansion: Kansas-Nebraska, 1854." *Kansas Historical Quarterly* 34 (1968).

Heer, David M. "Negro-White Marriages in the United States." *Journal of Marriage and The Family* 28 (August 1966). Analyzes trends in those marriages in California, Hawaii, Michigan and Nebraska.

Klem, Mary J. "The Kansas-Nebraska Slavery Bill and Missouri's Part in the Conflict." *Mississippi Valley Historical Association Proceedings* 9 (1919).

Laurie, Clayton D. "The U.S. Army and the Omaha Race Riot of 1919." *Nebraska History* 72 (Fall 1991).

Lawson, Michael. "Omaha, a City in Ferment: Summer of 1919." *Nebraska History* 58 (Fall 1977). Information about the September race riot.

Levy, Daniel S. "The Cantor and the Klansman." *Time,* 17 February 1992. The KKK in Nebraska.

"Lynching in Omaha." Chapter in *Racial Violence in the United States*, ed. Allen D. Grimshaw. Chicago: Aldine, 1969. Originally published in the *New York Times*, 30 September 1919, titled "700 Federal Troops Quiet Omaha; Mayor Recovering; Omaha Mob Rule Defended by Most of the Population."

McKenna, Clare V., Jr. "Seeds of Destruction: Homicide, Race, and Justice in Omaha, 1880–1920." *Journal of American Ethnic History* 14 (Fall 1994). Author, using detailed records, contends Southern Blacks brought with them a "subculture of violence" to Omaha.

Menard, Orville D. "Tom Dennison, the Omaha Bee, and the 1919 Race Riot." *Nebraska History* 68 (1987). The Omaha race riot.

Mihelich, Dennis N. "Boom or Bust: Prince Hall Masonry in Nebraska during the 1920s." *Nebraska History* 79 (Summer 1998).

————. "The Formation of the Lincoln Urban League." *Nebraska History* 68 (Summer 1987).

————. "The Lincoln Urban League: The Travail of Depression and War." *Nebraska History* 70 (Winter 1989).

————. "The Origins of the Prince Hall Mason Grand Lodge of Nebraska." *Nebraska History* 76 (1995).

————. "A Socioeconomic Portrait of Prince Hall Masonry in Nebraska, 1900–1920." *Great Plains Quarterly* 17 (1997).

————. "World War II and the Transformation of the Omaha Urban League." *Nebraska History* 60 (Fall 1979).

"New Jersey, Nebraska, and Detroit Feature Negro History Projects." *Library Journal* 90 (15 March 1965).

"Official Says Questioning of Black Students Mishandled." *Black Issues in Higher Education* 9 (3 December 1992). University of Nebraska, Lincoln.

"Omaha." *Nation* 109 (11 October 1919). Race riots.

"Omaha: Riots in the Nebraska City." *Literary Digest* 63 (11 October 1919).

"One of the Advocates of 'The League of Nations.'" *Crusader* 2 (November 1919). Mississippi senator Williams approves of the Omaha lynchings.

Overturf, Wayne. "John Brown's Cabin at Nebraska City." *Nebraska State Historical Society* 21 (April-June 1940).

Parker, George Wells. "The Omaha Mob." *Crusader* 2 (November 1919). Mob lynches Black accused rapist Will Brown and attempted to lynch the mayor during attack on the jail.

Paul, Justus F. "The Ku Klux Klan in the Midwest: A Note on the 1936 Nebraska Elections." *North Dakota Quarterly* 39 (Autumn 1971). Ties the Nebraska Protective Association (the Klan) to the Republican campaign of 1936.

Paz, D. G. "John Albert Williams and Black Journalism in Omaha, 1895–1929." *Midwest Review* 10 (Spring 1988).

Potts, James B. "Nebraska Statehood and Reconstruction." *Nebraska History* 69 (Summer 1988). Some concerns over Blacks.

Powell, F. C. , and James A. Thorson. "Political Behavior: Voting Participating of Inner-City Elderly Blacks Compared to Other Populations in a Medium-Sized City." *Psychological Reports* 67 (1990). Participation was the same or better than other elderly and higher when compared to all ages.

"Race Prejudice in Nebraska." *World Tomorrow* 13 (January 1930).

Ray, Marcia. "Sandhills Settlement that Lived and Died...DeWitty." *Nebraska Farmer* [Special Issue] (January 17 1959).

"The Real Causes of Two Race Riots." *Crisis* 19 (December 1919). Riots in Phillips County, Arkansas and in Omaha, Nebraska. A man named Brown was lynched in Omaha.

"The Riots at Charleston, Longview, Omaha and Knoxville." Section in *Negro Year Book...1921–1922*, ed. Monroe N. Work. Tuskegee Institute: Negro Year Book Publishing Company, 1922.

Roberts, Randy. "Heavyweight Champion Jack Johnson: His Omaha Image, Public Reaction Study." *Nebraska History* 57 (1976).

Schubert, Frank N. "The Fort Robinson YMCA, 1902–1907: A Social Organization in a Black Regiment." *Nebraska History* 55 (Summer 1974). The importance of the YMCA for the 10th Cavalry.

_____. "Ten Troopers: Buffalo Soldier Medal of Honor Men Who served at Fort Robinson." *Nebraska History* 78 (Winter 1997).

_____. "Troopers, Taverns, and Taxes: Fort Robinson, Nebraska, and Its Municipal Parasite, 1886–1911." Chapter in *Soldiers and Civilians: The U.S. Army and the American People*, eds. Garry D. Ryan and Timothy K. Nenninger. Washington, DC: National Archives and Records Administration, 1987.

Schuyler, Michael W. "The Ku Klux Klan in Nebraska, 1920–1930." *Nebraska History* 66 (Fall 1985).

Scrimsher, Lila Gravatt, ed. "The Diaries and Writings of George A. Matson, Black Citizen of Lincoln, Nebraska, 1901–1913." *Nebraska History* 52 (1971). Though Matson lived in Lincoln from 1901–1913, the years covered are mostly from 1869–1898 when he lived in Ohio and Missouri.

Simons, John. "Paid to Leave, but Wanting to Stay." *U.S. News and World Report*, 11 July 1994. Blacks of North Omaha do not want to use HUD rent subsidy vouchers because they would be placed in neighborhoods that are at least 65% white.

Suzuki, Peter T. "The Denouement of an Institution in a Black Urban Community: The Jitney Taxicabs of Omaha, Nebraska." *International Bulletin of Urgent Anthropological and Ethnological Research* 23 (1981).

_____. "Omaha's Black Vernacular-Cab Driver and His Fare: Facets of a Symbiotic Relationship." *Western Journal of Black Studies* 15 (Summer 1991). Illegal or "gypsy" cab operations.

_____. "Vernacular Cabs: Jitneys and Gypsies in Five Cities." *Transportation Research* 19 (1985).

"Three White Men Discharged from Air Force for Racial Incident, Other Problems." *Jet*, 13 April 1998. Whites parade in building on Offutt Air Force Base (Nebraska) with pillowcases over their heads, imitating Klansmen.

Valentine, C. "The Man Whom They Lynched." *Crusader* 2 (November 1919). Lynching of Will Brown in Omaha.

Wax, Darold D. "The Odyssey of an Ex-Slave: Robert Ball Anderson's Pursuit of the American Dream." *Phylon* 45 (Spring 1984).

_____. "Robert Ball Anderson, Ex-Slave, A Pioneer in Western Nebraska, 1884–1930." *Nebraska History* 64 (Summer 1983).

Williams, Eric. "Police vs. Blacks in Nebraska." *The Progressive* 58 (January 1994). Police mass-arrest Black teenagers in downtown Omaha.

Wilson, Major L. "Of Time and the Union: Kansas-Nebraska and the Appeal from Prescription to Principle." *Midwest Quarterly* 10 (1968). Examines the act and the debate in Congress.

Books:

Anderson, Robert Ball. *From Slavery to Affluence: Memoirs of Robert Anderson, Ex-Slave*, ed. Daisy Anderson Leonard.   Hemingford, NE:

Hemingford Ledger, 1927; reprinted, Steamboat Springs, CO: Steamboat Pilot, 1967.

[Bayard, William]. *Comments on the Nebraska Bill with Views on Slavery in Contrast with Freedom; Respectfully Addressed to the Free States, by One Acquainted with Southern Institutions.* Albany: J. Munsell, 1854.

Bazaar, Mona. *Black Fury.* Oakland, CA: n.p., 1970. Omaha race relations.

Bigotry and Violence on Nebraska's College Campuses. Washington, DC: U.S. Commission on Civil Rights, 1990.

Calloway, Bertha W. *Visions of Freedom on the Great Plaines: An Illustrated History of African Americans in Nebraska.* Virginia Beach, VA: Donning Company, 1998.

Crowell, John. *The Wickedness of the Nebraska Bill. A Sermon Preached in the Second Presbyterian Church, Orange, N.J., February 26th, 1854.* New York: M. W. Dodd, 1854.

Hale, Edward Everett. *Kansas and Nebraska.* Black Heritage Library Collection Series. Freeport, NY: Books for Libraries Press, 1972.

Inman, William E. *Size and State School System Organization.* Lincoln: Great School System Organization Project, 10 May 1968.

Lief, Alfred. *Democracy's (George W.) Norris: The Biography of A Lonely Crusade.* New York: Stackpole Sons, 1939. U.S. Senator fights the Klan.

Lowitt, Richard. *George W. Norris: The Triumph of A Progressive, 1933–1944.* Urbana: University of Illinois Press, 1978. U.S. Senator fights the Klan.

Malin, James C. *The Nebraska Question, 1852–1854.* Lawrence: University Press of Kansas, 1953.

McConkey, Clarence. *A Burden and an Ache.* Nashville: Abington Press, 1970. Omaha poor.

NAACP Administrative File. Subject File. Lynching...Nebraska, 1919, 1929. Frederick, MD: University Publications of America, 1986.

Nebraska Urban League. *The State of Black Nebraska.* Omaha: Nebraska Urban League, 1980.

Nebraska Writers' Project (Works Progress Administration). *The Negroes of Nebraska.* Lincoln, NE: Woodruff Printing, 1940.

Norris, George W. *Fighting Liberal, The Autobiography of George W. Norris.* New York: Macmillan Company, 1945. U.S. Senator fights the Klan.

Omaha School Community Advisory Board. *Your Right to Know: The Closed Hearing of Eddie Chambers Before the Omaha School Board,* 2d ed. Omaha: School Community Advisory Board, 1972. Discrimination and Black teachers.

Omaha's Riot in Story and Picture. Omaha: Educational Publishing Company, 192? Omaha riot of 1919.

Polk, Donna Mays. *Black Men and Women of Nebraska.* Lincoln: Nebraska Black History Preservation society, 1981. Biography.

Proceedings of a Public Meeting of the Citizens of Providence Held in the Beneficent Congregational Church, March 7, 1854, to Protest Against Slavery in Nebraska; with the Address of the Speakers. Providence, RI: Knowles, Anthony, 1854.

Rawick, George P., ed. *The American Slave: A Complete Autobiography.* Westport, CT: Greenwood Publishing Company, 1972. Transcriptions of narratives for the 1936–1938 Federal Writers' Project. Vol. I.

Schubert, Frank N. *Buffalo Soldiers, Braves, and the Brass: The Story of Fort Robinson, Nebraska.* Shippensburg, PA: White Mane Publishing Company, 1993.

State Government Affirmative Action in Mid-America: An Update: A Report. Prepared by the Iowa, Kansas, Missouri, and Nebraska Advisory Committees to the United States Commission on Civil Rights. Washington, DC: The Commission, 1982.

Sullenger, Thomas Earl, and James H. Kearns. *The Negro in Omaha: A Social Study of Negro Development.* Omaha: Municipal University of Omaha and Omaha Urban League, 1931.

Thompson, Joseph Parrish. *The Voice of God Against Nature Crime.* New York: Ivison and Phinney, 1854. Call for "No Slavery in Nebraska."

Todd, Ralph H. *Changing Income Patterns of the Omaha Metropolitan Area Black Population.* Omaha: University of Nebraska at Omaha, Center for Public Affairs Research, 1972.

United States Commission on Civil Rights. Nebraska Advisory Committee. *Private Sector Affirmative Action, Omaha: A Report.* Washington, DC: The Commission, 1979.

Writers' Program. *The Negroes of Nebraska, Written and Compiled by Workers of the Writers' Program, Work Projects Administration in the State of Nebraska.* Lincoln, NE: Woodruff Printing Company, 1940. Sponsored by the Omaha Urban League Community Center.

Theses and Dissertations:

Age, Arthur V. "The Omaha Riot of 1919." Master's thesis, Creighton University, 1964.

Bish, James D. "The Black Experience in Selected Nebraska Counties, 1854–1920." Master's thesis, University of Nebraska, Omaha, 1989.

Brown, Obbie Zonnie. "Attendance and Achievement of Negro Students at the University of Nebraska." Master's thesis, University of Nebraska, 1948.

Butler, Millard Elwin. "A Follow-Up Study of the Negro Children Who Entered the Lincoln High Schools from 1932–33 to 1937–37." Master's thesis, University of Nebraska, 1940.

Cecil, Harriet Mildred. "A Study of Attitudes and Behavior Patterns of Black Parents toward Education and Schooling." Ph.D. diss., University of Nebraska, 1985.

Chandler, Vera Adrienne. "A Study of 100 Adolescent Negro Children in Omaha with Especial Reference to the Family." Master's thesis, University of Nebraska, 1940.

Collins, Talma Ree Bell. "A Survey of the Present Educational Vocational Status of the Negro Youth in Lincoln, Nebraska." Master's thesis, university of Nebraska, 1951.

Davies, Mary Emily, and Genevieve Marsh. "A Study of the Negro in Lincoln." Master's thesis, University of Nebraska, 1904.

Deeb, Norma Jean. "An Analysis of the Implemented Desegregation Plan of the Elementary Schools of Omaha, Nebraska." Ph.D. diss., University of Nebraska, 1988.

Hess, Eldora Frances. "The Negro in Nebraska." Master's thesis, University of Nebraska, 1932.

Partridge, Gaines R. "The Effect on Negro Youth in Nebraska High Schools of Their Practices of Identification." Ph.D. diss., University of Nebraska Teachers College, 1961.

Schubert, Frank N. "Fort Robinson, Nebraska: The History of a Military Community, 1874–1916." Ph.D. diss., University of Michigan, 1977.

Black Newspapers:[1]

LINCOLN

Colored People's Advocate. Lincoln. 1919.

Lincoln Leader. Lincoln. 1899–1900.

Review. Lincoln. 1920.

Urban League Informer. Lincoln. 193?

Voice. Lincoln. 1946–1953. Weekly.

Weekly Review. Lincoln. 1933.

OMAHA

Afro-American Sentinel. Omaha. 1893–1911.

American Record. Omaha. 1945–1948.

Enterprise. Omaha. 1893–1914.

Everybody. Omaha. 1959–1981.

Everyone. Omaha. 1959–1974.

Monitor. Omaha. 1915–1928.
Omaha Monitor. Omaha. 1928–1929.

New Era. Omaha. 1920–1926.

Omaha Advocate. Omaha. 1923–1925.

Omaha Chronicle. Omaha. 1934–1936.

Omaha Guide. Omaha. 1927–1958.

Omaha Journal. Omaha. 1934–1936.

Omaha Star. Omaha. 1938–199?

Progress. Omaha. 1889–1904.

[1] Double-lined boxed items indicate change in masthead names.

Progressive Age. Omaha.
    1913–1915.
Tan Pride. Omaha. 1968–1981.

VARIOUS COMMUNITIES

American Record. Plattsmouth.
    1946–?

Fort Robinson Weekly Bulletin.
    Crawford. 1884–1894.
Mode. Farnum. 1961–1962.
Urban League Informer. Linden.
    1930s.
Western Post. Hastings. 1876. Ne-
    braska's first Black news-
    paper.

Other:

Black on Black: Forever Free. KMTV Omaha, James A.; Nelson, producer,
    1981. Review of exhibit "Forever Free," art by Black women,
    1862–1980, Omaha's Josyln Museum. Videorecording.
Kaleidoscope: The Word of Allah Behind Bars. KETV Omaha, Bettie Shapiro,
    producer, 1979. Positive look at the impact of Islam on the inmates of
    the Nebraska State Penitentiary.
A Time for Burning. Lutheran Film Associates, Robert E. A. Lee, producer,
    1966. Augustana Lutheran Church in Omaha reaches out to the city's
    Blacks in 1966.

Nevada

Articles:

Blackburn, George M. , and Sherman L. Richards. "The Prostitute." Section in "The Prostitutes and Gamblers of Virginia City, Nevada: 1870." *Pacific Historical Review* 48 (1979). Four of the 138 prostitutes were Black, and are profiled.

Bracey, Earnest N. "The Moulin Rouge Mystique: Blacks and Equal Rights in Las Vegas." *Nevada Historical Society Quarterly* 39 (Winter 1996).

Colcord, R. K. "Reminiscences of Life in Territorial Nevada." *California Historical Society Quarterly* 7 (1928).

Coray, Michael S. "African-Americans in Nevada." *Nevada Historical Society Quarterly* 35 (Winter 1992). Covers 1860s through 1990s.

_____. "'Democracy' on the Frontier: A Case Study of Nevada Editorial Attitudes on the Issue of Nonwhite Equality." *Nevada Historical Society Quarterly* 21 (1987). Racial attitudes in newspapers.

Crowley, Joseph N. "Race and Residence: The Politics of Open Housing in Nevada." Chapter in *Sagebrush and Neon*, ed. Eleanore Bushnell. Reno: Bureau of Governmental Research, University of Nevada, 1973.

Davis, Mike. "Racial Caldron in Las Vegas." *Nation* (6 July 1992).

Dobbs, William T. "Southern Nevada and the Legacy of Basic Magnesium, Inc." *Nevada Historical Society Quarterly* 24 (1991).

Earl, Phillip I. "Nevada's Miscegenation Laws and the Marriage of Mr. and Mrs. Harry Bridges." *Nevada Historical Society Quarterly* 37 (Spring 1994). Though focused on a white male and Asian female, still provides a glimpse into those laws.

Fitzgerald, Roosevelt. "Blacks and the Boulder Dam Project." *Nevada Historical Society Quarterly* 24 (1981).

_____. "The Evolution of a Black Community in Las Vegas, 1905–1940."
    Nevada Public Affairs Review 2 (1987).

Hanchett, William. "Yankee Law and the Negro in Nevada, 1861–1869." *West-
    ern Humanities Review* 10 (Summer 1956). Racist Republicans ratify
    the 15th Amendment only to toe the party line.

Hawkins, Leland Stanford. "Boulder Dam" *Crisis* 41 (March 1934). Recounts
    efforts of Walter Hamilton of Las Vegas to secure jobs for Blacks.

Hickson, Howard, ed. "Black Wrangler: Reminiscences of Lawrence Jackson."
    Northeastern *Nevada Historical Society Quarterly* 77 (1977).

Hulse, James W. "The Blacks, or African-Americans." Section in "The Strug-
    gle for Equal Rights." Chapter in *The Silver State: Nevada's Heritage
    Reinterpreted.* Reno: University of Nevada Press, 1991. A couple
    pages on discrimination against Blacks.

Johnson, Ed, and Elmer R. Rusco. "The First Black Rancher: Ben Palmer and
    Other Blacks Made Their Marks in the 1800s." *Nevada* 49 (January
    1989).

Lewis, Georgia. "The Black Ranchers of Lincoln County." *Nevadan* 18 (July
    1971).

"Michael Douglas Elected Nevada District Court Judge." *Jet*, 23 December
    1996.

Patrick, Elizabeth Nelson. "Notes and Documents: The Black Experience in
    Southern Nevada, Pt. 1." *Nevada Historical Society Quarterly* 22
    (Summer 1979). Review of 12 interviews of Blacks.

_____. "Notes and Documents: The Black Experience in Southern Nevada,
    Pt. 2." *Nevada Historical Society Quarterly* 22 (Fall 1979).

Pettit, Arthur G. "Mark Twain's Attitude Toward the Negro in the West,
    1861–1867." *Western Historical Quarterly* 1 (January 1970). Though
    he changed his slavery stance in Nevada from 1861–1864, he didn't
    change his Negrophobia.

Robinson, Louie. "Las Vegas: Entertainment Capital of the World." *Ebony*,
    April 1972. Article about Black entertainers and their opportunities in
    Las Vegas.

_____. "Lola Falana." *Ebony*, October 1979. Las Vegas entertainer recalls
    her path to stardom.

Rusco, Elmer R. "African Americans in Nevada, 1860s–1920s." Chapter in
    Peoples of Color in the American West, eds. Sucheng Chan, et al.
    Lexington, MA: D. C. Heath and Company, 1994. Argues that
    Blacks were recipients of little racism until the end of Reconstruction,
    when it greatly increased.

_____. "The Civil Rights Movement in Nevada." *Nevada Public Affairs
    Review: Ethnicity and Race in Nevada* 2 (1987).

St. James, Nicole. "Grabbing Another Slice." *Black Enterprise*, December
    1997. Black company PacPizza L. L. C. becomes Pizza Hut's second
    largest franchiser with restaurants in northern California, southern Ore-
    gon and western Nevada.

Swallow, Craig F. "The Ku Klux Klan in Nevada during the 1920s." *Nevada Historical Society Quarterly* 24 (Fall 1981).

Titus, A. Costandina. "Howard Cannon, the Senate and Civil Rights Legislation, 1959–1968." *Nevada Historical Society Quarterly* 33 (Winter 1990). U.S. Senator and his civil rights history.

Williams, Franklin H. "Sunshine and Jim Crow." *Crisis* 61 (April 1954). Jim Crow in Las Vegas.

Books:

Can We All Get Along? Las Vegas: *Las Vegas Review-Journal*, 1993. Collection of newspaper articles that ran from 25 April to 30 April, 1993.

Coughtry, Jamie, ed. *Lubertha Johnson: Civil Rights Efforts in Las Vegas, 1940's–1960's*. Reno: Oral History Program, 1988.

Coughtry, Jamie, and R. T. King, eds. *Lubertha Johnson: Civil Rights Efforts in Las Vegas: 1940's–1960*. Reno: University of Nevada Oral History Program, 1988.

————. *Woodrow Wilson: Race, Community and Politics in Las Vegas, 1940s–1980s*. Reno: University of Nevada Oral History Program, 1990.

Lisby, Lee Henry. *Oral Interview of Lee Henry Lisby*, eds. Elizabeth Nelson Patrick and Rita O'Brien. Las Vegas: James R. Dickinson Library, University of Nevada, 1978. Black experience in southern Nevada.

Nevada, Bureau of Governmental Research. *Minority Groups in Nevada*. Carson City: The Bureau, 1966.

Nevada. University. Bureau of Governmental Research. *Voices of Black Nevada*. Reno: The Bureau, University of Nevada, 1971.

Rusco, Elmer R. *"Good Time Coming?" Black Navadans in the Nineteenth Century*. Contributions in Afro-American and African Studies, no. 15. Westport, CT: Greenwood Press, 1975.

————. *Minority Groups in Nevada*. Reno: Bureau of Governmental Research, University of Nevada, 1966. Race discrimination.

————. *Voices of Black Nevada*, *Governmental Research Newsletter*, Bureau of Governmental Research. Reno: University of Nevada, 1971.

————. *Voting Patterns of Racial Minorities in Nevada*. Reno: Bureau of Governmental Research, University of Nevada, 1966.

Shelden, Randall G. *Blacks, Crime and Criminal Justice in America and Nevada: The Social and Economic Context*. n.p., 1990. First presented as a paper at the Nevada Chapter of the National Association of Blacks in Criminal Justice, North Las Vegas, Nevada.

Theses and Dissertations:

Kaufman, Perry. "The Best City of Them All: A History of Las Vegas, Nevada, 1930–1960." Ph.D. diss., University of California, Santa Barbara, 1974. One chapter concerning Blacks and West Las Vegas.

White, Claytee D. "The Roles of African American Women in the Las Vegas Gaming Industry, 1940–1980." Master's thesis, University of Nevada, Las Vegas, 1997.

Black Newspapers:[1]

Las Vegas Sentinel-Voice. Las Vegas. 1980–199?

Voice. North Las Vegas.
    1963–1977.
Las Vegas Voice. Las Vegas.
    1964–1969.

Nevada Observer. Reno. 1915–1919.
Reno Observer. Reno. 1975–1983.

---

[1] Double-lined boxed items indicate change in masthead names.

New Mexico

Articles:

Banks, Roger W. "Between the Tracks and the Freeway: The Negro in Albuquerque." Chapter in *Minorities in Politics*, ed. Henry Jack Tobias. Albuquerque: University of New Mexico Press, 1969.

Bennett, Charles. "The Buffalo Soldiers and the Apache War Chief." *El Palacio* 101 (Summer 1996). Native American reactions to Black troops in New Mexico Territory.

Billington, Monroe Lee. "Black Cavalrymen and Apache Indians in New Mexico Territory." *Fort Concho and the South Plains Journal* 22 (Summer 1990).

_____. "Black History and New Mexico's Place Names." *Password* 24 (Fall 1984).

_____. "Black Soldiers at Fort Selden, New Mexico, 1866–1891." *New Mexico Historical Review* 62 (1987).

_____. "Civilians and Black Soldiers in New Mexico Territory, 1866–1900: A Cross-Cultural Experience." *Military History of the Southwest* 19 (Spring 1989).

_____. "A Profile of Blacks in New Mexico on the Eve of Statehood." *Password* 32 (Summer 1987).

Bloom, L. B., ed. "Lt. John Bourke's Description of a Lynching in Tucson, N.M., in 1873." *New Mexico Historical Review* 19 (July 1944).

Bustamante, Adrian. "'The Matter Was Never Resolved': The Casta System in Colonial New Mexico, 1693–1823." *New Mexico Historical Review* 66 (1991). How those with "Black blood" began to identify themselves as Indian, mestizo, or Spanish.

Chambers, R. L. "The Negro in New Mexico." *Crisis* 59 (March 1952).

Chávez, Fray Angélico. "De Vargas' Negro Drummer." *El Palacio* 56 (1949); reprinted in *The Black Military Experience in the American West*, John M. Carroll. New York: Liveright Publishing, 1971.

Coleman, Anita Scott. "Arizona and New Mexico—The Land of Esperanza." *Messenger* 8 (September 1926). The status of Blacks in those places.

Colton, Ray Charles. *The American Civil War in the Western Territories of New Mexico, Arizona, Colorado and Utah.* Norman: University of Oklahoma Press, 1959.

Conner, Veda N. "There's a Big We in New Mexico." *Crisis* 61 (1954).

Creamer, Winifred. "Re-examining the Black Legend: Contact Period Demography in the Rio Grande Valley of New Mexico." *New Mexico Historical Review* 69 (July 1994).

DeMark, Judith L. "Occupational Mobility and Persistence Within Albuquerque Ethnic Groups, 1880–1910." *New Mexico Historical Review* 68 (1993).

Ellis, Margretta. "The Negro Enemy." *Crisis* 58 (November 1951). Problems with Blacks and whites working together.

Fleming, Elvis E. "Collins Family." In *Roundup on the Pecos*, eds. Elvis E. Fleming and Minor S. Huffman. Roswell, NM: Chaves County Historical Society, 1978. Story of Monroe and Mary Collins and family, homesteaders of Blackdom and Roswell.

Flipper, Henry O. "Did a Negro Discover Arizona and New Mexico?" 1896; reprinted, Chapter in *Black Frontiersman: The Memoirs of Henry O Flipper: First Black Graduate of West Point*, ed. Theodore D. Harris. Fort Worth: Texas Christian University Press, 1997.

Ganaway, Loomis Morton. "New Mexico and the Sectional Controversy, 1846–1861." *New Mexico Historical Review* 18 (1943); and 19 (1944).

Gibson, Daniel. "Blackdom." *New Mexico Magazine* 64 (February 1986). History of the small community of Blackdom which lasted from 1901 until almost 1930.

Gilliand, Frank D., Thomas M. Becker, and Charles R. Key. "Contrasting Trends of Prostate Cancer Incidence and Mortality in New Mexico's Hispanics, Non-Hispanic Whites, American Indians, and Blacks." *Cancer: Diagnosis, Treatment, Research* 73 (15 April 1994).

Hall, Martin H. Letter to the Editor in "Historical Notes." *Password* 13 (Fall 1968). Story of a slave who went to New Mexico with his master, a Confederate soldier.

————. "Negroes With Confederate Troops in West Texas and New Mexico." *Password* 13 (Spring 1968). Slaves with Confederate masters in 1861 and 1862.

Hardwickhall, Martin. Letter to the Editor, "Historical Notes" section. *Password* 13 (Fall 1968). Information found after following article was published.

Heath, Jim F., and Frederick M. Nunn. "Negroes and Discrimination in Colonial New Mexico: Don Pedro Bautista Pino's Startling Statements of 1812 in Perspective." *Phylon* 31 (1970). In spite of the facts, Governor stated that there were no people of African origin in New Mexico.

"Hidden Histories." *Quantum* 13 (Spring 1996). Blacks with the Conquistadors in New Mexico.

Kammer, David J. "TKO in Las Vegas: Boosterism and the Johnson-Flynn Fight." *New Mexico Historical Review* 61 (October 1936). Jack Johnson fight in Las Vegas, New Mexico.

Kurtz, Don. "Vado: Refuge on the Rio." *New Mexico Magazine* 58 (July 1980).

Long, George. "How Albuquerque Got its Civil Rights Ordinance." *Crisis* 60 (November 1953).

McDonald, Dedra S. "Intimacy and Empire: Indian-African Interaction in Spanish Colonial New Mexico, 1500–1800." *American Indian Quarterly*, Winter 1988.

Milbauer, John A. "Population Origins and Ethnicity in the Silver City Mining Region of New Mexico, 1870–1890." *International Social Science Review* 60 (1985).

Murphy, Lawrence R. "Reconstruction in New Mexico." *New Mexico Historical Review* 43 (1968). Reconstruction ends opposition to abolish slavery and debt peonage.

Myers, Lee. "Mutiny at Fort Cummings." *New Mexico Historical Review* 46 (1971).

Nash, Horace Daniel. "Community Building on the Border: The Role of the 24th Infantry Band at Columbus, New Mexico, 1916–1922." *Fort Concho and the South Plains Journal* 22 (Summer 1990).

"New Mexico State University Diverse, But Still Facing Diversity Problems." *Black Issues in Higher Education* 10 (3 June 1993). Challenges of multiculturalism.

Stephenson, Richard. "Race in the Cactus State." *Crisis* 61 (April 1954).

Sunseri, Alvin R. "A Note on Slavery and the Black Man in New Mexico, 1846–1861." *Negro History Bulletin* 38 (October 1975); reprinted as "Slavery and the Black Man in New Mexico." Chapter in *Seeds of Discord: New Mexico in the Aftermath of the American Conquest, 1848–1861*. Chicago: Nelson-Hall, 1979.

"A Symposium: The Negro and the Jew." *Burning Bush* 3 (Summer 1965). Fifteen San Francisco Bay-area residents discuss inter-relationships.

Theisen, Lee Scott, ed. "The Fight in Lincoln, N.M., 1878: The Testimony of Two Negro Participants." *Arizona and the West* 12 (Summer 1970). Testimony regarding an incident in the Lincoln County War during July 1878.

Tjarks, Alicia V. "Demographic, Ethnic and Occupational Structure of New Mexico, 1790." *The Americas: A Quarterly Review of Inter-American Cultural History* 35 (1978).

Vigil, Maurilio E. "A New Remedy for an Old Ailment: Cumulative Voting as an Alternative to the Single Member District in Minority Voting Rights." *Latino Studies Journal* 3 (1992).

Welsh, Michael S. "Often Out of Sight, Rarely Out of Mind: Race and Ethnicity at the University of New Mexico." *New Mexico Historical Review* 71 (April 1996).

Wilson, Raymond. "Another White Hope Bites the Dust: The Jack Johnson–Jim Flynn Heavyweight Fight in 1912." *Montana: The Magazine of Western History* 29 (Winter 1979). Johnson's last fight as champion in the U.S.

Wright, Richard R. "A Negro Discovered New Mexico." *AME Review* 13 (July 1896).

Books:

American and Foreign Anti-Slavery Society. *Address to the Inhabitants of New Mexico and California, on the Omission by Congress to Provide Them with Territorial Governments, and on the Social and Political Evils of Slavery*. New York: The Society, 1849.

Baton, Maisha. *A History of Blackdom, N.M. in the Context of the African American Post Civil War Colonization Movement*. Santa Fe, NM: Historic Preservation Division, Office of Cultural Affairs, 1997.

Bell, John. *The Compromise Bill: Speech of Hon. John Bell, of Tennessee, in the Senate of the United States, July 3 and 5, 1850, on the Bill for the Admission of California into the Union, the Establishment of Territorial Governments for Utah and New Mexico, and Making Proposals to Texas for the Settlement of Her Northern and Western Boundaries*. Washington, DC: Congressional Globe Office, 1850. Extension of slavery.

Billington, Monroe Lee. *New Mexico's Buffalo Soldiers, 1866–1900*. Niwot, CO: University Press of Colorado, 1991.

Bingham, John Armor. *Bill and Report of John A. Bingham: And Vote on Its Passage, Repealing the Territorial New Mexican Laws Establishing Slavery and Authorizing Employers to Whip "White Persons" and Others in Their Employment, and Denying Them Redress in the Courts*. Washington, DC: n.p., 1860.

Burr, Marjorie. *Increasing Participation and Success of Minorities and Women at Dona Ana Branch Community College. Submitted to the New Mexico Commission on Higher Education*. Las Cruces: New Mexico State University, 1992. ERIC. ED 356 025. Academic persistence and achievement.

DeBlassie, Richard R., and Gary W. Healy. *Self Concept: A Comparison of Spanish-American, Negro, and Anglo Adolescents Across Ethnic, Sex, and Socioeconomic Variables*. Las Cruces: Clearinghouse on Rural

Education and Small Schools, 1970. ERIC. ED 037 287. Study conducted in New Mexico.

Dolman, Geoffrey, Jr., and Norman S. Kaufman. *Minorities in Higher Education: The Changing Southwest—New Mexico*. Princeton, NJ: College Entrance Examination Board; and Boulder, CO: Western Interstate Commission for Higher Education, 1984. ERIC. ED 276 561. Academic persistence, educational attainment, etc.

Eastern New Mexico University Library. *An Introduction Bibliography of Black Study Resources in Eastern New Mexico Library*. Portales: The Library, 1970.

Fowler, Orin. *Slavery in California and New Mexico. Speech of Mr. Orin Fowler, of Massachusetts, in the House of Representatives, March 11, 1850*. Washington, DC: Buell and Blanchard, Printers, 1850.

Ganaway, Loomis Morton. *New Mexico and the Sectional Controversy, 1846–1861*. Albuquerque: University of New Mexico Press, 1944.

Kustaa, Friedrich Freddy. *A Description and Analysis of the Perspectives on Leadership Effectiveness of African-American Student Leaders at the University of New Mexico: A Qualitative Study*. 1993. ERIC. ED 364 619. Student interviews regarding leadership styles.

Lekson, Stephen H. *Nana's Raid: Apache Warfare in Southern New Mexico, 1881*. El Paso: Texas Western Press, 1987. 9th Cavalry.

Lopez, Andrew. *Minority Groups in New Mexico*. Albuquerque: New Mexico Employment Security Commission, 1969. ERIC. ED 035 457. Socioeconomic data.

Mann, Horace. *Horace Mann's Letters on the Extension of Slavery into California and New Mexico; and on the Duty of congress to provide the trial by Jury for alleged fugitive slaves*. Washington, DC: Buell and Blanchard, 1850.

Mock, Charlotte K. *Bridges: New Mexican Black Women, 1900–1950*. Albuquerque: New Mexico Commission on the Status of Women, 1985.

Murphy, Lawrence R. *Antislavery in the Southwest: William G. Kephart's Mission to New Mexico, 1850–53*. Southwestern Studies Monograph, no. 54. El Paso: Texas Western Press, 1978.

Murray, Betty. *A National Study of Minority Group Barriers to Allied Health Professions Education in the Southwest. Final Report*. San Antonio: Southwest Program Development Corporation, 1975. ERIC. ED 118 297. A two year study conducted in California, Colorado, New Mexico, Oklahoma and Texas.

NAACP 1940–55. General Office File. Civil Rights—Bills. Frederick, MD: University Publications of America, 1993.

NAACP Administrative File. Subject File. Lynching—New Mexico, 1926, 1928. Frederick, MD: University Publications of America, 1986.

Richardson, Barbara J. *Black Directory of New Mexico: Black Pioneers of New Mexico, Documentary and Pictorial History*. Rio Rancho, NM: Panorama Press, 1976.

_____. *Black Pioneers in New Mexico*. Albuquerque: Panorama Press, 1977.

Smith, Truman. *Speech of Mr. Smith, of Conn." On the Bill "To Admit California into the Union, to Establish Territorial Governments for Utah and New Mexico, Making Proposals to Texas for the Establishment of the Western and Northern Boundaries"...Delivered in the Senate of the United States, July 8, 1850*. Washington, DC: Gideon and Company, Printers, 1850. Extension of slavery.

Stegmaier, Mark J. *Texas, New Mexico, and the Compromise of 1850: Boundary Dispute and Sectional Crisis*. Kent, OH: Kent State University Press, 1996.

Tobias, Henry J., and Charles E. Woodhouse. *Minorities and Politics*. Albuquerque: University of New Mexico Press, 1969. Minorities and Albuquerque.

U.S. Commission on Civil Rights. New Mexico State Advisory Committee. *The Civil Rights Status of Minority Groups in Clovis, New Mexico*. n.p.: The Commission, 1969.

U.S. Congress. House of Representatives. House Reports Committee. *Slavery in the Territory of New Mexico*. 36th Cong., 1st sess., 1859–60.

Theses and Dissertations:

Nash, Horace Daniel. "Blacks on the Border: Columbus, New Mexico, 1916–1922." Master's thesis, New Mexico State University, 1988.

_____. "Town and Sword: Black Soldiers in Columbus, New Mexico, in the Early Twentieth Century." Ph.D. diss., Mississippi State University, 1996.

Onwubu, Chukwuemeka. "Black Ideologies and the Sociology of Knowledge: The Public Response to the Protest Thoughts and Teachings of Martin Luther King, Jr. and Malcolm X." Ph.D. diss., Michigan State University, 1975. Albuquerque attitudes.

Spriggs, Haroldie K. "Minority Group Education in New Mexico Prior to 1954." Master's thesis, Howard University, 1967.

Young, Brian A. "The History of the Blacks in New Mexico from the Sixteenth Century through the Nineteenth Century Pioneer Period." Master's thesis, University of New Mexico, 1969.

Black Newspapers:

ALBUQUERQUE

Albuquerque American. Albuquerque. 1896–?

Cornish-Russwurm Chronicle #1. Albuquerque. 1989–1991.

Cornish-Russwurm Chronicle #2. Albuquerque. 1993–199?

Mountain States Recorder. Albuquerque. 193?–19??

New Age. Albuquerque. 1911–1915.

New Mexico State News. Albuquerque. 1950–19??

Southwest Review. Albuquerque. 1922–1932.

Southwestern Plaindealer. Albuquerque. 1924–192?
Western Star. Albuquerque.
 1940–1941.

EL RITO

Pulse. El Rito. 1970–? Interracial
 political and literary publication.

LAS CRUCES

The Blackboard. Las Cruces. 1990.
 Monthly. Black Programs,
 New Mexico State Univer-
 sity.
Harambee. Las Cruces. 1972–1973.
Western Voice. Las Cruces.
 1938–1940.

Other:

Cowboys, Soldiers and Settlers: Blacks in the History of New Mexico. Chaves
 County Historical Society, 1982. Videocassette.

Library of Congress and National Archives. *The General Education Board: The
 Early Southern Program*, microfilm. No. 80.

NAACP 1904–55. General Office File. Labor Cases—New Mexico, 1955.
 Papers of the NAACP. Part 13, NAACP and Labor, 1940–1955. Series A, Subject Files on Labor Conditions and Employment Discrimination, 1940–1955; Reel 12, FR. 0439–0446. Frederick, MD: University Publications of America, 1991. Microform.

"Oral History Interview of Willie and Clara Simms." Colorado Historical Society, 1981. The Sims talk about experiences in Oklahoma, New Mexico and Colorado.

Schools. New Mexico, 1940, 1943. Papers of the NAACP. Part 3, Campaign
 for Educational Equality. Series B, Legal Department and Central Office Records, 1940–1950; Reel 3, FR. 0113–0167. Frederick, MD:
 University Publications of America, 1986. Microform.

North Dakota

Articles:

Anderson, Kathie Ryckman. "Era Bell Thompson: A North Dakota Daughter." *North Dakota History* 49 (Fall 1982). Account of the childhood of an editor for *Ebony*.

Bender, Mike. "Civil Rights: Race and Sex Discrimination in Refusal to Train Correctional Officers Is Not Excused by Contract under North Dakota Human Rights Act." *North Dakota Law Review* 66 (Summer 1990).

Bernson, Sarah L., and Robert J. Eggers. "Black People in South Dakota History." *South Dakota History* 7 (Summer 1977). Also discusses slavery and franchise issues in the Dakota Territory.

Lewis, Earl. "Pioneers of a Different Kind." *Red River Valley Historian* (Winter 1978–79). Traces Blacks moving to the Red River Valley area in 1879.

Lounsberry, C. A. "Early Development of North Dakota." North Dakota State Historical Society Collections, Vol. I (1908).

McDermott, John D. "The Frontier Scout: A View of Fort Rice in 1865." *North Dakota History* 61 (1994).

Otto, Solomon, and John Solomon Otto. "I Played Against 'Satchel' for Three Seasons: Blacks and Whites in the 'Twilight' Leagues." *Journal of Popular Culture* 7 (1974). Solomon Otto of the Dickinson Cowboys.

Roper, Stephanie Abbot. "From Military Forts to 'Nigger Towns': African Americans in North Dakota, 1890–1940." *Heritage of the Great Plains* 27 (Winter 1994).

Sherman, William C. "Ethnic Distribution in Western North Dakota." *North Dakota History* 46 (Winter 1979).

Vyzralek, Frank E. "Murder in Masquerade: A Commentary on Lynching and Mob Violence in North Dakota's Past, 1882–1931." *North Dakota*

History 57 (Winter 1990). Depicts the lynching of a Black man, Charles Thurber.

Books:

Daul, Jennifer, et al. *Racial Minority Groups in North Dakota, 1970–1980: A Statistical Portrait.* North Dakota Census Data Center Report Series, no. 6. Fargo: North Dakota State University, 1986. ERIC. ED 292 604.

NAACP Administrative File. Subject File. Lynching—North Dakota, 1926. Frederick, MD: University Publications of America, 1986.

NAACP Legal File. Cases Supported. Charlie Simpson, 1931–1939. Frederick, MD: University Publications of America, 1988. Murder trial.

Newgard, Thomas, William C. Sherman, and John Guerrero. *African Americans in North Dakota.* Bismark, ND: University of Mary Press, 1994.

Newgard, Thomas, and William Sherman. *Plain Folks: North Dakota Ethnic History.* Fargo: North Dakota State University Press, n.d.

Sherman, William C. *Prairie Mosaic: An Ethnic Atlas of Rural North Dakota.* Fargo: North Dakota Institute for Regional Studies, 1983.

Thompson, Era Bell. *American Daughter.* St. Paul, MN: Minnesota Historical Society Press, 1946; reprinted, 1986. Social life and customs in North Dakota and Iowa from a future editor at *Ebony*.

Torrence, Jackie. *The Importance of Pot Liquor.* August House, 1994. Folk tales.

Thesis:

Harwood, William L. "The Ku Klux Klan in Grand Forks." Honors thesis, University of North Dakota, 1968.

Other:

"Duke Ellington at Fargo, 1940." Book-of-the-Month Records, 1978. Ellington and orchestra play Fargo in 1940. Soundrecording.

Interview, Era Bell Thompson, 16 September 1975. State Historical Society of North Dakota, Oral History Project, Bismarck.

Oklahoma (Indian Territory)

Articles:

Abbott, L. J. "Race Question in Oklahoma." *Independent* 63 (25 July 1907).

————. "Race Question in the Forty-Sixth State." *Independent* 63 (25 February 1907).

Andrews, Thomas F. "Freedmen in Indian Territory: A Post Civil-War Dilemma." *Journal of the West* 4 (June 1965).

"The Anita Hill Chair: A New Chapter in the Long Racial History of the University of Oklahoma College of Law." *Journal of Blacks in Higher Education* 11 (Spring 1996).

"Anita Hill Resumes Teaching Post at University of Oklahoma Law School." *Jet*, 11 September 1995.

"Anita Hill Sabbatical Raises ire of Oklahoma Republicans." *Black Issues in Higher Education* 9 (10 September 1992).

"Anita Hill to Resign as Law Professor at Univ. of Oklahoma." *Jet*, 3 April 1995.

Bagnall, Robert. "An Oklahoma Lynching." *Crisis* 37 (August 1930). Mob attacks jail in Chickasha, Oklahoma, and kill Black teenager Henry Argo in May 1930.

Balyeat, Frank A. "Segregation in the Public Schools of Oklahoma Territory." *Chronicles of Oklahoma* 39 (1961).

Bilger, Burkhard. "The Blacks in Oklahoma." *Oklahoma Today* 44 (March 1994). Stories of resolve and bravery.

————. "My Eyes Have Seen the Glory." *Oklahoma Today* 47 (February 1997). Black towns.

Billington, Monroe Lee. "Black Slavery in Indian Territory: The Ex-Slave Narratives." *Chronicles of Oklahoma* 60 (1982).

————. "Public School Integration in Oklahoma." *Historian* 26 (1964).

Bittle, William Elmer. "The Desegregated All-White Institution...The University of Oklahoma." *Journal of Educational Sociology* 32 (February 1959).

Bittle, William Elmer., and Gilbert L. Geis. "Alfred Charles Sam and an African Return: A Case Study in Negro Despair." *Phylon* 23 (1962). Return to Africa scheme ends in failure.

_____. "Racial Self-fulfillment and the Rise of an All-Negro Community in Oklahoma." *Phylon* 18 (Fall 1957). The establishment and destruction of political power in Boley.

"Black Oklahoma Lawmaker Recalls His Narrow Escape from Federal Building Blast." *Jet*, 29 May 1995.

Blake, Aldrich. "Oklahoma's Klan-Fighting Governor." *Nation*, 3 October 1923.

Bliven, Bruce. "From the Oklahoma Front." *The New Republic*, 17 October 1923. Spotlight on the Klan.

"Blood and Oil." *Survey* 46 (11 June 1921). Racial strife.

Bogle, Lori. "Black Arkansas." *Chronicles of Oklahoma* 72 (Summer 1994). As civil rights in Oklahoma deteriorated, Blacks look to Oklahoma.

Bond, Horace Mann. "Langston Plan: Curriculum for Negro Teacher-Training Schools." *School and Society* 20 (27 December 1924).

Bonner, Mary Winstead, and B. R. Belden. "Comparative Study of the Performance of Negro Seniors of Oklahoma City High Schools on the Wechsler Adult Intelligence Scale and the Peabody Picture Vocabulary Test." *Journal of Negro Education* 39 (Fall 1970).

Brown, Karen F. "The Oklahoma Eagle: A Study of Black Press Survival." *Howard Journal of Communications* 1 (June 1988).

Brown, Thomas Elton. "Seminole Indian Agents, 1842–1874." *Chronicles of Oklahoma* 51 (1973).

Brown, Willis L., and Janie M. McNeal Brown. "Langston University." *Chronicles of Oklahoma* 74 (Spring 1996). Profile of the school created in 1897.

Burbank, Garin. "Agrarian Radicals and their Opponents: Political Conflict in Southern Oklahoma, 1910–1924." *Journal of American History* 58 (June 1971). Klan activities.

Busby, Mark. "Ralph Ellison." Chapter in *Updating the Literary West*. Fort Worth: Texas Christian University Press, 1997.

Carney, George O. "All Black Towns." *Chronicles of Oklahoma* 69 (Summer 1991). Reviews the "bold experiment."

_____. "Historic Resources of Oklahoma's All-Black Towns: A Preservation Profile." *Chronicles of Oklahoma* 69 (Summer 1991).

Casey, Orben J. "Governor Lee Cruce, White Supremacy and Capital Punishment, 1911–1915." *Chronicles of Oklahoma* 52 (Winter 1974–1975). Pro-Black actions by a white-supremacist governor.

Chapman, Berlin B. "Freedmen and the Oklahoma Lands." *Southwestern Social Science Quarterly* 29 (September 1948).

Chase, Henry. "Boley's Bank Robbed!" *American Visions*, December 1994.

_____. "Sooner or Later: Touring Black Oklahoma." *American Visions*, December-January 1997. Travel information.

"Chief Sam and the Negro Exodus." *Literary Digest* 48 (21 March 1914).

"Constitution Week in Oklahoma." *Literary Digest* 79 (13 October 1923). Klan activities.

Crabb, Beth. "May 1930: White Man's Justice for a Black Man's Crime." *Journal of Negro History* 75 (Winter, Spring 1990). Mob violence in the deaths of George Hughes and Sam Johnson of Texas and Henry Argo of Oklahoma.

"Crime." *Crisis* 11 (February 1916). Contains account of armed Blacks rescuing two others from a lynching in Muskogee, Oklahoma.

Crockett, Norman L. "Witness to History: Washington Visits Boley." *Chronicles of Oklahoma* 67 (Winter 1989). Booker T. Washington's two visits to Boley.

Crouch, Stanley. "The Oklahoma Kid." *The New Republic*, 9 May 1994. Reflection on writer Ralph Ellison.

Dann, Martin. "From Sodom to the Promised Land: E. P. McCabe and the Movement for Oklahoma Colonization." *Kansas Historical Quarterly* 40 (Autumn 1974). Examines McCabe's role in that effort.

"Democracy or Invisible Empire?" *Current Opinion* 75 (November 1923). The Klan in Oklahoma.

Derrick, W. Edwin, and J. Hershal Barnhill. "With 'All' Deliberate Speed: Desegregation of the Public Schools in Oklahoma City and Tulsa, 1954 to 1972." *Red River Valley Historical Review* 6 (Spring 1981).

Dervarics, Charles. "Langston's Role Threatened in Oklahoma Post-Adams Debate." *Black Issues in Higher Education* 6 (25 May 1989). University under scrutiny.

Douglas, W. A. S. "Ku Klux." *American Mercury* 13 (March 1928).

Dulan-Wilson, Gloria. "Douglass High School of Oklahoma City: A Century of Excellence." *Crisis* 98 (October 1991).

Edmunds, Edwin R. "The Myrdalian Thesis: Rank Order of Discrimination." *Phylon* 15 (Summer 1954). Study of the Myrdalian hypothesis in Texas and Oklahoma indicates it is inaccurate to use in the Southwest.

Ellison, Ralph. "On Becoming a Writer." *Commentary* 38 (1964). Observations on growing up Black between W.W.I and the Depression.

"Fisher, Ada." *Jet*, 13 November 1995. Obituary of Ada (Sipuel) Fisher, who integrated the University of Oklahoma Law School.

Forbes, G. "Part Played by Indian Slavery in Removal of Tribes to Oklahoma." *Chronicles of Oklahoma* 9 (June 1938).

Frank, Kenny A. "The California Overland Express Through Indian Territory and Western Arkansas." *Arkansas Historical Quarterly* 33 (Spring 1974). A traveler observes surroundings, including slavery.

Frost, Stanley. "Behind the White Hoods: The Regeneration of Oklahoma." *Outlook* 135 (21 November 1923).

_____. "The Klan, the King, and a Revolution: The Regeneration of Okla-
homa. *Outlook* 135 (28 November 1923).

_____. "Night Riding Reformers: The Regeneration of Oklahoma." *Out-
look* 135 (14 November 1923).

_____. "The Oklahoma Regicides Act." *Outlook* 135 (7 November 1923).

Goode, Stephen. "Picture Profile." *Insight* 12 (16 December 1996). The election of Black conservative J. C. Watts from rural Oklahoma.

"Grandfather Clause in Oklahoma." *Outlook* 95 (20 August 1910).

Graves, Carl R. "The Right to be Served: Oklahoma City's Lunch Counter
Sit-ins, 1958–1964." *Chronicles of Oklahoma* 59 (Summer 1981).

Grimshaw, Allen D. "Three Major Cases of Colour Violence in the United
States." *Race* 5 (July 1963). Tulsa riot of 1921 is one of the studies.

Grinde, Donald, and Quintard Taylor. "Red vs. Black: Conflict and Accommodation in the Post Civil War Indian Territory, 1865–1907." *American
Indian Quarterly* 8 (Summer 1984).

Guess, John F., Jr. "Featured Politico: Julius Caeser (J. C.) Watts, Candidate,
4th Congressional District, Oklahoma." *National Minority Politics* 11
(November 1994).

Gwaltney, William W. "The Story of the Seminole-Negro Indian Scouts." *Lest
We Forget* 4 (October 1996).

Halliburton, Janet. "Black Slavery in the Creek Nation." *Chronicles of Oklahoma* 56 (1978).

Halliburton, R., Jr. "Black Slave Control in the Cherokee Nation." *Journal of
Ethnic Studies* 3 (1975).

_____. "Origins of Black Slavery among the Cherokees." *Chronicles of
Oklahoma* 52 (1974–1975).

_____. "The Tulsa Race War of 1921." *Journal of Black Studies* 2 (Sep-
tember 1972).

Hamilton, Kenneth Marvin. "The Origins and Early Developments of Langston,
Oklahoma." *Journal of Negro History* 62 (July 1977).

_____. "Townsite Speculation and the Origin of Boley, Oklahoma."
Chronicles of Oklahoma 55 (1977).

Haslam, G. "Oil Town Rumble: The Young Men of Taft: Conflict Between
Residents and Negro Football Players." *Nation* 221 (13 September
1975).

Hawkins, Homer C. "Trends in Black Migration from 1863 to 1960." *Phylon*
34 (June 1973). Black migration to southwestern U.S., then to Oklahoma Territory, then north.

Henslick, Harry E. "Abraham Jefferson Seay: Governor of Oklahoma Territory,
1892–1893." *Chronicles of Oklahoma* 53 (1975). Seay faced opposition when he attempted to extend civil rights to Blacks.

Hill, Mozell C. "The All-Negro Communities of Oklahoma: The Natural History of a Social Movement." *Journal of Negro History* 31 (July 1946).

Hill, Mozell C., and Eugene Richards. "Demographic Trends of the Negro in
Oklahoma." *Southwestern Journal* 2 (Winter 1946).

Hill, Mozell C., and Thelma D. Ackins. "Culture of a Contemporary All-Negro Community: *Langston University Bulletin* (July 1943).

Hubbell, John T. "The Desegregation of the University of Oklahoma, 1946–1950." *Journal of Negro History* 57 (October 1972).

————. "Some Reactions to the Desegregation of the University of Oklahoma, 1946–1950." *Phylon* 34 (June 1973).

"Jack, the Klan-Fighter in Oklahoma." *Literary Digest* 79 (20 October 1923).

Jones, Joyce. "High Wattage." *Black Enterprise*, March 1999. Congressman J. C. Watts.

Krogman, Wilton Marion. "The Racial Composition of the Seminole Indians of Florida and Oklahoma." *Journal of Negro History* 19 (1934).

"Ku Klux Klan in Oklahoma." *Current Opinion* 75 (November 1923).

Lammen, A. "Chief Sam en Zijn 'Back-to-Africa' Beweging [Chief Sam and his 'Back-to-Africa' Movement]." *Spiegel Historiael* [Netherlands] 14 (1979).

Langley, J. Ayo. "Chief Sam's African Movement and Race Consciousness in West Africa." *Phylon* 32 (Summer 1971). Recruits for this 1914–1916 "back-to-Africa" movement came primarily from Oklahoma.

Larsen, Jonathan Z. "Tulsa Burning." *Civilization: the Magazine of the Library of Congress* 4 (February 1997).

"Legal Lynching Disapproved." *International Juridical Association Monthly Bulletin* 1 (October 1932). Reversal of convictions of Blacks in Oklahoma and Missouri.

Lehman, Paul. "The Edwards Family and Black Entrepreneurial Success." *Chronicles of Oklahoma* 64 (Winter 1986/1987).

"Lessons of Tulsa." *Outlook* 128 (15 June 1921). Tulsa racial strife.

Lewallen, Kenneth A. "'Chief' Alfred C. Sam" Black Nationalism on the Great Plains, 1913–1914." *Journal of the West* 16 (January 1977).

Littlefield, Daniel F., Jr., and Ann Littlefield. "The Beams Family: Free Blacks in Indian Territory." *Journal of Negro History* 61 (January 1976). The antebellum family faced murder, enslavement, and forced flight to Mexico.

Littlefield, Daniel F., Jr., and Lonnie E. Underhill. "Black Dreams and 'Free' Homes: The Oklahoma Territory, 1891–1894." *Phylon* 34 (December 1973). Efforts by Blacks to make Oklahoma a haven.

————. "The 'Crazy Snake Uprising' of 1909: A Red, Black, or White Affair?" *Arizona and the West* 20 (1978).

————. "Negro Marshals in the Indian Territory." *Journal of Negro History* 54 (April 1971).

————. "Slave 'Revolt' in the Cherokee Nation, 1842." *American Indian Quarterly* 3 (Summer 1977).

Logue, Barbara J. "Race Differences in Long-Term Disability: Middle-Aged and Older American Indians, Blacks, and Whites in Oklahoma." *Social Science Journal* 27 (1990).

"The Lynching at Wewoka." *Crisis* 7 (January 1914). In November 1913, John Cudjo lynched in Seminole County, Oklahoma.

Malcomson, Scott L. "Having Their Say: Residents of Boley, Oklahoma Describe Conditions in the All-Black Town." *The New Yorker*, 29 April 1996.

"Martial Law in Oklahoma." *Outlook* 135 (26 September 1923). Klan activity.

"Masked Floggers of Tulsa." *Literary Digest* 78 (22 September 1923). Klan activity.

McAuley, William J. "History, Race, and Attachment to Place Among Elders in the Rural All-Black Towns of Oklahoma." *Journals of Gerontology-Series B* 53 (January 1998).

McLoughlin, William G. "The Choctaw Slave Burning: A Crisis in Mission Work Among the Indians." *Journal of the West* 13 (January 1974). Black slave commits suicide over a murder and mistress is burned at the stake.

_____. "Indian Slaveholders and Presbyterian Missionaries, 1837–1861." *Church History* 42 (1973). How missionaries converted the Native People.

_____. "Red Indians, Black Slavery and White Racism: America's Slaveholding Indians." *American Quarterly* 26 (1974). Complexities of relationships between Blacks and their Indian owners.

Mellinger, Philip. "Discrimination and Statehood in Oklahoma." *Chronicles of Oklahoma* 49 (Autumn 1971).

Menig, Harry. "Woody Guthrie: The Oklahoma Years, 1912–1929." *Chronicles of Oklahoma* 53 (1975). How the Black community in Okemah affected Guthrie's life.

Meredith, Howard L. "Agrarian Socialism and the Negro in Oklahoma, 1900–1918." *Labor History* 11 (Summer 1970). Relationships between Blacks, the Socialist Party, and the 1910 Grandfather Clause.

Moon, F. D. "Higher Education and Desegregation in Oklahoma." *Journal of Negro Education* 27 (Summer 1958).

_____. "Negro Public College in Kentucky and Oklahoma." *Journal of Negro Education* 31 (Summer 1962).

Moses, V., et al. "A Thirty-Year Review of Maternal Mortality in Oklahoma, 1950 through 1979." *American Journal of Obstetrics and Gynecology* 157 (November 1987).

"Move to Endow Anita Hill Professorship at Oklahoma." *Black Issues in Higher Education* 9 (18 June 1992).

Mundende, D. Chongo. "Black Immigration to Canada." *Chronicles of Oklahoma* 76 (Fall 1998). Near the beginning of the 20th century, Black Oklahomans immigrated to Canada for opportunities

"The Negro in Oklahoma." *Outlook* 95 (18 June 1910).

Neilson, John C. "Indian Masters, Black Slaves: An Oral History of the Civil War in Indian Territory." *Panhandle-Plains Historical Review* 65 (1992).

Nelson, Llewellyn. "The K.K.K. for Boredom." *The New Republic*, 14 January 1925. Oklahoma and the Klan.

Neuringer, Sheldon. "Governor Walton's War on the Ku Klux Klan: An Episode in Oklahoma History, 1923–1924." *Chronicles of Oklahoma* 45 (Summer 1967). Examines why the popular governor eventually turned against the Klan.

"New Chance for a Black Man: Poverty and Decay Were Destroying Boley, a Negro Town in Oklahoma: Its New Industry May Save it." *Business Week,* 9 August 1969.

N'Namdi, Carmen A. "A Play in Three Acts: A Town You Could Bank On." *Learning* 19 (February 1991). Excerpt of a play about Boley to assist students in learning about Black history.

Norton, Wesley. "Religious Newspapers in Antebellum Texas." *Southwestern Historical Quarterly* 769 (1975). Most white religious newspapers supported slavery and secession.

O'Beirne, Kate Walsh. "Bread and Circuses." *National Review*, 21 April 1997. Role of Black conservative congressman J. C. Watts of Oklahoma and Jim Talent of Missouri and bi-partisan support of their proposed American Community Renewal Act.

"Okla. Youth Buried, KKK Recruiting Mission Fails." *Jet*, 21 February 1980.

"Oklahoma City: Separate and Equal." *The Atlantic* 268 (1 September 1991). Desegregation and resegregation of Oklahoma City schools.

"Oklahoma Grandfather Clause Annulled." *Outlook* 110 (30 June 1915).

"Oklahoma Kingless, Not Klanless." *Literary Digest* 79 (8 December 1923).

"The Oklahoma Lynching." *Crisis* 2 (August 1911). Governor's letter about the lynching of a Black woman and her child in Okemah.

"Oklahoma State Makes History by Choosing First Black Coach in Prestigious Big Eight Conference." *Jet*, 9 January 1995.

Olson, Carol, and Joe Hagy. "Achieving Social Justice: An Examination of Oklahoma's Response to Adams v. Richardson." *Journal of Negro Education* 59 (Spring 1990).

Perdue, Theda. "Cherokee Planters, Black Slaves, and African Colonization." *Chronicles of Oklahoma* 60 (Fall 1982).

Perry, Thelma Ackiss. "The Education of Negroes in Oklahoma." *Journal of Negro Education* 16 (Summer 1947).

_____, and Julius H. Hughes. "Educational Desegregation in Oklahoma." *Journal of Negro Education* 25 (Summer 1956).

Pew, Thomas W., Jr. "Boley, Oklahoma: Trial in American Apartheid." *American West* 17 (November-December 1980).

Phillips, Andrew. "Black, Proud and Republican." *Maclean's*, 11 August 1997. Profile of J. C. Watts, Jr., conservative member of Congress.

Phillips, Waldo B. "Jim Noble: Oklahoma's Negro Governor." *Phylon* 20 (Spring 1959).

Prentice, Frances W. "Oklahoma Race Riot." *Scribner's Magazine* 90 (April 1931).

Rampp, Lary C. "Negro Troop Activity in Indian Territory, 1863–1865." *Chronicles of Oklahoma* 47 (1969). Includes exploits of the 1st Kansas Colored Volunteer Infantry Regiment.

"Rep. Watts' Ex-College Coach lauds Him for Making It Big in D.C." *Jet*, 12 June 1995. Oklahoma politics.

Richard, Eugene Scott. "Negro Higher Education and Professional Education in Oklahoma." *Journal of Negro Education* 17 (1948).

————. "Trends of Negro Life in Oklahoma as Reflected by Census Reports." *Journal of Negro History* 33 (1948).

Robbins, Louise S. "Racism and Censorship in Cold War Oklahoma: The Case of Ruth W. Brown and the Bartlesville Public Library." *Southwestern Historical Quarterly* 100 (1996).

Roberson, Jerri. "Edward McCabe and the Langston Experiment." *Chronicles of Oklahoma* 51 (Fall 1973).

Rogers, Patrick. "Calling His Play." *People Weekly*, 24 March 1997. Profile of conservative congressman J. C. Watts, Jr., his admission to having an illegitimate daughter, his failure to pay some income taxes, and his involvement with welfare reform.

Savage, W. Sherman. "Jazz and the American Frontier: Turner Webb, and the Oklahoma City Blue Devils." *Journal of the West* 28 (July 1989).

————. "The Role of Negro Soldiers in Protecting the Indian Territory from Intruders." *Journal of Negro History* 36 (1951).

Shepard, R. Bruce. "The Origins of the Oklahoma Black Migration to the Canadian Plaines." *Canadian Journal of History* 23 (April 1988).

————. "Plain Racism: The Reaction Against Oklahoma Black Immigration to the Canadian Plains." *Prairie Forum* 10 (Autumn 1985).

"Six Women." *Crisis* 8 (May 1914). Includes a Black woman lynched in Wagoner, Oklahoma.

Smith, Joy McDougal. "Elliott Memorial Academy." *Chronicles of Oklahoma* 72 (Fall 1994). Boarding school for Choctaw Freedmen and other Black children.

Spivey, Donald. "Crisis on a Black Campus: Langston University and Its Struggle for Survival." *Chronicles of Oklahoma* 59 (1981–1982).

St. John, Craig, and Nancy A. Bates. "Racial Composition and Neighborhood Evaluation." *Social Science Research* 19 (March 1990). Focus on Oklahoma City.

Sullins, William S., and Paul Parsons. "Roscoe Dunjee: Crusading Editor of Oklahoma's Black Dispatch, 1915–1955." *JQ: Journalism Quarterly* 69 (Spring 1992).

Tolson, Arthur L. "Black Towns of Oklahoma." *Black Scholar* 1 (April 1972).

Traub, James. "Oklahoma City: Separate and Equal." *Atlantic* 268 (1 September 1991). Desegregation of the city schools during the 1970s and their resegregation.

Troper, Harold M. "The Creek-Negroes of Oklahoma and Canadian Immigration, 1901–1911." *Canadian Historical Review* 53 (September 1972).

"Tulsa." *Nation* 112 (15 June 1921). Racial strife.

"Tulsa Race Riots." *Independent* 105 (7 June 1921).

"University of Oklahoma and the Ku Klux Klan." *School and Society* 16 (7 October 1922).

Waldman, Amy. "The GOP's Great Black Hope." *Washington Monthly*, October 1996. Focus on J. C. Watts, Jr., Black conservative Republican from Oklahoma, and his proposed American Community Renewal Act.

Washington, Booker T. "Boley: A Negro Town in the West." *Outlook* 88 (4 January 1908).

White, Walter F. "Eruption of Tulsa." *Nation* 112 (29 June 1921). Tulsa race riot.

————. "A Town Owned by Negroes." *World's Work* 14 (July 1907).

Whitson, Edward, and Paul A. Brinker. "The Housing of Negroes in Oklahoma." *Phylon* 19 (Spring 1958).

Williams, Nudie E. "Bass Reeves: Black Lawman on Trial." *Chronicles of Oklahoma* 68 (Summer 1990).

————. "George Napier Perkins." *Chronicles of Oklahoma* 70 (Winter 1993). Civil rights advocate known as the "African Lion."

Wilson, L. D., ed. "Reminiscences of Jim Tomm." *Chronicles of Oklahoma* 44 (Fall 1966). Born a slave in 1859, Tomm describes his life, including observations of Indian culture.

Wilson, Walt. "Freedmen in Indian Territory During Reconstruction." *Chronicles of Oklahoma* 49 (Summer 1971).

Woodward, James E. "Vernon: An All Negro Town in Southeastern Oklahoma." *Negro History Bulletin* 27 (1964). Town founded in 1911.

Books:

Aldrich, Gene. *Black Heritage of Oklahoma*. Edmond, OK: Thompson Book and Supply Company, 1973.

Bailey, Minnie Thomas. *Reconstruction in Indian Territory: The Story of Avarice, Discrimination, and Opportunism*. Port Washington, NY: Kennikat Press, 1972.

Baker, T. Lindsay, and Julie P. Baker, eds. *The WPA Oklahoma Slave Narratives*. Norman: University of Oklahoma Press, 1996. Interviews of former slaves.

Bittle, William Elmer, and Gilbert L. Geis. *The Longest Way Home: Chief Alfred C. Sam's Back-to-Africa Movement*. Detroit: Wayne State University Press, 1964.

Brill, H. E., comp. *Story of the Methodist Episcopal Church in Oklahoma*. Oklahoma City: Oklahoma City University Press, 1939.

Burton, Arthur T. *Black, Red, and Deadly: Black and Indian Gunfighters of the Indian Territory, 1870–1907*. Austin: Eakin Press, 1991.

Calhoun, Sharon C., and Billie J. English. *Oklahoma Heritage*. Maysville, OK: Holt, Calhoun & Clark Publishers, 1984.

Campbell, J. B. *Campbell's Abstract of Creek Freedman Census Cards and Index*. Muskogee: Phoenix Job Printing Company, 1915.

Cross, George Lynn. *Blacks in White Colleges: Oklahoma's Landmark Cases*. Norman: University of Oklahoma Press, 1975.

Davis, James P. *Success Story: Negro Farmers*. Little Rock: U.S. Department of Agriculture, 1952. U.S. Production and Marketing Administration booklet covering seventeen states.

Ellsworth, Scott. *Death in a Promised Land: The Tulsa Race Riot of 1921*. Baton Rouge: Louisiana State University Press, 1982.

Estes, Mary. *Bass Reeves: Deputy U.S. Marshal 1873–1902*, ed. Mary Williamson. Houston: Larksdale, 1997.

Everett, Syble Ethel Byrd. *Adventures With Life: An Autobiography of a Distinguished Negro Citizen*. Boston: Meador Publishing, 1945. Recounts being raised in Oklahoma where she became a teacher. Also tells of experiences while a student at the University of Utah.

Federal Writers' Project. *Oklahoma and Mississippi Narratives*. Westport, CT: Greenwood Publishing Company, 1972. Slave narratives.

Federal Writers' Project. Work Projects Administration. *Slaves Narratives: A Folk History of Slavery in the United States from Interviews with Former Slaves*. Vol. 14, *Oklahoma*. Washington, DC: Work Projects Administration, 1941.

Fisher, Ada Lois Sipuel, and Danny Goble. *A Matter of Black and White: The Autobiography of Ada Lois Sipuel Fisher*. Norman: University of Oklahoma Press, 1982; reprinted, 1996.

Flickinger, Robert Elliott. *The Choctaw Freedmen and the Story of Oak Hill Industrial Academy, Valliant, McCurtain County, Oklahoma, Now Called the Alice Lee Elliott Memorial; Including the Early History of the Five civilized Tribes of Indian Territory, the Presbytery of Kiamichi, Synod of Canadian, and the Bible in the Free Schools of the American Colonies, but Suppressed in France, Previous to the American and French Revolutions*. Pittsburgh: The Presbyterian Board of Missions for Freedmen, 1914.

Franklin, Jimmie Lewis. *The Blacks in Oklahoma*. Norman: University of Oklahoma Press, 1982.

————. *Journey Toward Hope: A History of Blacks in Oklahoma*. Norman: University of Oklahoma Press, 1982.

Gaskin, J. M. *Black Baptists in Oklahoma*. Oklahoma City: Messenger, 1992.

Gates, Eddy. *They Came Searching: How Blacks Sought the Promised Land in Tulsa*. El Cajon, CA: Sunbelt, 1997. Race relations in Black frontier and pioneer life.

Halliburton, R., Jr. *Red Over Black: Black Slavery among the Cherokee Indians*. Contributions in Afro-American and African Studies, no. 27. Westport, CT: Greenwood Press, 1977.

_____. *The Tulsa Race War of 1921*. San Francisco: R&E Research Associates, 1975.

Hendricks, Leo E. *Unmarried Adolescent Fathers: Problems They Encounter and the Ways They Cope With Them: The Tulsa, Oklahoma Sample, Final Report*. Washington, DC: Mental Health Research and Development Center, Institute for Urban Affairs and Research, Howard University, 1979.

Knight, Thomas. *Sunset on Utopian Dreams: An Experiment of Black Separatism on the American Frontier*. Washington, DC: University Press of America, 1977.

Langston University Diamond Anniversary Founders Week. Langston: Langston University Press, 1972.

Littlefield, Daniel F., Jr. *The Cherokee Freedmen: From Emancipation to American Citizenship*. Contributions to Afro-American and African Studies, no. 40. Westport, CT: Greenwood Press, 1978.

Luper, Clara. *Behold the Walls*. Oklahoma City: Jim Wire, 1979. Civil rights and rights workers.

McBee, William D. *The Oklahoma Revolution*. Oklahoma City: Modern Publishers, 1956. Governor John Walton and the Klan.

Memorial and Other Papers of Caesar F. Simmons, Formerly Postmaster at Boley, Okfuskee County, Okla., to the 69th Congress of the United States. Boley: n.p., 1933.

Mulroy, Kevin: *Freedom on the Border: The Seminole Maroons in Florida, the Indian Territory, Coahuila, and Texas*. Lubbock: Texas Tech University Press, 1993.

Murray, Betty. *A National Study of Minority Group Barriers to Allied Health Professions Education in the Southwest. Final Report*. San Antonio: Southwest Program Development Corporation, 1975. ERIC. ED 118 297. A two year study conducted in California, Colorado, New Mexico, Oklahoma and Texas.

NAACP Administrative File. Financial Papers. Tulsa, Oklahoma, Riot Fund, 1921. Frederick, MD: University Publications of America.

NAACP Administrative File. Subject File—Discrimination. Voting, Oklahoma, 1928. Frederick, MD: University Publications of America, 1986.

NAACP Administrative File. Subject File—Lynching—Oklahoma, 1914–1936. Frederick, MD: University Publications of America, 1986.

NAACP Branch Files. Oklahoma State Conference, 1931–1939. Frederick, MD: University Publications of America, 1991. Civil Rights.

NAACP Branch Files. Oklahoma State Conference, Feb.–Nov. 1933. Frederick, MD: University Publications of America, 1986.

NAACP Legal File. Cases Supported—Lane vs. Wilson, 1934–1940, Undated, News Clippings. Frederick, MD: University Publications of America, 1986.

National Urban League. Community Relations Project. *Report of the Health Consultant for Oklahoma City, Oklahoma.* Oklahoma City: Council of Social Welfare, 1946.

_____. *Study of the Social and Economic Conditions of the Negro Population of Tulsa, Oklahoma.* Tulsa: Tulsa Council of Social Agencies, 1946.

_____. *A Study of the Social and Economic Conditions of the Negro Population of Oklahoma City, Oklahoma.* Oklahoma City: National Urban League, 1945.

_____. *A Study of the Social and Economic Conditions of the Negro Population of Tulsa, Oklahoma, Conducted for the Tulsa Council of Social Agencies by the National Urban League, Community Relations Project: J. Harvey Kerns, Survey Director.* Tulsa: National Urban League, 1946.

Page, Jo Ann Curls. *Index to the Cherokee Freedmen Enrollment Cards of the Dawes Commission, 1901–1906.* Bowie, MD: Heritage Books, 1995.

Parrish, Mary E. *Events of the Tulsa Disaster.* Chicago: Third World Press, 1992.

Patterson, Zella I. Black, and Lynette L. Wert. *Churches of Langston.* Norman: University of Oklahoma Press, 1979; reprinted, Oklahoma City: Western Heritage Books, 1982.

_____. *Langston University: A History.* Norman: University of Oklahoma Press, 1979; reprinted, 1993.

Perdue, Theda. *Slavery and the Evolution of Cherokee Society, 1548–1866.* Knoxville, TN: University of Tennessee Press, 1979; reprinted, Knoxville, TN: University of Tennessee Press, 1988.

Rader, Brian F. *The Political Outsiders: Blacks and Indians in a Rural Oklahoma County.* San Francisco: R&E Research Associates, 1978. Blacks, Native Americans and politics in McIntosh County.

Rampp, Lary C., and Donald L. Rampp. *The Civil War in the Indian Territory.* Austin: Presidial Press, 1975.

Randall, Lawanda. *Nelson Jackson-Cowboy.* Washington, DC: Directions, Production Services, Inc., 1997. Juvenile. Current cowboy traced historically.

Rawick, George P., ed. *The American Slave: A Complete Autobiography.* Westport, CT: Greenwood Publishing Company, 1972. Transcriptions of narratives for the 1936–1938 Federal Writers' Project. Vol. 8.

_____. *The American Slave*, supplement, Series 1, Vol. 12, *The Oklahoma Narratives.* Westport, CT: Greenwood Press, 1979.

Reese, Linda Williams. *Women of Oklahoma, 1890–1920.* Norman: University of Oklahoma Press, 1997. Profiles some minority women.

Salerno, Dan, Kim Hooper, and Ellen Baxter. *Hardship in the Heartland: Homelessness in Eight U.S. Cities.* New York: Community Service Society of New York, Institute for Social Welfare Research, 1984. Tulsa is one of the cities.

Shepard, R. Bruce. *Deemed Unsuitable: Blacks from Oklahoma Move to the Canadian Prairies in Search of Equality in the Early 20ᵗʰ Century, Only to Find Racism in Their New Home.* Toronto: Umbrella Press, 1997. Blacks in Oklahoma and Saskatchewan.

Smallwood, James M. *Crossroads Oklahoma: The Black Experience in Oklahoma.* Stillwater, OK: Crossroads Oklahoma Project, Oklahoma State University, 1981.

Smith, Leon E. *Hidden Heroes on the Checkerboard Plains: All Black Town's Bank Trap Terminated Notorious Bandits...The Pretty Boy Floyd Gang.* Detroit: Diversified, 1980.

_____. *High Noon at the Boley Corral (An Autobiographic Documentary).* Detroit: The Author, 1980. Confrontation with Pretty Boy Floyd gang.

A Study of the Social and Economic Conditions of the Negro Population of Oklahoma City, Oklahoma. New York: National Urban League, Community Relations Project, 1945,

A Study of the Social and Economic Conditions of the Negro Population of Tulsa, Oklahoma. Tulsa: National Urban League, Community Relations Project, 1946.

Teall, Kaye M., ed. *Black History in Oklahoma: A Resource Book.* Oklahoma City: Oklahoma City Public Schools, 1971.

Tolson, Arthur L. *The Black Oklahomans, a History: 1541–1972.* New Orleans: Edwards Printing Company, 1973.

Tucker, Howard A. *History of Governor Walton's War on Ku Klux Klan, the Invisible Empire.* Oklahoma City: Southwest Publishing, 1923.

Walton-Raji, Angela Y. *Black Indian Genealogy Research: African-American Ancestors among the Five Civilized Tribes.* Bowie, MD: Heritage Books, 1993.

Washington, Nathaniel Jason. *Historical Development of the Negro in Oklahoma.* Tulsa: Dexter Publishing Company, 1948.

Williams, Lee E., and Lee E. Williams III. *Anatomy of Four Race Riots: Racial Conflict in Knoxville, Elaine (Ark.), Tulsa, and Chicago.* Jackson, MI: University and College Press of Mississippi, 1972. Riots following W.W.I.

Wilson, Jay Jay, and Ron Wallace. *Black Wallstreet: A Lost Dream.* Tulsa: Black Wallstreet Publishing Company, 1992.

Witcher, Walter C. *The Reign of Terror in Oklahoma, a Detailed Account of the Klan's Barbarous Practices and Brutal Outrages Against Individuals; its Control Over Judges and Juries and Governor Walton's Heroic Fight, Including a General Exposure of Klan Secrets, Sham and Hypocrisy.* Fort Worth: Witcher, 1923.

Theses and Dissertations:

Alexander, Charles C. "Invisible Empire in the Southwest: The Ku Klux Klan in Texas, Louisiana, Oklahoma, and Arkansas, 1920–1930." Ph.D. diss., University of Texas, 1962.

Anderson, Edison H., Sr. "The Historical Development of Music in the Negro Secondary Schools of Oklahoma and at Langston University." Ph.D. diss., State University of Iowa, 1957. From 1878 to 1954.

Anderson, William E. "The Reading Interest of 347 Negro High School Pupils, Dunbar High School, Okmulgee, Oklahoma." Ed.D. thesis, University of Northern Colorado, 1943.

_____. "A Study of the Personality Characteristics of 153 Negro Pupils, Dunbar High School, Okmulgee, Oklahoma." Ed.D. thesis, University of Northern Colorado, 1944.

Ashley, Velma D. "A History of Boley, Oklahoma." Master's thesis, Kansas State College, 1940.

Bagley, Asa W. "The Negro of Oklahoma." Master's thesis, University of Oklahoma, 1926.

Baker, Ben. "Some Aspects of Segregation Law in Oklahoma." Master's thesis, University of Tulsa, 1952.

Baker, June A. "Patterns of Black Residential Segregation in Oklahoma City, 1890–1960." Master's thesis, University of Oklahoma, 1970.

Bateman, Rebecca Belle. "'We're Still Here': History, Kinship, and Group Identity Among the Seminole Freedmen of Oklahoma." Ph.D. diss., Johns Hopkins University, 1991.

Beeson, Ronald Max. "Desegregation and Affirmative Action in Higher Education in Oklahoma: A Historical Case Study." Ph.D. diss., Oklahoma State University, 1986.

Bell, J. D. "A Study of a Negro City." Master's thesis, University of Kansas, 1930. Boley, Oklahoma.

Bond, Jon. "The Impact of Judicial Policy in a Local Community: School Desegregation in Oklahoma City." Master's thesis, Oklahoma State University, 1973.

Bonner, Mary Winstead. "A Comparative Study of the Performance of Negro Seniors of Oklahoma City High Schools on the Wechsler Adult Intelligence Scale and the Peabody Picture Vocabulary Test." Ed.D. thesis, Oklahoma State University, 1968.

Brown, Bobby Joe. "The Relationship of Selected Biographical and Psychometric Characteristics for Disadvantaged Adolescent Females to Success in a Compensatory Education Program for Office Occupations." Thesis, University of Oklahoma, 1973. Vocational education of women of Guthrie.

Burke, Francis D. "A Survey of the Negro Community of Tulsa, Oklahoma." Master's thesis, University of Oklahoma, 1936.

Cayton, Leonard Bernard. "A History of Black Public Education in Oklahoma." Ed.D. thesis, University of Oklahoma, 1976.

Christian, James Earl. "A Study of Policies and Practices Which Demonstrate a Commitment to the Achievement of Racial Integration in Selected Oklahoma High Schools." Ed.D. thesis, University of Oklahoma, 1979.

Clark, Carter Blue. "A History of the Ku Klux Klan in Oklahoma." Ph.D. diss., University of Oklahoma, 1976.

Clark, Karen Marie Scott. "The Contributions of African-American Women to Education in Oklahoma." Ph.D. diss., Oklahoma State University, 1996.

Clubb, Inez. "A History of the Ku Klux Klan in Oklahoma from 1920 to the Present." Master's thesis, Oklahoma State University, 1941.

Coleman, Annie Laurie. "Some Educational and Social Effects of Closing Negro High Schools in Oklahoma." Ed.D. thesis, Oklahoma State University, 1968.

Coleman, John W. "Criteria for Evaluating a Program of Education for Professional Workers in Oklahoma Metropolitan Negro Baptist Churches." Ph.D. diss., Oklahoma A&M University, 1956.

Crossley, Mildred M. "A History of the Negro Schools of Oklahoma City, Oklahoma." Master's thesis, University of Oklahoma, 1939.

Cudjoe, Freddie Foshe. "Black Student Dropout Rate and the Racial Composition of the School." Thesis, University of Oklahoma, 1974. School integration in Oklahoma.

Davis, Elmyra Richardson. "A Comparative Study of Langston University Freshmen Who Graduated from Integrated High Schools and Those from Predominantly Negro High Schools." Ed.D. thesis, University of Oklahoma, 1970.

Elahi, Larry. "A History of Boley, Oklahoma, to 1915." Master's thesis, University of Chicago, 1968.

Estes, Mary. "An Historical Survey of Lynchings in Oklahoma and Texas." Master's thesis, University of Oklahoma, 1942.

Etter, Earl T. "A Study of Negro Operated Farms in Oklahoma." Master's thesis, Oklahoma State university, 1940.

Fulkerson, Fred G. "Social Forces in a Negro District in Oklahoma City, Oklahoma." Master's thesis, University of Oklahoma, 1946.

Gandy, Lenouliah E. "Educational Opportunities in Oklahoma for Preparing Colored Home Economics Trained Persons for Professional and Occupational Advancement." Master's thesis, Colorado State University, 1942. Teaching home economics to Blacks in Oklahoma.

Gill, Loren. "The Tulsa Race Riot." Master's thesis, University of Tulsa, 1946.

Griffin, Jack Leo. "The Effects of Integration on the Academic Aptitude, Classroom Achievement, Self-Concept, and Attitudes toward the School En-

vironment of a Selected Group of Negro Students in Tulsa, Oklahoma."
Ed.D. thesis, University of Tulsa, 1969.

Grissom, Thomas William. "Occupational Opportunities and Vocational Education for Negroes in Oklahoma." Master's thesis, Arizona State University, Tempe, 1940.

Hammons, Myrna Adcock. "Aspects of Written Language of College Freshmen
in Oklahoma, According to Race and Sex: Negro, American Indian, and
Caucasian." Thesis, University of Tulsa, 1973.

Hatcher, Ollie Everett. "The Development of Legal Controls in Racial Segregation in the Public Schools of Oklahoma, 1865–1952." Master's thesis,
University of Oklahoma, 1954.

Hickman, Gerald. "Disfranchisement in Oklahoma: The Grandfather Clause of
1910–1916." Master's thesis, University of Tulsa, 1967.

Hill, Mozell C. "The All-Negro Society in Oklahoma." Ph.D. diss., University of Chicago, 1946.

Humphrey, Charles Allen. "Socio-Economic Study of Six All-Black Towns in
Oklahoma." Thesis, Oklahoma State University, 1974.

Jackson, Nellie B. "Political and Economic History of the Negro in Indian Territory." Master's thesis, University of Oklahoma 1960.

Jelz, Wyatt F. "The Relations of Negroes and Choctaw and Chickasaw Indians."
Journal of Negro History 33 (1948).

Knight, Thomas. "Black Towns in Oklahoma: Their Development and Survival." Ph.D. diss., Oklahoma State University, 1975.

LeSure, Lessie Lois Fowler. "Willa A. Strong: An Historical Study of Black
Education in Southeastern Oklahoma." Ph.D. diss., University of
Oklahoma, 1982.

Miller, Maggie Ullery. "A Study of the Movement for the Advancement of Negroes in Oklahoma." Master's thesis, University of Southern California, Los Angeles, 1947.

Moon, Mary Carletta. "Frederick Douglass Moon: A Study of Black Education
in Oklahoma." Ed.D. thesis, University of Oklahoma, 1978. Black
school principals.

Peniston, Eugene Gilbert. "Levels of Aspiration of Black Students as a Function of Significant Others in Integrated and Segregated Schools." Thesis, Oklahoma State University, 1972. Focus on Oklahoma secondary
schools.

Pollard, Gloria Jean. "The Role of Higher Education in African-American
Community Development: Perceptions from Green Pastures." Ph.D.
diss., University of Oklahoma, 1993.

Reese, Linda Williams. "Race, Class, and Culture: Oklahoma Women,
1890–1920." Ph.D. diss., University of Oklahoma, 1991.

Roethler, Michael D. "Negro Slavery among the Cherokee Indians,
1540–1866." Ph.D. diss., Fordham University, 1964.

Saxe, Allan A. "Protest and Reform: The Desegregation of Oklahoma City."
Ph.D. diss., University of Oklahoma, 1969.

Sharp, Wanda F. "The *Black Dispatch*: A Sociological Analysis." Master's thesis, University of Oklahoma, 1951.

Simpson, Clay Eddie, Jr. "Comparisons of Pregnancy Outcome Related to Prenatal Care between Private and Service Negro Patients in Oklahoma County." Ph.D. diss., University of Oklahoma, 1968.

Smith, Lee Rand. "A Comparative Study of the Achievement of Negro Students Attending Segregated Junior High Schools and Negro Students Attending Desegregated Junior High Schools in the City of Tulsa." Ed.D. diss., University of Tulsa, 1971.

Steers, Nina A. "The Ku Klux Klan in Oklahoma during the 1920's." Master's thesis, Columbia University, 1965.

Stephens, Louise C. "The Urban League of Oklahoma City, Oklahoma." Ph.D. diss., University of Oklahoma, 1957.

Stout, Charles O. "A Comparison between Vocational Offerings and Job Placement in Five Vocational Schools for Negroes and Five Vocational Schools for Whites in Oklahoma." Ph.D. diss., Indiana University, 1950.

Strong, Evelyn Richardson. "Historical Development of the Oklahoma Association of Negro Teachers: A Study in Social Change." Ph.D. diss., University of Oklahoma, 1961.

Strong, Willa A. "The Origin, Development, and Current Status of the Oklahoma Federation of Colored Women's Clubs." Ph.D. diss., University of Oklahoma, 1957.

Tata, Elizabeth Juanita. "Delinquency Among the Negro Youth in Tulsa, Oklahoma." Master's thesis, Colorado State University, 1939.

Taylor, George Shedrick. "A Comparative Study of Differentials and Similarities Between Rural and Urban Juvenile Delinquency Recidivism." Thesis, Oklahoma State University, 1972. Focus on Oklahoma.

Thomas, Chleyon Decatur. "Boley: An All-Black Pioneer Town and the Education of Its Children." Ph.D. diss, University of Akron, 1989.

Thomas, Pamela D. "The Oklahoma City School Board's 1984 Decision to Curtail Busing and Return to Neighborhood Elementary Schools." Ph.D. diss., University of Oklahoma, 1990.

Thompson, John. "The Little Caesar of Civil Rights: Roscoe Dunjee in Oklahoma City, 1915 to 1955." Ph.D. diss., Purdue University, 1990.

Tolson, Arthur L. "A History of Langston, Oklahoma, 1890–1950." Master's thesis, Oklahoma State University, 1953.

_____. "The Negro in Oklahoma Territory, 1889–1907: A Study in Racial Discrimination." Ph.D. diss., University of Oklahoma, 1966.

Washington, Nathaniel Jason. "The Historical Development of the Negro in Oklahoma." Master's thesis, University of Arizona, Tucson, 1947.

Whitson, Edward. "Selected Characteristics of Negro Housing in Oklahoma, 1950." Master's thesis, University of Oklahoma, 1957.

Williams, Nudie E. "A History of the American Southwest: Black United States Marshall in the Territory, 1875–1907." Master's thesis, Oklahoma State University-Stillwater, 1973.

Black Newspapers:[1]

ARDMORE

┌───┐
│ *Ardmore Sun.* Ardmore. 1901–1911.   │
│ *Sun.* Ardmore. 1906.   │
└───┘

Avalanche. Ardmore. 1901.
Baptist Rival. Ardmore.
        1902–1917.
Chickasaw Rival. Ardmore.
        1902–1907.
Indian Territory Sun. Ardmore.
        1901–1907.
Oklahoma Sun. Ardmore. 1906.
Sun. Ardmore. 1908–1912.
Western World. Ardmore.
        1902–1904.
World Sun. Ardmore. 1902–1904.
World. Ardmore. 1907–1908.

BOLEY

Boley Beacon. Boley. 1907.
Boley Elevator. Boley. 1920–1926.
Boley News. Boley. 1918–1938.

┌───┐
│ *Boley Progress.* Boley. 1905–1926.   │
│   Published in Guthrie until   │
│   1907.   │
│ *Watchman Lantern.* Muskogee.   │
│   1901–1943.   │
│ *Weekly Progress.* Boley. 1926.   │
│ *Weekly Progress.* Muskogee. 1926.   │
│   Continues previous paper.   │
│ *Informer.* Clearville. 1909–1911.   │
│ *Boley Informer.* Boley. 1911–1912.   │
└───┘

Express. Boley. 1920–1922.
Greater Boley Area Newsletter.
        Boley. 1975–1976.
Marriott's Advertiser. Boley.
        1917–1925.

Star. Boley. 1913–1914.
Tribune. Boley. 1926–1928.
Trumpet. Boley. 1926–1927.

CLEARVILLE (LINCOLN)

┌───┐
│ *Clearview Patriarch.* Clearview.   │
│   1911–1913.   │
│ *Patriarch.* Clearview. 1913–1926.   │
│ *Lincoln Tribune.* Clearview.   │
│   1904–1905.   │
│ *Clearview Tribune.* Clearview. 1904.   │
└───┘

Informer. Clearville. 1909–1911.

GUTHRIE

Avalanche. Guthrie. 1901.
Baptist Safeguard. Guthrie.
        1917–1919.
Constitution. Guthrie. 1892.

┌───┐
│ *Guthrie Progress.* Guthrie.   │
│   1902–1914.   │
│ *Labor Advocate.* Guthrie.   │
│   1902–1903.   │
└───┘

Health Bulletin. Guthrie.
        1918–1921.
Little Missionary. Guthrie. 1905.
Oklahoma Enterprise. Guthrie.
        1908.

┌───┐
│ *Oklahoma Guide.* Guthrie.   │
│   1892–1925.   │
│ *Oklahoma Safeguard.* Guthrie.   │
│   1894–1915.   │
│ *Peoples Elevator.* Guthrie.   │
│   1900–1923. Began publi-   │
│   cation in Wichita in 1924.   │
└───┘

────────────────────────────

[1] Double-lined boxed items indicate change in masthead names.

Oklahoma School News. Guthrie.
    1910.
Russell's Review. Guthrie.
    1899–1904.
Taborian Monitor. Guthrie.
    1904–1921.
Twice-A-Week Sun. Guthrie.
    1911–1914.
Western World. Guthrie.
    1902–1904.

KINGFISHER

Kingfisher Constitution. Kingfisher.
    1894–1899.
Oklahoma Constitution. Kingfisher.
    1891–1894.
Russell's Review. Kingfisher. 1898.
Western Home. Kingfisher.
    1907–1908.
Western World. Kingfisher.
    1902–1904.

LANGSTON CITY

Church and State. Langston City.
    1911.
Church Review. Langston City.
    1902.
Headlight. Langston City. 1904.

Langston City Herald. Langston
    City. 1891–1902. Okla-
    homa's first Black weekly
    newspaper.
Western Age. Langston City.
    1904–1909.

Living Age. Langston City. ?–1904.
    Monthly.
Negro School Journal. Langston
    City. 1913.
New Constitution. Langston City.
    1898.
Oklahoma Church and State News.
    Langston City. 1911.
Southwestern Journal. Langston
    City. 1944–1951.

Western Age. Langston City.
    1904–1909.

MUSKOGEE

Baptist College Searchlight.
    Muskogee. 1899–1912.
Baptist Informer. Muskogee.
    1909–1925.
Blade. Muskogee. 1906.
Cimeter. Muskogee. 1899–1932.
Creek Baptist Herald. Muskogee.
    1911–192?
Daily Republican. Muskogee.
    1909–1910.
Daily Searchlight. Muskogee.
    1905–1906. Oklahoma's
    first Black daily.
Dispensation. Muskogee.
    1905–1906.
Enterprise. Muskogee. 1910–1913.
Herald. Muskogee. 1932–1968.
Ministerial Voice. Muskogee.
    1919–1922.
Muskogee Comet. Muskogee. 1904.
Oklahoma Eagle. Muskogee. 1978.
    Weekly edition of the Tulsa
    Oklahoma Eagle.
Oklahoma Independent. Muskogee.
    1932–1965.
Our Brother in Black #1. Muskogee.
    1880–1883.
Our Brother in Black #2. Muskogee.
    1890–1891.
Pioneer. Muskogee. 1898–1907.
Republican. Muskogee. 1905–1913.
Saturday Evening Tribune.
    Muskogee. 1913–1915.
Searchlight. Muskogee.
    1905–1907.
Southwestern World. Muskogee.
    1904–1905.
Southwesterner. Muskogee. 1905.

Star. Muskogee. 1912–1913.
Tulsa Star. Tulsa. 1912–1921.

Tulsa Daily Star. Tulsa. 1918–1921.

Sun. Muskogee. 1893–1895.
Tattler. Muskogee. 1915–1917.
Tribune. Muskogee. 1926–1928.

Weekly Progress. Muskogee.
    1926–1932.
Lantern. Muskogee. 1901–1943.
    Also published as *Watch-
    man-Lantern.*
Western World. Muskogee.
    1903–1905. Moved from
    Oklahoma City.
Unionist. Muskogee. 1904–1905.

YMCA Bulletin. Muskogee. 1914.

OKLAHOMA CITY
Black Chronicle. Oklahoma City.
    1979–current.
Black Dispatch. Oklahoma City.
    1915–1981.
Black Voices Magazine. Oklahoma
    City. 1971–?
Ebony Tribune. Oklahoma City.
    1986–current.
Gazette. Oklahoma City. ?–1970.
Occidental Lighthouse. Oklahoma
    City. 1899–1907.
Oklahoma Defender. Oklahoma City.
    1936–1942.
Oklahoma Eagle. Oklahoma City.
    1936.

Oklahoma Guide. Oklahoma City.
    1889–1922. Monthly.
    Oklahoma's first Black
    newspaper.
Guide. Oklahoma City. 1897–1903.

Oklahoma Traveler. Oklahoma City.
    1939.
Oklahoma Tribune. Oklahoma City.
    1907–1915.
Oracle. Oklahoma City.
    1921–current. Omega Psi
    Phi fraternity.

Western World. Oklahoma City.
    1903–1905.

TAFT (TWINE)
Informer. Taft. 1910–1912.
News. Taft. 1910–1912.
Taft Enterprise. Taft. 1910–1915.
Twine Enterprise. Taft. 1910.
Western Age. Taft. 1904–1910.

TULSA
Appeal. Tulsa. 1938–1955.
Call. Kansas City (Tulsa edition).
    1933–19??

Muskogee Star. Muskogee.
    1912–1918.
Tulsa Star. Tulsa. 1912–1921.
Tulsa Daily Star. Tulsa. 1918–1921.

Oklahoma Eagle. Tulsa.
    1921–current.
Oklahoma Sun. Tulsa. 1921.
Tulsa Guide. Tulsa. 1906–1912.

VARIOUS COMMUNITIES
Afro-American. Muldrow.
    1902–1903.
American. Wagoner. 191?
Bookertree Searchlight. Bookertree.
    1919.
Castle News. Okfuskee. 1908.
Chandler and Falls Express. Chan-
    dler. 1904.
Cherokee Advocate. Tahlequah.
    1856–1906.
Citizen. Fort Gibson. 1897–1900.
Clarksville. Muskogee County.
    1905.
Community Guide. Lawton.
    1971–1980. Special edi-
    tion of the Tulsa Oklahoma
    Eagle.
Fallis Blade. Fallis. 1904–1905.
Garvin Pioneer. Garvin.
    1908–1912.

Informer. Eufaula. 1902–1903.

Lantern. Wagoner. 1908–1913.

Missionary Baptist of Oklahoma. 1900.

Mulhall Enterprise. Mulhall. 1893–1911.

Oklahoma Freeman. Watonga. 1901–1903.

Oklahoma Hornet. Waukomis. 1899–1908.

Oklahoma Negro News. Bartlesville. 1937–1940.

Oklahoma Star. Enid. 1903–1905.

Oklahoma Trumpet. Newkirk. 1925–1928.

Okmulgee Observer. Okmulgee. 1927–1963.

Paden Times. Paden. 1904–1908.

Paden Press. Paden. 1908–1909.

People's Protector. Atoka. ?–1915.

Pythian Monitor. 1907.

Redbee. Redbird. 1912–1914.

Rentiesville News. Rentiesville. 1913–1926.

Southwestern Journal. Lawton. 1944–?

Voice of the People. McAlester. 1900–1905.

Voice. Bartlesville. 1936–1938.

Western Advocate. Fort Gibson. 1906.

Western World. Chandler. 1904–1904.

Western World. Shawnee. 1902–1904.

Other:

African-American Baptist Annual Reports, 1865–1990s: Oklahoma. National Archives, microfilm. Books, pamphlets, periodicals, statistics, biographies, etc.

Black Wallstreet. Latressa Walloe and Annette Wilson, producers, 1991. Traces the 1921 demise of Tulsa's Black community.

Education. Elk City, Okla., 1929. Papers of the NAACP. Part 3, Campaign for Educational Equality. Series A, Legal Department and Central Office Records, 1913–1940; Reel 21, FR. 1063–1096. Frederick, MD: University Publications of America, 1986. Microform.

"Interview with Juanita Kidd Stout." Stout describes discrimination she experienced. Schomburg Center Oral History [audio] Tape Collection, 197?

National Negro Business League. Afro-American Film Company, 1914. Newsreel featuring the National Negro Business League in Muskogee, plus businesses in Boley, Oklahoma.

Oklahoma: Alive and Well. Nebraska ETV Network, 1979. Videorecording.

"Oral History Interview of Willie and Clara Sims." Colorado Historical Society, 1981. The Sims talk about experiences in Oklahoma, New Mexico, and Colorado. Audiorecording.

Library of Congress and National Archives. *The General Education Board: The Early Southern Program*, microfilm. Nos. 98.

School Cases. Oklahoma Schools, 1937–39. Papers of the NAACP. Part 3, Campaign for Educational Equality. Series A, Legal Department and

Central Office Records, 1913–1940; Reel 9, FR. 0533–0637. Frederick, MD: University Publications of America, 1986. Microform.

Schools. Oklahoma, 1945–48. Papers of the NAACP. Part 3, Campaign for Educational Equality. Series B, Legal Department and Central Office Records, 1940–1950; Reel 4, FR. 0429–0439. Frederick, MD: University Publications of America, 1986. Microform.

Teachers' Salaries. Oklahoma, 1941–42. Papers of the NAACP. Part 3, Campaign for Educational Equality. Series B, Legal Department and Central Office Records, 1940–1950; Reel 9, FR. 0325–0339. Frederick, MD: University Publications of America, 1986. Microform.

Teachers' Salaries. Oklahoma, Freeman v. Board of Education, 1947–48. Papers of the NAACP. Part 3, Campaign for Educational Equality. Series B, Legal Department and Central Office Records, 1940–1950; Reel 9, FR. 0340–0434. Frederick, MD: University Publications of America, 1986. Microform.

Oregon

Articles:

"Accessions to the Museum of Oregon Historical." *Oregon Historical Quarterly* 4 (March 1946). Proceedings to expel a Negro from Oregon in 1851.

"Act by Provisional Government in 1844 Provides for Forced Hiring of Free Negroes at Public Bidding Under Certain Conditions." *Oregon Statesman* (26 July 1853).

"Act Preventing Negroes or Mulattoes Coming to or Residing in Oregon Passed by Territory Legislature in 1849." *Oregon Spectator* 20 February 1851; 27 February 1851; and 6 March 1851).

"Address of Judge George H. Williams." *Oregon Statesman* (28 July 1857).

"African Students Charge Prejudice in Rent Denial." *The Journal* (6 September 1962).

"Albina: The Dream and the Reality." *Portland Observer* (6 January 1972).

American Association of University Professors. *The Negro and Higher Education in Oregon.* University of Oregon chapter, Research Council. Eugene, 1964.

"Anti-Negro Legislation-Letter of September 29, 1862." Scrapbook #112, Oregon Historical Society.

Ayer, John Edwin. "George Bush, the Voyageur." *Washington Historical Quarterly* 4 (March 1946).

Bell, S. Leonard. "W. O. Bush from Bush Prairie." *Black World* (July 1970).

Bergquist, James M. "The Oregon Donation Act and National Land Policy." *Oregon Historical Quarterly* 8 (March 1957).

"Bill Giving Negroes Equal Rights Losses." *The Oregonian* (21 February 1919).

Black Potential. Portland: Urban League of Portland, June 1973.

Bledsoe, John Craig. "An Overview of Black Status in Oregon in the 1850's." Unpublished Seminar Paper, History Department, Portland State University, 1971.

Bogle, Kathryn Hall. "Document: Kathryn Hall Bogle's 'An American Negro Speaks of Color.'" *Oregon Historical Quarterly* 89 (1988).

Bogle, Kathryn Hall, and Rick Harmon. "Interview: Kathryn Hall Bogle on the Writing of 'An American Negro Speaks of Color.'" *Oregon Historical Quarterly* 89 (1988).

Branigar, Thomas. "The Murder of Cyrenius C. Hooker." *Oregon Historical Quarterly* 75, no. 4 (1974). Outcome of a murder case involving Blacks.

"Bring Negroes to Oregon." *The Oregonian* (21 March 1908).

Broussard, Albert S. "McCants Stewart: The Struggles of a Black Attorney in the Urban West." *Oregon Historical Quarterly* 89 (Summer 1988).

Brown, William Compton. "Old Fort Okanogan and the Okanogan Trail." *The Quarterly of the Oregon Historical Society* 15 (March 1914).

Brownell, Jean B. "Negroes in Oregon Before the Civil War." Oregon Historical Society Vertical File.

Bureau of Labor, Civil Rights Division. *A Decade of Progress Under Oregon's Civil Rights Legislation 1949–1959.* Portland, 1960.

Carter, William. "Civil Rights-Discrimination in Public Accommodation and Housing-State and Federal Remedies Available in Oregon." *Oregon Law Review* 44 (February 1965).

"The Case of Robin Holmes vs. Nathaniel Ford." *Oregon Historical Society Quarterly* 23 (June 1922).

Clark, Malcolm, Jr. "The Bigot Disclosed: 90 Years of Nativism." *Oregon Historical Quarterly* 75 (1974). About half of the article focuses on the Ku Klux Klan.

Clark, Robert Carlton. "The Last Step in the Formation of a Provisional Government for Oregon in 1845: Speech of Mr. Eli Thoyer on the Admission of Oregon as a State." *Oregon Historical Quarterly* 16 (December 1915).

"Collections: Oral History Interview: Kathryn Hall Bogle on the African-American Experience in Wartime Portland." *Oregon Historical Quarterly* 93 (Winter 1992).

"Colored Peoples' Suffrage." *Oregon Voter* (16 April 1927).

"Crime in Albina Area and Crime by Race." Research Memorandum, Subcommittee on Community and Home Environment, October 23, 1963.

Crowell, Evelyn Miller. "Twentieth Century Black Women in Oregon." *Northwest Journal of African and Black American Studies* I (Summer 1973).

Davenport, Timothy W. "The Late George Williams." *Oregon Historical Quarterly* 2 (March 1914).

_____, and G. H. William's. "Oregon Agitation up to 1801." *Oregon Historical Society Quarterly* 8 (September 1908).

Davis, Harry E. "John Malvin, a Western Reserve Pioneer." *Journal of Negro History* 23 (October 1938).

Davis, Lenwood G. "Black Educational Bookstore: A Community Asset." *Portland Observer* (22 February 1973).

_____. "Judge Diez: A Woman of Compassion." *Portland Observer* (16 March 1972).

_____. "Oregon Black Caucus, NAACP, Urban League and Others." *Portland Observer* (17 August 1972).

_____. "Oregon's Black Inmates: The Forgotten Men." *Portland Observer* (9 March 1972).

_____. "Sources for the History of Blacks in Oregon." *Oregon Historical Quarterly* 73 (September 1972).

_____. "Toran: Oregon's 1st Black Representative?" *Portland Observer* (2 March 1972).

_____. "White Businesses in the Black Community." *Portland Observer* (1–14 July 1972).

Douglas, Jesse S. "Origins of the Population of Oregon in 1850." *Pacific Northwest Quarterly* 41 (April 1950).

Elliott, T. O. "The Earliest Travelers on the Oregon Trail." *The Quarterly of the Historical Society* 13 (1912).

Franklin, Joseph. "Black Pioneers: George Washington and George Washington Bush." *Pacific Northwest Forum* 14 (1976).

Friedman, Carol. "Historiographical Essay on the Negro in Oregon During the Twentieth Century." *Oregon Historical Society*, 1969.

"George Winslow was the First Colored Man to Reach Oregon." *Oregon Statesman* (13 August 1892).

Hamscom, John. "Company Coal Town: Franklin and the Oregon Improvement Company." *Columbia* 8 (1994).

Harrell, Jerry D. "The Fight for Recognition." *Crisis* 61 (March 1954). The NAACP at the University of Oregon.

Henry, Francis. "George Bush," *Oregon Pioneer Association Transaction*, Fifteenth Annual Reunion, Portland, Oregon, June 15, 1887.

Hill, Daniel Grafton. "The Negro as a Political and Social Issue in the Oregon Country." *Journal of Negro History* 33 (April 1948).

Hogg, Thomas C. "Black Man in White Town." *Pacific Northwest Quarterly* 63 (January 1972). Blacks in Eugene since 1943.

_____. "Negroes and Their Institutions in Oregon." *Phylon* 30 (Fall 1969). From the 18th century to 1969.

Holland, M. Edward. "Oregon Civil Rights Litigation, 1964–1984: The Struggle for Equal Opportunity in the Marketplace." *Journal of the West* 25 (October 1986).

Holsinger, M. Paul. "The Oregon School Bill Controversy, 1922–1925." *Pacific History Review* 37 (August 1968). KKK influences state legislature.

Horowitz, David A. "The Klansman as Outsider: Ethnocultural Solidarity and Antielitism in the Oregon Ku Klux Klan of the 1920's." *Pacific Northwest Quarterly* 80 (January 1989).

————. "Social Morality and Personal Revitalization: Oregon's Ku Klux Klan in the 1920's." *Oregon Historical Quarterly* 90 (1989).

Hult, Ruby E. "The Saga of George W. Bush, Unheralded Pioneer of the Northwest Territory." *Negro Digest* 11(September 1962).

"Intolerance in Oregon." *Survey* 49 (15 October 1922).

Johannsen, Robert W. "A Breckinridge Democrat on the Succession Crisis: Letters of Isaac I. Stevens, 1860–1861." *Oregon Historical Quarterly* 55 (December 1954).

————. "The Kansas-Nebraska Act and the Pacific Northwest Frontier." *Pacific Northwest Review* 21 (1953).

————. "The Oregon Legislature of 1868 and the Fourteenth Amendment." *Oregon Historical Quarterly* 51 (March 1950).

————. "Specters of Disunion: The Pacific Northwest and the Civil War." *Pacific Northwest Quarterly* 44 (July 1953).

Johnson, Jalmar. "Michael T. Simmons and George Washington Bush, Who Went Where They Wished." Chapter in *Builders of the Northwest*. New York: Dodd, Mead, 1963.

Karolevitz, Bob. "George Washington, Northwest City Builder." *Negro Digest* 12 (September 1953).

————. "Northwest City Builder: George Washington." *Black World* 12 (September 1963).

Keith, Richard K. "Unwelcome Settlers: Black and Mulatto Oregon Pioneers," Part I. *Oregon Historical Quarterly* 84 (1984).

————. "Unwelcome Settlers: Black and Mulatto Oregon Pioneers," Part II. *Oregon Historical Quarterly* 84 (1984).

"KKK in Oregon." *Survey* 49 (1922).

"Klan Victories in Oregon and Texas." *Literary Digest* 75 (25 November 1922).

"Ku Klux Klan." *Oregon Voter* 31 (11 November 1922).

"Ku Klux Klan in Politics." *Literary Digest* 73 (10 June 1922). The Klan in Oregon.

Leiser, Sidney. "A Pioneer Judge of Oregon, Matthew P. Deady." *Oregon Historical Quarterly* 44 (March 1943).

————. "The Second Chief Justice of Oregon Territory, Thomas Nelson." *Oregon Historical Quarterly* 48 (September 1947).

Loveless, Dawn. "Lynch Law in Oregon." *Labor Defender* 10 (April 1934). Oregon Supreme Court grants a rehearing for a Black person sentenced to hang.

Lovrich, Nicholas P., Charles H. Sheldon, and Erik Wasmann. "The Racial Factor in Nonpartisan Judicial Elections: A Research Note." *Western Political Quarterly* 41 (1988).

McClintock, Thomas C. "James Saules, Peter Burnett, and the Oregon Black Exclusion Law of June 1844." *Pacific Northwest Quarterly* 86 (Summer 1995).

Miller, Clifford R. "The Old School Baptists in Early Oregon." *Oregon Historical Quarterly* 58 (December 1957).

"Negro Brought to Oregon by Mr. Vanderpool to be Banished From Territory." *Oregon Spectator* (12 September 1850).

"Negro Hanged to Tree, Then Told to Skip." *The Journal* (3 February 1922).

"Negro Pioneers of the Northwest." *Oregon Native Son.* Scrapbook #125.

"Negro Pioneers: Their Page in Oregon History." *Oregon Native Son* (January 1900).

"Negro Suffrage." *Oregon Voter* (4 November and 16 December 1916).

O'Hara, Edwin V. "The School Question on Oregon." *Catholic World* 116 (January 1923).

Ogburn, William F. "Social Legislation of the Pacific Coast." *Popular Science Monthly* 86 (January-June 1915).

Oliver, Egbert S. "Obed Dickinson and the 'Negro Question' in Salem." *Oregon Historical Quarterly* 92 (Spring 1991). Dickinson's contribution to the debate during his ministry in Salem.

Operation Step-Up Newsletter. Portland: A Negro Industries Project (1972–1973).

Oregon School Study Council. *Selected Oregon Population Characteristics: 1900–1960. Special Emphasis Upon Growth and Racial Composition of the Population.* Eugene, 1964.

Oregon: 1961 Report to the Commission on Civil Rights from the State Advisory Committee.

Peterson, Edwin J. "The Oregon Supreme Court Task Force on Racial Issues in the Courts: A Call for Self-Determination." *Willamette Law Review* 32 (Summer 1996). Black law students and discrimination in justice administration in Oregon.

Pintarich, Dick. "Even Black Cowboys Get the Blues." *Oregon Times* 8 (July 1978).

Platt, Robert Treat. "Oregon and its Share in the Civil War." *Oregon Historical Quarterly* 4 (1897).

Pollard, Lancaster. "Oregon Constitution Anti-Negro Until Referendum in 1927." *The Sunday Oregonian* (19 April 1959).

Poole, Kenneth A. "The Fair Employment Practices Act—Oregon." *Oregon Law Review* 32 (February 1953).

————. "Statutory Remedies for the Protection of Civil Rights." *Oregon Law Review* 32 (April 1953).

"Rampages of Ku Klux Klan on the Pacific Coast." *Messenger* 4 (June 1922). The Klan in Bakersfield and Oregon.

"Residential Attitudes Toward Negroes as Neighbors." Urban League Survey, 1950. Pamphlet.

Richard, K. Keith. "Unwelcome Settlers: Black and Mulatto Oregon Pioneers." *Oregon Historical Quarterly* 84, no. 1 and no. 2 (1983).

Roberts, Waldo. "The Ku Kluxing of Oregon." *Outlook* 133 (14 March 1923).

Rockwood, Eleanor Rugh. "Oregon Document Checklist II: Committee Reports," 1866 Prohibition of Negroes and Mulattoes from Residing in the State. *Senate Journal 1866. Oregon Historical Quarterly* (1944).

Saling, Ann. "George Washington Bush." *Columbia* 6, no. 4 (1993-1993).

Schwarz, K. Robert. "Black Maestros on the Podium, But No Pedestal" *New York Times* (11 October 1992). Includes James DePriest, music director of the Oregon Symphony.

"Slim Jim: Negro Cattle Rustler (from Oregon) Hanged at Walla Walla." Scrapbook #112, Oregon Historical Society (2 May 1864).

St. James, Nicole. "Grabbing Another Slice." *Black Enterprise*, December 1997. Black company PacPizza L. L. C. becomes Pizza Hut's second largest franchiser with restaurants in northern California, southern Oregon and western Nevada.

Stowell, George. "Enoch Pinkney Henderson." *Oregon Historical Quarterly* 19 (June 1918).

Teiser, Sidney. "Life of George H. Williams: Almost Chief Justice." *Oregon Historical Quarterly* 47 (September 1946).

Toll, William. "Black Families and Migration to a Multiracial Society: Portland, Oregon, 1900–1924." *Journal of American Ethnic History* 17 (Spring 1998).

_____. "Progress and Piety: The Ku Klux Klan and Social Change in Tillamook, Oregon." *Pacific Northwest Quarterly* 69 (April 1978).

Toy, Eckard V. "The Ku Klux Klan in Oregon." Chapter in *Experiences in a Promised land: Essays in Pacific Northwest History*, eds. G. Thomas Edwards and Carlos A. Schwantes. Seattle: University of Washington Press, 1986.

_____. "The Ku Klux Klan in Tillamook, Oregon." *Pacific Northwest Quarterly* 2 (March-December 1981).

_____. "The Ku Klux Klan in Tillamook, Oregon." Chapter in *The Northwest Mosaic*, eds. James A. Halseth and Bruce Alden Glasrud. Boulder: Pruett Publishing, 1977.

Tyack, David B. "Perils of Pluralism: The Background of the Pierce Case." *American Historical Review* 74 (October 1968). Oregon and the Klan.

"White Students Sentenced for Harassing Black Student." *Jet*, 22 April 1996. Two white Oregon State University students plead guilty to the charge.

Wiggins, David K. "The Future of College Athletics Is at Stake: Black Athletes and Racial Turmoil on Three Predominantly White University Campuses, 1968–1972." *Journal of Sport History* 15 (1988). UC-Berkeley, Syracuse, and Oregon State University.

Williams, George H. "The 'Free-State Letter' of the Judge George H. Williams." *Oregon Historical Society* 9 (September 1908).

_____. "Slavery in Oregon." *Quarterly of the Oregon Historical Society* 9 (1908).

"Winslow Anderson Declared Notorious, Ordered from Oregon Territory." *Oregon Spectator* (2 September 1861).

"Wiping Out Oregon's School Law." *Literary Digest* 81 (26 April 1924). Oregon and the Klan.

Portland

Agger, Robert E., and Clyde Edward De Barry. "School and Race in Portland." *Integrated Education* 3 (April-May 1965).

Allen, Rosemary. "Reminiscences of Early Portland: Mrs. Marie Smith." *Observer's Periscope* [Special edition of *Portland Observer*] (14 February 1974).

_____. "Portland Fire Bureau: Opportunity for Blacks?" *Portland Observer* (31 January 1974).

Berry, Edwin C. "Intercultural Education in Portland." *Opportunity* 24 (October-November 1946).

Bogle, Kathryn Hall, and Rick Harmon. "Oral History Interview: Kathryn Hall Bogle on the African -American Experience in Wartime Portland." *Oregon Historical Quarterly* 93 (1992).

Boyd, George Felix. "The Levels Aspiration of White and Negro Children in Non-Segregation Elementary School." *Journal of Social Psychology* 36 (1952). Study of a Portland school.

"Brotherhood Calling on Portland Negroes to be Men and Women of Purpose: Announcement of the First Annual Negro Race Conference for Portland." *The Advocate* (11 May 1929).

City Club of Portland. "Civil Rights." *Portland City Club Bulletin* 31 (22 September 1950).

_____. "Report on the Negro in Portland: A Progress Report 1945–1957." *Portland City Club Bulletin* (1 April 1966).

_____. "Report on Problems of Racial Justice." *Portland City Club Bulletin* (14 June 1968).

"Clara Mae Peoples of Portland, Oregon." *Ebony*, December 1971.

Davis, Lenwood G. "Portland's Black Caucus: An Assessment." *Portland Observer* (2 March 1972).

_____. "Portland's Black Middle Class: A Disappointment." *Portland Observer* (4–18 May 1972).

Flournoy, Liz. "Roy Jay: Making Portland the Place for People of Color: Expanding the Network in Conventions and Tourism." *Black Issues in Higher Education* 12 (August 24, 1995).

Portland City Club, Committee on Race Relations. "The Negro in Portland." *Portland City Club Bulletin* 26 (20 July 1945).

"A Salute: To Portland's Black Community." *The Press* (11 February 1970).

Taylor, Quintard. "The Great Migration: The Afro-American Communities of Seattle and Portland During the 1940s." *Arizona and the West* 23 (Summer 1981).

Toll, William. "Black Families and Migration to a Multiracial Society: Portland, Oregon, 1900–1924." *Journal of American Ethnic History* 17 (Spring 1998).

"When the Klan Rode in Portland." *Portland Observer* (15 February 1973).

Slaves and Slavery

"Bill to Protect Rights of Slave Holders Indefinitely Postponed in House of Representatives." *Oregon Statesman* (22 December 1857).

"Black Republican Convention at Lafayette Advocated Throwing Question of Slavery on the Democratic Party: Editor Denies the Party Taking Any Action on Subject." *Oregon Statesman* (24 February 1857),

Davenport, Timothy W. "Slavery Question in Oregon: Recollections and Reflections of a Historical Nature having Special Relation to the Slavery Agitation in the Oregon Territory and Including the Political Status up to the Beginning of Secession in 1861." *Oregon Historical Society Quarterly* 8 (September 1908 and December 1908).

"Debate Between Free State and Pro-Slavery Men Held in Eugene City During Democratic Convention, Vote about 30 to Pro-Slavery." *Oregon Statesman* (21 April 1857).

"G. H. Williams Sets Forth Reasons Why Oregon Should be Non-Slave State." *Oregon Statesman* (28 July 1857).

"Gov. Whiteaker in Message Says John Brown's Raid Hastens Settlement of Slavery Question." *Oregon Statesman* (21 October 1860).

Graebner, Norman A. "Politics and the Oregon Compromise." *Pacific Northwest Quarterly* 52, no. 1 (1961). In the Oregon Territory compromise of U.S. and Great Britain, slavery was a factor.

"Habeas Corpus Proceedings in Oregon Supreme Court to Release Negroes at Dallas, Polk County Who Were Once 'Held as Slaves in Missouri'." *Oregon Statesman* (5 July 1853).

"History of Attempts to Legalize Slavery in Oregon." *The Oregonian* (14 February 1899).

"Lane County Democratic Convention Passes Pro-Slavery Resolution." *Oregon Statesman* (27 December 1859).

Lee, R. Alton. "Slavery and the Oregon Territorial Issue: Prelude to the Compromise of 1850." *Pacific Northwest Quarterly* 64 (July 1973).

"Letter from 'Posted' Advocates Limited Form of Slavery for Training Indians." *Oregon Statesman* (6 December 1859).

"Letter Signed 'Anti-Niggerphobia' Says Let Democratic Conventions Nominate Good and True Men Without Reference to Their Views Upon Slavery in Oregon." *Oregon Statesman* (3 March 1857).

Lockley, Fred. "The Case of Robin Holmes vs. Nathaniel Ford." *Oregon Historical Society Quarterly* 23 (June 1922). Former slave sues for freedom of his children.

_____. "Facts Pertaining to Ex-Slaves in Oregon and Documentary Record of the Case of Robin Holmes vs. Nathaniel Ford." *Quarterly of the Oregon Historical Society* 23 (March 1922).

_____. "Oregon Slavery Documentary Records." *Oregon Historical Society Quarterly* 17 (June 1916).

_____. "Race Feeling Arose Very Early in Oregon." *The Journal* (6 January 1920).

_____. "Some Documentary Records of Slavery in Oregon." *Oregon Historical Society Quarterly* 17 (March 1916). Account of slave Mommia Travers.

"Luteshio Ceusar, Woman Slave in Missouri Brought to Oregon, Sues Estate of Master for Back Wages." *Oregon Statesman* (17 October 1854).

McArthur, Scott. "The Polk County Slave Case." *Oregon Historical Society* (August 1970).

"Oregon City a Slave Mart in a Small Way." Scrapbook #85, Oregon Historical Society (8 January 1920).

Rockwood, Eleanor Rugh. "Oregon Document Checklist II: Committee Reports," Protection to Slave Property, *House Journal 1858–1859*, pp. 174–179. *Oregon Historical Quarterly* 45 (September 1944).

"'S' Urges Oregonians to Buy Negroes in South and Free Them in Oregon." *Oregon Spectator* (9 September 1851).

"Slavery Agitation in Oregon up to 1861." *Oregon Historical Quarterly* 8 (September 1908).

"Slavery in Oregon: A Matter of Personalities and Issues." *Northwest Magazine* (20 September 1970).

"Some Documentary Records of Slavery in Oregon." *Oregon Historical Quarterly* 17 (June 1916).

"Starting of Jacksonville Herald Pro-Slavery Paper." *The Oregonian* (22 August 1857).

Sutton, Jacob. "Slavery in Oregon: A Matter of Personalities and Issues." *Northwest Magazine* (September 20, 1970).

Taylor, Quintard. "Slaves and Free Men: Blacks in the Oregon Country, 1840–1860." *Oregon Historical Quarterly* 83 (Summer 1982).

Books:

American Association of University Professors. *The Negro and Higher Education in Oregon.* Eugene, OR: University of Oregon, Research Council, 1964.

Atwood, Kay. *Minorities of Early Jackson County, Oregon.* Medford, OR: Jackson County Intermediate Education District, Instructional Media Center, 1976. Chinese, Blacks and Jews.

Blacks in Oregon: A Statistical and Historical Report. Portland: Black Studies Center and Center for Population Research and Census, Portland State University, 1978.

Broussard, Albert S. *The Stewarts: Three Generations of an African-American Family.* Lawrence: University of Kansas Press, 1998.

Bureau of Labor, Civil Rights Division. *A Decade of Progress Under Oregon's Civil Rights Legislation 1949–1959.* Portland, 1960.

Carey, Charles H. *History of Oregon.* Chicago: Pioneer Historical Publishing Company, 1922. Some history on early Blacks.

Casey, Helen Marie. *Portland's Compromise: The Colored School, 1867–1872.* Portland: Portland Public Schools, Public Information Department, 1980.

Collier, Mary A., and David D. Weitz. *Blacks Making History in Portland: A Project for Black History Week.* Portland: Sabin Elementary School, 1971.

Davis, Lenwood G.. *Blacks in the State of Oregon, 1788–1974: A Bibliography of Published Works and of Unpublished Source Materials on the Life and Achievements of Black People in the Beaver State.* Monticello, IL: Council of Planning Librarians, 1974. Bibliography.

_____. *Blacks in the State of Oregon, 1788–1971.* Monticello, IL: Council of Planning Librarians, 1971.

Davis, Lenwood G., and Mary Vance, comps. *Blacks in the State of Oregon: 1788–1974,* 2^d ed. Monticello, IL: Council of Planning Librarians, 1974. Bibliography.

Dees, Morris, and Steve Fiffer. *Hate on Trial: The Case Against America's Most Dangerous Neo-Nazi.* New York: Villard Books, 1993. Tom Metzger and hate crimes.

Eugene Human Rights Commission. *Survey of the Black Community: Report to the Human Rights Commission.* Eugene: City of Eugene, 1970.

Goldhammer, et al. *The Politics of De Facto Segregation, a Case Study.* Eugene: University of Oregon, Center for the Advanced Study of Educational Administration, 1969.

Grant, Richard D. *The Economic Condition of Minority Enterprise in the Portland, Oregon Model Cities Areas.* Western Interstate Commission for Higher Education, Portland State University Urban Studies Center.

Heflin, John F., and Marcia Douglas. *School Desegregation: Portland Style.* Paper prepared for the Annual Meeting of the American Educational Research Association and a Symposium on "Exploration of School Desegregation Impact on Black Communities: A View From the Western States," Boston, 10 April 1980. ERIC. ED 197 041. Focuses on the interaction between the Portland Public School Board with the Community Coalition for School Integration and the Black United Front.

Heikel, Iris White. *The Wind-Breaker: George Washington Bush, Black Pioneer of the Northwest.* New York: Vantage, 1980.

Hill, E. Shelton. *The Occupational Status of the Negro Worker in the Portland Area.* Portland Urban League, December 7, 1950.

HIV Risk and Oregon People of Color: A Data Source Book. Portland, OR: Oregon Health Division, Center for Disease Prevention and Epidemiology, HIV Program, 1993.

It's Not All Black and White. Portland, OR: League of Women Voters, 1968.

Johannsen, Robert W. *Frontier Politics and the Sectional Conflict on the Eve of the Civil War.* Seattle: University of Washington Press, 1955. Chapter on settlers and slavery.

League of Women Voters of Eugene, Oregon. *The Negro in Eugene.* Eugene: The League, 1951.

Little, William A., and James E. Weiss, eds. *Blacks in Oregon: A Statistical and Historical Report.* Portland: Black Studies Research Center, 1978.

Lynch, Vera Martin. *Free Land for Free Men: A Story of Clackamas County.* Oregon City: 1973.

Mahan, Milo. *Mr. Mahan's Speech.* n.p.: 1862. Slavery and the church.

McLagan, Elizabeth. *A Peculiar Paradise: A History of Blacks in Oregon, 1778–1940.* Portland, OR: Georgian Press, 1980. Oregon Black History Project.

Mitchell, Stephanie. *Whitney M. Young Learning Center in the Portland Public Schools. 1986–87. Evaluation Report.* Portland, OR: Portland Public Schools, 1987. ERIC. ED 292 826. After school programs for students in grades 6–12 in north and northeast Portland.

Multicultural Health: Mortality Patterns by Race and Ethnicity, Oregon, 1986–1994. Portland, OR: Oregon Department of Human Resources, Health Division, Center for Disease Prevention and Epidemiology, Center for Health Statistics, 1997. Mortality and race statistics.

Multnomah County, Or. School District No. 1. Board of Education. Committee on Race and Education. *Race and Equal Educational Opportunity in Portland's Public Schools: A Report.* Portland, OR: Multnomah County School District no. 1, 1964.

Oregon. Supreme Court. Task Force on Racial/Ethnic Issues in the Judicial System. *Report of the Oregon Supreme Court Task Force on Racial/Ethnic Issues in the Judicial System.* Salem, OR: Office of the State Court Administrator, Oregon Judicial Department, 1994.

Portland Committee on Race and Education. *Race and Equal Educational Opportunity in Portland's Public Schools: A Report to the Board of Education, Multnomah School District No. 1 by its Committee on Race and Education.* Portland: Metropolitan Printing Company (October 1964).

Rist, Ray C. *The Invisible Children: School Integration in American Society.* Cambridge: Harvard University Press, 1979. Oregon case studies.

Saalfield, Lawrence J. *Forces of Prejudice in Oregon, 1920–1925.* Portland, OR: Archdiocesan Historical Commission, 1984. Ku Klux Klan in Oregon.

Sawyer, Reuben H. *The Truth About The Invisible Empire, Knights of the Ku Klux Klan.* Portland, OR: Northwest Domain, 1922. Klan pamphlet.

A Statistical Portrait of the Multicultural/Multiethnic Student Population in the Portland Public Schools. Portland: Portland Public School, 1987. Key statistics on the status of culturally diverse children during the 1986–1987 school year.

The Status of Blacks in Oregon. Corvallis: Calmax Corporation, 1975.

Turnbull, George H. *An Oregon Crusader.* Portland, OR: Binfords and Mort, Publishers, 1955. Newspaper reporter George Putnam opposes the Klan.

United States Commission on Civil Rights. *School Desegregation in Portland, Oregon: A Staff Report of the U. S. Commission on Civil Rights,* by Roberta Jones-Booker. Washington, DC: The Commission, 1977.

Wahab, Zaher. *The Portland Public School System: From Panacea to Battleground.* Paper presented at the Annual Meeting of the Comparative and International Education Society, Tallahassee, 18–21 March 1981. ERIC. ED 236 789. Traces school segregation from 1867 through the emergence of the Black United Front

Theses and Dissertations:

Bonaparte, Lawson Gregg. "Opinions and Characteristics of Portland Community College Black Students." Ed.D. thesis, Oregon State University, 1971.

Boyd, George Felix. "The Levels Aspiration of White and Negro Children in Non-Segregation Elementary School." Master's thesis, University of Oregon, 1950.

Bryant, Janet. "The Ku Klux Klan and the Oregon Compulsory School Bill of 1922." Master's thesis, Reed College, 1970.

Canfield, Dana William. "An Approach to the Placement of Negro Teachers in the Portland Suburban Area." Master's thesis, University of Oregon, 1950.

Ciliberti, Patricia. "An Innovative Family Preservation and Support Program in an African-American Community: Analysis of Six-And Twelve-Month Follow-Up Data." Program to retain maltreated children with the natural family.

Clark, William R. "A Study of the Academic and Non-Academic Characteristics of the Negro Graduates of a Portland, Oregon, Secondary School." Ph.D. diss., University of Portland, 1967.

Farrell, Bernard Joseph. "A Survey and Analysis of the Attitudes of Non-Negro Parents in Selected Portland Elementary Schools." Ph.D. diss., Oregon State University, 1971.

Henderson, Archie Maree. "Introduction of the Negroes into the Pacific Northwest, 1788–1842." Master's thesis, University of Washington, 1949.

Herndon, Ronald D. "Racism in the Portland Schools." BA thesis, Reed College, 1970.

Herzog, June. "A Study of the Negro Defense Worker in the Portland-Vancouver Area." BA thesis, Reed College, 1944.

Hill, Daniel Grafton. "The Negro in Oregon: A Survey." Master's thesis, University of Oregon, Eugene, 1932.

Hopkins, Oznathylee Alverdo. "Black Life in Oregon, 1899–1907: A Study of the Portland *New Age*." BA thesis, Reed College, 1974.

Johnson, Frederick. "An Analysis of Negro News and Non-News Matters Appearing in Four Oregon Daily Newspapers During the Years, 1931, 1936, 1941, 1945, and 1948." Master's thesis, University of Oregon, 1949.

Kaplan, Richard B. "The Housing Authority of Portland and its Critics: A Study of Controversy over De Facto Segregation." BA thesis, Reed College, 1964.

Kingsbury, Helen. "Attitudes, Opportunities and Environment of Negro Grade School Children at Couch School." Master's thesis, Oregon State University, 1951.

Kippling, Paul Frank. "Constitutional Arguments Regarding Slavery in the Territories and the Organization of the Oregon Territorial Government." Master's thesis, University of Washington, 1969.

Leonard, Helen Carol Louise. "The Oregon Constitutional Convention of 1857." BA thesis, Reed College, 1951.

MalaRoff, Marion. "Tendencies Toward Bureaucratization in the Portland Urban League." BA thesis, Reed College, 1951.

Pearson, Rudy N. "African-Americans in Portland, Oregon, 1940–1950. Work and Living Conditions: A Social History." Ph.D. diss., Washington State University, 1996.

Poulton, Helen Jean. "The Attitude of Oregon Toward Slavery and Secession, 1843–1865." Master's thesis, University of Oregon, 1946.

Rhodes, Ethel C. "Negroes in Pacific Coast History Prior to 1865." Master's thesis, Howard University, 1940.

Rothwell, Charles Easton. "The Ku Klux Klan in the State of Oregon." BA thesis, Reed College, 1924.

Saalfield, Lawrence J. "Forces of Prejudice in Oregon, 1920–1925." Master's thesis, Reed College, 1924. Ku Klux Klan in Oregon.

Schneider, Franz M. "The Black Laws of Oregon." Master's thesis, University of Santa Clara, 1970.

Standard, Ellen Mae. "The Racial Composition of College Students in Oregon." Master's thesis, Willamette University, 1931.

Thomas, Paul F. "George Bush." Master's thesis, University of Washington, 1965.

Toy, Eckard V. "The Ku Klux Klan in Oregon." Master's thesis, University of Oregon, 1959.

Wade, Joseph Downey. "Effects of Improved Self-Concept on Retention of
     Black Students at the University of Oregon." Ph.D. diss., University
     of Oregon, 1982.
Walls, Florence. "The Letters of Ashel Bush to Matthew P. Deady,
     1851–1863." BA thesis, Reed College, 1941.
Wingfield, Harold Lloyd. "Affirmative Action: The Shoot-Out over Racism and
     Sexism at the Academy. The Case of Minority (Black) Faculty Re-
     cruitment and Hiring at the University of Oregon, 1973–1975." Ph.D.,
     University of Oregon, 1982.

Black Newspapers: [1]

PORTLAND

Advocate. Portland. 1903–1937.

African-American Journal. Portland.
     1989–current.

Clarion Defender. Portland.
     1953–197?

Inquirer. Portland. 1900–1946.

Interracial Progress. Portland.
     1952–1957.

Negro Times. Portland. 1909–1924.

New Age. Portland. 1896–1905.
Portland New Age. Portland.
     1905–1907.

Newspaper. Portland. 1967–1970.

Northwest Clarion Defender. Port-
     land. 1944–1973.

Northwest Clarion. Portland.
     1944–1967.

Observer. Portland. 1900–1903.

Oregon Advance Times. Portland.
     1968.

Pacific Dispatch. Portland.
     1946–1947.

Portland Challenger. Portland. 195?

Portland New Age. Portland.
     1905–1907.

Portland Northwest Defender. Port-
     land. 1962.

People's Observer. Portland.
     1941–1951.
Portland Observer #1. Portland.
     1939–1940.
Portland Observer #2. Portland.
     1970–current.

Portland Oregon Advance Times.
     Portland. 1968.

Portland Oregon Mirror. Portland.
     196?

Portland Skanner. Portland.
     1975–current.

Progress. Portland. 195?–? Urban
     League of Portland.

Times. Portland. 1911–1912.

Ujima. Portland. 1975. Black Stud-
     ies Program, Portland State
     University serial.

SALEM

Uhuru Messenger. Salem, Oregon
     State Penitentiary.

[1] Double-lined boxed items indicate change in masthead names.

Other:

Death in the Hood. Lanita Duke, producer, 1997. Documentary focusing on the drug trade and homicides among Black youth.

National Association for the Advancement of Colored People—Portland Oregon. Official documents of the NAACP from 1953–1959. Oregon Historical Society Collection.

Oregon Committee for Equal Rights. Official records of O.C.E.R., 1953–1959. Oregon Historical Society Collection.

Portland Citizen Committee on Racial Imbalance in the Public Schools—Portland Oregon. Official records, 1962–1965. Oregon Historical Society Collection.

South Dakota

Articles:

Bernson, Sarah L., and Robert J. Eggers. "Black People in South Dakota History." *South Dakota History* 7 (Summer 1977).

"Blacks Prominent in State [South Dakota] History." *Rapid City Journal* (January 1972).

Buecker, Thomas R. "Confrontation at Sturgis: An Episode in Civil-Military Race Relations, 1885." *South Dakota History* 14 (Fall 1984).

Elder, Arlene. "Oscar Micheaux: The Melting Pot on the Plains." *Old Northwest* 2 (1976).

Gatewood, Willard B., Jr. "Kate D. Chapman Reports on 'The Yankton Colored People,' 1889." *South Dakota History* 7 (Winter 1976). Author and poet reports on Blacks in Yankton and encourages others to settle there.

Hebert, Janis. "Oscar Micheaux: A Black Pioneer." *South Dakota Review* 11 (Winter 1973–74). Homesteader turned independent filmmaker.

Hunhoff, Bernie. "Simple Splendor: The Simplicity of Yankton's Century-old Black Church." *South Dakota Magazine* (July 1985). South Dakota's only Black AME church.

Johnson, M. K. "'Strangers in a Strange Land': An African American Response to the Frontier Tradition in Oscar Micheaux's *The Conquest: The Story of a Negro Pioneer*." *Western American Literature* 33 (Fall 1998). Micheaux's literary attempt to demonstrate that legends of the West can be Black legends, and challenges anti-Black racism.

Mashek, Carol Martin. "Looking Back—The Ku Klux Klan's Early County (Minnehaha) Roots." South Dakota Historical Society (n.d.).

Peterson, Susan C. "Discrimination and Jurisdiction: Seven Civil Rights Cases in South Dakota, 1976–1982." *Journal of the West* 25 (October 1986).

Rambow, Charles. "The Ku Klux Klan in the 1920's: A Concentration on the Black Hills." *South Dakota History* 4 (Winter 1973). The Klan in South Dakota.

Books:

NAACP Administrative File. Subject File. Lynching—South Dakota, 1930, 1933. Frederick, MD: University Publications of America, 1986.

United States Commission on Civil Rights, South Dakota Advisory Committee. *Negro Airmen in a Northern Community: Discrimination in Rapid City, South Dakota. Report of the South Dakota Advisory Committee to the Commission*. Washington, DC: U.S. Government Printing Office, 1963.

Black Newspapers:

Bystander. Iowa. Covered South Dakota Black issues.
Chicago Defender. Chicago. Covered South Dakota Black issues.
Spokesman. Minneapolis. 1934. Covered South Dakota Black issues through its "Sioux Falls News" column.

Texas

Articles:

Abramowitz, Jack. "John B. Rayner—A Grass-Roots Leader." *Journal of Negro History* 36 (April 1951).

Adams, Ephriam Douglass, ed. Correspondence from the British Archives Concerning Texas, 1837–1846." *Southwestern Historical Quarterly* 17 (October 1913).

"African American Lawyers: A Voice for Unification." *Texas Bar Journal* 57 (September 1994). Black attorneys in Texas.

"African American Lawyers Organize." *Texas Bar Journal* 55 (October 1992). Interview of Sheila Jackson Lee, chair of the African American Section of the Texas State Bar.

Alexander, Charles C. "Secrecy Bids for Power: The Ku Klux Klan in Texas Politics in the 1920s." *Mid-America* 46 (January 1964).

"Alexander Vernon to Lead Texas State VFW." *Jet*, 1 July 1996. First Black state commander named.

Allen, Lee N. "The Democratic Presidential Primary Election of 1924 in Texas." *Southwestern Historical Quarterly* 61 (April 1958). Texas and the Klan.

"An American Atrocity." *Independent* 87 (31 July 1916). Black teenager is lynched in Waco.

Amin, Julius. "Black Lubbock: 1955 to the Present." *West Texas Historical Association Year Book* 65 (1989).

Anders, Evan. "Boss Rule and Constituent Interests: South Texas Politics During the Progressive Era." *Southwestern Historical Quarterly* 84 (January 1981). Some Black involvement.

"Anderson County: Foster Cemetery (Black)." *East Texas Family Records* 18 (Fall 1994).

Anderson, John Q. "Old John and the Master." *Southern Folklore Quarterly* 25 (September 1961).

Arthur, Charles M. "All for a Dollar: Trade Extension Classes for Negroes, Fort Worth, Texas." *Scholastic Life* 22 (November 1936).

"Auto-da-fe in Tyler, Texas." *Crisis* 4 (September 1912). The burning of a Black man. "Auto-da-fé" means the burning of a heretic.

Baeza, Abelardo. "*La Escuela Escondida*: History of the Morgan School in Alpine, Texas, 1929–1954." *Journal of Big Bend Studies* 6 (1994).

Baggett, James Alex. "Origins of Early Texas Republican Party Leadership." *Journal of Southern History* 40 (July 1974).

Bailey, Anne J. "A Texas Cavalry Raid: Reaction to Black Soldiers and Contrabands." *Civil War History* 35 (June 1989).

Bales, Mary Virginia. "Some Negro Folk-Songs of Texas." Chapter in *Follow de Drinkin' Gou'd*, ed. Frank Dobie. Dallas: Southern Methodist University Press, 1965.

Barr, Alwyn "African Americans in Texas: From Stereotypes to Diverse Roles. Chapter in *Texas Through Times*, eds. Walter L. Buenger, and Robert A. Calvery. College Station: Texas A&M University Press, 1991.

————. "Black Texans." Chapter in *A Guide to the History of Texas*, eds. Light Townsend Cummins and Alvin R. Bailey, Jr. Westport, CT: Greenwood Press, 1988.

————. "The Texas 'Black Uprising' Scare of 1883." *Phylon* 41 (1980).

Beil, Gail K. "James Leonard Farmer: Texas' First African American Ph.D." *East Texas Historical Journal* 36, no. 1 (1998).

Bentley, Max. "The Ku Klux Klan in Texas." *McClure's* 57 (May 1924).

————. "A Texan Challenges the Klan." *Collier's*, 3 November 1923.

Billington, Monroe Lee "Lyndon B. Johnson and Blacks: The Early Years." *Journal of Negro History* 62 (January 1977). Johnson and early efforts for Blacks in Texas.

"Black Graduate Feted by U. of Texas Architecture School." *The Chronicle of Higher Education* 40 (30 March 1994).

"Black Law School Enrollments: A Virtual Eviction in Texas and California." *The Journal of Blacks in Higher Education* 16 (Summer 1997).

Bliss, David. "Antiwar Movement Attacks Links of Houston Police to Ku Klux Klan." *Militant* 34 (27 November 1970).

Borrud, Lori G., Patricia C. Pillow, and Pamela K. Allen. "Food Group Contributors to Nutrient intake in Whites, Blacks, and Mexican American in Texas." *Journal of the American Dietetic Association* 89 (August 1989). Targeted dietary planning.

Bourgeois, Christie L. "Stepping over Lines: Lyndon Johnson, Black Texans, and the National Youth Administration, 1935–1937." *Southwestern Historical Quarterly* 91 (October 1987).

Bradley, John Ed. "Once Upon a Time." *Sports Illustrated*, 28 August 1995. Features Prairie View A&M, formerly a powerhouse, and it 46 straight losses in football.

Brandenstein, Sherilyn. "*Sepia Record* as a Forum for Negotiating Women's Roles." Chapter in *Women and Texas History: Selected Essays*, eds.

Fane Downs and Nancy Baker Jones. Austin: Texas State Historical Association, 1993.

Britten, Thomas A. "The Dismissal of the Seminole-Negro Indian Scouts, 1880–1914." *Fort Concho and the South Plains Journal* 24 (Summer 1992).

_____. "The Seminole-Indian Scouts in the Big Bend." *Journal of Big Bend Studies* 5 (1 January 1993).

Brokow, John W. "The Minstrel Show in the Hoblitzelle Theatre Arts Library." *Library Chronicle of the University of Texas* 4 (1972). Describes the collection.

Brophy, William J. "Black Business Development in Texas Cities, 1900–1950." Red River Valley Historical Review 6 (Spring 1981).

_____. "Black Texans and the New Deal." Chapter in *The Depression in the Southwest*, ed. Donald W. Whisenhunt. Port Washington, NY: Kennikat, 1980.

Broyles, William. "The Making of Barbara Jordan." *Texas Monthly*, October 1976.

Bryan, Marilyn T. "The Economic, Political and Social Status of the Negro in El Paso." *Password* 13 (Fall 1968).

Bryant, Ira B. "The Need for Negro History in the Schools of Texas." *Negro History Bulletin* 20 (January 1957).

_____. "News Items About Negroes in White Urban and Rural Newspapers." *Journal of Negro Education* 4 (1935).

_____. "Vocational Education in Negro High Schools in Texas." *Journal of Negro Education* 18 (Winter 1949).

Bucholtz, Michael. "Racial References in the Texas Press, 1813–1836." *Journalism Quarterly* 67 (Autumn 1990).

Bullock, Charles S., and Susan A. MacManus. "Voting Patterns in a Tri-Ethnic Community: Conflict or Cohesion?" *National Civic Review* 79 (January 1990). Blacks and Latinos struggle for power in Austin.

Bullock, Henry Allen. "The Availability of Education in the Texas Separate School." *Journal of Negro Education* 16 (Summer 1947).

_____. "Expansion of Negro Suffrage in Texas." *Journal of Negro Education* 26 (Summer 1957).

_____. "Racial Attitudes and the Employment of Negroes." *American Journal of Sociology* 56 (March 1951).

_____. "Some Readjustments of the Texas Negro Family to the Emergency of War." *Southwestern Social Science Quarterly* 25 (September 1944).

"The Burden." *Crisis* 11 (January 1916). Article and photographs of the burning of Will Stanley at Temple, Texas.

Burka, Paul. "Jewel of the Forest." *Texas Monthly*, August 1998. Report on Jasper, Texas, following he murder of James Byrd, Jr.

_____. "Major Barbara [Jordan]." *Texas Monthly,* March 1996.

_____. "What's Black and White and Red-Faced All Over?" *Texas Monthly*, December 1997. Comments of white professor Lino Graglia of the

University of Texas at Austin, who stated that Blacks and Hispanics are not on an academic par with whites.

Burran, James A. "Violence in an 'Arsenal of Democracy': The Beaumont Race Riot, 1943." *East Texas Historical Review* 14 (Spring 1976).

Byrne, Kevin, and Oliver Houghton. "Texas Klan Rally: Cow Pasture Politics." *Space City* 3 (31 August 1971).

Calvert, Robert A. "The Civil Rights Movement in Texas." Chapter in *The Texas Heritage*, eds. Ben Proctor and Archie P. McDonald. Arlington Heights, IL: Forum, 1980.

_____, ed. "The Freedmen and Agricultural Prosperity." *Southwestern Historical Quarterly* 76 (April 1969). Labor contracts, freedmen, and white immigrants.

Cantrell, Gregg. "'Dark Tactics': Politics in the 1887 Texas Prohibition Campaign." *Journal of American Studies* 25 (April 1991).

Cantrell, Gregg, and D. Scott Barton. "Texas Populists and the Failure of Biracial Politics." *Journal of Southern History* 55 (November 1989).

Carlson, Paul H. "William R. Shafter, Black Troops, and the Opening of the Llano Estacado, 1870–1875." *Panhandle-Plains Historical Review* 47 (1974). Opening the Texas Panhandle for settlement.

Carstarphen Meta G. "Rare Films: The Tyler, Texas Treasure Trove." *American Visions*, June 1989. Rescue of Black films of the 1930s and 1940s.

Casdorph, Paul Douglas. "Norris Wright Cuney and Texas Republican Politics, 1883–1896." *Southwestern Historical Quarterly* 68 (April 1965). Republican Party leader in Texas.

Chase, Henry. "Juneteenth in Texas." *American Visions*, June-July 1997.

Chenoweth, Karin. "Texas Twister." *Black Issues in Higher Education* 13 (11 July 1996). The successful Graduate Opportunities Program (GOP) at the University of Texas at Austin and the *Hopwood* v. *Texas* decision.

Christian, Garna L., and Marvin E. Fletcher. "Black Soldiers in Jim Crow Texas, 1899–1917." *The American Historical Review* 102, no. 1 (1997).

Clary, David A. "The Role of the Army Surgeon in the West: Daniel Weisel at Fort Davis, Texas, 1868–1872." *Western Historical Quarterly* 3 (January 1972). The 9th Cavalry and the 41st (later the 25th) Infantry were stationed there.

Colloff, Pamela. "The Wrong Man." *Texas Monthly*, December 1997. Kevin Byrd spent 12 years in prison for a rape he did not commit, despite the weak case.

Cox, Patrick. "Nearly a Statesman": LBJ and Texas Blacks in the 1948 Election." *Social Science Quarterly* 74 (June 1993).

Crabb, Beth. "May 1930: White Man's Justice for a Black Man's Crime." *Journal of Negro History* 75 (Winter, Spring 1990). Mob violence in the deaths of George Hughes and Sam Johnson of Texas and Henry Argo of Oklahoma.

Crane, R. C. "D. W. Wallace ('80 John'): A Negro Cattleman on the Texas Frontier." *West Texas Historical Association Year Book* 28 (1952).

Cravens, John N. "Felix 'Zero' Erwin: Louisiana Negro Slave and East Texas Freedman." *East Texas Historical Journal* 10 (Fall 1972).

Crawford, Ann Fears, and Crystal Sasse Ragsdale. "Congresswoman from Texas." Chapter in *Women in Texas: Their Lives, Their Experiences, Their Accomplishments*. Burnet, TX: Eakin Press, 1982.

"Crime." *Crisis* 2 (May 1911). Information on twenty Blacks murdered by mobs in Palestine, Texas, during July 1910.

Cripps, Thomas R. *"The Birth of a Race*: A Lost Film Rediscovered in Texas." *Texas Humanist* 5 (March/April 1983).

Cross, Cora M. "Early Days in Texas. Reminiscences by an Old-Time Darkly." *Texas Monthly*, October 1929.

Crouch, Barry A. "'All the Vile Passions': The Texas Black Code of 1866." *Southwestern Historical Quarterly* 97 (July 1993).

_____. "Black Dreams and White Justice." *Prologue* 6 (1974). Black communities in Texas.

_____. "The 'Chords of Love': Legalizing Black Marital and Family Rights in Postwar Texas." *Journal of Negro History* 79 (Fall 1994).

_____. "Freedmen's Bureau Records: Texas, a Case Study." Chapter in *Afro-American History: Sources for Research*, ed. Robert L. Clarke. Washington, DC: Howard University Press, 1981.

_____. "Guardian of the Freedpeople: The Texas Freedman's Bureau Agents and the Black Community." *Southern Studies* 3 (Fall 1992).

_____. "Hidden Sources of Black History: The Texas Freedmen's Bureau Records as a Case Study." *Southwestern Historical Quarterly* 83 (January 1980).

_____. "Self-Determination and Local Black Leaders in Texas." *Phylon* 39 (1978).

_____. "A Spirit of Lawlessness: White Violence, Texas Blacks, 1865–1868." *Journal of Social History* 18 (Winter 1984).

Crouch, Barry A., and Larry Madaras. "Reconstructing Black Families: Perspectives from the Texas Freedmen's Bureau Records." *Prologue* 18 (Summer 1986).

Crouch, Barry A., and L. J. Schultz. "Crisis in Color: Racial Separation in Texas During Reconstruction." *Civil War History: A Journal of the Middle Period* 16 (March 1970).

Crowell, Evelyn Miller. "My Father and the Klan." *The New Republic*, 1 July 1946. The Klan in Texas.

Cullen, James, and Carol Countryman. "Dividing Line: Police vs. Blacks in East Texas." *The Texas Observer* 84 (19 June 1992).

Curriden, Mark. "In Defense of KKK: Texas Lawyer Anthony Griffin Fights for KKK's First Amendment Right." *Barrister* 21, 1994 Annual. "Profiles of the Profession 1994" features Black attorney.

Curtis, Gregory. "A Case of Murder." *Texas Monthly*, April 1995. Writer supports the death penalty for 21-year-old Black woman, Erica Sheppard, for the murder of Marilyn sage Meagher.

_____. "The First Protester." *Texas Monthly*, June 1997.

Daniel, Wayne. "The Many Trials of Captain Armes." *Fort Concho Report* 13 (Fall 1981).

_____. "The 10th at Fort Concho, 1875–1882." *Fort Concho Report* 14 (Spring 1982).

"Daniel James III, Son of the Nation's First Black Four-Star General, Recently Was Installed as Commander of the Texas National Guard during a Ceremony in Austin." *Jet*, 18 December 1995.

_____. "More About the Klan." *Survey* 48 (8 April 1922).

Davis, Marilyn B. "Local Approach to the Sweatt Case." *Negro History Bulletin* 23 (Spring 1948).

De Shazo, Elmer Anthony. "An Equal Opportunities Committee at Work in Texas." *Social Science* 41, no. 2 (1966). San Marcos and desegregation.

Devine, Edward T. "The Klan in Texas." *Survey* 48 (1 April and 13 May 1922).

Dew, Charles B. "Black Ironworkers and the Slave Insurrection Panic of 1856." *Journal of Southern History* 41 (August 1975). Lynchings, including those in Texas.

Dillon, Merton L. "Benjamin Lundy in Texas." *Southwestern Historical Quarterly* 63 (July 1959).

Dingus, Anne. "Angela Shelf Medearis." *Texas Monthly,* September 1997. Profile of Medearis, author of sixty children's books with Black themes.

Dodson, Jack. "Minority Group Housing in Two Texas Cities." Chapter in Nathan Glazer and Davis McEntire, *Studies in Housing and Minority Groups*. Berkeley: 1960.

Draper, Robert. "The Horse Killers." *Texas Monthly*, March 1996. Seven Black boys and a girl, ages 8 to 14, found guilty of beating a horse to death in Silsbee, Texas.

Dulaney, W. Marvin. "Long Ride to Blue." *Our Texas* (Summer 1992).

_____. "The Progressive Voters League." *Legacies: A History Journal for Dallas and North Central Texas* 3 (Spring 1991).

_____. "The Texas Peace Officers' Association: The Origins of Black Police Unionism." *Houston Review* 12 (1990).

Eastland, Terry. "The Yellow Pose of Texas: Hopwood Upheld Dooms Affirmative Action Admissions." *American Spectator* 29 (September 1996). The Supreme Court refuses to review the 5th Circuit Court of

Appeals ruling that the University of Texas Law School can not use race in admissions.

Edgley, E. K., et al. "Rent Subsidy and Housing Satisfaction: The Case of Urban Renewal in Lubbock, Texas." *American Journal of Economics and Sociology* 27 (April 1968).

Edmunds, Edwin R. "The Myrdalian Thesis: Rank Order of Discrimination." *Phylon* 15 (Summer 1954). Study of the Myrdalian hypothesis in Texas and Oklahoma indicates it is inaccurate to use in the Southwest.

Elliott, Claude. "The Freedmen's Bureau in Texas." *Southwestern Historical Quarterly* 56 (July 1952).

Ennis, Michael. "Shock Therapy: Austin Painter Michael Ray Charles." *Texas Monthly*, June 1997.

Everett, Mary. "A Texas Plantation: Then and Now." *Sewanee Review* 44 (October-December 1936).

"Family of 1991 Hate Slaying Victim Receives $900,000 Settlement." *Jet*, 28 August 1995. Settlement paid by company owning the convenience store where the three skinhead killers purchased beer.

Feid, Jan. "Milligan's Island." *Texas Monthly*, April 1997. Profile of blue-eyed Black albino Malford Milligan, soul singer.

Fickle, James E. "The Louisiana-Texas Lumber War of 1911–1912." *Louisiana History* 16 (Winter 1975). Study of struggle that also included Blacks.

"The Fight in Texas Against Lynching." *World's Work* 37 (April 1919).

Fischer, Waller A., and Dwight E. Breed. "Negro Health Week in Texas." *Survey* 45 (16 October 1920)."

Fisher, John E. "The Legal Status of Free Blacks in Texas, 1836–1861." *Texas Southern Law Review* 43 (1977).

Fleming, Robert E. "Sutton E. Griggs: Militant Black Novelist." *Phylon* 34 (1973).

Foster, Robert L., and Alwyn Barr. "Black Lubbock." *West Texas Historical Association Year Book* 54 (1978).

"Frank." *Crisis* 10 (October 1915). Included in the article is a report of the burning of a Black man in Temple, Texas, in front of a crowd of 10,000.

Friedsam, N. J., C. D. Whatley, and A. L. Rhodes. "Some Selected Aspects of Judicial Commitments of the Mentally Ill in Texas." *Texas Journal of Science* 6 (1954). Blacks are committed to institutions more than others, and also receive lesser quality of treatment.

Galloway, Joseph L. "Into the Heart of Darkness." *U.S. News and World Report*, 8 March 1999. Racist prison gangs may have led John William King to murder James Byrd, Jr., in Jasper, Texas.

Garcia, James E. "Hostile Words in Texas." *Black Issues in Higher Education* 14 (2 October 1997). White law professor under fire for racist remarks.

Gauss, John. "Give the Blacks Texas." *Civil War Times Illustrated* 29 (May 1990). U.S. Senate in 1863 proposed cutting Texas in half for Blacks and forming the "Territory of the Rio Grande."

Gergen, David. "Becoming 'Race' Savvy." *U.S. News and World Report*, 2 June 1997. Proposal to emulate U.S. Army's success in promoting racial equality in light of decreased Black admissions in the UCLA and University of Texas law schools.

Gill, Gale. "Texas Trail Ride, Negro Cowboys." *Ebony*, May 1963.

Gite, Lloyd. "Artfully Inspired." *Black Enterprise*, September 1996. Joyce Hunt, the owner of Mitchie's Fine Black Art in Austin, Texas.

_____. "Texas." *Black Enterprise*, June 1994. Texas is recovering from economic problems and Blacks have an array of opportunities.

_____. "Vanessa Gilmore: Stating Her Case in Texas." *Essence*, January 1995. The youngest federal judge in the country and the only Black woman on the federal bench in Texas.

Glasrud, Bruce A. "Black Texas Improvement Efforts, 1870–1929: Migration, Separatism, Nationalism." *Texas African-American History Journal* 3 (1998).

_____. "Blacks and Texas Politics During the Twenties." *Red River Valley Historical Review* 7 (Spring 1982). Segregation in Texas from the 1830s to the 1970s.

_____. "Child or Beast?: White Texas' View of Blacks, 1900–1910." *East Texas Historical Journal* 15 (1977).

_____. "Enforcing White Supremacy in Texas, 1900–1910." *Red River Valley Historical Review* 4 (Fall 1979).

_____. "From Griggs to Brewer: A Review of Black Texas Artists, 1899–1940." *Texas African-American History Journal* 1 (1997).

_____. "Jim Crow's Emergence in Texas." *American Studies* 15 (1974).

_____. "*Nixon* vs. *Condon*, 286 US 73 (1932)." In *Encyclopedia of African-American Civil Rights: From Emancipation to the Present*, eds. Charles D. Lowery and John F. Marszalak. Westport, CT: Greenwood Press, 1992.

_____. "William M. McDonald: Business and Fraternal Leader." Chapter in *Black Leaders: Texans for Their Times*, eds. Alwyn Barr and Robert A. Calvert. Austin: Texas State Historical Association.

Goode, Victor. "The Blackest Dirt, the Whitest People: An East Texas Municipal Election." *Journal of Ethnic Studies* 11 (Winter 1984).

_____. "Cultural Racism in Public Education: A Legal Tactic for Black Texans." *Harvard Law Review* 33 (Summer 1990).

_____. "The Possibility of Afro-Texan Unity." *Texas Bar Journal* 54 (October 1991). Planning by the Texas Association of African American Lawyers.

Goodwyn, Lawrence C. "Populist Dreams and Negro Rights: East Texas as a Case Study." *American Historical Review* 76 (December 1971). The power of the interracial Grimes County People's Party and its defeat by White Man's Union after 35 years.

Govenar, Alan B. "Musical Traditions of Twentieth-Century African-American Cowboys." Chapter in *Juneteenth Texas: Essays in African American*

Folklore, eds. Francis Edward Abernethy, Carolyn Fiedler Satterwhite, Patrick B. Mullen, and Alan B. Govenar. Texas Folklore Society Publication, no. 54. Denton, TX: University of North Texas Press, 1996. Black social life and customs.

Grandolfo, Jane. "Free Speech Becomes a Burning Cross to Bear." *In These Times* (19 August 1992). KKK Imperial Wizard James Stansfield.

Grann, David. "Firestarters." *New Republic*, 20 July 1998. Visit to Jasper, Texas, following the dragging to death of James Byrd, Jr.

Green, James. "The Brotherhood" *Southern Exposure* 4, no. 1/2 (1976). The interracial Brotherhood of Timber Workers of western Louisiana and eastern Texas.

_____. "Tenant Farmer Discontent and Socialist Protest in Texas, 1901–1917." *Southwestern Historical Quarterly* 81 (October 1977). Study includes Blacks.

Greenberg, Herbert, and Delores Hutto. "The Attitudes of West Texas College Students toward School Integration." *Journal of Applied Psychology* 42 (October 1958).

Grunbaum, Werner F. "Desegregation in Texas: Voting and Action Patterns." *Public Opinion Quarterly* 28 (Winter 1964). Investigates if demographic factors are associated with resistance to desegregation.

Gwynne, S. C. "Back to the Future." *Time*, 2 June 1997. Effects of ending affirmative action to law schools in Texas and California.

_____. "The Second Coming of a Nightmare." *Time*, 1 March 1999. Murder of James Byrd, Jr., in Jasper, Texas.

Hainsworth, Robert W. "The Negro and the Texas Primaries." *Journal of Negro History* 18 (October 1933).

Hall, Martin H. "Negroes With Confederate Troops in West Texas and New Mexico." *Password* 13 (Spring 1968). Slaves with Confederate masters in 1861 and 1862.

Hardwickhall, Martin. "Negroes with Confederate Troops in West Texas and New Mexico." *Password* (Spring 1968).

Harris, Trudier. "'The Yellow Rose of Texas': A Different Cultural View." Chapter in *Juneteenth Texas: Essays in African-American Folklore*, eds. Francis Edward Abernethy, et al. Publication of the Texas Folklore Society, no. 54. Denton: University of North Texas Press, 1996.

Hart, Norris. "You Must Go Home Again." *Center Magazine* 2 (July 1969). Black teacher advocates involvement in slums.

Hartley, Margaret L. "Black Boundaries in Big Texas." *Southwest Review* 37 (Winter 1952).

Hayes, Roland C. "Blacks in Texas." Chapter in *Texas: A Sesquicentennial Celebration*, ed. Donald W. Whisenhunt. Austin: Eakin Press, 1984.

Hendon, William S. "Discrimination Against Negro Homeowners in Property Tax Assessment." *American Journal of Economics and Sociology* 27 (April 1968). Fort Worth.

Higginbotham, A. Leon, Jr. "Breaking Thurgood Marshall's Promise." *Black Issues in Higher Education* 14 (5 February 1998). Former judge discusses *Hopwood* v. *Texas.*

"High Noon for Texas Education." *Black Issues in Higher Education* 10 (9 September 1993). Integration of white campuses conflicts with enhancement of Black and Latino colleges.

Hine, Darlene Clark. "Blacks and the Destruction of the White Primary, 1932–1944." *Journal of Negro History* 62 (January 1977).

_____. "The Elusive Ballot: The Black Struggle against the Texas Democratic White Primary, 1932–1945." *Southwestern Historical Quarterly* 81 (April 1978).

"Historical Document: An Address from the President of Bishop College, Marshall, Texas, 1901." *American Baptist Quarterly* 12 (March 1993). Albert Laughridge talks about American Baptists and Black higher education.

Holbrook, Abigail. "Cotton Marketing in Antebellum Texas." *Southwestern Historical Quarterly* 73, no. 4 (1970). How a frontier became a part of the cotton economy.

Hollandworth, Skip. "Does DaRoyce Mosley Deserve to Die?" *Texas Monthly*, February 1996. Investigation of a young Black man accused of killing four white men.

_____. "Refinery Woe." *Texas Monthly*, May 1995. Residents of Corpus Christi's "Refinery Row" blame pollution for high cancer rates and file suits.

Holloway, Harry. "The Negro and the Vote: The Case of Texas." *Journal of Politics* 23 (August 1961).

_____. "The Texas Negro as a Voter." *Phylon* 24 (Summer 1963). A study of Austin voters.

Holmes, Robert E. "The Last Days of the Texas Convention of 1836." *Texana* 8, no. 3 (1970). The convention declared independence from Mexico and dealt with slavery, among other issues.

Holtzman, W. H. "Attitudes of College Men toward Non-Segregation in Texas Schools." *Public Opinion Quarterly* 20 (Fall 1956).

"The Horizon. Ghetto" *Crisis* 13 (April 1917). Lawsuit against the Black Paul Quinn College by the husband of a murdered woman whose attacker was lynched. The student newspaper reported the husband was a murder suspect.

Hornsby, Alton, Jr. "The 'Colored Branch University' Issue in Texas—Prelude to *Sweatt* vs. *Painter*." *Journal of Negro History* 61 (January 1976). The 1940s creation of a "separate but equal" university for Blacks to avoid integration.

_____. "The Freedmen's Bureau Schools in Texas, 1865–1870." *Southwestern Historical Quarterly* 76 (April 1973).

Hwang, Sean-Shong, and Steve H. Murdock. "Segregation in Nonmetropolitan and Metropolitan Texas in 1980." *Rural Sociology* 48 (Winter 1983).

"Institutionalized Racism." *National Review*, 12 September 1992. Suit won by whites against the University of Texas School of Law.

Isaac, Paul E. "Municipal Reform in Beaumont, Texas, 1902–1909." *Southwestern History* 78 1975). Poll taxes and disfranchisement of the Black vote is mentioned.

Ivins, Molly. "In Memoriam: A Great Spirit (and Voice) Has Left Us." *Texas Tech Law Review* 27 (Fall 1996). Appreciation of Barbara Jordan.

Ivy, Charlotte. "Forgotten Color: Black Families in Early El Paso." *Password* 35 (1990).

Jackson, Bechetta A. "Racist Remarks, Death Threats, Crude Gestures Forced Blacks to Leave Texas Housing Complex." *Jet*, 4 October 1993.

Jackson, Jacquelyne Johnson. "Suzanne J. Terrell: This Other Kind of Doctors: Traditional Medical Systems in Black Neighborhoods in Austin, Texas." *Contemporary Sociology* 20 (September 1991).

Jackson, Kenneth. "Dallas: Dynamo of the Southwest." Chapter in *The Ku Klux Klan in the City, 1915–1930*. New York: Oxford University Press, 1967.

Jones, Douglas L. "The Sweatt Case and the Development of Legal Education for Negroes in Texas." *Texas Law Review* 47 (March 1969).

Jordan, Terry G. "A Century and a Half of Ethnic Change in Texas, 1836–1986." *Southwestern Historical Quarterly* 89 (April 1986). Black clues included.

_____. "The Imprint of the Upper and Lower South on Mid-Nineteenth Century Texas." *Annals of the Association of American Geographers* 57, no. 4 (1967). Social and economic development and relationship to population origins.

Karp, Hal. "Manufacturing Genius." *Black Enterprise*, September 1998. Profile of Roy Perry, vice president of operations for Dell Dimension, Latitude and Inspiron computers in Austin.

Keir. A. E. "The Texas Supreme Court and Trial Rights of Blacks, 1845–1860." *Journal of American History* 58 (December 1971).

Kerrigan, William T. "Race, Expansion, and Slavery in Eagle Pass, Texas, 1852." *Southwestern Historical Quarterly* 101 (January 1998).

Kirgan, Sadie E. "Tales the Darkies Tell of Ghosts that Walk in Freestone County, Texas." *Texas Monthly*, May 1930.

Kirk, W. Aston, and John Taylor Q. King. "Desegregation of Higher Education in Texas." *Journal of Negro Education* 27 (Summer 1958).

"Klan Victories in Oregon and Texas." *Literary Digest* 75 (25 November 1922).

Krapf, Kellie A., and Floyd B. Largent, Jr. "Black Seminole Indian Scouts in Texas." *Persimmon Hill* 24 (Winter 1996).

"The Ku Klux Klan Victory in Texas." *Literary Digest* 74 (5 August 1922).

"Ku Klux Violence to Teachers in the South." *American Missionary Magazine* 18 (September 1874).

Kuvlesky, William F., and George W. Ohlendorf. "A Rural-Urban Comparison of the Occupational Status Orientations of Negro Boys." *Rural Sociology* 33 (June 1968). Sampling of Texas high school youth.

Lack, Paul D. "Slavery and Vigilantism in Austin, Texas, 1840–1860." *Southwestern Historical Quarterly* 85 (July 1981).

Lamkin, Patricia E. "Blacks in San Angelo: Relations between Fort Concho and the City, 1875–1889." *West Texas Historical Association Year Book* 66 (1990).

Layden, Tim. "High Stakes Gambler." *Sports Illustrated*, 25 August 1997. Profile of Black Longhorn quarterback James Brown.

Leckie, William H. "Black Regulars on the Texas Frontier, 1866–85." Chapter in *The Texas Military Experience: From the Texas Revolution through World War II*, ed. Joseph G. Dawson III. College Station: Texas A&M University Press, 1995.

Ledbetter, Billy D. "White Over Black in Texas: Racial Attitudes in the Ante-Bellum Period." *Phylon* 34 (December 1973).

_____. "White Texans' Attitudes Toward the Political Equality of Negroes, 1865–1870." *Phylon* 40 (September 1979).

Lightfoot, Billy Bob. "The Negro Exodus from Comanche County, Texas." *Southwestern Historical Quarterly* 56 (January 1953).

Lind, Michael. "Obituary." *New Republic*, 12 February 1996. The death of Barbara Jordan.

Lipsitz, George. "'Goin' On': Afro-American Imagery in Texas Film and Folklore." *Southwest Media Review* 3 (Spring 1985).

Loewenstein, Gaither, and Lytlleton T. Sanders. "Bloc Voting, Rainbow Coalitions, and the Jackson Presidential Candidacy: A View from Southeast Texas." *Journal of Black Studies* 18 (September 1967).

Long, C. D. "Affirmative Action Struck Down at the University of Texas Law School." *Academe* (May/June 1996).

"The Looking Glass. As to Lynching in Texas." *Crisis* 16 (October 1918).

"The Looking Glass. Contrasts." *Crisis* 20 (June 1920). Includes the murder of a Black man named Price in St. Augustine, Texas.

Lucko, Paul M. "Dissertations and Theses Relating to African American Studies in Texas: A Selected Bibliography, 1904–1990." *Southwestern Historical Quarterly* 96 (1993).

"Lynched." *Crisis* 41 [sic 39] (June 1932). Black man, Dave Tillus, lynched in Crockett, Texas, for frightening a white woman.

"A Lynching? We're Too Busy." *New Masses* 10 (20 February 1934). Reaction of former governor Ferguson to the lynching of Black man David Gregory in Kountze, Texas.

"Lynching as a Japanese Sculptor Sees It." *Christian Century* 52 (13 February 1935). Isamu Noguchi's bronze statue of a Black man lynched in Sherman, Texas.

"The Lynching Horror." *Nation*, 29 August 1901. Blacks lynched, homes burned, and driven out in Pierce City, Missouri and Grayson County, Texas.

Marcello, Ronald E. "Reluctance versus Reality: The Desegregation of North Texas State College, 1954–1956." *Southwestern Historical Quarterly* 100 (1991).

Marshall, Thurgood. "The Rise and Collapse of the 'White Democratic Primary.'" *Journal of Negro Education* 26 (Summer 1957). The 1944 case Marshall argued before the Supreme Court.

Mathis, Annie Maie. "Negro Public Health Nursing in Texas." *Southern Workman* 56 (July 1927).

Maxwell, Madeline, and S. Smith Todd. "Black Sign Language and School Integration in Texas." *Language in Society* 15 (March 1986).

Maxwell, Robert S. "Lumbermen of the East Texas Frontier." *Forest History* 9, no. 1 (1965). Black labor in a timber region that was the size of Maine.

Mayer, Milton. "Deep in the Heart." *Progressive* 21 (July 1957). The White Citizens' Council in Texas.

McAdams, D. Claire. "Environmental Activism and the Intersection of Race, Class, and Gender: Patterns in Central Texas." *Sociological Abstracts* (August 1991, Supplement 167).

McCaslin, Richard B. "Steadfast in His Intent: John W. Hargis and the Integration of the University of Texas at Austin." *Southwestern Historical Quarterly* 95 (July 1991). First Black undergraduate at the University of Texas.

McDaniel, Vernon. "Negro Publicly-Supported Higher Institutions in Texas." *Journal of Negro Education* 31 (Summer 1962).

McGraw, Dan. "Justice Delayed." *U.S. News and World Report*, 1 March 1999. Jasper County, Texas, district attorney Guy James Gray to prosecute John William King for the murder of James Byrd, Jr. When a child, Gray's father told him of the murder of a Black man in the town square during the 1930s who was also dragged behind a truck.

Meeks, Walter A. "The Black American in Texas after the Civil War." *Negro History Bulletin* 37 (1974).

Merk, Frederick. "A Safety Valve Thesis and Texan Annexation." *Mississippi Valley Historical Review* 49, no. 3 (1962). The debate over the admission of Texas to the Union.

Miller, Kelly. "Art as a Cure for Lynching." *Christian Century* 52 (17 April 1935). Letter concerning article "Lynching as a Japanese Sculptor Sees It," above.

Miller, Mark, and Marc Peyser. "'We Live in Daily Fear.'" *Newsweek*, 2 September 1996. Blacks face arson in Greenville, Texas.

Min, Janice. "Hanging Tough." *People Weekly*, 15 May 1995. Feature on Miss USA Chelsi Smith, formerly Miss Houston and Miss Texas.

Moon, Henry Lee. "End of Night of Terror at TSU." *Crisis* 78 (1971). Charges dismissed against five students after an altercation in May 1967.

"More Texas Klansmen Indicted." *Militant* 35 (25 June 1971).

Morrow, Lance. "Something We Cannot Accept." *Time*, 8 March 1999. Implications of death sentence imposed on John William King for the murder of James Byrd, Jr., in Jasper, Texas.

Morse, Arthur D. "When Negroes Entered a Texas School: Del Mar College." *Harper's Monthly Magazine* 209 (September 1954).

Moseley, J. A. R. "The Citizens White Primary of Marion County, Texas, of 1898." *Southwestern Historical Quarterly* 69 (April 1946).

Muir, Andrew Forest. "The Free Negro in Fort Bend County, Texas." *Journal of Negro History* 33 (January 1948.

_____. "The Free Negro in Galveston County, Texas." *Negro History Bulletin* 22 (December 1958).

_____. "The Free Negro in Harris County, Texas." *Southwestern Historical Quarterly* 46 (January 1943).

_____. "The Free Negro in Jefferson and Orange Counties, Texas." *Journal of Negro History* 35 (April 1950).

_____. "The Free Negro in the Republic of Texas." *Southwestern History Quarterly* 41 (July 1937).

Mullen, Patrick B. "The Function of Folk Belief Among Negro Fishermen of the Texas Coast." *Southern Folklore Quarterly* 33 (June 1969).

_____. "A Negro Street Performer: Tradition and Innovation." *Western Folklore* 29, no. 2 (1970). Study of Galveston street entertainer George "Bongo Joe" Coleman.

_____. "The Prism of Race: Two Texas Folk Performers." *Southern Folklore* 54 (Spring 1997). Music of Lightnin' Hopkins and George Coleman (Bongo Joe).

Murphy, Lucretia P. "Black Women: Organizing to Lift...to Rise." *Texas Journal of Women and the Law* (4 (Summer 1995).

Nash, A. E. Keir. "The Texas Supreme Court and Trial Rights of Blacks, 1845–1860." *Journal of American History* 58 (December 1971). Five judges of the Texas supreme court who were sympathetic towards Blacks.

Nash, Sunny. "A Mission Completed for Doll." Chapter in *State Lines*, ed. Ken Hammond. College Station: Texas A&M University Press, 1993.

"Negro Primary Vote Barred by the Texas Democratic Party; Supreme Court Decision." *Literary Digest* 119 (13 April 1935).

Newell, Guy R., Lori G. Borrud, and R. Sue McPherson. "Nutrient Intakes of Whites, Blacks and Mexican Americans in Southeast Texas." *Preventive Medicine* 17 (September 1988). Targeted dietary planning.

Nieman, Donald G. "African Americans and the Meaning of Freedom: Washington County, Texas, as a Case Study, 1865–1886." *Chicago Kent Law Review* 70 (1994).

_____. "Black Political Power and Criminal Justice: Washington County, Texas, 1868–1884." *Journal of Southern History* 55 (August 1989).

"No Lynching in Texas, State Uses New Method." *Southern Frontier* 3 (January 1942). Using new tactics, an individual will kill a Black person or a gang might mutilate Black persons, but not kill them.

"Norris Wright Cuney: A Son of Texas." *Negro History Bulletin* 5 (March 1942).

Norton, Wesley. "The Methodist Episcopal Church and the Civil Disturbances in North Texas in 1859 and 1860." *Southwestern Historical Quarterly* 68 (January 1965).

Nye, Naomi Shihab. "Field Trip." Chapter in *State Lines*, ed. Ken Hammond. College Station: Texas A&M University Press, 1993.

Ohlendorf, George W., and William P. Kuvlesky. "Racial Differences in the Educational Orientation of Rural Youths." *Social Science Quarterly* 49 (September 1968). Study of Black and white youths in Texas.

Okolo, R. E., and J. P. Eddy. "A Job Satisfaction Study of Faculty at Historically Black Colleges and Universities in Texas." *College Student Journal* 28, no. 3 (1994).

Olson, James S., and Sharon Phair. "The Anatomy of a Race Riot: Beaumont, Texas, 1943." *Texana* 11 (Winter 1973). Describes how an incident escalated to a riot.

"On Being a Minority Student at the University of Texas." *Integrateducation* 17 (September-December 1979).

Ovington, Mary White. "Is Mob Violence the Texas Solution of the Race Problem?" *Independent* 99 (6 September 1919).

Owens, William A. "Writing a Novel—Problem and Solution." *Southwest Review* 40 (1955).

Pego, David. "Dos Culturas, One Pedagogy: Teaching History from Black and Hispanic Perspectives." *Black Issues in Higher Education* 13 (8 February 1996). Using history to raise ethnic identity.

Petersilia, Joan. "Racial Disparities in the Criminal Justice System: A Summary." *Crime and Delinquency* 31 (January 1985). Study of discrimination in the criminal justice system in California, Michigan and Texas.

Phillips, Edward Hake. "The Sherman Courthouse Riot of 1930." *East Texas Historical Journal* 25 (1987).

Pickens, William. "Death Detail: Trial and Execution of Thirteen Negro Soldiers at Fort Sam Houston, Texas, December, 1917." *World Tomorrow* 13 (April 1930).

_____. "Jim Crow in Texas." *The Nation* 117 (15 August 1923).

Porter, Kenneth Wiggins. "Negro Labor in the Western Cattle Industry, 1866–1900." *Labor History* 10 (Summer 1969).

_____. "Negroes and Indians on the Texas Frontier, 1831–1876: A Study in Race and Culture." *Journal of Negro History* 41 (July 1956 and October 1956). Study of relationships.

_____. "Negroes and Indians of the Texas Frontier, 1831–1876." *Southwestern Historical Quarterly* 53 (October 1949).

Posey, John R. "Ebony Voices Harmonizing across the Texas Prairie." Chapter in *New Texas 94: Poetry and Fiction*, eds. Kathryn S. McGuire and James Ward Lee. Denton: Center for Texas Studies, 1994.

Prairie View State Normal and Industrial College. *Proceedings of the Seventh Educational Conference, 1936.* Prairie View: The College, 1936.

Preece, Harold. "Texas Holiday." *Crisis* 43 (January 1936). In 1935, two Black teenagers are lynched in Columbus, Texas.

Price, John Ellis. "Needs and Problems of Minority-Owned Small Businesses." *The National Public Accountant* 37 (February 1992). Needs and problems of Black and Latino business communities in Texas.

Prince, Diane Elizabeth. "William Goyens, Free Negro on the Texas Frontier." Master's thesis, Stephen F. Austin State College, 1967.

Rabkin, Jeremy A. "Diversity Snobs." *American Spectator*, August 1997). Admissions decrease for Black students at Berkeley and the University of Texas law schools.

"Reading for Negroes: Resolution Adopted at Texas Conference of Negro Librarians." *Library Journal* 612 (1 May 1936).

Redwine, W. A. "Brief History of the Negro in Five Counties." Vol. 11, *Chronicles of Smith County.* Tyler, TX: 1972. First published as privately printed book, 1901.

Reese, James V. "The Early History of Labor Organizations in Texas, 1838–1876." *Southwestern Historical Quarterly* 72 (July 1968).

Reich, S. A. "Soldiers of Democracy: Black Texans and the Fight for Citizenship, 1917–1921." *Journal of American History* 82 (March 1996).

"A Reversion to Savagery." *Outlook* 110 (11 August 1915). The burning of Will Stanley in Temple, Texas.

Richardson, Susan. "Smaller Institutions Expect Increased Minority Presence as a Result of Hopwood Decision." *Black Issues in Higher Education* 14 (1 May 1997). Affirmative action in Texas education.

Richter, William L. "'The Revolver Rules the Day!': Colonel DeWitt C. Brown and the Freedman's Bureau in Paris, Texas, 1867–1868." *Southwestern Historical Quarterly* 93 (1990).

Ring, Harry. "Houston Election Campaign puts Socialists on the Map." *Militant* 35 (24 December 1971). The Klan in Texas.

"The Riots at Charleston, Longview, Omaha and Knoxville." Section in *Negro Year Book...1921–1922*, ed. Monroe N. Work. Tuskegee Institute: Negro Year Book Publishing Company, 1922.

Roberts, Randy. "Galveston's Jack Johnson: Flourishing in the Dark." *Southern Historical Quarterly* 87 (1983). First Black heavyweight champion.

Rodenberger, Lou Halsell. "A Developing Tradition: African-American Writers." Chapter in *Texas Women Writers: A Tradition of Their Own*, eds. Sylvia Ann Grider and Lou Halsell Rodenberger. College Station: Texas A&M University Press, 1997.

Rogers, B. Ann, and Linda Schott. "'My Mother Was a Mover': African American Seminole Women in Brackettville, Texas, 1914–1964." Chapter in *Writing the Range: Race, Class, and Culture in the Women's West*, eds. Elizabeth Jameson and Susan Armitage. Norman: University of Oklahoma Press, 1997.

Rose, Mark. "Odessa Branch of NAAP Wins Environmental Justice Case in Texas." *Crisis* 104 (July 1997). Texas branch wins settlement against Dynagen, Rexene and Shell Oil.

Rosen, Jeffrey. "Sandramandered." *New Republic*, 8 July 1996. Supreme Court justice O'Connor strikes down majority-Black congressional districts in Texas and North Carolina.

Russ, W. A., Jr. "Radical Disfranchisement in Texas, 1867–70." *Southwestern Historical Quarterly* 38 (July 1934).

Russell, Jan Jarboe. "We Will Never Surrender or Retreat." *Texas Monthly*, May 1994. Daughters of the Republic of Texas (DRT) have custody of the Alamo and its history, fight against inclusion of Blacks and others.

Saenz, Rogelio, and John K. Thomas. "Minority Poverty in Nonmetropolitan Texas." *Rural Sociology* 56 (1991).

San Miguel, Guadalupe, Jr. "From a Dual to Tri-Partite School System: The Origins and Development of Educational Segregation in Corpus Christi, Texas." *Integrateducation* 17 (September-December 1979).

Sanders, Charles L. "Barbara Jordan: Texan Is a New Power on Capitol Hill." *Ebony*, February 1975.

Santos, R. Chris. "Doris 'Dorie' Miller." *Texas Historian* 37 (May 1977). WWII naval hero from Texas.

Sapper, Neil Gary.. "Black Culture in Urban Texas: A Lone Star Renaissance." *Red River Valley Historical Review* 6 (Spring 1981).

Sargent, Frederic O. "Economic Adjustment of Negro Farmers in East Texas." *Southwestern Social Science Quarterly* 42 (June 1961).

Saunders, Robert. "Southern Populists and the Negro, 1893–1895." *Journal of Negro History* 54 (July 1969).

Savage, W. Sherman. "The Negro Cowboy of the Texas Plains." *Negro History Bulletin* 24 (April 1961). "Eighty" John Wallace, Emanuel Organ, and Matthew "Bones" Hooks profiled.

Schaffer, Ruth C. "The Health and Social Functions of Black Midwives on the Texas Brazos Bottom, 1920–1985." *Rural Sociology* 56 (Spring 1991).

Schecter, B. J. "Harry Flournoy, Texas Western Forward." *Sports Illustrated*, 6 April 1998. Profile of Flournoy, who was on the winning team at the 1966 NCAA basketball tournament for Texas Western (UTEP).

Schoen, Harold. "The Free Negro in the Republic of Texas: Legal Status." *Southwestern Historical Quarterly* 40 (January 1937).

_____. "The Free Negro in the Republic of Texas: Manumission." *Southwestern Historical Quarterly* 40 (1936).

_____. "The Free Negro in the Republic of Texas: Origin of the Free Negro in the Republic of Texas." *Southwestern Historical Quarterly* 39 (April 1936).

_____. "The Free Negro in the Republic of Texas: The Extent of Discrimination and Its Effects." *Southwestern Historical Quarterly* 41 (1937).

_____. "The Free Negro in the Republic of Texas: The Free Negro and the Texas Revolution." *Southwestern Historical Quarterly* 40 (1936).

_____. "The Free Negro in the Republic of Texas: The Law in Practice." *Southwestern Historical Quarterly* 40 (1937).

Scott, Alan. "Twenty-Five Years of Opinion on Integration in Texas." *Southwestern Social Science Quarterly* 48 (September 1967).

Shafter, W. R. "Shafter's Explorations in Western Texas, 1875, ed. Martin L. Crimmins. *West Texas Historical Association Year Book* 9 (1933).

Shange, Ntozake. "Recipes from the Gypsy Cowgirl." *American Visions*, February–March 1998. Historical discussions and recipes from noted poet/playwright.

Shaw, James, Jr. "Colonel of 7th United States Colored Troops." Section in *Our Last Campaign and Subsequent Service in Texas*. Providence: The Society, 1905.

Shook, Robert W. "Military Activities in Victoria." *Texana* 3, no. 4 (1965). Racial overtones during military occupation.

"Should Negroes Vote? Supreme Court Decision Denying the Negro the Right to Vote in Democratic Primary in Texas." *The New Republic*, 8 May 1935.

Sidanius, James. "Racial Discrimination and Job Evaluation: The Case of University Faculty." *National Journal of Sociology* 3 (1989). Study of the University of Texas.

Simon, Paul. "White Hood, Black Robes." *Black Issues in Higher Education* 13 (13 June 1996). Possible effects of *Hopwood* v. *Texas* at the University of Texas at Austin.

Simond, Ada DeBlanc. "The Discovery of Being Black: A Recollection." *Southwestern Historical Quarterly* 76 (1973).

Singer, Stu. "Armed Clansmen Threaten Socialists." *Militant* 39 (7 March 1975). The Klan in Texas.

Slaton, William J. "Negro Businesses in Texas." *Texas Business Review* 43 (July 1969).

Smallwood, James M. "Black Freedwomen after Emancipation: The Texas Experience." *Prologue: The Journal of the National Archives* 27 (Winter 1995).

_____. "Blacks in Antebellum Texas: A Reappraisal." *Red River Valley Historical* Review 2 (Winter 1975).

_____. "Emancipation and the Black Family: A Case Study in Texas." *Social Science Quarterly* 57 (1977).

_____. "Texas." Chapter in *The Black Press in the South, 1865–1985*, ed. Henry Lewis Suggs. Westport, CT: Greenwood Press, 1983.

_____. "The Woodward Thesis Revisited: The Origins of Social Segregation in Texas." *Negro History Bulletin* (1984).

Smith, Bryan L. "Desegregation in West Texas: The *United States* v. *Ector County ISD* Case." *West Texas Historical Association Year Book* 69 (1933).

Smith, Drifter, "Texas Women." *Journal of the Southwest* 33 (Summer 1991). Some slave stories included.

Smith, R. L. "Uplifting Negro Cooperative Society in Texas." *World's Work* 16 (July 1908).

Smith, Ralph A. "The Mamelukes of West Texas and Mexico." *West Texas Historical Association Year Book* 39 (1963).

Smith, Rhonda. "MOSES leads Winona, Texas, to Environmental Justice." *Crisis* 104 (July 1997). MOSES (Mothers Organized to Stop Environmental Sins) leads a successful fight against a polluting disposal service.

Smither, Harriet. "Effect of English Abolitionism on Annexation of Texas." *Southwestern Historical Quarterly* 32 (January 1929).

"Soldier in Texas." *Crisis* 1 (May 1911).

Solomon, Marva. "The Voices of Black Texans." *Texas Highways* 40 (September 1993).

Sonnichsen, C. L., and M. G. McKinney. "El Paso—From War to Depression." *Southwestern Historical Quarterly* 74 (January 1971). The Klan in Texas.

SoRelle, James M. "The 'Waco Horror': The Lynching of Jesse Washington." *Southwestern Historical Quarterly* 86 (April 1983).

Stanley, Oma. "Negro Speech of East Texas." *American Speech* 16 (February 1941).

Stern, Madelein B. "Stephen Pearl Andrews, Abolitionist, and the Annexation of Texas." *Southwestern Historical Quarterly* 67 (April 1964).

Strong, Donald S. "The Poll Tax: The Case of Texas." *American Political Science Review* 38 (August 1944).

_____. "The Rise of Negro Voting in Texas." *American Political Science Review* 42 (June 1948).

Sullivan, Mark. "Midsummer Politics and Primaries." *World's Work* 44 (July 1922). The Klan in Texas.

Swartz, Mimi. "Vidor in Black and White." *Texas Monthly*, December 1993. Story of a "notorious" East Texas city.

Temple, Frank M. "Colonel B. H. Grierson's Administration of the District of the Pecos." *West Texas Historical Association Year Book* 38 (1962).

_____. "Colonel B. H. Grierson's Victorio Campaign." *West Texas Historical Association Year Book* 35 (October 1959); reprinted in *The*

Black Military Experience in the American West, ed. John M. Carroll. New York: Liveright Publishing, 1971.

————. "Colonel Grierson in the Southwest." *Panhandle-Plains Historical Review* 30 (1957).

————. "Discipline and Turmoil in the Tenth U.S. Cavalry." *West Texas Historical Association Year Book* 17 (Winter 1985).

————. "The Tenth U.S. Cavalry in Texas." *Fort Concho Report* 17 (Winter 1985).

Terrell, J. C. "Lynch Law in Texas in the Sixties." *Green Bag* 14 (1902).

"A Texas Cavalry Raids: Reaction to Black Soldiers and Contrabands." *Civil War History* 35 (June 1989).

"Texas College Hopes the Turmoil Is Over." *The Chronicle of Higher Education* 41 (7 September 1994). Historical Black college fights for stability and accreditation.

"A Texas Horror." *Crisis* 24 (July 1932). Blacks lynched—three burned alive—following the murder of a white girl in Kirwin, Texas.

"The Texas Horror." *Public Opinion* 14 (11 February 1893). The lynching of Henry Smith.

"Texas Officials Approve Lynching of Negroes Too Young for Capital Punishment." *International Juridical Association Monthly Bulletin* 4 (November 1935). Victims Ernest Collins and Bennie Mitchell.

"Texas Remapping Woes May Be Seen Elsewhere." *Congressional Quarterly Weekly Report* 49 (17 August 1991). Drawing a new congressional map for the 1990.

Tharp, Mike. "Death in Black and White." *U.S. News and World Report*. Bill Simpson, one of the first Blacks to integrate Vidor, Texas, is murdered by young Blacks the evening he moved to Beaumont.

Thomas, Gates. "South Texas Negro Work-Songs: Collected and Uncollected." Chapter in *Rainbow in the Morning*, ed. J. Frank Dobie. Hatboro, PA: Folklore Association, 1965.

Thompson, Charles H. "Separate But Not Equal: The Sweatt Case." *Southwest Review* 33 (Spring 1948).

Thompson, Erwin N. "The Negro Soldiers on the Frontier: A Fort Davis Case Study." *Journal of the West* 7 (April 1968).

Thompson, Helen. "Black and White World." *Texas Monthly*, November 1994. Photographs of Blacks in Texas.

————. "Freedom fighter." *Texas Monthly*, March 1995. Profile of Black Galveston attorney Anthony Griffin, who represented the Ku Klux Klan at the same time he was pro bono counsel for the NAACP.

Tjarks, Alicia V. "Cooperative Demographic Analysis of Texas, 1777–1793." *Southwestern Historical Quarterly* 77 (1974).

"Torture and Lynching." *Outlook* 71 (28 June 1902). Black man burned at Lansing, Texas.

Totten, Herman, L. "The Wiley College Library, the First Library for Negroes West of the Mississippi." *Negro History Bulletin* 32, no. 1 (1969). Importance of the Wiley College Library from the 1870s.

Tower, John. "FEPC—Some Practical Considerations." *Federal Bar Journal* 24 (Winter 1964). Senator Tower and the illegality of discrimination.

Traub, James. "Testing Texas." *New Republic*, 6 April 1998. The *Hopwood v. Texas* decision and the University of Texas Law School.

Treat, Victor H. "William Goyens: Free Negro Entrepreneur." Chapter in *Black Leaders: Texans for Their Times*, eds. Alwyn Barr and Robert A. Calverts. Austin: Texas State Historical Association, 1981.

"Turning the Tide in Beaumont (Texas)." *Crisis* 91 (May 1984).

Tuttle, William M., Jr. "Violence in a 'Heathen' Land: The Longview Race Riot of 1919." *Phylon* 33 (Winter 1972). Also, the views of two participants.

"Two Black Churches Set on Fire; Brings Total to 32." *Jet*, 24 June 1996. Includes information about Greenville, Texas.

Utley, Robert M. "'Pecos Bill' On the Texas Frontier." *American West* 6 (January 1969). William Shafter, racist but effective commander of Black troops.

Valdez, A., Z. Yin, and C. D. Kaplan. "A Comparison of Alcohol, Drugs, and Aggressive Crime among Mexican-American, Black, and White Male Arrestees in Texas." *The American Journal of Drug and Alcohol Abuse* 23 (1997).

"Vidor's All-White Housing Complex Expected to Get More Blacks in by January." *Jet*, 27 December 1993. Housing desegregation.

Vlach, John Michael. "Afro-American Folk Crafts in Nineteenth Century Texas." *Western Folklore* 40 (1981).

————. "Black Folk Crafts in Antebellum Texas." Chapter in *Texana I: The Frontier. Proceedings of Humanities Forum Held at Round Top, Texas, May 1–3, 1980*, ed. LeRoy Johnson, Jr. Austin: Texas Historical Commission, 1983.

Wallace, Edward S. "General John Lapham Bullis, Thunderbolt of the Texas Frontier, I." *Southwestern Historical Quarterly* 54 (April 1951).

————. "General John Lapham Bullis, Thunderbolt of the Texas Frontier, II." *Southwestern Historical Quarterly* 55 (July 1951).

Wattris, Wendy. "Celebrate Freedom: Juneteenth." *Southern Exposure* 5, no. 1 (1977). Celebrates the landing of Union troops in Galveston on 19 June 1865.

Werlin, Herbert H. "The Victory in Slaton." *Negro History Bulletin* 25 (February 1962).

"When Men Become Beasts." *Frontier Times* 11 (June 1914). The lynching of Henry Smith in Paris, Texas.

White, Paula M. "Happy Juneteenth Day: African American 'Holiday' May Finally Receive Some National Recognition." *Black Enterprise*, June 1996.

Wiggins, William H., Jr. "Juneteenth: Tracking the Progress of an Emancipation Celebration." *American Visions*, June-July 1993.

Wilheim, Gene, Jr. "Dooryard Gardens and Gardening in the Black Community of Brushy, Texas." *Geographical Review* 65, no. 1 (1975).

Williams, J. Allen, Jr. "The Effects of Urban Renewal Upon a Black Community: Evolution and Recommendations." *Social Science Quarterly* 50 (December 1969).

Williams, L. V. "Teaching Negro Life and History in Texas High Schools." *Journal of Negro History* 20 (1935).

Williams, Patricia R. "Literary Traditions in Works by African-American Playwrights." Chapter in *Texas Women Writers: A Tradition of Their Own*, eds. Sylvia Ann Grider and Lou Halsell Rodenberger. College Station: Texas A&M University Press, 1997.

Winegarten, Ruthe, and Rosanne M. Barker. "Black Texas Women: 150 Years of Trial and Triumph." *The Mississippi Quarterly* 50 (1997).

Winegarten, Ruthe, and Merline Pitre. "Black Texas Women: 150 Years of Trial and Triumph." *The Journal of Southern History* 62 (1996).

Wood, W. D. "The Ku Klux Klan." *Quarterly of the Texas State Historical Association* 9 (April 1906).

Woods, Randall B. "George T. Ruby: A Black Militant in the White Business Community." *Red River Valley Historical Review* 1 (1974).

Woodson, Carter G. "The Cuney Family." *Negro History Bulletin* 11 (1948).

Woolfolk, George Ruble. "The Free Negro and Texas, 1836–1860." *Journal of Mexican-American History* 3 (1973).

_____. "Sources of History of the Negro in Texas, with Special Reference to Their Implications." *Journal of Negro History* 42 (January 1957).

_____. "Turner's Safety Valve and Free Negro Westward Migration." *Pacific Northwest Quarterly* 56 (July 1965). Analyzes Negro migration through the framework of Jackson's thesis between 1850 and 1860.

Wrinkle, Robert D., and Jerry L. Polinard. "Populism and Dissent: The Wallace Vote in Texas." *Social Science Quarterly* 54. Examines populism and racism.

Zirkel, Perry A. "Rights of Passage?" *Phi Delta Kappan* 80 (February 1999). Law suit filed by parents against a Livingstone, Texas, middle school on behalf of fifth-grader Charles Ryans

Brownsville Affray

"Affair at Brownsville." *Outlook* 84 (29 December 1906).

"Again the Black Battalion." *Current Literature* 42 (February 1907).

"Brownsville Again." *Outlook* 90 (26 December 1908).

"Brownsville Case Again." *Outlook* 88 (4 January 1908).

Buecker, Thomas R. "Prelude to Brownsville: The Twenty-Fifth Infantry at Fort Niobrara, Nebraska, 1902–66." *Great Plains Quarterly* 16 (Spring 1996).

Bumstead, Horace. "Marvel of Brownsville." *Independent* 68 (12 May 1910).

"Case of the Negro Battalion." *Current Literature* 42 (January 1907).

Christian, Garna L. "The Brownsville Raid's 168th Man: The Court-Martial of Corporal Knowles." *Southwestern Historical Quarterly* 93 (July 1989).

_____. "Rio Grande City: Prelude to the Brownsville Raid." *West Texas Historical Association Year Book* 57 (1981).

"Congress and the Brownsville Affray." *Outlook* 88 (21 March 1908).

"Debate on the Brownsville Affray." *Outlook* 85 (26 January 1907).

"Discharge of Colored Troops." *Review of Reviews* 35 (January 1907).

"Discharge of Three Companies of Negro Soldiers." *Outlook* 84 (17 November 1906).

"Discharge Without Honor of the Negro Battalions." *Charities and the Commons* 17 (5 January 1907).

"Discharged Negro Soldiers." *Independent* 61 (27 December 1906).

"Exit Brownsville." *Outlook* 91 (6 March 1909).

Foraker, Joseph Benson. "Testimony in the Brownsville Investigation." *North American Review* 187 (April 1908).

"'Judicial Lynching at Brownsville': November 9, 1906." *Crisis* 80 (January 1973).

"Just Act: Discharging Negro Troops." *Outlook* 84 (1 December 1906).

Paine, A. B. "Truth about the Brownsville, Texas, Affair, by Capt. 'Bill' McDonald." *Pearson's Magazine*, September 1908.

"Reinstatement of Negro Soldiers." *Independent* 64 (19 March 1908).

"Roosevelt and the Negro Soldiers." *Arena* 37 (January 1907).

"Senator Foraker, a Friend of the Negro." *Outlook* 88 (25 April 1908).

"Senator Foraker on Brownsville." *Outlook* 88 (25 April 1908).

"Soldier's View." *Outlook* 85 (2 February 1907).

"Taft on the Brownsville Affair." *Outlook* 84 (15 December 1906).

Terrell, Mary Church. "Taft and the Negro Soldiers." *Independent* 65 (23 July 1908).

Thornbrough, Emma Lou. "The Brownsville Episode and the Negro Vote." *Mississippi Valley Historical Review* 44 (1957). The discharge of the troops caused Blacks to remove support for Roosevelt.

Tinsley, James A. "Roosevelt, Foraker, and the Brownsville Affray." *Journal of Negro History* 41 (January 1956). Argues that Roosevelt was heavy-handed on the affair because of an unrelated episode involving Booker T. Washington.

U.S. Inspector General's Office. "The Brownsville Affray," 60th Cong., 1st Sess., Sen. Doc. 389, Washington, D.C.: Government Printing Office, 1908.

Wynne, Lewis N. "Brownsville—The Reaction of the Negro Press." *Phylon* 33 (Summer 1972). Reaction to the 1906 dishonorable discharge of a Black regiment.

Yeoman, G. Allen. "'Judicial Lynching at Brownsville': November 9, 1906."
    Crisis 80 (1973). Black soldiers' dishonorable discharge and their 1972
    Congressional vindication.
Young, Richard. "The Brownsville Affray." *American History Illustrated* 21
    (October 1986).

Dallas

Anjomani, Ardeshir, et al. "Racial Succession and Residential Mobility in Dal-
    las-Fort Worth and San Antonio." *Journal of Urban Affairs* 14 (1992).
"Beating of Black Businessman in Texas Gets Two White Attackers Sentenced to
    7 Years." *Jet*, 3 April 1995.
Bernstein, Robert A., and Jayne D. Polly. "Race, Class and Support for the
    Female Candidates." *Western Political Quarterly* 28, no. 4 (1975).
    The 1969 city council race in Dallas.
Biles, Roger. "The New Deal in Dallas." *Southwestern Historical Quarterly* 95
    (July 1991). Role of Blacks in the process.
Brophy, William J. "Active Acceptance—Active Containment: The Dallas
    Story." Chapter in *Southern Businessmen and Desegregation*, eds.
    Elizabeth Jacoway and David R. Colburn. Baton Rouge: Louisiana
    State University Press, 1982.
"Dallas Boy Born Without Hands Excels as a Gifted Artist." *Jet*, 1 March 1999.
    Desmond Blair, age 12, is outstanding artist at the Dallas W. E. Greiner
    Middle School and the Academy For the Exploratory Arts.
Dulaney, W. Marvin. "Whatever Happened to the Civil Rights Movement in
    Dallas, Texas?" Chapter in *Essays on the American Civil Rights
    Movement*, eds. W. Marvin Dulaney and Kathleen Underwood. College
    Station: Texas A&M University Press, 1993.
Edmiston, Dorothy. "A Ballet of the American Negro to be Performed in Dal-
    las, Texas." *Texas Monthly*, November 1940.
Engerand, Steven W. "Black and Mulatto Mobility in Dallas, Texas,
    1880–1910." *Phylon* 39 (1978).
Gite, Lloyd. "Texas: Are There Bigger Opportunities for Blacks in Dallas and
    Houston?" *Black Enterprise*, June 1994.
————. "The 'Pride' of Dallas No More: First Texas Bank of Dallas Sold to
    BOK Financial." *Black Enterprise*, July 1997. Dallas loses its only
    Black-owned bank.
Karp, Hal. "Gregory T. Davis: Riding the Airwaves of Success." *Black Enter-
    prise*, November 1996. Radio general manager increases ratings and
    profits.
"Little Gary Ferguson." *Ebony*, May 1966. Feature on the six-year-old singer
    and composer from Dallas.
Lowrey, Flora. "The Dallas Negro Players." *Southwest Review* 16 (Spring
    1931).

McEwen, Melanie, Pauline Johnson, and Jacque Neatherlin. "School-Based Management of Chronic Asthma Among Inner-City African-American Schoolchildren in Dallas, Texas." *Journal of School Health* 68 (May 1998).

Mitchell, Charles Dee. "F. L. 'Doc' Spellmon and Ruth Mae McCrane at the Museum of African-American Life and Culture." *Art in America* 84 (July 1996). Two Texas artists exhibit at the Dallas gallery.

Muhammad, Tariq K. "Shining in the Lone Star State." *Black Enterprise*, June 1998. Profile of Richard O. Davis of Davis Automotive—Stephens Oldsmobile Honda in Bloomington, Indiana, Davis Buick in Garland, Texas, and Davis Buick Hyundai GMC in Dallas.

Pipkin, Loretta. "Loretta Pipkin: Finding My Place." *International Review of African American Art* 13 (1996). Textile designer of Dallas.

"Racial Dynamism in Dallas: Negro Housing War." *The New Republic*, 24 March 1941. Segregation.

Rodriguez, Roberto. "Mamie McKnight: Promoting Education and Preserving Black Dallas History." *Black Issues in Higher Education* 10 (16 December 1993).

"Ron Kirk Elected the First Black Mayor of Dallas." *Jet*, 22 May 1995.

"The Week." *The New Republic*, 4 October 1933. Column reported police in Dallas prevent a double lynching.

Wilson, William H. "Desegregation of the Hamilton Park School, 1955–1975." *Southwestern Historical Quarterly* 95 (July 1991). Busing of white students to the Richardson Independent School District.

Womack, Ytasha L. "Teacher Gives Cues on Learning." *Emerge* 7 (September 1996). Actress Irma P. Hall of "A Family Thing" talks about teaching in Dallas.

Wright, Melanie. "Dallas Museum of Art: Showcasing African American Artists." *Time*, 18 January 1990.

Houston

Beeth, Howard. "Houston and History, Past and Present: A Look at Black Houston in the 1920s." *Southern Studies* 25 (Summer 1986).

"Black Arson Sleuths: A First for Houston." *Sepia* 20 (October 1970).

"Black Houston Physician Bernard Harris Makes Second Shuttle Flight." *Jet*, 20 February 1995.

"Black Public Universities Face Severe Adversity." *Black Issues in Higher Education* 13 (9 January 1997). Includes Texas Southern University.

Botson, Michael. "No Gold Watch for Jim Crow's Retirement: The Abolition of Segregated Unionism at Houston's Hughes Tool Company." *Southwestern Historical Quarterly* 101 (April 1998).

Broyles, Karen. "Chevron Set for Court Date to Answer Allegations of 'Environmental Racism.'" *The Oil Daily*, 13 May 1997. A suit brought by 2,500 Black residents of Kennedy Heights, Houston.

Bullard, Robert D. "Housing Problems and Prospects for Blacks in Houston."
    Review of Black Political Economy 19 (Winter-Spring 1991).
_____.   "Housing Problems and Prospects in Contemporary Houston."
    Chapter in *Black Dixie*, eds. Howard Beeth and Cary D. Wintz. Col-
    lege Station: Texas A&M Press, 1992.
_____. "Solid Waste Sites and the Black Houston Community." *Socio-
    logical Inquiry* 53 (Spring 1983).
Bullard, Robert D., ed. "Blacks in Heavenly Houston." Chapter in *In Search of
    the New South: The Black Urban Experience in the 1970s and 1980s*.
    Tuscaloosa, AL: University of Alabama Press, 1989.
Burke, John Francis. "A Twist in Houston." *Commonweal* 124 (5 December
    1997). Houston voters defeat an anti-affirmation action initiative.
Buzi, Ruth S., Weinman, Maxine L., and Smith, Peggy B. "Ethnic Differences
    in STD Rates Among Female Adolescents." *Adolescence* 33 (Summer
    1998). Sampling conducted at two family planning clinics in Houston.
Carr, Pat. "Black Like Them." *Texas Monthly*, May 1994. A graduate of all-
    white Rice becomes professor at all-Black Texas Southern.
Cohn, Samuel, and Mark Fossett. "What Spatial Mismatch? The Proximity of
    Blacks to Employment in Boston and Houston." *Social Forces* 75 (De-
    cember 1996).
Crouch, Barry A. "Seeking Equality: Houston Black Women during Recon-
    struction." Chapter in *Black Dixie: Afro-Texas History and Culture in
    Houston*, eds. Howard Beeth and Cary D. Wintz. College Station:
    Texas A&M University Press, 1992.
Crowell, Erbin, Jr. "HOPE in Houston." *Civil Rights Digest* I (Fall 1968).
Curtis, Gregory. "The First Protester." *Texas Monthly*, June 1997. Profile of
    Eldrewey Stearns, pioneer civil rights leader.
_____. "Getting Out." *Texas Monthly*, May 1998. Profile of "Fifth
    Ward," a low-budget film about that section of Houston—written, pro-
    duced and directed by Nestor Gregory Carter.
"Economic Advance of the American Negro." *Contemporary Review* 207 (Sep-
    tember 1965).
Fanning, Jerry, and Andy Bustin. "KKK Grand Dragon Indicted in Houston."
    Militant 35 (17 September 1971).
"Four Black Schools Make Best Colleges List." *Jet*, 6 November 1995. Texas
    Southern included.
Freiberg, H. Jerome, et al. "Turning Around At-Risk Schools through Consis-
    tent Management." *Journal of Negro Education* 58 (summer 1989).
Gite, Lloyd. "Affirmative Action Watch." *Black Enterprise*, November 1989.
_____. "Houston, Texas: Bucking the Trend." *Black Enterprise*, February
    1996. Affirmative action.
_____. "Texas." *Black Enterprise*, June 1992. Examines economic oppor-
    tunities for Blacks in Houston and other cities.
Gruening, Martha. "Houston: "An NAACP Investigation." *Crisis* 15 (No-
    vember 1917).

Gurwitt, Rob. "Rod Paige: Target of the Frustrated." *Governing* 8 (November 1994). Conservative Paige is Houston's first Black school superintendent and is subject of a lawsuit by Latinos.

Haynes, Robert. "Black Houstonians and the White Democratic Primary, 1920–45." Chapter in *Black Dixie: Afro-Texas History and Culture in Houston*, eds. Howard Beeth and Cary D. Wintz. College Station: Texas A&M University Press, 1992.

_____. "The Houston Mutiny and Riot of 1917." *Southwestern Historical Quarterly* 74 (April 1973). White provocation leads to largest court martial in history.

_____. "Unrest at Home: Racial Conflict between White Civilians and Black Soldiers in 1917." *Journal of the American Studies Association of Texas* 6 (1975).

Healy, Patrick. "A Public Black College Faces State Pressure to Improve Management or Lose Autonomy." *Chronicle of Higher Education*, 25 July 1997.

"Houston." *American Visions*, June-July 1997. Juneteenth celebrations in Houston.

"Houston Mutiny." *Outlook* 17 (5 September 1917).

"Houston Physician Is First Black to Walk in Space." *Jet*, 27 February 1995.

"Houston Socialist Candidate Debates Klan Leader." *Militant* 35 (18 June 1971).

Jackson, Susan. "Moving On: Mobility Through Houston in the 1850's." *Southwestern Historical Quarterly* 81 (January 1978).

_____. "Slavery in Houston: The 1850s." *Houston Review* 2 (1980).

Jensen, F. Kenneth. "The Houston Sit-In Movement of 1960–61." Chapter in *Black Dixie: Afro-Texas History and Culture in Houston*, eds. Howard Beeth and Cary D. Wintz. College Station: Texas A&M University Press, 1992.

Matthews, Frank L., and Joyce Mercer. "Dr. Marguerite Ross Barnett: The Newest Star in the Lone Star State." *Black Issues in Higher Education* 7 (31 January 1991).

McGraw, Dan. "Tackling Woes Others Won't." *U.S. News and World Report*, 27 November 1995. Patricia Hogan Williams, church leader with the Windsor Village United Methodist Church of Houston, tackles social problems.

Middleton, Lorenzo. "Troubled Texas Southern's Fight for Survival." *Chronicle of Higher Education* 20 (5 May 1980). Desegregation issues.

Morthland, John. "True Blues." *Texas Monthly*, May 1994. Houston blues scene.

Nimmo, Dan, and Clifton McCleskey. Impact of the Poll Tax System on Voter Participation: The Houston Metropolitan Area in 1966." *Journal of Politics* 31 (August 1969).

Noland, James R., Jerry Robinson, Jr., and Edward Martin. "How It Was in Houston, Texas." *Integrated Education* 7 (May-June 1969). Lack of progress in that school system.

Palmaffy, Tyce. "No Excuses." *Policy Review* 87 (January/February 1998). Profile of Thaddeus Lott, principal of the Mabel B. Wesley Elementary public charter school.

Peters, William. "Houston's Quiet Victory." *Negro History Bulletin* 23 (January 1960).

Pitre, Merline. "Black Houstonians and the 'Separate but Equal' Doctrine: Carter W. Wesley versus Lulu B. White." *Houston Review* 12 (1990).

————. "Richard Allen: The Chequered Career of Houston's First Black State Legislator." Chapter in *Black Dixie: Afro-Texas History and Culture in Houston*, eds. Howard Beeth and Cary D. Wintz. College Station: Texas A&M University Press, 1992.

"Recruiting Black Men for Higher Education." *The Chronicle of Higher Education* 41 (23 November 1994). Recruitment and retention efforts at Texas Southern University.

"Regional Reports: South." *National Minority Politics* 4 (January 1993). Law enforcement in Houston included.

Richardson, C. F. "Houston's Colored Citizens: Activities and Conditions among the Negro Population." *Southern Studies* 25 (Summer 1986).

Richardson, Susan. "Bail-Out Helps Texas Southern—At Least Temporarily." *Black Issues in Higher Education* 14 (3 April 1997). Texas' only independent public Black university seeks financial aid package from the state legislature.

Russell, Jan Jarboe. "Gwen and Willie Richardson." *Texas Monthly*, September 1995. Black conservative couple make the list of outstanding Texans of 1995.

"School Desegregation is Entering New Phase: Analysis of Houston and New Orleans." *New South* 15 (October 1960).

Schuler, Edgar A. "The Houston Race Riot, 1917." *Journal of Negro History* 29 (July 1944).

Sheeler, Reuben. "Negro History Week in the Houston Area." *Negro History Bulletin* 19 (October 1955).

Smith, C. Calvin. "The Houston Riot of 1917, Revisited." *Houston Review* 13 (1991).

————. "On the Edge: The Houston Riot of 1917 Revisited." *Griot* 10 (Spring 1991).

Smith, Robert G. "Fashioning Effective Solutions: The Promise of School Study Teams." *Equity and Excellence in Education* 29 (April 1996).

SoRelle, James M. "'An de Po Culled Man Is in de Wuss fix uv Awl': Black Occupational Status in Houston, Texas, 1920–1940." *Houston Review* 1 (Spring 1979).

————. "The Emergence of Black Business in Houston, Texas: A Study of Race and Ideology, 1919–45." Chapter in *Black Dixie: Afro-Texan*

History and Culture in Houston, eds. Howard Beeth and Cary D. Wintz. College Station: Texas A&M University Press, 1992.

————. "Race Relations in 'Heavenly Houston,' 1919–1945." Chapter in *Black Dixie: Afro-Texan History and Culture in Houston*, eds. Howard Beeth and Cary D. Wintz. College Station: Texas A&M University Press, 1992.

Sparks, Randy J. "'Heavenly Houston' or 'Hellish Houston'? Black Unemployment and Relief Efforts, 1929–1936." *Southern Studies* 25 (Winter 1986).

Story, Rosalyn M. "Guardians of Peace in Bronze." *American Visions*, October-November 1998. Freedman's Memorial burial site and sculpture park in Dallas, plus an article on its designer, sculptor David Newton.

"Texas Southern Law Professors Sue State Government." *Jet*, 31 May 1999. Suit alleges that the state discriminates against historically Black colleges.

"Thaddeus McCall: Impatient Young Artist." *Sepia*, August 1967. Profile of painter who owns Houston's Hemis Art Gallery.

Thomas, Lorenzo. "Gathering Like Heat: Black Writing in Texas." *Texas Humanist* 2 (April 1980).

Waide, C. D. "When Psychology Failed: An Unbiased Fact-Story of the Houston Race Riot of 1917." *Houston Gargoyle* (15, 22 and 29 May; plus 5 and 12 June 1928).

Willis, Margaret E. "Lauren Anderson: Joie de Ballet!" *Dance Magazine*, April 1999. Cover story on Houston Ballet's principal dancer.

Wintz, Cary D. "Blacks." Chapter in *The Ethnic Groups of Houston*, ed. Fred R. von der Mehden. Houston: Rice University Studies, 1984.

————. "The Emergence of a Black Neighborhood: Houston's Fourth Ward, 1865–1915." Chapter in *Religion and the Life of the Nation: American Recoveries*, ed. Rowland A. Sherill. Urbana, IL: University of Illinois Press, 1990; Chapter in *Urban Texas: Politics and Development*, eds. Char Miller and Heywood T. Sanders. Texas A&M Southwestern Studies, no. 8. College Station: Texas A&M University Press, 1990.

Reconstruction

Baenziger, Ann P. "The Texas State Police during Reconstruction: A Reconsideration." *Southwestern Historical Quarterly* 72 (April 1969).

Barr, Alwyn. "Black Legislators of Reconstruction Texas." *Civil War History* 32 (December 1986).

Brown, Arthur Z. "The Participation of Negroes in the Reconstruction Legislatures of Texas." *Negro History Bulletin* 20 (January 1957). Achievements of Black legislators.

Cantrell, Gregg. "Racial Violence and Reconstruction Politics in Texas, 1867–1868." *Southwestern Historical Quarterly* 93 (1990).

Crouch, Barry A. "The Freedmen's Bureau of the 30ᵗʰ Sub-District in Texas: Smith County and Its Environs during Reconstruction." *Chronicles of Smith County, Texas* 11 (Spring 1972).

————. "Seeking Equality: Houston Black Women during Reconstruction." Chapter in *Black Dixie: Afro-Texas History and Culture in Houston*, eds. Howard Beeth and Cary D. Wintz. College Station: Texas A&M University Press, 1992.

Crouch, Barry A., and Leon J. Schultz. "Crisis in Color: Racial Separation in Texas During Reconstruction." *Civil War History* 16 (March 1970).

Elliott, Claude. "The Freedmen's Bureau in Texas." *Southwestern Historical Quarterly* 56 (1952).

Greene, A. C. "The Durable Society: Austin in the Reconstruction." *Southwestern Historical Quarterly* 72 (April 1969).

Moneyhon, Carl H. "George T. Ruby and the Politics of Expediency in Texas." Chapter in *Southern Black leaders in the Reconstruction Era*, ed. Howard N. Rabinowitz. Urbana: University of Illinois Press, 1982.

————. "Public Education and Texas Reconstruction Politics, 1871–1874." *Southwestern Historical Quarterly* 92 (January 1989).

Pitre, Merline. "The Evolution of Black Political Participation in Reconstruction Texas." *East Texas Historical Journal* 26 (Spring 1981).

Ramsdell, Charles W. "Presidential Reconstruction in Texas." *Quarterly of the Texas State Historical Association* 11 (1907–1908); and *Quarterly of the Texas State Historical Association* 12 (1908-1909).

Ricter, William L. "The Army and the Negro during Reconstruction, 1865–1870." *East Texas Historical Journal* 10 (Spring 1972).

————. "'It's Best to go in Strong-Handed.': Army Occupation of Texas, 1865–1866." *Arizona and the West* 27 (Summer 1985).

————. "Spread-Eagle Eccentricities: Military-Civilian Relations in Reconstruction Texas." *Texana* 8, no. 4 (1970). Civilians react to U.S. troops, particularly Blacks.

————. "'We Must Rubb Out and Begin Anew': The Army and the Republican Party in Texas Reconstruction, 1867–1870." *Civil War History* 19 (December 1973).

Singletary, Otis. "The Texas Militia during Reconstruction." *Southwestern Historical Quarterly* 60 (July 1956). The biracial "Negro Militia" of 1870.

Smallwood, James M. "Black Education in Reconstruction Texas: The Contributions of the Freedmen's Bureau and Benevolent Societies." *East Texas Historical Journal* 19 (1981).

————. "The Black Family during Reconstruction: Texas, a Case Study." *Social Science Quarterly* 57 (March 1977).

————. "Early 'Freedom Schools': Black Self-Help and Education in Reconstruction Texas: A Case Study." *Negro History Bulletin* 41 (1978).

_____. "The Freedman's Bureau Reconsidered: Local Agents and the Black Community." *Texana* 11 (1973).

_____. "Perpetuation of Caste: Black Agricultural Workers in Reconstruction Texas." *Mid-America* 61 (January 1979).

_____. "When the Klan Rode: White Terror in Reconstruction Texas." *Journal of the West* 25 (October 1986).

Sneed, Edgar P. "A Historiography of Reconstruction in Texas: Some Myths and Problems." *Southwestern Historical Quarterly* 72 (1969). Examines Reconstruction Texas.

Work, Monroe Nathan, comp. "Some Negro Members of Reconstruction Legislatures: Texas." *Journal of Negro History* 5 (1920).

San Antonio

Anjomani, Ardeshir, et al. "Racial Succession and Residential Mobility in Dallas-Fort Worth and San Antonio." *Journal of Urban Affairs* 14 (1992).

Bailey, Herbert J. "Charles Bellinger and Jim Crow in San Antonio, Texas, 19051937." *South Texas Studies* 4 (1993).

Baker, F. M., et al. "Black, Middle-Class Women in San Antonio, Texas." *Journal of the National Medical Association* 84 (June 1992). Mechanisms through which women handled stress.

Barr, Alwyn. "Occupational and Geographical Mobility in San Antonio, 1870–1900." *Social Science Quarterly* 51, no. 2 (1970). Using city directories and census material, the study traces the mobility of various groups over thirty years, including Blacks.

Dickerman, George S. "The Negroes of San Antonio." *Southern Workman* 43 (April 1914).

Dingus, Anne. "Jo Long." *Texas Monthly*, September 1997. Profile of Long, community-arts organizer of the Carver Community Cultural Center.

Goldberg, Robert A. "Racial Change on the Southern Periphery: The Case of San Antonio, Texas, 1960–1965." *Journal of Southern History* 49 (August 1983).

Rowe, Alan. "Note on Education and Self-Worth among AngloAmerican, Black American, and Mexican-American Men in San Antonio." *Perceptual and Motor Skills* 73 (1991).

Williams, Mary L. "Fort Davis, Texas: Key Defense Post on the San Antonio—El Paso Road." *Password* 31 (1986).

Slaves and Slavery

Addington, Wendell C. "Slave Insurrections in Texas." *Journal of Negro History* 35 (October 1950).

Ashburn, Karl E. "Slavery and Cotton Production in Texas." *Southwestern Social Science Quarterly* 14 (December 1933).

Baker, F. M., et al. "The Influence of Slavery in the Colonization of Texas." Southwestern Historical Quarterly 28 (July 1924).

Barker, Eugene C. "The African Slave Trade in Texas." *Southwestern Histori-cal Quarterly* 6 (October 1902).

————. "The Influence of Slavery in the Colonialization of Texas." *Missis-sippi Valley Historical Review* 11 (June 1924); also in *Southwestern Historical Quarterly* 28 (June 1924).

————. "Slave Trade in Texas." *Texas Historical Association Quarterly* 6 (1903).

Brauer, Kinley J. "The Massachusetts State Texas Committee: A Last Stand Against the Annexation of Texas." *Journal of American History* 51, no. 2 (1964).Abolitionists against the admission of Texas and slavery.

Bugbee, Lester G. "Slavery in Early Texas." *Political Science Quarterly* 13 (1898).

Campbell, Randolph B. "Human Property: The Negro Slave in Harrison County, 1850–1860." *Southwestern Historical Quarterly* 76 (April 1973).

————. "Intermittent Slave Ownership: Texas as a Test Case." *Journal of Southern History* 51 (1985).

————. "Local Archives as a Source of Slave Prices: Harrison County, Texas as a Test Case." *Historian* 36 (August 1974).

————. "Planters and Plain Folk: Harrison County, Texas, as a Test Case, 1950–1960." *Journal of Southern History* 40 (1974). Addresses the slavery question.

————. "Political Conflict With the Southern Consensus: Harrison County, Texas, 1850–1860." *Civil War History* 26 (September 1980). Role of slavery included.

————. "The Productivity of Slave Labor in East Texas: A Research Note." *Louisiana Studies* 13 (1974).

————. Research Note: Slave Hiring in Texas." *American Historical Re-view* 43 (February 1988). Slave hiring in rural areas and small towns.

————. "Slave Hiring in Texas." *American Historical Review* 93 (1988).

————. "Slaveholding in Harrison County, 1850–1860." *East Texas His-torical Journal* 11 (Spring 1973).

————. "Texas and the Nashville Convention of 1850." *Southwestern His-torical Quarterly* 76 (1972). Attempt to unify slaveholders.

Campbell, Randolph B., and Donald K. Pickens. "'My Dear Husband': A Texas Slave's Love Letter, 1862." *Journal of Negro History* 65 (Fall 1980). Letter from a wife (Fannie) to her husband (Norfleet).

Curlee, Abigail. "The History of a Texas Slave Plantation, 1861–63." *South-western Historical Quarterly* 26 (October 1922).

Downs, Fane. "Tryels and Trubbles: Women in Early Nineteenth-Century Texas." *Southwestern Historical Quarterly* 90 (July 1986). Includes slave women.

Eighmy, John Lee. "The Baptists and Slavery: An Examination of the Origins and Benefits of Segregation." *Social Science Quarterly* 44 (December 1968).

Faust, Drew Gilpin. "Trying to Do a Man's Business: Gender Violence and Slaves Management in Civil War Texas." Chapter in *Southern Stories in Peace and War*, ed. Drew Gilpin Faust. Columbia: University of Missouri Press, 1992.

Fernell, Earl W. "The Abduction of Free Negroes and Slaves in Texas." *Southwestern Historical Quarterly* 56 (January 1957). Kidnapping and sale of free Blacks.

_____. "Agitation in Texas for Reopening the Slave Trade." *Southwestern Historical Quarterly* 60 (1956). Proslavery agitation in Texas newspapers and politics.

Fuller, John D. P. "Slavery Propaganda during the Mexican War." *Southwestern Historical Quarterly* 38 (1934–1935).

Hall, Martin H. "Negroes with Confederate Troops in West Texas and New Mexico." *Password* 13 (Spring 1968). Slaves and Confederate masters, 1861 and 1862.

Harper, Cecil, Jr. "Slavery without Cotton: Hunt County, Texas, 1846–1864." *Southwestern Historical Quarterly* 88 (April 1985).

Haygood, Tamara Miner. "Use and Distribution of Slave Labor in Harris County, Texas, 1836–60." Chapter in *Black Dixie: Afro-Texas History and Culture in Houston*, eds. Howard Beeth and Cary D. Wintz. College Station: Texas A&M University Press, 1992.

Holbrook, Abigail. "A Glimpse of Life on Antebellum Slave Plantations in Texas." *Southwestern Historical Quarterly* 76 (1973).

Jackson, Susan. "Slavery in Houston: The 1850s." *Houston Review* 2 (Summer 1980).

Lack, Paul D. "Slavery and the Texas Revolution." *Southwestern Historical Quarterly* 89 (October 1985).

_____. "Slavery and Vigilantism in Austin, Texas, 1840–1860." *Southwestern Historical Quarterly* 85 (July 1981).

_____. "Urban Slavery in the Southwest." *Red River Valley Historical Review* 4 (Spring 1981).

Ledbetter, Billy D. "Slave Unrest and White Panic: The Impact of Black Republicanism in Ante-Bellum Texas." *Texana* 10 (1972). Antislavery sentiments before the 1860 election

"Letters to Dr. William E. Channing on Slavery and the Annexation of Texas." *New England Quarterly* 5 (July 1932).

Marten, James. "Slaves and Rebels: The Peculiar Institution in Texas, 1861–1865." *East Texas Historical Journal* 28 (1990).

_____. "What is to Become of the Negro? White Reaction to Emancipation in Texas." *Mid-America* 73 (April-July 1991).

Neal, Diane, and Thomas W. Kremm. "'What Shall We Do with the Negro?' The Freedman's Bureau in Texas." *East Texas Historical Journal* 27 (1989).

Reynolds, Donald E. "Smith County and Its Neighbors during the Slave Insur-
        rection Panic of 1860." *Chronicles of Smith County, Texas* 10 (Fall
        1971).
_____. "Vigilante Law During the Texas Slave Panic of 1860." *Locus* 2
        (1990).
Robbins, Fred. "The Origin and Development of the African Slave Trade in
        Galveston, Texas, and Surrounding Areas from 1816 to 1836." *East
        Texas Historical Journal* 9 (October 1971).
Schroeder, John H. "Annexation or Independence: The Texas Issue in American
        Politics, 1836–1845." *Southwestern Historical Quarterly* 89 (October
        1985).
Shively, Charles. "An Option for Freedom in Texas, 1840–1844." *Journal of
        Negro History* 50 (April 1965). Stephen Pearl Andrews and his plan to
        enlist England in the emancipation of Texas slaves.
Tyler, Ronnie C. "The Callahan Expedition of 1855: Indians or Negroes?"
        Southwestern Historical History 70 (April 1967). Expedition into
        Mexico for the recovery of slaves
White, William W. "History of a Slave Plantation." *Southwestern Historical
        Quarterly* 26 (October 1922).
_____. "The Texas Slave Insurrection of 1860." *Southwestern Historical
        Quarterly* 52 (January 1949).
Who's Who among the Blacks of Abilene, 2^{d} ed. Abilene: Copy Shop, 1991.
        Biography.
Winningham, Mrs. David. "Sam Houston and Slavery." *Texana* 3 (Summer
        1965).
Woolfolk, George Ruble. "Cotton Capitalism and Slave Labor in Texas."
        Southwestern Social Science Quarterly 37 (1956).
_____. "Sources of the History of the Negro in Texas with Special Refer-
        ence to Their Implications for Research on Slavery." *Journal of Negro
        History* 42 (1957).
_____. "Sources of the History of the Negro in Texas with Special Refer-
        ence to Their Implications for Research in Slavery." *Negro History
        Bulletin* 20 (1957).

Books:

Abernethy, Francis Edward, Carolyn Fiedler Satterwhite, Patrick B. Mullen, and
        Alan B. Govenar, eds. *Juneteenth Texas: Essays in African American
        Folklore.* Texas Folklore Society Publication, no. 54. Denton, TX:
        University of North Texas Press, 1996. Black social life and customs.
Adams, Effie Kay. *Tall Black Texans: Men of Courage.* Dubuque: Ken-
        dall/Hunt, 1972.
Adele, Lynne. *Black History/Black Vision: The Visionary Image in Texas.*
        [Austin] The Gallery: University of Texas at Austin, 1989. Exhibi-
        tion catalog. Videorecording also available.

Ainslie, Ricardo. *No Dancin' in Anson: An American Story of Race and Social Change*. Northvale, NJ: Jason Aronson Incorporated, 1995. Race discrimination in Anson, Texas.

Alexander, Charles C. *Crusade for Conformity: The Ku Klux Klan in Texas, 1920–1930*. Houston: Texas Gulf Coast Historical Association, 1962.

Allen, Bertram Leon. *Blacks in Austin*. n.p.: The Author, 1989.

Allen, Ruth. *The Labor of Women in the Production of Cotton*. Austin: University of Texas, 1931. Comparative study of "Negro," "Mexican," and "American" women.

Asbaugh, Carolyn. *Lucy Parsons, American Revolutionary*. Chicago: Kerr, 1976.

Atkins, Jasper Alton. *The Texas Negro and His Political Rights*. Houston: n.p., 1932.

Atkinson, Mary Jourdan. *Creolism and Racism on the Gulf Coast*. Houston: Roots, 1977.

Balester, Valerie M. *Cultural Divide: A Study of African-American College-Level Writers*. Portsmouth, NH: Boynton/Cook, 1993. Case studies in Texas.

Banks, Melvin James. *The History of the New Hope Baptist Church: A Century of Faith*. Dallas: New Hope Baptist Church, 1967.

Barnes, Marian E. *Black Texans: They Overcame*. Austin: Eakin Press, 1996.

Barr, Alwyn. *Black Texans: A History of African Americans in Texas, 1528–1995*, 2[d] ed. Norman, OK: University of Oklahoma Press, 1996.

————. *Black Texans: A History of Negroes in Texas, 1528–1995*. Austin: Jenkins Publishing, 1973.

————. *Reconstruction to Reform; Texas Politics, 1876–1906*. Austin: University of Texas Press, 1971.

Barr, Alwyn, and Robert A. Calvert. *Black Leaders: Texans for Their Times*. Austin: Texas State Historical Association, 1981; reprinted, 1990.

Barrett, Anna P. *Juneteenth*, ed., Frances B. Goodman. Houston: Larksdale, 1993.

Beasley, Ellen. *The Alleys and Back Buildings of Galveston: An Architectural and Social History*. Houston: Rice University Press, 1966; reprinted, College Station: Texas A&M University Press, 1994.

Benjamin, R. C. O. *Southern Outrages: A Statistical Record of Lawless Doings*. Los Angeles: The Author, 1894. Black author details deaths in Paris, Texas, Texarkana, Arkansas, and other places.

Beyond Desegregation: The Problem of Power: A Special Study in East Texas. Washington, DC: National Education Association of the United States, National Commission on Professional Rights and Responsibilities, 1970.

Black Cinema Treasures. Denton: University of North Texas Press, 1991.

Blackwelder, Julia Kirk. *Women of the Depression: Caste and Culture in San Antonio, 1929–1939*. College Station, TX: Texas A&M University Press, 1984.

Blocksom, Augustus P., et al. *Affray at Brownsville, Texas, August 13 and 14, 1900, Investigation of the Conduct of U.S. Troops*. Washington, DC: U.S. Government Printing Office, 1906.

Blue, Rose, and Corinne Naden. *Barbara Jordan: Politician*. Broomall, PA: Chelsea House, 1992.

Boatright, Mody Coggin, Wilson M. Hudson, and Allen Maxwell, eds. *Texas Folk and Folklore*. Dallas: Southern Methodist University Press, 1954.

Braddy, Haldeen. *Pershing's Mission in Mexico*. El Paso: Texas Western Press, 1966.

Branch, Hettye Wallace. *The Story of "80 John," A Biography of One of the Most Respected Negro Ranchmen in the Old West*. New York: Greenwich Book Publishers, 1960. Story of Daniel Webster Wallace.

Breed, Warren. *Beaumont, Texas: College Desegregation Without Popular Support*. New York: Anti-Defamation League, 1957.

Brewer, John Mason. *Aunt Dicy Tales: Snuff-Dipping Tales of the Texas Negro*. Austin: n.p., 1956.

————, ed. *An Historical Outline of the Negro in Travis County*. Austin: The College, 1940.

————. *Dog Ghosts, and Other Texas Negro Folk Tales*. Austin: University of Texas Press, 1958. Drawings by John T. Biggers.

————, ed. *Heralding Dawn: An Anthology of Verse by Texas Negroes*. Dallas: June Thomason, 1936.

————. *Negro Legislators of Texas and Their Descendants*. San Francisco: R&E Research Associates, 1970.

————. *Negro Legislators of Texas and Their Descendants: A History of the Negro in Texas-Politics From Reconstruction to Disfranchisement*. Dallas: Mathis Publishing Company, 1935.

————. *The Word on the Brazos: Negro Preacher Tales from the Brazos Bottoms of Texas*. Austin: University of Texas Press, 1953. Blacks and their ministers.

Bryant, Ira B. *Barbara Charline Jordan: From the Ghetto to the Capitol*. Houston: D. Armstrong Company, 1977.

Bryson, Conrey. *Dr. Lawrence A. Nixon and the White Primary*. El Paso: Texas Western Press, 1974; reprinted, Southwestern Studies no. 42. University of Texas at El Paso: Texas Western Press, 1992.

Buford, Michael Dwain. *Up from Cotton: A Pictorial History Book of Blacks in the Brazos Valley*. Bryan, TX: The Author, 1980.

Bundy, William Oliver. *Life of William Madison McDonald, Ph.D.* Fort Worth: Bunker Printing and Book Company, 1925. Biography.

Byrd, James W. *J. Mason Brewer: Negro Folklorist*. Austin: 1967.

Campbell, Randolph B. *An Empire for Slavery: The Peculiar Institution in Texas, 1821–1865*. Baton Rouge: Louisiana State University, 1989.

_____. *Grass-Roots Reconstruction in Texas, 1865–1880*. Baton Rouge: Louisiana State University, 1997.

_____. *A Southern Community in Crisis: Harrison County, Texas, 1850–1880*. Austin: Texas State Historical Association, 1983.

Christian, Garna L. *Black Soldiers in Jim Crow Texas, 1899–1917*. Centennial Series of the Association of Former Students no. 57. College Station: Texas A&M University Press, 1995.

Christian Education for Negroes Under Baptist Auspices: Proceedings of an Unofficial Inter-racial Conference of One Hundred Texas Baptist Leaders, November 14, 1941, Baptist Building Dallas, Texas. Marshall, TX: Board of Trustees, Bishop College, 1941. Black church colleges.

Civil Rights During the Johnson Administration: A Collection from the Holdings of the Lyndon Baines Johnson Library, Austin, Texas. Austin: University Publications of America.

Clayton, Sheryl H., ed. *Black Women Role Models of Waco, Texas*. East St. Louis, IL: Essai Seay Publishers, 1986.

_____. *Black Women Role Models of Waco and Hillsboro, Texas*. East St. Louis, IL: Essai Seay Publishers, 1986.

Cole, Everett B., and Jakie L. Pruett. *As We Lived*. Eakins Publications, 1982. Biography and social customs.

Conference of Texas Negro Librarians (1937: Prairie View, Texas). *A Survey of Negro Public School Library Facilities in Texas, 1936–1937*. Prairie View: The Conference, 1937.

Conference on Education for Negroes in Texas. Proceedings of the Annual Session. Prairie View: Prairie View State College, 1930.

Conference on Education for Negroes in Texas. Proceedings of the Fifth Educational Conference, 1934. Prairie View: Prairie View State Normal and Industrial College, 1934.

Conference on Education for Negroes in Texas. Proceedings of the Sixth Educational Conference, 1935. Prairie View: Prairie View State Normal and Industrial College, 1935.

Corpus Christi, Texas Department of Planning and Urban Development. Long Range Planning Section. *Blacks in Corpus Christi*. Corpus Christi: The Department, 1974.

Cotrell, Charles Lee. *Status of Civil Rights in Texas*, Vol. 1, *A Report on the Participation of Mexican Americans, Blacks and Females in the Major Political Institutions and Processes of Texas, 1968–78*. Austin: The Committee, 1980.

Cotton, Walter F. *History of Negroes of Limestone County From 1860–1939*. Mexia: 1939.

Craft, Juanita. *A Child, the Earth, and a Tree of Many Seasons: The Voice of Juanita Craft*. Dallas: Halifax Publishing, 1982. Houston NAACP leader.

Crouch, Barry A. *Cullen Montgomery Baker, Reconstruction Desperado*. Baton
    Rouge: Louisiana State University Press, 1997.
_____. *The Freedmen's Bureau and Black Texans*. Austin: University of
    Texas Press, 1992.
Croxdale, Richard and Melissa Hied, eds. *Women in the Texas Workforce: Yes-
    terday and Today*. Austin: People's History of Texas, 1979.
Cuney-Hare, Maud. *Norris Wright Cuney: A Tribute of the Black People*.
    Austin: Steck-Vaughan Company, 1968; reprinted, New York: G. K.
    Hall: 1995. Prominent Texas politician.
Cuninggim, Merrimon. *Perkins Led the Way: The Story of Desegregation at
    Southern Methodist University*. Dallas: Perkins School of Theology,
    Southern Methodist University, 1994.
Dahir, James. *Region Building: Community Development Lessons from the
    Tennessee Valley*. New York: Harper, 1955. Regional planning,
    Bakewell Negro community.
Davidson, Chandler. *Biracial Politics; Conflict and Coalition in the Metropoli-
    tan South*. Baton Rouge: Louisiana State University Press, 1972.
_____. *Race and Class in Texas Politics*. Princeton: Princeton University
    Press, 1990.
Davies, Nick. *White Lies: Rape, Murder, and Justice, Texas Style*. New York:
    1991.
Davis, James P. *Success Story: Negro Farmers*. Little Rock: U.S. Depart-
    ment of Agriculture, 1952. U.S. Production and Marketing Admini-
    stration booklet covering seventeen states.
Davis, John Preston. *The Negro and the TVA: A Report to the National Asso-
    ciation for the Advancement of Colored People*. New York: n.p.,
    1935.
Davis, William R. *The Development and Present Status of Negro Education in
    East Texas.*, New York: Teachers College, Columbia University,
    1934.
Day, Walter E. *Remembering the Past with Pride: Organized High School
    Basketball for Blacks in Texas, 1940–1970*. Fort Worth: W. E. Day,
    1994.
Delta Sigma Theta Sorority, Inc., Austin Alumnae Chapter. *Pictorial History
    of Austin, Travis County, Texas' Black Community, 1839–1920*.
    Austin: Delta Sigma Theta, 1972.
Dobie, J. Frank, ed. *Rainbow in the Morning*. Hatboro, PA: Folklore Associ-
    ates, 1926; reprinted, Southern Methodist University Press, 1965.
    Black folk songs, work songs, social life, and customs.
Dobie, J. Frank, et al, eds. *Texian Stomping Grounds*. 1941; reprinted, Austin:
    University of Texas Press, 1967. Black folk lore.
Du Bois, W. E. B. *What the Negro Has Done for the United States and Texas*.
    Texas: Texas Centennial Commission, 1936.

Duren, Almetris M., and Louise Iscoe. *Overcoming: A History of Black Integration at the University of Texas at Austin*. Austin: University of Texas at Austin, 1979.

Emerson, C., and Gwendolyn M. Jackson. *The History of the Negro, Wichita Falls, Texas, 1880–1988*. Wichita Falls, TX: Antioch Baptist Church, 1989.

Emmons, Martha. *Deep Like the Rivers: Stories of My Negro Friends*. Austin: 1969.

Federal Writers' Project, Work Projects Administration. *Slaves Narratives: A Folk History of Slavery in the United States from Interviews with Former Slaves*. Vol. 17, *Texas*. Washington, DC: Work Projects Administration, 1941.

Foley, Neil. *The White Scourge: Mexicans, Blacks, and Poor Whites in the Cotton Culture of Central Texas*. Berkeley: University of California Press, 1997.

Foraker, Joseph Benson. *The Black Battalion: They Ask No Favors Because They Are Negroes, But Only for Justice Because They Are Men, Speech of Hon. Joseph B. Foraker of Ohio in the Senate of the United States, January 12, 1909*. Washington, DC: n.p., 1909.

_____. *Notes of a Busy Life*. American Studies Series. Cincinnati: Stewart and Kidd, 1916. Autobiography of U.S. senator involved in the Brownsville Affray.

Fort Worth Public Schools. *African Studies*. Fort Worth: Humanities Department, Fort Worth Public Schools, 1972. Curriculum bulletin.

Gibbs, Warmoth T. *President Matthew W. Dogan of Wiley College: A Biography*. Marshall: Firmin-Greer, 1930. Profile of the former president.

Gillette, Michael. "The Rise of the NAACP in Texas." *Southwestern Historical Quarterly* 81 (April 1978).

Gómez, Arthur R. A Most Singular Country: A History of Occupation in the Big Bend. Provo: Charles Redd Center for Western Studies, Brigham Young University, 1990.

Govenar, Alan B. *The Life and Poems of Osceola Mays*. Racine, WI: Arcadian Press, 1989. Biography of a Texan woman.

_____. *Living the Blues*. Dallas: Dallas Museum of Art, 1985.

_____. *Meeting the Blues: The Rise of the Texas Sound*. Dallas: Taylor, 1988.

_____, compiler. *Portraits of Community: African American Photography in Texas*. Austin: Texas State Historical Association, 1996.

Graham, Katheryn Campbell. *Under the Cottonwood: A Saga of Negro Life in Which the History, Traditions and Folklore of the Negro of the Last Century are Vividly Portrayed*. New York: W. Malliet and Company, 1941.

Griffin, John Howard. *A Time to be Human*. New York: Macmillan. Race relations, juvenile.

Griffin, John Howard, and Theodore Freedman. *Mansfield, Texas: A Report of the Crisis Situation Resulting from Efforts to Desegregate the School System*. New York: Anti-Defamation League, 1957.

Griffin, Marvin C. *Texas African-American Baptists: The Story of the Missionary Baptist General Convention of Texas*. Austin: Publisher's Marketing House, 1994.

Hallman, Patsy. *A Psalm of Life—A Story of a Woman Whose Life Made a Difference—Willie Lee Campbell Glass*. Austin: Sunbelt Media, 1990. Blacks and education in Texas.

Hamilton, Jeff. *"My Master," The Inside Story of Sam Houston and His Times, by His Former Slave, Jeff Hamilton, as Told to Lenoir Hunt; with a Foreword by Franklin Williams*. Dallas: Manfred, Van Nort and Company, 1940.

Hancock, Ian F. *Creole Featu4res in the Afro–Seminole Speech of Brackettville, Texas*. Society for Caribbean Linguistics Occasional Papers, No. 3. Mona, Jamaica: Society for Caribbean Linguistics, 1975.

————. *Further Observations on Afro-Seminole Creole*. Society for Caribbean Linguistics Occasional Papers, No. 7. Mona, Jamaica: Society for Caribbean Linguistics, 1977.

————. *The Texas Seminoles and Their Language*. Austin: University of Texas African and Afro-American Studies and Research Center, 1980.

Hare, Maud Cuney. *Norris Wright Cuney: A Tribune of the Black People*. Austin: Steck-Vaughn, 1968. Biography of Republican party leader.

Hathcock, Louise. *True Stories of Little Dixie*. San Antonio: Naylor Company, 1962. Afro-American tales, illustrated by Donald M. Yena.

Heintz, Michael R. *Private Black Colleges in Texas, 1865–1954*. College Station, TX: Texas A&M University Press, 1985.

Hine, Darlene Clark. *Black Victory: The Rise and Fall of the White Primary in Texas*. Millwood, NY: KTO Press, 1979.

Holland, Ada Morehead. *No Quittin' Sense*. Austin: University of Texas Press, 1969.

Home Cookin'. Fort Worth: Allen Chapel AME Church, 1996. Cookbook prepared as fundraiser to save Allen Chapel AME Church.

Horton, Eliza. *My Visions From Eliza Horton (Colored Lady)*. Oakland, CA: 1916. Religious experiences in Texas, 1874–1899, located in the East Bay Negro Historical Society.

Hunt, Annie Mae, and Ruthe Winegarten. *I Am Annie Mae: An Extraordinary Woman in Her Own Words: The Personal Story of a Black Texas Woman*. Austin: Rosegarden Press, 1984; reprinted, Austin: University of Texas Press, 1996.

Institute of Texan Cultures, Melvin M. Sance, Jr., principal researcher. *The Afro-American Texans*, 2[d] ed. Texas and Texans Series. San Antonio: University of Texas-San Antonio, 1975; revised, San Antonio: University of Texas Institute for Texan Culture at San Antonio, 1987; reprinted, 1992.

Jackson, A. W. *A Sure Foundation: A Sketch of Negro Life in Texas.* Houston: Yates Publishing Company, 1940.

Jackson, Bruce, ed. *Wake up Dead Man: Afro-American Worksongs from Texas Prisons.* Cambridge: Harvard University Press, 1972.

Jeffrey, Laura S. *Barbara Jordan: Congresswoman, Lawyer, Educator.* Springfield, NJ: Enslow Publisher, 1997.

Johnson, Eugene. *The Beginnings.* New York: Vantage Press, 1984. Biography of Black Texans.

Johnson, Ozie Harold. *Price of Freedom.* Houston?: 1954.

Jones, Allene, Henry Lee Brown, Jr. and Michelle R. Brown. *The Memoirs of Elnora Brown.* Moab Community (Lexington), Texas: Mount Nebo African Methodist Episcopal Church, 1993. Brown's writings and recipes collected and printed to help with the renovation of the church she attended.

Jordan, Barbara, and Shelby Hearon. *Barbara Jordan, A Self-Portrait.* Garden City, NY: Doubleday, 1979.

Jordan, Terry G. *Germans and Blacks in Texas.* Philadelphia, PA: German Society of Pennsylvania, 1989.

Joseph, Harriett Denise. *The Brownsville Raid.* Brownsville: Texas Southmost College, 1976.

Justice, Blair. *Detection of Potential Community Violence; Final Report to Office of Law Enforcement Assistance, U.S. Department of Justice.* Washington, DC: Office of Law Enforcement Assistance, U.S. Department of Justice, 1968.

————. *Violence in the City.* Fort Worth: Leo Potishman Fund, 1969.

Kealing, H. T. *History of African Methodism in Texas.* Waco: 1885.

Kinevan, Marcos E. *Frontier Cavalryman: Lieutenant John Bigelow with the Buffalo Soldiers in Texas.* El Paso: Texas Western Press, 1998. Bigelow and the 10th Cavalry.

King, Edward. *Texas: 1874: An Eyewitness Account of Conditions in Post-Reconstruction Texas,* ed. Robert S. Gray. Houston: Cordovan Press, 1974. Travel description with sketches by J. Wells Champney.

Ladd, Jerrold. *Out of Madness: From the Projects of a Life of Hope.* New York: Warner Books, 1994. Black journalist.

————, comp. *Gone to Texas: Genealogical Abstracts from "The Telegraph & Texas Register," 1835–1841.* Bowie, MD: Heritage Books, 1994.

Ladino, Robyn Duff. *Desegregating Texas Schools: Eisenhower, Shivers, and the Crisis at Mansfield High.* Austin: University of Texas Press, 1996. How white and Black Southerners viewed desegregation of the Mansfield school.

Lane, Ann J. *The Brownsville Affair: National Crisis and Black Reaction.* Port Washington, NY: Kennikat Press, 1971.

Lay, Shawn. *War, Revolution, and the Ku Klux Klan: A Study of Intolerance in a Border City.* El Paso: Texas Western Press, 1985.

Ledbetter, Barbara A. Neal. *Fort Belknap Frontier Saga: Indians, Negroes, and Anglo-Americans on the Texas Frontier*. Burnet, TX: Eakin Publications, 1982.

Ledé, Naomi W. *Precious Memories of a Black Socialite: A Narrative of the Life and Times of Constance Houston Thompson*. Houston: D. Armstrong, 1991.

Lomax, John A., and Alan Lomax, eds. *Negro Folksongs as Sung by Lead Belly*. New York: New York: 1936.

Lovingood, Penman. *A Negro Seer: The Life and Work of Dr. R. S. Lovingood, Educator, Churchman and Race Leader, by Penman Lovingood*. Compton: The Lovingood Company, 1963. Biography of Lovingood, Wiley College instructor at Marshall, Texas.

Lundy, Benjamin. *The Life, Travels, and Opinions of Benjamin Lundy, Including His Journeys to Texas and Mexico*. Philadelphia: William D. Parrish, 1847.

Maier, Howard. *Undertow*. Garden City, NY: Doubleday, Doran and Company, 1945. White soldiers who failed to prevent the lynching of a Black soldier develop mental problems.

Malone, Ann Patton. *Women on the Texas Frontier: A Cross-Cultural Perspective*. El Paso: Texas Western Press, University of Texas at El Paso, 1983.

Marquart, James W., Sheldon Ekland-Olson and Jonathan R. Sorensen. *The Rope, the Chair, and the Needle*. Austin: University of Texas Press, 1998. Examines capital punishment and the role of racism.

Martinello, Marian L., and Melvin A. Sauce. *A Personal History: The Afro-American Texans*. University of Texas Institute of Texan Culture, Young Readers Series. San Antonio: University of Texas Institute of Texas Culture at San Antonio, 1982. Juvenile.

Mason, Kenneth. *African Americans and Race Relations in San Antonio, Texas, 1867–1937*, Studies in African American History Culture Series. New York: Garland Publishing, 1998.

McCleskey, Clifton. *The Government and Politics of Texas*. Boston: 1969.

The Mexican-Americans of Brazos County, the Black Americans of Brazos County. College Station: The Class, 1972. Planning by students in Texas A&M University Department of Urban Regional Planning.

Miller, Vickie Gail. *Doris Miller: A Silent Medal of Honor Winner*. Austin: Eakin Press, 1997. WWII naval hero.

Moneyhon, Carl H. *Republicanism in Reconstruction Texas*. Austin: 1980.

Montejano, David. *Race, Labor Repression, and Capitalist Agriculture: Notes from South Texas, 1920–1930*. Berkeley, CA: Institute for the Study of Social Change, 1977.

Morgan, Leon. *Public Education for Blacks in Galveston, 1838–1968*. Galveston: Old Central Cultural Center, 1978.

Morland, J. Kenneth. *Lunch-Counter Desegregation in Corpus Christi, Galveston, and San Antonio, Texas.* Atlanta: Southern Regional Council, 1960.

Morrison, Dorothy, and Rebecca Buard. *The Black Citizen in American Democracy: Black Culture in Harrison County, Past, Present and Future.* 2 vols. Marshall: Marshall Public Library, 1976; reprinted, 1979.

Mulroy, Kevin. *Freedom on the Border: The Seminole Maroons in Florida, the Indian Territory, Coahuila, and Texas.* Lubbock: Texas Tech University Press, 1993.

Murdock, Steven H. *Patterns of Ethnic Change in Texas 1980 to 1990: The 1990 Census.* College Station: Department of Rural Sociology, Texas Agricultural Experiment Station, Texas A&M University System, 1991.

Murphy, DuBose. *A Short History of Protestant Episcopal Church in Texas.* Waco: n.p., 1885.

Murray, Betty. *A National Study of Minority Group Barriers to Allied Health Professions Education in the Southwest. Final Report.* San Antonio: Southwest Program Development Corporation, 1975. ERIC. ED 118 297. A two year study conducted in California, Colorado, New Mexico, Oklahoma and Texas.

Museum of African-American Life and Culture. *They Showed the Way: An Exhibit of Black Texas Women, 1836–1986.* Dallas: Museum of African-American Life and Culture, 1986.

NAACP 1940–55. General Office File. Lynching. Willie Vinson, Texarkana, Texas, 1942. Frederick, MD: University Publications of America, 1986.

NAACP 1940–55. Legal File. Crime—Lindsay, Harvey W., 1939. Frederick, MD: University Publications of America, 1988. Texas murder trial.

NAACP 1940–55. Legal File. Crime—White, Robert, 1937–39. Frederick, MD: University Publications of America, 1986.

NAACP 1940–55. Legal File. Discrimination—Galveston, Texas Pier, 1941. Frederick, MD: University Publications of America, 1992.

NAACP 1940–55. Legal File. Smith v. Allwright (Texas Primary). Frederick, MD: University Publications of America, 1986.

NAACP Administrative File. Subject File. Lynching—Texas, 1916–1939. Frederick, MD: University Publications of America, 1986.

NAACP Administrative File. Subject File—Discrimination. Voting, Texas, 1934. Frederick, MD: University Publications of America, 1986.

NAACP Branch Files. El Paso, Tex., 1913–1932. Frederick, MD: University Publications of America, 1986.

NAACP Branch Files. Texas Sate Conference, 1937–1939. Frederick, MD: University Publications of America, 1986. Civil Rights.

NAACP Legal File. Cases Supported—Nixon vs. Condon, 1930–1933. Frederick, MD: University Publications of America, 1986.

NAACP Legal File. Cases Supported—Nixon vs. Herndon, 1924–1929. Frederick, MD: University Publications of America, 1986.

NAACP Legal File. Cases Supported—Texas Primary, 1934–1935. Frederick, MD: University Publications of America, 1986.

Nash, Kwame M. *Cologne: The History and Anthropology of a Rural Texas African American Community.* San Antonio, M. C. Nash, 1990.

Nash, Sunny. *Bigmama Didn't Shop at Woolworth's.* College Station: Texas A&M University Press, 1996.

National Association for the Advancement of Colored People. *Burning at Stake in the United States. A Record of the Public Burning by Mobs of Six Men During the First Six Months of 1919 in the States of Arkansas, Florida, Georgia, Mississippi and Texas.* New York: NAACP, 1919; reprinted, Baltimore: Black Classic Press, 1986.

National Education Association. *Beyond Desegregation: The Problem of Power; A Special Study in East Texas.* Washington: 1979.

Neville, A. W. *The History of Lamar County.* Paris, TX: n.p., 1937.

Nunn, W. Curtis. *Texas Under the Carpetbaggers.* Austin: University of Texas Press, 1962.

Olmsted, Frederick Law. *Journey Through Texas.* New York: 1857.

Overton, Volma. *Volma—My Journey: One Man's Impact on the Civil Rights Movement in Austin, Texas.* Austin: Sunbelt Media, 1998. The NAACP in Austin.

Parks, H. B. *Follow de Drinkin' Gou'd.* Publications of the Texas Folk Lore Society, ed. J. Frank Dobie, no. 7. Austin: Texas Folk Lore Society, 1928; reprinted, Austin: Proceedings of the Texas Folk-Lore Society, 1965. Discussion of the song and its origins.

Passon, W. H. *The Historical and Bibliographical Souvenir and Program of the 25th Anniversary of Metropolitan A.M.E. Church, Austin, Texas, 1882–1907, May 6th to 14th, 1907.* Austin: Delta Sigma Theta, 1971.

Pemberton, Doris Hollis. *Juneteenth at Comanche Crossing.* Austin: Eakin Publications, 1983. Black history of Limestone County.

Pitre, Merline. *In Struggle Against Jim Crow: Lulu B. White and the NAACP, 1900–1957.* The Centennial Series of the Association of Former Students, Texas A&M University. College Station: Texas A&M University Press, 1999.

————. *Through Many Dangers, Toils, and Snares: The Black Leadership of Texas, 1868–1900.* Austin: Eakin Press, 1985.

Prather, Patricia Smith, and Jane Clements Monday. *From Slave to Statesman: The Legacy of Joshua Houston, Servant to Sam Houston.* Denton: University of North Texas Press, 1993. The life of one of the first Black city aldermen.

Proceedings of the State Convention of Colored Men of Texas, Held at the City of Austin, July 10–12, 1883. Houston: n.p., 1983.

Ramsdell, Charles W. *Reconstruction in Texas.* New York: 1910; reprinted, Austin: University of Texas Press, 1970.

Rand, Earl Wadsworth. *The Journey of Earl Wadsworth Rand: From There to Here, From Then until Now*. New York: Vintage Press, 1992.

Rice, Lawrence D. *The Negro in Texas 1874–1900*. Baton Rouge: Louisiana State University Press, 1971.

Richter, William L. *The Army in Texas During Reconstruction, 1865–1870*. College Station: Texas A&M University Press, 1987.

Robinson, Dorothy Redus. *The Bell Rings at Four: A Black Teacher's Chronicle of Change*. Austin: Madrona Press, 1978. Biography of Black teacher.

Sanchez, Ray. *Basketball's Biggest Upset: Texas Western Changed the Sport with Win Over Kentucky in 1966*. Mesa Publishing, 1991. Five Black starters and how they changed the game.

Scarborough, Dorothy. *On the Trail of the Negro Folksong*. Cambridge: Harvard University, 1925; reprinted, Hatboro, PA: Folklore Associates, 1963.

Schmidt, May. *Sources of Information Relating to Blacks in the Austin-Travis County Collection of the Austin Public Library*. Austin: Austin Public Library, 1979. Bibliography.

Schutze, Jim. *The Accommodation: The Politics of Race in an American City*. Secaucus, NJ: Citadel Press, 1986.

Second Baptist Church of San Antonio. *100 Years: A Century of Progress, 1879–1979*. San Antonio: n.p., 1979.

Shackles, Chrystine I. *Reminiscences of Huston-Tillotson College*. Austin: n.p., 1973. Historical Black college.

Shufeldt, Robert W. *The Negro: A Menace to American Civilization*. Boston: Richard G. Badger, 1907. Includes photographs of the lynching of Henry Smith at Paris, Texas.

Silverthorne, Elizabeth. *Plantation Life in Texas*. College Station: Texas A&M University Press, 1986.

Simond, Ada DeBlanc. *Looking Back: A Black Focus on Austin's Heritage*. Austin: Austin Independent School District and *Austin American-Statesman*, 1984.

Simpson, Julie. *The Clever Leader: Dr. L. H. Simpson, D. D.* Houston: J. Simpson, 1963.

Singletary, Otis. *Negro Militia and Reconstruction*. Austin: University of Texas Press, 1957.

Sivad, Doug. *The Black Seminole Indians of Texas*. Boston: American Press, 1984.

Smallwood, James M. *A Century of Achievement: Blacks in Cooke County, Texas*. Test Publishers, 1975.

————. *The Struggle for Equality: Blacks in Texas*. Boston: American Press, 1983.

————. *Time of Hope, Time of Despair: Black Texans During Reconstruction*. Port Washington, NY: Kennekat Press, 1981.

Soukup, James R., Clifton McCleskey, and Harry Holloway. *Party and Factional Division in Texas*. Austin: 1964.

Southwestern Historical Quarterly 76 (April 1973). Special issue on Blacks in Texas.

Stanley, William David. *The Impact of the TV Event "Roots": A Case Study of East Texas Nonmetropolitan Black Women*. College Station, TX: Texas A&M University, 1979.

Stimpson, Eddie. *My Remembers: A Black Sharecropper's Recollections of the Depression*. Denton: University of North Texas Press, 1995. A stable Black family during the Depression.

Sul Ross State University. *Five-Year Plan to Increase the Rates of Participation of Blacks and Hispanics in Enrollments, Degrees Conferred, and Employment, 1982–1986*. Alpine: Sul Ross State University, 1991.

Terrell, Suzanne J. *The Other Kind of Doctors: Traditional Medical Systems in Black Neighborhoods in Austin, Texas*. Immigrant Communities and Ethnic Minorities in the U.S. and Canada Series. New York: AMS Press, 1990.

Texas. Governor. *Message of Governor J. S. Hogg, of Texas, to the Twenty-Third Legislature, on the Subject of Lynch Law*. Austin: Governor's Office, 1893.

Texas Constitutional Convention. *The Minority Report, in Favor of Extending the Right of Suffrage, with Certain Limitations, to All Men Without Distinction of Race or Color/Made in the Texas Reconstruction Convention by E. Degener, February 24, 1866*. Austin: Southern Intelligence Office, 1866.

Texas Department of Education. *Negro Education in Texas*. Austin: The Department, 1927.

Thomas, Jesse O. *Negro Participation in the Texas Centennial Exposition*. Boston: Christopher Publishing House, 1938.

Thomas, Matt. *Hopping on the Border (The Life Story of a Bellboy)*. San Antonio: Naylor, 1951.

Thompson, Charles H. *Separate but not Equal: The Sweatt Case*. Dallas: n.p., 1948; reprinted from *Southwest Review* (1948).

Thraser, Max Bennett. *A Texas Experiment: An Institution from New England Planted in Texas: Robert Smith's Great Work Among the Colored Farmers: the Typical Freedman's Town*. Atlanta: n.p., 190?

Tillman, Benjamin R. *The Race Problem. The Brownsville Raid*. Speech of Benjamin R. Tillman of South Carolina in the Senate of the United States, Saturday, January 12, 1907. Washington, DC, 1907.

Turner, Martha Anne. *The Life and Times of June Long*. Waco: Texian, 1969.

————. *The Yellow Rose of Texas: Her Saga and Her Song*. Austin: Shoal Creek Publishers, 1976.

_____. *The Yellow Rose of Texas: The Story of a Song*. El Paso: Texas Western Press, 1971. Recounts the story of Emily, a slave woman captured by Mexican general Santa Ana, and how she inspired the song.

Two Years of Work with Libraries in Negro Public Schools. Prairie View: Prairie View A&M College, 1949. Blacks and libraries.

U.S. War Department. *Names of Enlisted Men Discharged on Account of Brownsville Affray, with Application for Reenlistment: Letter from Acting Secretary of War*. Senate Documents No. 430, 60th Cong., 1st sess. Washington, DC: Government Printing Office, 1908.

United States Commission on Civil Rights. *Public Schools: Southern States: Texas*. Washington: 1964.

_____. Texas State Advisory Committee. *Status of Civil Rights in Texas*. Austin: The Committee, 1980. Rights of women and minorities in Texas.

Vera, Ronald T. *Texas Responds to the Office of Civil Rights: Progress Made Under the Texas Equal Educational Opportunity Plan for Higher Education*. Claremont, CA: Tomas Rivera Center, 1989.

Vyas, Avni P. *1987–1992 Fort Worth Health Statistics: With Emphasis on the African-American Community in Forth Worth*. Fort Worth: Health Statistics and Information Services, 1994.

Weatherford, Carole Boston. *Juneteenth Jamboree*. New York: Lee & Low, 1995.

Weaver, John D. *The Brownsville Raid*. New York: Kennikat Press, 1970; reprinted, New York: Norton, 1973; reprinted, College Station: Texas A&M University Press, 1992.

_____. *The Senator and the Sharecropper's Son: Exoneration of the Brownsville Soldiers*. College Station: Texas A & M University Press, 1997. Race relations in Brownsville.

White, Charley C. *No Quittin' Sense*. Austin: University of Texas Press, 1969. Story of Rev. C. C. White of Jacksonville, TX.

Williams, David Alvernon, ed. *Bricks Without Straw: A Comprehensive History of African Americans in Texas*. Austin: Sunbelt Media, 1997. History of Blacks and Texas.

Williams, James Henry. *Equalization of School Support in Texas*. Los Angeles: University of Southern California Press, 1944.

Williams, Joyce E. *Black Community Control: A Study of Transition in a Texas Ghetto*. New York: Praeger, 1973.

Winegarten, Ruthe. *Black Texas Women: A Sourcebook: Documents, Biographies, Timeline*, eds. Janet G. Humphrey and Frieda Werden. Austin: University of Texas Press, 1996.

_____. *Black Texas Women: 150 Years of Trial and Triumph*. Austin: University of Texas Press, 1995.

_____. *Brave Black Women: From Slavery to the Space Shuttle*. Austin: University of Texas Press, 1997. Adapted from *Black Texas Women*, juvenile.

Winfrey, Dorman H. *Julien Sidney Devereux and his Monte Verdi Plantation.*
    Waco: 1962.
*Women of Texas: A Brochure Honoring Miss Ellie Alma Walls, First Woman
    President of the Colored Teachers State Association of Texas.* 65th An-
    nual Convention, November 24, 25, 26, 1949, Houston.
Woods, L. A. *Negro Education in Texas, 1934–1935.* Austin: Texas Depart-
    ment of Education, 1935.
Wooldridge, Ruby A., and Robert B. Vezzetti. *Brownsville: A Pictorial His-
    tory.* Virginia Beach, VA: Donning, 1982.
Woolfolk, George Ruble. *The Free Negro in Texas, 1800–1860: A Study in
    Cultural Comparison.* Ann Arbor: Published for *Journal of Mexican-
    American History* by University Microfilms International, 1976.
_____. *Prairie View: A Study in Public Conscience, 1878–1946.* New
    York: Pageant Press, 1962.
Wooster, Ralph A. *Civil War Texas: A History and a Guide.* College Station:
    Texas A&M University Press, 1999. Overview of Texas' involvement
    in that war, and the location of historical sites.

Dallas

Blacks and the 1984 Republican National Convention: A Guide. Washington,
    DC: Joint Center for Political Studies, 1984.
Carmack, William R., and Theodore Freedman. *Factors Affecting School De-
    segregation.* New York: Anti-Defamation League of B'nai B'rith,
    1963. Problems in Dallas.
Dallas, Texas: Negro City Directory, 1941–1942. Dallas: Dallas Negro
    Chamber of Commerce, 1942.
Gee, Sadye, comp., and Darnell Williams, ed. *Black Presence in Dallas, His-
    toric Black Dallasites.* Dallas: Museum of African-American Life and
    Culture, 1986.
Hickman, R. C. *Behold the People: R. C. Hickman's Photographs of Black
    Dallas, 1949–1961.* Barker Texas History Center Series no. 3. Austin:
    Texas State Historical Association, 1994.
Jordan, Julia K. Gibson, in collaboration with Charlie Mae Brown Smith.
    *Beauty and the Best: Frederica Chase Dodd, the Story of a Life of Love
    and Dedication.* Dallas: Delta Sigma Theta Sorority, Dallas Alumnae
    Chapter, 1985. Texan educator, social worker, and sorority leader.
Kinfolks: A Collection of Art by Afro-American Artists: An Exhibition. Dal-
    las: South Dallas Cultural Center, Art Gallery, 1990. Exhibition cata-
    logue.
Linden, Glenn M. *Desegregating Schools in Dallas: Four Decades in the Fed-
    eral Courts.* Dallas: 1995.
*Look at Me! Experiences of Children of Children of Dallas Told by Them-
    selves.* Dallas: Dallas Public Library, 1973.

McKnight, Mamie L., and Black Dallas Remembered Editorial Board, eds. *African-American Families and Settlements of Dallas: On the Inside Looking Out*. 2 vols. Dallas: Black Dallas Remembered, 1990.

McKnight, Mamie L., ed. *First African-American Families of Dallas: Creative Survival*, Vol. 1. Dallas: Black Dallas Remembered Steering Committee, 1987.

Museum of African-American Life and Culture. *The Showed the Way: An Exhibit of Black Texas Women, 1836–1986*. Dallas: Museum of African-American Life and Culture, 1986.

NAACP Branch Files. Dallas, Tex., Feb.–Sept. 1938. Frederick, MD: University Publications of America, 1986.

Runnels, Gerald D. *Blacks Who Wear Blue*. Forney, TX: Alexanders Publications, 1989. Black police in Dallas.

Wilson, William H. *Hamilton Park: A Planned Black Community in Dallas*. Baltimore: Johns Hopkins University Press, 1998.

Houston

Bailey, Eric J. *Urban African American Health Care*. Lanham, MD: University Press of America, 1991. Urban Health case studies in Michigan and Texas.

Beeth, Howard, and Cary D. Wintz, eds. *Black Dixie: Afro-Texan History and Culture in Houston*. Centennial Series of the Association of Former Students, no, 41. College Station: Texas A&M University Press, 1992.

Biggers, John Thomas, Carroll Simms, and John Edward Weems. *Black Art in Houston: The Texas Southern University Experience*. College Station: Texas A&M University Press, 1978.

Bryant, Ira B. *The Development of the Houston Negro Schools*. Houston: Informer Publishing Company, 1935.

Bullard, Robert D. *Invisible Houston: The Black Experience in Boom and Bust*. College Station: Texas A&M University Press, 1987. Economic and social conditions.

———. *Issues Surrounding Blacks in the Housing Market: A Focus on Housing Discrimination Complaints in Houston, 1975–1978*. Houston: Texas Southern University, 1979.

Bullock, Henry Allen. *Pathways to the Houston Negro Market*. Houston: J. W. Edwards, 1957. Includes maps.

Clayton, Sheryl H., ed. *Black Women Role Models of Houston, Texas*. East St. Louis, IL: Essai Seay Publishers, 1986.

Cole, Thomas R. *No Color is My Kind: The Life of Eldrewey Stearns and the Integration of Houston*. Austin: University of Texas Press, 1997. Biography of Houston civil rights leader, his confinement to a mental hospital, and issues of power and authority.

Davidson, Chandler. *Biracial Politics: Conflict and Coalition in the Metropolitan South*. Baton Rouge: Louisiana State University Press, 1972. Blacks in Houston.

Gallagher, Arthur, Jr. *The Negro and Employment Opportunities in the South—Houston*. Atlanta: Southern Regional Council, 1961.

Gloster, Jesse E. *Minority Business Enterprise in Houston, Texas*. Houston: Department of Economics, Texas Southern University, 1969.

Govenar, Alan B. *The Early Years of Rhythm and Blues: Focus on Houston*. Houston: Rice University Press, 1990.

Haynes, Robert. *A Night of Violence: The Houston Riot of 1917*. Baton Rouge: Louisiana University Press, 1976.

Hecht, James L. *Because it is Right: Integration in Housing*. Boston: Little, Brown and Company, 1970.

Houston 1991: Where We Are. Paragon Publishing Company, 1992.

James, Franklin J., et al. *Discrimination, Segregation, and Minority Housing Conditions in Sunbelt Cities: A Study of Denver, Houston, and Phoenix*. Denver: Center for Public-Private Sector Cooperation, University of Colorado-Denver, 1983.

Joe Overstreet. Houston: Rice University, 1972. Exhibition catalogue.

Jones, Howard. *The Red Diary: A Chronological History of Black Americans in Houston and Some Neighboring Harris County Communities—122 Years Later*. Austin: Nortex Press, 1991.

Justice, Blair. *Detection of Potential Community Violence: Final Report to Office of Law Enforcement Assistance, U.S. Department of Justice*. Washington, DC: Office of Law Enforcement Assistance, Department of Justice, 1968. Blacks and Houston police.

Keller, William Henry. *Make Haste Slowly: Moderates, Conservatives, and School Desegregation in Houston*. The Centennial Series of the Association of Former Students, Texas A&M University. College Station: Texas A&M University Press, 1999. The fight to desegregate the nation's largest segregated school system.

Kittrell, Norman Goree. Old "Miss" and "Mammy": *Address Delivered on Memorial Day, April 26, 1924, in First Presbyterian Church, Houston, Texas*. Houston: The Author, 1924. "The entire proceeds of the sale of this booklet will go to the Home for Aged Ex-Slaves at Houston, Texas."

Ledé, Naomi W. *Precious Memories of a Black Socialite: A Narrative of the Life and Times of Constance Houston Thompson*. Houston: D. Armstrong Company, 1991. Life of a Houston socialite.

Montgomery, Ellie Walls. *A Survey of Negro Youths Not in School—Houston, Texas*. Houston: Houston College for Negroes, 1936.

NAACP Branch Files. Houston, Tex., 1915–1923, 1925–1939. Frederick, MD: University Publications of America, 1991.

National Urban League. Community Relations Project. *Report on the Field Services of the Specialist in Health.* Houston: Council of Social Agencies, 1945. Public health of Houston Blacks.

————. *Report on the Field Services of the Specialist in Social Group Work and Recreation in Houston, Texas, November 3–December 20, 1945.* Houston: Community Relations Project, National Urban League, 1945.

————. *A Review of the Economic and Cultural Problems of Houston, Texas; as They Relate to Conditions in the Negro Population.* New York: National Urban League, 1945.

Recent Additions to the Heartman Negro Collection [Texas Southern University Library]. Houston: Texas Southern University, 1955. Continuing series, University Library News Notes.

The Red Book of Houston: A Compendium of Social, Professional, Religious, Educational and Industrial Interests of Houston's Colored Population. Houston: Sotex Publishing Company, 1915.

Report of Special Committee on Negro Masonry. Houston: Freemasons, Grand Lodge of Texas, 1898.

Simpson, Julie. *The Clever Leader: Dr. L. H. Simpson, D.D.* Houston: J. Simpson, 1963. Biography of Black minister.

Thomas, Jesse O. *A Study of the Social Welfare Status of the Negroes in Houston, Texas.* Houston: National Urban League, 1929.

Tillman, Robert. *Case of United States vs. Corporal Robert Tillman, et al., 24th U.S. Infantry: Copy of Proceedings of Trial by General Court-Martial at Fort Sam Houston, Texas, February-March, 1918.* San Antonio: Alamo Printing Company, 1918. Trial relating to Houston Riot, 1918.

Walker, May. *The History of Black Police Officers in the Houston Police Department, 1878–1980.* Houston: Houston Police Department, 1993.

Wardlow, Alvia J. *The Art of John Biggers: View from the Upper Room.* Houston: Museum of Fine Arts and Harry N. Abrams, 1995. Exhibition book.

Wintz, Cary D. *Blacks in Houston.* Houston: Center for Humanities, 1982.

Juneteenth

Abernethy, Francis Edward, et al., eds. *Juneteenth Texas: Essays in African-American Folklore.* Texas Folklore Society Publication, Vol. 54. Denton, TX: University of Texas Press, 1996. Black social life and customs.

Barrett, Anna P. *Juneteenth,* ed., Frances B. Goodman. Houston: Larksdale, 1993.

————. *Juneteenth! Celebrating Freedom in Texas.* Austin: Sunbelt Media, 1998.

Branch, Muriel M. *Juneteenth: Freedom Day.* NY: NAL-Dutton, 1998.

Frieda, Carroll. *Juneteenth Celebration Cookbook*. n.p.: The Author, 1997.

Juneteenth: A Celebration of Freedom. Madison, WI: Praxis Madison, 1995.

Juneteenth Food Festival: A Story Rhyme with Recipes. Denver: Story Time, 1995.

Pemberton, Doris Hollis. *Juneteenth at Comanche Crossing*. Austin: Eakin Publications, 1983. Black history of Limestone County.

Weatherford, Carole Boston. *Juneteenth Jamboree*. New York: Lee & Low, 1995.

Slavery

Baker, T. Lindsay, and Julie P. Baker, eds. *Till Freedom Cried Out: Memories of Texas Slave Life*. Clayton Williams Texas Life Series no. 6. College Station: Texas A&M University Press, 1997. WPA slave narratives illustrated by Kermit Oliver.

Bell, John. *The Compromise Bill: Speech of Hon. John Bell, of Tennessee, in the Senate of the United States, July 3 and 5, 1850, on the Bill for the Admission of California into the Union, the Establishment of Territorial Governments for Utah and New Mexico, and Making Proposals to Texas for the Settlement of Her Northern and Western Boundaries*. Washington, DC: Congressional Globe Office, 1850. Extension of slavery.

Campbell, Randolph B. *An Empire for Slavery: The Peculiar Institution in Texas, 1821–1865*. Baton Rouge: Louisiana State University Press, 1989.

Corder, Mrs. Claude. *1850–1860 Census of Henderson County, Texas, Including Slave Schedule and 1846 Tax List*. Athens, TX: Henderson County Historical Society, 1984.

Dewey, Orville. *A Discourse on Slavery and the Annexation of Texas*. New York: Charles S. Francis, 1844.

Federal Writer's Project. Texas. *Texas Narratives*. Westport, CT: Greenwood Publishing Company, 1972. Slave narratives.

Fontaine, Jacob III, and Gene Burd. *Jacob Fontaine: From Slavery to the Greatness of the Pulpit, the Press, and Public Service*. Austin: University of Texas Press, 1983.

Jollivet, Adolphe. *Documents Americains, Annexion du Texas, Emancipation des Noirs, Politique de l'Angeleterre*. Paris: Imprimerie de Bruneau, 1845.

Lewis, J. Vance. *Out of the Ditch: A True Story of an Ex-Slave*. Houston: Rein and Sons, 1910.

Massachusetts State Anti-Texas Committee. *Report of the Massachusetts Committee to Prevent the Admission of Texas as a Slave State*. n.p, 1845.

Merk, Frederick. *Slavery and the Annexation of Texas*. New York: Knopf, 1963.

Phillips, Stephen C. *An Address on the Annexation of Texas, and the Aspect of Slavery in the United States, in Connection Therewith. Delivered in Boston, November 14 and 18, 1845.* Boston: William Crosby and H. P. Nichols, 1845.

Prather, Patricia Smith, and Jane Clements Monday. *From Slave to Statesman: The Legacy of Joshua Houston, Servant to Sam Houston.* Denton: University of North Texas Press, 1993.

Rawick, George P., ed. *The American Slave: A Composite Autobiography.* Westport, CT: Greenwood Publishing Company, 1972. Transcriptions of narratives for the 1936–1938 Federal Writers' Project. Vol. 5, parts 1 and 2; Vol. 6, parts 3 and 4.

————. *The American Slave: A Composite Autobiography,* Vol. 4, *The Texas Narratives.* Westport, CT: Greenwood Publishing Company, 1972.

Reagan, John Heninger. *Speech of Hon. John H. Reagan, of Texas, in the House of Representatives, February 29, 1860.* Washington, DC: T. McGill, 1860. Speech.

Smith, Truman. *Speech of Mr. Smith, of Conn.: On the Bill "To Admit California into the Union, to Establish Territorial Governments for Utah and New Mexico, making Proposals to Texas for the Establishment of the Western and Northern Boundaries."...Delivered in the Senate of the United States, July 8, 1850.* Washington, DC: Gideon and Company, Printers, 1850. Extension of slavery.

Tyler, Ronnie C., and Lawrence R. Murphy, eds. *The Slave Narratives of Texas.* Austin: Encino Press, 1974; reprinted, Austin: State House Press, 1997.

Theses and Dissertations:

Abney, Lucille A. "Black Mothers' Perceptions of their Child-rearing Practices from 1945 to 1955: A Cohort of Southern Black Mothers Born in the 1930's." Ph.D. diss., Texas Woman's University, 1991. Galveston County, Texas.

Adams, Bonnie J. "The Political and Economic Status of Texas Blacks, 1868–1874." Master's thesis, Texas Woman's University, 1979.

Adams, Thomas Richard. "The Houston Riot of 1917." Master's thesis, Texas A&M University, 1972.

Albers, Margaret Irene. "Linguistic Variation in Situational Context: An Ethnographic Analysis of the Speech of Black University Students and Working Class Blacks in Austin, Texas." Master's thesis, University of Texas at Austin, 1973.

Albrecht, Winnell. "The Black Codes of Texas." Master's thesis, Southwest Texas State University, 1969.

Alexander, Charles C. "Invisible Empire in the Southwest: The Ku Klux Klan in Texas, Louisiana, Oklahoma, and Arkansas, 1920–1930." Ph.D. diss., University of Texas, 1962.

Alexander, Genevieve T. "An Historical Analysis of Catholic Educational Integration in Texas." Master's thesis, University of Texas, 1959.

Allen, Irving Henry. "A Comparative Study of Alumni Attitudes Toward Their Alma Mater at Selected Small Black Church Related Colleges in Texas." Ph.D. diss., Kansas State University, 1981.

Allen, Juna S. "The Communication Channels used by Blacks and Hispanics to Obtain Health Information." Master's thesis, Texas Southern University, 1987. Health attitudes in Houston.

Arendell, Evan McCarty. "Crossing Into Bounty: Blacks, Women, Mexicans and the Texas NYA." Master's thesis, Tarleton State University 1994.

Ashbury, Doris T. "Negro Participation in the Primary and General Elections in Texas." Master's thesis, Boston University, 1951.

Austin, Lettie Jane. "Programs of English in Representative Negro High Schools of Texas." Ph.D. diss, Stanford University, 1952.

Baker, Margaret Bouland. "The Texas Negro and the World War." Master's thesis, University of Texas, 1938.

Bales, Mary Virginia. "Negro Folk-Songs in Texas, Their Definition and Origin." Master's thesis, Texas Christian University, 1927.

Banks, Melvin James. "The Pursuit of Equality: The Movement for First Class Citizenship Among Negroes in Texas, 1920–1950." D.S.S. diss, Syracuse University, 1962.

Barriffe, Eugene, Jr. "Some Aspects of Slavery and Anti-Slavery Movements in Texas, 1830-1860." Master's thesis, University of Southwestern Louisiana, 1968.

Barth, Shell, Jr. "A History of the Negro Presbyterian Church U.S. in Texas." Master's thesis, University of Texas, 1965.

Batts, William Malcolm. "Prospects for Blacks in Texas Management: A 1971 Survey." M.B.A. professional report, University of Texas at Austin, 1971. Black business executives in Texas.

Berardi, Gayle K., and Thomas W. Segady. "Community Identification and Cultural Formation: The Role of African-American Newspapers in Texas, 1868–1970." Ph.D. diss., University of Texas at Austin, 1989.

Bessent, Nancy Ruth. "The Publisher: A Biography of Carter W. Wesley." Ph.D. diss., University of Texas, 1981.

Boggess, George. "Political Activities of Negroes in the Reconstruction of Texas." Master's thesis, Howard University, 1938.

Boswell, John David. "Negro Participation in the 1936 Texas Centennial Exposition." Master's thesis, University of Texas at Austin, 1969.

Brandenstein, Sherilyn. "Prominent Roles of Black Womanhood in *Sepia Record*, 1952–1954." Master's thesis, University of Texas at Austin, 1989.

Brewington, Paulette F. "The Colored Page: A History of the African-American Communities of Bethel, Texas, and Happy Holler in Kannapolis, North Carolina: An Account Based on Oral Narratives and Other Sources." Master's thesis, North Carolina Agricultural and Technical State University, 1996.

Briggs, Ibim I. "Indicators of Cultural Transformation of African Kalabari Students at Southern University and Texas Southern University." Master's thesis, Southern University, 1987.

Brophy, William J. "The Black Texan, 1900–1950: A Quantitative History." Ph.D. diss., Vanderbilt University, 1974.

Brown, Patsy McGee. "The Effects of Cultural Deprivation on the Achievement of American Blacks at Mary E. Scroggins Elementary School in Houston, Texas." Master's thesis, Texas Southern University, 1973. Segregation in Texas.

Bryant, Ira B. "Administration of Vocational Education in Negro High Schools of Texas." Ph.D. diss., University of Southern California, Los Angeles, 1948.

Budd, Harrell. "The Negro in Politics in Texas, 1867–1898." Master's thesis, University of Texas, 1925.

Chambers, Bill. "The History of the Texas Negro and His Development Since 1900." Master's thesis, North Texas State College, 1940.

Chapman, David L. "Lynching in Texas." Master's thesis, Texas Tech University, 1973.

Christopher, Nehemiah McKinley. "The History of Negro Public Education in Texas, 1865–1900." Ed.D. diss., University of Pittsburgh, 1948.

Chumley, Leo Betrice. "Negro Labor and Property Holdings in Shelby County, Texas, 1870–1945." Master's thesis, Prairie View Agricultural and Mechanical College, 1948.

Chunn, Prentis W., Jr. "Education and Politics, A Study of the Negro in Reconstruction Texas." Master's thesis, Southwest Texas State Teachers College, 1957.

Clay, S. C. "Brief Survey of Guidance Work in Blackshear High School, San Angelo, Texas." Master's thesis, Prairie View Agricultural and Mechanical College, 1948.

Cobb, William Lenox. "Provisions for Vocational Education for Negroes in the High Schools of Texas." Master's thesis, University of Southern California.

Colby, Ira C. "The Freedmen's Bureau in Texas and Its Impact on the Emerging Social Welfare System and Black-White Social Relations, 1865–1885." Ph.D. diss., University of Pennsylvania, 1984.

Collins, William M. "A Study to Determine Practices in Secondary Student Teaching Programs in Nine Negro Colleges and Universities in Texas and the Improvements That are Needed." Ph.D. diss., Cornell University, 1957.

Blacks in the American West

Cook, Lawrence Hugh. "The Brownsville Affray of 1906." Master's thesis, University of Colorado, 1942.

Cooper, Matthew N. "To Determine the Nature and Significance, If Any, of Certain Differences in the Social and Personal Adjustment of Fifty-One Successful and Fifty-One Non-Successful College Students at Texas Southern University." Ph.D. diss., New York University, 1955.

Crook, Carland Elaine. "San Antonio, Texas, 1846–1861." M. A. thesis, Rice University, 1964. Urban slavery.

Crump, Oliver Wendell. "Community Activities of Negro Rural Teachers in Texas." Ed.D. thesis, University of Northern Colorado, 1945.

Curlee, Abigail. "A Study of Texas Slave Plantations." Ph.D. diss., University of Texas at Austin, 1932.

Dailey, Nancy. "History of the Beaumont, Texas, Chapter of the National Association for the Advancement of Colored People, 1918–1970." Master's thesis, Lamar University, 1971.

Davidson, Chandler. "Negro Politics and the Rise of the Civil Rights Movement in Houston, Texas." Ph.D. diss., Princeton University, 1968.

Davis, William R. "The Development and Present Status of Negro Education in East Texas." Ph.D. diss., Columbia University, Teachers College, 1935.

Dickens, Edwin Larry. "The Poll Tax in Texas." Master's thesis, Texas College of Arts and Industries, 1963.

Dittmar, Nancy Jo Dawson. "A Comparative Investigation of the Predictive Validity of Admissions Criteria for Anglos, Blacks, and Mexican-Americans." Ph.D. diss., University of Texas at Austin, 1977.

Dorsett, Jesse. "Blacks in Reconstruction Texas, 1865–1877." Ph.D. diss., Texas Christian University, 1981.

Durvan, Katherine I. Greene. "Status of Guidance in the Thirteen Negro Colleges of Texas with a Proposed Program for St. Phillip's Junior College." Master's thesis, University of Colorado, 1940.

Echols, Jack W. "Criteria for Evaluating Teacher Education in the Negro Colleges of Texas." Ph.D. diss., University of Denver, 1955.

Egar, Emmanuel E. "Development and Termination of Bishop College between 1960 to 1988." Ph.D. diss., University of Oklahoma, 1989. Black Texas college.

Eilers, William A. "Negro Education in Lavaca County, Texas." Master's thesis, Southwest Texas State Teachers College, 1938.

Elam, Richard Lee. "Behold the Fields: Texas Baptists and the Problem of Slavery." Ph.D. diss., University of North Texas, 1993.

Ellard, Charles John. "An Investigation of the Influence of the In-School Neighborhood Youth Corps on Earning Capacity in Houston, Texas." Thesis, University of Houston, 1975.

Ellison, William M. Jr. "Negro Suffrage in Texas and Its Exercise." Master's thesis, Colorado State College of Education, 1943.

Engelking, Johanna Rosa. "Slavery in Texas." Master's thesis, Baylor University, 1933.

Estes, Mary. "An Historical Survey of Lynchings in Oklahoma and Texas." Master's thesis, University of Oklahoma, 1942.

Fennell, Romey, Jr. "The Negro in Texas Politics, 1865–1874." Master's thesis, North Texas State University, 1963.

Findley, James Lee, Jr. "Lynching and the Texas Anti-Lynching Law of 1897." Master's thesis, Baylor University, 1974.

Foley, Neil Francis. "The New South in the Southwest: Anglos, Blacks, and Mexicans in Central Texas, 1880–1930." Ph.D. diss., University of Michigan, 1990.

Foster, Robert L. "Black Lubbock: A History of Negroes in Lubbock, Texas, to 1940." Master's thesis, Texas Tech University, 1974.

Fuller, William. "The Definition, Etiology and Treatment of Mental Illness Among Adult Black Males with Middle and Low Socioeconomic Backgrounds." Ed.D. thesis, University of Northern Colorado, 1982. Black mental health in Texas study.

Gallaway, Steven Kent. "A History of the Desegregation of the Public Schools in Abilene, Texas, During the Wells Administration, 1954–1970." Ed.D. diss., University of North Texas, 1995.

Gillette, Michael. "The NAACP in Texas, 1937–1957." Ph.D. diss., University of Texas at Austin, 1984.

Ginn, Duane E. "Racial Violence in Texas, 1884–1900." Master's thesis, University of Houston, 1974.

Glasrud, Bruce A. "Black Texans, 1900–1930: A History." Ph.D. diss., Texas Tech University, 1969.

Gooden, Burnice R. "The Development of Negro Life in Madisonville, Texas, since 1900." Master's thesis, Prairie View A&M University, 1949.

Gooden, John Eddie. "Negro Participation in Civil Government with Emphasis on Public Education in Texas." Ph.D. diss., University of Southern California, Los Angeles, 1950.

Gordon, John Ramsey. "The Negro in McLennan County, Texas." Master's thesis, Baylor University, 1932.

Grant, Boston Phillip. "An Evaluation of the Vocational Guidance Program in the San Marcos, Texas, Negro High School." Master's thesis, Colorado State College, 1943.

Greene, Carrie Etta. "The History of Education Provided for Negroes in San Angelo, Texas, from Inception to Integration, September, 1955." Master's thesis, Texas Southern University, 1956.

Grose, Charles William. "Black Newspapers in Texas, 1868–1970." Ph.D. diss., University of Texas at Austin, 1972.

Grossman, Beth. "Ethnic Identity and Self Esteem: A Study of Anglo, Chicano, and Black Adolescents in Texas." Ph.D. diss., New School for Social Research, 1981. Ethnic identity and self esteem.

Guidry, Francis W. W. "Reaching the People Across the Street: An African-American Church Reaches Out to Its Hispanic Neighbors." D.Min. diss., Drew University, 1997. Boyton Chapel United Methodist Church in Houston.

Gulley, Steve D. "M. M. Rodgers, the Politician, 1877–1909." Master's thesis, Prairie View Agricultural and Mechanical College, 1966.

Hagood, Louise Wimberley. "Negroes in Northeast Texas, 1850–1875." Master's thesis, East Texas State College, 1966.

Hall, John Arlis. "The Influence of School Desegregation on the Work Values and Occupational Aspiration Levels of Twelfth-Grade Negro Males in Texas Public High Schools." Ph.D. diss., East Texas State University, 1971.

Hardman, Peggy Jane. "The Anti-Tuberculosis Crusade and the Texas African-American Community, 1900–1950." Ph.D. diss., Texas Tech University, 1997. The first study on efforts to control TB in the Black community.

Harrison, General L. "A Program of Teacher Training by Prairie View State College for the Improvement of the Rural Negro Schools of Texas." Ph.D. diss., Ohio State University, 1937.

Hawkins, Marjorie Browne. "Runaway Slaves in Texas From 1830 to 1860." Master's thesis, Prairie View A&M University, 1952.

Hayman, Bettie. "A Short History of the Negro of Walker County, 1860–1942." Master's thesis, Sam Houston State College, 1942.

Haynes, Rose Mary F. "Some Features of Negro Participation in Texas History through 1879." Master's thesis, Texas A&I University, 1948.

Hedgepath, Donald R. "The Plan of San Diego: A Border Conspiracy." Master's thesis, Southwest Texas State College, 1969.

Heintz, Michael R. "A History of the Black Private Colleges in Texas, 1865–1954." Ph.D. diss., Texas Tech University, 1981.

Heinze, Virginia Neal. "Norris Wright Cuney." Master's thesis, Rice University, 1965.

Hendricks, Harry G. "The Full-Time Negro Principalship in Texas." Ph.D. diss., University of Colorado-Boulder, 1960. Evaluation of the status of the Black principal.

Hennigan, Charles Taylor. "An Inquiry into the Oral Communication Patterns of Eight Disadvantaged Pre-School Negro Boys in Houston, Texas, 1966." Ed.D. thesis, University of Houston, 1967.

Hill, Artis. "'Jim Crow-ism' in Several Areas of Twentieth-Century Texas Life Relative to the Negro: Transportation, Eating and Lodging Places, Public Parks, and Movie Theaters." Master's thesis, Abilene Christian College, 1969.

Hill, Forest Garrett. "The Negro in the Texas Labor Supply." Master's thesis, University of Texas at Austin, 1946.

Hill, John Thomas. "The Negro in Texas During Reconstruction." Master's thesis, Texas Christian University, 1965.

Hinton, William H. "History of Howard Payne College with Emphasis on the Life and Administration of Thomas H. Taylor." Ph.D. diss., University of Texas, 1957.

Hinze, Virginia Neal. "Norris Wright Cuney." Master's thesis, Rice University, 1965. Black politician.

Holbrook, Abigail. "A Study of Texas Slave Plantations, 1822 to 1865." Ph.D. diss., University of Texas, 1932.

Hollingsworth, James S. "An Analysis of Selected Demographic Characteristics of the Texas Nonwhite Population." Master's thesis, Texas A&M University, 1964.

Hollins, Arntie Edward. "The Colored Teachers State Association of Texas as Revealed in the Texas Press." Master's thesis, Prairie View Agricultural and Mechanical College, 1948.

Hornsby, Alton, Jr. "Negro Education in Texas, 1865–1917." Master's thesis, University of Texas at Austin, 1962.

Housewright, George Maxwell. "The Changing Economic Status in Texas of the Latin-American and the Negro: 1959–1960." Ph.D. diss, University of Arkansas, 1972.

Houston, Faye Ruff. "A Process Evaluation of an American Heart Association Hypertension Program for Black Churches Entitled 'Hypertension: Life or Death, It's Your Choice.'" M.P.H. thesis, University of Texas Health Science Center at Houston, School of Public Health, 1992.

Hutchinson, Janis Faye. "Understanding Condom Use among Young Adult African-American Women in Houston, Texas." M.P.H. thesis, University of Texas Health Science Center at Houston, School of Public Health, 1997.

Jackson, Charles Christopher. "A Southern Black Community Comes of Age: Black San Antonio in the Great Depression, 1930–1941." Master's thesis, Texas A&M University, 1989.

Jackson, Robena Estelle. "East Austin: A Socio-Historical View of a Segregated Community." Master's thesis, University of Texas at Austin, 1979.

James, Allie Winifred. "The Homemaking Activities of a Selected Group of Negro Homemakers in East Texas." Master's thesis, Kansas State College, Manhattan, 1939.

Jamison, Glenn Parker. "An Exploratory Study of the Perceptions, Preferences, and Participation Patterns in Recreation by Blacks and Whites in a North Texas City." Master's thesis, Texas A&M University, 1984.

Johnson, Norman J. "Comparative Study of the Interest Patterns of Students Enrolled in Selected Curricula at Prairie View Agricultural and Mechanical College, Texas, 1956–1958." Ph.D. diss., University of Michigan, 1961.

Jones, Beverly Jane. "A Study of Oral Language Comprehension of Black and White, Middle and Lower Class, Pre-School Children Using Standard

English and Black Dialect in Houston, Texas, 1972." Thesis, University of Houston, 1972.

Jones, Michael Alan. "Local Television Coverage of Blacks and Hispanics: A Study of KTBC-TV in Austin, Texas." Master's thesis, University of Texas at Austin, 1983.

Jones, Nancy Nell Alsobrook. "Be in Dallas Black English." Thesis, North Texas State University, 1972.

Junkins, Enola. "Slave Plots, Insurrections, and Acts of Violence in the State of Texas, 1828–1865." Master's thesis, Baylor University, 1969.

Keener, Charles V. "Racial Turmoil in Texas, 1865–1874." Master's thesis, North Texas State University, 1971.

Kellar, William Henry. "Make Haste Slowly: A History of School Desegregation in Houston, Texas." Ph.D. diss., University of Houston, 1994.

Kerr, George R. "An Investigation of the Pica Practices of Pregnant Women in Houston and Prairie View, Texas." Ph.D. diss., University of Texas Health Science Center at Houston, 1996. A study of pica or craving for nonnutritive substances such as starch (Subjects were 88.6% Black).

Kilgore, Linda Elaine. "The Ku Klux Klan and the Press in Texas—1920–1927." Master's thesis, University of Texas, 1964.

Kilmer, Rita Kathryn. "Residential Movement of Blacks in Austin, Texas, 1950–1970." Master's thesis, University of Texas at Austin, 1974.

Kimble, Westerfield T. "An Analysis of the Methods of Teaching History in the Seventeen High Schools for Negroes in Texas Accredited by the Southern Association of Colleges and Secondary Schools." Master's thesis, Prairie view University, 1952.

Kinsey, Winston Lee. "Negro Labor in Texas, 1865–1876." Master's thesis, Baylor University, 1965.

Kirk, Rita G. "Barbara Jordan: The Rise of a Black Woman Politician." Master's thesis, University of Arkansas, 1978.

Kirven, Lamar L. "A Century of Warfare: Black Texans." Ph.D. diss., Indiana University Press, 1974.

Krawczynski, Keith. "The Agricultural Labor of Black Texans as Slaves and Freedmen." Ph.D. diss., Baylor University, 1990.

Kremm, Thomas Wesley. "Race Relations in Texas, 1865 to 1870." Master's thesis, University of Houston, 1970.

Kroutter, Thomas E., Jr. "The Ku Klux Klan in Jefferson County, Texas, 1921–1924." Master's thesis, Lamar University, 1972.

Kumler, Donna J. "They Have Gone From Sherman: The Courthouse Riot of 1930 and its Impact on the Black Professional Class." Ph.D. diss., University of North Texas, 1995.

Lack, Paul D. "Urban Slavery in the Southwest." Ph.D. diss., Texas Tech University, 1973.

LaGrone, Cyrus Wilson. "A Sociological Study of the Negro Population of Marshall, Texas." Master's thesis, University of Texas, 1932.

Laine, Alice K. "An In-Depth Study of the Black Political Leadership in Houston, Texas." Ph.D. diss., University of Texas at Austin, 1978.

Lamkin, Patricia E. "A History of Blacks in San Angelo, 1869–1930." Master's thesis, Angelo State University, 1990.

Lancaster, Lucila. "The Effectiveness of School-Based Prenatal Care for the Prevention of Low Birthweight." M.P.H. thesis, University of Texas Health Science Center at Houston, School of Public Health, 1996.

Landon, Johnnie A., Jr. "The N.A.A.C.P. in El Paso: An Instrument for Political Involvement." Master's thesis, University of Texas at El Paso, 1972.

Lane, Ann J. "The Brownsville Affair." Ph.D. diss., Columbia University, 1906.

Lane, Harry B. "The Present Status of Secondary Education for Negroes in Texas." Master's thesis, University of Southern California, Los Angeles, 1932.

Lanier, Raphael O. "The History of Higher Education for Negroes in Texas, 1930–1955, with Particular Reference to Texas Southern University." Ph.D. diss., New York University, 1957.

Lanier, Roy H. "Church-Related Colleges for Negroes in Texas." Master's thesis, Hardin-Simmons University, 1950.

Lavine, Margaret Singleton. "The Distribution of Organ Donors and Organ Recipients among Caucasians, Blacks, and Hispanics." M.S.N. thesis, University of Texas, 1992.

Leavitt, Urban J. D. "Desegregation and Attendance Zoning in Austin." Master's thesis, University of Texas, 1956.

Ledbetter, Billy D. "Slavery, Fear, and Disunion in the Lone Star State: Texas' Attitude toward Secession and the Union, 1856–1861." Ph.D. diss., North Texas State University, 1972.

Lindsey, Walter. "Black Houstonians Challenge the White Democratic Primary, 1921–1944." Master's thesis, University of Houston, 1969.

Linton, Delores Burton. "The Growth and Development of the West San Antonio Heights School in District I." Master's thesis, Our Lady of the Lake College, 1952.

Livingston, David W. "The Lynching of Negroes in Texas, 1900–1925." Master's thesis, East Texas State University, 1972.

Lockhart, W. E. "The Slave Code of Texas." Master's thesis, Baylor University, 1929.

Lott, Mabel Smith. "The Extra-Curricular Activities Program: A Case Study of Booker T. Washington High School, Houston, Texas." Ph.D. diss., University of California, Berkeley, 1953.

Lovett, Leslie Anne. "The Jaybird-Woodpecker War: Reconstruction and Redemption in Fort Bend County, Texas, 1869–1889." Master's thesis, Rice University, 1994.

Lumpkins, Josephine. "Antislavery Opposition to the Annexation of Texas, with Special Reference to John Quincy Adams." Ph.D. diss., Cornell University, 1941.

Margot, Louis III. "The *Dallas Express*: A Negro Newspaper: Its History, 1892–1971, and Its Point of View." Master's thesis, East Texas State University, 1971.

Mason, Kenneth. "Paternal Community: African Americans and Race Relations in San Antonio, Texas, 1867–1937." Ph.D. diss., University of Texas at Austin, 1994.

McClendon, Joyce Rae. "Attitudes of Minority and Nonminority Students Toward Nonskill Aspects of Office Work." Thesis, Arizona State University, 1973. Psychological testing in Fort Worth.

McDavid, Percy Hiram. "A Social and Economic Survey of the Community Served by the Phillis Wheatley High School in Houston, Texas." Master's thesis, University of Southern California, Los Angeles, 1940.

McDonald, Jack Arthur. "Higher Education for Negroes in Texas." Master's project report, University of Southern California, Los Angeles, 1947.

McDonald, Jason John. "Race Relations in Austin, Texas, c. 1917–1929." Ph.D. diss., University of Southampton [United Kingdom], 1993.

McDowell, Neil Allen. "A Status Study of the Academic Capabilities and Achievements of Three Ethnic Groups: Anglo, Negro, and Spanish Surname, in San Antonio, Texas." Ph.D. diss., University of Texas at Austin, 1966.

McGowan-Johnson, Cernoria. "A Study in the History and Development of the Urban League Program in Forth Worth, Texas, 1944–1945." Master's thesis, Atlanta University, 1946.

Meador, Bruce S. "Minority Groups and their Education in Hays County, Texas." Ph.D. diss., University of Texas, 1959.

Meltzer, Mildred Huber. "Chapters in the Struggle for Negro Rights in Houston, 1944–1962." Master's thesis, University of Houston, 1963.

Merseburger, Marion. "A Political History of Houston, Texas, during the Reconstruction Period as Recorded by the Press: 1868–1873." Master's thesis, Rice University, 1950.

Miles, Charles M. "Voting Habits and Political Attitudes of Negroes in Austin, Texas." Master's thesis, North Texas State University, 1963.

Miles, Merle Yvonne. "'Born and Bred' in Texas: Three Generations of Black Females: A Critique of Social Science Perceptions on the Black Female." Ph.D. diss., University of Texas at Austin, 1986.

Miller, Norman Theodore. "Attitudes of a Selected Group of Black and White Secondary School Students Toward White and Black Teachers in a Newly Desegregated High school in Austin, Texas." Thesis, University of Houston, 1974.

Mindiola, Tatcho, Jr. "The Cost of Being Mexican American and Black in Texas, 1960–1979." Ph.D. diss., Brown University, 1978.

Moorer, Virginia C. "The Free Negro in Texas, 1845–1860." Master's thesis, Lamar State College of Technology, 1969.

Moring, Margaret Carol. "Brave Nigger Brit." Master's thesis, University of Texas at Austin, 1972. Focus on a work of fiction.

Munchus-Forde, Lady George. "History of the Negro in Fort Worth—Syllabus for a High School Course." Master's thesis, Fisk University, 1941.

Murphy, Leonard B. "A History of Negro Segregation Practices in Texas, 1865–1958." Master's thesis, Southern Methodist University, 1958.

Neeley, Saran LeVahn. "A Study of the Rehabilitation Program at Crockett State School for Girls." Master's project, Texas Southern University, 1958.

Nelum, Junior Nathaniel. "A Study of the First Seventy Years of the Colored Teachers State Association of Texas." Ed.D. diss., University of Texas, 1955.

Newsom, Zoie Odom. "Anti-slavery Sentiment in Texas, 1821–1861." Master's thesis, Texas Technological College, 1968.

Nichols, Ruby Marion. "An Appraisal of the Educational Program of Selected Consolidated Rural High Schools for Negroes in Texas." Master's thesis, University of Southern California, Los Angeles, 1948.

Noe, Minnie Alice. "History of Jarvis Christian College." Master's thesis, Texas Christian University, 1966.

Norris, Clarence Windzell. "A Comparative Study of Selected White and Negro Youth of San Antonio, Texas, With Special Reference to Certain Basic Social Attitudes." Ph.D. diss., University of Southern California, Los Angeles, 1951.

Notebaert, Eugene J. "The Development, Present Status, and Future Needs of Catholic Education for Blacks in the Diocese of Dallas, Texas." Master's thesis, University of Dallas, 1978.

Nwachie, Judy Carol Flakes. "An Evaluation: The Texas Equal Educational Opportunity Plan for Higher Education on the Representation of Black and Hispanic Women Administrators." Ph.D. diss., University of Texas at Austin, 1993.

O'Brien, Florence Bradshaw. "Adequacy of Texas History Texts in Reporting Negro Achievements." Master's thesis, Stephen F. Austin State Teachers College, 1939.

Odell, Arabella Gertrude. "Reopening the African Slave Trade in Texas." Master's thesis, University of Texas, 1946.

Olmos, Sandra De La Garza. "Interracial Marriage and Dating Preferences among Anglos, Hispanics, and Blacks." Master's thesis, Texas A&I University, 1981. Interracial dating and marriage among college students at Kingsville, Texas.

Olube, Friday K. "A Comparative Study of Mass Media Use by Elderly Blacks and Elderly Whites in Houston." Master's thesis, Texas Southern University, 1984.

Park, Phocion Samuel, Jr. "The Twenty-Fourth Infantry Regiment and the Houston Riot of 1917." Master's thesis, University of Houston, 1971.

Passey, M. Louise. "Freedmantown: The Evolution of a Black Neighborhood in Houston, 1865–1880." Master's thesis, Rice University, 1993.

Pender, William M. "Curriculum and Instructional Problems of the Smaller Secondary Schools for Negroes in East Texas." Ed.D. diss., University of Texas, 1960.

Perpener, John O. "The Effects of the Gilmer-Aikin Laws Upon Fifteen Schools in Texas That Have Negro Superintendents or Supervising Principals." Ph.D. diss., University of Colorado-Boulder, 1953.

Perry, Douglas Geraldyne. "Black Populism: The Negro in the People's Party in Texas." Master's thesis, Prairie View University, 1945.

Perry, James O. "A Study of a Selective Set of Criteria for Determining Success in Secondary Student Teaching at Texas Southern University." Ph.D. diss., University of Texas, 1962.

Perry, Willhelmina Elaine. "The Urban Negro..." Ph.D. diss, University of Texas, 1967. Houston Negroes, 1967.

Phelps, Ralph A., Jr. "The Struggle for Public Higher Education for Negroes in Texas." Ph.D. diss., Southwestern Baptist Theological Seminary, 1949.

Platter, Allen A. "Educational, Social, and Economic Characteristics of the Plantation Culture of Brazoria County, Texas." Ph.D. diss., University of Houston, 1961.

Polk, Travis Ray. "The Status of the Teaching of Negro History in the Public Schools of Texas." Ed.D. thesis, North Texas State University, 1972.

Pratt, Alexander T. M. "Free Negroes in Texas to 1860." Master's thesis, Prairie View Agricultural and Mechanical College, 1963.

Prince, Diane Elizabeth. "William Goyens, Free Negro on the Texas Frontier." Master's thesis, Stephen F. Austin State College, 1967.

Pruden, Durward. "A Sociological Study of a Texas Lynching." Master's thesis, Southern Methodist University, 1935.

Rainville, Alice Johannah. "An Investigation of the Pica Practices of Pregnant Women in Houston and Prairie View, Texas." Ph.D. diss, University of Texas Health Science Center at Houston, 1997. Study of craving of nonnutritive substances among pregnant Black women.

Ray, Ruth Dunn. "Selected Graduate Programs of Professional Education in the Spanish Southwest, with Curricular Emphases on Blacks, Indians, and Spanish Americans." Thesis, North Texas State University, 1980. Teacher training and higher education in Texas.

Reynolds, James Talmadge. "The Preretirement Educational Needs of Retired Black Women Who Were Domestic Workers in Dallas, Texas." Ph.D. diss., East Texas State University, 1981.

Reynolds, Lois Arnell. "Sustenance Position of Texas negro Domestic Servants in the Texas Economy." Master's thesis, Prairie View State Normal and Industrial College, 1942.

Rice, Lawrence D. "The Negro in Texas, 1874–1900." Ph.D. diss., Texas Tech University, 1967.

Robbins, Fred. "The Origins and Development of the African Slave Trade into Texas, 1816–1860." Master's thesis, University of Houston, 1972.

Roberson, Alberta Carl. "A Survey of Certain Aspects of the Negro High Schools in Leon County, Texas." Master's thesis, University of Southern California, Los Angeles, 1941.

Roberts, Faye E. Campbell. "A Proposal for a Case Control Study of Risk Factors for Unintended Childbearing among African-American Teens in Houston, Texas, 1995." M.P.H. thesis, University of Texas Health Science Center at Houston, School of Public Health, 1995.

Robinson, Richard R. "Racism as an Aspect of the Violent History of the State of Texas in the 1830s and 1840s." Master's thesis, Kean College of New Jersey, 1979.

Rudoff, Judith Kidd. "The Poll Tax in Texas: Political Panacea." Master's thesis, East Texas State University, 1968.

Sapper, Neil Gary. "A Survey of the History of the Black People of Texas, 1930–1954." Ph.D. diss., Texas Tech University, 1972.

Schoen, Harold. "The Free Negro in the Republic of Texas." Ph.D. diss., University of Texas, 1938.

Schupack, Charles W. "A Comparative Study of White and Negro Schools in Fayette and Eight Adjoining Counties." Master's thesis, University of Texas, 1953.

Shannon, Mary Gamble. "An Occupational Study of Negro Maids in Dallas." Master's thesis, Southern Methodist University, 1941.

Sherpell, Branda K. "Racial and Gender Integration Patterns of Professional Librarians in Texas Academic Libraries, 1972–1992." Ph.D. diss., Texas Women's University, 1992.

Siler, Benjamin T. "The Brownsville, Texas, Affray of August 13–14, 1906, and Subsequent Proceedings (A Historical Interpretation)." Master's thesis, North Carolina College of Durham, 1963.

Smallwood, James M. "Black Texans During Reconstruction, 1865–1874." Ph.D. diss., Texas Tech University, 1974.

Smith, Ann Crowley. "Whites, Blacks and Hispanics as Candidates in Local Elections." Ph.D. diss., University of Texas at Arlington, 1988.

Smith, Bryan L. "The Desegregation of Ector County (Odessa) Independent School District, 1965–1985." Master's thesis, University of Texas-Permian Basin, 1992.

Smith, L. B. "A Survey of Negro Schools in Wood County, Texas." Master's thesis, University of Southern California, Los Angeles, 1936.

Smith, Rogers Melton. "The Waco Lynching of 1916: Perspectives and Analysis." Master's thesis, University of Texas, 1936.

Smyrl, Frank. "Unionism, Abolitionism, and Vigilantism in Texas, 1856–1865." Master's thesis, University of Texas, 1961.

Snow, Laura. "The Poll Tax in Texas: Its Historical, Legal, and Fiscal Aspects." Master's thesis, University of Texas, 1936.

SoRelle, James M. "The Darker Side of 'Heaven': The Black Community in Houston, Texas, 1917–1945." Ph.D. diss., Kent State University, 1980.

Spurlin, Virginia Lee. "The Conners of Waco: Black Professionals in Twentieth Century Texas." Ph.D. diss., Texas Tech University, 1991.

Stanley, William David. "Southern Black Women's Orientation toward Interracial Relations: Study of a Small Nonmetropolitan-Urban East Texas Town, 1970–1977." Master's thesis, Texas A&M University, 1982.

Stewart, Jacob Thomas. "Characteristics of Negro-owned and Operated Business Establishments in Houston." Ph.D. diss., University of Texas, 1956.

Stiles, Jo Ann P. "The Changing Economic and Educational Status of Texas Negroes, 1940–1960." Master's thesis, University of Texas at Austin, 1966.

Stoker, Winfred M "A Comparison of White and Negro Elementary School Teachers in Galveston County." Ph.D. University of Houston, 1958. "Based on a 30-minute visit to class and questionnaire."

Strange, Tempie Virginia. "The Dallas Negro Chamber of Commerce: A Study of a Negro Institution." Master's thesis, Southern Methodist University, 1945.

Tang, Rosa A. "Development of an Interviewer-Administered Survey of Adherence Related to Glaucoma Regimen among African-American Patients in Houston." M.P.H. thesis, University of Texas Health Science Center at Houston, School of Public Health, 1995.

Taylor, Barbara Bryan. "Voluntary Metropolitan Councils: Lubbock's Adaptation to Changing Urban Needs." Master's thesis, Texas Technological College, 1969.

Teel, Robert Eli. "Discrimination Against Negro Workers in Texas: Extent and Effect." Master's thesis, University of Texas, 1947.

Telford, Margaret Joan Agnes. "Slave Resistance in Texas." Master's thesis, Southern Methodist University, 1975.

Thompson, Esther Lane. "The Influence of the Freedmen's Bureau on the Education of the Negro in Texas." Master's thesis, Texas Southern University, 1972.

Thompson, Hortense Smith. "A Study of the Status of Negro Education in Liberty County, Texas." Master's thesis, Southern Methodist University, 1935.

Thompson, Lloyd Kay. "The Origins and Development of Black Religious Colleges in East Texas." Ph.D. diss., North Texas State University, 1976.

Thompson, Thomas Lycurgus. "Institutional Racism in the Housing Market: A Study of Growth Poles and Investment Patterns." Ph.D. diss., University of Texas at Arlington, 1981.

Thornton, Peter B. "Analysis of the Counselor-Training Program at Texas Southern University." Ph.D. diss., Colorado State University, 1963.

Tinsley, James A. "The Brownsville Affray." Master's thesis, University of North Carolina, 1948.

Tollerson, Tandy III. "The Negro in Politics in Houston, Texas." Master's thesis, Texas Southern University, 1952.

Torrance, Lois F. "The Ku Klux Klan in Dallas, 1915–1928: An American Paradox." Master's thesis, Southern Methodist University, 1948.

Trantham, Carrie P. "An Investigation of the Unpublished Negro Folk-Songs of Dorothy Scarborough." Master's thesis, Baylor University, 1941.

Travis, Ray Polk. "The Status of the Teaching of Negro History in the Public High Schools of Texas." Ed.D. diss., North Texas State University, 1972.

Truett, Luther J. "The Negro Element in the Life and Work of Dorothy Scarborough." Master's thesis, Baylor University, 1967.

Tullis, David S. "A Comparative Study of Negro, Latin, and Anglo Children in a West Texas Community." Ph.D. diss., Texas Technological College, 1964.

Tyler, Ronnie C. "Slave Owners and Runaway Slaves in Texas." Master's thesis, Texas Christian University, 1966.

Ulrich, Ora Emma. "A Study of the Expenditure of Urban Negro Work Relief Families in Travis County, Texas, as compared to an Adequate Diet." Master's thesis, University of Texas, 1935.

vanBolden, Vernon. "Faculty Participation in the Decision-Making Process in Small Private Black Colleges of Texas." Ed.D. thesis, North Texas State University, 1983.

Walker, Myrtle Lee Garner. "The Portrayal of Blacks, Mexican-Americans, and Indians in Selected Texas-Adopted Secondary American Literature Textbooks." Ed.D. thesis, East Texas State University, 1982.

Ware, Ural F. "The History of the Church of the Living God from 1906 to 1971." Master's thesis, Texas Southern University, 1972.

Watkins, Jocelyn Henderson. "The History and Development of Colored State Teachers' Association of Texas." Master's thesis, University of Southern California, Los Angeles, 1941.

Watley, Sarah Beal. "The Power Structure in the Negro Sub-Community in Lubbock, Texas." Master's thesis, Texas Tech University, 1970.

Weatherby, Norman L. "Racial Segregation in Dallas Public Housing, 1970–1976." Master's thesis, north Texas State University, 1978.

Weaver, Thomas Pritchett. "A History of the North Texas Conference of the Methodist Episcopal Church, South, 1866–1889." Master's thesis, University of Texas at Austin, 1927.

Webb, Hertha Auburn. "D. W. '80 John' Wallace: Black Cattleman, 1875–1939." Master's thesis, Prairie View A&M College, 1957.

Webb, John Compton. "Personal Problems on Negro Students in High Schools of East Texas." Ph.D. diss., Texas A&M University, 1971.

Webber, Carolyn Cott. "The Negro in the Texas Industrial Labor Market, 1940–1947." Master's thesis, University of Texas, 1948.

Weisel, Jonathan Edward. "The Cosmopolitan-Local Orientation of Aged Blacks and Whites in Denton, Texas." Master's thesis, North Texas State University, 1973.

Whisenhut, Donald Wayne. "Texas in the Depression, 1929–1933." Ph.D. diss., Texas Technological College, 1966.

White, Leslie J. "A Study of Recent Efforts to Equalize Educational Opportunities for Negroes in Texas." Master's thesis, Fisk University, 1945.

Whittaker, Jeweleane Wilma Parker. "Effects of the Application of Linguistics on Reading Comprehension of Black Freshmen Students at Texas Southern University." Thesis, University of Houston, 1974.

Williams, David Alvernon. "The History of Higher Education for Black Texans, 1872–1977." Ph.D. diss., Baylor University, 1978.

Williams, James Henry. "Equalization of School Support in Texas." Ph.D. diss., University of Southern California, Los Angeles, 1943.

Williams, Joyce E. "Black Community in Transition: Issues and Leadership in a Texas Ghetto" Ph.D. diss., Washington University, St. Louis, Missouri, 1971.

Williams, Mabel Crayton. "The History of Tillotson College, 1881–1952." Master's thesis, Texas Southern University, 1967.

Wilson, Leonard. "Texas and the Kansas Fever, 1897–1888." Master's thesis, University of Houston, 1973.

Wilson, Samuel Paschal, Jr. "The White Primary Laws in Texas from 1923–1953." Master's thesis, Southwest Texas State University, 1971.

Woods, Sister Frances Jerome. "Negro Suffrage under the Texas Direct Primary System." Master's thesis, Catholic University, 1945.

Wortham, Sue Clark. "The Role of the Negro on the Texas Frontier, 1821–1836." Master's thesis, Southwest Texas State University, 1970.

Wright, Leola Marie. "An Historical Account of African-American Life in the Kingsville, Texas Community, Especially during the Early Years, 1904–1975." Ph.D. diss., Union Institute, 1997.

Xie, Jinjing. "The Black Community in Waco, Texas: A Study of Place, Family, and Work, 1880–1900." Master's thesis, Baylor University, 1988.

Yancy, C. C. "Negro Participation in the Agricultural Adjustment Agency Program in Texas." Master's thesis, Colorado A&M College, 1946.

Yerwood, Ada Marie. "Certain Housing Conditions and Activities of Negro Girls Enrolled in Federally Aided Schools in Texas as One Index of Their Educational Needs." Master's thesis, Iowa Sate College, 1936.

Young, Horace Alexander, Jr. "A History and Appraisal of the Colored Teachers' State Association of Texas." Master's thesis, University of New Mexico, 1949.

Yousuf, Hasan Mohammed. "The Prevalence and Risks of Human Immunodeficiency Virus (HIV) Infection among High Risk African American Persons in Houston, Texas." M.P.H. thesis, University of Texas Health Science Center at Houston, School of Public Health, 1995.

Black Newspapers:[1]

AUSTIN

Austin Informer. Austin. 1905–19??
Austin Mirror. Austin. 1958–1961.
Austin Sun. Austin. 1993–current.
Colored Alliance. Austin. 1890–1891.
Express. Austin. 1912–1915.

Freedman's Press. Austin. 1868.
Free Man's Press. Austin 1868–1869.
Free Man's Press. Galveston. 1868-1869.

Gold Dollar. Austin. 1876.
Herald. Austin. 1890–1931.*Illustrated News*. Austin. 1923–1937.
Informer. Austin. 1939–1946.
Interracial Review. Austin. 1970–1976.
Monitor. Austin. 1921–1922.
National Union. Austin. 1890–1892.
Nokoa: The Observer. Austin. 1987–current.
People's Mouthpiece. Austin. 1920–1928.
Ram's Voice. Austin. 1948–1973.
Searchlight. Austin. 1896–1909.
Silver Messenger. Austin. 1897.
Sunday School Herald. Austin. 1891–1893.
Texas Blade. Austin. 1886–1889.
Texas Headlight. Austin. 1895–1903.

Texas Illuminator. Austin. 189?

Texas Interracial Review. Austin. 1941–1969.
Capital City Argus. Austin. 1962–current.
Capital City Argus and Interracial Review. Austin. 1969–1971.

Tilloston Tidings. Austin. 1912–1922.
Tribune. Austin. 1970–1983.
Villager and Tribune. Austin. 1973–1974.
Villager. Austin. 1973–current.
Watchman. Austin. 1901–1926.
Weekly Bulletin. Austin. 1900–1922.

BEAUMONT

Advertiser. Beaumont. 1896–1898.
Echo. Beaumont. 1893–1897.
Industrial Era. Beaumont. 1903–1949.
Monitor. Beaumont. 1920–1926.
Progress Reporter. Beaumont. 1969.
Recorder. Beaumont. 1889–1891.

BRAZORIA

Advocate of the People's Rights. Brazoria. 1934.

BRENHAM

Register. Brenham. 1903–1905.

---

[1] Single-lined boxed items were published by the same publisher. Double-lined boxed items indicate change in masthead names.

Watchword. Brenham. 1913–1917.

CALVERT
Alliance Vindicator. Calvert.
    1892–1893.
Bugle. Calvert. 1912–1932.
Calvert Eagle. Calvert. 1922.
Seven Mansions. Calvert.
    1885–1888.

COLMESNEIL
Republican. Colmesneil.
    1889–1893.
Trinity Valley Baptist. Colmesneil.
    1900–1903.
United States Republican.
    Colmesneil. 1889–1893.

CONROE
Taborian Banner. Conroe.
    1902–1914.
Visions of Missions. Conroe.
    1909–1911.

CORSICANA
Baptist Journal. Corsicana.
    1878–1887.
Oil City Afro-American. Corsicana.
    1898–1902.
Taborian Banner. Corsicana.
    1900–1942.

DALLAS
African Herald. Dallas. 1992–?
Applause. Dallas. 1933.
Baptist Journal. Dallas. ?–1915.
Black Tennis Magazine. Dallas.
    1977–current.
Brotherhood Eyes. Dallas.
    1930–1939.
Christian Messenger. Dallas. ?
Christian Star. Dallas. 1881–1888.
Colored Methodist. Dallas.
    1884–1888.
Daily Metropolitan. Dallas. 1912.
Dallas Appeal. Dallas. ?–1915.

Dallas Examiner. Dallas.
    1986–current.
Dallas Express. Dallas. 1892–1972.
Dallas Leaflet. Dallas. ?–1915.
Dallas Post Tribune. Dallas.
    1947–current.
Post Tribune. Dallas. 1948–1987.
Star Post. Dallas. 1950–1964.
Dallas Weekly Newspaper. Dallas.
    1955–current.
Echo. Dallas. 1884.
Elite News. Dallas. 1966–1972.
Enterprise. Dallas. 1887–1889.
Freedoms' Journal. Dallas.
    1978–1983.
Gazette. Dallas. 1930–1938.
Great Circle West. Dallas.
    1971–1976.
Herald of Truth. Dallas. 1885–1887.
In Sepia. Dallas. 1953–1971.
Informer. Dallas. 1939–1945.
Item. Dallas. 1891–1901.
Key News. Dallas. 198?–1986.
Link. Dallas. 19??–198?
Mahogany. Dallas. 1972–1987.
Metropolitan. Dallas. 1906–1910.
Mutual Enterprise. Dallas.
    1889–1890.
National Baptist Bulletin. Dallas.
    1902–1905.
Oak Cliff Eagle. Dallas. 1977–1978.
Odd Fellows Budget. Dallas.
    1919–1922.
Our Texas. Dallas. 199?
Post Tribune. Dallas. 1950–1987.
Preacher and Teacher. Dallas.
    ?–1915.
Reporter. Dallas. 1900–1912.
Star Post. Dallas. 1950–1964.
Texas Baptist Star. Dallas.
    1888–1900.
Texas Protest. Dallas. 1894–1896.
Texas Recorder. Dallas. 1904–1907.
Tribune. Dallas. 1887–1891.

Western Index. Dallas. 1912–1943.
Western Star of Zion. Dallas.
      1902–1917.
World #1. Dallas. 1902–1905.
World #2. Dallas. 1976.

DENISON

Colored Farmer. Denison.
      1920–1922.
Gate City Bulletin. Denison.
      1913–1931.
Gem City Bulletin. Denison. 191?
Living Age. Denison. 1891–?
      Monthly.
Texas Reformer. Denison.
      1890–1894.

FORT WORTH

Afro-American. Fort Worth.
      1902–1903.
Black Dispatch. Fort Worth.
      1898–1901.
Bronze Texan News. Fort Worth.
      1965–1974.
Bronze Thrills. Fort Worth. 1951–
      1978.
Brown Texan. Forth Worth.
      1964–1965.
Church Week. Fort Worth. 1976.
Como Weekly. Fort Worth.
      1940–1978.
Defender and Baptist Herald. Fort
      Worth. 1950.
Defender. Fort Worth. 1944–1951.
Eagle Eye. Fort Worth. 1930–1944.
Ebony Mart. Fort Worth. 197?–19??
Fort Worth Bronze Texan News.
      Forth Worth.
Fort Worth Como Monitor. Fort
      Worth. 1940–current.
Fort Worth Mind. Fort Worth.
      1931–1980.
Forth Worth LaVida. Fort Worth.
Hep. Fort Worth. 1951–1975.
Hornet. Fort Worth. 1918–1926.

Item. Fort Worth. 1890–1912.
Jive. Fort Worth. 1951–1975.
La Vida. Fort Worth. 1958–current.
Lake Como News. Fort Worth.
      1940–1959.
Light. Fort Worth. 1930–1932.
Masonic Quarterly. Fort Worth.
      1919–1922.
Metro Cities News. Fort Worth.
      1965–1981.
Negro Achievements. Fort Worth.
      1947–1951.
Negro Progress. Fort Worth.
      1968–1979.
Organizer. Fort Worth. 1895–1897.
People's Contender. Fort Worth.
      1930–1932.
Sepia. Fort Worth. 1954–1982.
Soul Teen. Fort Worth. 1957–1982.
Sport News. Fort Worth.
      1945–1946.
Texas Standard. Fort Worth. 1926.
Texas Times. Fort Worth.
      1973–current.
Times. Fort Worth. 1980–1987.
Torchlight Appeal. Forth Worth.
      1886–1894.
URE News in Sports. Fort Worth.
      1945–1946.
Weekly. Fort Worth. 1966–1987.
Western Star. Fort Worth.
      1924–1944.
White Man and the Negro Magazine.
      Fort Worth. 1939.
Woman's World. Fort Worth.
      1900–190?
World. Fort Worth. 1912–1976.
World's Messenger. Fort Worth.
      1944–1951.

GALVESTON

Argus. Galveston. 1890–1893.
Banner. Galveston. 1925–1936.
City Times. Galveston. 1898–1931.
Colored American. Galveston.
      1920–1926.
Examiner. Galveston. 1938–1940.

Free Man's Press. Galveston. 1868-
    1869.
Freeman's Journal. Galveston.
    1887–1894.
Galveston Sentinel. Galveston.
    1932–1940.
Galveston Voice. Galveston.
    1931–1949.
Informer. Galveston. 1939–1946.
New Idea. Galveston. 1896–1932.
Spectator. Galveston. 1873–1887.
Test. Galveston. 1890–1892.
Texas Blade. Galveston.
    1886–1889.

HENDERSON
Colored Methodist. Henderson.
    1884–1890.
Educator. Henderson. 1886–1888.

HOUSTON
Afro-American. Houston. 1897.
Altitudes Magazine. Houston.
Baptist Headlight. Houston.
    1891–1893.
Christian Examiner. Houston.
    1943–1946.
Citizen. Houston. 1881–1888.
Dallas Express. Houston. 1948.

Forward Times. Houston.
    1960–1977.
Houston Forward Times. Houston.
    1977–?

Free Lance. Houston. 1898–1899.
Freedmen's Journal. Houston.
    1983–?
Globe-Advocate. Houston.
    1965–1983.
Griot. Houston. 1981–?
Guide. Houston. 1936–1938.
Guiding Star of Truth. Houston.
    1922.
Headlight. Houston. 1894.
Herald. Houston. 1947–1992. Bi-
    monthly by Texas Southern
    University.
Hoo-Doo. Houston. 1973.
Houston Call. Houston. 1969–1972.

Houston Defender. Houston.
    1930–current.
Houston Freeman. Houston.
    1893–1966.
Houston Newspages. Houston.
    198?–current.
Houston Observer. Houston.
    1916–1932.
Houston Sentinel. Houston.
    1927–1932.
Houston Sun. Houston.
    1886–current.
Independence Heights Record. Hous-
    ton. 1902–1926.
Independent. Houston. 1898–1906.
Metropolitan Civic News. Houston.
    1946.
Metropolitan. Houston. 1961.
National Alliance. Houston.
    1889–1893.
Negro Labor News. Houston.
    1931–1976.
Negro Life. Houston. 1944–?
New Age. Houston. 1981–1990.
New Orleans Informer and Sentinel.
    Houston. 1948.
Old Ironsides' Monthly. Houston.
    1947–1950.
San Antonio Informer. Houston.
    1948–1949.
Southern Guide. Houston.
    1879–1881.
Southwestern Banner. Houston.
    1901–1903.
Space City. Houston. 1975–1976.
Sunnyside Digest. Houston.
    1966–1967.
Tempo. Houston. 1965–1977.
Texas Citizen. Houston.
    1881–1889.
Texas Courier. Houston.
    1913–1915.
Texas Examiner. Houston. 194?

There were several temporary name changes, mergers, and re-namings among this group of newspapers. Therefore, they are listed from the first year a name was used.

Texas Freeman. Houston. 1893–1930.

The Houston Informer. Houston. 1893–1930.

The Houston Informer and the Texas Freeman. Houston. 1893–1947.

The Houston Informer. Houston. 1934.

The Informer. Houston. 1934–1941.

The Informer and Texas Freeman. Houston. 1941–1947.

Houston Informer. Houston. 1947.

Houston Informer and Texas Freeman. Houston. 1964–current.

Thurgood Marshall Law Review. Houston. Thurgood Marshall School of Law, Texas Southern University. 1991–current.

Tips News Illustrated. Houston. 1973–1976.

TSU Herald. Houston. 1947–1973.

Van. Houston. 1879–1903.

Voice of Hope. Houston. 1966–1978.

Western Index. Houston. 1938. Moved from Topeka, Kansas.

Western Star #1. Houston. 1881–1932.

Western Star #2. Houston. 191?

Witness. Houston. 1905–1912.

HUNTSVILLE

Bugle. Huntsville. 1897–1900.

East Texas Messenger. Huntsville. 1935.

Free Lance. Huntsville. 1898–1900.

LONGVIEW

Flyer. Longview. 1901–1902.

Great Circle News. Longview. 1969.

Informer. Longview. 1939–1946.

Reporter. Longview. 1900–1902.

Western Christian Advocate. Longview. 1878–1883.

LUBBOCK

Lubbock Digest. Lubbock. 1977–1983.

Lubbock Southwest Digest. Lubbock. 1977–current.

Manhattan Heights Times. Lubbock. 1961–1965.

Manhattan Heights Times and West Texas Times. Lubbock. 1965.

West Texas Times. Lubbock. 1960–1987.

Southwest Digest. Lubbock.

MANOR

Manor Appeal. Manor. ?–1915.

Voice. Manor. 1910–1912.

MARLIN

Colored Texan. Marlin. 1895–1898.

Republican Appeal. Marlin. 1902–1903.

MARSHALL

Baptist Journal. Marshall. 1877–1883.

Campus Lens. Marshall. 1940–1946.

Christian Advocate. Marshall. 1878–1882.

Informer. Marshall. 1939–1946.

People's Union. Marshall. 1913–1919.

Texas and Louisiana Watchman. Marshall. 1904–1913.
Traveler. Marshall. 195?
Tribune. Marshall. 1935.
Wiley Reporter. Marshall. 1904–1973. Wiley College monthly.

NAVASOTA
Bugle. Navasota. 1897–1906.
Colored Knights of Liberty Alliance. Navasota. 1893–1896.
Texas Messenger. Navasota. 1895–1898.

PALESTINE
Colored American Journal. Palestine. 1882–195? Monthly.
Informer. Palestine. 1939–1947.
Plaindealer. Palestine. 1894–1915.
Texas Guide. Palestine. 1910–1915.

PARIS
Helping Hand. Paris. 1896–1911.
Living Age. Paris. 1891–1893.
People's Informer. Paris. 1882–1883.

PORT ARTHUR
Flash. Port Arthur. 1940.
Herald. Port Arthur. 1930–1932.
Review. Port Arthur. 1923–1927.

PRAIRIE VIEW
Panther. Prairie View. 1946–1973. Prairie View University.
Prairie View Standard. Prairie View. 1912–1951.

SAN ANTONIO
Alamo Eagle. San Antonio. 1907.
Conservator. San Antonio. 1900–1901.
Express. San Antonio. 1884–1891.
Guard. San Antonio. 1940–1946.

Hephzibah Herald. San Antonio. 1920–1924.
Hustler. San Antonio. 1910–1918.
Informer. San Antonio. 1939–1949.
Inquirer. San Antonio. 1906–1942.
National S.N.C.C. San Antonio. 1968.
Negro American Magazine. San Antonio. 1922–?
New Generation. San Antonio. 1972–1976.
Our Heritage. San Antonio. 1994–current.
People's I Opener. San Antonio. 1930–1932.
San Antonio Informer. San Antonio. 1988–current.
San Antonio Reformer. San Antonio. 1946.
San Antonio Register. San Antonio. 1931–current.
Sentinel. San Antonio. 1920–1932.
Snap News. San Antonio. 1947–current.
Texas Illuminator. San Antonio. 1892.
Tonguelet. San Antonio. 1892–1892.

SEALY
Austin County Enterprise. Sealy. 1898.
Texas Christian Recorder. Sealy. 1909–1913.

SEGUIN
New American. Seguin. 1913–1927.
Texas News. Seguin. 1895–1900.

TEXARKANA
Afro-American Voice. Texarkana. 1892–1944.
Appreciator. Texarkana. 1898–1922.

Courier. Texarkana. 1975–1983.
Texarkana Courier. Texarkana.
1975–1987.

Informer. Texarkana. 1939–1946.
Inter-State Blade. Texarkana.
1897–1900.
Texarkana Sun. Texarkana.
1888–1890.

TIMPSON
Progressive Age. Timpson.
1898–1900.
Union. Timpson. 1904–1905.

TYLER
Caret. Tyler. 1971–1976.
East Texas Guard. Tyler.
1906–1908.
Informer. Tyler. 1939–1946.
Texas Steer. Tyler. 1973.
Tyler Leader. Tyler. 1962–1973.

VICTORIA
Guard. Victoria. 1912–1925.
Guide. Victoria. 1894–1909.
Southwestern Herald. Victoria.
1900–1904.
Texas Guide. Victoria. 1894–1922.

WACO
Baptist Journal. Waco. 1880–1884.
Baptist Pilot. Waco. 1884–1889.
Cen-Tex Reflections. Waco. 1984.
Clarion. Waco. 1921–1936.
Colored Observer. Waco.
1915–1921.
Conservative Counselor. Waco.
1909–1922.
Enterprise. Waco. 1898–1900.
Helping Hand. Waco. 1912–1939.

Paul Quinn Monthly. Waco.
1886–1900.
Paul Quinn Weekly. Waco.
1900–1916.

Social Gleaner. Waco. 1894–1900.
Southern Herald. Waco. 1894–1900.
Texas Interracial Review. Waco.
1940.
Texas Searchlight. Waco.
1893–1895.
Waco Good News. Waco. 1880.
Waco Messenger. Waco. 1929–?
Waco Spectator. Waco.

WHARTON
Elevator. Wharton. 1897–1899.
Pilot. Wharton. 1896–1898.
Southern Monitor. Wharton.
1887–1890.

VARIOUS COMMUNITIES
Avinger Advance. Avinger.
1919–1922.
Banner. Mexia. 1925.
Colony Leader. The Colony.
1992–current.
Conservative Counselor. Gonzales.
1908–1911.
Consolidated Colored Alliance. Gid-
dings. 1889–1890.
Enterprise. San Angelo.
1936–1938.
Herald. Amarillo. 1936–1938.
Indicator. Sour Lake. 1919–1923.
Informer. Corpus Christi.
1937–1946.
Informer. Galena Park. 1966–1967.
Informer. Lovelady. 1939–1946.
Journal. Center. 1910–1912.
La Vida News. La Vida. 199?
Liberator. Cameron. 1907–1908.
Messenger. Kendleton. 1966–1987.
National Negro Retailers Journal.
Mineral Wells.
1940–1942.
New Test. Lockart. 1893–1899.
Reformer. Bellville. 1899–1901.
Scimitar. Ennis. 1910–1920.

Silhouette. Bryan. 19??–19??
Southwestern Torch. El Paso.
   1941–1944.
Texas Colored Citizen. Luling.
   1907–1908.
Texas Hornet. Forney. 1891–1893.

Texas Reformer. Sherman.
   1890–1894.
West Texas Voice. Galena.
   1966–1967.
Western Star. Temple. 1924–1933.

Other:

African-American Baptist Annual Reports, 1865–1990s: Texas. National Archives, microfilm. Books, pamphlets, periodicals, statistics, biographies, etc.

The Buffalo Soldiers of West Texas: A History of the Buffalo Soldiers. Tucson, AZ: Blue Horse Productions, 1987. Videorecording.

Ella Reid Public Library Records (includes microfilm), 1941-1969. The Negro Public Library was chartered in 1941 and quartered in the basement of the Bethlehem Baptist Church in Tyler, Texas. Established for the "colored children residing in the vicinity," it was supported entirely by donations of money, books, and furnishings. It became a city tax-supported institution ca. 1950, and its name was changed in 1961 to the Ella Reid Public Library. Located at the Balch Institute.

Guts, Gumption and Go-Ahead: Annie Mae Hunt Remembers. Dallas: Media Projects, 1992. Videorecording.

Library of Congress and National Archives. *The General Education Board: The Early Southern Program,* microfilm. Nos. 132–139.

Library of Congress and National Archives. *Records of the Assistant Commissioner, Bureau of Refugees, Freedmen, and Abandoned Lands. 1865–1869,* microfilm. M821.

Library of Congress and National Archives. *Records of the Superintendent of Education, Bureau of Refugees, Freedmen, and Abandoned Lands. 1865–1870,* microfilm. M822.

"Mance Lipscomb: Texas Sharecropper and Songster." Soundrecording.

Marshall, Texas. Washington, DC: PBS Video, 1984. Videorecording.

"Poor Whites, Poor Blacks and Integration." Films for the Humanities and Sciences: Multimedia Entertainment, 1993. Segment (1992) from the Phil Donahue television show concerning proposed integration of federally-funded housing in all-white Vidor, Texas. Videorecording.

"Ragtime Texas." Henry Thomas [Complete Recorded Works, 1927–1929]. Sound recording.

Records of the Assistant Commissioner, Bureau of Refugees, Freedmen, and Abandoned Lands: Texas, 1865–1869. National Archives, microfilm.

Records of the Superintendent of Education, Bureau of Refugees, Freedmen, and Abandoned Lands: Texas, 1865–1870. National Archives, microfilm.

Schools. Texas, Brown, Julius v. Board of Trustees of La Grange School District 1947–48. Frederick, MD: University Publications of America, 1986. Microform. NAACP archives.

Schools. Texas, Corpus Christi: Lawton, W. B. et al. v. Corpus Christi Independent School District, 1943. Frederick, MD: University Publications of America, 1986. Microform. NAACP archives.

Schools. Texas, General, 1945–54. Frederick, MD: University Publications of America, 1986. Microform. NAACP archives.

Schools. Texas, Jennings v. Board of Trustees of Hearne Independent School District, 1947–48. Frederick, MD: University Publications of America, 1986. Microform. NAACP archives.

The Strange Demise of Jim Crow: How Houston Desegregated its Public Accommodations, 1959–1963. Austin: University of Texas Press, 1997. Videorecording.

Teachers' Salaries. Gilmer, Texas, 1945. Frederick, MD: University Publications of America, 1986. Microform. NAACP archives.

Teachers' Salaries. Texas, Dallas, 1942–43. Frederick, MD: University Publications of America, 1986. Microform. NAACP archives.

Teachers' Salaries. Texas—General, 1940–41. Frederick, MD: University Publications of America, 1986. Microform. NAACP archives.

Teachers' Salaries. Texas, Houston, 1943. Frederick, MD: University Publications of America, 1986. Microform. NAACP archives.

Wake Up Dead Man: Black Convict Worksongs from Texas Prisons. Cambridge, MA: Rounder Records 2013, 1975. Soundrecording.

Utah and Mormonism

Articles:

Alexander, Thomas G., and Leonard J. Arrington. "The Utah Military Frontier, 1872–1912: Forts Cameron, Thornburgh, and Duchesne." *Utah Historical Quarterly* 32 (Fall 1964).

"Aunt Jane James, Joseph Smith, The Prophet." *Young Women's Journal* 16 (December 1905).

Barnhill, J. Herschel. "Civil Rights in Utah: The Mormon Way." *Journal of the West* 25 (October 1986).

Beller, Jack. "Negro Slaves in Utah." *Utah Historical Society Quarterly* 2 (October 1929).

Bringhurst, Newell G. "An Ambiguous Decision: The Implementation of Mormon Priesthood Denial for the Black Man—A Reexamination." *Utah Historical Quarterly* 46 (1978).

————. "The 'Descendants of Ham' in Zion: Discrimination Against Blacks Along the Shifting Mormon Frontier, 1830–1920." *Nevada Historical Society Quarterly* 24 (Winter 1981).

————. "Elijah Abel and the Changing Status of Blacks within Mormonism." *Dialogue: A Journal of Modern Thought* 12 (Summer 1979). Abel joined the church in 1832 and was ordained a priest.

————. "Forgotten Mormon Perspectives: Slavery, Race, and the Black Man as Issues among Non-Utah Latter-Day Saints, 1844–1873." *Michigan History* 61 (1977).

————. "The Mormons and Slavery—a Closer Look." *Pacific Historical Review* 50 (1981).

Bush, Lester E., Jr. "A Commentary on Stephen G. Taggart's *Mormonism's Negro Policy: Social and Historical Origins.*" *Dialogue: A Journal of Mormon Thought* 4 (Winter 1969). In both articles, Bush attributes the denial of the priesthood to Blacks to Brigham Young, not Joseph Smith.

————. "Mormonism's Negro Doctrine: An Historical Overview." *Dialogue: A Journal of Mormon Thought* 8 (Spring 1973).

Caldwell, Gaylon L. "Utah Has Not Seceded: A Footnote to Local History." *Utah Historical Quarterly* 21 (1953).

Christensen, James B. "Negro Slavery in Utah Territory." *Phylon* 13 (October 1957). The first slaves were in Utah in 1847.

Clark, Michael J. "Improbable Ambassadors: Black Soldiers at Fort Douglas, 1896–99." *Utah Historical Quarterly* 46 (Summer 1978).

Coleman, Ronald G. "Blacks in Utah History: An Unknown Legacy." Chapter in *The Peoples of Utah*, ed. Helen Papanikolas. Salt Lake City: Utah State Historical Society, 1976.

————. "The Buffalo Soldiers: Guardians of the Uintah Frontier, 1886–1901." *Utah Historical Quarterly* 47 (Fall 1979).

————. "Utah's African American Community and Politics, 18901910." *Beehive History* 19 (1978).

————. "Utah's Black Pioneers: 1847–1869." *UMOJA: A Scholarly Journal of Black Studies* 2 (Summer 1978).

Cooley, Everett L. "Carpetbag Rule Territorial Government in Utah." *Utah Historical Quarterly* 26 (April 1958).

Embry, Jessie L. "Separate but Equal?: Black Branches, Genesis Groups, or Integrated Wards?" *Dialogue; a Journal of Mormon Thought* 23 (Spring 1990).

England, Eugene. "Are All Alike Unto God: Prejudice Against Blacks and Women in Popular Mormon Theology." *Sunstone* 14 (1 April 1990).

————. "The Mormon Cross." *Dialogue: A Journal of Mormon Thought* 8 (Spring 1973). Blacks and the Mormon church.

Esplin, Ronald K. "Brigham Young and Priesthood Denial to the Blacks: An Alternate View." *BYU Studies* 19 (1979).

Flake, Osmer D. "Life of William Jordan Flake." n.p., 1948. Early Black settler. Located in Church of Jesus Christ of Latter-Day Saints Genealogical Society Library, Salt Lake City.

"Free People of Color." *Evening and Morning Star*. Independence, Missouri, 1 and 16 July 1833.

Garrett, H. Dean. "The Controversial Death of Gobo Fango." *Utah Historical Quarterly* 57 (1989). Death of a Black Mormon.

Gerlach, Larry R. "Ogden's Horrible Tragedy: The Lynching of George Segal." *Utah Historical Quarterly* 49 (Spring 1981).

Hubbard, George U. "Abraham Lincoln As Seen By the Mormons." *Utah Historical Quarterly* 31 (Spring 1963).

Hyda, Orson. "Slavery Among the Saints. *Millennial Star* 13, 1851.

Jennings, Warren A. "Factors in the Destruction of the Mormon Press in Missouri, 1833." *Utah Historical Quarterly* 35 (1967). An 1833 article in the Mormon newspaper precipitates their expulsion from the county.

Jenson, H. Bert. "Where Dreams Become Destiny: General Benjamin O. Davis, Sr." *Military Review* 75 (1994–95).

Jonas, Frank H. "A Matter of Opinion: Mormonism's Negro Policy." *American West* 8 (November 1971).

Jones, Stacy. "Ethics of Racial Identification." *Editor and Publisher*, 21 December 1996. Two Salt Lake City newspapers debate over racial identification when one reported the race (Black) of two murder suspects.

Kunz, Phillip R., and Oheneba-sakyi Yaw. "Social Distance: A Study of Changing Views of Young Mormons toward Black Individuals." *Psychological Reports* 65 (1989).

Launius, Roger D. "A Black Woman in a White Man's Church: Amy E. Robbins and the Reorganization." *Journal of Mormon History* 19 (Fall 1993).

————. "One Man's Air Force: The Experience of Byron Dussler at Wendover Field, Utah, 1941–1946." *Utah Historical Quarterly* 54 (Spring 1986). Aspects of social history.

"The Lynching of a Black Man." *New Advocate*, 18 June 1925.

Lythgoe, Dennis L. "Negro Slavery and Mormon Doctrine." *Western Humanities Review* 21(Fall 1967). A historical survey of positions on Blacks and the Mormon Church.

————. "Negro Slavery in Utah." *Utah Historical Quarterly* 39 (Winter 1971).

Mauss, Armand L. "Mormonism and the Negro: Faith, Folklore, and Civil Rights." *Dialogue: A Journal of Mormon Thought* 4 (Winter 1967). Defense of Mormon Church's policy of not allowing Blacks to the lay priesthood.

————. "Mormonism and Secular Attitudes toward Negroes." *Pacific Sociological Review* 9 (1966).

————. "Negro Slavery in Utah." *Utah Historical Quarterly* 39 (Winter 1971).

Merrill, Jerald H. "Fifty Years With a Future: Salt Lake's Guadalupe Mission and Parish." *Utah Historical Quarterly* 40 (Spring 1972). Some account of reaction to Blacks.

"Mormonism's Negro Doctrine." *Dialogue: A Journal of Mormon Thought* 8 (1973).

"Mrs. Romney's Quandary." *Christian Century* 84 (8 February 1967). Treatment of Blacks by Mormons.

Murphy, Miriam B. "The Black Baseball Heroes of '09." *Beehive History* 7 (1981).

————. "Those Pioneering African Americans." *Beehive History* 22 (1996).

Nibley, Hugh. "The Best Possible Test." *Dialogue: A Journal of Mormon Thought* 8 (Spring 1973). Blacks and the Mormon church.

Papanikolas, Helen Zeese. "The Greeks of Carbon County." *Utah Historical Quarterly* 22 (April 1954). Klan Activities in Utah and the lynching of a Black man.

_____. "Tragedy and Hate." *Utah Historical Quarterly* 38 (Spring 1970). Klan activities plus description and photo of a lynching.

_____. "Utah's Ethnic Legacy." *Dialogue* 19 (1986).

Poll, Richard. "The Political Reconstruction of Utah Territory, 1886–1890." *Pacific Historical Review* 27 (May 1958).

Russell, William D. "A Priestly Role for a Prophetic Church: The RLDS and Black Americans." *Dialogue: A Journal of Mormon Thought* 12 (1979).

"Saint Without Priesthood: The Collected Testimonies of Ex-Slave Samuel D. Chambers." *Dialogue: A Journal of Mormon Thought* 12 (1979). Chambers, though denied the priesthood, remained faithful to the church from 1844 until his death in 1929.

Shipps, Jan. "Second-Class Saints." *Colorado Quarterly* 11 (1962). Notes that Joseph Smith was an abolitionist, defended slavery while the Mormons were in Missouri, and then was an abolitionist in 1844.

"The Slave Trade." *Salt Lake Tribune*, 31 May 1939.

"Slavery Among the Saints." *Millennial Star,* 15 February 1851.

Smith, Joseph. "Slaves and Slavery." *Messenger and Advocate* (April 1836).

Thomasson, Gordon C. "Lester Bush's Historical Overview: Other Perspectives." *Dialogue: A Journal of Mormon Thought* 8 (Spring 1973). Response to the Bush article above.

Thurman, Wallace. "Quoth Brigham Young: This is the Place." *Messenger* 8 (August 1926). The status of Blacks.

Trank, Douglas M. "The Negro and the Mormons: A Church in Conflict." *Western Journal of Speech Communication* 35 (Fall 1971).

Ulibarri, Richard O. "Blacks: Servitude and Service." Section in "Utah's Ethnic Minorities: A Survey." *Utah Historical Quarterly* 4 (1972).

_____. "Utah's Ethnic Minorities." *Utah Historical Quarterly* 4 (Summer 1972).

"What Ku Klux Klan Stands For." *News Advocate*, 16 July 1922, 16 November 1922, and August 1923.

White, O. K. "Mormonism's Anti-Black Policy and Prospects for Change." *Journal of Religious Thought* 29 (Fall-Winter 1972).

Wolfinger, Henry J. "A Test of Faith: Jane Elizabeth James and the Origins of the Utah Black Community." In. *Social Accommodations in Utah*, ed. Clark Knowlton. Salt Lake City: University of Utah American West Center, 1975. Portrait of a devout member of the Church of Latter-Day Saints, servant of Joseph Smith.

Wyman, Walker D., and John D. Hart. "The Legend of Charlie Glass." *Colorado Magazine* 46 (1969); reprinted as a pamphlet *The Legend of Charlie Glass, Negro Cowboy on the Colorado-Utah Range*. River Falls, WI: River Falls State University Press, 1970.

Young, Levi Edgar. "The Spirit of the Pioneers." *Utah Historical Quarterly* 14 (1946). Brief description of Blacks as among the first to enter Salt Lake Valley.

Books:

Bell, John. *The Compromise Bill: Speech of Hon. John Bell, of Tennessee, in the Senate of the United States, July 3 and 5, 1850, on the Bill for the Admission of California into the Union, the Establishment of Territorial Governments for Utah and New Mexico, and Making Proposals to Texas for the Settlement of Her Northern and Western Boundaries.* Washington, DC: Congressional Globe Office, 1850. Extension of slavery.

Berrett, William E. *The Church and the Negroid People.* Orem, UT: Community Press, 1960.

Bowles, Carey C. *A Mormon Negro Views the Church.* Newark: n.p., 1968.

Bringhurst, Newell G. *Saints, Slaves, and Blacks: The Changing Place of Black People Within Mormonism.* Contributions to the Study of Religion, no. 4. Westport, CT: Greenwood Press, 1981.

Bush, Lester E., Jr., and Armand L. Mause, eds. *Neither Black nor White: Mormon Scholars Confront the Race Issue in a Universal Church.* Midvale, UT: Signature Books, 1984.

Carter, Kate B. *The Negro Pioneer.* Salt Lake City: Utah Printing Company, 1965. Covers the years 1848–1964.

————. *The Negro Pioneers.* Salt Lake City: Utah Printing Company, 1965.

————. *The Story of the Negro Pioneer.* Salt Lake City: Daughters of Utah Pioneers, 1965.

————. *Utah During Civil War Years.* Salt Lake City: n.p., 1956. Pamphlet.

Cherry, Alan Gerald. *It's You and Me, Lord!* Provo: Trilogy Arts, 1970.

Clark, Michael J. *U.S. Army Pioneers: Black Soldiers in Nineteenth Century Utah.* Fort Douglas, UT: Fort Douglas Military Museum, 1981.

Colton, Ray Charles. *The American Civil War in the Western Territories of New Mexico, Arizona, Colorado and Utah.* Norman: University of Oklahoma Press, 1959.

Davis, France A. *Light in the Midst of Zion: Calvery Missionary Baptist Church and a History of Black Baptists in Utah, 1892–1996.* Salt Lake City: University Publishing, 1997.

Davis, Lenwood G., and Mary Vance *Blacks in the State of Utah: A Working Bibliography.* Monticello, IL: Council of Planning Librarians, 1974.

Douglas, Stephen A. *Remarks of the Hon. Stephen A. Douglas, on Kansas, Utah, and the Dred Scott Decision; Delivered at Springfield, Illinois, June 12, 1857.* Chicago: Daily Times Book & Job Office, 1857.

Embry, Jessie L. *Black Saints in a White Church: Contemporary African American Mormons.* Salt Lake City: Signature Books, 1994.

Fogel, Jacqueline L., and Joanne Yaffe. *Ethnic Minority and Caucasian Student Experiences at the University of Utah and Recommendations for Institutional Response. AIR 1992 Annual Forum Paper.* Paper presented at

the Annual Forum of the Association for Institutional Research, Atlanta, 10–13 May 1992. ERIC. ED 349 874. Academic persistence,
racial discrimination, etc.

Freeman, Joseph. *In the Lord' Due Time*. Salt Lake City: Bookcraft, 1979.

Gerlach, Larry R. *Blazing Crosses in Zion: The Ku Klux Klan in Utah*.
Logan: Utah State University Press, 1982.

Green, Thomas A. *The Negro Revelation*. Salt Lake City: n.p., 19?? Blacks
and the Mormon Church.

Hawkins, Chester L. *Selected and Annotated Bibliography of the History and
Status of Blacks in the Church of Jesus Christ of Latter-Day Saints,
1830–1985*. n.p.: 1985.

Heywood, Yates. *The Negro Question Resolved*. Salt Lake City: Paragon
Press, 1964.

Jenson, Andrew. *Latter-Day Saint Biographical Encyclopedia*. Salt Lake City:
1901–1936. Biography of Elijah Able, Black Priest, Elder, and representative of the Mormon Church.

Lacy, Steve. *The Lynching of Robert Marshall*. Prince, UT: Castle Press,
1978. Marshall, a Black man, lynched near Price, Utah.

LeBaron, E. Dale. *All Are Alike Unto God*. Salt Lake City: Bookcraft, 1990.
Black Mormon converts.

Logan, Rayford Whittingham. *The New Theologians of Doom for Negroes*.
Salt Lake City, 1971.

Lund, John Lewis. *The Church and the Negro: A Discussion of Mormons,
Negroes and the Priesthood*. Salt Lake City: Paramount Publishers,
1967.

Lythgoe, Dennis L. *Slavery in Utah*. Salt Lake City: n.p., 1966.

Martin, Wynetta Willis. *Black Mormon Tells Her Story*. Salt Lake City:
Hawkes Publishers, 1972.

Martinez, Luciano S. *Report on the Ethnic Minority at the University of Utah
with a Specific Look at the Health Sciences*. Salt Lake City: University of Utah, 1978. ERIC. ED 149 940. Student recruitment, enrollment, etc.

McMurrin, Sterling M. *The Negroes Among the Mormons*. Salt Lake City:
Salt Lake City chapter of the NAACP, 1968. Annual address to the
NAACP delivered June 21, 1968.

NAACP Administrative File. Subject File. Lynching...Utah, 1925. Frederick,
MD: University Publications of America, 1986.

Oliver, David H. *A Negro on Mormonism*. n.p.: The Author, 1963.

Petersen, Mark Edward. *Race Problems—As They Affect the Church*. Salt
Lake City: n.p., 1970.

Petty, Wayne G. *The Reverence of Black Literature to the Mormon Culture*.
Salt Lake City, 1969. Essay, Department of English, University of
Utah.

Richardson, Arthur M. *"That Ye May Not Be Deceived": Discussion of the Racial Problem; Segregation or Integration?* Salt Lake City: n.d. Rare book collection, University of Utah.

Salt Lake Community Mental Health Center. *Needs Assessment of the Salt Lake Black Community.* Salt Lake City: The Center, 1977.

Samuels, Willfred D. *Raymond Lark: American Artist of Tradition and Diversity.* Salt Lake City: Utah Museum of Fine Arts, 1989. Catalog of exhibitions.

The Seed of Cain: Being a Collection of Statements Made by the Prophet Joseph Smith and Others, Taken from Public Documents, Concerning Cain, the Brother of Abel, and the Son of Adam and Eve, and His Descendants. Murray, UT: Gems Publishing Company, 1970. Blacks and Mormon theology. Note: "This book is not for public sale or distribution.

Smith, Elmer Richard. *The Status of the Negro in Utah.* Salt Lake City: NAACP, Salt Lake City Branch, 1956.

Smith, Truman. *Speech of Mr. Smith, of Conn.: On the Bill "To Admit California into the Union, to Establish Territorial Governments for Utah and New Mexico, making Proposals to Texas for the Establishment of the Western and Northern Boundaries."...Delivered in the Senate of the United States, July 8, 1850.* Washington, DC: Gideon and Company, Printers, 1850. Extension of slavery.

Stewart, John J. *Mormonism and the Negro: An Explanation and Defense of the Doctrine of the Church of Jesus Christ of Latter-Day Saints in Regard to Negroes and Others of Negroid Blood.* Orem, UT: Community Press Publishing Company, 1960; reprinted, 1964. Defense of the policies regarding Blacks and traces them to Joseph Smith.

Taggart, Stephen G. *Mormonism's Negro Policy: Social and Historical Origins.* Salt Lake City: University of Utah Press, 1970. Traces antiblack policies to Joseph Smith, but believes they were expedient measures and therefore, the church should reverse them.

Tanner, Jerald *The Negro in Mormon Theology.* Salt Lake City: Modern Microfilm Co., 1963.

Tanner, Jerald, and Sandra Tanner. *Joseph Smith's Curse Upon the Negro.* Salt Lake City: University of Utah Press, 1970.

_____. *Mormons and Negroes.* Salt Lake City: Modern Microfilm Co., 1970.

_____. *The Negro in Mormon Theology.* Salt Lake City: Modern Microfilm Co., 1967.

Turner, Wallace. *The Mormon Establishment.* Boston: Houghton Mifflin, 1966. Some information on Blacks and Mormons.

University of Utah, Marriott Library. *Black Bibliography.* Salt Lake City: Marriott Library, 1974.

_____. *Supplement to Black Bibliography.* Salt Lake City: Marriott Library, 1977.

Utah Academy of Sciences, Arts and Letters. Social Sciences Section. *Symposium on the Negro in Utah*, 1954.

Walton, Brian. *BYU and Race; Where We Are Now*. Provo: Brigham Young University, 1970.

Woodbury, Naomi Felicia. *A Legacy of Intolerance: Nineteenth Century Pro-Slavery Propaganda and the Mormon Church Today*. Los Angeles: University of California, 1966.

Wyman, Walker D., and John D. Hart. "The Legend of Charlie Glass." *Colorado Magazine* 46 (1969); reprinted as a pamphlet *The Legend of Charlie Glass, Negro Cowboy on the Colorado-Utah Range*. River Falls, WI: River Falls State University Press, 1970.

Young Blacks on Blackness: Central City Youth on Being Black. Salt Lake City: n.p., 1972.

Theses and Dissertations:

Ainsworth, Charles Harold. "Religious and Regional Sources of Attitudes toward Blacks among Southern Mormons." Ph.D. diss., Washington State University, 1982.

_____. "Southern Mormon Attitudes toward Jews and Blacks." Ed.D. thesis, University of Sarasota, 1975.

Brewer, David Leslie. "Utah Elites and Utah Racial Norms." Ph.D. diss., University of Utah, 1966.

Bringhurst, Newell G. "A Servant of Servants...Cursed as Pertaining to the Priesthood: Mormon Attitudes Toward Slavery and the Black Man, 1830–1880." Ph.D. diss., University of California–Davis, 1975.

Christensen, James B. "A Social Survey of the Negro Population of Salt Lake City, Utah." Master's thesis, University of Utah, 1948.

Clark, Michael J. "A History of the Twenty-Fourth United States Infantry Regiment in Utah, 1896–1900." Ph.D. diss., University of Utah, 1979.

Coleman, Ronald G. "A History of Blacks in Utah, 1825–1910." Ph.D. diss., University of Utah, 1980.

Douglas, Ella D. Lewis. "Negro Historiography with Special Emphasis on Negro Historians of the New School; and the Attitudes of Logan City, Utah, toward Ethnic Minority Groups with Special Emphasis on the Negro." Master's thesis, Utah State University, 1968.

Kirkham, John Spencer. "A Study of Negro Housing in Salt Lake County." Master's thesis, University of Utah, 1968.

Lythgoe, Dennis L. "Negro Slavery in Utah." Master's thesis, University of Utah, 1966.

Maag, Margaret Judy. "Discrimination against the Negro in Utah and Institutional Efforts to Eliminate It." Master's thesis, University of Utah, 1971.

Mauss, Armand L. "Mormonism and Minorities." Ph.D. diss., University of California, Berkeley, 1970.

Ramjoue, George. "The Negro in Utah; A Geographical Study in Population." Master's thesis, University of Utah, 1968.

Trank, Douglas M. "A Rhetorical Analysis of the Rhetoric Emerging from the Mormon-Black Controversy." Ph.D. diss., University of Utah, 1973.

Woodbury, Naomi Felicia. "A Legacy of Intolerance: Nineteenth Century Pro-Slavery Propaganda and the Mormon Church Today." Master's thesis, University of California-Loa Angeles, 1966.

Black Newspapers:

The Advisory. Salt Lake City, 1992–? Quarterly.

Broad Ax. Salt Lake City. 1895–1899.

Eagle. Ogden. 1946–1947.

Mountain West Minority Reporter and West Valley City Sentinel. West Valley City. 1990–?

Tri-City Oracle. Salt Lake City. 1902–1903.

Utah Plain Dealer. Salt Lake City. 1895–1909.

Other:

The Advisory. Salt Lake City: Department of Community and Economic Development. Office of Black Community Affairs, 1992. Quarterly serial.

Flake, William J. File, Latter-Day Saint Church Historian's Library, Salt Lake City, 1894.

The Faces of Utah. KUED, Salt lake City, 1992. Videocassette.

Register of the papers of Lowry Nelson. Special Collections Division, University of Utah Library. Contains information concerning Mormon attitudes toward Blacks.

Washington

Articles:

"Allah Be Praised." *Seattle Magazine* 2 (December 1965). Black Muslims in Seattle.

"An Eloquent Epitaph for Ed Pratt—Spoken in His Own Words." *Seattle Magazine* 6 (March 1969). Murdered civil rights leader.

Anderson, Larry. "We Need Acceptance Where We Are: A Central Area Negro Leader Gives Her Views." *Seattle Times Magazine*, 18 September 1966.

Ayer, John Edwin. "George Bush, the Voyager." *Washington Historical Quarterly* 7 (January 1916).

Barth, Ernest A. T., and Sue March. "Research Note on the Subject of Minority Housing." *Journal of Intergroup Relations* 3 (1962).

Bell, S. Leonard. "W. O. Bush from Bush Prairie." *Black World* (July 1970).

Bettis, William J. "George W. Bush: First Black Man in Washington." *True West* 37 (June 1990).

"Black Backlash." *Seattle Magazine* 1 (October 1964).

Bowker, Gordon. "A Town Divided: Pasco, Wash. Is Full of Tumbleweeds and Trouble." *Seattle Magazine* 75 (June 1970).

Brewster, David. "Solidarity Forever: Black Demands for Construction Jobs Have Revived Labor's Old Fighting Spirit—Not on Behalf of All Workers, But *White* Workers." *Seattle Magazine* 6 (December 1969).

Bunzel, Peter D. "The Clubs: Bastions of Racial Bigotry." *Seattle Magazine* 4 (September 1967).

Campbell, Robert A. "Blacks and the Coal Mines of Western Washington, 1888–1896." *Pacific Northwest Quarterly* 73 (October 1982).

Carle, Glenn L. "The First Kansas Colored." *American Heritage* 43 (February 1992).

"Charles M. Stokes, Pioneering Judge, Dies at 93." *Jet*, 13 January 1997. Obituary of Seattle judge.

"Charles Z. Smith, Prosecuting Attorney, Now With the U.S. Justice Department." *Jet*, 16 March 1961.

"Civil Rights Roundtable." *Seattle Magazine* 3 (November 1966).

Colley, N. S., and M. L. McGhee. "The California and Washington Fair Housing Cases." *Law in Transition* 22 (Summer 1962).

Colon, Aly. "New Data shows that Washington State's Affirmative Action helps More Whites than Blacks." *Black Issues in Higher Education* 13 (30 May 1996)

Crane, Warren Eugene. "Interesting Westerners." *Sunset* 45 (December 1920). John Cragwell, Seattle barber.

Davis, Lenwood G. "Sources for History of Blacks in Washington State." *Western Journal of Black Studies* 2 (March 1978).

Douglas, Patrick. "The Family of Two Revolutions: The Gaytons." *Seattle Magazine* 5 (January 1969).

_____. "New Stirrings in the Central Area. Yeah, Baby You Almost got Burned" *Seattle Magazine* 4 (October 1967).

_____. "'Yeah, Baby, You Almost Got Burned': Must Act II of Our Negro Revolution Produce as It Did in Watts—a 'Reign of Terror'?" *Seattle Magazine* 4 (October 1967).

Dricker, Gerand, and Theodore Shouldberg. "A Locational Analysis of Low Income Housing in Seattle and King County. *Washington University Urban Law Annual.* (1970).

Droker, Howard Alan. "Seattle Race Relations during the Second World War." *Pacific Northwest Quarterly* 67 (October 1976).

Egan, Timothy, Sara Mosle and Linda Greenhouse. "Type-A Gandhi." New *York Times Magazine*, 4 January 1998. Spokane civil rights attorney Carl Maxey.

"Eloquent Epitaph for Ed Pratt—Spoken in His Own Words." *Seattle Magazine* 6 (March 1969). Slain civil rights leader.

Fitzgerald, Mark. "Soul Searching Over Seattle as Unity '99 Site." *Editor and Publisher*, 11 July 1998. The National Association of Black Journalists, the state initiative on affirmative action and the proposed site for Unity '99.

Floyd, G. Douglas. "A Sacrifice for Civic Journalism." *American Journalism Review* 19 (July-August 1997). The need for ethnic diversity.

Franklin, Joseph. "Black Pioneers: George Washington and George Washington Bush." *Pacific Northwest Forum* 14 (1976).

"George Washington Bush, First Black Man to Homestead in Washington." *The Kansas City Genealogist* 34 (Winter 1994).

Gould, William B. "The Seattle Building Trades Order: The First Comprehensive Relief Against Employment Discrimination in the Construction Industry." *Stanford Law Review* 26 (April 1974).

Granberg, W. J. "Appreciation from Knowledge." *Crisis* 56 (August–September 1949). African American history course taught by Ralph Johnston, University of Puget Sound.

Haley, Fred T. "Tacoma Faces School Segregation." *Integrated Education* 2 (April-May 1964).

Halpin, James. "Discrimination by Whites Has Kept Negroes Locked in Jobs that Lead Nowhere." *Seattle Magazine* 5 (June 1968).

_____. "You Gotta Have Soul." *Seattle Magazine* 4 (September 1967). Negro radio station KYAC.

Halseth, James A. "Black Americans in a New Society: Washington State during the Formative Years." *Liberal Arts Review* 1 (Winter 1975).

Hankin, Janet R. "FAS Prevention Strategies: Passive and Active Measures." *Alcohol Health and Research World* 18 (1994). Research on alcohol beverage warning labels and prevention methods conducted in Tuba City, Arizona and King County, Washington.

Harris, Joanne. "Portfolio." *American Visions*, August–September 1996. Profiles of artists Barbara Thomas and Marita Dingus of Seattle and Kira Lynn Harris of Los Angeles.

Hart-Nibbrig, Nand Engie. "Policies of School Desegregation in Seattle." *Integrated Education* 17 (January-April 1979).

Houston, Eric. "Seattle: The Nation's 'Gateway to Asia'." *Black Enterprise*, May 1994. Blacks attempting to benefit from business opportunities.

Hueber, D. F. "Reality or Misinformation?" *Community* 25 (May 1966). Minorities in Spokane.

Hungerford, Thomas W. "An Exercise in Understanding." *Puget Soundings* (December 1964). Seattle interracial home visit day.

Hynding, Alan A. "The Coal Miners of Washington Territory Labor Troubles in 1888–1889." *Arizona and the West* 12 (Autumn 1970). Includes Black experiences.

"In Washington State, Whites Benefit More From Affirmative Action than Blacks." *Black Issues in Higher Education* 13 (30 May 1996).

Karolevitz, Bob. "George Washington, Northwest City Builder." *Negro Digest* (September 1963).

_____. "Northwest City Builder: George Washington." *Black World* 12 (September 1963).

Lippman, Leopold. "Public Relations for Better Race Relations." *Public Relations Journal* 16 (February 1960). Written for the Seattle Urban League.

MacDonald, Norbert. "Population Growth and Change in Seattle and Vancouver, 1880–1960." *Pacific Historical Review* 39 (August 1970). Refers to Black population of Seattle.

Marks, Carole. "Split Labor Markets and Black-White Relations, 1865–1920." *Phylon* 42 (December 1981).

Maynard, C. "Characteristics of Black Patients Admitted to Coronary Care Units in Metropolitan Seattle: Results from the Myocardial Infarction

Triage and Intervention Registry." *American Journal of Cardiology* 67 (1 January 1991).

Moffitt, Donald. "Business-Backed 'Fair' in Seattle Aims to Open More Jobs to Negroes." *Wall Street Journal* (29 January 1965). Report on Chamber of Commerce project.

Morrill, Richard L. "The Negro Ghetto: Problems and Alternatives." *Geographical Review* (July 1965). Focus on Seattle.

Morris, Arval A., and Daniel B. Ritter. "Racial Minority Housing in Washington." *Washington Law Review* 37 (Summer 1962).

"Mrs. Mary Ray, Celebrant of 101st Birthday." *Colored American Magazine* 14 (April 1908). Seattle resident.

Mumford, Esther Hall. "Seattle's Black Victorians—Revising a City's History." *Portage* 2 (Fall/Winter 1980–81).

_____. "Washington's African American Communities." Chapter in *Peoples of Washington: Perspectives on Cultural Diversity*, eds. Sid White and S. E. Solberg. Pullman, WA: Washington State University Press, 1989.

"Nation's NAACP Chapters on Alert After Recent Attacks on West Coast." *Jet*, 16 August 1993> Examines situations in Sacramento and Tacoma.

Nein, Robert M. "Don't Be Fooled by This Lady's Laughter—White Man, She'll Pin Your Tail to the Wall." *Seattle Magazine* 3 (December 1966).

"Negro Founder of Centralia, Washington." *Negro History Bulletin* 27 (November 1963). George Washington.

"A Negro Pioneer in the West." *Journal of Negro History* 8 (July 1923). George Bush and his son.

"New Life in Seattle: In the Biggest, Fastest-Growing City in the Northwest, Negroes Have Found a New Frontier." *Our World* 6 (August 1951).

O'Brien, Robert W. "The Changing Cast Position of the Negro in the Northwest." *Research Studies* 10 (March 1942).

_____. "George Washington, Founder of Centralia." *Negro History Bulletin* 5 (June 1942). Washington (1817–1902), son of a slave father and a white mother, founded Centralia.

_____. "Seattle: Race Relations Frontier, 1949: Trends in Race Relations on the West Coast—a Symposium." *Common Ground* 9 (Spring 1949).

Peterson, Joe. "The Great Ku Klux Klan Rally in Issaquah, Washington." *Pacific Northwest Forum* 2, no. 4 (1977).

Pierce, Kingston. "Amazing Grace: The Gospel According to Seattle's Black Churches." *Washington: The Evergreen State Magazine* 4 (March—April 1988).

Pieroth, Doris Hinson. "With All Deliberate Caution: School Integration in Seattle, 1954–1968." *Pacific Northwest Quarterly* 73 (April 1982).

"A Pioneer's Lonely Path: Setting His Sights on Suburbia, He Made It to Bellevue the Hard Way." *Seattle Magazine* 1 (April 1964).

"Roundup Report: How Schools Meet Desegregation Challenges." *Nation's Schools* 78 (November 1966). Includes Seattle.

Rousseve, Ronald J. "A Negro American's Reflections on Some Aspects of Education." *Washington Education* 77 (October 1965). Professor of education reflects.

Rowe, Mary Ellen. "The Early History of Fort George Wright: Black Infantrymen and Theodore Roosevelt in Spokane." *Pacific Northwest Quarterly* 80 (July 1989).

Savage, W. Sherman. "George Washington of Centralia, Washington." *Negro History Bulletin* 27 (November 1963).

_____. "Negro Founder of Centralia, Washington." *Negro History Bulletin* 27 (November 1963). George Washington, founder of Centralia.

_____. "The Negro Pioneer in the State of Washington." *Negro History Bulletin* 21 (January 1958).

Schear, Rillmond. "How the Ghetto Looks from the Inside." *Seattle Magazine* 2 (November 1965). Seattle Black community, part II.

_____. "The World that Whites Don't Know." *Seattle Magazine* 2 (October 1965). Seattle Black community.

Schwab, Heidi. "Four Black Activists Speak: What We Want from the White Establishment." *Puget Soundings* (January 1969).

Seattle University Magazine I (July 1968). Issue devoted to racism and implications for Seattle.

"Slim Jim: Negro Cattle Rustler (from Oregon) Hanged at Walla Walla." Scrapbook #112, Oregon Historical Society (2 May 1864).

Stern, Mark. "Black Strikebreakers in the Coal Fields: King County, Washington, 1891." *Journal of Ethnic Studies* 5 (1977).

Taylor, Quintard. "Black Urban Development—Another View: Seattle's Central District, 1910–1940." *Pacific Historical Review* 58 (November 1989).

_____. "Blacks and Asians in a White City: Japanese Americans and African Americans in Seattle, 1890–1940." *Western Historical Quarterly* 22 (November 1991).

_____. "The Civil Rights Movement in the American West: Black Protest in Seattle, 1960–1970." *Journal of Negro History* 80 (Winter 1995).

_____. "The Emergence of Black Communities in the Pacific Northwest, 1865–1910." *Journal of Negro History* 64 (Fall 1979).

_____. "The Great Migration: The Afro-American Communities of Seattle and Portland During the 1940s." *Arizona and the West* 23 (Summer 1981).

_____. "Migration of Blacks and Resulting Discriminatory Practices in Washington State between 1940 and 1950." *Western Journal of Black Studies* 2 (March 1978).

_____. "The Question of Culture: Black Life and the Transformation of Black Urban America, Seattle's Central District, 1900–1940." *Essays in History: The Journal of the Historical Society of the University of Lagos, Nigeria* 6 (December 1989).

Tilton, James. "Echo of the Dred Scott Decision, Letter, September 30, 1860 to H. M. McGill, Acting Governor of Washington Territory, Regarding British Removal of a Slave from a Mail Steamer at Victoria." *Washington Historical Quarterly* 1 (October 1906).

Valentine, Bettylou. "The Black Homefront in Seattle and King County during World War II." *Portage* 6 (Summer 1985).

"Washington State Board Against Discrimination Upholds Charge of Discrimination of Negro Couple Against White Owners of FHA Financed Home." *Race Relations Law Reporter* (Fall 1959).

"Washington State Helps Minority Faculty Gain Tenure." *Black Issues in Higher Education* 15 (9 July 1998). The university offers an academic enrichment program, plus implements an exit interview to Black employees.

Watts, Lewis G. "Racial Trends in Seattle, 1958." *Crisis* 65 (June-July 1958).

_____. "Social Integration and the Use of Minority Leadership in Seattle, Washington." *Phylon* 21 (Summer 1960).

"White Racism in Seattle." *Seattle Magazine* 5 (June 1968). Special issue.

Williams, Guy. "Seattle's History-Making Negro Theater." *Federal Theater* 2 (1936).

Yang, Dori Jones. "Lots of Love—and No Excuses." *Business Week*, 8 May 1995. Zion Preparatory Academy in Seattle.

Books:

Banner, Warren M. *A Survey of Community Patterns Related to the Program of the Seattle Urban League.* New York: National Urban League, March 1954.

Barth, Ernest A. T. *Case Studies of the Process of Integration in Neighborhoods of Seattle, Washington.* Seattle: Greater Seattle Housing Council, 1960.

Black-King County Project. Washington (State), Division of Archives and Records Management. Interviews with Blacks on economic and social conditions, 1900–1945.

Cayton, Horace Roscoe. *Long Old Road.* New York: Trident Press, 1965. Autobiography includes early life in Seattle.

_____. *Cayton's Year Book: Seattle's Colored Citizens.* Seattle: H. R. Cayton and son, 1923. Included in *Black Biographical Dictionaries, 1790–1950*, no. 61, 1987. Year book of 1923's Black citizens.

Central Area Committee for Peace and Improvement, Seattle. *Final Report to Economic Development Administration, Technical Assistance Project, U.S. Department of Commerce.* Seattle: Central Area Committee for Peace and Improvement, 1970.

Congress of Racial Equality (CORE), Washington Branch. *Washington's Negro Pioneer: George Washington Bush.* CORE: Seattle, 1967.

Debarros, Paul. *Jackson Street After Hours: The Roots of Jazz in Seattle.* Seattle: Sasquatch Books, 1993.

Final Report to Economic Development Administration, Technical Assistance Project, U.S. Department of Commerce. Seattle: Central Area Committee for Peace and Improvement, 1970. Economic conditions.

Franklin, Joseph. *All through the Night: The History of Spokane Black Americans, 1860–1940.* Fairfield, WA: Ye Galleon Press, 1989.

Griffiths, Keith S. *An Audit of Intergroup Relations in the City of Seattle.* Seattle: Health and Welfare Council, 1950.

Harris, William M. *A Design for Desegregation Evaluation.* n.p.: RF Publishing, 1976. School integration in Seattle.

Heikel, Iris White. *The Wind-Breaker: George Washington Bush: Black Pioneer of the Northwest.* New York: Vantage Press, 1980.

Henry, Mary T. *Tribute: A Guide to Seattle's Public Parks and Buildings Named for Black People: With Brief Biographical Sketches.* Seattle: Statice Press, 1997. Seattle guidebook.

Hobbs, Richard Stanley, ed. *The Autobiography of Horace Cayton, Sr.* Manama, Bahrain: Delmon Press, 1987. Member of a Black Seattle family. Cayton and wife, daughter of Senator Hiram R. Revels.

Institute of Labor Economics. *Job Opportunities for Racial Minorities in the Seattle Area.* Seattle: University of Washington Press, 1948.

Jackson, Joseph Sylvester. *What to Tell Them: A Booklet Designed to be of Special Service to Counselors, Guidance Workers and Agencies with Reference to Negro Girls and Boys in Seattle; and for the Use of Students Themselves.* Seattle: Seattle Urban League, 1938.

Mills, Hazel E., and Nancy B. Pryor. *The Negro in the State of Washington: 1788–1969: A Bibliography.* Olympia: Washington State Library, 1972.

Mumford, Esther Hall. *Calabash: A Guide to the History, Culture, and Art of African Americans in Seattle and King County, Washington.* Seattle: Ananse Press, 1993.

————. *The Man Who Founded a Town.* Seattle: Ananse Press, 1990. George Washington, founder of Centralia, Washington. Juvenile.

————. *Seattle's Black Victorians, 1852–1915.* Seattle: Ananse Press, 1981.

————, ed. *Seven Stars and Orion: Reflections of the Past.* Seattle: Ananse Press, 1986. Biography.

National Association of Colored Women. *The 26th National Convention: 10th Biennial Session of the National Association of Colored Girls.* Seattle: Garfield High School, July 31–August 7, 1948. Souvenir program with photographs of past and present officers.

Northwest Black Pioneers: A Centennial Tribute. Seattle: BON, 1989. Black historical perspectives in the Pacific Northwest.

Northwood, Lawrence K., and Ernest A. T. Barth. *Urban Desegregation: Negro Pioneers and their White Neighbors*. Seattle: University of Washington Press, 1965. Interviews of Black and white families in six Seattle neighborhoods.

Plummer, Nellie Arnold. *Out of the Depths, or, the Triumph of the Cross*. New York: G. K. Hall, 1997. Plummer family in the Washington region.

Race and Violence in Washington State: Report of the Commission of the Causes and Prevention of Civil Disorder. Olympia: Washington Commission on the Causes and Prevention of Civil Disorder, 1969.

Ray, Emma P. *Twice Sold, Twice Ransomed: Autobiography of Mr. and Mrs. L. O. Ray*. Chicago: Free Methodist Publishing House, 1926. Southern and Western experiences of couple who became missionary workers in Seattle.

Schmid, Calvin F. and Wayne W. McVey, Jr. *Growth and Distribution of Minority Races in Seattle, Washington*. Seattle: Seattle Public Schools, 1964.

Schmid, Calvin F., and Vincent A. Miller. *Impact of Recent Negro Migration on Seattle Schools*. Seattle: Office of Population Research, University of Washington, 1959.

Schmid, Calvin F., Charles E. Nobbe, and Arlene E. Mitchell. *Non-White Races: State of Washington*. Olympia: Washington State Planning and Community Affairs Agency, 1968.

Schmid, Calvin F., Laura Hildreth Hoffland, and Bradford H. Smith. *Social Trends in Seattle*. Seattle: University of Washington Press, 1944. Minority groups in Seattle.

Seattle City Council. *Seminar on Equal Opportunities and Racial Harmony, March 22 and April 6, 1968: Summary of Proceedings and Recommendations*. Seattle: City of Seattle, 1968.

Seattle Public Schools. *A Report of Racial Distribution Among Pupils and Employees*. Seattle: Seattle Public Schools, 1968.

_____. *The Report of the Citizens' Advisory Committee for Equal Educational Opportunity*. Seattle: Seattle Public Schools, 1964.

_____. Research Department. *The Garfield Leaver Study. Seattle Public Schools, April 1950*. Seattle: Seattle Public Schools, 1950. Study of high school dropouts.

_____. Research Office. *Racial Distribution: Distribution and Change Among Pupils and Employees of the Seattle Public Schools, Seattle, Washington, 1957 to 1966*. Seattle: Seattle Public Schools, 1966.

Seattle-King County Economic Opportunity Board. *Central Area Motivation Program: A Preliminary Evaluation Report*. Seattle: The Board, 1968.

Seattle-King County Health and Welfare Council. Committee on Intergroup Relations. *A Report on Recreational Facilities and Services for Negro Servicemen in the Seattle Area*. Seattle: The Committee, 1950.

Seattle School District. *Racial Distribution in Seattle Schools, 1957–1968.* Seattle: Seattle School District, 1969.

Seattle University Magazine I (July 1968). Entire issue devoted to racism as a local and national problem.

Seattle Urban League. *Seattle's Racial Gap: 1968.* Seattle: Seattle Urban League, 1968.

_____. *"The Silver Scoreboard."* Seattle: Seattle Urban League, 1935.

_____. *Who's Available? A Listing of Black College Students in the State of Washington.* Seattle: Seattle Urban League, 1969.

Smith, Herndon. *Centralia, the First Fifty Years, 1845–1900.* Centralia, n.p., 1941. Section on George Washington, founder of Centralia.

Spokane Bethel African Methodist Episcopal Church. *50 Years of Progress.* n.p., 1940.

Spokane Community Action Council. *Spokane Community Action Anniversary Report.* Spokane: The Council, May 1968.

Suchman, E. A., L. Dean, and R. Johnson. *Desegregation: Some Propositions and Research Suggestions.* Seattle: Anti-Defamation League of B'nai B'rith, 1958.

Taylor, Quintard. *The Forging of a Black Community: Seattle's Central District, from 1870 through the Civil Rights Era.* Seattle: University of Washington Press, 1994.

University of Washington. *A Survey of Racial Attitudes in the Broadview District.* Seattle: The University, 1968.

_____. Institute of Labor Economics. *Job Opportunities for Racial Minorities in the Seattle Area.* Seattle: University of Washington Press, 1948.

Valentine, Charles. *DEEDS: Background and Basis, a Report on Research Leading to the Drive for Equal Employment in Downtown Seattle.* Seattle: CORE, 1964.

Washington. Commission on the Causes and Prevention of Civil Disorder. *Race and Violence in Washington State: Report of the Commission on the Causes and Prevention of Civil Disorder. Presented to the Urban Affairs Council and Governor Daniel J. Evans, Feb. 1969.* Olympia: The Commission, 1969.

Washington State Board Against Discrimination: Annual Report, 1951. Olympia: State Printing Office, 1952.

Washington State Library. *The Negro in the State of Washington: 1788–1969: A Bibliography of Published and of Unpublished Source Materials on the Life and Achievements of the Negro in the Evergreen State,* eds. Hazel E. Mills and Nancy B. Pryor. Olympia: Washington State Library, 1970.

Washington's Negro Pioneer...George Washington Bush. Seattle: Congress of Racial Equality, 1967.

Watson, Walter B. *Seattle's Negro Population, A Statistical Profile, 1963.* Seattle: Seattle Urban League, 1964.

Whitman, Winslow. *Study of Racial Tension in Tacoma*. Olympia: Washington State Board Against Discrimination, 1970.

Whitman, Winslow, and Isabelle G. Rosenfeld. *Study and Evaluation of Racial Tension at Pasco High School*. Olympia: Washington State Board Against Discrimination, 1969.

Who's Who in Religious, Fraternal, Social, Civic and Commercial Life on the Pacific Coast, State of Washington. Seattle: Searchlight Publishing Company, 1926–27. Source of biographical information on Blacks of the 1920s and earlier.

Wilson, Lyle Kenai. *Sunday Afternoons at Garfield Park: Seattle's Black Baseball Teams, 1911–1951*. Everett: Lowell Printing and Publishing, 1997.

Theses and Dissertations:

Adair, Harriet Elaine. "Trends in School Desegregation: A Historical Case Study of Dayton, Denver, Los Angeles and Seattle." Ed.D. diss., Brigham Young University, 1986.

Amdur, Reuel Seeman. "An Exploratory Study of Nineteen Negro Families in the Seattle Area Who Were First Negro Residents in White Neighborhoods, of Their White Neighbors, and of the Integration Process, Together With a Proposed Program to Promote Integration in Seattle." MSW thesis, University of Washington, 1963.

Bleeg, Joanne Wagner. "Black People in the Territory of Washington, 1860–1880." Master's thesis, University of Washington, 1970.

Brimmer, Andrew Felton. "Some Economic Aspects of Fair Employment." Master's thesis, University of Washington, 1951.

Burgess, Margaret Elaine. "A Study of Selected Socio-Cultural and Opinion Differentials Among Negroes and Whites in the Pasco, Washington Community." Master's thesis, Washington State University, 1949.

Campbell, Robert A. "An Added Objection: The Use of Blacks in the Coal Mines of Washington, 1880–1896." Master's thesis, University of British Columbia, 1978.

Droker, Howard Alan. "The Seattle Civic Unity Committee and the Civil Rights Movement, 1944–1964." Ph.D. diss., University of Washington, 1974.

Fei, John Chang Han. "Rent Differentiation Related to Segregated Housing Markets for Racial Groups—With Special Reference to Seattle, Washington." Master's thesis, University of Washington, Seattle, 1949.

Finley, Jarvis M. "Fertility Trends and Differentials in Seattle." Ph.D. diss., University of Washington, 1958. Analyzed by economic class, race, and education.

Friedman, Ralph. "The Attitudes of West Coast Maritime Unions in Seattle Toward Negroes in the Maritime Industry." Master's thesis, Washington State University, 1952.

Garrity, Frederick Dennis. "The Civic Unity Committee of Seattle, 1944–1964." Master's thesis, University of Washington, 1971.

Griffiths, Keith S. "The Measurement of Intergroup Tensions in the State of Washington and the City of Seattle: Analysis of Two Surveys Conducted Under the Auspices of the Washington Public Opinion Laboratory." Ph.D. diss., University of Washington, 1952.

Henderson, Archie Maree. "Introduction of the Negroes into the Pacific Northwest 1788–1842." Master's thesis, University of Washington, 1949.

Hobbs, Richard Stanley. "The Cayton Legacy: Two Generations of a Black Family, 1859–1976." Ph.D. diss., University of Washington, 1989.

Jackson, Joseph Sylvester. "The Colored Marine Employees Benevolent Association of the Pacific, 1921–1934, or Implications of Vertical Mobility for Negro Stewards in Seattle." Master's thesis, University of Washington, 1939.

Jahn, Julius Armin. "Principles and Methods of Area Sampling Applied to a Survey of Employment, Housing and Place of Residence of White and Non-White Ethnic Groups in Seattle, Washington, July to October 1947." Ph.D. diss., University of Washington, 1949.

Johnson, Evamarii Alexandria. "A Production History of the Seattle Federal Theater Project Negro Repertory Company: 1935–1939." Ph.D. diss., University of Washington, 1981.

Jones, James Beauregard. "Character Education for the Prevention of Negro Criminality, Based Upon a Study of the Character Deficiencies of Negro Inmates at the Federal Penitentiary, McNeil Island, Washington." Master's thesis, University of Washington, 1947.

Little, William A. "Community Organization and Leadership: A Case Study of Minority Workers in Seattle." Ph.D. diss., University of Washington, 1976.

Pieroth, Doris Hinson. "Desegregating the Public Schools, Seattle, Washington, 1954–1968." Ph.D. diss., University of Washington, 1979.

Pitts, Robert Bedford. "Organized Labor and the Negro in Seattle." Master's thesis, University of Washington, 1941.

Richardson, Larry S. "Civil Rights in Seattle: A Rhetorical Analysis of a Social Movement." Ph.D. diss., Washington State University, 1975.

Riordan, Timothy B. "The Relative Economic Status of Black and White Regiments in the Pre-World War I Army: An example from Fort Walla Walla, Washington." Ph.D. diss., University State University, 1995.

Roy, Donald Francis. "Hooverville: A Study of a Community of Homeless Men in Seattle." Master's thesis, University of Washington, 1935.

Royster-Horn, Juana Racquel. "The Academic and Extracurricular Undergraduate Experiences of Three Black Women at the University of Washington, 1935–1941." Ph.D. diss., University of Washington, 1980.

Sever, David Arthur. "Comparison of Negro and White Attitudes in a Washington Community." Master's thesis, Washington State University, 1967. City of Pasco.

Smith, Charles U. "Social Change in Certain Aspects of Adjustment of the Negro in Seattle, Washington." Ph.D. diss., Washington State University, 1951.

Smith, Stanley H. "Social Aspects of the Washington State Law against Discrimination in Employment." Ph.D. diss., Washington State College, 1953.

Taylor, Quintard. "A History of Blacks in the Pacific Northwest, 1788–1970." Ph.D. diss., University of Minnesota, 1977.

Thomas, Paul F. "George Bush." Master's thesis, University of Washington, 1965.

Walker, Diane Louise. "The University of Washington Establishment and the Black Student Union Sit-In of 1968." Master's thesis, University of Washington, 1980.

Wiley, James T. "Race Conflict as Exemplified in a Washington Town." Master's thesis, Washington State University, 1949. A study of Pasco.

Williams, Charles R. "Adaptations of the Black-White Mixed Racial Child." Ed.D. thesis, University of Northern Colorado, 1981. Race relations in Tacoma, Washington.

Black Newspapers:[1]

EVERETT

Riding Sun. Everett. 191?

OLYMPIA

Washington State Board Against Discrimination, Quarterly Newsletter. Olympia. 1967–?

SEATTLE

Afro-American Journal. Seattle. 1967–1971.

Black View. Seattle. 1970–?

Cayton's Weekly. Seattle. 1916–1921.
Cayton's Monthly. Seattle. 1921–1922.

Facts. Seattle. 1961–current. Also known as *Facts News* and *Northwest Facts*.

Fair Play. Seattle. 1950–?

Impulse. Seattle. 1964–?
K-ZAM Kazette. Seattle. 1962.
Messenger. Seattle. 1964.
Metro House Maker. Seattle. 1992–?
New Frontiers. Seattle. 1974–?
Northwest Bulletin. Seattle. 1937–1940.
Northwest Herald #1. Seattle. 1935–1946.
Northwest Herald #2. Seattle. 1970–1992.
Northwest Illuminator. Seattle. 1898–?

Pacific Dispatch. Seattle. 1946–1947.
Seattle Dispatch. Seattle. 1947–1949.

Pacific Leader. Seattle. 1952–1956
Pacific Northwest Bulletin. Seattle. 1944–1948.
Progressive Herald. Seattle. 1933.

---

[1] Single-lined boxed items were published by the same publisher. Double-lined boxed items indicate change in masthead names.

Puget Sound Observer. Seattle.
    1954–1966.
Puget Sound and Inland Empire Ob-
    server. Seattle. 1959.

Red Dragon. Seattle. 19??–1982.
Renaissance Courier. Seattle. 1969.

Republican. Seattle. 1893–1915.
Seattle Republican. Seattle. ?–1915.

Score. Seattle. 1960–1961.
Searchlight. Seattle. 1904–1925.
Seattle Bee #1. Seattle. 189?–1900.
Seattle Bee #2. Seattle. 1906–?
Seattle Builder. Seattle. ?–1954.
Seattle Dispatch. Seattle.
    1947–1949.

Seattle Enterprise. Seattle.
    1920–192?
Enterprise. Seattle. 1920–1930.
Northwest Enterprise. Seattle.
    1920–1962.

Seattle Medium #1. Seattle.
    1935–1946.
Seattle Medium #2. Seattle.
    1970–199?
Seattle Observer. Seattle.
    1954–1964.
Seattle Progressive Herald. Seattle.
    1933–?
Seattle Republican. Seattle.
    1894–1915.
Seattle Skanner. Seattle. 1992–?
Seattle Standard. Seattle.
    1891–1902.
Soul Town Review. Seattle. 1992–?
Trumpet. Seattle. 1966–1967.
Western Sun. Seattle. 1898–1900.
World. Seattle. 1898–1903.

SPOKANE

Citizen. Spokane. 1908–1915.
Northwest Echo. Spokane. 1896–?
Northwest Review-Bulletin. Spo-
    kane. 1936–?
Voice of the West. Spokane.
    1912–1915.

TACOMA

Fact News. Tacoma. 1969–1979.
Facts. Tacoma. 1970–1980.
Forum. Spokane. 1908–1912.
Forum. Tacoma. 1903–1920.
Kitsap County Dispatch. Tacoma.
    1988–1992.
Northwest Courier. Tacoma.
    1969–1972.
Northwest Dispatch. Tacoma.
    1981–199?
Northwest Journal Reporter. Tacoma.
    1970.
Pacific Northwest Review Bulletin.
    Tacoma. 1940–1949.
Progress Messenger. Tacoma.
    1970–1971.

Reporter. Tacoma. 1966–1967.
Journal-Reporter. Tacoma. 1967–?

Star. Spokane. 1946.
Sunday Morning Echo. Tacoma.
    1907–1909.
Tacoma New Courier. Tacoma.
    1969–1973.
Tacoma Northwest Courier. Tacoma.
Tacoma True Citizen #1. Tacoma.
    1974–199?
Tacoma True Citizen #2. Tacoma.
    1975–199?
Thurson County Dispatch. Tacoma.
    1989–199?

Other:

African-American Baptist Annual Reports, 1865–1990s: Washington. National Archives, microfilm. Books, pamphlets, periodicals, statistics, biographies, etc.

Blacks in the Pacific Northwest: The Clayton Family. Dramatization. KWSU-TV, Pullman, 1980. Videorecording.

Blacks in the Pacific Northwest: The Roslyn Migration. Dramatization. KWSU-TV, Pullman, 1979. Videorecording. Black migration to Roslyn, 1880.

Newspaper clippings: 1888 importation of Blacks to break a miners strike in the Roslyn, Washington coal fields. British Columbia Archives, 197?. Microfiche.

Wyoming

Articles:

Adams, Gerald M. "The Casper Army Field in World War II." *Annals of Wyoming* 64 (Summer/Fall 1992). Mention of the 377th Aviation Squadron.

Berwanger, Eugene H. "William J. Hardin: Colorado Spokesman for Racial Justice, 1863–1873." *Colorado Magazine* 52 (1975).

Brown, Amanda Hardin. "A Pioneer in Colorado and Wyoming." *Colorado Magazine* 35 (1958).

Bullock, Clifford A. "Fired by Conscience: The Black 14 Incident at the University of Wyoming and Black Protest in the Western Athletic Conference, 1968–1970." *Wyoming History Journal* 68 (Winter 1996).

Burns, Robert H. "Beefmakers of the Laramie Plains." *Annals of Wyoming* 36 (October 1964). Information on cowboy Samuel Stewart.

Guenther, Todd. "Y'All Call Me Nigger Jim Now, But Someday You'll Call Me Mr. James Edwards: Black Success on the Plains of the Equality State." *Annals of Wyoming* 61 (Fall 1989). Biography of Jim Edwards and wife Lethel Dawson of Denver.

Hardaway, Roger D. "Prohibiting Interracial Marriage: Miscegenation Laws in Wyoming." *Annals of Wyoming* 52 (Spring 1980). The 1869 and 1913 laws.

————. "William Jefferson Hardin: Wyoming's Nineteenth Century Black Legislator." *Annals of Wyoming* 63 (Winter 1991). Hardin was twice elected to the Wyoming Territorial Legislature.

Lamb, David. "Home on the Range—Where Blacks Are Finding a Haven." *Los Angeles Times* (8 April 1993).

"The Last Days of Jim Edwards." *Ebony*, March 1949. Profile of Edwards, a rancher, that may be exaggerated.

Murray, Robert A. "The United States Army in the Aftermath of the Johnson County Invasion." *Annals of Wyoming* 38 (April 1966); reprinted in *The Black Military Experience in the American West*, ed. John M. Carroll. New York: Liveright Publishing, 1971.

Schubert, Frank N. "Black Soldiers on the White Frontier: Some Factors Influencing Race Relations." *Phylon* 32 (Winter 1971). Author surmises that the proximity of Native Americans may have affected how the troops were embraced in Wyoming.

————. "The Suggs Affray: The Black Cavalry in the Johnson County (Wyoming) War." *Western Historical Quarterly* 4 (January 1973). The 9th Cavalry.

"U. of Wyoming Seeks Federal Help in Addressing Racial Tensions." *Black Issues in Higher Education* 8 (25 April 1991).

"University of Wyoming Asks Justice Department to Assess Campus Racial Climate." *Black Issues in Higher Education* 8 (25 April 1991).

Whittlesey, Lee. "A Brief History of Black Americans in the Yellowstone National Park Area, 1872–1907." *Annals of Wyoming* 69 (Fall 1997).

Williams, Jennie Winona. "Allen and Winona Williams: Pioneers of Sheridan and Johnson Counties." *Annals of Wyoming* 14 (1942). Mention of Black cowboy Jim Simpson.

Zollo, Richard P. "General Francis S. Dodge and His Brave Black Soldiers." *Essex Institute Historical Collections* 122 (July 1986). Wyoming in 1879.

Books:

Civil Rights Enforcement in Wyoming. Washington, DC: Commission on Civil rights, 1988.

Corporate Reactions to Workplace Conditions in Wyoming: A Statement of the Wyoming Advisory Committee to the U.S. Commission on Civil Rights. Washington, DC: The Commission, 1982.

The Employment of Minorities and Women by Wyoming State Government. Cheyenne, WY: Wyoming Advisory Committee to the Wyoming State Government, 1994.

Gugliotta, Bobette. *Nolle Smith: Cowboy, Engineer, Statesman.* New York: Dodd, Mead, 1971. Born and raised in Wyoming, he eventually moved to Hawaii where he served in the territorial legislature. Juvenile.

NAACP Administrative File. Subject File. Lynching Green River, Wyoming, 1918. Frederick, MD: University Publications of America, 1986.

Theses and Dissertations:

Guenther, Todd. "At Home on the Range: Black Settlement in Rural Wyoming, 1850–1950." Master's thesis, University of Wyoming, 1988.

Schubert, Frank N.   "The Black Regular Army Regiments in Wyoming, 1885–1912." Master's thesis, University of Wyoming-Laramie, 1970.

Other:

Interview, Sudie Rhone, 8 November 1979.   University of Wyoming Heritage Center, Laramie.
O'Mahoney, Joseph.   Collection of papers that include "fragments of primary sources" on Black history.   University of Wyoming.
Parkhill, Forbes.   Collection of papers that include "fragments of primary sources" on Black history.   University of Wyoming.

Canada

Articles:

"Background on the Ku Klux Klan." Nova Scotia Human Rights Commission. n.d.

Baily, Marilyn. "From Cincinnati, Ohio to Wilberforce, Canada: A Note on Antebellum Colonization." *Journal of Negro History* 58 (October 1973).

Baxter, Michael St. Patrick. "Black Bay Street Lawyers and Other Oxymora." *Canadian Business Law Journal* 30 (July 1988). Prestigious Bay Street law firms tend not to hire Blacks.

Beaton, E. "An African-American Community in Cape Breton, 1901–1904." *Acadiensis* 25 (Spring 1995).

Berry, J. W., and Kalin, R. "Multicultural and Ethnic Studies in Canada: An Overview of the 1991 National Survey." *Canadian Journal of Behavioral Science* (July 1995).

"Big Break for Crystal Joy." *Ebony*, October 1959. The musical career of Canadian-born singer Crystal Joy, and her sponsorship by Steve Allen.

"Black Education Gets Better." *Contrast* 4 (1972).

"Black Organizations of Black People, by Black People for Black People." *Expression* 3 (1969).

"Black School Booming." *Contrast* 4 (1972).

"Blacks Need a Better Deal: Hard Look at Canadian Racist." *Contrast* 2 (1974).

Blockson, Charles and Henry Chase. "Canada." *American Visions*, April–May 1995. The Underground Railroad.

Boehm-Hill, Charles. "Empowering an Endangered Species: The African-Caribbean/Canadian Male." *Education Canada* 33 (Summer 1993).

Boyd, Herb. "Canada." *Crisis* 93 (1986).

"Breakthrough: Community Body Gets Okay to Work with Black Prisoners." *Contrast* 4 (1972).

Brown, Dick. "The Coloring of Canada." *Quest* 4 (1975).

Brown, Lloyd W. "Beneath the North Star: The Canadian Image in Black Literature." *Dalhousie Review* 50, no. 3 (1970).

Cahill, Barry. "The 'Colored Barrister': The Short Life and Tragic Death of James Robinson Johnston, 1876–1915." *Dalhousie Law Journal* 15 (Fall 1992).

Calbreath, D. "Kovering the Klan." *Columbia Journalism Review* (March/April 1981).

Calliste, Agnes. "Blacks on Canadian Railways." *Journal of Ethnic Studies* 20 (1988).

————. "Sleeping Car Porters in Canada: An Ethnically Submerged Split Labour Market." *Canadian Ethnic Studies* 19 (1987).

————. "The Struggle for Employment Equity by Blacks on American and Canadian Railroads." *Journal of Black Studies* 25 (1995).

"Campaign Against Blacks." *Contrast* 2 (1970).

"Canada: Police and Black Wageless." *Race Today* 7 (1975).

"Canada's 'Keep-Out' to Klanism." *Literary Digest* 76 (3 February 1923).

Carey, S. H. D. "The Church of England and the Colour Question in Victoria, 1860." *Journal of the Canadian Church Historical Society* 24 (1982).

Chigbo, Okey. "Pride of Place." *West Africa* 3778 (22–28 January 1990). Black Canadians growing identification with Africa.

Christensen, Carole Pigler, and Morton Weinfeld. "The Black Family in Canada: A Preliminary Exploration of Family Patterns and Inequality." *Canadian Ethnic Studies* 25 (1993).

Clark, Debbie. "Problems of Growing up in Canada...Black!" *Contrast* 2 (1970).

Clarke, George Elliott. "Contesting a Model Blackness: A Mediation on African-Canadian African Americanism, or the Structure of African Canadianite." *Essays on Canadian Writing*, no. 63 (Spring 1998). African Canadians have developed their own forms of art and literature.

————. "Must All Blackness be American? Locating Canada in Borden's 'Tightrope Time,' or Nationalizing Gilroy's *The Black Atlantic*." *Canadian Ethnic Studies* 28, no 3 (1996).

Cooper, Afua. "The Search for Mary Bibb." Chapter in *We Specialize in the Wholly Impossible: A Reader in Black Women's History*, eds. Darlene Clark Hine, Wilma King, and Linda Reed.

————. "The Search for Mary Bibb, Black Woman Teacher in Nineteenth-Century Canada West." *Ontario History* 83 (March 1991).

De Arman, Charles. "The Black Image in the Black Mind; Or, Flight to Canada." *CLA Journal* 33 (December 1989).

Dei, George J. Sefa. "Narrative Discourses of Black/African-Canadian Parents and the Canadian Public School System." *Canadian Ethnic Studies* 25 (1993).

————. "The Role of Afrocentricity in the Inclusive Curriculum in Canadian Schools." *Canadian Journal of Education* 21 (Spring 1996). The need for a more inclusive curriculum.

Diebel, Linda. "Black Women in White Canada." *Chatelaine* 46 (1973).

Elliott, Lorrie. "Black Writing in Canada: The Problems of Anthologizing and Documenting." *Canadian Review of Comparative Literature* 16 (September 1989).

Erland, Anastasia. "The New Blacks in Canada." *Saturday Night* 85 (1970).

Fennell, T. "A Common Chord in Canada." *Maclean,* October 1995. Louis Farrakhan.

Fong, Eric. "A Comparative Perspective on Racial Residential Segregation: American and Canadian Experiences." *Sociological Quarterly* 37 (Spring 1996). Compares the experiences of Blacks and Asians in 404 American and 41 Canadian cities.

Forbes, Wendy. "Library of Black Literature Giving Blacks a Sense of Pride and Achievement." *Contrast* 4 (1972).

Foster, Cecil. "The March of Islam: Black Militant Louis Farrakhan targets Canada." *Maclean's*, 30 September 1996.

Frideres, J. "Racism in Canada: Alive and Well." *Western Canadian Journal of Anthropology* 6 (1976).

Geschwender, James. "Negro Education: The False Faith." *Phylon* 29 (1968).

Gillmor, D. "Promised Land." *Canadian Geographic* 115 (July/August 1995). A heritage tour.

Godard, Barbara. "A Writing of Resistance: Black Women's Writing in Canada." *Zora Neale Hurston Forum* 9 (Fall 1994).

"Grafton Tyler Brown: Black Artist in the West." Oakland Museum, Oakland, California. February 11–April 22, 1972. Catalogue.

Grey, F. W. "Race Question in Canada." *University Magazine*, April 1908.

Gulston, Felix. "Blacks Should Seek to Own Homes." *Contrast* 5 (1973). Home ownership.

Hancock, Harold B. "Mary Ann Shadd: Negro Editor, Educator, and Lawyer." *Delaware History* 15 (April 1973). Newspaper editor and advocate for Black immigration to Canada.

Henry, Annette. "African Canadian Women Teachers' Activism: Recreating Communities of Caring and Resistance." *Journal of Negro Education* 61 (Summer 1992).

————. "Missing: Black Self-Representations in Canadian Educational Research." *Canadian Journal of Education* 18 (Summer 1993).

"Hotels Told to Hire More Blacks." *Contrast* 4 (1972).

Irby, Charles C. "The Black Settlers on Saltspring Island in the Nineteenth Century." *Phylon* 35 (December 1974). Patterns of settlements in the late 1850s and early 1860s.

Jain, Prakash C. "Racism in Canada: Some Recent Surveys." *India Quarterly* 39 (1983).

James, Carl E. "Contradictory Tensions in the Experiences of African Canadians in a Faculty of Education with an Access Program." *Canadian Journal of Education* 22 (Spring 1997). Teacher education experiences.

Johnson, Clifton H. "Mary Ann Shadd: Crusader for the Freedom of Man."
    Crisis (April-May 1971). Brief biographical sketch.
Johnston, Thomas F. "Blacks in Art Music in Western Canada." *Canadian
    Journal of Anthropology* 19/2 (1981). Blacks in classical and jazz mu-
    sic.
_____. "Music and Blacks in 18th- and 19th-Century Canada." *Anthropo-
    logical Journal of Canada* 18/4 (1980).
Joyce, Gare. "SPORT: White Rules—If Black Athletes Need Some Help Es-
    caping 'Racist' Canada for Big-Time U.S. Colleges, Street Agents like
    Bob White are Happy to Assist." *Saturday Night* 107 (1 November
    1992).
Khan, Israel. "Two Weeks of Hostility: The Klan is Back!" *Contrast* 4 (1972).
Knight, Claudette. "Black Parents Speak: Education in Mid-Nineteenth-Century
    Canada West." *Ontario History* 89 (December 1997).
"Ku Klux Kanada." *Maclean's*, 4 April 1977. The Klan in Canada.
"Ku Klux Klan: Attempts to Establish Ku Klux Klan in Canada." *Canadian
    Forum* 10 (April 1930).
Ladson-Billings, Gloria, and Annette Henry. "Blurring the Borders: Voices of
    African Liberatory Pedagogy in the United States and Canada." *Journal
    of Education* 172, no. 2 (1990).
Lalonde, Richard N., Shilpi Majumder, and Roger D. Parris. "Preferred Re-
    sponses to Situations of Housing and Employment Discrimination."
    Journal of Applied Social Psychology 25 (1995). Black Canadians re-
    act to a scenario regarding discrimination and elect appropriate re-
    sponses.
Lawson, Bruce. "Being Negro." *Globe and Mail Magazine*, 12 November 1966.
Lindo, Louis. "The Black Crisis—Canada." *Expression* 3 (1969).
Lyons, Nancee L. "A Legacy of Black History in Canada." *American Visions*,
    April 1992.
MacDonald, Cheryl. "Last Stop on the Underground Railroad." *Beaver* 70
    (1990).
Martin, Ged. "British Officials and their Attitudes to the Negro Community in
    Canada, 1833–1861." *Ontario History* 66, no. 2 (1974). Blacks in
    Canada, not only fugitive slaves.
McClure, J. Derrick. "The Semantics of a Social Problem." *Revue de
    l'Université d'Ottawa* [Canada] 43, no. 1 (1973). Language used in dis-
    cussing Blacks.
Means, John E. "Human Rights and Canadian Federalism." *Phylon* 30, no. 4
    (1969). Canadian civil rights protections from 1865 to 1967.
Mundende, D. Chongo. "Black Immigration to Canada." *Chronicles of Okla-
    homa* 76 (Fall 1998). Near the beginning of the 20th century, Black
    Oklahomans immigrated to Canada for opportunities
"The Negro in Canada." *Chautauquan* 63 (July 1911).
O'Malley, Martin. "Black Pride? Well Not Quite." *Globe Magazine*, 15 Feb-
    ruary 1969.

_____. "Black, White and Canadian." *Globe Magazine*, 15 February 1969.

Palmer, Gwen. "Camperville and Duck Bay." *Manitoba Pageant* 18, no. 3 (1973). In part II of this series the role of a Black man, Bob Jones, is profiled for his part in development of Duck Bay.

Pease, William H., and Jane H. Pease. "Opposition to the Founding of the Elgin Settlement." *Canadian Historical Review* 38 (September 1957). Anti-Black sentiment.

_____. "Organized Negro Communities: A North American Experiment." *Journal of Negro History* 47 (January 1962). Examines some Canadian communities.

"Raw Deal in Canada: Blacks Face a Harsh System." *West Africa* 4106 (July 1, 1996).

Perry, Thelma D. "Race Conscious Aspects of the John Brown Affair." *Negro History Bulletin* 37, no. 6 (1974). The significance of Brown's 1858 meeting in Canada.

"Police and Black People: Vicious Plot to Antagonize Blacks?" *Contrast* 2 (1970).

Porter, Kenneth Wiggins. "Negroes in the Fur Trade." *Minnesota History* 15 (1934).

Potter, Harold H. "Negroes in Canada." *Race* 103 (1961).

Proudfoot, Dan. "The Negro in the C.F.L." *Canadian Magazine*, 18 November 1967. Inside the Canadian Football League.

Richmond, A. "Black and Asian Immigrants in Britain and Canada: Some Comparisons." *New Commentary* 4 (1975).

Roach, Charles. "Minorities and Police Racism." *Prometheus*, no. 2 (1980).

Robbins, Arlie C. "Census of Kent County, Canada West, 1851." *Journal of the Afro-American Historical and Genealogical Society* 5 (1984).

Rosenberg, Neil V. "Ethnicity and Class: Black Country Musicians in the Maritimes." *Journal of Canadian Studies* 23 (1988).

Samson, Jacques, and Magdeleine Yerlès. "Racial Differences in Sports Performance." 18th Annual Meeting of the Canadian Association of Sport Sciences (1985, Quebec, Canada). *Canadian Journal of Sport Sciences* 13 (1988).

Shadd, Adrienne. "Special Feature: 300 Years of Black Women in Canadian History." *Tiger Lily* 1 (1987).

Simms, Glenda P. "Diasporic Experiences of Blacks in Canada: A Discourse." *Dalhousie Review* 73 (Fall 1993).

Spray, W. A. "The Settlement of the Black Refugees in New Brunswick, 1815–1836." *Acadiensis* [Canada] 6 (Spring 1977). Though 371 U. S. Blacks were granted land in 1816, they still faced racial discrimination from the government.

Stouffer, Allen P. "Black Abolitionists in Britain and Canada." *Canadian Review of American Studies* 19 (1988).

Strange, Carolyn, and Tina Loo. "Spectacular Justice: The Circus on Trial and the Trial as Circus, Picton, 1903." *Canadian Historical Review* 77 (1996).

Timberlake, Constance. "The Canadian Black Experience." *Crisis* 88 (March 1981).

Troper, Harold M. "The Creek-Negroes of Oklahoma and Canadian Immigration, 1901–1911." *Canadian Historical Review* 53 (September 1972). Creek Indian Negro and conflicts with Southern Blacks, plus development of Canadian anti-Negro immigration restrictions.

Tunteng, P. "Racism and the Montreal Computer Incident of 1969." *Race* 14 (1973). Black student refused scholarship she won.

Walker, W. James St. G. "Historical Study of Blacks in Canada: The State of the Discipline." Chapter in *Black Presence in Multi-Ethnic Canada*, ed. V. D'Oyley. Vancouver: University of British Columbia; and Toronto: Ontario Institute for Studies in Education, 1978.

Wayne, Michael. "The Black Population of Canada West on the Eve of the American Civil War: A Reassessment Based on the Manuscript Census of 1861." *Histoire Sociale/Social History* 28 (November 1995).

Winks, Robin W. "Canada: Black and White Relationships." *Negro History Bulletin* 35, no. 8 (1970).

_____. "The Canadian Negro: A Historical Assessment—Part I." *Journal of Negro History* 53 (October 1968).

_____. "The Canadian Negro: A Historical Assessment—Part II." *Journal of Negro History* 54 (January 1969).

_____. "The Canadian Negro: The Problem of Identity." Chapter in *Minority Canadians*, ed. Elliott Jean Leonard. Scarborough, ON: Prentice-Hall, 1971.

Woolfson, Peter. "A Question of Identity: A Review of Recent Work on Blacks in Canada." *American Review of Canadian Studies* 7, no. 1 (1977). Blacks in Canada have fared no better than their counterparts in the U.S.

Yee, Shirley J. "Finding a Place: Mary Ann Shadd Cary and the Dilemmas of Black Migration to Canada, 1850–1870." *Frontiers: A Journal of Women Studies* 18, no. 3 (1997).

Zeldis, Nancy. "U.S.-Canada Group Meet on Judicial Minority Issues." *New York Law Journal* 200 (13 December 1988). Black judges and social aspects of the legal profession.

Alberta

Grow, Stewart. "The Blacks of Amber Valley: Negro Pioneering in Northern Alberta." *Canadian Ethnic Studies* 6 (1974).

Henson, T. "Ku Klux Klan in Western Canada." *Alberta History* 25, no. 4 (1977).

Palmer, Howard, and Tamara Palmer. "Urban Blacks in Alberta." *Alberta History* 29 (Summer 1981).

Ponting, J. Rick, and Richard A. Wanner. "Blacks in Calgary: A Social and Attitudinal Profile." *Canadian Ethnic Studies* 15 (1983).

Thompson, Colin A. "Dark Spots in Alberta." *Alberta History* 25 (1977).

British Columbia

Edwards, Malcolm. "'The War of Complexional Distinction': Blacks in Gold Rush California and British Columbia." *California Historical Quarterly* 56 (Spring 1977). Racial discrimination against Blacks in California caused 800 to move to British Columbia, where they continued to encounter discrimination.

Foner, Philip S. "The Colored Inhabitants of Vancouver Island." *British Columbia Studies* 8 (Winter 1970-1971).

Howay, F. W. "The Negro Immigration into Vancouver Island in 1858." *British Columbia Historical Quarterly* 3 (April 1939).

_____. "Negro Immigration to Vancouver Island in 1858." *Transactions of the Royal Society of Canada* (May 1935).

O'Brien, Robert W. "Victoria's Negro Colonists—1858–1866." *Phylon* 3 (Spring 1942).

Ralston, H. Keith. "John Sullivan Deas: A Black Entrepreneur in British Columbia Salmon Canning." *BC Studies* 32 (1976–1977). Tinsmith Deas went from making cans to owning a cannery, making him a founder of the canning industry.

Reid, Patricia H. "Segregation in British Columbia." *Bulletin of the United Church of Canada* 16 (1963). Issues of segregation within the Congregational Unions.

Weber, Ralph E. "Documents—Riot in Victoria, 1860." *Journal of Negro History* 56 (April 1971). Growth of anti-Negro feelings leading to the Vancouver Island riot of 1860.

Nova Scotia

Blakeley, Phillis R. "Boston King: A Negro Loyalist Who Sought Refuge in Nova Scotia." *Dalhousie Review* 48, no. 3 (1968).

_____. "William Hall, Canada's First Naval V. C." *Dalhousie Review* 37, no. 3 (1957). Black Nova Scotian wins the Victoria Cross in 1857.

Cahill, Barry. "Stephen Blucke: The Perils of Being a 'White Negro' in Loyalist Nova Scotia." *Nova Scotia Historical Review* 11 (1991).

Creighton, Helen. "Collecting Songs of Nova Scotia Blacks." *Folklore Studies in Honour of Herbert Halpert: A Festschrift*. Published by St. John's Memorial University of Newfoundland, 1980.

Davis, Morris. "Results of Personality Tests Given to Negroes in the Northern and Southern United States and in Halifax, Canada." *Phylon* 25, no. 4

(1964). Comparative study of the results of the Tomkins-Horn Picture Arrangement Test administered to white and Black youth.

Dillard, J. L. "The History of Black English in Nova Scotia: A First Step." *Review Interamericana* [Puerto Rico] 2, no. 4 (1973). Africa the source of Black English in the U.S. South and Nova Scotia.

_____. "The West African Day-Names in Nova Scotia." *Names* 19, no. 4 (1971). A study of day-names from African slave sources.

Grant, John N. "Black Immigrants into Nova Scotia, 1776–1815." *Journal of Negro History* 58 (July 1973). Discusses three waves of Black immigration to 1812.

_____. "The 1821 Emigration of Black Nova Scotians to Trinidad." *Nova Scotia Historical Quarterly* 2, no. 3 (1972). British attempts to resettle Blacks to its Caribbean colony for Canadian Blacks, including runaway slaves from the U.S. border states.

Griffin-Allwood, Philip G. A. "The Reverend James Thomas and 'Union of All God's People': Nova Scotian African Baptist Piety, Unity and Division." *Nova Scotia Historical Review* 14 (1994).

Fingard, J. "From Sea to Rail: Black Transportation Workers and Their Families in Halifax, c.1870–1916." Montreal: *Acadiensis* 25 (Spring 1996).

Hamilton, Sylvia. "Our Mothers Grand and Great—Black Women of Nova Scotia." *Canadian Woman Studies/les cashiers de la femme* 11 (Spring 1991).

Harvey, Evelyn B. "The Negro Loyalist." *Nova Scotia Historical Quarterly* 1, no. 3 (1971). The 500 Blacks who were members of the United Empire Loyalists of 1789 to 1792.

Jones, B. "Nova Scotia Blacks: A Quest for Place in the Canadian Mosaic." Chapter in *Black Presence in Multi-Ethnic Canada*, ed. V. D'Oyley. Vancouver: University of British Columbia; and Toronto: Ontario Institute for Studies in Education, 1978.

Kolemaine, R. S. "Black Operators in Heritage Touring." *American Visions*, April-May 1994. Profiles Black heritage tours in California, Nova Scotia and Ontario.

Lennox, Brian. "Nova Scotia's Forgotten Boxing Heroes: Roy Mitchell and Terrence 'Tiger' Warrington." *Nova Scotia Historical Review* 12 (1992).

Morton, Suzanne. "Separate Spheres in a Separate World: African-Nova Scotian Women in Late-19th-Century Halifax County." *Acadiensis* 22 (1993).

Nova Scotia Human Rights Commission. "Background on the Ku Klux Klan." n.d.

Oliver, W. P. "Cultural Progress of the Negro in Nova Scotia." *Dalhousie Review* 29 (October 1949).

Pachai, Bridglal. "The African Presence in Nova Scotia." *Dalhousie Review* 68 (1988).

Power, Jim. "To Nova Scotia in Search of Liberty." *American Visions*, 1988.

Rawlyk, George A. "The Guysborough Negroes: A Study in Isolation." *Dalhousie Review* 48, no. 1 (1968). Loyalist Blacks who settled in Nova Scotia.

Saney, Isaac. "Commentary: Canada: The Black Nova Scotian Odyssey: A Chronology." *Race and Class* 40 (1 July 1998).

Tudor, Kathleen. "David George: Black Loyalist." *Nova Scotia Historical Review* 3 (1983).

Winks, Robin W. "A History of Negro School Segregation in Nova Scotia and Ontario." *Canadian Historical Review* 52, no. 2 (1969). From 1850s to the 1960s.

Ontario

Armstrong, F. H. "The Toronto Directories and the Negro Community in the Late 1840's." *Ontario History* 61, no. 2 (1969). Uses two city directories of 1846–1847 and 1850–1851 for data.

"Black Studies, White Students: An Ontario Experiment that May Open New Areas of Understanding." Contrast 4 (1972).

Braithwaite, Rella. "Ontario's First Black Woman Minister." *Contrast* 4 (1972).

"Canada." *Maclean's*, 14 January 1992. Push for national unity juxtaposed against Black critic of police.

Cooper, J. I. "Mission to Fugitive Slaves at London." *Ontario History* 46 (April 1954).

Dobson, V. Paul. "Working in the Black Community of Downtown Toronto as a Detached Worker." Chapter in *Human Rights Administration: Current Problems and Future Development: Summary of Proceedings of the Fourth Annual Workshop, Canadian Administrators of Human Rights Legislation*. Toronto: Ontario Department of Labour, Human Rights Commission, 1971.

Green, Ernest. "Upper Canada's Black Defenders." *Ontario History Society Papers and Records* 27 (1931).

Hale, Barrie. "Toronto: Does Colour Really Make a Difference." *Globe Magazine*, 8 May 1971.

Helling, Rudolf A. "The Position of Negroes, Chinese and Italians in the Social Structure of Windsor, Ontario." *Interracial Review* 39 (1966).

Hill, Daniel Grafton. "Negroes in Toronto." *Expression* 1 (1965).

_____. "Negroes in Toronto, 1793–1865." *Ontario History* 55 (1963). History beginning with the migration of fugitive slaves in the 1830s.

Kolemaine, R. S. "Black Operators in Heritage Touring." *American Visions*, April-May 1994. Profiles Black heritage tours in California, Nova Scotia and Ontario.

Landon, Fred. "Agriculture Among the Negro Refugees in Upper Canada." *Journal of Negro History* 21 (July 1936).

_____. "History of the Wilberforce Refugee Colony in Middlesex County." *Proceedings and Transactions: London and Middlesex Historical Society*, Part 9, 1918.

_____. "Negro Colonization Schemes in Upper Canada Before 1860" *Transactions of the Royal Society of Canada* 23, 3rd Series, Section 2, 1929.

_____. "Refugee Negroes from the United States in Ontario." *Dalhousie Review* 5 (January 1926).

_____. "Social Conditions Among the Negroes in Upper Canada." *Ontario Historical Society Papers and Records* 22 (1925).

Lewis, James K. "Religious Nature of the Early Negro Migration to Canada and the Amherstburg Baptist Association." *Ontario History* 58, no. 2 (1966).

Littlewhite, Lenny. "Most Toronto Blacks are Snobs." *Contrast* 5 (1973).

Marston, Wilfred G. "Social Class Segregation with Ethnic Groups in Toronto." *Canadian Review of Sociology and Anthropology* 6, no. 2 (1969). Segregation by social class in Toronto ethnic groups is the same as among Blacks.

O'Malley, Martin. "Blacks in Toronto." Chapter in *The Underside of Toronto*, ed. W. E. Mann. Toronto: McCelland and Stewart, 1970.

Peck, P. M. "Northern Exposure: Toronto-North American African Studies Convention." *African Arts* (Spring 1995).

Rhodes, Jane. "Race, Money, Politics and the Antebellum Black Press." *Journalism History* 20 (Autumn-Winter 1994). History of the Ontario's *Provincial Freeman*.

Rieke, Tom. "Triumph Over Tragedy: The Story of the Sons and Daughters of Buxton, Canada." *American Visions*, 1991.

Sefa Dei, George J. "Examining the Case for 'African-Centered' Schools in Ontario." *McGill Journal of Education* 30 (Spring 1995). Argument for such schools on an experimental basis.

Silverman, Robert A., Marc Riedel and Leslie W. Kennedy. "Murdered Children: A Comparison of Racial Differences Across Two Jurisdictions." *Journal of Criminal Justice* 18 (September-October 1990). Comparative demographics for Illinois and Ontario.

Stouffer, Allen P. "A 'Restless Child of Change and Accident': The Black Image in Nineteenth Century Ontario." *Ontario History* 76 (1984).

Swisher, Jacob A. "The Rise and Fall of Buxton." *Palimpsest* 26 (June 1945).

"Toronto Black School Opens." *Contrast* 2 (1970).

Wilson, Ruth Danenhower. "Negro-White Relations in Western Ontario." *Negro History Bulletin* 18, no. 5 (1955(. Contrasts discrimination from 1793 to recent times.

Winks, Robin W. "A History of Negro School Segregation in Nova Scotia and Ontario." *Canadian Historical Review* 52, no. 2 (1969). From 1850s to the 1960s.

Yee, Shirley J. "Gender Ideology and Black Women as Community-Builders in Ontario, 1850–70." *Canadian Historical Review* 75 (March 1994). Uses the career of Mary Ann Shadd Cary to illustrate both sex role ideology and participation.

Saskatchewan

"Activities of the Ku Klux Klan in Saskatchewan." *Queen's Quarterly* 35 (Autumn 1928).

Anon. "Activities of Ku Klux Klan in Saskatchewan." *Queen's Quarterly* 35 (Autumn 1928).

Calderwood, William. "The Decline of the Progressive Party in Saskatchewan, 1925–1930." *Saskatchewan History* 21 (Autumn 1968).

_____. "Religious Reactions to the Ku Klux Klan in Saskatchewan." *Saskatchewan History* 26 (Autumn 1973).

_____. "Pulpit, Press, and Political Reactions to the Ku Klux Klan in Saskatchewan." Chapter in *Prophecy and Protest*, eds. S. Clark, J. Grayson and L. Grayson. Toronto: Gage, 1975.

"The Ku Klux Klan in Saskatchewan." *Queen's Quarterly* 35 (August 1928).

Kyba, P. "Ballots and Burning Crosses—The Election of 1929." Chapter in *Politics in Saskatchewan*, eds. Norman Ward and Duff Spafford. Toronto: Longmans, Canada, Ltd., 1968.

Shepard, R. Bruce. "The Little 'White' Schoolhouse: Racism in a Saskatchewan Rural School." *Saskatchewan History* 39 (1986).

_____. "North to the Promised Land: Black Migration to the Canadian Plains." *Chronicles of Oklahoma* 66 (Fall 1988).

_____. "The Origins of the Oklahoma Black Migration to the Canadian Plaines." *Canadian Journal of History* 23 (April 1988).

_____. "Plain Racism: The Reaction Against Oklahoma Black Immigration to the Canadian Plains." *Prairie Forum* 10 (Autumn 1985).

Struhsaker, Virginia L. "Doc Shadd." *Saskatchewan History* 30 (Spring 1977).

Slaves and Slavery

Brown-Kubisch, Linda. "Researching Fugitive Slaves and Free African Americans in Canada West before 1860." *Families* 35 (1 November 1996).

Collison, Gary. "'Loyal and Dutiful Subjects of Her Gracious Majesty, Queen Victoria': Fugitive Slaves in Montreal, 1850–1866." *Quebec Studies* 19 (1994–95).

Dillard, J. L. "The West African Day-Names in Nova Scotia." *Names* 19, no. 4 (1971). A study of day-names from African slave sources.

Grant, John N. "The 1821 Emigration of Black Nova Scotians to Trinidad." *Nova Scotia Historical Quarterly* 2, no. 3 (1972). British attempts to resettle Blacks to its Caribbean colony for Canadian Blacks, including runaway slaves from the U.S. border states.

Hill, Daniel Grafton. "Negroes in Toronto, 1793–1865." *Ontario History* 55 (1963). History beginning with the migration of fugitive slaves in the 1830s.

Hite, Roger W. "Voice of a Fugitive: Henry Bibb and the Ante-Bellum Black Separatism." *Journal of Black Studies* 4 (1974). Bibb encouraged Black immigration to Canada.

Kelly, Wayne Edward. "Canada's Black Defenders: Former Slaves Answered the Call to Arms." *The Beaver: Exploring Canada's History* 77 (April–May 1997). The Coloured Corps of Canada.

Landon, Fred. "Anthony Burns in Canada." *Ontario Historical Society Papers and Records* 22 (1925). Famous runaway slave in Canada.

————. "Canada's Part in Freeing the Slaves." *Ontario Historical Society Papers and Records* 17 (1919).

————. "The Canadian Anti-Slavery Group Before the Civil War." *University Magazine*, December 1918.

————. "The Fugitive Slave in Canada Before the American Civil War." *University Magazine*, April 1919.

————. "The Negro Migration to Canada After the Fugitive Slave Act of 1850." *Journal of Negro History* 5 (January 1920).

————. "The Work of the American Missionary Association among the Negro Refugees in Canada West, 1848–64." *Ontario Historical Society Papers and Records* 21 (1924).

Law, Howard. "'Self Reliance is the True Road to Independence': Ideology and the Ex-Slaves in Buxton and Chatham." *Ontario History* 77 (1985).

"Letters of Hiram Wilson to Miss Hannah Gray: Missionary Work Among the Negro Fugitive in Canada." *Journal of Negro History* 14 (July 1929).

McCurdy, Alvin. "Henry Walton Bibb." *Negro History Bulletin* 12, no. 1 (1958). Profile of a fugitive slave who escaped to Canada and became a newspaper editor.

Murray, Alexander L. "The Extradition of Fugitive "Slaves from Canada: A Re-Evaluation." *Canadian Historical Review* 43, no. 4 (1962). Examines policies concerning fugitive slaves.

———— "The *Provincial Freeman*: A New Source for the History of the Negro in the United States and Canada." *Journal of Negro History* 60 (April 1959). Using the antislavery newspaper for research.

Paquet, L. A. "Slaves and Slavery in Canada." *Royal Society of Canada Proceedings and Transactions* 7 (1913).

"Petition for the Establishment of a Settlement in Canada, 1828: Text." *Journal of Negro History* 15 (January 1930).

Reid, Robie L. "How One Slave Became Free: An Episode in the old Days in Victoria." *British Columbia Historical Quarterly* 6 (October 1942).

Riddell, William R. "International Complications between Illinois and Canada arising out of Slavery." *Illinois State Historical Society Journal* 25 (April-July 1932).

_____. "Method of Abolition of Slavery in England, Scotland and Upper Canada Compared." *Ontario Historical Society Papers and Records* 27 (1931).

_____. "A Negro Slave in Canadian Detroit, 1795." *Michigan History Magazine* 18 (Winter 1934).

_____. "An Official Record of Slavery in Upper Canada." *Ontario Historical Society Papers and Records* 25 (1929).

Schweninger, Loren. "A Fugitive Negro in the Promised Land: James Rapier in Canada, 1856–1864." *Ontario History* 6, no. 2 (1975).

Silverman, Jason H. "The American Fugitive Slave in Canada: Myths and Realities." *Southern Studies* 19 (1980).

_____. "'We Shall Be Heard!': The Development of the Fugitive Slave Press in Canada." *Canadian Historical Review* 65 (1984).

Wilson, D. "Negro-White Relations in Western Ontario." *Negro History Bulletin* 18 (February 1955).

Books:

Alexander, Ken, and Avis Glaze. *Towards Freedom: The African-Canadian Experience.* Toronto: Umbrella Press, 1996.

Amherstburg, Ontario. Mayor's Committee on Race Relations. *A Summary Report.* August, 1966.

Baker, David, ed. *Reading Racism and the Criminal Justice System.* Toronto: Canadian Scholars, 1994.

Barrett, Stanley R. *Is God a Racist?: The Right Wing in Canada.* Toronto: University of Toronto Press, 1987. Racism and anti-Semitism.

Bearden, Jim, and Linda Jean Butler. *Shadd: The Life and Times of Mary Shadd Cary.* Toronto: N.C. Press, Ltd., 1977.

Beatty, Jessie Louise. *John Christie Holland, Man of the Year.* Toronto: Ryerson Press, 1956.

Bell, Dorothy, P. Jaison, K. Myers, and S. Day. *Canadian Black Studies Bibliography.* n.p.: n.p., 1971.

Berman, Jay. *The Black Man in Urban Canada: Equality, or "Polite Racism?"* n.p.: n.p., 1969.

Bertley, Leo W. *Black Tiles in the Mosaic.* Pierrefonds, QC: n.p., 1974. Day-by-day guide to events of Black Canadian history.

_____. *Blacks in Canada, 1867–1971.* Pierrefonds, QC: n.p., 1971.

_____. *Canada and its People of African Descent.* Pierrefonds, QC: Bilongo Publishers, 1977.

Best, Carrie M. *That Lonesome Road: The Autobiography of Carrie Best.* Nova Scotia: The Clarion Publishing Company Ltd., 1979.

Black, Ayanna, ed. *Daughters of the Sun, Women of the Moon: An Anthology of Canadian Black Women Poets.* South Bend: The Distributors, 1991.

_____. *Fiery Spirits: a Collection of Short Fiction and Poetry*. Toronto: HarperPerennial, 1994. By Canadian writers of African descent.

Black History: Kindergarten to Senior 4: A Bibliography of Resources Available from the Library, Instructional Resources Branch. Winnipeg: The Library, 1992.

Blacks in Canada: Representative Source Materials. Halifax: Dalhousie University Library, 1970. Bibliography.

The Blacks of Canada—A Special Survey. Toronto: Toronto Globe and Mail, 1969.

Bolaria, B., and P. Li. *Racial Oppression in Canada*. Toronto: Gramond Press, 1985.

Braithwaite, Karen S., ed. *Educating African Canadians*. Boston: Formac Distribution, n.d.

Braithwaite, Rella, ed. *The Black Woman in Canada: A Book of Profiles on Black Women*. n.p.: Sister Vision, 1976. Biography, Black women in Canada.

Braithwaite, Rella, and Tessa Benn-Ireland. *Some Black Women: Profiles of Black Women in Canada*. n.p.: Sister Vision, 1993.

Bramble, Linda. *Black Fugitive Slaves in Early Canada*. Vanwell History Project Series. St. Catherines: Vanwell, 1988.

Bristow, Peggy, et al. *We're Rooted Here and They Can't Pull Us Up: Essays in African Canadian Women's History*. Toronto: University of Toronto Press, 1994.

Buck, D. D. *The Progression of the Race in the United States and Canada: Treating of the Great Advancement of the Colored Race*. Chicago: Atwell Printing and Binding Company, 1907.

Canada. Department of Labour. Economics and Research Branch. *Discrimination in Employment: A Selected Annotated Bibliography*. Ottawa: n.p., 1970.

Carter, Velma, and Leah Carter. *The Window of Our Memories*. Vol. 1, *Black Cultural Research*. n.p.: 1980.

_____. *The Window of Our Memories*. Vol. 2, *The New Generation*. n.p.: 1990.

_____, and Levero Carter. *The Black Canadians: Their History and Contributions*. Edmonton: Reidmore Books, 1993. Juvenile history and biography.

Clarke, Austin. *Nine Men Who Laughed*. Markham: Penguin Books, 1986.

_____. *Public Enemies: Police Violence and Black Youth*. Toronto: HarperCollins Publishers, 1992. Black complaints against police.

Cochran, Jo, et al., eds. *Gathering Ground: New Writing and Art by Northwest Women of Color*. Seattle: Seal Press, 1984. A cross-cultural anthology.

Coles, Howard W. *The Cradle of Freedom: A History of the Negro in Rochester, Western New York and Canada*. Rochester, NY: Oxford Press, 1942.

Consultative Conference on Discrimination Against Natives and Blacks in the Criminal Justice System and the Role of the Attorney General. *Consultative Conference on Discrimination Against Natives and Blacks in the Criminal Justice System and the Role of the Attorney General: Edited Transcript of Proceedings: November 24–26, 1988.* Halifax: Royal Commission on the Donald Marshall, Jr. Prosecution, 1989.

_____. *Innovations in Black Education in Canada.* Toronto: Umbrella Press, 1994.

Cooke, Britton. *The Black Canadian.* Toronto: Maclean's Magazine, 1911.

D'Oyley, Enid, and Rella Braithwaite, eds. *Women of Our Times.* Toronto: Canadian Negro Women's Association for the National Congress of Black Women, 1973. Biographies, Black women of Canada.

D'Oyley, Vincent, ed. *Black Presence in Multi-Ethnic Canada.* Vancouver: University of British Columbia; and Toronto: Ontario Institute for Studies in Education, 1978.

_____. *Innovations in Black Education in Canada.* Toronto: Umbrella Press, 1994.

Dabydeen, Cyril, ed. *A Shapely Fire: Black Writers in Canada.* Buffalo, NY: Mosaic Press, 1987. History and criticism.

Dalhousie University. *Blacks in Canada. Representative Source Materials.* Halifax: Dalhousie University Library, 1970.

Dalhousie University Library Bibliographies. *Blacks in Canada: Representative Source Materials.* Halifax, NS: n.p., 1970. Bibliography.

Denby, Charles. *Indignant Heart: A Black Worker's Journal.* Montreal: Black Rose, 1979.

Doyle-Marshall, William. *A Mandate for Educating African-Canadians.* Toronto: Calypso House, 1994. Black students and education in Canada.

Dungy, Hilda. *Planted by the Waters: A Family History of the Jones-Carter Family.* n.p.: The author, 1977.

Elgersman, Maureen G. *Unyielding Spirits: Black Women and Slavery in Early Canada and Jamaica.* New York: Garland, 1999.

Ferguson, T. *A White Man's Country.* Toronto: Doubleday Canada, 1975.

Ffrench, Robert. *Black Canadian Achievement: Out of the Past Into the Future.* n.p.: Pride, 1994.

Foggo, Cheryl. *Pourin' Down Rain.* Calgary: Detselig Enterprises, 1990. The Foggo family of Alberta.

Forsythe, Dennis, ed. *Let the Niggers Burn: The Sir George Williams University Affair and it Caribbean Aftermath.* Montreal: Our Generation Press, 1971.

Foster, Cecil. *A Place Called Heaven: The Meaning of Being Black in Canada.* Toronto: HarperCollins, 1996. Race and racism in Canada.

Furnas, J. C. *Goodbye to Uncle Tom.* New York: William Sloane Associates, 1956. Slaves running to the North or Canada frequently returned South for their families.

Gorrell, Gena K. *North Star to Freedom: The Story of the Underground Railroad.* n.p.: Stoddart Publishing, 1996.

Govia, Francine, and Helen Lewis. *Blacks in Canada: In Search of the Promise: A Bibliographical Guide to the History of Blacks in Canada.* Edmonton: Harambee Centres Canada, 1988.

Greaves, Ida C. *National Problems of Canada: The Negro in Canada.* Economic Studies no. 16. Montreal: McGill University, 1930.

Gysin, Brion. *To Master—A Long Goodnight: The Story of Uncle Tom, A Historical Narrative.* New York: Creative Age, 1946. Abolitionist and former slave.

Hay, Frederick J. *African-American Community Studies from North America: A Classified, Annotated Bibliography.* New York: Garland Publishing, 1991. Social conditions of Blacks in Canada.

Head, Wilson A. *The Black Presence in the Canadian Mosaic.* Ontario: Ontario Human Rights Commission, 1975.

————. *A Life on the Edge: "Experiences in Black and White" in North America.* Willowdale, ON: A. R. Sandy Head, 1995. Memoirs.

Henry, Annette *Taking Back Control: African Canadian Women Teachers' Lives and Practice.* SUNY Identity in the Classroom Series. Albany: State University of New York Press, 1998.

Henry, Franklin J. *The Experience of Discrimination: A Case Study Approach.* San Francisco: A&E Research Associates, 1974. Blacks and Japanese in Canada.

Hill, Daniel Grafton. *The Freedom-Seekers: Blacks in Early Canada.* Agincourt, Canada: Book Society of Canada, 1981; reprinted, Stoddart Publishing, 1996; reprinted, Buffalo, NY: General Distribution Services, 1996. History and race relations.

————. *Human Rights in Canada: A Focus on Racism.* Canadian Labour Congress, 1977.

Hill, Lawrence. *Trials and Triumphs: The Story of African-Canadians.* Toronto: Umbrella Press, 1993.

————. *Women of Vision: The Story of the Canadian Negro Women's Association, 1951–1976.* Toronto: Umbrella Press, 1996.

History and Culture of Black People: A Selected Bibliography for Elementary Schools. Toronto: TBE, Library Services Department, 1990. Juvenile literature.

Hornby, Jim. *Black Islanders: Prince Edward Island's Historical Black Community.* Charlottetown, PE: Institute of Island Studies, 1991.

Identity: The Black Experience in Canada, ed. Patricia Thorvaldson. Toronto: ON: Educational Communications Authority: Gage Educational Publishing Ltd., 1979.

Ijaz, M. *Study on Ethnic Attitudes of Elementary School Children toward Blacks and East Indians.* Scarborough, ON: Scarborough Board of Education, 1981.

Jain, Sushil Kumar, comp. *The Negro in Canada*. Regina, SK: University of Saskatchewan, 1967.

James, Carl E. *Making It: Black Youth, Racism and Career Aspirations in a Big City*. Buffalo, NY: Mosaic Press, 1990.

Johnson, Homer Uri. *From Dixie to Canada: Romance and Realities of the Underground Railroad*, Vol. 1. O. Orwell and H. U. Johnson. Buffalo: C.W. Moulton, 1894; reprinted, Louisville, KY: Lost Cause Press, 1977.

Kallen, Evelyn. *Ethnicity and Human Rights in Canada*, 2nd ed. Toronto: Oxford University Press, 1995.

Krauter, Joseph F., and Morris Davis. *Minority Canadians: Ethnic Groups*. Ontario: Methuen, 1978.

Kwamdela, Odimumba. *Niggers...This is Canada*. Toronto: 21st Century Book, 1971.

Lind, Jane. *The Underground Railroad*: Ann Maria Weems. Toronto: Grolier Ltd., 1990.

MacEwan, Grant. *John Ware's Cow Country*. Saskatoon, SK: Western Producer. Prairie Books, 1972.

McClain, Paula Denice. *Alienation and Resistance: The Political Behavior of Afro-Canadians*. Palo Alto: R&E Research Associates, 1979.

National Congress of Black Women of Canada. *Impetus, the Black Woman: Proceedings of the Fourth National Congress of Black Women of Canada*, ed. Joella H. Gipson. n.p.: National Congress of Black Women of Canada, 1978.

National Strategy on Race Relations. Ottawa: Multiculturalism in Canada, n.d.

Nelson, Gersham. *The Life and Works of Rudolph James: Black Adventism in Canada*. Frostburg: G. Aston Nelson Books, 1998.

Ngatia, Therese. *The Blacks in Canada: A Selective Annotated Bibliography*. Edmonton: T. Ngatia, 1984.

Nourbese Philip, Marlene. Showing Grit: *Showboating North of the 44th Parallel*. n. p.: Poui, 1996.

Palmer, Howard, and Tamara Palmer. *Peoples of Alberta*. Saskatoon, SK: Western Producer. Prairie Books, 1985.

Potter, Harold H. *Negro Settlement in Canada, 1628–1965: A Survey*. Ottawa: n.p., 1966.

Ramcharan, S. *Racism: Nonwhites in Canada*. Toronto: Butterworths, 1982.

Ripley, C. Peter, ed. *The Black Abolitionist Papers: Canada, 1830–1865*. Chapel Hill: University of North Carolina Press, 1987. Canada's anti-slavery movement.

Robin, Martin. *Shades of Right: Nativist and Fascist Politics in Canada, 1920–1940*. Buffalo: University of Toronto Press, 1992.

Robson, Arthur. *A Minority Group Study: A Demographic Study of the Black Community in Saint John, N.B.* Frederiction: New Brunswick Human Rights Commission, Department of Labour, 1970. Blacks and social conditions.

Ruck, Calvin W. *The Black Battalion: 1916–1920: Canada's Best Kept Military Secret.* Halifax: Nimbus Publishing, 1987. Canadian Blacks in W.W.I.

————. *Canada's Black Battalion.* Halifax: Numbus Publishing, 1987.

————. *Canada's Black Battalion: No. 2 Construction Battalion, 1916–1920.* Halifax: Black Cultural Centre, 1986.

Sadlier, Rosemary. *Leading the Way: Black Women in Canada.* Toronto: Umbrella Press, 1994. Biography, Black Canadian women.

Scott, Victoria. *Sylvia Stark, a Pioneer: A Biography.* Seattle: Open Hand Publishing, 1991. Juvenile.

Sefa Dei, George J., et al. *Reconstructing "Dropout": A Critical Ethnography of the Dynamics of Black Students' Disengagement from School.* Toronto: University of Toronto Press, 1997.

Shadd (Cary), Mary Ann. *A Plea for Emigration, or, Notes of Canada West: In its Moral, Social, and Political Aspect; with Suggestions Respecting Mexico, West Indies, and Vancouver's Island, for the Information of Colored Emigrants.* Detroit: n.p., 1852; reprinted, Toronto: Mercury Press, 1998.

————. *A Scholarly Edition of Mary A. Shadd's "A Plea for Emigration, or, Notes of Canada West."* Ottawa: National Library of Canada/Bibliotheque nationale du Canada, 1997.

Shepard, R. Bruce. *Deemed Unsuitable: Blacks from Oklahoma Move to the Canadian Prairies in Search of Equality in the Early 20th Century, Only to Find Racism in Their New Home.* Toronto: Umbrella Press, 1996. Blacks in Oklahoma and Saskatchewan.

Sher, J. *White Hoods: Canada's Ku Klux Klan.* Vancouver: New Star Books, 1983.

Shreve, Dorothy Shadd. *The AfriCanadian Church: A Stabilizer.* Jordan Station, ON: Paideia Press, 1983. Blacks and Canadian church history.

Siegfried, Andre. *The Race Question in Canada.* Toronto: McClelland and Stewart, 1970.

Silvera, Makeda, ed. *Silenced: Talks with Working Class West Indian Women About Their Lives and Struggles as Domestic Workers in Canada.* Toronto: Sister Vision, 1989.

Social Planning Council of Metropolitan Toronto. *The Adoption of Negro Children: A Community Wide Approach.* Toronto: The Social Planning Council, 1966.

Solomon, R. Patrick. *Black Resistance in High School: Forging a Separatist Culture.* Frontiers in Education Series. Albany: State University of New York Press, 1992. Blacks and education in Canada.

Some Missing Pages: The Black Community in the History of Quebec and Canada: Primary and Secondary Source Materials. Montreal: Services à la communauté anglophone, Direction des politiques et des projects, 1995.

Songs Sung by the Famous Canadian Jubilee Singers, the Royal Paragon Male Quartette and Imperial Orchestra: Five Years' Tour of Great Britain, Three Years' Tour of United States. Hamilton, ON: Duncan Lithograph Company, 189? Black spirituals and plantation melodies.

Spray, W. A. *The Blacks of New Brunswick.* Frederiction, NB: Brunswick Press, 1972.

Sterling, Dorothy. *Freedom Train: The Story of Harriet Tubman.* Garden City: Doubleday, 1954.

Talbot, Carol. *Growing Up Black in Canada.* Toronto: Williams-Wallace, 1984.

Thomson, Colin A. *Blacks in Deep Snow: Black Pioneers in Canada.* Don Mills, ON: J. M. Dent and Sons, 1979. Biography.

Thorvaldson, Patricia. *Identity: The Black Experience in Canada.* Toronto: Ontario Educational Communications Authority: Gage Educational Publishing Ltd., 1979.

Tulloch, Headly. *Black Canadians: A Long Line of Fighters.* Toronto: New Canada Press, 1975.

Ullman, Victor. *Look to the North Star: A Life of William King.* Boston: Beacon Press, 1969. Elgin Settlement, Raleigh, Ontario.

Viger, Jacques. *De L'esclavage en Canada.* Montréal, Imprimé par duvernay frères, 1859. Issue of Société historique de Montréal. Mémoires et documents relatifs à l'histoire du Canada. Livr. 1–2, 1859.

Walcott, Rinaldo. *Black Like Who?: Writing Black Canada.* Toronto: Insomniac Press, 1997. Blacks and races identity.

Walker, W. James St. G. *A History of Blacks in Canada: A Study Guide for Teachers and Students.* Hull, QC: Minister of State, Multiculturalism, 1980.

————. *"Race," Rights and the Law in the Supreme Court of Canada: Historical Case Studies.* Waterloo, ON: Osgoode Society for Canadian Legal History: Wilfrid Laurier University Press, 1997.

————. *Racial Discrimination in Canada: The Black Experience.* Ottawa: Canadian Historical Association, 1985.

Ward, Samuel Ringgold. *Autobiography of a Fugitive Negro: His Anti-Slavery Labours in the United States, Canada, and England.* New York: Arno Press, 1968.

Winks, Robin W. *Blacks in Canada: A History.* New Haven, CT: McGill-Queen's University Press, 1971; reprinted, Toronto: University of Toronto Press, 1997.

————. *The Negro in Canada.* New Haven, CT: Yale University Press, 1969.

British Columbia

Carter, Velma and Wilma Leffler Akili. *The Window of Our Memories.* St. Albert, AB: B.C.R. Society of Alberta, 1981.

Cartwright, Peggy. *Black Pioneers in Gold Rush Days*. Canada: Manning Press, 1993. Blacks in British Columbia.

Directory of British Columbia Black Owned Businesses and Services. Vancouver: BC Black Action Coalition, 1994.

D'Oyley, Vincent, ed. *Black Presence in Multi-Ethnic Canada*. Vancouver: Centre for the Study of Curriculum and Instruction, Faculty of Education, University of British Columbia, 1982. Collection of addresses and essays.

Garraway, Garbette. *Blacks in British Columbia, 1990–1991 Calendar*. Vancouver, BC: Black History Month Committee, 1983; reissued 1990.

————. *A Handbook on Blacks in British Columbia: Accomplishments and Contributions*. Vancouver, BC: Black Theatre West, 1990. Biography for Black History Month.

Kilian, Crawford. *Go So Some Great Thing: The Black Pioneers of British Columbia*. Vancouver: Douglas and McIntyre, 1978.

McAlpine, J. *Report Arising out of the Activities of the Ku Klux Klan in British Columbia*. Presented to the Honourable Minister of Labour for the Province of British Columbia, 1981.

Muszynski, Alieja. *Cheap Wage Labour: Race and Gender in the Fisheries of British Columbia*. Montreal: McGill-Queen's University Press, 1996.

Victoria Black People's Society. *Blacks in British Columbia: A Catalog of Information and Sources of Information Pertaining to Blacks in British Columbia*. Victoria, BC: Victoria Black People's Society, 1978.

Walhouse, Freda. *The Influences of Minority Ethnic Groups on the Cultural Geography of Vancouver*. Vancouver, BC: University of British Columbia Archives, 1961.

Nova Scotia

Abucar, Mohamed Hagi. *Struggle for Development: The Black Communities of North and East Preston and Cherry Brook, Nova Scotia, 1784–1987*. Dartmouth: Black Cultural Centre for Nova Scotia, 1988.

Africville Genealogical Society, ed. *The Spirit of Africville*. Halifax: Formac Press, 1992.

Africville: A Spirit That Lives On. Halifax, NS: Art Gallery, Mount Saint Vincent University and the Black Cultural Centre for Nova Scotia, Africville, 1989. From the exhibition, 20 October–19 November 1989.

Appelt, Pamela G. *Citizenship, Culture and the Black Community*. Dartmouth: Clack Cultural Centre for Nova Scotia, 1988.

A Black Community Album Before 1930. Halifax: Art Gallery, Mount Saint Vincent University, 1983. Photographic exhibition. Organized by Henry Bishop and Frank Boyd of the Black Cultural Centre for Nova Scotia.

Black Community Profile: A Survey of the Black Population of New Glasgow, Nova Scotia, Summer 1973, Bette Skinner, et al., comp. Halifax: Nova Scotia Human Rights Commission, 1973.

Black Cultural Centre of Nova Scotia. *Traditional Lifetime Stories: A Collection of Black Memories*, 2 vols. Halifax: Black Cultural Centre, 1987 and 1990.

Bymmer, D. *The Jamaican Maroons: How They Came to Nova Scotia: How They Left It.* 1898. Reprint, Toronto: Canadian House, 1968.

Clairmont, Donald H., and Dennis W. Magill. *Africville, Relocation Report.* Halifax, NS: Institute of Public Affairs, Dalhousie University, 1971.

―――――. *Africville Relocation Report and Supplement.* Halifax, NS: Institute of Public Affairs, Dalhousie University, 1973.

―――――. *Africville: The Life and Death of a Canadian Black Community.* Toronto: McClelland and Stewart, 1974; reprinted, Toronto: Canadian Scholars' Press, 1987; reprinted, 1997. Blacks and social conditions in Halifax.

―――――. *Nova Scotian Blacks: An Historical and Structural Overview.* Halifax, NS: Dalhousie University, 1970.

Clifford, Mary Louise. *From Slavery to Freetown: Black Loyalists After the American Revolution.* Jefferson, NC: McFarland, 1999. Runaway American slaves evacuated to Nova Scotia and then transported to West Africa.

Collins, A. William, N. Patrick Kakembo, and Anne Martell. *BLAC Report on Education: Redressing Inequity—Empowering Black Learners.* Halifax: Black Learners Advisory Committee, 1994. Discrimination in education in Nova Scotia.

The Condition of the Negroes of Halifax City, Nova Scotia: A Study. Halifax: The Institute of Public Affairs, 1962. The Institute's study of social conditions.

A Documentary Study of the Establishment of the Negroes in Nova Scotia Between the War of 1812 and the Winning of Responsible Government. Halifax: Public Archives of Nova Scotia, 1948.

Extracts and Copies of Letters from Sir John Wentworth, Lieutenant Governor of Nova Scotia, to His Grace the Duke of Portland, Respecting the Settlement of the Maroons in the Province. London: n.p., 1797. Maroons in Nova Scotia volume in the National Library of Canada.

Gibson, Ethel L. *My Journey through Eternity: An Autobiography.* Dartmouth: Black Cultural Centre for Nova Scotia, 1988. Blacks in Nova Scotia.

Grant, John N. *Black Nova Scotians.* Halifax: Nova Scotia Museum, 1980.

―――――. *The Immigration and Settlement of the Black Refugees of the War of 1812 in Nova Scotia and New Brunswick.* Halifax: Black Cultural Centre, 1990.

Henry, Frances. *Forgotten Canadians: The Blacks of Nova Scotia.* Ontario: Longman, 1973.

Hodges, Graham Russell, Susan Hawkes Cook and Alan Brown, eds. *The Black Loyalist Directory: African Americans in Exile After the American Revolution*. Garland Reference Library to the Humanities Series. New York: Garland, 1995. Profiles Blacks who went to Nova Scotia following the Revolutionary War.

McKerrow, P. E. *A Brief History of the Coloured Baptists of Nova Scotia and Their First Organization as Churches, A.D. 1832*. Halifax: Nova Scotia Printing Company, 1895.

Oliver, W. P. *Brief Summary of Nova Scotia Negro Communities*. n.p., 1964. Blacks in Nova Scotia.

Pachai, Bridglal. *Beneath the Clouds of the Promise Land*. Vol. I, *1660–1800: The Survival of Nova Scotia's Blacks*. Halifax: Black Educators Association of Nova Scotia, 1987.

_____. *Beneath the Clouds of the Promise Land*. Vol. II, *1800–1989: The Survival of Nova Scotia's Blacks*. Halifax: Black Educators Association of Nova Scotia, 1987.

Saunders, Charles R. *Share and Care: The Story of the Nova Scotia Home for Colored Children*. Halifax: Nimbus, 1994. History of the home.

The Spirit of Africville. Halifax, NS: Formac Publishing Company, 1992.

The Spirit of Africville and Remember Africville. Halifax, NS: Maritext, 1993.

Thomas, Carolyn G., ed. *Reflections*. East Preston, NS: East Preston United Baptist Church 150th Anniversary Committee, 1995. Frontier and pioneer life in Nova Scotia.

Traditional Lifetime Stories: A Collection of Black Memories. Dartmouth: Black Cultural Centre for Nova Scotia, 1987.

Walker, W. James St. G. *The Black Loyalists: The Search for a Promised Land in Nova Scotia and Sierra Leone, 1783–1870*. Irving Place, NY: Holmes and Meier, 1976; reprinted, Toronto: University of Toronto Press, 1992.

_____. *A History of Blacks in Canada: A Study Guide for Teachers and Students*. Hull: Canadian Government Publishing Centre, 1980.

_____. *Identity: The Black Experience in Canada*, ed. Patricia Thorvaldson. Toronto: Ontario Educational Communications Authority and Gage Educational Publishing, Ltd., 1979.

_____. *Racial Discrimination in Canada: The Black Experience*. Ottawa: The Canadian Historical Association, 1985.

_____. *The West Indians in Canada*. Toronto: The Canadian Historical Association, 1984.

Wylie, William Newman Thomas. *Prospective Sites Relating to Black History in Canada: A Study*. Ottawa: The Historic Sites and Monuments Board of Canada, 1994. Black Canadian history of Nova Scotia and Ontario.

Ontario

Black Dial Directory. Toronto: T. Sessing, 1975/77. Blacks in Ontario.

Brand, Dionne, Lois De Shield, et al. *No Burden to Carry: Narratives of Black Working Women in Ontario 1920s to 1950s*. Toronto: University of Toronto Press, 1991.

Breyfogle, Donna, ed. *Blacks in Ontario: A Selected Bibliography, 1965–1976*. Toronto: Ontario Ministry of Labour, Research Library, 1977.

Brown, George A. *Community Tensions and Conflicts Among Youths of Different Ethnic and Racial Backgrounds in Wards 3, 4, 5 and 6 in Downtown Toronto*. Toronto: Ontario Department of Labour, Human Rights Commission, 1968.

————. *Community Tensions and Conflicts Among Youths of Different Ethnic and Racial Backgrounds in Wards 3, 4, 5 and 6 in Downtown Toronto: Appendix to a Report Submitted to the Ontario Human Rights Commission*. Toronto: Ontario Department of Labour, Human Rights Commission, 1968.

Brown, Rosemary. *Being Brown: A Very Public Life*. Mississauga: Random House, 1989.

Colonial Church and School Society, West London Branch. *Mission to the Free Colored Population in Canada*. London: Macintosh, 1855. United Church of England and Ireland missions to Ontario Blacks.

Commission on Systemic Racism in the Ontario Criminal Justice System. *Racism Behind Bars: The Treatment of Black and Other Racial Minority Prisoners in Ontario Correctional Institutions: Interim Status Report of the Commission on Systemic Racism in the Ontario Criminal Justice System*. Toronto: The Commission, 1994.

D'Oyley, Vincent, ed. *Black Students in Urban Canada*. Toronto: Ministry of Culture and Recreation, 1976.

Fisher, William Allen. *Legend of the Drinking Gourd*. Barrie, ON: W. A. and M. W. Fisher, 1973. Blacks in Ontario history.

French, Gary E. *Men of Color: An Historical Account of the Black Settlement on Wilberforce Street and in Oro Township, Simcoe County, Ontario, 1819–1949*. Stroud, ON: Kaste Books, 1978.

Gairey, Harry. *A Black Man's Toronto 1914–1980: The Reminiscences of Harry Gairey*, ed. Donna Hill. Toronto: The Multicultural History Society of Ontario, 1981.

Head, Wilson A. *The Black Presence in the Canadian Mosaic: A Study of Perception and the Practice of Discrimination Against Blacks in Metropolitan Toronto Submitted to The Ontario Human Rights Commission*. Ontario: Ontario Human Rights Commission, 1975.

Henry, Franklin J. *The Dynamics of Racism in Toronto*. Don Mills, ON: Longman, Canada Ltd., 1973.

_____. *Perception of Discrimination Among Negroes and Japanese-Canadians in Hamilton: A Report Submitted to the Ontario Human Rights Commission.* Hamilton: McMaster University, 1965.

Henry, Franklin J., and E. Ginzberg. *Who Gets the Work: A Test of Racial Discrimination in Employment.* Toronto: The Urban Alliance of Race Relations and the Social Planning Council of Metropolitan Toronto, 1985.

Henry, Keith S. *Black Politics in Toronto since World War I.* Occasional Papers in Ethnic and Immigration Studies Series. Toronto: Multicultural History Society, 1981.

Hubbard, Stephen L. *Against All Odds: The Story of William Peyton Hubbard, Black Leader and Municipal Reformer.* Toronto: Dundrun Press, 1987.

Landon, Fred *Negro Colonization Schemes in Upper Canada Before 1860.* Ottawa: Royal Society of Canada, 1929.

Larrie, Reginald. *Makin' Free: African-Americans in the Northwest Territory.* Detroit: B. Ethridge Books, 1981. Ontario and Michigan.

Lewis, James K. *Religious Life of Fugitive Slaves and Rise of the Coloured Baptist Churches, 1820–1865, in What is Now Ontario,* ed. Edwin S. Gausted. Salem, NH: The Baptist Tradition, 1980.

McIntyre, Paul. *Black Pentecostal Music in Windsor.* Ottawa: National Museums of Canada, 1976.

Mitchell, William M. *The Underground Railroad.* London: W. Tweedie, 1860. Fugitive slaves in the United Sates and Ontario.

Ontario. Department of Labour. *Human Rights Commission. A Brief Pictorial History of Blacks in Nineteenth Century Ontario.* Toronto: Human Rights Commission, 1971.

Perry, Charlotte Bronte. *The History of the Coloured Canadian in Windsor, Ontario, 1867–1967.* Windsor: Summer Printing and Publishing, 1967.

_____. *The Long Road,* Vol. 1. Windsor, ON: Sumner Printing and Publishing, 1967. The history of Blacks in Windsor.

Riendeau, Roger. *An Enduring Heritage: Black Contributions to Early Ontario.* Toronto: Dundurn Press, 1984.

Robbins, Arlie C. *Legacy to Buxton.* Chatham, ON: Ideal Printing, 1883; reprinted, North Buxton, ON: A. C. Robbins, 1983. Black community of North Buxton, Ontario.

Robbins, Vivian. *Musical Buxton.* Windsor: Art Gallery of Windsor, 1966.

Ross, Alexander Milton. *Recollections and Experiences of an Abolitionist, from 1855 to 1865.* Toronto: Rowsell and Hutchison, 1875. Slaves and the Underground Railroad in the United States and Ontario.

Simpson, Donald George. *Negroes in Ontario From Early Times to 1870: A Bibliography.* London: University of Western Ontario, 1971.

Stouffer, Allen P. *The Light of Nature and the Law of God: Antislavery in Ontario, 1833–1877.* Montreal: McGill-Queen's University Press, 1992. Antislavery, fugitive slaves, and race relations in Ontario.

Tanser, Harry A. *The Settlement of Negroes in Kent County, Ontario, and a Study of the Mental Capacity of Their Descendants.* Chatham, ON: Shepherd, 1939, reprinted, Westport, CT: Greenwood Publishing Group, 1970. Psychological Tests.

Wylie, William Newman Thomas. *Prospective Sites Relating to Black History in Canada: A Study.* Ottawa: The Historic Sites and Monuments Board of Canada, 1994. Black Canadian history of Nova Scotia and Ontario.

York University. Department of Sociology. *The Extent and Pattern of Residential Segregation in Toronto According to Social Rank, Ethnicity and Housing and Family Status.* Toronto: York University, 1970.

_____. *Research on Immigrants and Ethnic Groups in Metropolitan Toronto: A Bibliography Covering the Period 1930–1965.* Toronto: York University, 1966.

York University. Institute for Behavioural Research. *Ethnic Research Programme. Ethnic Residential Segregation in Metropolitan Toronto,* ed. Anthony H. Richmond. Toronto: York University, 1972.

Quebec

Bertley, Leo W. *Montreal's Oldest Black Congregation: Union Church 3007 Deslisle Street.* Pierrefonds: Bilongo Publishers, 1976.

Black History Month: February 1993. Montreal: The Ville, 1993. History and social conditions of Blacks in metropolitan Montreal.

DeJean, Paul. *Les Haitiens au Quebec.* Montreal: Presses de l'University du Quebec, 1978.

_____. *Haitians in Quebec.* Ottawa: Tecumseh Press, 1980.

Gay, Daniel. Des empreintes noires sur la neige blanche: les noires au Quebec (1750–1900): Rapport final. Quebec: Quebecois de la Recherche Sociale, 1988.

Gilmore, John. *Swinging in Paradise: The Story of Jazz in Montreal.* Montreal: Vehicle Press, 1988.

Some Missing Pages: The Black Community in the History of Quebec and Canada: Primary and Secondary Source Materials. Montreal: Services à la communauté anglophone, Direction des politiques et des projects, 1995.

Williams, Dorothy W. *Blacks in Montreal, 1628–1986: An Urban Demography.* Cowansville: Editions Yvon Blais, 1989.

_____. *The Road to Now: A History of Blacks in Montreal.* Montreal: Véhicule Press, 1996.

Slaves and Slavery

Bramble, Linda. *Black Fugitive Slaves in Early Canada.* St. Catherine's, ON: Vanwell Publishing Company, 1988.

Clarke, Austin. *When He Was Free and Young and He Used to Wear Silks*. Toronto: House of Anansi Press Ltd., 1971.

Colonial and Continental Church Society. *Mission to the Coloured Population in Canada: Late Fugitive Slave Mission, Being a Branch of the Operations of the Colonial and Continental Church Society*. London: Society's Offices, 1866.

Drew, Benjamin. *A North-Side View of Slavery. The Refugee: Or the Narratives of Fugitive Slaves in Canada; Related by Themselves, with an Account of the History and Condition of the Colored Population of Upper Canada*. Boston: J. P. Jewett and Company; Cleveland, OH: Jewett, Proctor and Worthington; New York: Sheldon, Lamport and Blakeman, 1856; reprinted, New York: Johnson Reprint Corporation, 1969; reprinted, Toronto: Coles Publishing Company, 1972.

Hallam, Lillian Gertrude Best. *Slave Days in Canada*. Toronto: n.p., 1919.

Hamilton, James Cleland. *Slavery in Canada*. Toronto: n.p., 1890. Abstract from Canadian Institute's *Transactions*, Vol. 25.

Henson, Josiah. *An Autobiography of the Rev. Josiah Henson: From 1789 to 1876, with Preface by Harriet Beecher Stowe; and an Introductory Note by George Sturge and S. Morley*, ed. John Lobb. London: Christian Age, 1876. A fugitive slave in Canada.

_____. *Father Henson's Story of his Own Life: With an Introduction by H. B. Stowe*. Boston: J. P. Jewett, 1858. Henson, a runaway slave, lived in Canada.

_____. *The Life of Josiah Henson, Formerly a Slave, Now an Inhabitant of Canada—as Narrated by Himself*. Boston: Arthur D. Phelps, 1849.

Howe, Samuel G. *The Refugees from Slavery in Canada West: Report to the Freedmen's Inquiry Commission*. Boston, Wright and Potter, 1864, reprinted, Stratford, NH: Ayer, 1968.

Jamieson, Annie Straith. *William King, Friend and Champion of Slaves*. Toronto: Missions of Evangelism, 1925; reprinted, New York: Negro Universities Press, 1969.

Landon, Fred. *Canada's Part in Freeing the Slave*. n.p., 1919. Blacks, fugitive slaves, and the Underground Railroad in Canada.

Lewis, James K. *Religious Life of Fugitive Slaves and Rise of the Coloured Baptist Churches, 1820–1865, in What is Now Ontario*, ed. Edwin S. Gausted. Salem, NH: The Baptist Tradition, 1980.

Mitchell, William M. *The Underground Railroad*. London: W. Tweedie, 1860. Fugitive slaves in the United Sates and Ontario.

Refugee's Home Society. *Thirty Thousand Refugees*. Detroit: Refugee's Home Society, 1852. Fugitive slaves.

Riddell, William R. *The Slave in Upper Canada, 1852–1865*. Lancaster, PA: n.p., 1919.

Ross, Alexander Milton. *Recollections and Experiences of an Abolitionist, from 1855 to 1865*. Toronto: Rowsell and Hutchison, 1875. Slaves and the Underground Railroad in the United States and Ontario.

Silverman, Jason H. *Unwelcome Guests: Canada West's Response to American Fugitive Slaves, 1800–1865.* Millwood, NY: Associated Faculty Press, 1985.

Smith, T. Watson. *The Slave in Canada.* Halifax: Nova Scotia Historical Society Collection, Vol. 10, 1899.

Steward, Austin. *Twenty-Two Years a Slave, and Forty Years a Freeman: Embracing a Correspondence of Several Years While President of Wilberforce Colony, London, Canada West.* Rochester, NY: Allings and Cory, 1859.

Stouffer, Allen P. *The Light of Nature and the Law of God: Antislavery in Ontario, 1833–1877.* Montreal: McGill-Queen's University Press, 1992. Antislavery, fugitive slaves, and race relations in Ontario.

Thoreau, Henry David. *A Yankee in Canada, with Anti-Slavery and Reform Papers*, 12th ed. New York: Haskell House, 1969.

United States. American Freedmen's Inquiry Commission. *Report to the Freedmen's Inquiry Commission, 1864: The Refugee from Slavery in Canada.* New York: Arno Press, 1969.

Ward, Samuel Ringgold. *Autobiography of a Fugitive Negro, His Anti-Slavery Labors in the United States, Canada and England.* 1855. Reprinted as *Autobiography of a Fugitive Negro.* New York: Arno Press, 1968; reprinted, Chicago: Johnson Publishing Company, 1970.

Theses and Dissertations:

Almonte, Richard. "A Scholarly Edition of Mary A. Shadd's 'A Plea for Emigration; or, Notes of Canada West.'" Master's thesis, Concordia University (Canada), 1996.

Austin, Bobby William. "The Social Status of Blacks in Toronto." Ph.D. diss., McMaster University, 1972.

Avakame, Frank Edem. "Homicide Among Blacks in Canada." Master's thesis, University of Alberta, 1990.

Basham, Richard Dalto. "Crisis in Blanc and White: Urbanization and Ethnic identity in French Canada." Ph.D. diss., University of California, Berkeley, 1972.

Bertley, Leo W. "The Universal Negro Improvement Association of Montreal, 1971–1979." Ph.D. diss., Concordia University, 1980.

Calderwood, William. "The Rise and Fall of the Ku Klux Klan in Saskatchewan." Master's thesis, University of Saskatchewan, 1968.

Carlesimo, Peter. "The Refugee Home Society: Its Origins, Operations, and Results." Master's thesis, University of Windsor, 1973.

Etoroma, Efajemue Enenajor. "Blacks in Hamilton: An Analysis of Factors in Community Building." Ph.D. diss., McMaster University, 1993.

Farrall, John Kevin. "The History of the Negro Community in Chatham, Ontario, 1787–1865." Ph.D. diss., University of Ottawa, 1977.

Herzog, June. "A Study of the Negro Defense Worker in the Portland-Vancouver Area." BA thesis, Reed College, 1944.

Hill, Daniel Grafton. "Negroes in Toronto—A Sociological Study of a Minority Group." Ph.D. diss., University of Toronto, 1961.

Jensen, Carole. "History of the Negro Community in Essex County, 1850–1860." Master's thesis, University of Windsor, 1966.

Magill, Dennis William. "The Relocation of Africville: A Case Study of Planned Social Change." Ph.D. diss., Washington University, 1974.

Mannette, Joy Anne. "'Making Something Happen': Nova Scotia's Black Renaissance, 1968–1986." Ph.D. diss., Carleton University, 1988.

Moreau, Bernice Mary. "Black Nova Scotian Women's Educational Experience, 1900–1945: A Study in Race, Gender and Class Relations." Ph.D. diss., University of Toronto, 1996.

Morton, William J. "Fair Accommodation Practices in Ontario: A Study of the Negro Complainants' and Leaders' Knowledge of and Attitudes Toward the Ontario Human Rights Code and Commission." Master's thesis, University of Toronto, 1966.

Murray, Alexander L. "Canada and the Anglo-American Anti-Slavery Movement: A Study in International Philanthropy." Ph.D. diss., University of Pennsylvania, 1960. Efforts to aid fugitive slaves in Canada.

Pilton, James William. "Negro Settlement in British Columbia, 1858–1871." Master's thesis, University of British Columbia, 1951.

Rhodes, Jane. "Breaking the Editorial Ice: Mary Ann Shadd Cary and the Provincial Freeman." Ph.D. diss., University of North Carolina, Chapel Hill, 1992.

Scott, Nolvert Preston, Jr. "The Perception of Racial Discrimination by Negroes in Metropolitan Winnipeg, Manitoba, Canada." Ph.D. diss., Pennsylvania State University, 1971.

Sharon, Roger A. "'Slaves No More': A Study of the Buxton Settlement, Upper Canada, 1849–1861." Ph.D. diss., State University of New York at Buffalo, 1995.

Simpson, Donald George. "Negroes in Ontario from Early Times to 1870." Ph.D. diss., University of Western Ontario, 1971.

Spencer, Hildreth Houston. "To Nestle in the Mane of the British Lion: A History of Canadian Black Education, 1820 to 1870." Ph.D. diss., Northwestern University, 1970.

Uneke, Okori Akpa. "Inter-Group Differences in Self-Employment: Blacks and Chinese in Toronto." Ph.D. diss., University of Toronto, 1994.

Utendale, Kent Alan. "Race Relations in Canada's Midwest: A Study of the Immigration, Integration, and Assimilation of Black Minority Groups." Ph.D. diss., Pacific Western University, 1985.

Walker, W. James St. G.. "The Black Loyalist in Nova Scotia and Sierra Leone." Ph.D. diss., Dalhousie University, 1973.

Walton, Jonathan William. "Blacks in Buxton and Chatham, Ontario, 1830–1890: Did the 49th Parallel Make a Difference?" Ph.D. diss., Princeton University, 1979.

Black Newspapers and Magazines:[1]

CHATHAM

Canadian Freeman and Kent General Advertiser. Chatham. 1847–1848. *Kent Advertiser*. Chatham.

Provincial Freeman. Chatham. 1852–1855.*Provincial Freeman and Weekly Advertiser*. Chatham. 1852–1855.

HALIFAX

Black Focus. Halifax. 1995–?

The Black Insight. Halifax, NS. 1971.

Ebony Express. Halifax. 1979–1981. *The Black Express*. Halifax. 1981–1982.

LONDON

Dawn of Tomorrow. London. 1923–1931. 1932–1972.

MONTREAL

Afro-Can Communications. Montreal. 1981–1982. *Afro-Can*. Montreal. 1982.

The Afro-Canadian. Montreal. 1984–1990?

The Black I: A Canadian Journal of Black Expression. ?

Black Voice. Montreal. 1972–?

Expression. Montreal quarterly. 1965.

The Oracle. Montreal. 1976. *Montréal Oracle*. Montreal.

Transatlantique. Montreal. 1989–?

Uhuru: Black Community News. Montreal. 1969–1970.

NEW GLASGOW

Negro Citizen. New Glasgow. 1934.

TORONTO

Africa Speaks: The Voice of the Colored Man in Canada. Toronto 1950–? Monthly.

The Afro-Beacon. Toronto. ? Monthly.

Anglo-American Magazine. Toronto. 1852–1855.

Black Business and Professional Association Newsletter. Toronto. Biannual.

Black Images: A Critical Quarterly on Black Culture. Toronto. 1972–1975. Quarterly.

Black Liberation News. Toronto. 1969–1970.

Black Voice. Toronto 1970–197?

Bumble Bee. Toronto. 1991. Juvenile monthly.

Canadian Negro. Toronto. 1953–1956.

---

[1] Single-lined boxed items were published by the same publisher. Double-lined items indicate change in masthead names.

Contrast. Toronto. 1969–1975;
    1980–1991. Weekly.
Cultural Times International. To-
    ronto. 1989–? Monthly.

> *Provincial Freeman.* Toronto.
>   1853–1855.
> *Provincial Freeman and Weekly Ad-*
>   *vertiser.* Toronto. 1855–?

Share. Toronto. 1978–? Weekly.
Spear: Canadian Magazine of Truth
    and Soul. Toronto.
    1971–1987? Monthly.
Talking Drums. Toronto. 1975.
    Weekly.
Third World News. Toronto. ?

> *West Indian News.* Toronto. 1966.
> *West Indian News Observer.* Toronto.
>   1967–1991.
> *Contrast.* Toronto. 1969–1975;
>   1980–1991.
> *The Islander.* Toronto. 1973.

WINDSOR

Provincial Freeman. Windsor.
    1853–1858.
Unity Press (Black Unity Press).
    Windsor. 1970.

VARIOUS COMMUNITIES

> *The Dawn of Tomorrow.* London.
>   1923–1931; 1932–1972.
>   Official organ of the Cana-
>   dian League for the Ad-
>   vancement of Colored Peo-
>   ple.

Diaspora. Vancouver. 1993.
Negro Citizen. New Glasco, NS.
    1934.
Soul Magazine. Edmonton. Quar-
    terly.
Tiger Lily: The Magazine for Women
    of Color. Stratford, ON.,
    1986–1989.
Voice of the Fugitive.

Other:

Against the Tides: The Jones Family, Nova Scotia. Almeta Speaks Produc-
    tions with Sleeping Giant Productions. Videorecording.
The Black Canadians: Their History and Contributions. Produced by Velma
    Carter and LeVero Carter. Edmonton: Alberta Education, 1991.
    Audiorecording. Juvenile.
Black Cultural Centre for Nova Scotia Library. Dartmouth East.
Black Cultural Research Society of Alberta. Edmonton.
Black Mother, Black Daughter. Montreal: National Film Board of Canada,
    1990. Testament to Black women of Nova Scotia. Videorecording.
Black Music Association of Canada. Toronto.
Fields of Endless Day. National Film Board of Canada, Terrance Macartney-
    Filgate, 1978. History of Blacks in Canada. Videorecording.
Go Do Some Great Thing: The Black Pioneers of British Columbia, by Craw-
    ford Kilian. Vancouver, BC: Crane Memorial Library, 1979.
    Audiorecording.
Home Feeling. National Film Board of Canada, Jennifer Hodge. Blacks in To-
    ronto. Videorecording.

Hymn to Freedom: The History of Blacks in Canada. Almeta Speaks, producer, four-part series featuring British Columbia, Nova Scotia, Ontario, and Quebec. 1997. Slavery, freedom, escaped U.S. slaves, and Black influences in Canada. Videorecording.

In the Key of Oscar. National Film Board of Canada, William R. Cunningham and Sylvia Sweeney, 1992. Biography of musician Oscar Peterson. Videorecording.

Older, Stronger, Wiser. By Dione Band and Claire Prieto. National Film Board of Canada, 1989. Life stories of five women document the history of Black women in Canada. Videorecording.

Remember Africville. National Film Board of Canada, Shelagh Mackenzie, 1991. Residents of Halifax Black community discuss Africville's demolition and their relocation. Videorecording.

The Right Candidate for Rosedale. National Film Board of Canada, Bonnie Sherr Klein and Ann Henderson, 1979. Focus on Anne Cools and her bid for the Liberal Party nomination in the Rosedale area of Toronto. Videorecording.

Seven Shades of Pale. National Film Board of Canada under the auspices of the Government of Canada Multiculturalism Program. Montreal: National Film Board, 1994. Blacks in Nova Scotia. Videorecording.

Slavery, A Canadian Story: The Packwood Family, Quebec. Almeta Speaks Productions and Sleeping Giant Productions. Mississauga, ON: International Tele-Film, 1994. Videorecording.

Speak It! From the Heart of Black Nova Scotia. National Film Board of Canada, 1993. Award-winning film about Black youth attending a Halifax high school. Videorecording.

Voice of the Fugitive. National Film Board of Canada, 1978. Drama about fugitive slaves moving north to Canada on the Underground Railroad. Videorecording.

Mexico

Articles:

"African Influence in Ancient Mexico: Some Say 'Yes,' Some Say 'No.'" *Black Issues in Higher Education* 9 (3 December 1992).

Aguirre Beltrán, Gonzalo. "The Integration of the Negro into the National Society of Mexico." Chapter in *Race and Class in Latin America*, ed. Magnus Morner. New York: Columbia University Press, 1970.

_____. "Races in Seventeenth Century Mexico." *Phylon* 6 (Third Quarter, 1945).

_____. "The Slave Trade in Mexico." *Hispanic American Historical Review* 24 (August 1944).

_____. "Tribal Origins of Slaves in Mexico." *Journal of Negro History* 31 (1945).

Aimes, Hubert H. S. "Coartación: A Spanish Institution for the Advancement of Slaves into Freedmen." *Yale Review* 17 (1909).

Alberro, Solange B. de. "Noirs et Mulatres dans la Societé Coloniale Mexicaine, D'Apres les Archives de L'Inquisition [Blacks and Mulattoes in Colonial Mexican Society According to the Archives of the Inquisition in the 16th and 17th Centuries]. *Cahiers des Amériques Latines* [France] 17 (1978).

Booker, Jackie R. "Needed but Unwanted: Black Militiamen in Veracruz, Mexico, 1760–1810." *Historian* 55 (1992).

Boyd-Bowman, Peter. "Negro Slaves in Early Colonial Mexico." *The Americas* 26 (October 1969).

Brack, Gene M. "Mexican Opinion, American Racism, and the War of 1846." *Western Historical Quarterly* 1 (1970). Slavery a factor in the 1846 war.

Brady, Robert La Don. "The Domestic Slave Trade in Sixteenth Century Mexico." *The Americas* 24 (January 1968).

Calhoun, Daniel H. "Strategy as Lived: Mixed Communities in the Age of New Nations." *American Indian Quarterly*, Winter 1988. Relationships in Mexico.

Clemence, Stella R. "Deed and Notes Covering Emancipation of a Negro Slave Woman in 1585." *Hispanic American Historical Review* 10 (February 1930).

Collins, John R. "The Mexican War: A Study in Fragmentation." *Journal of the West* 11, no. 2 (1972). The role of slavery in the war.

Crimmins, Martin L. "Colonel Buell's Expedition into Mexico in 1880." *New Mexico Historical Review* 10 (1935).

Davidson, David M. "Negro Slave Control and Resistance in Colonial Mexico, 1519–1650." *Hispanic American Historical Review* 46 (1966).

Diggs, Irene. "Color in Colonial Spanish America." *Journal of Negro History* 28 (1953).

Dusenberry, William H. "Discriminatory Aspects of Legislation in Colonial Mexico." *Journal of Negro History* 33 (1948).

Fleming, Mali Michele. "African Legacy: Afro-Americans in Mexico." *Hispanic* 7 (January-February 1984). Over 200,000 Africans brought to Mexico, leaving a large number of Mexicans with African heritage.

Foner, Eric. "The Wilmot Proviso Revisited." *Journal of American History* 56, no. 2 (1969). Van Burenite Democrats and the attempt to stop the expansion of slavery into Mexican territories.

Fuller, John D. P. "Effect of the Slavery Issue on the Movement to Annex Mexico." *Mississippi Valley Historical Review* 21 (June 1934).

————. "Slavery Propaganda during the Mexican War." *Southwestern Historical Quarterly* 38 (April 1935).

Hager, William M. "The Plan of San Diego: Unrest on the Texas Border in 1915." *Arizona and the West* 5 (1963). A "scheme" to create a white republic in the Southwest and a Black republic stretching from Oklahoma to Wyoming.

Hall, Paula. "Vaquero: The First American Cowboy." *Gilcrease Magazine of American History and Art* 13 (1991).

Harmon, G. D. "Stephen A. Douglas—His Leadership in the Compromise of 1850, Regarding Government and Question of Slavery in Territory Acquired from Mexico." *Illinois State Historical Society Journal* 21 (January 1929).

Harris, Theodore D. "Henry Flipper and Pancho Villa." *Password* 6 (Spring 1961).

Harstad, Peter T., and Richard W. Resh. "The Causes of the Mexican War: A Note on Changing Interpretations." *Arizona and the West* 6, no. 4 (1964). The role of slavery and its expansion in the Mexican War.

Hart, Charles Desmond. "The Natural Limits of Slavery Expansion: The Mexican Territories as a Test Case." *Mid-America—An Historical Quarterly* 52 (April 1972). Links the subject to the Civil War.

Hellwig, David J. "The Afro-American Press and Woodrow Wilson's Mexican Policy, 1913–1917." *Phylon* 48 (1987).

Jacoby, Karl. "From Plantation to Hacienda: The Mexican Colonization Movement in Alabama." *Alabama Heritage* 35 (1995).

Johnson, Robert B. "The Punitive Expedition: A Military, Diplomatic, and Political History of Pershing's Chase after Pancho Villa, 1916–1917." Ph.D. diss., University of Southern California, 1964.

King, James Ferguson. "Descriptive Data on Negro Slaves in Spanish Importation Records and Bills of Sale." *Journal of Negro History* 28 (April 1943).

_____. "Evolution of the Free Slave Principle in Spanish Colonial Administration." *Hispanic American Historical Review* 23 (February 1942).

_____. "Negro History in Continental Spanish America." *Journal of Negro History* 29 (January 1944).

Lack, Paul D. "Slavery and the Texas Revolution." *Southwestern Historical Quarterly* 89 (October 1985).

Landers, Jane. "New Research on the African Experience in Spanish America and the Caribbean." *Colonial Latin American Historical Review* 3 (1994).

LeFalle-Collins, Lizzetta. "The Mexican Connection: The New Negro and Border Crossings." *American Visions*, December 1996. Black artists and their debt to Mexican artists such as José Clemente Orozco and Diego Rivera. Description of show "In the Spirit of Resistance: African-American Modernists and the Mexican Muralist School."

Lewis, L. A. "Colonialism and its Contradictions: Indians, Blacks and Social Power in Sixteenth and Seventeenth Century Mexico." *Journal of Historical Sociology* 9, no. 4 (1996).

Lodge, Michelle. "Due South: Mexico's African Legacy." *Essence* 25 (November 1994).

Love, Edgar F. "Afro-Spanish Marriages in the Parish of Santa Veracruz, Mexico City, 1646–1747." *Journal of the Afro-American Historical and Genealogical Society* 5 (1984).

_____. "Legal Restrictions on Afro-Indian Relations in Colonial Mexico." *Journal of Negro History* 55 (April 1970).

_____. "Marriage Patterns of Persons of African Descent in a Colonial Mexico City Parish." *Hispanic American Historical Review* 51 (1971).

_____. "Negro Resistance to Spanish Rule in Colonial Mexico." *Journal of Negro History* 52 (April 1967).

May, Robert E. "Invisible Men: Blacks and the U.S. Army in the Mexican War." *Historian* 49 (1987).

Melzer, Richard. "On Villa's Trail in Mexico: The Experiences of a Black Cavalryman and a White Infantry Officer, 1916–1917." *Military History of the Southwest* 21 (Fall 1991).

Miranda, Gloria E. "Racial and Cultural Dimensions of *Gente de Razón* Status in Spanish and Mexican California." *Southern California Quarterly* 70 (Fall 1988).

Morey, Lewis S. "The Cavalry Fight at Carrizal." *Journal of U.S. Cavalryman* (January 1917).

"Negro-Indian Mixtures in Mexico." *Science* 79 (12 January 1934).

Palmer, Colin A. "From Africa to the Americas: African Slaves in Mexico City and Their Cultural Survival: Ethnicity in the Early Black Communities of the Americas." *Journal of World History* (Autumn 1995). Insights into cultural roles of Africans in the early Americas.

Pattee, Richard. "Negro Studies in Latin America." *American Council of Learned Societies* (Bulletin No. 32, 1931–1933).

Pi-Sunyer, Oriol. "Historical Background to the Negro in Mexico." *Journal of Negro History* 42 (October 1957).

Porter, Kenneth Wiggins. "The Creek Indian-Negro Tradition: The Hawkins Negroes go to Mexico." *Chronicles of Oklahoma* 24 (Spring 1946). Red-Black Indians.

————. "The Seminole in Mexico, 1850–1861." *The Hispanic American Historical Review* 31 (1951).

————. "The Seminole in Mexico, 1850–1861." *Chronicles of Oklahoma* 29 (1951).

Rippy, J. Fred. "Border Troubles along the Rio Grande, 1848–1860." *Southwestern Historical Quarterly* 23 (1919).

————. "A Negro Colonization Project in Mexico, 1895." *Journal of Negro History* 6 (1921).

————. "The Negro and the Spanish Pioneer in the New World." *Journal of Negro History* 6 (1921).

————. "Some Precedents of the Pershing Expedition into Mexico." *Southwestern Historical Quarterly* 60 (July 1956).

Roncal, Joaquin. "The Negro Race in Mexico: A Statistical Study." *Hispanic American Historical Review* 24 (August 1944).

Schoonover, Thomas. "Misconstrued Mission: Expansionism and Black Colonization in Mexico and Central America During the Civil War." *Pacific Historical Review* 49 (1980).

Seed, Patricia. "Social Dimensions of Race: Mexico City, 1753." *Hispanic American Historical Review* 62 (November 1982).

Shankman, Arnold. "The Image of Mexico and the Mexican-American in the Black Press, 1890–1930." *Journal of Ethnic Studies* 3 (Summer 1975). Writer uncovers areas of conflict.

Smith, Ralph A. "The Mamelukes of West Texas and Mexico." *West Texas Historical Association Year Book* 39 (1963).

Stenberg, R. R. "The Motivation of the Wilmot Proviso to a Bill for the Purchase of Mexican Territory, Prohibiting Slavery Therein." *Mississippi Valley Historical Review* 18 (March 1932).

Stoddard, Ellwyn R.   "Negro (Black) Americans."   Chapter in *Borderlands Sourcebook: A Guide to the Literature on Northern Mexico and the American Southwest*, eds. Ellwyn R. Stoddard, Richard L. Nostrand, and Jonathan P. West. Norman: University of Oklahoma Press, 1983.

"Tale of Two Towns: Runaway Slaves and Indians Find Freedom in Mexico." *Black Issues in Higher Education* 9 (December 1992).

Thurman, Sue Bailey. "How Far From Here to Mexico." *Crisis* 42 (September 1935). Advice for Black travelers.

Troxel, Erwin N. "The Tenth Cavalry in Mexico." *U.S. Cavalry Journal* (October 1916).

Tyler, Ronnie C.   "The Callahan Expedition of 1855: Indians or Negroes?" *Southwestern Historical History* 70 (April 1967).   Expedition into Mexico for the recovery of slaves.

————. "Fugitive Slaves in Mexico." *Journal of Negro History* 57 (January 1972). Recounts the history of the thousands of slaves who escaped to Mexico before the Civil War and their retrieval.

Utley, Robert M.   "'Pecos Bill' On the Texas Frontier."   *American West* 6 (1969). Lieutenant Colonel William R. Shafter, commander of Negro troops in Texas.

Valdés, Dennis N.   "The Decline of Slavery in Mexico." *The Americas* 44 (1987).

VanDenBerghe, Pierre L.   "The African Diaspora in Mexico, Brazil, and the United States." *Social Forces* 54, no. 3 (1976).

Vigil, Ralph H.   "Negro Slaves and Rebels in the Spanish Possessions, 1503–1558." *The Historian* 33 (August 1971).

Vincent, Ted. "The Blacks Who Freed Mexico." *Journal of Negro History* 79 (Summer 1994).

————. "Black Hopes in Baja California: Black American and Mexican Co-operation, 1917–1926." *Western Journal of Black Studies* 21 (Fall 1997).

Vinson, Ben III. "Free Colored Voices: Issues of Representation and Racial Identity in the Colonial Mexican Militia." *Journal of Negro History* 80 (Fall 1995).

Weber, David J. "A Black American in Mexican San Diego: Two Recently Recovered Documents." *Journal of San Diego History* 20 (Spring 1974). The 1835 arrival of Allen B. Light, a sea otter hunter.

————. "Mestizaje: The First Census of Los Angeles, 1781." Chapter in *Foreigners in Their Native Land: Historical Roots of the Mexican Americans*, David Weber. Albuquerque: University of New Mexico Press, 1973.

Wharfield, H. B. "The Affair at Carrizal: Pershing's Punitive Expedition." *Montana, the Magazine of Western History* 18 (October 1968). The 10th Cavalry at Chihuahua, Mexico.

Yeager, Timothy J. "*Encomienda* or Slavery? The Spanish Crown's Choice of Labor Organization in Sixteenth-Century Spanish America." *Journal of Economic History* 55 (1995).

Young, Karl. "A Fight That Could Have Meant War." *American West* 3 (Spring 1966). The 10th Cavalry in New Mexico and Mexico.

Wallace, Andrew. "The Sabre Retires: Pershing's Cavalry Campaign in Mexico, 1916." *Smoke Signal* 9 (Spring 1964).

Zimmerman, Karl H. "Drummer for De Vargas." *New Mexico Magazine* 45 (August 1967).

Books:

Aguirre Beltrán, Gonzalo. *Cujila, Esbozo Etnográfico de un Pueblo Negro.* México: Fondo de Cultura Económica, 1958. Blacks in Mexico.

_____. *La población negra de México: Estudio Ethnohistórico,* 3d ed. Jalapa, México: Fondo de Cultura Económica, 1989.

Alonso, Vincenta Cortés. *La Esclavitud de Valencia durante el reino de los reyes católicos.* Valencia: n.p., 1964. The early Spanish slave trade.

Andrade Torres, Juan. *El Comercio de Esclavos en la Provincia de Tabasco (Siglos XVI–XIX).* Villahermosa, Tabasco: Universidad Juárez Autónoma de Tabasco, División Académica de Ciencias Económica-Administrativas, Centro de Investigación, 1994. Slavery in Tabasco, Mexico.

Aparicio Prudente, Francisca, Adela García Casarrubias, and María Cristina Díaz Pérez, eds. *Cállate Burrita Prieta: Poética Afromestiza.* Chilpancingo, Gro., México: Consejo Nacional Para la Cultura y las Artes, 1993. Black Mexican poets.

Archivo General de la nación (Mexico). *Los cimarrones de Mazateopan.* Xalapa, Veracruz: Gobierno del Estado de Veracruz-Llave, 1992. Maroons in Veracruz.

Archivo Notarial de Xalapa (Veracruz, Mexico). *Esclavos en el Archivo Notarial de Xalapa, Veracruz, 1700–1800,* comp. Fernando Winfield Capitaine. Xalapa, Ver.: Universidad Veracruzana, Museo de Antropología, 1984.

Barnes, Thomas C., Thomas H. Naylor, and Charles W. Polzer. "Racial Terminology." Chapter in *Northern New Spain: A Research Guide.* Tucson: University of Arizona Press, 1981.

Barrett, Ward J. *The Sugar Hacienda of the Marqueses del Valle.* Minneapolis: University of Minnesota Press, 1970. Sugar trade and slavery in Mexico.

Bradley, Michael Anderson. *Dawn Voyage: The Black African Discovery of America.* Toronto: Summerhill Press, 1987. African influences in the early Americas.

Brockington, Lolita Gutiérrez. *The Leverage of Labor: Managing the Cortés Haciendas in Tehuantepec, 1588–1688.* Durham: Duke University Press, 1989.

Cabeza de Vaca, Alvar Núñez. *The Journey of Alvar Núñez Cabeza de Vaca and his companions from Florida to the Pacific, 1528–1536; translated from his own narrative by Fanny Bandelier, together with the report of Father Marcos of Nizza and a letter from the Viceroy Mendoza.* New York: A. S. Barnes and Company, 1905. Estevanico included in this account.

Canté Corro, Jos. *La esclavitud en el mundo y en Méjico: Estudio sobre.* México: Escuela Tip. Salesiana, 1925. Slavery and the church in Mexico.

Cardosa, Geraldo Da Silva. *Negro Slavery in the Sugar Plantations of Veracruz and Pernambuco, 1550–1680.* Washington, DC: University Press of America, 1983.

Carroll, Patrick James. *Blacks in Colonial Veracruz: Race, Ethnicity, and Regional Development.* Austin: University of Texas Press, 1991.

Chance, Joseph E. *Mexican War Journal of Captain Franklin Smith,* 2^d ed. University Press of Missouri, 1991. Race relations and politics.

Cruz Carretero, Sagrario. *El Carnaval en Yanga: Notas y Comentarios Sobre Una Fiesta de la Negritud.* Veracruz: Consejo Nacional para la Cultura y las Artes, Dirección General de Culturas Populares, Unidad Regional Centro de Veracruz, 1990. Black social life and customs, Yanga, Mexico.

El rostro colectivo de la nación mexicana. Morelia, Michoacán, México: Universidad Michoacana de San Nicolás de Hidalgo, Instituto de Investigaciones Históricas, 1997. Blacks and African influences in Mexico. Papers from the 5th Encuentro de Afromexicanistas of October 25–27, 1995.

Encuentro Nacional de Afromexicanistas. *Memoria del III Encuentro Nacional de Afromexicanistas.* Colima, col., México: Gob. del Estado, Instituto Colimense de Cultura: Culturas Populares, Nuestra Tercera Raiz, Consejo Nacional para la Cultura y las Artes, 1993. Black congresses in Mexico.

Featherstonhaugh, George William. *Excursion Through the Slave States, From Washington on the Potomac, to the Frontier of México; with Sketches of Popular Manners and Geological Notices.* New York: Harper, 1844. Travel and social customs.

Fernández Repetto, Francisco, and Genny Negroe Sierra. *Una Población en la Memoria: Los Negros de Yucatán.* Mérida, Yucatán, México: Universidad Autónoma de Yucatán, Dirección General de Extensión, 1995. Blacks in Yucatán.

Gálvez Jiménez, Mónica Leticia. *Celaya: sus ráices africanas.* Guanajuato: Ediciones La Rana, 1995. History of Blacks and slavery in Celaya (Guanajuato).

Gleaton, Tony. *Africa's Legacy in Mexico.* Washington, DC: Smithsonian Institution Traveling Exhibition Service, 1993. Photographs by Tony Gleaton.

Goded, Maya. Tierra Negra. *Fotografías de la Costa Chica en Guerrero y Oax-aca, México*. México: Consejo Nacional para la Cultura y las Artes, 1994.

Gutiérrez Avila, Miguel Angel. *Corrido y Violencia Entre los Afromestizos de la Costa Chica de Guerrero y Oaxaca*. Chilpancingo, Gro.: Universidad Autónoma de Guerrero, 1988. Blacks and violence in Guerrero, Mexico.

Heizer, Robert F., and Alan J. Almquist. *The Other Californians: Prejudice and Discrimination Under Spain, Mexico, and the United States to 1920*. Berkeley: University of California Press, 1971.

Herrera Casasús, María Luisa. *Presencia y Esclavitud del Negro en la Huasteca*. México: M.A. Porrúa, 1989. Slavery in the Huasteca Region of Mexico.

Hill, Leslie, and Peter C. Hogg. *Black Corps D'elite: An African Slave Battalion of the Second Empire in México*. East Lansing: Michigan State University Press, 1994.

Hispanic American Historical Review 24 (August 1944). Special Issue: *The Negro on the Spanish-American Main Land*. Blacks in Latin America, including Mexico.

Israel, Jonathan. *Race, Class and Politics in Colonial Mexico*. London: n.p., 1975.

LaTorre, Felipe A., and Dolores L. LaTorre. *The Mexican Kickapoo Indians*. Austin: University of Texas Press, 1976. Red-Black Indians.

Lon, Nicol S. *El negrito poeta mexicano y sus populares versos*. México: Impr. del Museo Nacional, 1912.

Lundy, Benjamin. *The Life, Travels, and Opinions of Benjamin Lundy, Including His Journeys to Texas and Mexico*. Philadelphia: William D. Parrish, 1847.

[Lundy, Benjamin]. *The War in Texas; a Review of the Facts and Circumstances, Showing that this Contest is a Crusade against Mexico, set on Foot and Supported by Slaveholders, Land Speculators, etc., in order to Reestablish, Extend and Perpetuate the System of Slavery and the Slave Trade*. Philadelphia: Merridew and Gunn, 1837.

Martínez Montiel, Luz María. *Presencia Africana en México*. México, D.F.: Consejo Nacional para la Cultura y las Artes, 1994. African influences.

————. *Presencia Africana en México*. México, D.F.: Consejo Nacional para la Cultura y las Artes, 1994. African influences.

Mayer, Vincent, Jr. *The Black on New Spain's Northern Frontier: San José de Parral, 1631 to 1641*. Occasional Papers of the Center of Southwest Studies no. 2. Durango, CO: Center of Southwest Studies, 1974. Slave trade in Mexico.

Melville, Eleanor. *A Plague of Sheep*. Cambridge: University Press, 1994. Slavery in Mexico.

Morner, Magnus. *Race Mixture in Latin America*. Boston: Little, Brown and Company, 1967.

Mulroy, Kevin. *Freedom on the Border: The Seminole Maroons in Florida, the Indian Territory, Coahuila, and Texas*. Lubbock: Texas Tech University Press, 1993.

Naveda Chávez-Hita, Adriana. *Esclavos negros en las haciendas azucareras de Córdoba, Veracruz, 1690–1830*. Xalapa, Ver., México: Universidad Veracruzana, Centro de Investigaciones Históricas, 1987. Slavery in Veracruz.

Palmer, Colin A. *Slaves of the White God: Blacks in Mexico, 1570–1650*. Cambridge: Harvard University Press, 1976.

Pan American Institute of Geography and History. *El mestizaje en la historia de Ibero-América*. México: The Institute, 1961. Black-Indians of Latin America.

Pérez Fernández, Rolando Antonio. *La Música Afromestiza Mexicana*. Xalapa, Ver., México: Universidad Veracruzana, 1990.

Pérez-Rocha, Emma, and Gabriel Moedano Navarro. *Aportaciones a la Investigación de Archivos del México Colonial y a la Bibliohemerografía Afromexicanista*. México, D.F.: Instituto National de Antropología e Historia, 1992.

Powell, Phillip Wayne. *Soldiers, Indians, and Silver: The Northward Advance of New Spain, 1550–1600*. Berkeley: University of California Press, 1952.

Reynolds, Alfred W. *The Alabama Negro Colony in Mexico, 1894–1896*. Auburn, AL: Alabama Polytechnic Institute, 1953.

Rout, Leslie B., Jr. *The African Experience in Spanish America: 1502 to Present Day*. New York: Cambridge University Press, 1976. Blacks in Latin America.

Rumeu de Armas, Antonio. *España en la Africa Atlántica*, 2 vols. Madrid: n.p., 1956. General history of the Spanish slave trade.

Saco, José Antonio. *Historia de la Esclavitud*, 5 vols. Paris: n.p., 1875–1893. Vols. 2 and 3 are about Spain and African slavery.

Sagrera, Martín. *Los racismos en América "Latina."* Buenos Aires: Ediciones la Bastilla, 1974. Race relations in Latin America, including Mexico.

Scelle, Georges. *La traite negrière aux Indes de Castille*, 2 vols. Paris: n.p., 1906. General history of the Spanish slave trade.

Schwartz, Rosalie. *Across the Rio to Freedom: U.S. Negroes in Mexico*. Southwestern Studies Monograph no. 44. El Paso: Texas Western Press, 1975.

Shaw, Elton Raymond. *The Conquest of the Southwest: A Discussion of the Charges that the Colonization of Texas and the Revolution Against Mexico were the Results of a Movement of the "Slavocracy" to Increase Slave Territory, or of the Activity of Andrew Jackson, through Samuel Houston, to Accomplish the Same Result*. Berwyn, IL: Shaw Publishing Company, 1924.

Testimonios de la esclavitud en la Nueva Galicia. Guadalajara, Jalisco, México: Gobierno de Jalisco, Secretaría General, Unidad Editorial, 1985. Slavery in Mexico.

Torres Cerdán, Raquel, and Dora Elena Careaga Gutiérrez. *La Cocina Afromestiza en Veracruz.* Veracruz, Veracruz, México: Instituto Veracruzano de Cultura, 1995. Blacks and cooking in Veracruz.

Troxel, O. C., et al, eds. *Narrative of Service of the Tenth U.S. Cavalry in the Punitive Expedition.* Tucson: Acme Printing Company, 1921. Pamphlet.

United States. Congress. Senate. Select Committee of Thirteen. *Report (To Accompany Bill S. no. 225 and S. no. 226) by the Senate's Select Committee of Thirteen to Whom Were Referred Various Resolutions Relating to California, to Other Portions of the Territory Recently Acquired by the United States from the Republic of Mexico, and Other Subjects Connected with the Institution of Slavery.* Washington, DC: n.p., 1850.

Utley, Robert M. *Fort Davis National Historic Site.* Historic Handbook 38, U.S. Department of Interior, National Park Service, Washington, DC: 1965. Home to Black troops.

Valdés, Carlos Manuel. *Esclavos Negros en Saltillo* (Siglos XVII–XIX). Saltillo: R. Ayuntamiento de Saltillo: Universidad Autónoma de Coahuila, 1989. Slavery in Saltillo, Coahuila, Mexico.

Valdéz Aguilar, Rafael. *Sinaloa: Negritud y Olvido.* Culiacán, Sinaloa: El Diario de Sinaloa, 1993. Race Relations, Sinaloa, Mexico.

Van Sertima, Ivan, ed. *African Presence in Early America.* New Brunswick, NJ: Transaction Books, 1987. Pre Columbus African contacts and influences.

Wiener, Leo. *Africa and the Discovery of America,* 3 vols. Philadelphia: Innes and Cons, 1920–22. Early African contact and influences in the New World.

Williams, Morris. *Lo llevo en la sangre: las memorias de Morris "Moe" Williams, Jr.* Puebla, Pue, Mexico: Familia Williams, 1988. Biography of a Black basketball coach.

Wilson, James. *Speech of Mr. James Wilson, of N. Hampshire, on the Political Influence of Slavery, and the Expediency of Permitting Slavery in the Territories Recently Acquired from Mexico: Delivered in the House of Representatives of the United States, February 16, 1849.* Washington, DC: J. and G. S. Gideon, 1849.

Theses and Dissertations:

Bennett, Herman Lee. "Lovers, Family and Friends: The Formation of Afro-Mexico, 1580–1810." Ph.D. diss., Duke University, 1993.

Brady, Robert La Don. "The Emergence of a Negro Class in Mexico, 1524–1640." Thesis, State University of Iowa, 1965. Blacks and slavery in Mexico.

Brockington, Lolita Gutiérrez. "The Haciendas Marquesanas in Tehuantepec: African, Indian and European Labor and Race Relations, 1588–1683." Ph.D. diss., University of North Carolina, Chapel Hill, 1982.

Cardosa, Geraldo Da Silva. "Negro Slavery in the Sugar Plantations of Veracruz and Pernambuco, 1550–1680: A Comparative Study." Ph.D. diss., University of Nebraska, 1975.

Carroll, Patrick James. "Mexican Society in Transition: the Blacks in Veracruz, 1750–1830." Ph.D. diss., University of Texas at Austin, 1975.

Chance, John Keron. "Race and Class in a Colonial Mexican City: A Social History of Anteguera, 1521–1800." Thesis, University of Illinois at Urbana-Champaign, 1974. Oaxaca, Mexico.

Fain, Samuel S. "The Pershing Punitive Expedition and Its Diplomatic Battlegrounds." Master's thesis, University of Arizona, 1951.

Gonzalez-El Hilali, Anita. "Performing Mestizaje: Official Culture and Identity in Veracruz, Mexico." Ph.D. diss., University of Wisconsin-Madison, 1997. Mixed-race heritage in Mexico as demonstrated through theater and dance.

Johnson, Robert B. "The Punitive Expedition: A Military, Diplomatic, and Political History of Pershing's Chase after Pancho Villa, 1916–1917." Ph.D. diss., University of Southern California, 1964.

Mayer, Vincent, Jr. "The Black Slave on New Spain's Northern Frontier: San José de Parral, 1632–1676." Ph.D. diss., University of Utah, 1975.

Miller, Susan A. "Wild Cat and the Origins of the Seminole Migration to Mexico." Master's thesis, University of Oklahoma, 1988. Red-Black Indians.

Palmer, Colin A. "Negro Slavery in Mexico, 1570–1650." Ph.D. diss., University of Wisconsin, 1970.

Rios-Bustamante, Antonio. "Los Angeles, Pueblo and Region, 1781–1850: Continuity and Adaptation on the North American Periphery." Ph.D. diss., University of California, Los Angeles, 1985.

Schwartz, Rosalie. "Runaway Negroes: Mexico as an Alternative for United States Blacks, 1825–1860." Master's thesis, San Diego State University, 1974.

Shadley, Frank W. "The American Punitive Expedition Into Mexico, 1916–1917." Master's thesis, College of the Pacific, 1952.

Black Periodical:

Afroamerica. Mexico. 1945–1946.

Other:

"The African Struggle in Mexico: A First Hand Report from the Quintro Encuentro de Afromexicanistas in Michoacán." KPFK-FM radio, Los Angeles, broadcast on 9 January 1996. Interviews and papers, 180 minutes. Sound recording.

Afro-American Colonization Company of Mexico. Articles of Incorporation, San Diego, 1891. Located in the California State Archives.

The Black Heritage of Ancient Mexico. Los Angeles: Golden Legacy, 1990. Archaeological evidence that Blacks were in the Americas during the Olmec period. Videocassette.

Colored Mexican Colonization Company. Articles of Incorporation, San Diego, 1891. Located in the California State Archives.

General History

Books:

African American Almanac, 7th ed. Detroit: Gale, 1996.

African American History in the Press, 1851–1899, 2 Vols. Detroit: Gale, 1996.

Afro-Americana, 1553–1906: Author Catalog of the Library Company of Philadelphia and the Historical Society of Pennsylvania. Boston: G. K. Hall, n.d.

Aguirre Beltrán, Gonzalo. *La poblacion negra de Mexico, 1519–1810.* Ediciones Fuente cultural, Mexico, D.F., 1946. Estudio etno-historico

Alan, John, ed. *Black, Brown and Red: The Movement for Freedom Among Black, Chicano, Latino, and Indian.* News and Letters, 1975.

Anderson, William. *Narrative of a Ride to the Rocky Mountains in 1834.* Missoula, MT: Montana State University, 1938.

Aptheker, Herbert, ed. *A Documentary History of the Negro People in the United States.* New York: Citadel Press/Carol, 1992.

Ashe, Arthur R., Jr. *Hard Road to Glory.* New York: Warner Books, 1988.

Atwood, Albert. *Glimpses in Pioneer Life on Puget Sound.* Seattle: Denny-Coryell, Company, 1903.

Balty, Joseph. *Over the Wilds to California.* Leeds, England: J. Parrott Company, 1867.

Bancroft, Hubert Howe. *History of British Columbia, 1792–1887.* San Francisco: The History Company, 1887.

_____. *History of California*, 7 Vols. San Francisco: The History Company, 1888.

_____. *History of Oregon*, 2 Vols. San Francisco: The History Company, 1888.

_____. *History of the North Mexican States*, 7 Vols. San Francisco: The History Company, 1888.

_____. *History of the Northwest Coast*, 2 Vols. San Francisco: The History Company, 1888.

_____. *History of Utah*. San Francisco: The History Company, 1891.

_____. *History of Washington, Idaho and Montana*. San Francisco: The History Company, 1880.

Bard, Floyd C. *Horse Wrangler: Sixty Years in the Saddle in Wyoming and Montana*. Norman, OK: University of Oklahoma Press, 1960.

Barnaby, William H. *Life and Labour in the Far, Far West*. New York: Cassell and Company, 1894.

Bennett, Lerone, Jr. *Before the Mayflower: A History of Black America*, 6th ed. New York: Penguin, 1993.

Berwanger, Eugene H. *The Frontier Against Slavery: Western Anti-Negro Prejudice and Slavery Extension Controversy*. Urbana: University of Illinois Press, 1967.

Billington, Ray Allen. *Westward Expansion*. New York: Macmillan, 1967.

Black Enterprise. Journal.

Black Music Research Journal.

Black Scholar. Journal.

Black Studies Journal.

Blockson, Charles L. *Black Genealogy*. Baltimore: Black Classic, 1992.

Bontemps, Arna. *Story of the Negro*. New York: Knopf, 1958.

Brebner, John. *Explorers of North America 1492–1806*. New York: Macmillan and Company, 1935.

Breyfogle, William A. *Make Free: The Story of the Underground Railroad*. Philadelphia: Lippincott, 1958.

Bullock, Penelope L. *The Afro-American Periodical Press 1838–1909*. Baton Rouge: Louisiana State University Press.

Callaloo: A Journal of African-American and African Arts and Letters.

Campbell, Walter S. *Dodge City: Queen of the Cattle Towns*. New York: Harper, 1952.

Cantor, George. *Historic Landmarks of Black America*. Detroit: Gale, 1991.

Carroll, Charles. *"The Negro a Beast;" or, "In the Image of God;" the Reasoner of the Age, the Revelator of the Century! The Bible as It Is! The Negro and His Relation to the Human Family."* St. Louis: American Book and Bible House, 1900. This and the following are pseudo-scientific, pseudo-religious works of racism.

_____. *The Tempter of Eve; or the Criminality of Man's Social, Political, and Religious Equality with the Negro, and the Amalgamation to Which These Crimes Inevitably Lead*. St. Louis: Adamic, 1902.

Carter, Kate B. *Utah During Civil War Years*. Salt Lake City: 1956. Pamphlet.

Chalmers, David M. *Hooded Americanism: The History of the Ku Klux Klan*. Chicago: Quadrangle Books, 1968.

Churchill, Ward, and Jim Vander Wall. *Agents of Repression: The FBI's Secret War Against the American Indian Movement and the Black Panther Party*. Boston: South End Press.

Cleland, Robert G. *This Reckless Breed of Men: The Trappers and Fur Traders of the Southwest*. New York: Alfred A. Knopf, 1950.

Coues, Elliott. *New Light on the Early History of the Greater Northwest*. New York: Francis F. Harper, 1893.

Cowan, Tom, and Jack Maguire. *Timelines of African-American History: 500 Years of Black Achievement*. New York: Roundtable Press/Perigee, 1994.

Crawford, Lewis F. *History of North Dakota*. New York: American Historical Society, 1931.

Daniel, Cletus. *Bitter Harvest: A History of California Farmworkers, 1870–1941*. Ithaca, NY: Cornell University Press.

Davis, Abraham L., and Barbara Luck Graham. *The Supreme Court, Race, and Civil Rights*. Thousand Oaks, CA: Sage, 1995.

Davis, Marianna W., ed. *Contributions of Black Women to America: The Arts, Media, Business, Law, Sports*, Vol. 1. Columbia, SC: Kenday Press, 1982.

_____. *Contributions of Black American Women to America: Civil Rights, Politics and Government, Education, Medicine, Sciences*, Vol. 2. Columbia, SC: Kenday Press, 1982.

Dimsdale, Thomas J. *The Vigilantes of Montana*. Butte: McKee Printing Company, 1949.

Donaldson, Thomas. *Idaho of Yesterday*. Caldwell, ID: The Caxton Printer, 1941.

Drury, Clifford Merrill. *Marcus Whitman, M.D. Pioneer and Martyr*. Caldwell, ID: The Caxton Printer, 1937.

Dunn, John. *History of the Oregon Territory*. London: Edwards and Hughes, Publishers, 1844.

Evans, Walter O. *The Walter O. Evans Collection of African American Art*. Detroit, MI: W. O. Evans Collection, 1991.

Finney, James E. *The Long Road to Now: A Bibliography of Material Relating to the American Black Man*. New York: Charles W. Clark, 1969.

Foner, Eric, ed. *America's Black Past: A Reader in Afro-American History*. New York: Harper and Row, 1971.

Franklin, John Hope, and Alfred A. Moss, Jr. *From Slavery to Freedom: A History of African Americans*, 7th ed. New York: McGraw-Hill, 1994.

Frazier, Robert W. *Forts of the West*. Norman: University of Oklahoma Press, 1965.

Frazier, Thomas R., ed. *Afro-American History: Primary Sources*. Chicago: Dorsey Press, 1988.

Gardds, Wayne. *Frontier Justice*. Norman: University of Oklahoma Press, 1949.

Garwood, Alfred N., ed. *Black America: A Statistical Source Book.* Boulder: Numbers & Concepts, 1990.

Gatewood, Willard B., Jr. *"Smoked Yankees" and the Struggle for Empire: Letters from Negro Soldiers, 1898–1902.* Urbana, IL: University of Illinois Press, 1971.

Gilbert, Edmund W. *Exploration of Western America 1800–1850.* Cambridge, England: University Press, 1933.

Gould, Stephen Jay. *The Mismeasure of Man.* New York: W. W. Norton, 1981.

Hafen, LeRoy R. *Fort Laramie and the Pageant of the West.* Glendale, CA: Arthur H. Clark Company, 1938.

_____, ed. *The Mountain Men and the Fur Trade*, 6 Vols. Glendale, CA: Arthur H. Clark Company, 1938. Includes profiles of Cyrus Alexander, James Beckwourth and Moses "Black" Harris.

Ham, Debra Newman, ed. *The African American Mosaic: A Library of Congress Resource Guide for the Study of Black History and Culture.* Washington, DC: Library of Congress, 1993.

Hamilton, James M. *From Wilderness to Statehood: A History of Montana, 1805–1900.* Portland, OR: Binfords and Mort, 1957.

Harrison, Maureen, and Steve Gilbert, eds. *Civil Rights Decisions of the United States Supreme Court: The 19th Century.* San Diego: Excellent Books, 1994.

_____. *Civil Rights Decisions of the United States Supreme Court: The 20th Century.* San Diego: Excellent Books, 1994.

Historical Statistics of Black America. Detroit: Gale, 1995.

A History and Analysis of the Planning Process in Three Cities: Atlanta, Georgia; Seattle, Washington; Dayton, Ohio. Department of Housing and Urban Development, Washington, DC; U.S. Government Printing Office, 1969.

hooks, bell. *Black Looks: Race and Representation.* Boston: South End Press, 1992.

Horan, James D., and Paul Sann. *Pictorial History of the Wild West: A True Account of the Bad Men, Desperadoes, Rustlers and Outlaws of the Old West-and the Men Who Fought Them to Establish Law and Order.* New York: Crown Publishers, 1954.

Hornsby, Alton, Jr. *Chronology of African-American History.* Detroit: Gale, 1996.

In Black and White, 3d ed. 2 Vols. Detroit: Gale, 1980. Biographical information on 25,000 Blacks in the U.S., Africa, and elsewhere.

Jackson, Kenneth. *The Ku Klux Klan in the City, 1915–1930.* New York: Oxford University Press, 1967.

Jansen, Andrew. *Latter-Day Saint Biographical Encyclopedia*, 4 Vols. Salt Lake City: 1901–1936. See Vols. III and IV.

Jazz Educators Journal.

Johnson, Charles. *African American Soldiers in the National Guard: Recruitment and Deployment During Peacetime and War*. Westport, CT: Greenwood Press, 1992.

Journal of Black Music Research.

Journal of Black Music.

Journal of Black Studies.

Journal of Blacks in Higher Education.

Journal of Negro History.

Junne, George H., Jr. *Afroamerican History: A Chronicle of People of African Descent in the United States*. Dubuque, IA: Kendall/Hunt, 1996.

Katz, William Loren. *Eyewitness: The Negro in American History*. New York: Pitman Publishing Corporation, 1967.

Krash, Ronald, et al. *Black America: A Research Bibliography*. St. Louis: St. Louis University Library, 1972.

Kujoory, Parvin. *Black Slavery in America: An Annotated Mediagraphy*. Lanham, MD: Scarecrow Press, 1995.

Leeson, Michael A., ed. *History of Montana, 1739–1885*. Chicago, 1885.

Lewis, Floyd. *African American Art and Artists*. Berkeley: University of California Press, 1990.

Limerick, Patricia Nelson. *The Legacy of Conquest: The Unbroken Past of the American West*. New York: Norton, 1987.

Lincoln, C. Eric, and Lawrence Mamiya. *The Black Church in the African American Experience*. Durham: Duke University Press, 1990.

Living Blues: A Journal of the African American Blues Tradition.

Macleod, William Christie. *The American Indian Frontier*. New York: Alfred A. Knopf, 1923.

McAdoo, Harriette Pipes. *Black Families*. Thousand Oaks, CA: Sage, 1996.

Miller, Elizabeth W. *The Negro in America: A Bibliography*. Cambridge, MA: Harvard University Press, 1966.

Moebs, Thomas T. *Black Soldiers—Black Sailors: Research Guide on African-Americans in U.S. Military History, 1526–1900*. 4 vols. Chesapeake Bay: Moebs, 1994.

Myers, Walter Dean. *Now is Your Time!: The African-American Struggle for Freedom*. New York: HarperTrophy, 1991. Juvenile.

National Advisory Commission on Civil Disorders. *The Report of the National Advisory Commission on Civil Disorders*. Washington, DC: U.S. Government Printing Office, 1968.

Negro History Bulletin.

Negro Population in the United States, 1790–1915. Washington, DC: U.S. Government Printing Office, 1918; reprinted, New York: Arno Press, 1968.

Northwood, Lawrence K., and Ernest A. Barth. *Urban Desegregation: Negro Pioneers and Their White Neighbors*. Seattle: University of Washington Press, 1965.

Patterson, Orlando. *The Sociology of Slavery.* Rutherford, NJ: Fairleigh Dickinson Press, 1967.

Phylon. Journal.

Ploski, Harry A., and James Williams. *Reference Library of Black America,* 5 Vols. Detroit: Gale Research, 1990.

Pomeroy, Earl. *The Pacific Slope: A History of California, Oregon, Washington, Idaho, Utah and Nevada.* New York: Alfred A. Knopf, 1965; reprinted, 1991.

Porter, Dorothy B. *The Negro in the United States: A Selected Bibliography.* Washington, DC: Library of Congress, 1970.

_____. *The Negro in the United States: A Working Bibliography.* Ann Arbor: University of Michigan Press, 1969.

Potter, Joan, and Constance Claytor. *African-American Firsts.* Elizabethtown, NY: Pinto Press, 1994.

Pride, Armistead S. *The Black Press: A Bibliography.* Madison: Association for Education in Journalism, 1968.

Prosser, William Ferrand. *A History of the Puget Sound Country; Its Resources, Its Commerce and Its People,* 2 Vols. New York: Lewis Publishing Company, 1903.

Querol y Roso, Luis. *Negros y mulatos de nuevo Espana.* Imprenta Hijo F. Vives Mora, Valencia, 1935. Historia de su alzamiento en Méjico en 1612.

Ray, Verne F. *Cultural Relations in the Plateau of Northwestern America.* Los Angeles: The Southwest Museum Administration of the Fund.

Rees, John. *Idaho: Chronology, Nomenclature Bibliography.* Chicago: W. B. Conkey Company, 1918.

Rollins, Philip A. *The Cowboy: His Characteristics, His Equipment, and His Part in the Development of the West.* New York: Charles Scribner's and Sons, 1922.

SAGE: A Scholarly Journal of Black Women.

Sandoz, Mari. *The Buffalo Hunters: The Story of the Hide Men.* New York: Hastings House, 1954.

_____. *The Cattlemen: From the Rio Grande Across the Far Marias.* New York: Hastings House, 1958.

Schmid, Calvin F. *Social Trend in Seattle.* Seattle: University of Washington Press, 1944.

Sefton, James E. *The United States Army and Reconstruction, 1865–1877.* Baton Rouge: Louisiana State University Press, 1967.

Shaw, James C. *North From Texas: Incidents in the Early Life of a Range Cowman in Texas, Dakota, and Wyoming, 1852–1883.* Evanston, IL: Branding Iron Press, 1952.

Smith, Jessie Carney. *Black Firsts: 2,000 Years of Extraordinary Achievement.* Detroit: Visible Ink Press, 1994.

_____, ed. *Notable Black American Women.* Detroit: Gale Research, 1992.

Sterling, Dorothy, ed. *We Are Your Sisters: Black Women in the Nineteenth Century*. New York: W;. W. Norton and Company, 1984.

Thompson, Edgar T., and Alma M. Thompson. *Race and Region: A Descriptive Bibliography Compiled With Special Reference to the Relations Between Whites and Negroes in the U.S.* Chapel Hill: University of North Carolina Press, 1949.

Toll, Robert C. *Blacking Up: The Minstrel Show in Nineteenth-Century America*. London: Oxford University Press, 1977.

Vandiveer, Clarence. *The Fur Trade and Early Western Exploration*. Cleveland: Arthur H. Clark, 1929.

Vaz, Kim Marie. *Black Women in America*. Thousand Oaks, CA: Sage, 1995.

Walker, Tacotta B. *Stories of Early Days in Wyoming*. Casper: Prairie Publishing Company, 1936.

Wesley, Charles H., and Patricia W. Romero. *Negro Americans in the Civil War: From Slavery to Citizenship*. New York: Publishers Company, 1968.

Western Journal of Black Studies.

White, William Bruce. "The Military and the Melting Pot: The American Army and Minority Groups, 1865–1924." Ph.D. diss., University of Wisconsin, 1968.

Whitman, Sidney E. *The Trooper: An Informal History of the Plains Cavalry, 1865–1890*. New York: Hastings House Publishers, 1962.

Wilkins, Charles. *Narrative of the U.S. Exploring Expedition During the Year 1838, 1840, 1841, 1842*. Philadelphia: Lea and Blanchard, 1845.

Williams, Ethel L., and Clifton F. Brown. *Afro-American Religious Studies: A Comprehensive Bibliography*. Metuchen, NJ: Scarecrow, 1972.

Williams, George Washington. *A History of the Negro Troops in the War of the Rebellion, 1861–1865*. New York: Harper and Brothers, 1888; reprinted, New York: Greenwood, Negro Universities Press, 1969.

Wilson, Carter A. *Racism*. Thousand Oaks, CA: Sage, 1996.

Woodson, Carter G., and Charles H. Wesley. *The Negro in Our History*. Washington, DC: Associated Publishers, 1962.

Zinn, Howard. *A People's History of the United States*. New York: Harper and Row, 1980.

Zornow, William Frank. *Kansas: A History of the Jayhawk State*. Norman: University of Oklahoma Press, 1957.

Other:

African-American Newspapers: The 19th Century, Part I. Wilmington, DE: Scholarly Resources. CD-ROM.

Ethnic Notions. Traces evolution of Black stereotypes, by Marlon Riggs. 56 min., 1987. Videorecording.

Related Bibliographies

Abajian, James de T., comp. *Blacks and Their Contributions to the American West: A Bibliography and Union List of Library Holdings Through 1970.* Boston: G. K. Hall, 1974.

Blazek, Ron, Janice Fennell, and Frances Masterson McKinney, eds. *The Black Experience: A Bibliography of Bibliographies, 1970–1975.* Chicago: Adult Services Division, American Library Association, 1978.

Breyfogle, Donna, ed. "Blacks in Ontario: A Selected Bibliography, 1965–1976."

Dalhousie University Library Bibliographies. *Blacks in Canada: Representative Source Materials.* Halifax, NS: n.p., 1970. Bibliography.

Davis, Lenwood G. *The Black Woman in American Society: A Selected Annotated Bibliography.* Boston: G. K. Hall, 1975.

_____. *Blacks in the American West: A Working Bibliography*, 2^d ed. Exchange Bibliography, no. 661. Monticello, IL: Council of Planning Librarians, 1974.

_____. *Blacks in the Pacific Northwest: 1788–1972. A Bibliography of Published Works and of Unpublished Source Materials on the Life and Contributions of Black People in the Pacific Northwest.* Monticello, IL: Council of Planning Librarians, 1972.

_____ *Blacks in the State of Oregon, 1788–1974: A Bibliography of Published Works and of Unpublished Source Materials on the Life and Achievements of Black People in the Beaver State.* Monticello, IL: Council of Planning Librarians, 1974.

_____. *Blacks in the State of Oregon, 1788–1971.* Monticello, IL: Council of Planning Librarians, 1971.

Davis, Lenwood G., and George Hill, comps. "Blacks in the American West." Chapter in *Blacks in the American Armed Forces, 1776–1983: A Bibliography.* Westport, CT: Greenwood Press, 1985.

Davis, Lenwood G., and Mary Vance, comps. *Blacks in the State of Utah: A Working Bibliography*. Monticello, IL: Council of Planning Librarians, 1974.

————. *Blacks in the State of Utah: A Working Bibliography*. Monticello, IL: Council of Planning Librarians, 1974.

Devejian, Pat, and Jacqueline J. Etulain. "African Americans." Chapter in *Women and Family in the Twentieth-Century American West: A Bibliography*. Albuquerque: Center for the American West, 1990.

Glasrud, Bruce A., comp. *African Americans in the West: A Bibliography of Secondary Sources*. Center for Big Bend Studies, Occasional Papers no. 2. Alpine, TX: Sul Ross State University, 1998.

Hardaway, Roger D. *A Narrative Bibliography of the African-American Frontier: Blacks in the Rocky Mountain West, 1535–1912*. Studies in American History Series, Vol. 9. Lewiston, NY: Edwin Mellen Press, 1995.

Hawkins, Chester L. "Selective Bibliography on African-Americans 1830–1990." *Dialogue* 25 (Winter 1992).

Hay, Frederick J. *African-American Community Studies from North America: A Classified, Annotated Bibliography*. New York: Garland Publishing, 1991. Social conditions of Blacks in Canada.

History and Culture of Black People: A Selected Bibliography for Elementary Schools. Toronto: TBE, Library Services Department, 1990. Juvenile literature.

Junne, George H., Jr., comp. *The Black American West: A Bibliography*. Occasional Paper Series, no. 2. Greeley, CO: University of Northern Colorado, 1999.

Krash, Ronald, et al. *Black America: A Research Bibliography*. St. Louis: St. Louis University Library, 1972.

Lucko, Paul M. "Dissertations and Theses Relating to African American Studies in Texas: A Selected Bibliography, 1904–1990." *Southwestern Historical Quarterly* 96 (1993).

Matthews, Miriam. *The Negro in California from 1781–1910*. Los Angeles: 1944. Bibliography.

Miller, Elizabeth W. *The Negro in America: A Bibliography*. Cambridge, MA: Harvard University Press, 1966.

Mills, Hazel E., and Nancy B. Pryor. *The Negro in the State of Washington: A Bibliography*. Olympia: Washington State Library, 1972.

Ngatia, Therese. *The Blacks in Canada: A Selective Annotated Bibliography*. Edmonton: T. Ngatia, 1984.

Porter, Dorothy B. *The Negro in the United States: A Selected Bibliography*. Washington, DC: Library of Congress, 1970.

Pride, Armistead S. *The Black Press: A Bibliography*. Madison: Association for Education in Journalism, 1968.

————. *The Negro in the United States: A Working Bibliography*. Ann Arbor: University of Michigan Press, 1969.

Rees, John. *Idaho: Chronology, Nomenclature Bibliography*. Chicago: W. B. Conkey Company, 1918.

Reichard, Maximilian. *The Black Man in St. Louis: A Preliminary Bibliography*. Monticello, IL: council of Planning Librarians, 1974.

Sampson, F. A., and W. C. Breckenridge. "Bibliography of Slavery in Missouri." *Missouri Historical Review* 2 (April 1908).

Snapp, Elizabeth, and Harry F. Snapp, eds. "African American Women." Chapter in *Read All about Her!: Texas Women's History, a Working Bibliography*. Denton: Texas Woman's University Press, 1995.

Socolofsky, Homer, and Virgil Dean, comps. "Blacks." Chapter in *Kansas History: An Annotated Bibliography*. Westport, CT: Greenwood Press, 1992.

Thompson, Edgar T., and Alma M. Thompson. *Race and Region: A Descriptive Bibliography Compiled With Special Reference to the Relations Between Whites and Negroes in the U.S.* Chapel Hill: University of North Carolina Press, 1949.

Thompson, Lucille Smith, and Alma Smith Jacobs. *The Negro in Montana 1800–1945: A Selective Bibliography*. Helena: Montana State Library, 1970.

University of Utah, Marriott Library. *Black Bibliography*. Salt Lake City: Marriott Library, 1977.

———. *Supplement to Black Bibliography*. Salt Lake City: Marriott Library, 1977.

Washington State Library. *The Negro in the State of Washington: 1788–1969: A Bibliography of Published and of Unpublished Source Materials on the Life and Achievements of the Negro in the Evergreen State*, eds. Hazel E. Mills and Nancy B. Pryor. Olympia: Washington State Library, 1970.

Williams, Ethel L., and Clifton F. Brown. *Afro-American Religious Studies: A Comprehensive Bibliography*. Metuchen, NJ: Scarecrow, 1972.

Work, Monroe Nathan., comp. *A Bibliography of the Negro in Africa and America*. New York: H. W. Wilson Company, 1928.

Films and Videos

Title	Director or Producer	Year	Running Time
Absent	Rosebud Films	1928	
Adios Amigos	Fred Williamson	1975	87m
Afro-American Work Songs/Texas Prison	Documentary	1966	29m
Anatomy of a Riot	Documentary	1992	47m
Another 48 Hours	Walter Hill	1990	98m
Ashes and Embers	Haile Gerima	1985	120m
The Betrayal	Oscar Micheaux	1948	180m
Beverly Hills Cop	Martin Brest	1984	107m
Beverly Hills Cop 2	Tony Scott	1987	102m
Beverly Hills Cop 3	John Landis	1994	104m
Beyond Hate Trilogy: Hate on Trial	Tatgel/Lasseur	1992	146m
Birth of a Nation	M. McDaniel	1992	60m
Black Belt Jones	Robert Clouse	1974	87m
Black Canadian Experience	L. Little-White	1972	
The Black Cowboy	WOW-TV, NB	1993	25m
The Black Cowboys	TBS Productions	1987	50m
Black Gold	Norman Films	1928	
Black Panthers: Huey Newton	Documentary	1968	53m
Black Pioneers: True Faces of the West	UWTV	1995	
Black Rodeo	Jeff Kanew (Doc)	1972	87m
Black Sister's Revenge	Jamaa Fanaka	1976	100m
Black Warriors of the Seminole	Documentary	1990	28m
The Black West	William Miles	1994	60m
Blacula	William Crain	1972	92m
Blood of Jesus	Spencer Williams	1941	50m
Boyz N The Hood	John Singleton	1991	107m
Bronze Buckaroo	Hollywood Prds.	1939	57m

Buck and the Preacher	Sidney Poitier	1971	103m
Buffalo Soldiers	Charles Haid	1997	95m
The Buffalo Soldiers	BA Productions	1992	50m
The Bull-Dogger (Bill Pickett)	Normal Film Co.	1923	
Bush Mama	Haile Gerima	1976	100m
California Suite	Herbert Ross	1978	103m
A Chocolate Cowboy	Cyclone Comedy	1925	
Charlie-One-Eye	Don Chaffey	1973	107m
Colors	Dennis Hopper	1988	120m
Come On Cowboy	Goldmax Prdts.	1948	
Condor, El	John Guillermin	1970	102m
Cowboy Canteen	Lew Landers	1944	72m
The Cowboys	Mark Rydell	1972	128m
The Crimson Skull (Bill Pickett)	Norman Films	1921	
Death of a Gunfighter	Robert Totten	1969	100m
Devil in a Blue Dress	Carl Franklin	1995	86m
Don't Leave Out the Cowboys			22m
Duel at Diablo	Ralph Nelson	1966	103m
Fass Black	D'Urville Martin	1977	105m
Fields of Endless Day	Macartney-Fligate	1978	59m
Flaming Crisis	Colored Players	1924	
48 Hours	Walter Hill	1982	97m
Frontier Scout	Franklin Warner	1938	
The Ghost Rider	William Steiner	1925	
The Grasshopper	Jerry Paris	1970	
Harlem on the Prairie	Associated Picts.	1938	54m
Harlem Rides the Range	Hollywood Prds.	1939	58m
Held in Trust: The True Story of			
Lt. Henry O. Flipper	PBS		60m
A Hero Ain't Nothin' But a Sandwich	Ralph Nelson	1978	107m
Hollywood Shuffle	Robert Townsend	1987	82m
Hollywood Vice Squad	Penelope Spheeris	1986	101m
Home Feeling	Jennifer Hodge (Can)		58m
The Homesteader	Micheaux Films	1919	
Joshua	Larry Spangler	1976	75m
Juke Joint	Spencer Williams	1947	70m
Kenny and Georgia: The Story of a			
Homeless African-American Couple	Claire Burch	1994	58m
Killer of Sheep	Charles Burnette	1977	87m
Landmark Spiritual Church	Documentary	1968	25m
The Learning Tree	Gordon Parks	1969	107m
The Legend of Nigger Charley	Martin Goldman	1972	115m
Long Train Running: Oakland Blues	Marlon Riggs	1983	30m
Look Out Sister	Astor Pictures	1948	64m

The Mack	Michael Camus	1973	110m
Man and Boy	E. W. Swackhamer	1971	98m
The Man from Texas	Ben Roy Prods.	1921	
Marching On	Spencer Williams	1943	83m
The McMasters	Alf Kjellin	1970	89m
Menace II Society	Hughes Brothers	1993	97m
Mother, Jugs and Speed	Peter Yates	1976	98m
My Brother's Wedding	Charles Burnett	1983	116m
The Nation Erupts	Not Channel Zero	1992	60m
One Dark Night	Million Dollar	1939	
One False Move	Carl Franklin	1991	103m
100 Rifles	Tom Gries	1969	105m
The Petrified Forest	Archie Mayo	1936	
Poetic Justice	John Singleton	1993	109m
Posse	Mario Van Peebles	1993	109m
Power Versus the People	William Greaves	1970	36m
Prairie Comes to Harlem	Toddy Pictures	194?	61m
Rainbow Rangers	William Steiner	1924	
Rapping	Frith-Doc.	1969	14m
Rhythm Rodeo	George Randol	1938	20m
Rifles	Marvin Schwartz	1969	100m
Rio Conchos	Gordon Douglas	1964	107m
The River Niger	Krishna Shah	1976	105m
Rodney King Case: What the Jurors Saw	D. Palumbo	1992	116m
A Ropin' Ridin' Fool	William Steiner	1925	
Saddle Daze	Wild West Rodeo		
The Scalphunters	Sydney Pollack	1968	102m
Scream, Blacula, Scream	Bob Kelljan	1973	95m
Sell 'em Cowboy	Ben Wilson Prod.	1924	
Sergeant Rutledge	John Ford	1960	118m
Sergeants 3	John Flynn	1962	
The Sheriff		1971	90m
Shoot 'em up, Sam	Black Western	1922	
Silverado	Laurence Kasdan	1985	132m
Soul of Nigger Charley	Larry Spangler	1973	109m
Soul Soldier	John Cardos	1970	83m
South Central	Steve Anderson	1992	99m
South Central Los Angeles: Inside Voices	Maxi Cohen	1996	46m
Sun Tan Ranch	Norwanda Pcts.	1948	
Sweet Potato Ride	Greene/Tucker	1994	41m
Sweet Sweetback's Baadasssss Song	M. Van Peebles	1971	90m
Symbol of the Unconquered	Micheaux Films	1921	
Take a Hard Ride	Anthony Dawson	1975	103m
Take This Hammer [James Baldwin]	NET		45m
The $10,000 Trail	Booker T. Films	1921	

Thomasine and Bushrod	Gordon Parks, Jr.	1975	95m
To Sleep With Anger	Charles Burnett	1990	95m
Trial [Pts 1–4, *Denver* v. *Lauren Watson*]	NET	1970	6hrs.
Trooper of Company K	Lincoln	1916	
Two-Gun Man From Harlem	Merit Pictures	1938	60m
The Untold West: The Black West	Documentary		
Vanishing Point	Robert Sarafian	1972	107m
Virgin of the Seminole	Micheaux Films	1922	
Waiting to Exhale	Forest Whitaker	1995	124m
Watts!: Revolt or Riot?	CBS-TV	1966	45m
Watts Towers Theatre Workshop	ETS	1969	27m
Way Out West	Educational	1935	
Well Spent Life [Mance Lipscomb]	Les Blank	1971	44m
Western Vengeance	J. P. McDowan	1924	

Author Index

Subject Index

About the Author

GEORGE H. JUNNE, JR. is Associate Professor in the Africana Studies Department at the University of Northern Colorado and the author of *Afroamerican History: A Chronicle of People of African Descent in the United States* (1996).

ISBN 0-313-31208-7

EAN

90000>

9 780313 312083

HARDCOVER BAR CODE